R. VASSALOTTI
F.I.T.
2008

# THE DYNAMICS OF FASHION

THE **DYNAMICS** OF

Fairchild Books, Inc.
New York

# FASHION

## THIRD EDITION

**ELAINE STONE,** *professor emerita*
**FASHION INSTITUTE OF TECHNOLOGY, NEW YORK**

Director of Sales and Acquisitions: Dana Meltzer-Berkowitz

Executive Editor: Olga T. Kontzias

Development Editor and Senior Production Editor: Elizabeth Marotta

Associate Art Director and Photo Research: Erin Fitzsimmons

Production Director: Ginger Hillman

Senior Development Editor: Jennifer Crane

Creative Director: Adam B. Bohannon

Copyediting: Progressive Publishing Alternatives

Divine Illustrator: Jenny Green, shu shu design

Production Hazmat Specialist: Anne Sanow

All-Star Squadron: Kevin Brennan, Andrew Fargnoli, Ginger Hillman, Jeff Klingman, Suzie Q., Alexandra Rossomando, and Blake Royer

Cover design and interior design: Adam B. Bohannon

Text layout: Adam B. Bohannon, Erin Fitzsimmons

Cover photos: Stephen Sullivan

Cover model: Deon

Hair & makeup: Timmothy Olan for Vartali Salon, NYC

Styling: Collette LoVullo

Library of Congress Catalog Card Number: 2008924280

ISBN-13: 978-1-56367-686-4

GST R 133004424

Printed in China

TP17

# contents

# list of features

# extended contents

# preface

Fashion is fast and forward, challenging and changing, and constantly in motion. This new edition of *The Dynamics of Fashion* is presented to students and instructors so that they can be on the cutting edge of what is happening in the business known as *fashion*. This updated text will prepare students to learn and understand the innovation and challenge of careers in the global world of today's fashion business.

This third edition of *The Dynamics of Fashion* broadens, updates, and brings new perspectives of the fashion business to students' attention. It continues with the broadened scope of fashion and adds the newest and most up-to-date facts and figures used by professionals to keep the industry a vital and challenging career path.

All chapters have been substantially updated with new and current theories added. Recurring themes have been broadened, and the change in the future direction of fashion globalization, retail competition, theories of customer service, and career paths have been expanded. Technology and its impact on the movement of fashion, and the threat of confrontations among nations, are discussed in the context of the fashion business.

## Organization of the Text

This edition of *The Dynamics of Fashion* uses the successful classroom-tested organization of the previous editions. It is structured in the following sequential learning order:

### Unit One: The Changing World of Fashion

The first unit examines how and why fashion evolves and changes. It explains the principles around which fashion revolves and the role that economic, sociological, and psychological elements play in the cyclical nature of fashion. It also covers the business scope of the industry including recent growth and expansion. Chapter 1 is a new chapter on fashion history, which focuses on the development of fashion design and explains how it has grown into a major force for the future. There is a special project at the end of this chapter that helps students learn how designers relate to fashion and the decade to which they belong.

Fashion operates in a far different way today than it did years ago. It moves faster and reaches more people. And perhaps most important, it is more businesslike. To understand the changes that have occurred and will occur in the future of the fashion industry, you must first understand the dynamics that underlie the fashion business.

### Unit Two: The Primary Level: The Materials of Fashion

The growers and producers of the raw material of fashion, fibers, fabrics, trimming, leather, and fur are covered in this unit. New and fast-moving advances in these industries coupled with an increasing variety of fashion goods using these materials are explained. The difference between natural and manufactured fibers is explained, along with the worldwide impact of global warming, the sustainability of products made from "green" fibers, and the production process of most fabrics. Leather and fur are also covered in detail. Different categories of leather, special finishes, real and faux fur, the development of these industries, and the steps in producing and marketing are examined.

## Unit Three: The Secondary Level: The Producers of Apparel

The third unit begins with a chapter on product development. Students will learn about the six-stage process of developing and producing a line, the concept of Quick Response, and the major industry practices of licensing, private label, specification buying, offshore production, factors, and chargebacks. Industry trends in apparel are then broken down into separate chapters focusing on women's, men's, and children's apparel.

The history of the women's apparel industry is explained, along with the categories, size ranges, price zones, and brand and designer names used in marketing. The next chapter compares and contrasts all the factors that are common to both men's and women's apparel and explains the differences that exist in producing and marketing men's wear. For children's apparel, the impact of demographics is explained, along with the influence of fashion on children's wear, the impact of licensing, industry trends, and responses to social issues.

## Unit Four: The Secondary Level: The Other Fashion Producers

The producers of innerwear, accessories, cosmetics, fragrances, and home fashions no longer exist just to coordinate with apparel. These industries have become innovators and fashion trendsetters. This unit explains how each industry functions and covers current and future practices and trends.

Innerwear, bodywear, and legwear are all discussed in terms of history, merchandising, and marketing. The ever-expanding accessories industries—which today are taking advantage of the newest technology—are explored from their past to the present. Cosmetics and fragrances have become powerhouse industries, and students will engage with the "dreams versus science" debate and learn about new market segments. Another rapidly growing area is home fashions. The final chapter in this unit outlines the growing influence of top apparel designers who are increasingly expanding their range by producing looks for the home as well.

## Unit Five: The Retail Level: The Markets for Fashion

This unit focuses on the elements of fashion marketing and reveals how markets operate to help manufacturers sell their products and how retailers satisfy the needs of their target customer. It details both domestic and foreign markets and global sourcing. Different types of retailers are explained, and current trends and emerging retail strategies for the 21st century are detailed.

One chapter is devoted to global fashion markets and their unique offerings and personalities. We also take a closer look at global sourcing—both the advantages and disadvantages as American industries continue to expand into foreign markets. This chapter also discusses the single biggest problem confronting the American fashion industries today: the need to export American fashion around the world in order to reduce the trade deficit that has arisen from so many imports. The history and development of fashion retailing in the United States is explained, including the different types of retailers and changing retail patterns. Also discussed are current policies and strategies in fashion retailing and how they affect merchandising, operations, and location.

## Unit Six: The Auxiliary Level: The Supporting Services

Publicity is crucial for all areas of the fashion industry, and the final unit in this book covers the myriad fashion services and explains their interconnecting roles in the fashion business from design to consumer. Advertising and print media such as fashion magazines and newspapers are discussed, along with television, other broadcast media, and the Internet. The role of advertising agencies, fashion consultants, and public relations firms are explored. Visual merchandising and store design are also important aspects of promotion. Finally, we will have a look at the industry publications and organizations that work to provide information and other services.

## Text Features

*The Dynamics of Fashion* provides hundreds of new examples, color illustrations, and has many exciting special features that make the people, principles, practices, and techniques of the fashion business come alive in the minds of students. We believe that these features will help students to learn about the fashion business in an enjoyable manner. All these features are appropriate for class discussion, library research projects, and group projects.

## Fashion Focus

A popular feature, the "Fashion Focus," highlights interesting people, places, and/or products that impact on the subject matter. This feature is found in every chapter and makes the chapter material more relevant to the student.

## Then and Now

"Then and Now" is a feature that encourages the student to look to the past, present, and future of subjects that have a lasting imprint on fashion. Many are presented in exciting pictorial format.

## Famous Designers

This edition features a compilation of famous designers, including noteworthy elements of their designs.

## Glossary

The glossary has been updated and enlarged and now contains nearly 500 industry terms. A knowledge and understanding of the "language" of fashion gives students a firm footing upon which they can step out into the industry and know they are speaking the right language.

## Summary and Review

The chapters conclude with student-oriented activities designed to enrich and reinforce the instructional material. A summary gives a quick reminder of key concepts. A "Trade Talk" section explains fashion & merchandising terms introduced for the first time in that chapter. The student will recognize these terms when they appear in subsequent chapters. These terms are also defined in the glossary.

"For Review" asks questions about the key concepts of each chapter. These questions provoke thought, encourage classroom discussion, and develop recall of the material presented in the text.

"For Discussion" asks the student to explain the significance of a major concept and to support the explanation with specific illustrations. This activity affords the student an opportunity to apply theory to actual situations and to draw on his or her own background and experiences.

## Instructor's Manual and PowerPoint

An instructor's manual is available and includes a number of options for organizing the course and contains general suggestions for teaching the course. It also contains supplementary assignments for each unit. The key to the text includes answers to all end-of-chapter exercises.

A useful feature is a test bank containing material for the individual units, and a final examination. The tests are composed of 100 objective questions each and are ready to duplicate.

A PowerPoint presentation is included as a supplemental teaching tool for the classroom, featuring art and text from the book.

## Acknowledgments

I am grateful to the many educators and business-people who have given me encouragement, information, and helpful suggestions. Among these are my teaching colleagues at the Fashion Institute of Technology, who have supported the writing of *The Dynamics of Fashion*, and the very helpful staff of professionals in the FIT library.

I am also indebted to the industry experts and professionals, both domestic and foreign, who gave of their time and expertise to ensure the timeliness and accuracy of the information in this book.

My heartfelt gratitude and sincere appreciation goes to the staff at Fairchild Publications. I particularly want to mention Elizabeth Marotta, the senior production editor at Fairchild and the person who really made this edition possible by her complete attention to every detail, and most of all for being a friend in need, who helped me on all phases of producing this book. To Adam Bohannon, the best art director ever, whose enthusiasm for this book, and unfailing artistic eye for design and color has made *Dynamics of Fashion* a real dynamic! To Erin Fitzsimmons for doing the photo research and bringing together the best photos to make this edition so wonderful. To Anne Sanow for her contributions to the new chapter. Thanks to Tania Grey of Stoneworks Design for her wonderful design and production of the PowerPoint presentation. Finally to the Executive Editor, Olga Kontzias, I say a heartfelt "thank you" for all the years we have worked together.

I regret that space does not permit me to personally list and thank my friends in all segments of the fashion business who supplied, throughout the development of this edition, their encouragement as well as significant amounts of current and trend trade information. As always, I welcome instructors' and students' comments. They can be sent to me through Fairchild Publications or to my e-mail address: elaine_stone@fitnyc.edu.

This book is dedicated to Minnie M. Stone, who served as a mentor, friend, and critic throughout my career. Best of all, she was a terrific mother.

THE DYNAMICS OF **FASHION**

unit one

FASHION—the very word conjures up excitement and interest in all of us. Fashion is the ultimate F word! It is faddish, familiar, fantasy, form, fatal, feasible, festive, finite, fit, fresh, and fun. Fashion is the most dynamic of American businesses. It thrives on change, and change is the engine that fuels it.

People long for excitement and variety in their lives and look to the fashion business to show them "what's new." Ever since Adam and Eve wore fig leaves, fashion has had the power to fascinate and excite. This power has been used by the trendsetters of history. Today, past eras conjure up images not only of the philosophy and social mores of the times, but also, in large part, the fashions of the times.

Designers, manufacturers, and retailers have enjoyed impressive growth. Press coverage has crossed over from the purely "passion for fashion" to become "hard news" in the *Wall Street Journal*, the *New York Times*, *Newsweek*, global television, and the Internet.

The fashion business is both an art and a science and at the same time both personal and incredibly public. Fashion can be viewed as an art because so much creativity is required to make its products. Unlike most other business where conformity is the norm, fashion nurtures innovation and creativity. Fashion has always been considered a science as well. Modern fashion manufacturing was born during the industrial revolution and has matured in the age of technology. Technology has revolutionized the way fashion is made.

Fashion, always a highly personal business, is in the process of becoming even more so. Mass customization has taken root in the fashion industry.

New fashion ideas now come from the world around us; the streets, innovative teenagers, film, a celebrity with his or her unique look. Shifts in the economy, sociological influences, and demographic changes all contribute to change in fashion and therefore affect the fashion business.

# THE CHANGING WORLD OF FASHION

# chapter one

*Everything you always wanted to know*

*about how fashion changes with the times,*

*and how changing times spark new fashion.*

KEY CONCEPTS
• The social and cultural conditions that affect fashion
• Major developments and trends, decade by decade
• The designers and other innovators who influence fashion

# A Century of Fashion

Turn on your television today, or log on to the Internet, and you're constantly being told what people are wearing. On the red carpet at the Oscars, every actress will be asked who designed her gown; less than a week later, she'll show up in *Star* or *People* magazine on either the best-dressed or worst-dressed list, and a stylist will have written a sidebar telling you where you can buy an inexpensive replica of the dress—along with the shoes, jewelry, handbag, and cosmetics. When Katie Couric became the first woman to head up the CBS evening news broadcast in 2006, critics discussed her choice in suits as much as they did her reporting style. Suiting styles for men are worn with cool élan by actor George Clooney, rapper Jay-Z, and soccer star David Beckham. Socialites design clothing or handbag lines. Everyone is in on the act, it seems, from the reality show participants of *Project Runway* to those who want to laugh at it all by reading what the Fug Girls have to say online. The newest looks are seen and talked about and copied more quickly than ever—never before have we had so much information at our fingertips and so many options to choose from.

But how did we get here? It's true that we can see the latest from music videos, awards shows, and the fashion runway almost immediately. Almost 100 years ago, however, American women went wild for anything worn by the actress Mary Pickford, and newspapers and magazines hastened to provide photographs and drawings of her ingénue style as soon as they could roll them off the press. Factory and "office girls" from the turn of the 20th century had a role in shaping the apparel industry with their demands for functional, streamlined clothing, and the famous Rosie the Riveter poster from World War II boldly depicted fashion on duty: coveralls, along with a feminine swoosh of bright-red patriotic lipstick. Today's In and Out lists have their precedent in that wartime era, too, with the inauguration of the U.S.-based Best-Dressed List in 1940, formerly the domain of Paris. And one of the Best-Dressed's notable men was the suave Cary Grant—emulated by no other than Mr. Clooney today.

The point is that fashion has *always* been changing and evolving—and at any time in the past, though it may be history to us now, that change was usually dramatic. The evolution of fashion is an exciting one, full of innovations and imitations. Fashion history tells us where we've been and also suggests where fashion might be going. In this chapter, our focus is the last 100 years or so, from the turn of the twentieth century to the present day. There are different ways to determine when one decade "begins" and the former one "ends"—sometimes it's a momentous event, such as the stock market crash of 1929 or the end of World War II in 1945. Whatever the event may be, it's important to remember that there are many changes that occur over any 10-year period. In the following sections, we discuss an overview of the events of each decade—social, cultural, and economic; these events are related to major fashion trends and developments of the period, and the designers and other individuals who had a strong influence at the time are noted.

## Social and Cultural Conditions

You may have heard the old adage about hemlines going up when the stock market is on the rise—and falling when times get tough. Interestingly, this is often true: think of the miniskirts worn during the stock market boom of the 1980s, contrasted with the longer, more sedate skirts that were popular during the recession in the early 1990s. It isn't quite that simple, however, and examining other events in each decade provides more clues to what people were wearing and why. Significant issues are wars and revolutions; peacetime and prosperity; civil rights; travel; transportation; communication; literacy and education; developments in science, technology, and medicine; sports and recreation; and of course the entertainment industry, from vaudeville and theater to film and the Internet.

## Fashion Trends and Developments

It's said that for every action there's a reaction, and we'll see how this holds true for fashion. Sometimes the reactions are a response to horrific events: both the attack on Pearl Harbor in 1941 and the terrorist bombings on September 11, 2001, resulted in a trend for red, white, and blue clothing and accessories. Other times, fashion takes advantage of new technology and scientific breakthroughs, such as the invention of nylon. Along with apparel, trends include changes in accessories, hairstyles, and cosmetics. For every major trend that seems particular to its time— think flapper dresses from the 1920s, Jackie Kennedy's ladylike suits, bell-bottom pants from the 1970s—there is often a reinterpretation later on (contemporary Marc Jacobs or Michael Kors, the resurgence and refinement of low-slung pants). From the Gibson Girl's blouse to Twiggy's microminis, from the Man in the Gray Flannel Suit to Calvin Klein's underwear on display, the past 100 years has produced some memorable fashion moments. Some of them were a flash in the pan, but others influence us today—and will continue to do so in the future.

## Designers and Other Influences

Someone has to be the creative force behind all of this change, and this is where fashion designers take center stage. Twentieth-century modernization saw the rise of mass apparel production and the rise of designer as fashion arbiter—and fashion star. Many fashion staples in our closets today, such as the "little black dress," can be accredited to a particular designer (in this case, Chanel). Innovators, artists, and often followers too, designers have put their stamp on major fashion trends throughout the years. We will see also how other elements, such as urban or "street" culture, influence design.

Audrey Hepburn and Grace Kelly waiting backstage at the Academy Awards in 1958 (top) and Marion Cotillard on the red carpet at the Academy Awards in 2008 (bottom).

## PRELUDE TO THE 20TH CENTURY

Before we learn how fashion developed and evolved over the past century, we need to look at the state of things before that time—when the United States was a very young country, forging its own identity while still retaining close ties to Europe. In the mid-19th century, New York City's population was still under 1 million, and other prominent East Coast cities, such as Boston and Philadelphia, boasted only 137,000 and 121,000 respectively. The Western cities were much smaller outposts; St. Louis, famed as the "Gateway to the West," was the largest with nearly 80,000, and San Francisco had just 35,000 pioneering inhabitants. Contrast this with the 1.5 million citizens of Paris at the time, or London's 2.3 million—long-established urban centers of culture and industry that Americans hoped to emulate. The years leading up to 1900 brought enormous expansion and change to the United States, and with that, a new national identity.

## Social and Cultural Conditions

As the United States expanded, it experienced severe growing pains. The Civil War of 1861–1865 threatened the country's very survival, and the aftermath saw social upheavals in race and class. Industrialization brought improved modes of transportation such as safer railroads and electric trolleys; people could receive news faster because of the telegraph and telephone; and the cycle of the day (and therefore the workday) was altered forever with the widespread use of electric lights.

By the turn of the 20th century, there were nearly 3.5 million people living in New York City alone, and other urban centers were rapidly expanding as well. The Western part of the country gave way from frontier settlement to modernization, which was altogether different from the European-influenced East.

## Fashion Trends and Developments

During much of the 19th century, particularly the conservative Victorian era, clothing was straight-laced and bodies were covered up. While the wealthier population had always looked to Europe for aristocratic fashion design, the desire for gentility and refinement became a broader concern as Americans on the whole became more settled and established. Women's dress was carefully chosen to show their respectability. Restricted by corsets and hoop skirts, with layer upon layer of undergarments, inner and outer skirts, and flounces, the decorative aspect of dressing conveyed femininity.

The voluminous skirts of the mid-1800s were reduced to the slimmer bustle silhouette. The fashion cycle ebbed and flowed, with a continual struggle between gentility and practicality. A "respectable" wife from the East Coast accustomed to wearing corsets and heavy skirts might get rid of some layers should she migrate Westward overland, where such restrictions would be impractical for cooking over fires outdoors. Once settled in her new home, however, she'd be likely to resurrect her finery to show that she was a woman knowledgeable about fashion and culture.

The change from homemade to ready-made apparel was another significant fashion trend. Mass production of garments such as corsets and men's shirts began in the mid-1800s; by the mid-1890s, as more men—and also women—began working in factories and offices, the apparel industry responded to the demand for practical clothing by adapting the men's shirt for women in a blouselike form. The shirtwaist would keep manufacturers rushing to meet demand into the new century. Ready-made apparel became widespread, available from mail-order catalogs such as Sears, Roebuck and Co. and Montgomery Ward (popularized with the expansion of mail delivery) and the advent of department stores in major urban centers.

## Designers and Other Influences

Fashion before 1870 meant that every woman was essentially a dressmaker. For inspiration she would look to her friends and neighbors, most of whom would be concerned with some degree of respectability, just as she was. Influence from Europe found its way to the United States through publications such as *Godey's Lady's Book*, where the latest styles were illustrated.

Respectability meant looking to one's social betters—which meant, for all practical purposes, being somehow influenced by the designer Charles Frederick Worth. An Englishman who established the House of Worth in Paris in 1857, he dressed society women in Europe and the United States, along with royalty and others seeking social status. Along with Worth (who is often considered to be the father of haute couture), other designers based in Paris included Jeanne Paquin, a competitor, and Jacques Doucet of the House of Doucet, established in the mid-1800s as a producer of lingerie and men's clothing and accessories.

In addition to more widely available information about fashion (including *Vogue* magazine, which began publication in 1892), photography was a significant factor in fashion's development in the 19th century. First in use in the 1840s, technology continued to improve, and many Americans, particularly after the Civil War, had more opportunities to see what they—and other people—looked like. Comparison being a surefire way to encourage criticism or envy, no doubt more than one woman saw a photograph and thought, I want to wear *that*.

Conservative Victorian dress from 1902 (top); design by the House of Worth from 1930 (middle); and a cover of *Vogue* from 1894 (bottom).

## THE 1900S: THE BEAUTIFUL AGE

When Queen Victoria died in 1901, the new century had just turned and progress was evident. However, the first decade of the 20th century had more in common with the 19th; the so-called Edwardian Age, during the reign of King Edward VII, clung to the classical and opulent in dress and manner. Changes certainly occurred, and what was known as *La Belle Epoque* ("The Beautiful Age") would vanish in the upheaval of World War I.

## Social and Cultural Conditions

The U.S. population had reached 75.9 million by 1900—and it continued to grow, with immigrants pouring in through Ellis Island and other ports. In contrast to the opulence enjoyed by the wealthy, many of these new immigrants, mostly city-dwellers, lived in extreme poverty and hardship. As the divide between rich and poor became more pronounced, charities and other social institutions struggled to improve conditions as these new workers entered the U.S. economy. Women continued working, with 20 percent earning wages outside the home in 1902; by 1910, nearly 25 percent did so.

Mobility was increasing everywhere. Bicycling became a popular recreational pastime. Automobiles, a novelty in the late 1800s, were produced by the thousands by 1907, and Americans who could afford them were eager to get in the driver's seat. Wilbur and Orville Wright introduced the country to the possibility of air travel in 1903. Telephones became widespread, facilitating the ease of communication.

Aside from a brief economic downturn in 1907, most of the country was prospering during this decade—which means that more people had money to spend on entertainment. Theater, opera, and vaudeville were all enormously popular, and "mov-

ing pictures," which had sprouted up in the late 1890s, became a hit when *The Great Train Robbery*, the first movie with a real storyline, was shown in 1903. And while the devastation of the San Francisco earthquake in 1906 may have shocked the nation, the photographs and film reels of the city also served to unite it.

## Fashion Trends and Developments

The turn of the century featured a preference for a mature female silhouette compatible with the Edwardian fashions of the day. This pouter pigeon figure, accentuating a small waist with rounded curves above and below, required the S-bend corset (also known as the straight or erect form). Bodices were also boned, and bloused out above; sleeves were long, and skirts were worn close to the hip and featured gores that flared into a trumpet shape. Sleeves became shorter and fuller—including the famously exaggerated leg o' mutton look—but the basic components did not change drastically until the middle of the decade, when the princess shape slimmed the look down considerably. Still voluminous were hair and hats, the former piled and poufed, the latter wide, round, and elaborately decked out with ribbon, feathers, and bows.

Men's fashion tended toward a blockier shape, with three-piece suits and the sack coat with no waistline seams. Shirt tailoring was stiff and formal, with starched fronts; these later gave way to more relaxed styles, and men eventually began to omit vests and even jackets.

Recreation had an impact on fashion in this period too, most notably with the full, knee-length pants known as bloomers (for women) and knickers (for men) adopted for cycling. Modesty nevertheless prevailed in swimwear, with women's costumes featuring over-the-knee skirts and dark stockings. Though sportswear was in its infancy, the concept of practical clothing took hold.

## Designers and Other Influences

The overall formality of the decade kept the Paris designers in business, with Doucet responding to the art nouveau influences with decorative designs, and the house of Callot Soeurs specializing in lace. Paquin and the House of Worth remained prominent, with Jean-Philippe Worth taking over the business from his father.

Perhaps the most indelible fashion image of the early 1900s is the Gibson Girl, created by illustrator Charles Dana Gibson. Though she featured the popular curved figure of the day, the twist was that she was also a "new woman" who was independent and active in addition to being beautiful. Her counterpart was the Arrow Collar Man, fashioned as a clean-cut and sporty version of masculinity.

This was also a decade when fashion began to get into the streets. As more working-class men and women went to amusement parks, dance halls, and movie theaters, they had more opportunity to see what "the swells" were wearing and could attempt to imitate a frill on a blouse or the flip on the brim of a hat. The pace of fashion news picked up and spread from cities to towns and the country, paving the way for even more radical change with the advent of a war that would redraw the boundaries of the world.

Bicycling increased mobility everywhere and fashioned the "new woman" (top). Men's sack coat, 1850 (right). The Gibson Girl, as exemplified by Camille Clifford, is independent and active in addition to being beautiful (left).

## THE 1910S: NEW FASHIONS TAKE HOLD

The 20th century can be said to have really gotten underway after 1910, and the decade saw the full changeover to mass production of everything from clothing to foodstuffs to Model T Fords. Manufacturing continued to step up with the production of armaments and other supplies to assist the Allied European countries when World War I broke out in 1914. Long before the United States officially entered the war in 1917, the mood was one of preparation. The first income tax was introduced in 1913 as one way to cover war expenditures. Women took over jobs in heavy industry when men were drafted into the armed forces.

### Social and Cultural Conditions

Entertainment thrived in the United States, with a flourishing of popular songs and the public's new-found fascination with movies and movie stars. The film industry established itself in Hollywood, and the studio "star system" was born—along with movie fan magazines, which made household names of the players. Old-fashioned dances like the waltz and minuet were superseded by the new fox trot and "Castle Walk," made popular by the performing duo Irene and Vernon Castle.

### Fashion Trends and Developments

Even before the United States officially entered the war, the operating principle was about cutting back—and fashion followed suit. Manufacturers used lighter materials and construction, and the fussy silhouettes of the previous decade disappeared. Narrower lines and brighter colors prevailed. Styles gave a nod to modernism and other avant-garde influences, such as the theatrical costumes worn by the Ballet Russes troupe of dancers who performed to great acclaim in Paris. This resulted in some new and startling designs such as harem trousers, turbans, the hobble skirt, and the lampshade dress. These bohemian styles weren't for everyone, but the slimmed-down and sloping shapes carried over into more day-to-day styles as well.

Men's fashion followed a similar trend, with boxy suits replaced by a less full line and lighter fabrics. The war introduced the streamlined trench coat, which was then adopted by the general public, and remains a fashion classic today. War shortages included color dyes, and for the years 1914 to 1918 basic black, white, tan, and blue were popular. Hemlines crept up to conserve fabric. As utilitarian styles took hold, accessorizing became popular: exposed ankles showed off embroidered stockings, and eyes and lips were darkened with newly available cosmetics that complemented the new short bobbed or permed hairstyles under smaller hats. The first rubber-soled shoe or sneaker, called Keds, was introduced in 1917.

### Designers and Other Influences

Paris was the epicenter for innovation, and many designers started their businesses during this period, including Jean Patou, Coco Chanel, and Madeleine Vionnet. Forced to close briefly during the war, they would rise to prominence in the 1920s. Fashion leaders of the 1910s were Paul Poiret, who was dramatic and introduced the most cutting-edge styles; Jeanne Sacerdote, known as Madame Jenny, worked in a style that was simpler than Poiret's and was widely copied. Mariano Fortuny was known for his reinterpretation of classic Grecian draping and pleating used in gowns and robes. As the war brought more Americans overseas for the first time, interest in French designers increased, and American ready-to-wear manufacturers rushed to copy them.

The new American stars of stage and screen were also a significant influence during this time. Women were enthralled with the frilly ingénue dresses worn by Mary Pickford and the vampish look of Theda Bara, and men copied Charlie Chaplin or Rudolph Valentino.

Irene Castle, 1910 (top left). Madame Poiret in a dress by Paul Poiret, 1919 (top right). The Ballet Russes, 1916 (bottom).

## THE 1920S: FASHION GETS MODERN

Americans were ready to move on when the war ended, and move they did. The 1920s were a time when nostalgia for the past was pushed aside for the fast and fun pursuits of a younger generation—who delighted in shocking their elders. Jazz music and new dances became all the rage, and when Prohibition was passed in 1919, it provided another excuse to break the rules. Women responded to the ratification of suffrage in 1920 by taking liberties they felt were due to them, from smoking and cursing in public to wearing heavy makeup and baring their arms. These flappers and their loose, daring styles were imitated by anyone who wanted to appear young.

### Social and Cultural Conditions

The cinema—now a full-fledged industry—provided new idols to aspire to such as "It" girl Clara Bow, Myrna Loy, and Claudette Colbert, and for the men, the dashing, masculine ideal of Douglas Fairbanks. Ever fickle, the young population abandoned silent film stars who couldn't measure up when films with sound, dubbed "talkies," were introduced in 1927 (the same year the first Academy Awards were presented), and Americans became enamored of a talking mouse when Walt Disney introduced Mickey in 1928. Mass media continued its expansion with the first commercial radio station in 1920, and by the end of the decade, many, if not most, Americans owned or had access to radios of their own. Prosperity ended with the stock market crash of 1929, and the next 10 years would carry a more somber tone.

### Fashion Trends and Developments

As conventions fell away, so did restricting waistlines and skirts. To dance the Charleston, the Tango,

or the Black Bottom, spirited flappers wanted clothing that was loose, free, and above all, fun. The straight-cut chemise dress (often sleeveless) straightened the line of the body, and as hemlines rose to knee length, the dresses were augmented with fringe and beads that swung as one moved. The boyish silhouette was complemented by costume finery such as long necklaces and T-strap shoes for dancing, often with highly decorative heels. Hair became even shorter with the shingle bob, and hats were close-fitting cloches; makeup, now widely available, was worn dark around the eyes and emphasized a bow-pointed lip. The extremely short and bare styles changed again toward the end of the decade, as flappers grew up. By 1928, hemlines were longer again and pointed in back, and dresses at least skimmed the waistline again.

Men's fashions were still more conventional, with suits being the norm. There was a rise in sportswear for both men and women, and the layers of times past were streamlined to fit modern life. Clothing for tennis and golf popularized sleeveless shirts, argyle sweaters, and saddle oxfords. Women's swimwear utilized knits, became shorter, and revealed bare arms and legs, the better for achieving the now-desirable suntan—resulting in the arrest of young women at public beaches who sported the more daring styles.

### Designers and Other Influences

Parisian designers flourished in the postwar period. This was the heyday of Coco Chanel, who introduced the "little black dress" coveted by modern women everywhere, and pioneered the use of casual fabrics and chic sportswear separates. Also emphasizing new sportswear designs was Jean Patou, whose pleated skirts and pullover tops were a hit with sports stars and café society alike. Madeleine Vionnet created inventive styles with handkerchief and asymmetrical hems, geometric shapes, and cowl and halter necklines. More romantic interpretations from the period include those of Jeanne Lanvin, whose dresses were longer and fuller; her wide-ranging talent also led her to produce tubular dresses and coordinated separates. Also important among the Paris ateliers was Edward Molyneux, whose British heritage influenced his designs for modern, streamlined suits.

French designers also began to turn an eye to what American consumers were buying. As ready-to-wear apparel became more fashionable and desirable, U.S. manufacturers produced copies, or knockoffs, of popular Parisian looks.

Clara Bow, 1927 (top). Coco Chanel, 1937 (bottom). Design by Madeleine Vionnet (middle).

## THE 1930S: MAKING DO

If the previous 10 years had been freewheeling, the worldwide economic downturn that ushered in the 1930s brought a new frugality. The Depression era was a time when people were encouraged to "make do" with what they had—and many had little, with unemployment at an all-time high. In the United States, Franklin Delano Roosevelt was elected president in 1932 and instituted a wide-ranging program of social relief, from the Works Progress Administration and National Industrial Recovery Administration to the very practical repeal of Prohibition.

### Social and Cultural Conditions

As a relief from what seemed like constant bad news, Americans turned in droves to Hollywood, which provided the glamour of musicals, sharp-tongued comedies, and gangster films. The exploits of British royalty also provided a distraction, and when King Edward VIII gave up his throne for the love of divorcee Wallis Simpson, the media crowned them fashion icons. It was also a decade in which many literary classics were penned, including John Steinbeck's *The Grapes of Wrath* and Margaret Mitchell's *Gone with the Wind*. With Germany's invasion of Poland in 1939, the economic woes of the decade lessened, as industries in the United States and abroad began gearing up for war.

### Fashion Trends and Developments

Hemlines fell along with the stock market and stayed long throughout the decade. The overall look was softer and more feminine, with clothing fitting closer to the body. A slender silhouette still dominated, and the waistline returned, accentuated with belts. Both day and evening dresses were long and narrow, often offset by broader shoulders or draped necklines, emulating slinky Hollywood glamour

with bias cuts and light fabrics. Skirts were featured with yokes and gathers. The new rubberized Lastex fabric revolutionized the undergarment industry by introducing two-way stretch, and girdles and bras offered better shaping under clingy fabrics. Nylon stockings were introduced in 1938 and were an overnight sensation (though they would be rationed just short years later). Gloves and hats remained important accessories, and women favored the Marcel wave for hair and the platinum color of actress Jean Harlow. Men's clothing in the 1930s followed trends similar to those of women's apparel, streamlining throughout the decade and gradually acquiring broader, padded shoulders.

Casual styles continued to gain popularity for both men and women, as more people participated in sports. Here, too, Hollywood exerted an influence: as more starlets were wearing one-piece swimsuits or the snug dancing costumes of lavish musical productions, body-consciousness became widely accepted. Sportswear styles such as the cardigan coat or sweater were adopted for leisure time, and the 1932 Winter Olympics in Lake Placid, New York, encouraged sleeker trousers with stretch cuffs for many sports.

### Designers and Other Influences

Fewer American department store buyers made the trip to Paris during the 1930s, and American designers in New York and on the West Coast began to achieve prominence. Designers such as Elizabeth Hawes and Clare Potter addressed the growing demand for clothes to suit an active lifestyle, producing sportswear and softer, casual designs. Dressmakers such as Hattie Carnegie and Nettie Rosenstein ran highly successful businesses, and others, such as Muriel King, began their careers in art and illustration and designed costumes for films. Hollywood-influenced designs were epitomized by the flowing, ruffle-sleeved dress worn by Joan Crawford in *Letty Lynton* (designed by Adrian)—and a new kind of California glamour turned up in the form of the tailored men's trousers worn by Marlene Dietrich and Katharine Hepburn.

One American designer who successfully established himself in Paris was Mainbocher, whose elegant evening designs were favored by the Duchess of Windsor. There he joined a strong fashion group dominated at the time by Chanel and Elsa Schiaparelli, who experimented with the surrealist art of Salvador Dalí and Jean Cocteau to design wearable fashion. Molyneux remained a force, with his slimlined suiting, and Vionnet's bias cut was a signature look of the decade. Madame Grès was known for her intricate draped, wrapped, and pleated gowns.

Duchess of Windsor, 1937 (top). Elsa Schiaparelli, 1932 (middle). Joan Crawford, 1932 (bottom).

## THE 1940S: WAR AND DUTY

For the second time in the 20th century, the world was engaged in large-scale war. From the years 1939 to 1945, war was the dominating factor of life, most devastatingly in Continental Europe but also in Asia and the Pacific. While the United States avoided attacks on its mainland, Japan's surprise attack on the Hawaiian base of Pearl Harbor in December 1941 committed the country to a grueling 4 years. Wartime rationing affected food, transportation, and the apparel industry, with governmental controls over the amount of fabric that could be used for clothing. As men went off to battle, women—as they had during World War I—assumed industrial and other jobs formerly occupied by men.

### Social and Cultural Conditions

As the roles of men and women shifted, society moved toward a loosening of formality and convention—a trend that has continued to this day. Another westward migration (no less significant than the one that had occurred in the 1800s) took place with thousands of men and women relocating across the country to munitions plants and military bases. California's population grew by more than 70 percent during this time. The film industry still provided an escape from the wartime headlines, but Hollywood was pressed into patriotic duty with many stars spending time entertaining the troops or selling war bonds.

A return to traditional family values began to take hold after 1946, when returning soldiers completed college on the GI Bill and started families. Americans would experience a new prosperity and shift in values.

### Fashion Trends and Developments

Fashion for more than half of the decade was "on duty": subject to restrictions to conserve fabric and therefore shorter, sharper, and with a distinct military influence. Women's suits were tailored and mannish-looking, with padded shoulders and peplum jackets nipped in at the waist. Shoes were rationed and became more practical for walking (with gasoline rationed as well). To offset the sharp lines of clothing, accessories, hair, and makeup imitated the carefree glamour of stars like pinup girl Betty Grable. Hair was longer and rolled, lipstick a patriotic red, and hats, though small, were jauntily perched and often whimsically decorated. With more severe shortages in Europe, fashionable women in both Europe and the United States adopted the turban or scarf as a head covering.

Hawaiian shirts and other Pacific-inspired designs like the sarong enjoyed popularity. The growing teenage population in the United States adopted the bobbysoxer look, including slacks for girls.

When wartime restrictions were lifted, clothing began to become fuller and more formal again. French designer Christian Dior made a splash with the introduction of his full, feminine "New Look" in 1947. With this success, he was credited with rescuing French haute couture from obsolescence—though Parisian designers would now have to share fashion's stage with the Americans who had risen in prominence during the years of the war.

### Designers and Other Influences

Perhaps the biggest shift that occurred during the 1940s was that the designers in occupied Paris were effectively shut down. With a lack of European influence, American designers earned their due. Claire McCardell worked within rationing guidelines to produce dresses and play clothes that were simple in shape, including practical wardrobe staples like the dirndl skirt and popover dress. Other designers who successfully created clothes that were both stylish and practical were Tina Leser, Norman Norell, and Mildred Orrick, and Hattie Carnegie's ready-to-wear business thrived. Essential in shifting the focus from French to American designers was the appropriation of the Best-Dressed List from Paris, where it had originated as a publicity stunt for the venerable Mainbocher. As reinterpreted by publicist Eleanor Lambert, the annual list highlighted American women and an American sensibility of style.

In the later 1940s, Paris regained its foothold as a design center. Along with Dior were Pierre Balmain (who claimed credit for the New Look that Dior became celebrated for), Jacques Fath, and Nina Ricci, all of whom would make significant contributions to the feminine, more formal styles of the 1950s.

The turban headcovering was a popular trend in the 1940s (left). Dior "New Look" (top).

## THE 1950S: NEW PROSPERITY

Postwar was a boom period for Americans, who experienced an explosion in both the birth rate and the economy. All that wartime industry matured into the production of new consumer goods to fill the home: electric stoves and vacuum cleaners, toys, games, and gadgets. Televisions became the latest form of family entertainment, and shows such as *I Love Lucy* and *The Honeymooners* gave films stiff competition. With an overriding mood of conservatism, men and women reassumed more traditional masculine and feminine roles; many women who had worked outside of the home in the previous decade returned to homemaking, and the nuclear family was held up as the ideal.

### Social and Cultural Conditions

Bolstering the mood were film and television icons who seemed almost a throwback to the more independent icons of the wartime years: curvy sexpots like Marilyn Monroe and girl-next-door Doris Day, and well-dressed housewife models such as Donna Reed.

The West Coast lured Beat writers Allen Ginsberg and Jack Kerouac; Kerouac's road novel *On the Road* became a classic for the disaffected. Civil rights issues were brewing, and Rosa Parks's arrest in 1955 for refusing to relinquish her bus seat to a white passenger resulted in widespread protests. When the Civil Rights Act was passed in 1957, the struggle gained momentum. And though the majority of America's teenagers during the 1950s seemed happily and selfishly absorbed with their rock and roll (including parental shocker Elvis Presley), they were also drawn to films like *Rebel Without a Cause*. They would indeed rebel in earnest once they got a little older.

### Fashion Trends and Developments

The return to more traditional roles meant softer and fuller styles for women. Fashion also tended toward more conformity, with fashion editors in *Vogue* and *Harper's Bazaar* issuing decrees about the appropriate length and width for skirts. Full-skirted dresses as well as the narrower shirtwaist dress were available for daytime wear, but dressing for cocktails and other evening social events became more constructed for women again, with dresses featuring crinolines under wide skirts, boned bodices, and structured undergarments. When the stiletto heel was introduced in 1951, the thicker heels from the wartime era all but disappeared. Many of these feminine styles were worn by teenage girls too—though often given a more playful feel, with full poodle skirts and ballerina shoes. The twin set (cardigan and shell) was worn by women and teens alike, and matching mother–daughter dresses were popular as well.

For men, the 1950s was the time of the gray flannel suit, often accompanied by a fedora hat. While formality in the workplace was the accepted standard, leisure-time separates such as sports jackets and short-sleeved shirts were also worn. Casual clothes for all members of the family were given a boost with the invention of wash-and-wear fabrics such as acrylic and Orlon. Dungarees or jeans were another popular youth style, cuffed for after-school dress or, for truly rebellious types, worn with a white T-shirt and leather jacket like Marlon Brando.

### Designers and Other Influences

The trend toward formality brought French designers back into the spotlight, with Dior and Balmain leading the way. Jacques Fath introduced a slightly leaner silhouette and was known for his pointed collars; he also made inroads into the American ready-to-wear market before his death in 1954. Chanel reopened her atelier in that same year, and her collarless wool tweed suits, while not popular in France, achieved near-cult status in the United States. Italian designers arranged their first collective couture show in 1951 and started to become noticed; the House of Gucci, in particular, had a good deal of success with leather accessories. Other European influences included Queen Elizabeth II of England, who wore a dress by British designer Norman Hartnell at her 1953 coronation, and polished, ladylike film star Grace Kelly, who retired from films in 1956 when she married Prince Rainier of Monaco.

American designers like Claire McCardell continued to gain recognition—even earning coverage in the French fashion press. The generally less-structured styles being produced in New York and California were more appropriate for the ready-to-wear market. Norman Norell showed collections featuring a range of suits, day dresses, and formal wear. Charles James and Arnold Scaasi were known for their structured and dramatic clothing, while on the other end of the spectrum, Californian Bonnie Cashin, who had worked as a costume designer in Hollywood, specialized in layered, comfortable clothing for active women. Perhaps heralding the end of designer-dictated fashion, an unlikely fashion icon was introduced in 1959 in the form of Barbie, the doll who would come to incur both admiration and wrath for her idealized figure and fashion-forwardness.

James Dean (left). The gray flannel suit and fedora hat, as popularized by Gregory Peck, 1956 (right).

## THE 1960s: TIMES ARE A-CHANGING

The so-called Baby Boom generation came of age during the 1960s and set off a fast-forward "youthquake" surpassing even that of the 1920s. In a period of protests, antiwar demonstrations, and generational conflicts, the world seemed to be in constant chaos. The decade began on a note of progressiveness and optimism with the election of President John F. Kennedy but soured dramatically when he was assassinated in 1963. The conflict in Vietnam escalated and race riots dominated the evening news; 1968 was one of the most violent on record, with student revolts in France, Germany, Eastern Europe, and Mexico and, in the United States, the assassinations of civil rights leader Martin Luther King Jr. and favored Democratic presidential candidate Bobby Kennedy within two months of each other.

### Social and Cultural Conditions

Turmoil proved conducive to arts and music, however, and a cross-fertilization of styles emerged from the "British Invasion" of the Beatles and Rolling Stones to American homegrown talents such as Janis Joplin, Bob Dylan, and the Beach Boys. The San Francisco neighborhood of Haight-Ashbury became synonymous with "flower power" and hippies during the 1967 Summer of Love, and the Woodstock music festival in 1969 was a defining moment for youth culture. And it is important not to forget that the 1960s were a time when advances in science and technology outpaced anything seen before, with the introduction of the birth control pill igniting a sexual revolution and astronaut Neil Armstrong stepping out onto the moon in 1969.

### Fashion Trends and Developments

In the first years of the decade, conservatism was in evidence to a degree: women still wore full or longer skirts and fitted suits, although the teen crowd had already experimented with slightly higher hemlines. Men wore pressed slacks and sports jackets and were short-haired and clean-cut in the manner of "safe" pop and folk singers such as Pat Boone and the Kingston Trio. Women raced to copy First Lady Jackie Kennedy's suits with boxy little jackets and her signature pillbox hat. The Best-Dressed List continued to identify prominent socialites and actresses such as Audrey Hepburn as arbiters of American chic, although the concept of "dressing well" would change in interesting ways as the decade progressed.

The most visible fashions of the times were the most radical. Shift dresses climbed over the knee and then higher still, with the miniskirt making its debut in 1966 (and the even shorter micromini a few years later). Eastern influences showed up in caftans and Nehru jackets. Wild colors, op-art designs, and swirling Pucci prints became popular. Complimenting these shorter looks was the white mid-calf boot known as the go-go boot, and brightly colored and patterned tights completed the look. Other new shapes included the babydoll dress and bell-bottom pants and jeans. Beach and surf culture made the bikini a swimwear staple, though designer Rudi Gernreich's topless monokini was too wild for most.

More than in any other decade, the 1960s produced styles that demanded niche marketing to specific customers. More mature adults gravitated toward more tailored looks, while the fashionable youth crowd browsed trendy boutiques. And once the counterculture really got underway, young people ransacked Army-Navy stores, their grandmother's closet, and anywhere else to pull together their flower-child costumes—elements of which were then appropriated by haute couture at a much higher price.

This was also the decade for hair as fashion. From bouffants and falls to wigs, ironing, pixie cuts, or simply long and untamed, hair became an expression of individuality for women. The same applied to men as well. The Beatles' mop-top that had been considered too long in 1963 was, by the end of the 1960s, practically uptight. In 1968, the rock musical *Hair* gloried in long locks, the Age of Aquarius, and love beads.

## Designers and Other Influences

The big fashion story of the decade was swinging London, where Mary Quant introduced the miniskirt (cut shorter than in New York) and the Biba boutique sold a "total look" that coordinated dresses with tights and shoes. The rock group the Rolling Stones introduced the Carnaby Street "peacock" look for men to the United States. With styles that were easier to copy—and with rapid knockoffs being an increasing trend—French designers accustomed to the world of the atelier struggled to keep pace. Those influenced by futuristic design were Andre Courrèges, Paco Rabanne, Pierre Cardin, and Emanuel Ungaro. On the more conservative side of things, Hubert de Givenchy, known for dressing Jackie Kennedy and Audrey Hepburn, was successful with an older clientele. In the United States, designers such as Bill Blass and Oscar de la Renta succeeded in providing styles

that were updated but still ladylike, while up-and-comer Betsey Johnson catered to the youth market. Bonnie Cashin, working in California, continued her line of sportswear separates (including shorts, ponchos, and culottes), while another California designer, James Galanos, became known for the floaty chiffon evening look, a more formal turn.

Jackie Kennedy's signature pillbox hat, 1961 (left). Audrey Hepburn stars in *Breakfast at Tiffany's*, 1961 (right). Gernreich design, 1967 (top). Miniskirts, 1965–1966 (center).

## THE 1970S: FASHION AND THE "ME" DECADE

Social unrest remained a hallmark of the 1970s. Americans were divided by the war in Vietnam and the struggle of women and minorities to achieve equal rights. By the mid-1970s, the economy was at its lowest point since the Great Depression. Baby boomers, partly as a reaction to the chaos of the 1960s (and simply because they were getting older), set out to "find themselves" by whatever means possible.

### Social and Cultural Conditions

Television was quick to adapt, featuring shows depicting single working women who ran the gamut from *The Mary Tyler Moore Show* to *Charlie's Angels* and families who gave a nod to unconventionality, like the *Brady Bunch*. Magazines also saw change during this time. American *Vogue* featured a black model on the front cover for the first time in August 1974.

### Fashion Trends and Developments

Fashionwise, "anything goes" was the mantra of the 1970s. The hippie style of the counterculture continued to be popular with the younger generation (particularly those who had missed out on Woodstock), and also persisting throughout the decade were short skirts and long hair. Nobody could seem to make up their minds about skirt lengths, and along with minis there were midi and maxi lengths. (Many women, faced with confusing choices, gave up and simply wore pants instead; a more extreme choice were hot pants, or short shorts.) For men, the polyester leisure suit with pointed collars and open shirts were the stylish outfit of choice. Denim (especially designer jeans) soared in popularity for everyone, becoming acceptable for dress as well as casual wear. Platform shoes reached new heights and were worn by both sexes, and the 1970s might also be called the decade of the boot, which were produced in all kinds of leather, suede, vinyl, and patchwork prints.

Although there were many options, with influences ranging from ethnic designs to disco to glam rock and punk, the entrance of significant numbers of women into the professional workforce created a demand for appropriate office attire. With the publication of *Dress for Success* in 1975 and *The Woman's Dress for Success Book* in 1977, men's suits were feminized for women in slim, no-nonsense shapes.

### Designers and Other Influences

Designers responded to the times by introducing a variety of styles, but even fashion editors admitted that there were no longer "rules" to dictate one's choices. As a result, the business of French haute couture suffered. An exception was Yves Saint Laurent, whose often romantic designs and haute-bohemian looks were deemed easy enough to emulate with knockoffs. The Italian design team Missoni emerged with elegant, patterned knitwear. In London, British designer Vivienne Westwood brought the deconstructed, anarchist elements of punk style to the fore, while her compatriot Zandra Rhodes worked the aesthetic in a more glamorous mode.

With casual wear as the dominant mode, however, the 1970s was really a time for American designers to shine. In 1973, Eleanor Lambert produced a benefit fashion show at the palace of Versailles, which featured both French and American designers. The show was a hit, and this eventually lead to the spread of American fashion around the world. Ralph Lauren and Calvin Klein made their debuts, both producing wearable wardrobe separates with a nod to menswear. Klein became known for his neutral colors and minimalist approach to design, while Lauren traded in classic nostalgia (he designed the costumes for two popular films of the era, *Annie Hall* and *The Great Gatsby*). Diane von Furstenberg introduced her one-piece wrap dress in 1973, and its immediate success landed her on the cover of *Time* magazine. Anne Klein was another well-known designer of high-quality sportswear until her death in 1974; one of the design successors of her company was the young Donna Karan, who would make her mark in the 1980s. And no discussion of the 1970s would be complete without mention of Halston, whose simple, clinging dresses—a staple of the Studio 54 nightlife clique—became instant classics.

Fashion was influenced by popular culture more than ever. From John Travolta's white suit in *Saturday Night Fever* to Farrah Fawcett's feathered hair, trends in the 1970s came and went as fast as new media idols appeared. It's almost no wonder that nostalgia for this decade of self-expression didn't take long to come back around.

Beverly Johnson was the first black model to be featured on the front cover of American Vogue in 1974 (top left). Suits in the 1970s came in a variety of prints and color; from left, the leisure suit, evening suit, resort suit, and country suit (top right). A benefit fashion show at the palace of Versailles, France, 1973 (bottom).

## Eleanor Lambert
### *The Lady...*

**P**ublicity genius Eleanor Lambert, who died at 100 years of age in 2003, was the lady who made New York the world capital of fashion. Starting in 1940, she organized a biannual Press Week for Seventh Avenue (the forerunner of today's Fashion Week), founded the Costume Institute and the Council of Fashion Designers of America (CFDA), and started The List. Not bad for a petite pale blonde from Crawfordsville, Indiana, who was called a "hayseed" when she first arrived on the fashion scene.

Eleanor started the International Best-Dressed List in New York in 1940 at the beginning of World War II, basing it on a French Best-Dressed List that came to an end when France fell to the Nazis. The point of the list was to promote and publicize fashion and American designers. At the beginning, the list was made up of very rich women, socialites, members of royalty, and occasionally a movie star. Ten years later the number of movie stars had increased substantially and as times changed, so did The List. The international stars of fashion who had ruled for 30 years or more died and were replaced by younger people who had a far different feel and attitude toward fashion.

Over the more than 65 years that The List has been part of the social and fashion scenes it has been praised, denounced, and dissected, but never, never ignored. The List has survived war, revolutions, countercultures, and right now it may be more important than ever. As John Fairchild of *WWD* says, "We're more list minded these days than before, certainly more celebrity and publicity conscious. I believe the Best-Dressed List is more important now than it's ever been."

Eleanor Lambert, who maintained the International Best-Dressed List through a World War, periodic counterculture rebellions, 12 presidential administrations, and beyond, into a new century, and who single handedly captured the flag of fashion from Europe and planted it on American soil—would certainly agree with Mr. Fairchild. The List has maintained its importance because fashion is a phenomenal and a sociological barometer, and Eleanor called the Best-Dressed List a "piece of social history." "You cannot separate people, their yearnings, their dreams, and their inborn vanity from an interest in clothes."

In 2002, the year before she died, Eleanor Lambert chose to entrust *Vanity Fair* and four of its editors with the future of the list. Take a look at some other best-dressed people on the social and fashion scenes—past and present.

Actor Cary Grant (above left) was inducted into the International Best-Dressed List Hall of Fame in 1969 and actor George Clooney (above right) was honored in 2007.

Actress Audrey Hepburn (bottom left) earned her spot in the Hall of Fame in 1961, while author Marina Rust Connor (bottom right) was a recent addition in 2007.

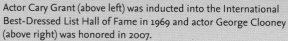

...And "The List" Then & NOW

## THE 1980S: POP CULTURE AND EXCESS

No other decade exemplifies excess quite like the 1980s. Although the decade began on a low note, with continued inflation and the continuing hostage crisis in Iran, the social landscape changed when Ronald Reagan came into office as president. He and his wife, Nancy, set a more glamorous stamp on the White House. Americans, eager for new wealth themselves, played along. This was the era of the "yuppie," or young urban professional, who engaged in conspicuous consumption—and many were women, primarily baby boomers who had worked their way up to executive-level positions and wanted to enjoy their newfound financial security. Food and fashion were status symbols, and it seemed that these yuppies couldn't get enough of sushi or arugula or the latest Gucci bag. The stock market was suddenly sexy—even middle-class investors joined the game. "Greed is good," went the tagline from the hit movie *Wall Street*—and most seemed to agree. The mood lasted until the stock market crashed in 1987.

### Social and Cultural Conditions

The corresponding advancements in technology had a profound effect on the way Americans spent their leisure time. Apple introduced the Macintosh in 1984, and by the end of the decade, they were used in offices, homes, and schools. Videocassette players (VCRs) and cable television brought movies into the home, and with your Sony Walkman, you could take music cassette tapes (and later, CDs) along on your commute or to the gym. Exercising became an industry in itself, with shiny new gyms boasting the latest in Nautilus fitness machines. But perhaps nothing revolutionized pop culture (and the emerging Generation X, born after the baby boomers) like the advent of MTV in 1981. The art of the music video was born, and it made international stars of those performers who could best exploit the medium: Madonna, Michael Jackson, and many more.

### Fashion Trends and Developments

There were a variety of fashion influences in the 1980s, but whatever the source of inspiration, the general idea was that bigger was better. Whether it was the shoulders on one of Nancy Reagan's red suits, the romantic style and signature hats of Princess Di, or the bleached, permed, ratted, and tied-up hair flaunted by pop star Madonna, this principle held true. More disposable income meant that conspicuous consumption was acceptable, and dressing for success took on a new meaning. Suits were slick and sharp, and the padded shoulder, for both women and men, was everywhere. "Power dressing" was the name of the game, and women embraced it in executive-style outfits featuring big shoulders, close-fitting skirts, and blouses with dolman or batwing sleeves. The sharp wedge cut (an inverted triangle) was popular for dresses. This was a style to aspire to, even if you hadn't yet worked your way up the executive ladder, and it gave birth to another trend (still sometimes visible today): white high-top Reebok athletic shoes (an 1980s staple) worn with the suits, over pantyhose, for the commute to the office. With pumps tucked safely in the briefcase. For nighttime, no amount of pouff or glitz was too much. As exemplified by actresses Joan Collins and Linda Evans in the nighttime television drama *Dynasty* (with costumes designed by Nolan Miller), fabrics were printed, shiny, threaded with gold, and often period-inspired.

Men had options as well—and there was more on the market for them to choose from. The emphasis on the yuppie lifestyle meant that owning at least one good suit was key, and those by Giorgio Armani were a favored choice. Wall Streeters (or those who wanted to look like them) also imitated the suspender look worn by actor Michael Douglas. As a casual alternative, the unstructured jackets worn over T-shirts and shoes without socks worn by Don Johnson and Philip Michael Thomas in the television show *Miami Vice* was the dominant look.

The pop music scene played an enormous part in 1980s fashion, due to the visibility of MTV. This was true especially for teenagers and those in their early twenties, who rushed out to shopping malls to imitate the short skirts, lace stockings, leggings, and see-through shirts worn by Madonna in her earliest incarnation. Later, when she changed her look to the more polished costumes of her "Material Girl" persona, accessorizing changed again. Other pop and synth-pop group members provided inspiration with deconstructed looks and big or wedge-cut hair. And perhaps no movie had such a fashion impact as *Flashdance*, which caused thousands of young women to don dancers' leg warmers and off-shoulder tops.

## Designers and Other Influences

The desire for luxury in the 1980s allowed French couture designers to make their mark with extravagant designs. Christian Lacroix's pouf skirt was one of the most widely copied designs. Jean-Paul Gaultier designed Madonna's famous conical bra and other gender-bending ensembles featuring tailored suits and corsetry. Thierry Mugler put his stamp on the power suit with broad-shouldered, nipped-waist versions that combined both historic and futuristic elements. Azzedine Alaïa redefined the little black dress as short, tight, and sexy, and Karl Lagerfeld reinvigorated the house of Chanel when he assumed the role of head designer in 1982 by updating the classic boxy suit in a modern mode—along with heaps of accessories.

The fashion world also began to take note of Japanese designers, such as Rei Kawakubo and Yohji Yamamoto—both of whom worked in avant-garde and often deconstructed styles. Kenzo Takada introduced colorful designs for both men and women. Issey Miyake, an innovator of experimental twists and pleats, created clothing that was always challenging, often more art than apparel.

Other significant designers, in addition to Armani (best known for his suiting looks), were fellow Italians Gianni Versace and Franco Moschino. London designer Vivienne Westwood shifted her focus from punk to pirate. Designers in the United States produced ready-to-wear collections that were less extravagant than their European counterparts: Calvin Klein

and Ralph Lauren expanded their range of sportswear and suiting, Donna Karan introduced a more feminine (yet practical) look for working women, and Liz Claiborne produced affordable women's separates.

MTV caused an explosion in pop culture in the 1980s (top). Princess Diana, 1983 (middle). Rosanna Arquette and Madonna in *Desperately Seeking Susan*, 1985 (bottom).

## THE 1990S: FASHION IN THE INFORMATION AGE

Faced with a new recession as Americans retrenched after the 1987 stock market crash, the Persian Gulf War in 1991 polarized the country and President George H.W. Bush was defeated by Democrat Bill Clinton in 1992. There was a rapid rise of new technologies, computer culture expanded to include email and the Internet, and cell phones became commonplace items (earlier in Europe and Asia, later in the United States).

### Social and Cultural Conditions

Generation X was now a significant part of the workforce, and they tried to define themselves against the previous decade's excesses. More technologically savvy than the baby boomers but less sure of pursuing high-pressure careers, this group—some of whom ironically tagged themselves with the moniker "slacker"—made their presence known in music and other areas of entertainment.

Digital know-how gave rise to a do-it-yourself style of filming and showed up too in the growing prominence of electronic and hip-hop music. But perhaps the loudest influence was from the "alternative" scene, when garage rock bands (many from the Seattle area) burst onto the music scene in the early 1990s. Bands such as Nirvana, Soundgarden, and Pearl Jam popularized the "grunge" aesthetic and shifted the terrain from pop to harder rock. As the economy rebounded in the late 1990s, brighter sounds in music came again, with manufactured pop stars such as the teenaged Britney Spears making their mark.

### Fashion Trends and Developments

The somber mood of the early 1990s reflected the way people dressed, with laid-back minimalism and informality. Office attire became more casual, as Gen Xers in their twenties showed up to work in casual separates at new high-tech companies, and "casual Fridays" relaxed the dress code for men and women at all but the stuffiest of firms. The classic chino pant was a beneficiary of these casual office environments and was offered in many variations for both men and women by newly prominent ready-to-wear companies such as the Gap, J. Crew, and Banana Republic. Fashion took its inspiration from many places, and individualism, rather than fashion rules, became the norm.

Layering was a popular look, with women often in longer skirts, jackets, and vests; more stretch fabrics were introduced, and styles were generally looser and flowing. The slip dress enjoyed a fairly long run of popularity—either worn over a T-shirt for a casual look, in sinuous silk for evening, and, for the "grunge" crowd, often worn with clunky combat-style boots such as Doc Martens. The grunge look also instigated a run on old plaid flannel shirts and ratty lingerie slips, worn as outerwear—though an attempt by young designer Marc Jacobs to bring this look to the runway was a failure. Clothing for active sports became more specialized, with some, like stretchy yoga pants, becoming acceptable for daywear. As the economy enjoyed an upswing in the late 1990s, more polished and playful clothing was desirable.

### Designers and Other Influences

Minimalist Calvin Klein's streamlined suits and slim, bias-cut slip dresses were a distinctive and widely copied look in the early 1990s. For those interested in a more deconstructed or avant-garde take on minimalism, Belgian designers Ann Demeulemeester and Dries Van Noten, along with German Jil Sander, filled the requirement. Classic styles in a new mix of neutrals and patterns were offered by Miuccia Prada, and the black nylon Prada backpack became a much-copied status item. France experienced a changing of the guard when British designers John Galliano and Alexander

McQueen were chosen to head up the venerable houses of Dior and Givenchy respectively. This started a trend toward internationalism, as increasingly design houses merged into large corporate groups and brought in talent from other countries to reinvigorate their products and image. American Tom Ford was hired as creative director of the Gucci group and made a splash with his high-cut, revealing long dresses. Michael Kors, another American, worked during the 1990s at Céline, and Marc Jacobs was hired by Louis Vuitton.

Branding, rather than the signature style of any one design house or designer, became the norm during this time, and "lifestyle" dressing was the operative term. This allowed designers to assume more than one identity. In the United States, Tommy Hilfiger initially made his mark with rap-inspired styles, later turning to a more casual American preppy look and jeans. Anna Sui caught the pulse of the retro trend and incorporated touches from the 1940s and 1960s—as well as "street" looks—into her designs. Isaac Mizrahi worked in the classic chic mode of Geoffrey Beene. And rap star Sean Combs became one of the first celebrities to launch a fashion line, with his Sean John line that took the hip-hop look high-class.

Calvin Klein, 1998 (left). The grunge look of the 90s (right).

## THE 2000S: INTO THE 21ST CENTURY

The effects of the economic downturn were still in evidence following the high-tech industry's peak and fall. The first year of the new millennium brought the election of George W. Bush in a hotly contested election that was only decided by the Supreme Court—setting off the age of voting recounts (which would be revisited in the 2004 election as well) and further polarizing the country into a bitter, two-party deadlock. But the most devastating event of the early decade was the terrorist attacks in the United States on September 11, 2001, which shattered Americans' perception of security and invulnerability. After an outpouring of sympathy worldwide, the global tide took a different turn after the U.S. invasions of Afghanistan in 2002 and, especially, the invasion of Iraq in 2003. Terrorist attacks also persisted in various parts of the world, from London to Madrid. At the same time, technology and industry continued to extend itself with the outsourcing of jobs to Asian countries such as China and India—both of which are becoming international economic contenders. Combined with the emergence of the euro and the subsequent fall of the dollar's power, Americans today find that globalization has both significant benefits and challenges.

### Social and Cultural Conditions

The new century has also seen the continued rise in technology, with cell phones now used by almost everyone and the Internet often the first stop for purchasing merchandise ranging from clothing to cosmetics to food. These days it's unthinkable for a retailer to be without a Web site to display the company's image and where products can be purchased and shipped overnight—often from manufacturing and packing sites halfway across the globe. The remarkable success of eBay has paved the way for almost anyone to set up a Web site and become a merchant.

Apple's introduction of the portable iPod has again revolutionized the entertainment industry by offering yet another way for users to personalize their choices. More and more people worldwide participate in Internet social networking sites such as Facebook and MySpace, and the ability to expose oneself to the masses is reflected in reality television and a watered-down celebrity culture where trivia is news and news is often trivial. And taking stock of what the last century of progress has brought us—and what it will cost us—concern for the very earth itself has reached a critical point, with global warming providing a new impetus for technology to find solutions.

It remains to be seen how these many choices will play out, but one thing is for certain: consumers are now accustomed to having more of a say in what they buy and from whom. This new level of individualism will lead to more challenges and opportunities.

### Fashion Trends and Developments

More than ever, celebrity culture provides the inspiration for how people want to dress. And the very idea of "celebrity" itself has become more attainable: socialites such as Paris Hilton are essentially famous for being famous, and reality television "stars" are watched for their style choices as well. The act of participating in fashion by attending runway shows is seen as a legitimizing factor, with many a young starlet fighting for prominent front-row seats. A hierarchy still exists, of course, with serious actresses such as Nicole Kidman, Cate Blanchett, and Gwyneth Paltrow embodying a more classic and glamorous approach to style. Glamour may have been put away abruptly after the 9/11 attacks, when the uniform of choice at the 2002 Academy Awards was a sober black suit for both men and women, accented with tasteful jewels in patriotic red, white, and blue, but it has enjoyed a resurgence since then. For example, the television show *Sex and the City* set off the popularity of feminine, ladylike styles for high-powered women. This look coexists with more casual, mix-and-match styles with a variety of textures and patterns.

The most notable change in proportion so far has been short over long, and boxy swing coats and trapeze jackets worn over blouses or long T-shirts, often with skinny jeans. The babydoll dress has resurfaced, as have minidresses and short tunics. The idea of organic or "sustainable" fashion is taking hold (as a more knowledgeable, modern version of the 1970s back-to-nature theme). Retro and vintage looks are inspiration too, with many twists on old designs given a fresh hand by young and often local designers who use the Internet as their main method of gaining a following, rather than being associated with a large fashion house. In addition to New York, the cities of Los Angeles and Austin, Texas, are fertile ground. In Europe, the 2000s have seen the emergence of Berlin as the choice city of cool for fashion and other art. One surefire way of taking a local design shop national (or international) is to offer up a variation on the T-shirt, which has emerged in this decade as a true fashion item with many interpretations and price levels: companies such as American Apparel, C&C California, and James Perse are well known, and Juicy Couture has expanded from T-shirts and velour loungewear to the production of a runway line.

## Designers and Other Influences

Celebrity culture has given us more celebrities as designers (in addition to Sean John, there are fashion lines by stars including singers Gwen Stefani, Jennifer Lopez, and Justin Timberlake, among others). And designers have become celebrities themselves—no longer secluded in a rarified atmosphere, they are household names. This democratization of fashion has led established designers to embrace the concept of "design for all" by associating themselves with retail chain stores looking for an image boost: Isaac Mizrahi has found a new niche designing classic-cut women's clothing for Target, and, in 2008, was signed as the creative director for Liz Claiborne.

The stars of *Sex and the City* (top). Viktor & Rolf, 2008 (middle). Designs by Roberto Cavalli for H&M, 2008 (above).

The trendy Scandinavia-based chain H&M introduced the idea of limited-edition lines of clothing from designers such as Karl Lagerfeld, Roberto Cavalli, and Stella McCartney. (Not to be outdone, Target brought in British designer Alice Temperley for the fall 2007 season.) Major fashion houses have continued to come under the corporate umbrella of large luxury-brand conglomerates such as the French-owned LMVH and the Gucci Group, and designers come and go. Recent pairings include Nicolas Ghesquière at Balenciaga and Alexander McQueen with the Gucci Group, after departing Givenchy. In Britain, Christopher Bailey has modernized the Burberry line. Donatella Versace, who assumed design control of the line after her brother Gianni's shocking murder in 1997, has not only kept the house alive but brought it up-to-date with a ready-to-wear line.

Ready-to-wear is indeed the predominant aspect of design today; couture is more widely understood to be something a designer does to create hype, but successful styles will be modified in a more casual vein. In the United States, both Michael Kors and Marc Jacobs have grasped this principle well by running both high-end and more affordable bridge lines. Among younger designers, those making their mark are Zac Posen, Behnaz Sarafpour, and the design teams Proenza Schouler and Viktor Rolf.

## Summary and Review

It is said that for every action there's a reaction—and this is very true for fashion. In the 1900s fashion began to be seen in the streets, as the public went to amusement parks, dance halls, and movie theaters. The indelible fashion image of the early 1900s was the Gibson Girl. Featured with a popular curved figure, she was considered a "new woman" who was independent, active, and beautiful. Jeanne Paquin and the House of Worth were leading designers and Charles Frederick Worth gained recognition as the father of haute couture.

During the 1910s, the operating principle was about cutting back—and fashion followed suit. Manufacturers used lighter materials and construction, and fussy silhouettes disappeared. Entertainment thrived in the United States, and the public had a new-found fascination with movies and Hollywood stars. Jean Patou, Coco Chanel, Madeleine Vionnet, and Paul Poiret were the fashion leaders, with Mariano Fortuny introducing classic draping and pleating.

The 1920s brought jazz music and flappers who wore loose and daring styles. Coco Chanel became famous for her "little black dress;" Jean Patou emphasized new sportswear designs; Jeanne Lanvin produced tubular dresses and coordinated separates; and Madeleine Vionnet created inventive styles with handkerchief and asymmetrical hems.

The 1930s and early 1940s were the Depression era and in the early 40s World War II encompassed Europe, Asia, and America. These years proved to be a boom to American design and creativity. Elizabeth Havens, Clare Potter, Hattie Carnegie, Nettie Rosenstein, and Claire McCardell were all successful designer entrepreneurs of the time. In Hollywood, Adrian, the famous designer for successful Hollywood films, came into the public eye. After the war's end, Christian Dior introduced the "New Look" in 1947. Along with Dior, Pierre Balmain and Nina Ricci helped Paris regain its foothold as a design center.

The 1950s and 1960s brought American design to the forefront of the fashion industry. The Baby Boom generation came of age during the 1950s and 1960s, wearing Pucci prints, baby doll dresses, and bell-bottom pants and jeans. Mary Quant, Paco Rabanne, Pierre Cardin, Emanuel Ungaro, and Hubert de Givenchy were popular French and English designers, while Bill Blass, Oscar de la Renta, and James Galanos were American stars.

The 1970s was the "anything goes" decade. Skirt lengths ranged from microminis, minis, midis, and maxi lengths. Fashion influences ranged from ethnic design to disco to glam rock and punk. This was the time of Yves Saint Laurent, Missoni suits, Vivienne Westwood, and Zandra Rhodes from Britain. Ralph Lauren and Calvin Klein made their debut; Diane von Furstenberg introduced her one-piece wrap denim in 1973, and Halston's simple, clinging dresses became instant classics.

Excess exemplifies the decade of the 1980s. There were a variety of fashion influences in the 1980s, but the general idea was that "bigger is better." For women, "power dressing" was the name of the game. The 1980s was a boon to French couture designers Christian Lacroix, Jean-Paul Gaultier, Thierry Mugler, Azzedine Alaïa, and Karl Lagerfeld, who designed new and exciting silhouettes. The fashion world began to take note of Japanese designers Rei Kawakubo, Yohji Yamamoto, Kenzo Takada, and Issey Miyake, who worked in avant-garde and deconstructed styles. Prominent Italian designers included Gianni Versace and Franco Moschino.

The somber mood of the 1990s reflected the way people dressed, with minimalism and informality prevalent. "Casual Friday" dress codes emerged; layering was a popular look, as was grunge. Belgian designers Ann Demeulemeester, Dries Van Noten, and German Jil Sander made their mark, as did Italian Miuccia Prada, whose black nylon Prada backpack became a much-copied status item.

The entry into the 21st century brought about technological advances, with more people participating in Internet social network sites and online shopping. The 2000s has become the decade of celebrities, socialites, and realty stars. Celebrity culture has given us more "designers," including Paris Hilton, Gwen Stefani, Jennifer Lopez, and Justin Timberlake, among others, while the fashion designers have become celebrities.

We now look to the future, and at the same time, the past. Where and how fashion will evolve will still be based upon hundreds of years of history—but it all depends on you!

## For Discussion

There seem to be definite correlations between fashion and the times. As times change, so do fashions, and when a fashion changes, the total look changes. Accessories, makeup, and hairstyles are all part of this total fashion look. When styles are revised, they are revived in new forms, adapted for new lifestyles and occasions.

Study Table 1.1 on the following pages and answer the questions below.

1. Find examples in magazines or draw, sketch, or photograph examples of one or more fashion items listed in the table.
2. What similarities in fashion and their causes can you find in the decades listed?
3. What environmental changes do you feel will have lasting effects over the next 10 to 20 years?
4. What examples from the decades listed can you find to support the theory that fashion is evolutionary?
5. During what time period was fashion closest to being revolutionary?
6. What additions can you make to the information on past decades listed?
7. From your interpretation of the information on past decades, what conclusions can you draw about the evolution of fashions and their relationship to current events?

| ERA | EVENTS TAKING PLACE | PUBLIC REACTIONS | INTERPRETATION IN APPAREL AND DRESS | DESIGNERS OF THE DECADES |
|---|---|---|---|---|
| 1920s | Post World War I, Paris influence<br>Voting rights for women<br>Women's Vote<br>Prohibition<br>Talking movies<br>Increasing prosperity<br>Modern art, music, literature<br>Birth of sportswear | Daring looks and behavior<br>Freedom for the body<br>Short hair styles<br>Women begin to smoke<br>Dancing (Charleston) | Chemise dresses<br>Short skirts<br>T-strap shoes<br>Cloche hats<br>Luxurious fabrics:<br>  silks,<br>  satins,<br>  crepes<br>Costume looks<br>Long strands of beads | Madeleine Vionnet<br>Jean Patou<br>Edward Molyneaux<br>Coco Chanel<br>Norman Hartnell<br>Jeanne Lanvin |
| 1930s | Depression era<br>Unemployment, little money<br>Hollywood influence:<br>  stars and designers<br>Rayon and acetate fabrics<br>Big bands, swing music | Frugality, conservatism<br>"The little woman"<br>"Make do" attitude | Soft looks: loose, light fabrics<br>Long hemlines, bias cuts<br>Big hats, big brims<br>The housedress<br>Fox fur-collared<br>  coats<br>Wraps<br>Platform shoes<br>Broad shouldered jackets | Jean Desses<br>Madame Grès<br>Elsa Schiaparelli<br>Vera Maxwell<br>Mainbocher |
| 1940s | World War II:<br>  government restrictions<br>Exit France as fashion source<br>Shortage of materials<br>Emergence of American designers<br>Radio, records<br>Crooners: Crosby, Sinatra<br>Dior—1947 "New Look" | Women take men's jobs<br>Glamour, pinup girls<br>Strong nationalism<br>Common cause philosophy | Tailored, mannish suits,<br>  peplum jackets<br>Padded shoulders<br>Knee-length straight skirts<br>Soft, shoulder-length hair<br>  (pageboy)<br>¾ length coats<br>Debut of bikini | Bonnie Cashin<br>Claire McCardell<br>Adrian<br>Norman Norell<br>Pauline Trigère<br>Christian Dior<br>Cristóbal Balenciaga<br>Hattie Carnegie<br>Adele Simpson<br>Charles James<br>Nina Ricci |
| 1950s | Population increasing; baby boom<br>Korean War<br>Films expand, go public, diversify<br>Move to suburbs<br>Incomes rising<br>More imports<br>Improved transportation<br>Improved communications: TV<br>Development of more<br>  synthetics, finishes<br>Birth of rock 'n' roll | Buy new homes,<br>  appliances,<br>  furnishings<br>Conformity<br>Improve quality<br>  of family life<br>Use of increased<br>  leisure time<br>  for sports and<br>  recreation<br>The station wagon | Classics: shirtwaist dress<br>At-home clothes<br>Mink coats<br>Sack dress (too quickly copied)<br>Sportswear<br>Ivy League look,<br>  gray flannel suit,<br>  skinny ties,<br>  button-down shirts<br>Car coats<br>Wash 'n' wear fabrics<br>Sweater sets<br>Unisex looks | Hubert de Givenchy<br>Mary Quant<br>Yves Saint Laurent<br>James Galanos<br>Ceil Chapman<br>Donald Brooks<br>Gucci<br>Anne Fogarty<br>Missoni |
| 1960s | Rise of shopping centers:<br>  boutiques<br>New technology: stretch fabrics,<br>  new knitting methods<br>Big business expansion; prosperity<br>Designer names<br>Civil rights movement<br>Woodstock<br>Vietnam war:<br>  youth rebellion,<br>  antiwar movement<br>London influence: The Beatles,<br>  Twiggy, Mod, Mary Quant,<br>  Carnaby<br>Peacock revolution, rock music,<br>  youth cult | New sexual freedom<br>Experimental in fashion<br>Antiestablishment<br>  attitudes<br>Generation gap<br>Identity seeking,<br>  new values<br>Divorce, singles<br>Drug experimentation | Street fashions: jeans<br>Vinyl, synthetics, wet-look<br>Miniskirts<br>Wild use of color patterns<br>Knits, polyester<br>Ethnic clothing and crafts<br>Fun furs<br>Long hair, wigs<br>Men: turtlenecks,<br>  wide ties,<br>  Nehru jackets,<br>  golf coordinates,<br>  nylon printed shirts | André Courrèges<br>Pierre Cardin<br>Anne Klein<br>Geoffrey Beene<br>Halston<br>Rudi Gernreich<br>Emilio Pucci<br>Emanuel Ungaro<br>Valentino<br>Mila Schon<br>Jean Muir |

| Era | Events Taking Place | Public Reactions | Interpretation in Apparel and Dress | Designers of the Decades |
|---|---|---|---|---|
| **1970s** | Equal rights, women's liberation movement<br>Women working outside the home<br>Watergate, disenchantment with politics<br>Recessions<br>Ecology, conversation; energy crisis<br>Stabilizing economy<br>End of Vietnam war<br>Disco dancing, clubs<br>Consumerism<br>Hostage crisis in Iran | Individualism<br>Return to sanity reaction to 1960s chaos<br>Back to nature, health foods, natural fibers<br>New conservatism<br>Urban renewal, interest in cities & their problems<br>Equal Rights Amendment<br>Minority organizations<br>Overseas manufacturing | Pantsuits (women), leisure suits (men)<br>Maxi and longuette (1970s disaster)<br>Jeans: bell bottoms, straight leg, tapered legs, peg leg; Denim acceptable for dress and casual wear<br>T-shirts, tank tops, boots<br>Eclecticism<br>Classic look: blazers, shirts, investment clothing<br>Separates, not coordinates<br>Hot pants<br>Romantic look: soft, feminine | Bill Blass<br>Ralph Lauren<br>Zandra Rhodes<br>Diane von Furstenberg<br>Giorgio Armani<br>Gianfranco Ferré<br>Vivienne Westwood<br>Calvin Klein<br>Kenzo<br>Betsey Johnson<br>Adolfo<br>Norma Kamali<br>Mary McFadden<br>Oscar de la Renta<br>Sonia Rykiel<br>Stephen Burrows<br>Bob Mackie<br>Paco Rabanne |
| **1980s** | Computer explosion<br>Music videos<br>Nuclear weapons buildup in Europe<br>Yuppy (Young Urban Professional)<br>Recessions and unemployment<br>Wars in Central America, Middle East<br>Movies: *Fame, E.T., Flashdance*<br>First black presidential and first woman vice-presidential candidates<br>Japanese fashion explosion<br>Executive level women; Two-income families<br>New baby boom<br>Licensing "arrangements"<br>Birth of MTV | Buy home computers<br>Michael Jackson, youth hero<br>Nuclear freeze movement<br>Entrepreneurship<br>Immigration legislation<br>Day-care centers<br>Graffiti art<br>London influence: Punk, Boy George and Culture Club<br>Patriotism flourishes<br>Convertibles return<br>Proliferation of malls | Return of chemise<br>Punk hairdos<br>Androgynous dressing<br>Tailored suits and classic dressing for men and women<br>Torn clothes fad<br>Return to pants in mid-decade<br>Hats return for everyone<br>Furs<br>Backpacks as fashion<br>Sneakers for everyday wear | Donna Karan<br>Perry Ellis<br>Rei Kawakubo<br>Christian Lacroix<br>Gianni Versace<br>Claude Montana<br>Adrienne Vittadini<br>Tommy Hilfiger<br>Stephen Sprouse<br>Issey Miyake<br>Yohji Yamamoto<br>Michael Kors<br>Thierry Mugler<br>Carolina Herrera<br>Franco Moschino<br>Karl Lagerfeld<br>Jean-Paul Gaultier<br>Liz Claiborne |
| **1990s** | Creation of the European Monetary Union<br>Gulf War<br>Economic recession<br>High-tech industry growth<br>NAFTA<br>GATT<br>Rise of terrorism<br>Cellular phones proliferate<br>Sports participation increases<br>*Sex and the City* | Expansion of companies overseas<br>Business failures, consolidations & takeovers<br>Casual Fridays<br>Proliferation of foreign manufacturing | Patriotic designs<br>Grunge<br>Retro<br>Chunky shoes<br>Rise of vintage<br>Layering<br>Innerwear as outerwear<br>The decade of the supermodel and fashion photographer<br>Sports gear becomes fashionable as each sport develops its own style<br>Image & branding becomes more important than seasonal style changes<br>Slip dresses<br>Chinos | Anna Sui<br>Josie Natori<br>Isaac Mizrahi<br>Todd Oldham<br>Tracy Reese<br>Nicole Miller<br>John Galliano<br>Vera Wang<br>Prada<br>Marc Jacobs<br>Donatella Versace<br>Martin Margiela<br>Ann Demeulemeester<br>Tom Ford<br>Jil Sander<br>Helmut Lang<br>Narciso Rodriguez<br>Alber Elbaz<br>Alexander McQueen<br>Patrick Kelly<br>Dries Van Noten<br>Dominico Dolce & Stefano Gabbana |
| **2000s** | Expansion of communication technology<br>September 11th terrorist attacks<br>Emergence of the Euro | Online shopping<br>Merchant/vendor data sharing | Mixing color, texture, and pattern<br>Short layers over long<br>End of haute couture influence | Zac Posen<br>Peter Som<br>Phillip Lim<br>Rodarte<br>Nicolas Ghesquière<br>Hussein Chalayan<br>Stella McCartney<br>Proenza Schouler<br>Ralph Rucci<br>Roberto Cavalli<br>Behnaz Sarafpour<br>Viktor & Rolf<br>Hedi Slimane |

# chapter two

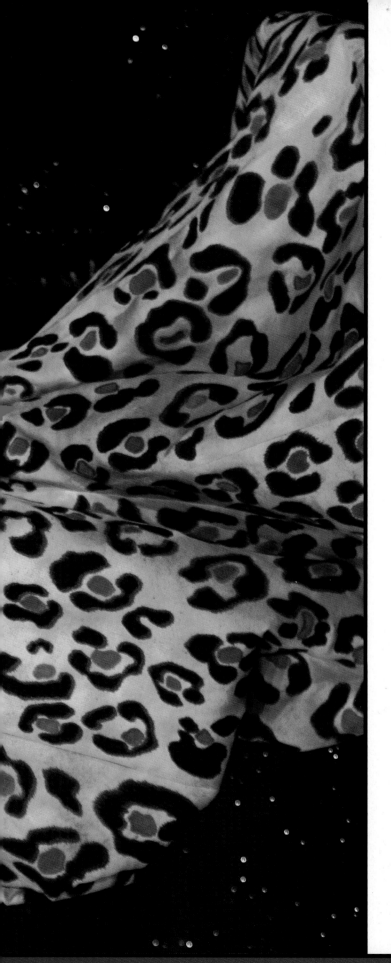

*Everything you always wanted to know*

*about the terminology, components, cycles,*

*and principles of fashion.*

**KEY CONCEPTS**
- Marketing and merchandising in the fashion business
- The stages of the fashion cycle
- The intangibles of fashion

# The Nature of Fashion

In 1850, in his book *Fashion: The Power That Influences the World*, George P. Fox said: "Fashion is and has been and will be, through all ages, the outward form through which the mind speaks to the universe. Fashion in all languages designs to make, shape, model, adapt, embellish, and adorn."[1]

In 2007, the famous designer Miuccia Prada pronounced, "People are losing the human dimension of fashion. I don't want to sound pretentious, but they are forgetting the importance of adornment and clothing, which is profound. They forget that even when people don't have anything, a way to express themselves is with their bodies and their clothing."[2]

Fashion involves our outward, visible lives. It involves the clothes we wear, the dances we dance, the cars we drive, and the way we cut our hair. Fashion also influences architecture, forms of worship, and lifestyles. It has an impact on every stage of life from the womb to the tomb.

People started covering their bodies with clothes to keep warm and to be modest, but adornment—decoration—was already an important part of dressing. Pressure from peer groups and changes in lifestyle influence the type of adornment considered acceptable in a particular time or for a particular group. Basically, the reasons people have for wearing clothes have not changed. Today, we still wear clothes to keep warm or cool and for the sake of modesty, but what we select for those purposes is very much influenced by a desire to adorn ourselves.

Because people are social animals, clothing is very much a social statement. By looking at the way a person dresses, you can often make good guesses about his or her social and business standing, sex-role identification, political orientation, ethnicity, lifestyle, and aesthetic priorities. Clothing is a forceful and highly visible medium of communication that carries with it information about who a person is, who a person is not, and who a person would like to be.

## The Importance of Fashion

During recent years, general interest in fashion has increased enormously. Fashion is one of the greatest economic forces in present-day life. To a great extent, it determines what people buy. Change in fashion is the motivating factor for replacing clothes, cosmetics, furniture, housewares, and automobiles. Fashion causes changes in consumer goods and at the same time makes people want the new products, since the thought of being unfashionable is a fate worse than death to many people!

Culturally, fashion impacts our architecture, music, and museums. In Spring 2007, a new exhibition at the Museum of Contemporary Art (MOCA) in Los Angeles explored the visual and conceptual principles connecting architecture with fashion design (see Figure 2.1). *Skin + Bones: Parallel Practices in Fashion and Architecture* featured more than 300 works by architects and fashion designers, works chosen to represent the growing similarities between the two disciplines. Among the famous architects were Frank Gehry, Zaha Hadid, and Future Systems, and among the fashion designers were Azzedine Alaïa, Alexander McQueen, Issey Miyake, and Yohji Yamamoto.

Historically, dwellings and clothing have been essential to humanity's survival, both providing protection from the environment in different ways. Items such as Hussein Chalayan's wearable living-room furniture—for example, a telescoping, wooden coffee table that becomes a skirt and slip-covered chairs that convert into dresses—emphasized the exhibition's theme of "body and identity," addressing the cross-disciplines of wrapping, folding, and draping. The exhibit also pointed out that the parallel between architecture and fashion extends to computer programs, industrial technology, and cutting-edge materials.[3]

Webster's Dictionary defines fashion as "prevail-

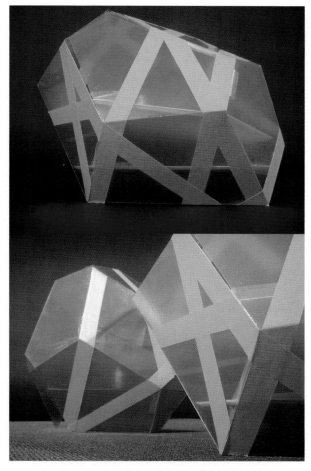

**FIGURE 2.1** Fashion is everywhere. The Museum of Contemporary Art (MOCA) featured (top) Testa & Weiser's "Carbon Beach House" and (bottom) Yoshiki Hishinuma's "Inside Out Two-Way Dress" in its *Skin + Bones* exhibit.

ing custom, usage, or style,"[4] and in this sense it covers a wide range of human activity. The term is used in this book in a narrower sense: **fashion** here means the style or styles of clothing and accessories worn at a particular time by a particular group of people. Fashion in cosmetics and fragrances and in home furnishings is also covered.

## The Fashion Business

Fashion today is big business; millions of people are employed in fashion-related activities. The **fashion industries** are those engaged in manufacturing the materials and finished products used in the production of apparel and accessories for men, women, and children. Throughout this book, references to fashion industries mean the manufacturing businesses, unless others are specifically mentioned. The broader term **fashion business** includes all the industries and services connected with fashion: design, manufacturing, distribution, marketing, retailing, advertising, communications, publishing, and consulting—in other words, any business concerned with fashion goods or services.

### Marketing

Marketing is a major influence in the fashion business. What does marketing mean? Most people think of marketing only as promotion and selling. However, promotion and selling are only two aspects of marketing. The process of **marketing** includes diverse activities that identify consumer needs; develop good products; and price, distribute, and promote those products effectively so that they will sell easily. "The aim of marketing is . . . to know and understand the customer so well that the product or service hits him [or her] and sells itself."[5]

### Fashion Marketing and Merchandising

The fashion business has been rather slow in adopting the marketing techniques that have been so successful in the growth of consumer goods such as automobiles, packaged foods, and health and beauty aids. For many years, fashion producers were concerned only with what was economical and easy to produce. They spent considerable time and money trying to convince the consumer that their products were what the consumer wanted. The producer had little or no interest in the wants and needs of the consumer.

Today, however, the total marketing process has been adopted by the fashion business and is being applied to the products and services of the fashion industries. The result is called *fashion marketing*: that is, the marketing of apparel, accessories, and other fashion-related products to the ultimate consumer.

We are also concerned with **fashion merchandising**, which is the *planning* required to have the right fashion-oriented merchandise at the right time, in the right place, in the right quantities, at the right prices, and with the right sales promotion for a specified target customer.

## Misconceptions about Fashion

As the power of fashion to influence our lives grows, three misconceptions about it continue to be widely held. The first and most common misconception is that designers and retailers dictate what the fashion will be and then force it upon helpless consumers. It has been said that the industry is composed of "obsolescence ogres." In reality, consumers themselves decide what the fashion will be by influencing new designs and by accepting or rejecting the styles that are offered. Consumers are, in truth, "variety vultures."

The second misconception is that fashion acts as an influence on women only. Today, men and children are as influenced by and responsive to fashion as women. Fashion is the force that causes women to raise or lower their skirt lengths from minis to maxis, straighten or frizz their hair, and change from casual sportswear to dressy clothes. Fashion is also the force that influences men to grow or shave off their mustaches and beards, choose wide or narrow ties and lapels, and change from casual jeans into three-piece suits. And fashion is the force that makes children demand specific products and styles.

The third misconception is that fashion is a mysterious and unpredictable force. Actually, its direction can be determined and its changes predicted with remarkable accuracy by those who study and understand the fundamentals of fashion. Fashion was once considered an art form controlled by designers who dictated its content. But fashion has now evolved into a science that can be measured and evaluated (see Figure 2.2).

**FIGURE 2.2** From wild to wacky: Designer John Galliano sends this radical look down the runway—not to sell to the public but to get "press buzz."

## The Terminology of Fashion

What is the difference between fashion, style, and design? Just what do high fashion, mass fashion, taste, classic, and fad mean? To avoid confusion when discussing fashion, we must first understand the meanings of these terms. The definitions that follow are based on the work of Dr. Paul H. Nystrom, one of the pioneers in fashion merchandising.[6]

### Style

The first step in understanding fashion is to distinguish between "fashion" and "style," words that most people use interchangeably despite the immense difference in their meanings. In general terms, a style is a characteristic or distinctive artistic expression or presentation. Styles exist in architecture, sculpture, painting, politics, and music, as well as in popular heroes, games, hobbies, pets, flirtations, and weddings.

In apparel, **style** is the characteristic or distinctive appearance of a garment—the combination of features that makes it unique and different from other garments. For example, T-shirts are as different from camp shirts as they are from peasant blouses. Riding jackets are as different from safari jackets as they are from blazer jackets.

Although styles come and go in terms of acceptance, a specific style always remains a style whether it is currently in fashion or not. Some people adopt a style that becomes indelibly associated with them and wear it regardless of whether it is currently fashionable. Carmen Miranda's platform shoes, Katharine Hepburn's pleated trousers, the Duchess of Windsor's jewelry, Marilyn Monroe's white halter dress, Michael Jackson's glove, Jennifer Lopez's signature hip-huggers and low-waisted pants, and Victoria "Posh" Beckham's oversized sunglasses and tailored look (see Figure 2.3) are all examples of personal style.

Some styles are named for the period of history in which they originated—Grecian, Roman, Renais-

**FIGURE 2.3** Victoria "Posh" Beckham shows off her personal style with oversized sunglasses and a reinterpretation of the tailored look.

sance, Empire, Gibson Girl era (early 1900s), flapper era (1920s). When such styles return to fashion, their basic elements remain the same. Minor details are altered to reflect the taste or needs of the era in which they reappear. For example, the flapper style of the 1920s was short, pleated, and body skimming. That style can be bought today but with changes for current fashion acceptance.

### Fashion

On the other hand, a fashion is a style that is accepted and used by the majority of a group at any one time, no matter how small that group. A fashion is always based on some particular style. But not every style is a fashion. A fashion is a fact of social psychology. A style is usually a creation from an artist or a designer. A fashion is a result of social emulation and acceptance. A style may be old or new, beautiful or ugly, good or bad. A style is still a style even if it never receives the slightest acceptance or even approval. A style does not become a fashion until it gains some popular acceptance. And it remains a fashion only as long as it is accepted. Miniskirts, square-toed shoes, mustaches, and theatrical daytime makeup have all been fashions. And no doubt each will again be accepted by a majority of a group of people with similar interests or characteristics—for example, college students, young career men and women, retired men and women.

Fashions appeal to many different groups and can be categorized according to the group to which they appeal. **High fashion** refers to a new style accepted by a limited number of fashion leaders who want to be the first to adopt changes and innovation in fashion. High-fashion styles are generally introduced and sold in small quantities and at relatively high prices. These styles may be limited because they are too sophisticated or extreme to appeal to the needs of the general public, or they are priced well beyond the reach of most people. However, if the style can appeal to a broader audience, it is generally copied, mass-produced, and sold at lower prices. The fashion leaders or innovators who first accepted it then move on to something new.

To contrast with high fashion, **mass fashion**, or **volume fashion**, consists of styles that are widely accepted. These fashions are usually produced and sold in large quantities at moderate to low prices and appeal to the greatest majority of fashion-conscious consumers. Mass fashion accounts for the majority of sales in the fashion business. Mass fashion is the "bread and butter" of the fashion banquet!

## Design

There can be many variations of detail within a specific style. A **design** is a particular or individual interpretation, version, or treatment of a style. A style may be expressed in a great many designs, all different, yet all related because they are in the same style. A sweatshirt, for example, is a distinctive style, but within that style, variations may include differ-

ent types of necklines, pockets, and sleeves. Another example is a satchel handbag, which may be interpreted with different closures, locks, or handles. These minor variations are the different interpretations that change the design of a style.

In the fashion industries, manufacturers and retailers assign a number to each individual design produced. This is the **style number**. The style number of a product identifies it for manufacturing, ordering, and selling purposes. In this instance, the term *style number* is used rather than *design number* even though a design is being identified.

## Taste

In fashion, **taste** refers to prevailing opinion of what is and what is not attractive and appropriate for a given occasion. Good taste in fashion, therefore, means sensitivity not only to what is artistically pleasing but also to what is appropriate for a specific situation. A style, such as an evening gown, may be beautiful. But if it is worn to a morning wedding, for example, it may not be considered in good taste.

Many styles are beautiful, but because they are not in fashion, good taste prevents their use. On the other hand, a present-day fashion may be inartistic or even ugly, but its common acceptance means that it is in good taste.

Nystrom described the relationship between good taste and fashion this way: "Good taste essentially is making the most artistic use of current fashion . . . bridging the gap between good art and common usage."[7]

Even during the height of acceptance of a particular fashion, it is considered in good taste only if it is worn by people on whom it looks appropriate. For example, miniskirts, tight pants, bikinis, and halter tops are considered in good taste only for slim people in good physical shape.

Timing, too, plays a part in what is considered good or bad taste. British costume authority James Laver saw the relationship between taste and fashion in terms of its acceptance level. A style, he said, is thought to be:

"indecent"     10 years before its time
"shameless"    5 years before its time
"outré"        1 year before its time
"smart"        in its time
"dowdy"        1 year after its time
"hideous"      10 years after its time
"ridiculous"   20 years after its time[8]

While the time an individual fashion takes to complete this course may vary, the course is always a cyclical one. A new style is often considered daring and in dubious taste. It is gradually accepted, then widely accepted, and finally gradually discarded.

For many decades, Laver's cycle has been accepted as the movement of most fashions. However, in the past few decades, some fashions have deviated from this pattern. The fashion cycles have become shorter and have repeated themselves within a shorter space of time. For the student of fashion, this shorter cycle presents an interesting challenge. What factors determine which fashions will follow the accepted cycles and which fashions will not? To understand the movement of fashion, it is important to understand that fashions are always in harmony with the times in which they appear. Since 1979, for example, Iranian law has specified that women and men must dress in a manner befitting Islam, and the law is interpreted very strictly. The law requires that women cover their hair and wear long, loose clothing. The black *chador*, a head-to-toe cloak, is considered the ideal dress. In April 2007, authorities launched Iran's annual crackdown on immodest dress, with teams of police officers stopping women in major squares to warn them about their attire (see Figure 2.4). The police and security authorities came under fire, but the crackdown has continued.[9]

## A Classic

Some styles or designs continue to be considered in good taste over a long period of time. They are

**FIGURE 2.4** Iranian policewomen in traditional dress warn a woman about her clothing and hair during a crackdown to enforce Islamic dress code in Tehran, Iran.

**46**

**FIGURE 2.5** The Chanel spring 2008 couture show featured classic styles that remain in fashion today. The Chanel cardigan suit jacket used as a giant backdrop for the 2008 couture show (top). The classic style integrated for today's fashion (bottom).

exceptions to the usual movement of styles through the fashion life cycle. A **classic** is a style or design that satisfies a basic need and remains in general fashion acceptance for an extended period of time (Figure 2.5).

Depending on the fashion statement a person wishes to make, he or she may have only a few classics or may have a wardrobe of mostly classics. A classic is characterized by simplicity of design that keeps it from being easily dated. The Chanel suit is an outstanding example of a classic. The simple lines of the Chanel suit have made it acceptable for many decades, and although it reappears now and then as a fashion, many women always have a Chanel suit in their wardrobes. Other examples of classics are blue denim jeans, blazer jackets, cardigan or turtleneck sweaters, and button-down oxford shirts. Among accessories, the pump-style shoe, the loafer, the one-button glove, the pearl necklace, and the clutch handbag are also classics. For young children, overalls and one-piece pajamas have become classics.

## A Fad

A fashion that suddenly sweeps into popularity, affecting a limited part of the total population, and then quickly disappears is called a **fad**. It comes into existence by the introduction of some feature or detail, usually exaggerated, that excites the interest of the customer. The fad starts by being quickly accepted and then quickly imitated by others.

Fads often begin in lower-price ranges, are relatively easy to copy, and therefore flood the market in a very short time. Because of this kind of market saturation, the public tires of fads quickly and they end abruptly.

Fads follow the same cycle as fashions do, but their rise in popularity is much faster, their acceptance much shorter, and their decline much more rapid than that of a true fashion. Because most fads come and go in a single season, they have been called *miniature fashions*. In recent decades we have had the "punk," multicolored hair, the "King Tut" design fad, the "Urban Cowboy" and the "grunge" fads. Fads, like fashions, invade every field: sports, literature, religion, politics, and education.

However, many things that begin as fads become fashions and can carry over for several seasons. In fact, it is very difficult to draw the line between fads and fashions. The chemise, or sack dress, is probably the outstanding example of this phenomenon. After an instant rise to popularity in the late 1950s, it quickly passed from the fashion scene. A few years later, the chemise reappeared as the shift. In 1974, the chemise again appeared in the Paris collections, modified to eliminate its former disadvantages. American manufacturers quickly reproduced it in several versions and in a wide price range. That the chemise, in its various manifestations, again appeared in the late 1980s and the mid-1990s, and flourished again in 2007 with the swingy shift

dress by Elie Tahari, providing strong evidence that the chemise has become a fashion classic (see Figure 2.6).[10]

## A Trend

A **trend** is a general direction or movement. For example, if you read in fashion magazines that "there is a trend toward shorter skirts," it means that several designers, including some leading ones, are showing shorter skirts, leading retailers are buying them, and fashion-forward customers are wearing them (see Figure 2.7). It is often difficult to tell a trend from a fad; even the experts get caught. However, marketers always want to know whether a new development is going to be a trend or a fad—because they want to cash in on trends but avoid getting burned by fads. A trend can originate anywhere and has a solid foundation that supports its growth; a fad does not.[11]

**FIGURE 2.6** Starting out as a fad, this swingy shift dress has turned into a fashion classic.

**FIGURE 2.7** Even the experts are unsure whether the ultra miniskirt is a trend or a fad.

**UNIT ONE**
**THE CHANGING WORLD OF FASHION**

## Components of Fashion

Fashion design does not just happen, nor does the designer wave a magic wand to create a new design. Fashion design involves the combination of four basic elements or components: silhouette, detail, texture, and color. Only through a change in one or more of these basic components does a new fashion evolve. This is true of any fashion-influenced product, from kitchen appliances to automobiles, from apartment houses to office buildings, and from accessories to apparel.

### Silhouette

The **silhouette** of a costume is its overall outline or contour. It is also frequently referred to as *shape* or *form*. It may appear to the casual observer that women have worn countless silhouettes throughout the centuries. In the 1930s, Agnes Brooke Young's research showed that there are actually only three basic forms—straight or tubular; bell-shaped or bouffant; and the bustle, or back fullness—with many variations.[12] Today, most fashion experts include four variations on the tubular silhouette: slim, rectangle, wedge, and A-line (see Figure 2.8).

### Details

The individual elements that give a silhouette its form or shape are called **details**. These include trimmings; skirt and pant length and width; and shoulder, waist, and sleeve treatment.

Silhouettes evolve gradually from one to another through changes in detail. When the trend in a detail reaches an extreme, a reversal of the trend takes place. For example, dresses and suits featured wide shoulders with much padding in the 1940s and 1950s. This detail was reversed in the late 1960s and 1970s, when the look became casual and unstructured. This casualness reached such extremes that by the start of the 1980s, structured clothing was back in fashion and dress and suit shoulders began once again to grow wider as padding was inserted. By the 1990s, the unstructured look was predominant again; and entering the 2000s, structured suits and wide shoulders were again seen on the runways, but by 2007, this look was softened and more unstructured.

Variations in detail allow both designer and consumer to express their individuality freely within the framework of the currently accepted silhouette. To emphasize a natural-waistline silhouette, for example, a slender woman might choose a simple wide belt, a decorated belt, or a belt in a contrasting color. To express his individuality, a man might emphasize the wide shoulder look with epaulets or heavy shoulder pads.

### Texture

One of the most significant components of fashion is texture. **Texture** is the look and feel of material, woven or nonwoven.

Texture can affect the appearance of a silhouette, giving it a bulky or slender look, depending on the

**FASHION SILHOUETTES**

A       B       C       D       E       F       G

**FIGURE 2.8** Silhouettes are categorized as belonging to one of three basic groups: (a) bell-shaped or bouffant, (b) bustle or back fullness, and (c) straight or tubular. Variations of the straight silhouette are (d) slim, (e) rectangle, (f) wedge, and (g) A-line.

roughness or smoothness of the materials (see Figure 2.9). A woman dressed in a rough tweed dress and a bulky knit sweater is likely to look larger and squarer than she does in the same dress executed in a smooth jersey and topped with a cashmere sweater.

Texture influences the drape of a garment. Chiffon clings and flows, making it a good choice for soft, feminine styles, while corduroy has the firmness and bulk suitable for more casual garments.

Texture affects the color of a fabric by causing the surface to either reflect or absorb light. Rough textures absorb light, causing the colors to appear flat. Smooth textures reflect light, causing colors to appear brighter. Anyone who has tried to match colors soon discovers that a color that appears extremely bright in a shiny vinyl, satin, or high-gloss enamel paint seems subdued in a rough wool, a suede, or a stucco wall finish.

## Color

Color has always been a major consideration in women's clothing. Since World War II, color in men's clothing has been regaining the importance it had in previous centuries. Today, color is a key factor in apparel selection for both sexes. Color is important in advertising, packaging, and store decor as well.

Historically, colors have been used to denote rank and profession. Purple, for instance, was associated with royalty, and in some periods could be worn only by those of noble birth (see Figure 2.10). Black became customary for the apparel of the clergy and for members of the judiciary.

Color symbolism often varies with geographical location. While white is the Western world's symbol of purity, worn by brides and used in communion dresses, it is the color of mourning in India.

Today, a fashion designer's color palette changes with consumers' preferences. In some seasons, all is

**FIGURE 2.9** Matthew Williamson layers different textures in his design, producing a rough and bulkier look. **FIGURE 2.10** London designers PPQ's design is fit for royalty, featuring the color purple and a gold crown.

# Fashion Focus

Fashion Focus

## "It's Just the Beginning"
### So Says Ralph Lauren

After over 40 years in the fashion business, Ralph Lauren is assuring the industry that "the company is just beginning"; Polo still has many more opportunities for growth. What began in 1967 with a collection of wide ties has grown into an entire world—redefining American style. Today, Ralph Lauren is the highest paid executive of an American vendor. He has topped the list four years in a row! He is the biggest-selling designer in the world. He has created some of fashion's greatest fashions, and his influence can be felt around the world. Not bad for a boy from the Bronx who had no formal designer education—but had a vision of what he saw as the American look and life and decided to make if available for all.

Lauren has built a multibillion dollar company by replicating preppy fashions, Art Deco sophistication, and Adirondack ease, and he wants to serve the public, "America straight up." He wants everyone to experience the rush of pleasure that luxurious objects provide.

Lauren, with his ability to envision a whole world in idealized form and then persuade others to buy into it, casts the design net far wider than almost any fashion designer in history. Most designers who have changed the course of history—whether Frank Lloyd Wright in architecture or Coco Chanel in fashion—have done it by breaking, often radically, with what came before. Lauren may be the first designer who has transferred the world by not doing anything new at all!

Since celebrating his 40th anniversary in 2007, and examining the growth and expansion of Polo in the first decade of the 21st century, there is little doubt that Polo Ralph Lauren is just beginning to plan and execute new, innovative ideas and concepts for continued successful growth in the second, third, and fourth decades of the 21st century.

Today, Lauren

is busy attending to the needs of over 400 stores and a multitude of brands: Purple Label, Blue Label, Black Label, Ralph Lauren Golf, Collection, Chaps, RRL, Polo Jeans Co., RLX, Ralph Lauren Home, and Ralph Lauren Fragrances, among others. Lauren may be one of the most famous names and personalities in the fashion business, but he and his family lead a quiet life and perform many charitable acts with little fanfare or publicity. In 1994, Lauren created Fashion Targets Breast Cancer, an organization that has become a global initiative and raised millions of dollars for breast cancer charities. In 2007, he designed the T-shirt to kick off the global partnership of the Council of Fashion

Left page: Designer Ralph Lauren on the runway, 2007 (top); Black Label and ready-to-wear designs, 2007 (bottom); right page: Advertisement for the designer's collection, 2008.

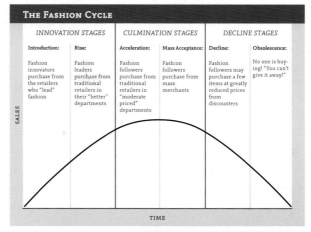

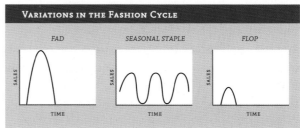

**FIGURE 2.11** The basic life cycle of fashion can be represented by a bell-shaped curve. Variations can occur to the height to which a fashion rises at its peak and the length of time it takes to get to that point and then to decline in popularity.

Designers of America (CFDA) and Net-a-Porter.com to bring more international attention to Fashion Targets Breast Cancer.

Among the many awards he has received recognizing and honoring his talent as a menswear and women's wear designer, he was most excited about the CFDA award as "American Fashion Legend." Jokingly, he said "Legend, I always love that. I could change my last name to it."

Lauren's odes to American style *are* American style to the rest of the world. Polo Ralph Lauren is the one American brand that has a significant international presence, on a par with Prada, Gucci, Chanel, and Louis Vuitton. Today, his products and designs can be bought worldwide at stores in London, Tokyo, Munich, Athens, as well as in Jedda, Riyadh, Kuwait City, Dubai, and Shanghai. His most recent international opening was in Moscow, where he successfully opened two stores to outstanding customer response and success. The Lauren stores are great advertisements for American fashion and lifestyle throughout the world.

A new initiative, American Living, a private label concept for JCPenney, began in 2008. The line is part of Polo's Global Brand Concepts, a business division in which the company works in partnerships with retailers to develop private brands. Lauren's idea is that everyone should have an equal opportunity to get rich—and that everyone should have an equal opportunity to look and feel rich, however much money they have. His genius is in selling the image of the upper classes to the masses without diluting its appeal to the people who made it in the first place. He has made aristocracy feel entirely democratic. What could be more American than that?

brightness and sharp contrast, and no color is too powerful to be worn. In other seasons, only subdued colors appeal. Fashion merchants must develop an eye for color—not only for the specific hues and values popular in a given season but also for indications of possible trends in consumer preference.

## The Fashion Cycle

All fashions move in cycles. The term **fashion cycle** refers to the rise, wide popularity, and then decline in acceptance of a style. The word *cycle* suggests a circle. However, the fashion cycle is represented by a bell-shaped curve (see Figure 2.11).

Some authorities compare the fashion cycle to a wave, which shows first a slow swell, then a crest, and finally a swift fall. Like the movement of a wave, the movement of a fashion is always forward, never backward. Like waves, fashion cycles do not follow each other in regular, measured order. Some take a short time to crest; others, a long time. The length of the cycle from swell to fall may be long or short. And, again like waves, fashion cycles overlap.

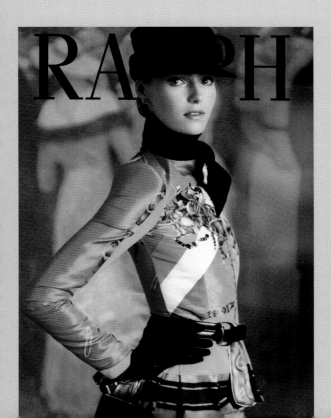

### *Stages of the Fashion Cycle*

Fashion cycles are not haphazard; they don't "just happen." There are definite stages in a style's development that are easily recognized. These stages can be charted and traced, and in the short run, accurately predicted. Being able to recognize and predict the different stages is vital to success in both the buying and the selling of fashion.

Every fashion cycle passes through five stages: (1) introduction, (2) rise, (3) culmination, (4) decline, and (5) obsolescence. A comparison of these stages to the timetable suggested by Laver looks like this:

| | |
|---|---|
| Introduction | "indecent/shameless" |
| Rise | "outré" |
| Culmination | "smart" |
| Decline | "dowdy/hideous" |
| Obsolescence | "ridiculous" |

The fashion cycle serves as an important guide in fashion merchandising. The fashion merchant uses the fashion cycle concept to introduce new fashion goods, to chart their rise and culmination, and to recognize their decline and obsolescence.

### Introduction Stage

The next new fashion may be introduced by a producer in the form of a new style, color, or texture. The new style may be a flared pant leg when slim legs are popular, vibrant colors when earth tones are popular, or slim body-hugging fabrics such as knit jersey when heavy-textured bulky looks are being worn.

New styles are almost always introduced in higher-priced merchandise. They are produced in small quantities, since retail fashion buyers purchase a limited number of pieces to test the new styles' appeal to targeted customers. This testing period comes at the beginning of the buying cycle of fashion merchandise, which coincides with the introduction stage of the fashion cycle. The test period ends when the new style either begins its rise or has been rejected by the target customer. Because there can be many risks, new styles must be priced high enough that those that succeed can cover the losses on those that fail. Promotional activities such as designer appearances, institutional advertising, and charity fashion shows, which appeal to the fashion leaders of the community and also enhance the store's fashion image, take place at this point.

### Rise Stage

When the new original design (or its adaptations) is accepted by an increasing number of customers, it is considered to be in its **rise stage.** At this stage, the buyer reorders in quantity for maximum stock coverage.

During the rise stage of a new original design, many retailers offer line-for-line copies or **knock-offs**, as they are called in the fashion industry. Knockoffs are versions of the original designer style duplicated by manufacturers. These copies look exactly like the original except that they have been mass-produced in less expensive fabrics. Because production of the merchandise is now on a larger scale, prices of the knockoffs are generally lower.

As a new style continues to be accepted by more and more customers, adaptations appear. **Adaptations** are designs that have all the dominant features of the style that inspired them but do not claim to be exact copies. Modifications have been made, but distinguishing features of the original, such as a special shoulder treatment or the use of textured fabric, may be retained in the adaptation. At this stage, the promotion effort focuses on regular price lines, full assortments, and product-type ads to persuade the customer of the store's superiority in meeting his or her fashion needs.

### Culmination Stage

The **culmination stage** of the fashion cycle is the period when a fashion is at the height of its popularity and use. At this stage, also called the **plateau**, the fashion is in such demand that it can be mass-produced, mass-distributed, and sold at prices within the range of most customers. This stage may be long or brief, depending on how extended the peak of popularity is. The quilted coat, which began as an expensive down-filled style in the late 1970s, reached its culmination stage when mass production in acrylic fill made a quilted coat available to practically every income level. At the culmination stage, the high–price line fashion buyer stops reordering the fashion and begins reducing stock.

The culmination stage of a fashion may be extended in two ways:

1. If a fashion becomes accepted as a classic, it settles into a fairly steady sales pattern. An example is the cardigan sweater, an annual steady seller.
2. If new details of design, color, or texture are continually introduced, interest in the fashion may be kept alive longer. Shoulder-strap handbags are a perfect example. Another example is the continued fashion interest in running shoes, fostered by new colors, designs, and comfort innovations.

## Decline Stage

When boredom with a fashion sets in, the result is a decrease in consumer demand for that fashion. This is known as the **decline stage**. It is a principle of fashion that all fashions end in excess.

As a fashion starts to decline, consumers may still be wearing it, but they are no longer willing to buy it at its regular price. The outstanding fashion merchandiser is able to recognize the end of the culmination stage and start markdowns early. At this point, production stops immediately or comes slowly to a halt. The leading fashion stores abandon the style; traditional stores take a moderate markdown and advertise the price reduction. A major price-slash clearance or closeout will probably follow in a short while. At this stage, the style may be found in bargain stores at prices far below what the style commanded in earlier stages.

## Obsolescence Stage

When strong distaste for a style has set in and it can no longer be sold at any price, the fashion is in its **obsolescence stage**. At this stage, the style can be found only in thrift shops, garage sales, or flea markets. However, by 2007, *obsolescence* had new meanings: recycled and sustainable fashion (see Figure 2.12). Opportunity to recycle clothes that are considered obsolete has become very important. At the Glasgow School of Art in Scotland, there is a project REJECT RAG-REBORN that takes obsolete clothes and rags and transforms them into funky high-fashion outfits. UNIQLO, a clothing store chain in Japan has a recycling program whereby customers may bring UNIQLO apparel they no longer use to UNIQLO for recycling and reuse. Reusable clothes are given to refugees and displaced people through the United Nations and other relief organizations, while waste garments are recycled into fuels, textiles, and other products.[13]

## Lengths of Cycles

Predicting the time span of a fashion cycle is impossible, since each fashion moves at its own speed. However, one guideline can be counted on. Declines are fast, and a drop to obsolescence is almost always steeper than a rise to culmination. At

**FIGURE 2.12** Scraps off the cutting room floor are no longer thrown in the trash, but rather made into dresses, as seen in these designs by From Somewhere.

this point, as they say in merchandising, "You can't give it away."

The speed with which products are moving through their cycles is accelerating. Rapid technological developments and "instant" communications have much to do with this speedup, as do fast-changing environmental factors. The result is an intense competition among manufacturers and retailers to provide consumers with what they want and expect—constantly changing assortments from which to choose.

American society accepts as routine live TV pictures of astronauts working in outer space, of battles being fought in various parts of the world, and of personalities participating in social occasions at every point of the globe. Our appetite for constant newness and change seems to be insatiable. The vast choice of new styles that consumers are offered continuously by the fashion world provides them with an important role in the movement of fashion cycles. Consumers either give a new style enough acceptance to get it started, or they immediately reject it. Since more new fashions are always ready to push existing ones out of the way, it is no wonder that with each passing year, the time required for a fashion to complete its cycle becomes shorter and shorter.

Women clear out their closets constantly with hopes of recouping a few dollars from clothes they no longer like—or just never wear. Thrift stores, resale shops, and flea markets have been the usual destination for these clothes, but thanks to television and the Internet, the market for reselling clothing is changing. Some of the least expensive clothes are seeing the biggest jumps in value, and online auction sites are letting shoppers sell hot items from H&M and Target in particular. Inexpensive clothes designed by Karl Lagerfeld, Victor and Rolf, Stella McCartney, Madonna, Proenza Schouler, and others were intended to give customers a chance to own designer duds. However, these limited-edition designer clothes made for Target and H&M can be sold on eBay and other auction sites

**FIGURE 2.13** A blue, silk bustier top (top), designed by the exciting Proenza Schouler team (bottom), was sold as an inexpensive design at Target but resold on eBay for top dollar.

for prices above their original values. Some items resold on eBay, for example, were a Stella McCartney sweater dress purchased at H&M in 2005 for $80 and sold on eBay for $500.44, and a Proenza Schouler blue silk bustier top purchased at Target in 2007 for $34.99 and sold on eBay for $255 (see Figure 2.13). Constance White, style director of eBay, says, "Logic isn't dictating the high prices. It's emotion."[14]

### Breaks in the Cycle

In fashion, as in everything else, there are always ups and downs, stops and starts. The normal flow of a fashion cycle can be broken or abruptly interrupted by outside influences. The influence can be simply unpredictable weather or a change in group acceptance. Or it can be much more dramatic and far-reaching—war, worldwide economic depression, or a natural disaster, for example.

Although no formal studies have been made of the phenomenon of the broken cycle, manufacturers and merchants have a theory about it. They believe that a broken cycle usually picks up where it has stopped once conditions return to normal or once the season that was cut short reopens. Consider the effect that a shortage of oil can have on the movement of manufactured fibers. Although the success of manufactured fibers—with all their easy-care attributes—is tremendous, their availability was interrupted by oil shortages in 1973, in 1979, in the late 1980s, and again through the early 2000s. However, when the oil supply increases, the popularity of these fibers return to what it had been.

Widespread economic depressions also temporarily interrupt the normal progress of a fashion cycle. When there is widespread unemployment, fashion moves much more slowly, resuming its pace only with economic recovery and growth.

Wars also affect fashion. They cause shortages that force designers, manufacturers, retailers, and consumers to change fashions less freely or to restrict styles. People redirect their interests, and fashion must take a back seat. When fashion apparel is in a cycle break, interest in cosmetics usually picks up. Women switch cosmetics or use them differently to satisfy their desire for something new. After wars have ended, interest in fashion picks up and flourishes once again.

### Long-Run and Short-Run Fashions

The length of time individual fashions take to complete their cycles varies widely. **Long-run fashions** take more seasons to complete their cycles than what might be considered average; **short-run fashions** take fewer seasons.

Some fashions tend to rise in popular acceptance more slowly than others, thereby prolonging their life. Some stay in popular demand much longer than others do. The decline in popular demand for some fashions may be slower than for others.

### Consumer Buying and the Fashion Cycle

Every fashion has both a consumer buying cycle and a consumer use cycle (see Figure 2.14). The curve of the consumer buying cycle rises in direct relation to that of the consumer use cycle. But when the fashion reaches its peak, consumer buy-

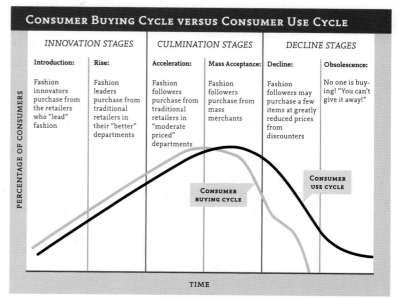

**FIGURE 2.14** Consumer use of a fashion product follows a cycle similar to the buying cycle, but the use cycle begins after the buying cycle and endures beyond the buying cycle's decline and obsolescence stages.

# Then & NOW

## Paul Poiret,
## the King of Fashion
### *Long Live the King*

Left page: Designer Paul Poiret (top); Poiret-inspired Proenza Schouler, 2007 (bottom left); "C'est Moi" fashion plate, 1911 (bottom right); right page: WWD published Poiret's design concepts for the year 2017.

More than any other designer of the 20th century, Paul Poiret—who is credited both with liberating women by making the corset disappear and with restricting their walk with narrow hemmed hobble skirts—elevated fashion to the status of art. Like the work of the artists with whom he collaborated, Poiret's work was inspired by the dominant discourses of the day, including classicism, orientalism, symbolism, and primitivism. The "Pasha of Paris," as he was known, was responsible for introducing the vivid colors of the Fauvists and the exotic references of the Ballets Russes to the haute couture.

A landmark exhibition at the Metropolitan Museum of Art in New York in 2007 celebrated the historic significance and influence of Poiret designs that exist to the present day. Harold Koda, curator in charge of the Metropolitan Museum's Costume Institute, says, "[Poiret] pioneered a self-confident modernity based on woman's seductive femininity and envisioned a 'total lifestyle' that extended from how she should dress to what fragrance she should wear and how she should decorate her home—an approach reflected in the strategies of many of today's fashion houses."

Evidence suggests that designers have been rediscovering their debt to Poiret for some time. Recent designer collections from Prada to Zac Posen to John Galliano to Marc Jacobs show that their blueprints were laid down a century ago by Poiret.

C'EST MOI

MANTEAU, DE PAUL POIRET

Poiret was a maverick, probably the world's first celebrity designer, who threw fabulous themed parties. The cognoscenti let their hair down at his famous, over-the-top "Thousand and Second Night" party he and his wife Denise threw in 1911 for 300 guests. He enforced a dress code of oriental costumes (and made those whose appearance fell short change into Poiret-designed Persian outfits or leave). He sent each guest home with a bottle of his Rosine fragrance—could this have been the first gift bag?

ing tends to decline more rapidly than consumer use. Different segments of society respond to and tire of a fashion at different times. So different groups of consumers continue to wear fashions for varying lengths of time after they have ceased buying them. While each group is using and enjoying a fashion, the producers and retailers serving that group are already abandoning the style and marketing something newer. Their efforts in this direction are most profitable when they anticipate, rather than follow, the trend of consumer demand. Consumer buying is often halted prematurely because producers and sellers no longer wish to risk making and stocking an item they believe will soon decline in popularity. Instead, they concentrate their resources on new items with better prospects for longevity. This procedure is familiar to anyone who has tried to buy summer clothes in late August or skiwear in March.

## The Intangibles of Fashion

Fashion itself is intangible. A style is tangible, made up of a definite silhouette and details of design. But fashion is shaped by such powerful intangibles as group acceptance, change, the social forces important during a certain era, and people's desire to relate to specific lifestyles.

### Group Acceptance

The fig leaf, the first fashion creation, was widely accepted, and since then we have come a long way. Basically, fashion is acceptance: group acceptance or approval is implied in any definition of fashion. Most people have a deep-seated wish to express themselves as individuals but also to be part of a group. To dress in the latest fashion means that they are trying to be individual yet also to belong.

However, acceptance need not be universal. A style may be adopted by one group while other segments of the population ignore it. As David Wolfe, creative director of Doneger Design Group, put it:

More people care about fashion than we think, but they don't care about trends. Fashion with a capital "F" is a game played by few people. More people care about presentation. Only 5 percent of Americans are passionate about fashion, while the majority moves at a slower pace.[15]

A style may also be accepted and become a fashion in one part of the world while it is ignored or rejected elsewhere. Each of the following is considered fashionable by its own inhabitants: the igloo of the Inuit, the thatched hut of some African tribes people, and the ranch-style house of many American suburbanites. Similarly, many ethnic and religious groups have distinctive styles of dress (see Figure 2.15).

The way we dress is a personal signature. The dress or suit we wear is not just a confirmation of the old adage that "Clothes makes the man . . . or woman," but rather an example of the fact that our need for acceptance is expressed largely in the way we dress. Acceptance also means that a fashion is considered appropriate to the occasion for which it is worn. Clothes considered appropriate for big-business boardrooms would not be considered acceptable for casual weekends.

If any of you should doubt the power of acceptance in fashion, try a simple experiment. Put on clothes worn 10 or 20 years ago, or totally different in style from what is considered the fashion. Then go out casually among your friends, acquaintances, or even strangers, and note their reactions toward you and then your feelings toward yourself. There will be quizzical looks, doubtful stares, and in some cases smirks and laughter. No one can really "belong" to a chosen group and at the same time choose to be completely "out" of present-day fashion. Such is the power of fashion acceptance.

## Change

Fashion changes because ideas about politics, religion, leisure, democracy, success, and age change. Fashion is also a complex means for facilitating orderly change within a mass society. This is particularly true when the society is no longer able to provide identity and maintain social order via custom or tradition. In the United States, where different immigrant and ethnic groups must adjust to one another, fashion is one means of providing a social bond.

Fashion is subject to change—both rapid and gradual. Modern communications play a major role in today's accelerated rate of fashion change. The mass media spreads fashion news across the face of the globe in hours, sometimes seconds. Live TV coverage of events around the world enables us to see not only what people are doing but also what they are wearing. Our morning newspapers show us what fashion leaders wore to a party the night before. Even slight fashion changes are given faster and wider publicity than

**FIGURE 2.15** Erykah Badu's traditional African head wrap is a distinctive and fashionable accessory for a red carpet event.

ever before. Consumers who like these changes demand them from merchants, who in turn demand them from manufacturers.

New technology is constantly producing new fibers and blends of fibers. Each seems to offer more than the one before and encourages the discarding of the old.

Clothing is also getting a lot smarter, and high-tech clothing is now an integral part of the world of wearable computers. They are so portable that their components are stored on the body in places like lapels, armbands, and eyeglass frames.

For most consumers, a cushion that doubles as a phone or a bulletproof USB memory stick equipped with an MP3 player and tourist tips for 37 countries would qualify as nonessential indulgences, but consumer wants many times outrank the needs.

These items, as well as a sleek, fashion-oriented Dolce & Gabbana cellphone (see Figure 2.16) with gold plating and a gold keychain, a GreenRider T-shirt that has a pocket for an iPod, a sewn seam to loop the headphones through, and a control panel on the shirt front were all on display at the CeBIT design technology trade fair in Hannover, Germany. Who knows what the years ahead will bring to the fashion world through technology?[16]

## The Futility of Forcing Change

Fashion expresses the spirit of the times and in turn influences it. Fashion designers are successful or not, depending on their ability to sense and anticipate changes if not to initiate them. Changes can be initiated, but there are as many examples of failures as there are of successful changes. Efforts have been made from time to time to force changes in the course of fashion, but they usually fail. Fashion is a potent force which by definition requires support by the majority.

As an example, in the late 1960s, designers and retailers decided that skirts had reached their limit in shortness and that women would soon be seeking change. So the designers designed and the retailers stocked and promoted the "midi," a skirt

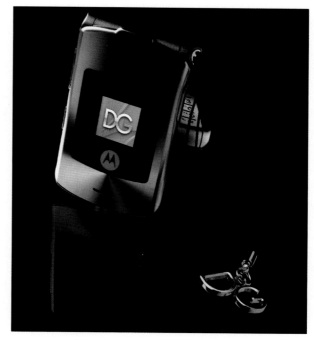

**FIGURE 2.16** Dolce & Gabbana's sleek Razr cell phone is fashion-oriented technology.

mid-calf in length. The designers and retailers were right in theory but wrong in timing and choice of skirt length. Consumers found the midi too sudden and radical a change and did not accept or buy the style in sufficient numbers to make it a fashion. In the late 1980s, designers and retailers did it again—this time they tried to force a change to very short skirts. Again, the public disliked the radical change and refused to buy miniskirts when they were first introduced. In the mid-1990s however, women were wearing both miniskirts and long skirts. By 2003, the runways were full of miniskirts once again.

Occasionally, necessity and government regulation can interrupt the course of fashion. During World War II, the U.S. government controlled the type and quantity of fabric used in consumer goods. One regulation prohibited anything but slit pockets on women's garments to avoid using the extra material that patch pockets require. Skirts were short and silhouettes were narrow, reflecting the scarcity of material.

## Meeting the Demand for Change

After World War II, a reaction to these designs was to be expected. A new French designer, Christian Dior, caught and expressed the desire for a freer line and a more feminine garment in his first collection, which achieved instant fashion success. Using fabric with a lavishness that had been impossible in Europe or America during the war years, he created his "New Look," with long, full skirts, fitted waistlines, and feminine curves.

Dior did not change the course of fashion; he accelerated it—from an evolutionary course to a revolutionary one. He recognized and interpreted the need of women at that time to get out of stiff, short, narrow, unfeminine clothes and into soft, free, longer, feminine ones. Consumers wanted the change, and the lifting of the very limiting wartime restrictions made it possible to meet their demand.

Another example of a consumer demand for change occurred in men's wear just before World War II. Year after year, manufacturers had been turning out versions of a style that had long been popular in England—the padded-shoulder draped suit. A number of young men from very influential families, who were attending well-known northeastern colleges, became tired of that look. They wanted a change. They took their objections to New Haven clothing manufacturers, and the result was the natural-shoulder Ivy League suit that achieved widespread popularity for the next 15 to 20 years.

## A Mirror of the Times

Fashion is a nonverbal symbol. It communicates that the wearer is in step with the times. Because fashions are shaped by the forces of an era, they in turn reflect the way we think and live. Each new fashion seems completely appropriate to its time and reflects that time as no other symbol does. A study of the past and careful observation of the present makes it apparent that fashions are social expressions that document the tastes and values of an era just as the paintings, sculpture, and architecture of the times do. The extreme modesty of the Victorian era was reflected in bulky and concealing fashions. The sexual emancipation of the flappers in the 1920s was expressed in their flattened figures, short skirts, "sheer" hosiery (the first time the bare leg was exposed), and short hair. The individualistic fashions of the 1990s and 2000s are a true reflection of the current freedom of expression and lifestyle.

## Social Class

Fashions mirror the times by reflecting the degree of rigidity in the class structure of an era. Although such ideas are difficult to imagine today, throughout much of history certain fashions were restricted to the members of certain rigidly defined social classes. In some early eras, royal edicts regulated both the type of apparel that could be worn by each group of citizens and how ornate it could be. Class distinctions were thus emphasized. Certain fashions have also been used as indications of high social standing and material success. During the 19th century, the constricted waists of Western women and the bound feet of high-caste Chinese women were silent but obvious evidence that the male head of the household was wealthy and esteemed.

Today, social classes are far more fluid and mobile than ever before. Because there is no universal way of life today, people are free to choose their own values and lifestyles—and their dress reflects that choice. Many fashions exist simultaneously, and we are all free to adopt the fashions of any social group. If we do not wish to join others in their fashion choices, we can create our own modes and standards of dress. The beatniks of the 1950s and the hippies of the 1960s had their typical fashions, as did the bohemians of the 1920s and the liberated groups of the 1970s. In the 1980s, the phenomenon of the punk rockers existed side by side with the yuppies. In the 1990s, hip-hop fashion coexisted with Ralph Lauren's Polo-Sport. Now in the 2000s, vintage has found a home alongside celebrity glamour.

## Lifestyle

Fashions also mirror the times by reflecting the activities in which people of an era participate. The importance of court-centered social activities in

17th- and 18th-century Europe was in evidence in men's and women's ornately styled apparel. Fashions became less colorful and more functional when a new working class was created by the industrial revolution.

Currently, our clothes also vary according to lifestyle. More casual and active sportswear in wardrobes reflect our interest in active sports and leisure pastimes. The difference in the lifestyle of an urban, career-oriented woman and that of a suburban housewife is totally reflected in their choice of wardrobes (see Figure 2.17).

## Principles of Fashion

Diversification of fashion has added new dimensions to the interpretation of the principles of fashion. While the intangibles of fashion can be vague and sometimes difficult to predict and chart, certain fundamental principles of fashion are tangible and precise. For many decades these principles served as the solid foundation for fashion identification and forecasting—they still do—but the astute student of fashion recognizes that in today's vibrant and changing atmosphere, the application of these principles becomes a more intricate and challenging task.

The five principles we discuss are the foundations upon which the study of fashion is based.

1. **Consumers establish fashions by accepting or rejecting the styles offered.** The popular belief that designers create artistic designs with little regard for the acceptance of these designs by the public is quite false. No designer can be successful without the support and acceptance of the customer.

   It is true that new fashions can be introduced by famous designers, but it is relatively rare. A few examples are the loose, boxy jacket of the Chanel suit, the famous bias cut clothes designed by Vionnet, and the New Look by Christian Dior. However, the designers who are

considered to be the "creators" of fashion are those who have consistently given expression to the silhouette, color, fabric, and design that are wanted and accepted by a majority of the consumers. Current examples include the looks introduced by Marc Jacobs (see Figure 2.18), Calvin Klein, Donna Karan, and Ralph Lauren.

A **customer** is a patron or potential purchaser of goods or services. Thus, a retail store's dress buyer is a customer of a dress manufacturer, and the dress manufacturer is a customer of a fabric producer. The consumer is the ultimate user, the person who uses the finished fashion garment.

Designers create hundreds of new styles each season, based on what they think may attract customers. From among those many

**FIGURE 2.17** Television's popular portrayal of housewives and their wardrobes: *Desperate Housewives* (top) and *The Real Housewives of Orange County* (bottom).

**FIGURE 2.18** Consumer response will determine if this new look by Marc Jacobs is a hit or not.

styles, manufacturers choose what they think will be successful. They reject many more than they select. Retailers choose from the manufacturers' offerings those styles they believe their customers will want. Consumers then make the vital choice. By accepting some styles and rejecting others, they—and only they—dictate what styles will become fashions.

2. **Fashions are not based on price.** Just because something is expensive, it does not follow that it will be successful. Although new styles that may eventually become fashions are often introduced at high prices, this is happening less and less today. What you pay for an item of apparel is not an indication of whether the item is considered to be fashionable.

    In the fashion diversity offered to consumers today, successful fashions are to be found at every price level. Upper income consumers will accept fashions at very low prices, and consumers at the opposite end of the income scale will often splurge and buy a very expensive item—if it is in fashion. In many cases, consumers coordinate fashions that are both inexpensive and expensive with little regard to the price. For example, an expensive piece of jewelry can be pinned to a inexpensive T-shirt, or conversely, a fashionable piece of costume jewelry can be pinned to an expensive designer suit.

3. **Fashions are evolutionary in nature; they are rarely revolutionary.** In these days of rapid cultural and national revolutions, it is hard to believe that a worldwide phenomenon such as fashion is evolutionary in nature—not revolutionary. To the casual observer it appears as though fashion changes suddenly. Actually, fashion change comes about as a result of gradual movements from one season to the next.

    Throughout history, there have probably been only two real revolutions in fashion styles. One of these occurred during the 20th century: the Dior New Look of 1947. The other was the abrupt change of styles brought about by the French Revolution when the fashion changed overnight from elaborate full skirts, low-cut daring bodices, and ornate and glamorous fabrics to simple, drab costumes in keeping with the political and moral upheaval.

    Fashions usually evolve gradually from one style to another (see Figure 2.19). Skirt lengths go up or down an inch at a time, season after season. Shoulder widths narrow or widen gradually, not suddenly. It is only in retrospect that fashion changes seem marked or sudden.

    Fashion designers understand and accept this principle. When developing new design ideas, they always keep the current fashion in mind. They know that few people could or would buy a whole new wardrobe every season, and that the success of their designs ultimately depends on sales. Consumers today buy apparel and accessories to supplement and update the wardrobe they already own, some of which was purchased last year, some the year before, some the year before that, and so on. In most cases, consumers will buy only if the purchase complements their existing wardrobe and does not depart too radically from last year's purchases.

4. **No amount of sales promotion can change the direction in which fashions are moving.** Promotional efforts on the part of producers or retailers cannot dictate what consumers will buy, nor can they force people to buy what they do not want. The few times that fashion merchants have tried to promote a radical change in fashion, they have not been successful.

As the women's liberation movement grew in the late 1960s, women rebelled against the constriction of girdles and bras. The overwhelming majority stopped wearing girdles and began wearing pantyhose instead. Various "counterculture" looks were adopted by some, and a more relaxed look was adopted by nearly everyone. Reflecting this change was the reemergence of the soft, no-seam natural bra. Regardless of promotion by the intimate-apparel industry, nothing could persuade the majority of American women to submit again to the rigid control of corsets and girdles.

Also, promotional effort cannot renew the life of a fading fashion unless the extent of change gives the fashion an altogether new appeal. This is why stores have markdown or clearance sales. When the sales of a particular style start slumping, stores know they must clear out as much of that stock as possible, even at much lower prices, to make room for newer styles in which consumers have indicated interest.

5. **All fashions end in excess.** This saying is sometimes attributed to Paul Poiret, a top Paris designer of the 1920s. Many examples attest to its truth. Eighteenth-century hoopskirts ballooned out to over eight feet in width, which made moving from room to room a complicat-

**FIGURE 2.19** Fashion is evolutionary, as seen in these designs by Christian Lacroix's pouf skirt from 1987 (top) and John Galliano's pouf skirt from 2008 (bottom).

**FIGURE 2.20** The principle that all fashion ends in excess is still demonstrated on the runway. These partially see-through dresses by designers Rodarte (top) and Alexander McQueen (bottom) prove this concept to be true.

ed maneuver. The French tried to accommodate these skirts and designed doors that could be opened to a width far beyond that of regular doors. They became known as "French doors" and can still be found in architecture today. Similarly, miniskirts of the 1960s finally became so short that the slightest movement caused a major problem in modesty. This same trend toward excess can be found in men's wear. Just think of the growth of the width of a tie. It will start as a thin string tie and become wider and wider until it becomes as wide as a bib!

Once the extreme in styling has been reached, a fashion is nearing its end (see Figure 2.20). The attraction of the fashion wanes, and people begin to seek a different look—a new fashion.

## Summary and Review

In its narrow sense, fashion is the prevailing way a group of people at a particular time and place dress themselves. The fashion industries, which manufacture the materials and finished products of clothing, also produce related goods, including cosmetics, fragrances, and home fashions. Fashion designers attempt to determine what styles—characteristic appearances of garments and other fashion items—will appeal to their target group of consumers. The designs that are offered to the public are versions of a style that are distinguished by their silhouette, details, texture, and color.

Public acceptance of a fashion follows a course called the fashion cycle, which includes the following stages: introduction, rise, culmination, decline, and obsolescence. A fashion that reaches the culmination stage and then declines over a brief period of time is called a fad. A classic, on the other hand, may not necessarily reach its peak of popularity very quickly, but its decline is gradual, and it never reaches the obsolescence stage.

Typically, the fashion leaders who buy a fashion at the introductory stage are the wealthy clientele of high-fashion designers. These consumers can afford to experiment with their wardrobes. When a fashion appears to gain acceptance, it can be mass-produced with less expensive materials for fashion followers. Some fashions have broad appeal, and others attract a smaller segment of the public, for example, a particular age group, an ethnic group, or people with a common lifestyle, such as casual sub-urbanites or more formally dressed businesspeople.

Any fashion evolves according to the demands of its market. Neither pricing nor promotion by the producers can force consumers to embrace a new fashion. Usually changes evolve gradually, building up to an extreme and then reversing and moving toward the other extreme. The success of fashion merchandisers depends on their ability to predict the changing tastes of their public with scientific accuracy and to use their artistic creativity to satisfy those tastes.

## Trade Talk

Define or briefly explain the following terms:

| | |
|---|---|
| adaptations | classic |
| consumer | culmination stage |
| customer | decline stage |
| design | details |
| fad | fashion |
| fashion business | fashion cycle |
| fashion industries | fashion merchandising |
| high fashion | knockoffs |
| long-run fashions | marketing |
| mass or volume fashion | obsolescence stage |
| plateau | rise stage |
| short-run fashions | silhouette |
| style | style number |
| taste | texture |
| trend | |

## For Review

1. What group ultimately decides whether a style will be "fashionable" or not? Explain your answer.

2. Apparel styles are often named for the period in history in which they were introduced. Name three such styles and the historic period in which they originated.

3. Give two examples of "classics" that are in style today for each of the following groups: (a) men, (b) women, and (c) children.

4. Distinguish between: (a) style, fashion, and design, and (b) classic and fad.

5. List and briefly explain the interrelationships among the four components of fashion.

6. Fashion apparel change has accelerated during the past 100 years. Which factors, in your opinion, have had the greatest influence on change? Why?

7. Fashions go through a five-stage life cycle. Name and explain each stage.

8. In what respects does the consumer buying cycle differ from the consumer use cycle? How is such information useful to fashion merchants?

9. Can designers, manufacturers, or retailers force unwanted fashion on consumers? Explain your answer.

10. What are the five basic principles relating to fashion? What are the implications for fashion merchants?

## For Discussion

The following statements are derived from the text. Discuss the significance of each, giving examples of how each applies to merchandising fashion goods.

1. Men today are as influenced by and responsive to fashion as women.

2. Predicting the time span of a fashion cycle is impossible, since each fashion moves at its own speed.

3. Because there is no universal way of life, people are free to choose their own values and lifestyles.

# chapter three

*Everything you always wanted to know*

*about the environmental factors affecting fashion,*

*as well as the geographic, demographic, psychographic,*

*and behavioral research tools for market segmentation.*

# The Environment of Fashion

A cardinal rule in any business is "know your customer." This rule is especially true in the fashion business. To satisfy the greatest number of customers and make them want to buy their products, every designer, manufacturer, and retailer must know the answers to the following questions:

- How many potential customers for your products and services are there in a given community?
- How old are these customers?
- How much are they willing to spend on your product?
- What level of service do they expect?
- Are they married or single, homeowners or renters?
- How many children do they have?
- What kind of work do they do?
- What is their annual income?
- What is more important to them: value or style? Prestige or price?
- How much do they have to spend on "extras"?
- Do they like to shop early or late in the day? Weekdays or weekends?
- What motivates them to shop in a particular store?
- How do they spend their leisure time?

In other words, *Who are your customers?*

Accurate facts about customers, properly interpreted, help designers, manufacturers, and retailers make important decisions about what to offer them. Guesswork and misinterpreted facts can lead to major business failures.

One major source of information about the consumer market is the U.S. Census Bureau, www.census.gov. The U.S. census produces more than 3 billion separate statistics about how many Americans there are, what work they do, where they live, and how they are doing as measured by income and creature comforts. These seemingly dull statistics are a treasure trove of vital information, not only for government but also for every business. They help businesspeople who are interested in translating the data and projections drawn from them into new product and profit opportunities.

Used properly, census data provide us with all-important information about conditions that affect our lives and influence our actions. Collectively, the conditions under which we live are called our **environment**. Just as the environment of one nation or society differs from that of another nation or society, so the environment of one neighborhood differs from that of another. In fashion merchandising, it is important to be aware of the conditions that affect a particular customer's environment and to know how the environment differs from one group to another.

Four major environmental factors that affect fashion interest and demand, which will be discussed in this chapter, are:

1. Market segmentation by geographics, demographics, psychographics, and behavior.
2. The degree of economic development and well-being of a country or society.
3. The sociological characteristics of the class structure.
4. The psychological attitudes of consumers.

## Market Segmentation

Both manufacturers and retailers try to identify and select target markets for their goods. **Target markets** are specific groups of potential customers that a business is attempting to turn into regular customers. Businesses attempt to determine who their customers are, what those customers want, how much the customers are willing to pay for goods, where potential customers are located, and how many targeted customers there are. Today, geographic, demographic, psychographic, and behavioral research studies are vital to determining these important factors.

Most manufacturers and designers are concerned with national trends. Retailers, however, must consider the impact of statistics in their local areas as well as statistics from national studies. **Market segmentation** is the separation of the total consumer market into smaller groups known as **market segments.** By identifying and studying each market segment, producers and retailers can target their goods and services to their special markets. Markets are divided or segmented in four main ways: by geographics, demographics, psychographics, and behavior.

## Geographics

Geographics are population studies that focus on where people live. These studies organize data by region of the country, by county or city size, by population density, and by climate. See Table 3.1 for geographic data on apparel spending.

## Demographics

**Demographics** are population studies that divide broad groups of consumers into smaller, more homogeneous market segments. The variables covered in a demographic study include:

- Age
- Sex
- Family size
- Stages in family life cycle
- Income
- Occupation
- Education
- Religion
- Race and ethnicity or nationality

## Psychographics

**Psychographics** are studies that develop fuller, more personal portraits of potential customers and their lifestyles. Psychographic studies more fully predict consumer purchase patterns and distinguish users of a product. The variables covered in a psychographic study include social class, values and lifestyle, and personality.

Sometimes researchers request information about the actual product benefits desired by consumers. These studies help greatly in matching the image of a company and its product with the type of consumer using the product.

Many research firms combine geographic and demographic studies for retailers and manufacturers. One such firm, Claritas, produces the PRIZM system, which divides and then clusters the U.S. population into sixty-six market segments or "clusters" based on postal zip codes, housing, and lifestyle choices. The clusters are then grouped into fourteen broader groups based on degree of urbanization and socioeconomic status. See the interesting group names in Table 3.2.[1]

PRIZM reveals what people buy, but not why. To get closer to that information, many people turn to another widely used research system that uses demographics and psychographics: the VALS system. The VALS (originally Values and Life Styles) system sorts customers into eight major categories based on psychological attributes. The categories are arranged into a framework that puts consumers

**TABLE 3.1** *Estimated Household Spending on Apparel*

| RANK | METROPOLITAN AREA | AVG. YEARLY SPENDING |
|---|---|---|
| 1 | New York–Northern New Jersey–Long Island; New York–New Jersey–Connecticut | $2,682 |
| 2 | Los Angeles–Long Beach, California | $2,514 |
| 3 | San Francisco–Oakland–San Jose, California | $2,321 |
| 4 | Philadelphia–Wilmington–Trenton; Pennsylvania–New Jersey–Delaware–Maryland | $2,310 |
| 5 | St. Louis–East St. Louis–Alton, Missouri–Illinois | $2,260 |
| | Average U.S. | $1,728 |

Source: U.S. Census Bureau, Statistical Abstract of the United States, 2007. Based on data from 2004.

**TABLE 3.2** *Marketing Segments*

| GROUP | SEGMENTS |
|---|---|
| Urban Uptown | Money & Brains, Young Digerati, Bohemian Mix |
| Midtown Mix | Urban Achievers, Close-In Couples |
| Urban Cores | Urban Elders, Big City Blues |
| Elite Suburbs | Blue Blood Estates, Movers and Shakers |
| The Affluentials | Executive Suites, Pools & Patios, Kids & Cul-de-Sacs |
| Middleburbs | Gray Power, Young Influentials |
| Inner Suburbs | New Beginnings, American Classics |
| Second City Society | Second City Elite, Upward Bound |
| City Centers | Up-and-Comers, White Picket Fences |
| Micro-City Blues | City Startups, Park Bench Seniors |
| Landed Gentry | Big Fish, Small Pond, Fast-Track Families |
| Country Comfort | Greenbelt Sports, New Homesteaders, Big Sky Families |
| Middle America | Heartlanders |
| Rustic Living | Young & Rustic, Bedrock America |

Source: Claritas Inc., 2007, www.claritas.com

with the high resources on the top and those with the low, on the bottom (see Figure 3.1). The main dimensions of the segmentation framework are primary motivation (the horizontal dimension) and resources (the vertical dimension).

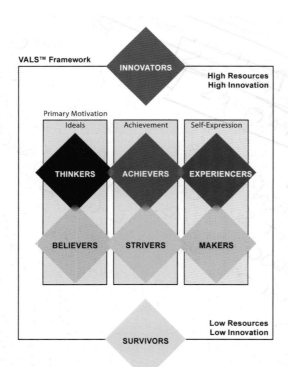

**FIGURE 3.1** In the VALS System, each diamond-shaped box represents one of the eight consumer markets.

## Primary Motivation

According to SRIC Business Intelligence (SRIC-BI), "Consumers buy products and services and seek experiences that fulfill their characteristic preferences and give shape, substance, and satisfaction to their lives. An individual's primary motivation determines what in particular about the self or the world is the meaningful core that governs his or her activities."[2]

SRIC-BI identifies three primary motivations that drive consumers' buying decisions: ideals, achievement, and self-expression. Consumers who are primarily motivated by ideals are guided by knowledge and principles. Consumers who are primarily motivated by achievement look for products and services that demonstrate success to their peers. Consumers who are primarily motivated by self-expression desire social or physical activity, variety, and risk.[3]

## Resources

We discuss resources more thoroughly in the next section, "The Economic Environment," but here we make the point that personality traits influence the way people use their resources. Conversely, consumers' level of resources—their income—influences the degree to which they can express, through purchasing decisions, their personality traits.

A person's tendency to consume goods and services extends beyond age, income, and education. Energy, self-confidence, intellectualism, novelty seeking, innovativeness, impulsiveness, leadership, and vanity play a critical role. These personality traits in conjunction with key demographics determine an individual's resources. Different levels of resources enhance or constrain a person's expression of his or her primary motivation.[4]

## *Behavior*

In an attempt to gather even more insight into customer preferences, some retailers and manufacturers use research on **behavior**. These studies group consumers according to (1) their opinions of specific products or services and (2) their actual rate of use of these products or services. Behavioral studies help companies understand and predict the behavior of present and potential customers. If you segment your market by behavior, you might be able to identify the reasons for one group's refusal to buy your product. Once you have identified the reason, you may be able to change the product enough to satisfy their objections. A more recent extension of VALS, GeoVALS, uses psychographics to identify where customers live and further explain their behavioral trends.

## The Economic Environment

The growth of fashion demand depends on a high level of economic development, which is reflected in consumer income, population characteristics, and technological advances. In his book *On Human Finery*,[5] Quentin Bell underscores the relationship between economics and fashion. He explains that most economically sophisticated countries discard their national costumes long before other nations begin to abandon theirs. England, for example, which led the Western world into the industrial revolution, was the first country to stop wearing traditional national dress. Bell points out that Greece, Poland, and Spain, countries with little in common except for being in similar stages of economic development, retained their national costumes when countries with more industrialized economies—Germany, Belgium, Denmark, and Japan—were abandoning theirs.

A striking example of how countries with swift economic development also move ahead in fashion is the People's Republic of China. Long restricted to the traditional blue Mao jacket and pants for both sexes, the Chinese have increased their interest in contemporary fashions with their increased economic growth, complete with fashion shows and boutiques (see Figure 3.2). With control of Hong Kong restored to China by Britain in 1997, the

**FIGURE 3.2** Asian fashion has embraced a contemporary style of dress. From top to bottom: a traditional look to fabulous new fashions.

# Fashion Focus

Fashion Focus

## Glamorous, Glamorous, Glamorous! Valentino, We Bid You Adieu, But Never Goodbye

Since 1962, when he started his own label in Rome, masterminding an empire of couture, ready-to-wear, and accessories, his only purpose was and is to make women beautiful! Valentino has used his inimitable talent for wrapping women up—like the greatest gifts in the world!

When he talks about couture, he is excited and brightens like a little schoolboy. Whether it was with his first red dress in 1959, his famed white collection in 1968, or Kate Winslet's mint gown at the 2007 Oscars, Valentino has had one goal: make the woman pop! "I love dresses that embellish the lady," he says.

Born in Voghera, Italy, Valentino, at age 17, convinced his parents to let him move to Paris, where he took drawing lessons at the Chambre Syndicale de la Couture Parisienne in 1950. He remained in Paris and worked for both Jean Desses and Guy Laroche, well-known Paris couturies of the time.

At the end of the 1950s, Valentino returned to Rome and, in 1962, presented his first couture collection at Palazzo Pitti in Florence. Critics and retailers alike described it as a triumph.

Because of his intense focus, he has been able to weather fashion's cycles and develop a broad perspective over the past five decades. "Fashion is an accordion—back and forth, up and down—you have to have your head firmly on your shoulders and remember who your customer is instead of wasting your time trying to design foolish things to catch the attention of the press," he said in 1989. (These are wonderful words for all the new young designers of today.)

Valentino's fame grew and stars

flocked to his couture house—Liz Taylor, Rita Hayworth, and Audrey Hepburn leading the way. The world's best-dressed socialites, including Marella Agnelli, Babe Paley, and Jackie Kennedy, weren't far behind. And after 1968, the year he showed his all-white collection and also designed Jackie Kennedy's ivory georgette dress for her wedding to Aristotle Onassis, he became an international star.

Valentino's reputation took off in America in the late 1960s. With actor's sideburns, a perennial tan, and macro sunglasses, he was his own best fashion advertisement.

Today, at the age of 75, he still is the golden boy who smiles at the world, knowing that it will smile right back. And that's why generations of Roman

Left page: Valentino with his signature red dresses (top); a classic red gown look (bottom left) and a recent update to the red look (bottom right).

aristocrats, Hollywood stars, and Park Avenue princesses have continued to go to him for beautifully constructed ball gowns and wedding dresses, as have all of the sheiks' daughters and hedge-fund manager's wives who finance his couture business.

Valentino and red go way back. To him, it's the color of love, passion, life, death—and the best remedy for sadness. "Valentino Red" has become a staple of the fashion lexicon, with nearly all of his collections featuring a flash of the fiery shade. "Even the most simple and normal dress becomes rich and meaningful if done in red," he explains, "It's the only strong color that I really love."

Valentino has been honored by the fashion centers of the world, starting in 1967 when he was awarded the Neiman Marcus Prize (the equivalent of an Oscar in the world of fashion). In 1984, he received an official award from the Ministry for Industry of Italy honoring his 25th year in business.

In 1986, he received the highest decoration possible in Italy, the Cavaliere di Gran Croce, from the President. In 1996, Valentino was named Cavaliere del Lavoro, and in 2006, French President Chirac awarded Valentino with the final jewel in the crown of achievements: Chevalier de la Legion d'Honneur from the country where he arrived as a 17-year-old Italian boy and fell in love with haute couture.

To celebrate the 45th anniversary of Valentino's career, a fashion extravaganza took place in Rome July 2007—A three-day, $10 million celebration of Valentino fashion. At the fashion show, the lineup of so many of Valentino's designer peers in one place explained the impact of his career in fashion. Donatella Versace, Giorgio Armani, Karl Lagerfeld, Diane von Furstenberg, Zac Posen, Manolo Blahnik, Tom Ford, and Carolina Herrera, among may others, stood with the rest of the audience and applauded as Valentino, in a white suit, led models down the runway for the finale—a fitting climax to a fabulous career and retirement.

As for his future, Valentino says it will be full of new commitments. "It is my intention to create and support institutions that promote design and that preserve the art of fashion. I think this would be the best continuation of this wonderful adventure that I had the privilege of living." So says Valentino!

Chinese fashion industry got a boost from Hong Kong–based companies that moved their manufacturing facilities to the mainland.

A notable example of the reverse situation occurred in Afghanistan in the mid- to late 1990s, when the fundamentalist Taliban faction rose to power and required strict adherence to traditional religious law, including prescribed dress. Men were required to grow their beards and women to wear only the most concealing traditional dress. These laws were a manifestation of a legal code that was particularly severe in its treatment of women, denying them even the right to an education. The political and economic climate of the country at the time of the takeover was one of turmoil, and the repressive regime cut Afghanistan off from participation in the global economy. In 2001, the country underwent a complicated and uncertain governmental transition that now tries to satisfy the needs of many ethnic and tribal groups, as well as the U.S. demand for stability and transparency in the region.

## Consumer Income

Consumer income can be measured in terms of personal income, disposable income, and discretionary income. Many groups of people use the amount of personal income as an indicator of "arriving" in their particular social set. The more personal income they have, the more socially acceptable they consider themselves to be.

At present, many U.S. families may be earning more personal income but enjoying it less. Statistics have shown sharp increases in personal income in the past decades but decreases in amounts of disposable and discretionary income.

### Personal Income

The total or gross income received by the population as a whole is called **personal income**. It consists of wages, salaries, interest, dividends, and all other income for everyone in the country. Divide personal income by the number of people in the population and the result is **per capita personal income.**

## Disposable Personal Income

The amount a person has left to spend or save after paying taxes is called **disposable personal income.** It is roughly equivalent to take-home pay and provides an approximation of the purchasing power of each consumer during any given year.

Disposable income per household and per capita varies according to age groups and sex (see Figure 3.3). While household after-tax income starts to drop after age 49, individual after-tax income does not peak until ages 60 to 64, showing that consumers in the 50- to 64-year-old age bracket often have the highest disposable income.

## Discretionary Income

The money that an individual or family can spend or save after buying necessities—food, clothing, shelter, and basic transportation—is called **discretionary income.** Of course, the distinction between "necessities" and "luxuries" or between "needs" and "wants" is a subjective one.

One definition of "middle class" is the middle 60 percent of U.S. households, ranked by income. The most commonly cited figures from the Census data are from all households mixed together. Median income among all U.S. households in 2006 was $48,201. The middle 60 percent ranged from about $20,000 to $97,000.[6] Although the economic gap is still growing, it is imperative to keep the middle class strong, for they are the key factor in fueling the American economy.

The lucky few are like consumer royalty, able to buy a wide variety of goods and services. Although marketers like to target these consumers, it may not be a wise long-term strategy. The super-rich have greater purchasing power, but they are declining in number. While middle-class households have less money, they still have overwhelming strength in numbers.

## Purchasing Power of the Dollar

Average income has been increasing each year, but people have not gained an equivalent increase in purchasing power because the value of the dollar—its **purchasing power,** or what it will buy—has steadily declined since 1950.

A decline in the purchasing power of money is caused by inflation. **Inflation** is an increase in available money and credit, with relative scarcity of goods, resulting in a significant rise in prices.[7] Inflation, therefore, is an economic situation in which demand exceeds supply. Scarcity of goods and services, in relation to demand, results in ever-increasing prices. Table 3.3 shows the changes in the purchasing power of the consumer dollar from 1950 to 2005.

When income taxes increase, the purchasing power of the family income drops; a decrease in income taxes has the reverse effect. With an inflationary economy, the working time required to acquire the necessities of life—basic food, clothing, transportation, and shelter—increases. The increase is not, however, uniform among all items.

In a **recession,** which represents a low point in a business cycle, money and credit become scarce, or

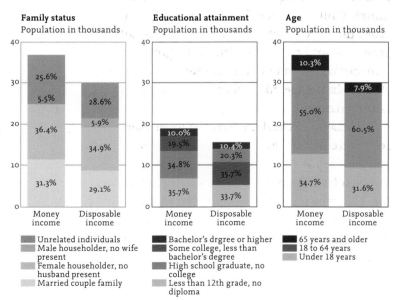

Source: U.S. Census Bureau, Current Population Survey, 2006 Annual Social and Economic Supplement.

**FIGURE 3.3** Personal and disposable incomes vary according to family status, educational attainment, and age.

**TABLE 3.3** *Purchasing Power of the Dollar: 1950–2005*

| YEAR | AVERAGE AS MEASURED BY CONSUMER PRICES |
|------|----------------------------------------|
| 1950 | $4.15 |
| 1955 | $3.73 |
| 1960 | $3.37 |
| 1965 | $3.16 |
| 1970 | $2.57 |
| 1975 | $1.85 |
| 1980 | $1.21 |
| 1985 | $0.92 |
| 1990 | $0.76 |
| 1995 | $0.65 |
| 2000 | $0.58 |
| 2005 | $0.51 |

Source: *Statistical Abstract of the United States*—2007, U.S. Department of Commerce, p. 493.

"tight." Interest rates are high, production is down, and the rate of unemployment is up. People in the lower-income groups are the hardest hit; those with high incomes are the least affected. Yet these groups are small when compared with the middle-income group. It is the reaction of these middle-income people to any economic squeeze that is the greatest concern of the fashion merchant. Not only is the middle-income group the largest, it is also the most important market for fashion merchandise.

Both inflation and recession affect consumers' buying patterns. Fashion merchants in particular must thoroughly understand the effects of inflation and recession when planning their inventory assortments and promotional activities. Manufacturers must also understand how consumers are affected by economic factors.

## Population

The majority of the population of the United States has some discretionary income and thus can influence the course of fashion. Two factors relating to population, however, have an important bearing on the extent of fashion demand:

1. The size of the total population and the rate of its growth
2. The age mix of the population and its projection into the future

## Size of Population

The size of the population relates to the extent of current fashion demand. The rate of population growth suggests what tomorrow's market may become. In 1920, the United States had a population of about 106 million. By 1950, that figure had reached 151 million, and by 1980, 227.6 million. In 2005, the population reached 296.4 million, showing the largest increase in one decade in U.S. history. By 2025, the U.S. population is estimated to reach 349.4 million![8]

## Age Mix

The age mix and its projection into the future affect the characteristics of current fashion demand and suggest what they may be in the future. While the overall population continues to grow, the growth rate is not the same for all age groups or for both sexes. Since each group has its own special fashion interests, needs, and reactions, changes in the age mix serve as vital clues to future fashion demand.

For example, children born between 1946 and 1964 were known as the **baby-boom generation**, because they were the largest group ever recorded. The first baby boomers reached age 55 in 2000, and the largest and fastest growing age group in the United States was graying. They were followed by the much smaller "baby bust" or **generation X** group. This group was in turn followed by the

**TABLE 3.4** *Guide to the Generations*

| GENERATION | BORN | LABELS OF THE TIMES | GENERATION TALK | FAMOUS PEOPLE AND THEIR GENERATION |
|---|---|---|---|---|
| G.I. Generation | 1900-1924 | War generation | They are high achievers; fearless, but not reckless; patriotic; idealistic; and morally conscience. | Christian Dior, Claire McCardell, Bonnie Cashin, Walt Disney |
| Silent Generation | 1925-1945 | Depression generation | They are categorized as being conventional, expecting disappointment but desiring faith; for women, there is the desire for both a career and a family. | Liz Claiborne, Sonia Rykiel, Betsey Johnson, Ralph Lauren |
| Baby Boomers | 1946-1964 | Love generation, the hippies | The end of World War II brought a baby boom to many countries, which gave this generation its name; they were the first to have televisions in their homes, which exposed them to news, shows, music, and marketers in a whole new way. | Diane von Furstenberg, Donna Karan, John Galliano, Marc Jacobs, Tom Ford |
| Generation X | 1965-1979 | Gap generation | This generation was originally known as "baby bust;" however, later in the UK the term Generation X was used and stuck. Generation X thinking has significant overtones of cynicism against things held dear to the previous generations. | Alexander McQueen, Nicolas Ghesquière, Kate Moss, Stella McCartney, Naomi Campbell |
| Generation Y or Millenials | 1980-2000 | iGeneration, the MyPod generation | This generation is described as "the digital age that heralded in its birth;" they grew up with more family breakdowns and divorces, which causes them to be more peer-oriented. | Zac Posen, Clare Tough, Christian Soriano |
| Generation Z or New Silent Generation | 2000–present | Internet generation | This generation numerically was the smallest of any other living generation. They are known to grow up faster, and are exposed to education earlier. They are also known as the Internet-savvy, technologically literate generation. | Who will the world see next? |

Source: http://geography.about.com/od/populationgeography/qt/generations.htm and the U.S. Census Bureau, http://www.census.gov. Accessed March 2008.

slightly larger "baby boomlet" or "echo-boom" group, known as **generation Y.** (See Table 3.4 for infomation about generations.)

Because both men and women are living longer, the over-age-65 group is steadily growing. Those 50 years old and older account for over one-half of all discretionary spending power. This mature group becomes increasingly important in the fashion world as their earlier retirement—and in many cases, increased retirement incomes—allows them to spend many active years wherever and however they choose. They are healthier, better educated, more active, and will live longer than the generations before them. Their interests and discretionary purchases vary radically from those of their younger counterparts, offering a real challenge to businesses to meet the demands of the "new old." The demand of older consumers for items such as package travel tours, cosmetic aids, and apparel that suits their ages and retirement lifestyles offer

growth opportunities for marketers, especially in fashion.

## The Sociological Environment

To understand fashion, we must understand the sociological environment in which fashion trends begin, grow, and fade away. The famous stage and screen designer Cecil Beaton saw fashion as a social phenomenon that reflects "the same continuum of change that rides through any given age." Changes in fashion, Beaton emphasized, "correspond with the subtle and often hidden network of forces that operate on society. . . . In this sense, fashion is a symbol."[9]

Simply stated, changes in fashion are caused by changes in the attitudes of consumers, which in turn are influenced by changes in the social patterns of the times (see Figure 3.4). The key sociological factors influencing fashion today are leisure time, ethnic influences, status of women, social and

**FIGURE 3.4** What a difference a decade makes! Top row from left to right: the covered-up 20s, the sturdy 40s, the flirty 50s; bottom row from left to right: the wild 60s, the "anything goes" 90s, and today, back to covering it up!

physical mobility, instant communications, and wars, disasters, and crises.

### Leisure Time

One of the most precious possessions of the average U.S. citizen today is leisure time, because it is also one of the most scarce. The demands of the workplace compete with the demands of family and home for much of people's waking hours, leaving less and less time for the pursuit of other activities, whether those activities be a fitness regimen, community work, entertainment, relaxation—or even shopping.

The ways in which people use their leisure time are as varied as people themselves. Some turn to active or spectator sports; others prefer to travel. Many seek self-improvement, while growing numbers improve their standard of living with a second job. The increased importance of leisure time has

# Then & NOW

## Sixty Years of New Looks
### *Then Dior*
### *and Now Galliano*

Since Christian Dior first dazzled the fashion world with the "New Look," the house he founded has had a bold and dramatic history.

From day one—February 12, 1947—Dior has left fashion watchers breathless. "A bright new star flashed into the couture firmament today when Christian Dior presented the first collection of his house to a three-rows deep audience," *Women's Wear Daily* reported from Paris. The New Look, as it was soon dubbed, became the must-have of the icons of the day—the Duchess of Windsor, Marlene Dietrich, Princess Margaret, Eva Perón, Gloria Guinness, and Babe Paley. In 1954, Dior addressed the era's stylish "every woman" with his *Little Dictionary of Fashion*, which included some of the following quips. *B* is for ballgown: "as necessary in a woman's wardrobe as a suit." *D* is for décolleté: "Nothing is more becoming, nothing is more feminine, nothing is more attractive." *H* is for handbags: "Don't forget, a bag is not a wastepaper basket." *S* is for sable: "the queen of all furs." *Z* is for zest: "This is a happy word with which to end my dictionary of fashion; anything you do, work or pleasure, you have to do it with zest."

For 10 years, from 1947 to 1957, Christian Dior ruled the world of couture and built a business unrivaled in his day. Sadly, in 1957, Dior died of a heart attack. Within months, a 21-year-old named Yves Saint Laurent, who had joined Dior's fashion house in 1953, took the helm, but by 1960, his tenure at Dior ended and he left to start his own couture house. The next designer to lead the house was Marc Bohan. Until 1989, the gentlemanly Bohan designed proper, discreet clothes for clients such as Princess Caroline of Monaco and Betsy Bloomingdale— clothes that fashion critics found much too conservative. Following Marc Bohan as the designer of Dior was Granfranco Ferré, an Italian designer who was not welcomed in the French design house, and critics called his Dior shows boring!

Now, on the contrary, no fashion watcher could call John Galliano galloping entrée a bore. The punk-meets-French romantic collections he staged under his own name in London in the mid-1980s became legendary. Like Dior's New Look, Galliano's nostalgic romance was something new in the early

Left page: Christian Dior with models at a fashion show, 1950 (top); 2008 collection inspired by John Singer Sargent's portrait "Madame X" (bottom left); Dior's Satin dress with linen jacket, 1947 (middle); right page: John Galliano with models in 2005.

1990s. In 1994, his polished, curvy ode to Dior was a wake-up call that resounded throughout the industry. "It was a strike back against the whole grunge movement and the undercurrent of deconstruction," said Galliano. "I wanted to be positive. I wanted to construct, and I wanted a return to glamour. That was my vision of Mr. Dior."

In 1995, Galliano was appointed head designer at Givenchy and remained there until 1997 when he was appointed head designer at Dior. Upon his appointment, he dove into the archives, pouring over photos and sketches and turning Monsieur Dior's samples inside out. Tapping into Dior's obsession with the Belle Epoque and his interest in Picasso and in African art, on the eve of the house's 50th anniversary, Galliano pulled off a stunning debut.

Since then, boundless imagination has informed his collections, often staged in elaborate settings. Many times, Galliano has faced off against critics who constantly accuse him of showing costumery.

The proof is in the profit. Pre-Galliano Dior owned thirty-two stores; today there are nearly two hundred. Bernard Arnault, owner of the LVMH luxury empire and of Dior house, stated, "John Galliano was criticized when he started, but thanks to him, we have built this luxury house into the best in the world." Galliano seduced a younger customer with a sexier silhouette and sleek advertising, and now he oversees all in-house collections, including accessories, costume jewelry, furs, kid's clothing, swimwear, lingerie, and perfume.

Along the way, stars such as Nicole Kidman, Gwen Stefani, Uma Thurman, and Charlize Theron have flocked to the house for its red-carpet perfection. But inside the fashion world, Galliano's own postshow runway bows spark nearly as much interest: Will he sport a bowler or a cowboy hat? Gypsy baubles or bandera stripes? Will he go oiled or bare-chested or Napoleonic? Years ago, Galliano's sensationalized looks convinced members of the old guard that Monsieur Dior would not approve. For his part, however, Galliano, who has now served at the house for nearly as long as its namesake, feels certain that Monsieur Dior has given his celestial blessing.

Then was then. Now is now!

brought changes to people's lives in many ways—in values, standards of living, and scope of activities. As a result, whole new markets have sprung up. Demand for larger and more versatile wardrobes for the many activities consumers can now explore and enjoy has mushroomed.

## Casual Living

A look into the closets of the American population would probably reveal one aspect that is much the same from coast to coast, in large cities and in small towns: most would contain an unusually large selection of casual clothes and sportswear. The market for casual apparel developed with the growth of the suburbs in the 1950s and has had a continuous series of boosts in the years since. The "do your own thing" revolution of the 1960s made a casual look for men and women acceptable in what had been more formal places and occasions. The 1970s saw a tremendous surge in the number of women wearing slacks and pantsuits and in the number of men and women wearing jeans just about everywhere.

Even with the return to more formal styles for many occasions in the 1980s, comfortable styling and casual influence continue to strongly influence dress in all segments of society. In the 1990s, "dress-down Fridays" at work became popular from coast to coast. The choice as to what is suitable for an activity is still largely left to the individual, and now a shift in the direction of casual dress has begun a reverse trend as an interest in "dressing up" starts to grow again.

## Active Sportswear

There is no doubt about it: the superstar of the fashion market in the 1970s, the 1980s, and the 1990s was sportswear. Its growth was phenomenal! While sports clothes have been around since the turn of the century, when they first appeared they were not particularly distinctive. Women's sport dresses for playing tennis or golf were not much different from their regular streetwear, and men's

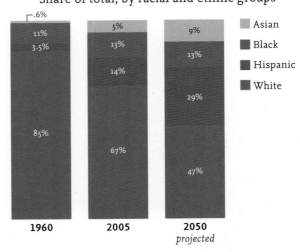

**U.S. Population 1960-2050**
Share of total, by racial and ethnic groups

**FIGURE 3.5** Projections show the proportion of the non-Hispanic white majority shrinking, the Hispanic population replacing African Americans as the largest minority, and the percentage of Asian Americans increasing at a fast rate.

outfits similarly varied little from business suits. By the 1920s, consumers began demanding apparel that was appropriate for active sports or simply for relaxing in the sunshine. But it is the emphasis on health and self in the past three decades that has caused the fantastic growth of the active sportswear market.

Today, sports-minded people play tennis in specially designed tennis fashions. Golfers want special golfwear. Joggers want only jogging outfits. And cyclists seem able to bike only in spandex biker shorts and high-tech helmets. Rollerbladers also want helmets, wrist and knee guards, and appropriate fashions. The same goes for ice-skaters, skiers, runners, hang gliders, sky divers, and climbers. Health clubs, exercise classes, and workout gyms exploded in popularity in the 1980s, and by 2007, membership in health clubs and gyms was considered to be a way of life. A whole new and vast world of leotards, exercise suits, warm-up suits, and other self-improvement fashions and accessories were born. Whatever the activity, the specialized fashions—from jogging suits to biker shorts—quickly followed and became de rigueur. Today, even those who do not participate in a particular sport beyond watching the pros on television feel the need to look the part!

## Ethnic Influences

In recent years, minority groups in the United States, representing over 30 percent of the nation's total population, have experienced vast population increases and sociological changes. The future holds even more change. By 2005, African Americans had slipped from the largest minority group in the United States to the second largest. Hispanics now outnumber African Americans, and the Asian population exhibits a rapid rate of growth (see Figure 3.5). This historic shift in the racial and ethnic composition of the U.S. population has many long-range implications. For example, the growth of the Hispanic and Asian populations has brought about

an increased demand for clothing in smaller sizes because both men and women in these groups are typically smaller in stature than people whose ethnic heritage is Northern European.[10]

## Hispanics

The Spanish-speaking market within the United States is growing so fast that market researchers cannot keep up with it. In 1987, there were an estimated 18 million Hispanics in the United States. In addition, 6 to 10 million undocumented Hispanics were estimated to be here. By 2005, the documented Hispanic population of the United States had increased to 42.6 million, making them the largest minority group in the nation.[11] Today, the United States follows only Mexico and Colombia in Hispanic population. By 2015, the Hispanic population is expected to be 16.6 percent of the total U.S. population, or more than 53 million people.[12]

Until 1930, immigration to the United States was almost exclusively from Europe and Asia. For the next three decades, Latin Americans, mostly from Mexico and Puerto Rico, comprised 15 percent of the immigrants. By 1970, that portion had grown to 40 percent, with an influx of people from Central and South America. Refugees from Cuba have been arriving since 1961; the annual number peaked at more than 120,000 during the Mariel boatlift in

1980 and has settled to 3,000 to 5,000 per year since the 1990s.[13]

The Hispanic population has made its impact on the fashion scene with the introduction of fiery colors and of prints reminiscent of lush South American rainforests. Dance and music styles from mariachi to macarena have been accepted by the entire American public.

## African Americans

At 13.0 percent of the population in 2005, African Americans were the second-largest minority in the United States, with a collective income of $543 billion.[14] They are better educated and hold higher-level jobs than they did in the past. With better education comes a stronger sense of oneself and one's heritage. Many black people show the pride they feel in their African heritage by wearing African styles, fabrics, and patterns. Other ethnic groups have adopted these styles as well. Fashion companies have acknowledged the changes that have occurred among the African American population and have reflected these changes in the products they market and the models they use. Cosmetics are available that emphasize rather than hide the beauty of dark skin. African American men and women have become world famous through modeling clothing and advertising various items in magazines and on television.

## Asians

Asian Americans are the fastest growing minority group in the United States, with a population that has doubled since 1975. This population, about 10.7 million in 2000, will more than triple again by 2050. But Asian Americans are not one homogeneous group. They come from more than a dozen countries and speak at least forty-one different languages!

About two-thirds of Asians in the United States are recent immigrants and have different characteristics from second-, third-, and fourth-generation U.S.-born Asian Americans.[15] These refugees joined other Asians who were already part of our country: Chinese, Filipinos, Japanese, and Koreans.

Asians in the United States are more geographically concentrated than blacks or Hispanics. The states that account for roughly half of the Asian population are New York, California, and Texas.[16]

The end of the Vietnamese war and the influx of thousands of refugees from Cambodia and Vietnam brought additional traditions and costumes to be shared. This stimulated interest in some of the more exotic fashions of the East and in the everyday comfort of the Chinese sandal and quilted jacket.

Immigration from many Asian countries is up sharply. The number of Koreans and Filipinos is growing rapidly. But the largest numbers of immigrants have come from India. At 2.5 million, the Asian Indian population in the United States has more than tripled between 1990 and 2005, fueled by the high demand for high-tech work as well as an increase in the number of immigrants.[17]

Most Asian Indians who came to the United States in the 1980s were affluent; 60 percent of those in the workforce were in professions, as opposed to 34 percent of all U.S. employees.[18] As with most recent immigrant groups, Asian Americans tend to live in and around major cities, like New York, Chicago, and Los Angeles.

## *Status of Women*

In the early 1900s, the American woman was, in many ways, a nonperson. She could not vote, serve on a jury, earn a living at any but a few occupations, own property, or enter public places unescorted. She passed directly from her father's control to her husband's control, without rights or monies. In both households, she dressed to please the man and reflect his status.

Profound changes began to occur during World War I and have accelerated ever since. The most dramatic advances have happened since the mid-

82

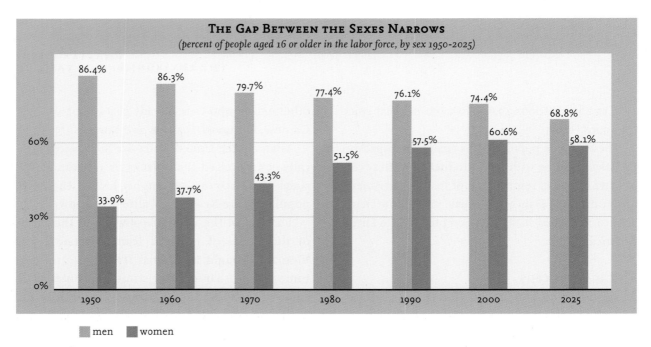

**THE GAP BETWEEN THE SEXES NARROWS**
*(percent of people aged 16 or older in the labor force, by sex 1950-2025)*

**FIGURE 3.6** The labor force has changed drastically since 1950, and the gap between the sexes is projected to narrow even further by 2025.

1960s, propelled by the women's movement. Women's demands for equal opportunity, equal pay, and equal rights in every facet of life continue to bring about even more change. These changes have affected not only fashion but the entire field of marketing.

## Jobs and Money

The number of women aged 16 and over who work has increased dramatically since 1975: a staggering 31.8 million women have entered the workforce since then. Although this figure has increased, women's salaries in 2005 were still, on average, only 77 percent of men's salaries. Both financial pressures and career satisfaction should keep the number of working women growing. As of 2005, roughly 60 percent of all women were working, and a growing number of women continue to enter the workforce each year (see Figure 3.6). [19]

The dramatic increase in the number of working women has led to a surge in fashion interest, because a woman who works is continuously exposed to fashion. It is everywhere around her as she meets people, shops during her lunch hour, or is on her way home. As a member of the workforce,

she now has the incentive, the opportunity, and the means to respond to fashion's appeal. Magazines such as *Ms.* and *Working Woman* make this market reachable.

Finally, women in general today have more money of their own to spend as they see fit. Approximately four women in every six have incomes, earned and unearned, of their own. These women and their acceptance or rejection of offered styles have new importance in the fashion marketplace.

## Education

Often, the better educated a woman becomes, the more willing she is to learn new things. She is also more willing to try new fashions, which of course serves to accelerate fashion change. And with more women today receiving more education than ever before, the repercussions on fashion are unmistakable. Today's educated women have had wider exposure than their mothers or grandmothers to other cultures and to people of different backgrounds. Consequently, they are more worldly, more discerning, more demanding, and more confident in their taste and feel for fashion.

No wonder Edward Sapir, a leading social scientist, considered education a major factor in fashion change. "Fashion is custom in the guise of departure from custom," said Sapir.[20] To him, fashion is a resolution of the conflict between people's revolt against adherence to custom and their reluctance to appear lacking in good taste.

## Social Freedom

Perhaps the most marked change in the status of women since the early 1900s is the degree of social freedom they now enjoy. Young women today are free to apply for a job and to earn, spend, and save their own money. They are free to go unescorted to a restaurant, theater, or other public place. Women travel more frequently than they did in the past. They travel to more distant locations at a younger age and often alone. Many own their own cars. If they can afford it, they may maintain an apartment or share one with others. It is difficult to imagine that the social freedoms and responsibilities that today's young women accept as normal were considered unfeminine or outrageous as recently as 30 years ago.

Short skirts, popular in the 1920s, the early 1940s, the 1960s, and the 2000s, are commonly interpreted as a reflection of women's freedom. So, too, is the simplicity of the styles that prevailed in those periods: chemises, sacks, tents, shifts, other variations of loose-hanging dresses, and pants.

Different theories exist about why these changes came about. Some people believe that stiff, unyielding corsets went out with a stiff, unyielding moral code. Others believe that the changes had no particular social significance. They believe that women rejected inflexible corsets not because of a change in the moral code but because the new materials were simply more comfortable. Similarly, pants may be viewed as an expression of women's freedom or merely as suitable garments for hopping in and out of the indispensable car.

Whatever the reasons, the lifestyles of American women and their opinions and attitudes about fashion have changed radically in the past three decades. American women have gained hard-won freedoms in their social and business lives. They are just as definite about their freedom of choice in fashion (see Figure 3.7). The thought of today's independent women accepting uncomfortable and constricting clothing or shoes just to follow the dictates of some fashion arbiter, as they did years ago, is ludicrous. Today's busy, active women, whether at home or at the office, have very carefully defined preferences for fashions that suit their own individual needs and comfort. Today's successful designers recognize these preferences and make sure that their drawing boards reflect them.

**FIGURE 3.7** Lindsay Price (right) is exercising her freedom to shop on the popular television show, *Lipstick Jungle*.

**TABLE 3.5** *The Six Major Social Classes in the United States*

| SOCIAL CLASS | CHARACTERISTICS |
|---|---|
| Upper-upper | These are the people in an area who represent "old families," who are locally prominent, and whose wealth is inherited. Such people usually occupy an old mansion and may have homes in other places. They are deeply interested in cultural events, usually travel extensively, serve on boards of charitable foundations, and are secure in their social position. |
| Lower-upper | The nouveau riches of the community constitute this class. Their wealth is not usually inherited but has been acquired by aggressive entrepreneurial activities. These people enjoy spending the wealth they have acquired, like publicity, and want to be seen at important events. They seek the news in purchases and lifestyles. |
| Upper-middle | These are moderately successful doctors, lawyers, and other professional people; owners of medium-sized businesses; and middle managers in large firms. They are concerned with status, live well, are usually substantial members of their communities, and have an enormous drive for success. |
| Lower-middle | To this group belongs the large segment of people who teach, work in offices, are small-business owners, successful salespeople, and blue-collar workers with good jobs. As a group, these people strive for success, are relatively conservative and respectable, either own their own homes or aspire to do so, and contribute to the overall stability of the country. |
| Upper-lower | People with limited education who may have fairly substantial incomes that are derived from semiskilled work or from work in small factories or retail shops, from jobs as police personnel, fire department employees, or sanitation workers, or from work as office clericals are classified in this group. These people often live from day to day, enjoy spending money (easy come, easy go), attend sporting events, and hang out at neighborhood recreation areas. |
| Lower-lower | This group comprises unskilled, uneducated, unemployed, and unassimilated people who are very poor, often on welfare, and sometimes even homeless. |

Source: Based on W. Lloyd Warner, Marchia Meeker, Kenneth Eells, *Social Class in America* (Chicago: Science Research Associates, 1949).

## Social Mobility

Almost all societies have classes, and individuals choose either to stand out from or to conform to their actual or aspired-to class. Bell viewed fashion as the process "whereby members of one class imitate those of another, who, in turn, are driven to ever new expedients of fashionable change."[21]

Bell considered the history of fashion inexplicable without relating it to social classes. He is not alone in his thinking. Other sociologists have related fashion change to changes in social mobility and to the effort to associate with a higher class by imitation.

The United States is sometimes called a classless society, but this concept is valid only in that there are no hereditary ranks, royalty, or untouchables. Classes do exist, but they are based largely upon occupation, income, residential location, education, or avocation, and their boundaries have become increasingly fluid. They range from the immensely wealthy (self-made millionaires or their descendants—the Vanderbilts, Whitneys, and Rockefellers, for example) at the top to the very wealthy (mostly nouveau riche) to the many middle-income levels and finally to the low-income and poverty levels. At the very bottom are the so-called hardcore unemployed and the homeless (see Table 3.5).

## Middle-Class Influence

Most fashion authorities agree that there is a direct relationship between the growth and strength of the middle class and the growth and strength of fashion demand. The middle class has the highest physical, social, and financial mobility. Because it is the largest class, it has the majority vote in the adoption of fashions. Members of the middle class tend to be followers, not leaders, of fashion, but the strength of their following pumps money into the fashion industry. And the persistence of their following often spurs fashion leaders to seek newer and different fashions of their own.

The United States has a very large middle class—roughly the middle 60 percent of U.S. households as ranked by their income.[22] They have both fashion interest and the money to indulge it. Despite fluctuations in the economy, this growth generally means a widespread increase in consumer buying power, which in turn generates increased fashion demand.

### Physical Mobility

Physical mobility, like social mobility, encourages the demand for and response to fashion. One effect of travel is "cross-pollination" of cultures. After seeing how other people live, travelers bring home a desire to adopt or adapt some of what they observed and make it part of their environment.

Marco Polo brought gunpowder, silks, and spices from the Orient, introducing new products to medieval Europe. In the 19th century, travelers brought touches of Asian and African fashions to Western dress and home furnishings. In the 20th century, Latin American and pre-Columbian influences were introduced into North America, dramatically changing the direction and emphasis of fashion in this country.

In the United States, people enjoy several kinds of physical mobility. For example, the daily routine for many people involves driving to work or to a shopping center, often in a different city. Among the broad range of influences they are exposed to during their daily trips are the fashions of others and the fashion offerings of retail distributors.

A second form of physical mobility popular among Americans is vacation travel. Whether travelers are going to a nearby lake or around the world, each trip exposes them to many different fashion influences, and each trip itself demands special fashions. Living out of a suitcase for a few days or a few months requires clothes that are easy to pack, wrinkle-resistant, suitable for a variety of occasions, and easy to keep in order.

A third form of physical mobility is change of residence, which, like travel, exposes an individual to new contacts, new environments, and new fashion influences.

### Faster Communications

Related to physical mobility is faster communications. Not many years ago, news of every sort traveled more slowly. This meant that life moved more slowly and fashions changed more slowly. It took weeks or months for people in one section of the country to learn what was being worn in another part of the country. Fashion trends moved at a pace that was as leisurely as the news.

Our electronic age has changed all that. Today, we enjoy rapid communication in ever-increasing quantities and infinite varieties. By means of satellites and round-the-clock broadcasting, television brings the world to our homes. It has become a most important medium for transmitting fashion information. Famous designers create special costumes for stars, and we all take note. Changes in the dress and hairstyles of our favorite newscasters, talk-show personalities, series characters, and even sports stars have a great impact on us. For instance, in the mid-1990s, the hip-hop look swept the coun-

**FIGURE 3.8** Famous model Christy Turlington's yoga line, which encourages people to be more active and fit.

try, as teenagers and young adults tried to emulate the style of their favorite rap stars.

Popular movies also influence fashion. Back in 1983, *Flashdance* caught the fancy of millions of young people. Soon the one-bare-shoulder look was seen everywhere. A few years later, *Top Gun* and its star Tom Cruise helped to popularize aviator-style sunglasses. Film after film shows sophisticated young stars surrounded by high-tech paraphernalia like cell phones, headsets, and high-powered computers, cruising the Internet at warp speed.

At the same time, a continuing enthusiasm for exercise has kept interest in fashions for fitness high. The support of major celebrities in this area influences the public as well. For instance, Jane Fonda has devoted ongoing promotion to her enormously popular workout program through exercise studios, a book, and DVDs, which were re-released in 2005. Today, the famous model Christy Turlington's Nuala yoga line is contributing to the appeal of being healthy and fit (see Figure 3.8). Other celebrities, such as Cher and Suzanne Somers, enhanced the appeal of exercise equipment and apparel by acting as spokespeople in "infomercials" (program-length advertising on television). While television informs us about fashion on national and international scales, radio also has a valuable function. Radio is an excellent medium through which local merchants can inform their audiences of special fashion events.

## War, Disaster, and Crisis

War, widespread disaster, and crisis shake people's lives and focus attention on ideas, events, and places that may be completely new. People develop a need for fashions that are compatible with changes in their attitudes and also changes in their environment.

Such changes took place in women's activities and in fashions as a result of the two world wars. World War I brought women into the business world in significant numbers and encouraged their desire for independence and suffrage. It gave them a reason to demand styles that allowed freer physi-

cal movement. World War II drew women into such traditionally masculine jobs as riveting, for which they previously had not been considered strong enough. It put them in war plants on night shifts. It even brought women other than nurses into the military services for the first time in the country's history. All these changes gave rise to women's fashions previously considered appropriate only for men, such as slacks, sport shirts, and jeans.

The Depression of the 1930s was a widespread disaster with a different effect on fashions. Because jobs were scarce, considerably fewer were offered to women than had been before. Women returned to the home and adopted more feminine clothes. And because money also was scarce, wardrobes became skimpier. A single style often served a large number of occasions. Women who did hold jobs felt pressure to look younger so they could compete with younger applicants, which encouraged an increased use of lipstick and cosmetics.

Even disruptions of lesser magnitude than war or economic depression can bring about a fashion trend. For example, in response to a transit strike in New York in 1981 businesspeople wore athletic shoes on their way to and from their offices because many of them had to walk great distances to reach alternative forms of transportation. Even after the strike was settled, the combination of athletic footwear and business suits remained a common sight on the streets of New York—and other cities as well. Perhaps the growing interest in physical fitness and the realization that walking provides good exercise helped to keep the trend alive. In the late 1970s and early 1980s, a combination of the energy crisis and exceptionally cold weather brought a mass of warm clothing to the marketplace. Thermal underwear, formerly seen only in sporting goods catalogs, was featured in department and specialty shops. Retailers stocked up on sweaters, tights, boots, mittens, leg warmers, scarves, coats, jackets, and down-filled vests. Not only the Northeast and West but the normally temperate Sun Belt was struck by bitter-cold weather.

Again in 1995, 1997, and 2003, record-breaking cold and unfamiliar snow and sleet created demand for warm clothing in areas formerly not interested in such apparel.

In the early 1990s, the rapid success of the U.S. forces in Operation Desert Storm led to young men wearing army fatigues as leisure wear on the street—whether they had military status or not. More recently, fashion worldwide reacted to the terrorist attacks on the United States in 2001. Many designers began to calm down, and the idea of comfort clothing resurfaced. Anything that suggested urban aggression was wiped away. New, roomy corduroys and bright sweaters by designers like Dolce & Gabbana and Versace became popular, and the emergence of a simple, classic style soothed the uncertainties of war.

## The Psychological Environment

"Fashion promises many things to many people," according to economist Dr. Rachel Dardis. "It can be and is used to attract others, to indicate success, both social and economic, to indicate leadership, and to identify with a particular social group."[23] Fashion interest and demand at any given time may rely heavily on prevailing psychological attitudes (see Figure 3.9).

The five basic psychological factors that influence fashion demand are boredom, curiosity, reaction to convention, need for self-assurance, and desire for companionship.[24] These factors motivate a large share of people's actions and reactions.

- *Boredom.* People tend to become bored with fashions too long in use. Boredom leads to restlessness and a desire for change. In fashion, the desire for change expresses itself in a demand for something new and satisfyingly different from what one already has.
- *Curiosity.* Curiosity causes interest in change for its own sake. Highly curious people like to experiment; they want to know what is around

**FIGURE 3.9** People's surroundings and desire for companionship can be the starting point for an outrageous fashion trend.

the next corner. There is curiosity in everyone, though some may respond to it less dramatically than others. Curiosity and the need to experiment keep fashion demand alive.

- *Reaction to Convention.* One of the most important psychological factors influencing fashion demand is the reaction to convention. People's reactions take one of two forms: rebellion against convention or adherence to it. Rebellion against convention is characteristic of young people. This involves more than boredom or curiosity: it is a positive rejection of what exists and a search for something new. However, acceptance by the majority is an important part of the definition of fashion. The majority tends to adhere to convention, either within its own group or class or in general.

- *Need for Self-Assurance.* The need for self-assurance or confidence is a human characteristic that gives impetus to fashion demand. Often the need to overcome feelings of inferiority or of disappointment can be satisfied through apparel. People who consider themselves to be fashionably dressed have an armor that gives them self-assurance. Those who know that their clothes are dated are at a psychological disadvantage.

- *Desire for Companionship.* The desire for companionship is fundamental in human beings. The instinct for survival of the species drives individuals to seek a mate. Humans' innate gregariousness also encourages them to seek companions. Fashion plays its part in the search for all kinds of companionship. In its broader sense, companionship implies the formation of groups, which require conformity in dress as well as in other respects. Flamboyant or subdued, a person's mode of dress can be a bid for companionship as well as the symbol of acceptance within a particular group.

## Summary and Review

Fashion marketers determine their customers' wants and needs by examining various market segments, identified by geographics, demographics, psychographics, and behavior. Each marketer identifies the group or groups within the general population that are its target customer. Determining the average customer's personal income helps marketers make pricing decisions and estimate sales, especially when population trends are matched with income figures. For example, businesses that target middle-age and retirement-age consumers know that their customers are increasing in number and that the average income for consumers in these age groups is also increasing. The teenage and young adult markets are a smaller portion of the population than they were earlier in the century, but they are an influential market segment, often spending their discretionary income on fashion merchandise. The growing value placed on leisure time and leisure-time activities has increased the market for casual clothing and active sportswear.

Marketers also track trends in the population of targeted ethnic groups. Changing patterns of immigration bring with them new influences from different parts of the world. The Hispanic market has become the largest ethnic-minority market in the United States in the 21st century, superseding the African American market in size. The Asian American market is the fastest growing minority. The non-Hispanic Caucasian population is expected to remain the majority, but by a reduced percentage.

The role of women in society changed dramatically in the 20th century, and their increased freedom, better education, and growing presence in the labor force increased their average income and changed their buying habits.

Other social forces that affect business include greater mobility and more rapid communication, which bring individuals wider choices in their purchases. Political, economic, and natural upheavals also affect fashion marketing, often leading to trends that last beyond the crisis. As consumers become more knowledgeable about their growing choices in their buying behavior, marketers are paying more attention to psychographic factors as they attempt to identify and meet the demands of their target customers.

## Trade Talk

Define or briefly explain the following terms.

| | |
|---|---|
| baby-boom generation | behavior |
| demographics | discretionary income |
| disposable personal income | environment |
| generation X | generation Y |

geographics

market segmentation

per capita personal income

psychographics

recession

VALS

inflation

market segments

personal income

purchasing power

target market

## For Review

1. Name the four major environmental influences on fashion interest and demand in any era.

2. Market segmentation is vitally important to producers and retailers of fashion merchandise. Explain why, giving at least two examples of how such information could be used by the fashion industry.

3. How does the size and age mix of a population affect current fashion demand? What does information about size and age mix today tell us about the future of fashion demand?

4. In what ways has increased availability of leisure time affected the fashion market?

5. How has the changing status of ethnic groups affected fashion interest and demand? Cite at least two examples.

6. How does a higher level of education affect fashion interest and demand?

7. What is social mobility? How does the degree of social mobility affect fashion interest and demand? Illustrate your answer with examples.

8. Upon what factors are classes in the United States usually based? Why is it more difficult to identify an individual's social class in this country than it is in other countries?

9. Describe three kinds of physical mobility that people in the United States enjoy today, explaining how each influences fashion demand.

10. Five basic psychological factors motivate much of human behavior. List them, explaining how each affects fashion interest and demand.

## For Discussion

1. Is discretionary income or disposable personal income the more significant figure to fashion producers and marketers? Why?

2. How did the status of women change during the 20th century? How have these changes affected fashion interest and demand?

# chapter four

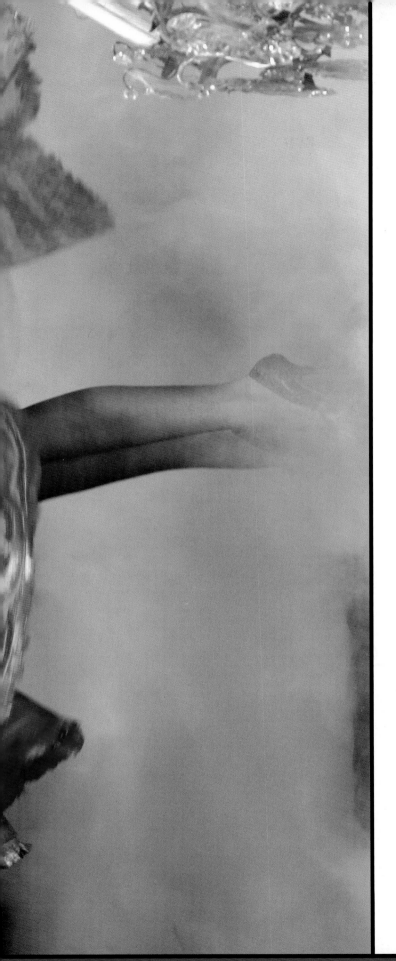

*Everything you always wanted to know*

*about the theories and identifications*

*of the movement of fashion.*

# The Movement of Fashion

Fashion is, in many ways, like a river. A river is always in motion, continuously flowing—sometimes it is slow and gentle, at other times rushing and turbulent. It is exciting, and never the same. It affects those who ride its currents and those who rest on its shores. Its movements depend on the environment.

All of this is true of fashion, too. The constant movements of fashion depend on an environment made up of social, political, and economic factors. These movements, no matter how obvious or how slight, have meaning and definite direction. There is a special excitement to interpreting these movements and estimating their speed and direction. Everyone involved in fashion, from the designer to the consumer, is caught up in the movement of fashion.

The excitement starts with the textile producers. Fully twelve to eighteen months before they offer their lines to manufacturers, the textile people must choose their designs, textures, and colors. From three to nine months before showing a line to buyers, the apparel manufacturers begin deciding which styles they will produce and in which fabrics. Then, two to six months before the fashions appear on the selling floor, the retail buyers make their selections from the manufacturers' lines. Finally, the excitement passes on to the consumers, as they select the garments that are versatile, appropriate, and suitably priced for their individual needs and wants.

How can all these people be sure their choices are based on reliable predictions? Successful designers, manufacturers, buyers, and consumers have a good understanding of basic cycles, principles, and patterns that operate in the world of fashion. Their predictions are based on this understanding.

## Factors Influencing Fashion Movement

At the beginning of this chapter, the movement of fashion was likened to the movement of a river. As James Laver said, in comparing the fashion cycle to a force of nature, "Nothing seems to be able to turn it back until it has spent itself, until it has provoked a reaction by its very excess."[1] However, just as a river can swell to turbulent flood stage or be slowed or diverted by a dam, so the movement of fashion can be accelerated or retarded by a variety of factors.

### Accelerating Factors

There are seven general factors that speed up fashion cycles. These influences are, themselves, ever growing and accelerating in the 21st century as the pace of life becomes increasingly rapid and geographically all-encompassing. The accelerating factors are:

- Widespread buying power
- Leisure time
- More education
- Improved status of women
- Technological advances
- Sales promotion
- Seasonal change

### Widespread Buying Power

Widely diffused discretionary income means there are more people with the financial means to respond to a fashion change. The more consumers flock to a new fashion, the sooner it will reach its culmination. The more widespread the financial ability of consumers to turn to yet a newer fashion, the sooner the current fashion will plunge into obsolescence.

### Leisure Time

In the past, long hours of work and little leisure permitted scant attention to fashion for the great majority of the population. More leisure time usually means more time to buy and enjoy fashion of many kinds. Since 1900, decreases in working hours and increases in paid vacations have encouraged more use of at-home wear, casual clothes, sports apparel, travel clothes, and different types of ordinary business dress. Increased purchases of these types of apparel give impetus to their fashion cycles.

One result of today's frantic pace has been the return to catalog buying and the emergence of other forms of nonstore retailing. Catalog buying originally evolved because people in farming societies lived far from stores and had little leisure time for shopping. Today's leisure time has allowed people to add new physical and mental activities to their lives, such as sports and hobbies, leaving little time for shopping once again. Realizing that their customers are using leisure time in other pursuits, retailers are bringing shopping into the consumers' homes with catalogs, cable TV shopping channels, and Web sites. Consumers can browse at any time of day, and with customer service telephone lines and computer connections available all day, every day, customers can place their orders whenever they wish.

## More Education

The increasingly higher level of education in the United States helps to speed up fashion cycles in two ways. First, more people's horizons have been broadened to include new interests and new wants. And second, more people are equipped by education to earn the money to satisfy those wants. These two factors provide significant impetus to the adoption of new fashions.

## Improved Status of Women

In a society with few artificial social barriers, women with discretionary income can spend it as they choose. No law or custom prevents any woman from buying the newest and most prestigious styles in dresses, hats, or shoes if she can afford to—thus giving impetus to a fashion cycle in its earliest phases. Sex discrimination in the job market has steadily decreased, and social acceptance of women who manage both homes and jobs has steadily increased. As a result, today's women have more discretionary income and are influencing the speed of fashion cycles in the way they use that income.

## Technological Advances

Today we live in an "instant" world. The stunning advances in technology in almost every area have put us in immediate possession of facts, fantasies, and fashions. We see news as it happens around the world. Goods are sped to retail stores by land, air, and sea more rapidly than would have been dreamed of just a few decades ago.

New fibers, finishes, and materials with improved qualities are constantly being developed. Computer technology has improved production techniques and statistical control and analysis for more efficient product marketing. The result has been control of price increases, and in many cases, reduced prices on fashion goods. All of these technological advances combine to make goods available almost at the instant the consumer is psychologically and financially ready to buy (see Figure 4.1). Thus, the cycle of fashion becomes more and more accelerated.

## Sales Promotion

The impact of sales promotion is felt everywhere in the fashion world today. Magazines, television, newspapers, billboards, and direct mail all expose the public to new fashions in a never-ending procession. While there is no way to force consumers to accept new fashions, nor any way to save a fashion if consumers reject it, sales promotion can

**FIGURE 4.1** Sometimes different accelerating factors work together. Here, Nicole Miller's Web site uses both technology and sales promotion.

greatly influence a fashion's success by telling peo-ple it exists. Sales promotion can help to speed up acceptance of a new fashion or sometimes extend its peak or duration. Promotion, therefore, can fre-quently help a fashion reach its culmination more speedily.

### Seasonal Change

Nothing is so consistent in bringing about change in fashions as the calendar. As the seasons change, so do consumer demands. After months of winter, peo-ple want to shed their heavy clothing for lightweight spring and summer fashions. In climates where there are radical seasonal changes, this is only natu-ral, even though our homes, schools, cars, and places of business are kept at desired temperatures through central heating and air conditioning. How-ever, even in areas such as Florida and Hawaii, where the weather is moderate year-round, people change their wardrobes with the seasons. Even if the 21st century brings complete climate control, people will never accept the boredom of a year-round wardrobe.

Because people today are so geared to travel at all times of the year to all types of climates, the season-al changes are accelerated and a kind of preseason testing can go on. Resort wear appears in retail stores in time for selection by the public for winter vacations in tropical areas. The late-June appear-ance of the first fall fashions in leading stores makes it possible for the style-conscious to make their selections well in advance of the first cold wind. Consumer responses to these early offerings allow manufacturers and retailers alike to know what does and does not appeal.

### *Retarding Factors*

Factors that retard the development of fashion cycles either discourage people from adopting incoming styles or encourage them to continue using styles that might be considered on the decline. Retarding factors include the opposites of the accelerating factors—for example, decreased

buying power during recessionary periods. Major retarding factors are habit and custom, religion and sumptuary laws, the nature of the merchandise, and reductions in consumers' buying power.

### Habit and Custom

By slowing acceptance of new styles and prolonging the life spans of those already accepted, habit and custom exert a braking effect on fashion movement. Habit slows the adoption of new skirt lengths, sil-houettes, necklines, or colors whenever shoppers unconsciously select styles that do not differ per-ceptibly from those they already own. It is easy for an individual to let habit take over, and some con-sumers are more susceptible to this tendency than others. Their loyalty to an established style is less a matter of fashion judgment than a natural attrac-tion to the more familiar.

Custom slows progress in the fashion cycle by per-mitting vestiges of past fashions, status symbols, taboos, or special needs to continue to appear in modern dress. Custom is responsible for such details as buttons on the sleeves of men's suits, vents in men's jackets, and the sharp creases down the front of men's trousers. Custom usually requires a degree of formal-ity in dress for religious services. The trend toward similarity of dress for men and women in the United States has permitted women to wear trousers, but cus-tom still discourages men from wearing skirts.

A classic example of the influence of custom is the placement of buttons. They are on the right side for men, originating with the need to have the weapon arm available while dressing and undress-ing. And they are on the left for women, who tend to hold babies on that side and can more conveniently use the right hand for buttons. The stitching on the backs of gloves is another example; it dates back to a time when sizes were adjusted by lacing at these points.

### Religion

Historically, religious leaders have championed custom, and their ceremonial apparel has demonstrated their respect for the old ways. In the past, religious leaders tended to associate fashion with temptation and urged their followers to turn their backs on both. Religion today, however, exerts much less of a restraining influence on fashion. Examples of the new relaxation may be found in the modernization of women's dress in most religious orders and that most women no longer consider a hat obligatory when in church.

Today, a countertrend to religion's diminishing impact on fashion has reoccurred. It is particularly evident in the adoption of ancient dress in countries such as Afghanistan and Iran that are ruled by religious fundamentalists; and with the growth of the Muslim population in the United States and Europe, Muslim religious leaders have decreed that wearing modern fashions leads to temptation and corruption.

## Sumptuary Laws

**Sumptuary laws** regulate what we can and cannot purchase. Today, there are sumptuary laws that, for example, require children's sleepwear to be flame-retardant. In the past, sumptuary laws have regulated extravagance and luxury in dress on religious or moral grounds. Height of headdress, length of train, width of sleeve, value and weight of material, and color of dress have all at times been restricted by law to specific classes. Such laws were aimed at keeping each class in its place in a rigidly stratified society.[2]

Other laws, such as those of the Puritans, attempted to enforce a general high-mindedness by condemning frippery. An order passed in 1638 by the General Court of Massachusetts stated:

No garment shall be made with short sleeves, and such as have garments already made with short sleeves shall not wear same unless they cover the arm to the wrist; and hereafter no person whatever shall make any garment for women with sleeves more than half an ell wide.[3]

**FIGURE 4.2** In the 1920s, women were stopped on the beach to check that their bathing suits were not more than six inches above their knees.

And in the 18th century, a bill was proposed (but rejected) that stated:

All women of whatever age, rank, profession, or degree, whether virgin, maid, or widow, that shall impose upon, seduce, and betray into matrimony any of His Majesty's subjects by scents, paints, cosmetic washes, artificial teeth, false hair, Spanish wool, iron stays, hoops, high-heeled shoes, or bolstered hips, shall incur the penalty of the law now in force against witchcraft and the like demeanours, and that marriage, upon conviction, shall stand null and void.[4]

People have a way of ignoring local ordinances, however, if they conflict with a fashion cycle that is gathering strength. In New York in the 1920s and 1930s, fines could be imposed on individuals who appeared on the streets wearing shorts, or whose bathing-suit shoulder straps were not in place on public beaches. At the Washington Bathing Beach, bathing suits could not be shorter than six inches above the knee (see Figure 4.2). What was considered indecent exposure then is commonplace today.

School uniforms in public schools were common before the 1960s, but they were largely abandoned in the free-spiritedness of that decade. However, when school violence and classroom disruption increased across the country, uniforms became popular once again. In his State of the Union address in 1996, President Bill Clinton endorsed uniforms as a way to keep kids "from killing each other over designer jackets."

People in favor of uniforms argue that they promote a sense of discipline and belonging. Today, the number of schools requiring uniforms continues to increase (see Figure 4.3). The strongest opposition to uniforms comes from two groups: civil libertarians and older students (ages 12–14). Civil libertarians argue that uniforms violate students' free expression rights, while students resent that uniforms make all students look alike. Marshal Cohen, chief industry analyst of the NPD Group, reports that "many children may not like wearing school uniforms, but mothers and a select few kids can find peace of mind knowing that it takes [away] peer pressure and competition of buying and wearing brand name designer clothes."[5]

## Nature of the Merchandise

Not all merchandise moves at the same pace through a fashion cycle. Often, the very nature of the merchandise is responsible for the rate of movement. Over the years, it has been accepted as normal that men's fashion cycles move more slowly than women's. In recent years, however, the changing lifestyles of the male population have resulted in accelerating men's wear cycles. Women's apparel generally moves in slower cycles than accessories, though some accessories now have full-run cycles comparable to those of apparel.

## Reductions in Consumers' Buying Power

Consumers' buying power has a powerful effect on the movement of fashion cycles. When buying power increases, fashion cycles often speed up. Decreased buying power, conversely, can retard the movement of fashion cycles. During economic recessions and

**FIGURE 4.3** School uniforms are increasing globally. Some students oppose them but others are relieved that they don't have to worry about what to wear.

resultant high unemployment, consumers' buying power is sharply reduced. Many people make do with clothes they have, buying only necessities. A similar caution is shown by consumers affected by strikes, inflation, high taxes, or high interest rates. All these factors have a slowing influence on fashion cycles. The poorer people are, the less impact they have on fashion's movements. They become bystanders in matters of fashion, and as a result do not keep cycles moving. Laver emphasized the importance of buying power when he said that nothing except poverty can make a style permanent.[6]

## Recurring Fashions

In the study of fashion history, we see that styles reoccur, with adaptations that suit the times in which they reappear. Occasionally, an entire look is reborn. The elegant, simple look of the late 1940s and early 1950s, for example, was born again for the generation of the 1980s. Nostalgia influenced choices not only in apparel but also in hairstyles and makeup.

Sometimes a single costume component or a minor detail that had exhausted its welcome stages a comeback, such as the "chandelier" earring. At other times, a single article of clothing, like the sandals of the ancient Greeks, returns to popularity.

An outstanding example of a recurring men's fashion is the T-shirt. T-shirts originated in France as cotton underwear. They were discovered during World War I by American soldiers who preferred them to their own itchy wool union suits. In the 1940s, they reemerged as "tee" shirts for golfing and other active sports. In the 1960s they became part of the women's fashion scene as well.

Today, the T-shirt has put ego into fashion (see Figure 4.4). T-shirts are bought for both fashion and antifashion reasons, and in both cases, they announce to all what the wearer stands for and where he or she has been. A T-shirt can feature a country or city, a rock concert tour, a traveling art exhibition, the uniform number of the wearer's

**FIGURE 4.4** Today's T-shirt puts ego into fashion and announces to the world what the wearer stands for. Here, a sketch of Karl Lagerfeld's face and signature is displayed.

favorite baseball player, or the name of a designer (Tommy Hilfiger) or manufacturer (Nike). T-shirt wearers can identify themselves outright by names, initials, telephone numbers, or even blown-up photographs of themselves transferred onto the T-shirt.[7] Organizations offer T-shirts as promotional items (Hard Rock Cafe T-shirts featuring the names of cities where the theme restaurant is located) and souvenirs of conventions (corporate sales meetings and class reunions).

Research indicates that in the past, similar silhouettes and details of design in women's apparel have recurred with remarkable regularity. In *Recurring Cycles of Fashion*,[8] Agnes Brooke Young studied skirt silhouettes and their variations in connection with her interest in theatrical costumes. From data she collected on the period from 1760 to 1937, she concluded that despite widely held opinions to the contrary, there were actually only three basic silhouettes—bell-shaped, backfullness, and straight—which always followed each other in the same 100-year sequence. (See Chapter 2 for variations on this

Fashion
Focus

## Little Boy Lost—
## and Found
### *Marc Jacobs*

The most important person in Marc Jacobs's life, through thick and thin, is Robert Duffy. He is part business partner, part brother, part father figure, part soul mate. Jacobs and Duffy met at a dinner thrown by Parsons School of Design, Jacobs' alma mater in 1984. Duffy was looking for a creative partner at the time, and something about Jacobs's take on fashion clicked with him.

The belief that united them was that no one was making high fashion for young, cool people and so they launched Jacob Duffy Designs, Inc., out of a small studio in the garment district. What kept Jacobs and Duffy afloat was the support of key people: Anna Wintour and the buying teams at Bergdorf Goodman and Bloomingdale's, who began placing big orders; and models such as Naomi, Christy, and Tyra, who worked the runway for free!

In 1986, the designer Perry Ellis died, and the company's promotion of two in-house assistants to the top design job proved disastrous. In 1988, acting on fashion industry buzz, the Perry Ellis Company hired Jacobs as creative director and Duffy as president. Finally, they had the money and infrastructure they needed, even if it meant designing under the name of Perry Ellis.

In 1992, Jacobs showed a landmark collection, one that people still marvel at over almost two decades later. Jacobs was into grunge, and he decided to put it on the runway. The press was very impressed and raved about the collection. However, the powers at Perry Ellis were *not*! Jacobs and Duffy were fired shortly thereafter.

Jacobs and Duffy

rented a store on Mercer Street in downtown New York City, but because of money, or lack of it, they did not do well. But in 1996 a call came from Bernard Arnault. He wanted to meet Jacobs and Duffy to see their clothes, and soon the two were flown to Paris. When they arrived, Arnault brought up the top jobs at Christian Dior and Givenchy. "We didn't want to have to follow another designer; we'd done that at Perry Ellis," Duffy explained. Duffy suggested Louis Vuitton, which, though internationally famous for its handbags, had no ready-to-wear. Negotiations lasted eighteen months. Eventually, Arnault agreed to have Jacobs design for Louis Vuitton and to finance Jacobs's own line. LVMH Group put up the money to open the Mercer Street store and produce the clothes and a few runway shows.

Their contract renewal, finally signed in 2004, and phenomenal sales gave them leverage, and mass globalization is well underway.

Early on, the smart money bet that neither the partnership nor the house of Marc Jacobs and Robert Duffy could last. But 25-plus years have proven the smart money very wrong. Together, Jacobs and Duffy have endured trials and tribulations almost too hard to imagine—failed financial backing, grunge backlash, and Jacobs's battle with substance abuse, to name a few. Yet through it all, the two have directed a stunning climb to the pinnacle of fashion from two distinct seats of power.

With this swift transformation of the stuffy leather-goods giant Louis Vuitton into a remarkable trend-spawning one confirmed worldwide that Jacobs is a wildly talented, quietly fearless creator capable of impacting international fashion in a major way. While Paris, which Jacobs now calls home, provided the international stage, the New York-based Marc Jacobs company remains a hotbed of influence both creatively and in its novel approach to growth under Duffy's supervision. Case in point: the flourishing secondary line Marc by Marc Jacobs has become a mecca for fashion types from assistants to actresses. Marc by Marc Jacobs is expanding on all fronts; it operates eighty-two stores around the world, and plans to open many more from Moscow to Chicago.

Among Jacobs's many honors, the Council of Fashion Designers (CFDA) has awarded him numerous awards starting in 1987 when he was the youngest designer to win the Womenswear Perry Ellis Award for New Fashion Talent. He received the CFDA Womenswear Designer of the Year Award in 1992 and 1997; the Menswear Designer of the Year in 2002; and Accessories Designer of the year in 1999, 2003, and 2005.

Not bad for a little boy lost—and look what he has found: success and happiness.

theory.) Each silhouette with all its variations dominated the fashion scene for a period of approximately 35 years. Having reached an excess in styling, it then declined in popularity and yielded to the next silhouette in regular sequence.

The anthropologist A. L. Kroeber studied changes in women's apparel from the early 1600s to the early 1900s. His conclusions confirm Young's findings that similar silhouettes recur in fashion acceptance approximately once every 100 years. In addition, Kroeber found that similar neck widths recurred every 100 years, and similar skirt lengths every 35 years.[9]

## Playing the Apparel Fashion Game

According to Madge Garland, a well-known English fashion authority, "Every woman is born with a built-in hobby: the adornment of her person. The tricks she can play with it, the shapes she can make of it, the different portions she displays at various times, the coverings she uses or discards" all add up to fashion.[10]

Many clothing authorities read a clear message into the alternate exposure and covering of various parts of the body—sex. J. C. Flügel cited sexual attraction as the dominant motive for wearing clothes.[11]

Laver explained fashion emphasis in terms of the sexuality of the body. "Fashion really began," he said, "with the discovery in the fifteenth century that clothes could be used as a compromise between exhibitionism and modesty."[12] Laver also suggested that those portions of the body no longer fashionable to expose are "sterilized" and are no longer regarded as sexually attractive. Those that are newly exposed are **erogenous**, or sexually stimulating. He viewed fashion as pursuing the emphasis of ever-shifting erogenous zones but never quite catching up with them. "If you really catch up," he warned, "you are immediately arrested for indecent exposure. If you almost catch up, you are celebrated as a leader of fashion."[13]

Men's apparel has long played the fashion game, too, but, since the industrial revolution, in a less dramatic manner than women's. Women's fashions have tended to concentrate mainly on different ways to convey sexual appeal. Men's fashions have been designed to emphasize such attributes as strength, power, bravery, and high social rank. When a male style does emphasize sex, it is intended to project an overall impression of virility.

### Pieces of the Game

The pieces with which the women's fashion game is played are the various parts of the female body: waist, shoulders, bosom, neckline, hips, derriere, legs, and feet, as well as the figure as a whole (Figure 4.5). Historically, as attention to a part of the anatomy reaches a saturation point, the fashion spotlight shifts to some other portion.

In the Middle Ages, asceticism was fashionable. Women's clothes were designed to play down, rather than emphasize, women's sexuality. The Renaissance was a period of greater sexual free-

**FIGURE 4.5** Viktor & Rolf's "eye-popping" design plays with a tuxedo look for women and reveals just enough of the neckline and shoulders.

dom. Women's apparel during this period highlighted the breasts and the abdomen, particularly the latter.

By the 18th century, however, the abdomen had lost its appeal. Although the bosom continued to be emphasized, a flatter abdomen was fashionable, and heels were raised to facilitate upright carriage. The Empire period, with its high waistline, also stressed the bosom. But the entire body was emphasized with sheer and scanty dresses—some so sheer they could be pulled through a ring. Some advocates of this fashion even wet their apparel so that it would cling to the figure when worn.

During the 19th century, fashion interest shifted to the hips, and skirts billowed. Later, the posterior was accented with bustles and trains.

Early in the 20th century, emphasis switched from the trunk to the limbs, through short skirts and sleeveless or tight-sleeved dresses. Flügel interpreted accent on the limbs, together with the suggestion of an underdeveloped torso, as an idealization of youth. He foresaw continued emphasis on youth and boyishness as a result of women's participation in varied activities, the steady march of democracy, and increasing sexual freedom.[14]

In the 1960s, fashion interest was focused on short skirts and the legs. As the sixties drew to a close, interest shifted from legs to bosom. By the early 1970s, the natural look of bosoms was in. The unconstructed, natural look was followed by the "no-bra" look. This fashion reached its culmination and began its decline when bosoms were only slightly concealed beneath see-through fabrics or plunging necklines. As this excess led to obsolescence, the 1980s ushered in a reemergence of the 1950s bosom. Manufacturers of bras and inner wear featured soft-sided bras, strapless bras, T-back bras, and sports bras to once again give a firmly supported look to the bosom.

According to Garland, the fashions of the 1950s and early 1960s showed off the entire figure (Figure 4.6):

The modern girl manages at the same time to bare her shoulders, accentuate her bust, pull in her waist, and show her legs to above the knees. It is a triumph of personal publicity over the taboos of the past and the previous limitations of fashion.[15]

Until the late 1960s brought the "youth cult" and its attendant revolt against conventional sexual and political attitudes, previous fashion eras had centered attention only on parts of the body. The "triumph of personal publicity" achieved in the late 1960s and early 1970s broke all records for calling attention to just about every area of the human body. It was, indeed, an allover feast for the eye of the observer.

### Rules of the Game

In the game of emphasizing different parts of the female body at different times, as in any game, there are rules. The first and strongest rule is that fashion emphasis does not flit from one area to another! Rather, a particular area of the body is emphasized until every bit of excitement has been exhausted. At this point, fashion attention turns to another area. For example, as has been noted, when miniskirts of the 1960s could go no higher and still be legal, the fashion emphasis moved on.

The second rule of the fashion game may well be, as Garland suggested, that only certain parts of the body can be exposed at any given time.[16] Dozens of examples throughout fashion history back up this theory: floor-length evening gowns with plunging necklines, high necklines with miniskirts, turtlenecks on sleeveless fashions.

A third rule of the fashion game is that, like fashion itself, fashion attention must always go forward. Dwight E. Robinson said, "A fashion can never retreat gradually and in good order; like a dictator, it must always expand its aggressions or collapse. Old fashions never fade away; they die suddenly and arbitrarily."[17]

**FIGURE 4.6** Full-skirted and colorful, summer dresses from the 1950s showed off a woman's entire figure.

### Predicting the Movement of Fashion

Producing and selling fashion merchandise to consumers at a profit are what fashion merchandising is all about. To bring excitement and flair to their segment of merchandising, producers and retailers must have a well-defined plan and must follow the movement of general fashion preferences.

The success of fashion merchandising depends on the correct prediction of which new styles will be accepted by the majority of consumers. The successful forecaster of fashion must:

1. Distinguish what the current fashion trends are.
2. Estimate how widespread they are.
3. Determine when these fashions will appeal to the firm's target customer groups.

With information on these three points, projections—a prime requisite in successful fashion merchandising—become possible.

## Identifying Trends

A fashion trend, as discussed in Chapter 2, is a direction in which fashion is moving. Manufacturers and merchants try to recognize each fashion trend to determine how widespread it is and whether it is moving toward or away from maximum fashion acceptance. They can then decide whether to actively promote the fashion to their target customers, to wait, or to abandon it.

For example, assume that wide-leg pants have developed as a fashion trend. At the introduction and rise stages, retailers will stock and promote more and more wide-leg pants. When customer response begins to level off, retailers will realize that a saturation point is being reached with this style and will begin introducing narrower pants into their stocks in larger numbers. If the retailers have correctly predicted the downturn in customer demand for wide-leg pants, they will have fewer on hand when the downturn occurs. And while some customers may continue to wear the wide-leg style, they will not be buying new wide-leg pants, and certainly not at regular prices.

## Sources of Data

Modern fashion forecasters bear little resemblance to the mystical prognosticators of old. Their ability to predict the strength and direction of fashion trends among their customers has almost nothing to do with what is often called a "fashion sense." Nor does it depend on glances into the future via a cloudy crystal ball. Today's successful fashion forecasters depend on that most valuable commodity—information. Good, solid facts about the willingness of customers to accept certain goods are the basis of successful merchandising decisions.

In today's computerized business world, merchants can keep "instant" records on sales, inventories, new fashion testing, and myriad other contributing factors that aid the fashion merchandising process. In addition, wise merchants keep their eyes open to see what is being worn by their own cus-tomers as well as by the public as a whole. They are so familiar with their customers' lifestyles, economic status, educational level, and social milieu that they can determine at just what point in a fashion's life cycle their customers will be ready to accept or reject it. Merchants turn to every available source for information that will help ensure success. They use their hard-earned sales experience but don't just rely on their own judgment; they rely on the judgment of others, too. From the producers of fashion, from resident buying/merchandising/developing offices, and from special fashion groups they learn about the buying habits of customers other than their own (see Figure 4.7). Successful merchants look at the larger fashion picture to predict more ably just where their local scene fits in.

## Interpreting Influential Factors

An old theater saying goes, "It's all in the interpretation." In other words, written or spoken words gain their importance by the way they are presented to the audience. That is where the special talents of the performer come in. The same is true of fashion forecasting. All the data in the world can be collected by merchants, producers, or designers, but it is of little importance without interpretation. That is where the forecasters' knowledge of fashion and fashion principles comes into the picture. From the data they have collected, they are able to identify certain patterns. Then they consider certain factors that can accelerate or retard a fashion cycle among their target group of customers. Among these factors are current events, the appearance of prophetic styles, sales promotion efforts, and the canons of taste currently in vogue.

### Current Events

The news of what is going on in the country or the world can have a long-term or short-term influence on consumers and affect their response to a fashion (see Figure 4.8). For example, in the mid-1980s, many newspapers, magazines, and TV shows were discussing opportunities for women at mid- and upper-management levels. Success in responsible positions in the business world demanded "dressing for success," and career-minded women responded by adopting the severely tailored business suit look. By their very appearance, these women indicated their determination to succeed in the still male-dominated world of business. A reaction to this male-dominated, strictly tailored look occurred in the early 1990s, when women turned to a softer, less tailored look and many men abandoned the business suit "uniform" that had been de rigueur for generations. Today, men and women can choose what "fashion" is right for them.

## Prophetic Styles

Good fashion forecasters keep a sharp watch for what they call **prophetic styles**. These are particularly interesting new styles that are still in the introduction phase of their fashion cycle. Taken up enthusiastically by the socially prominent or by the flamboyant young, these styles may gather momentum very rapidly or they may prove to be nonstarters. Whatever their future course, the degree of acceptance of these very new styles gives forecasters a sense of which directions fashion might go in.

## Sales Promotion Efforts

In addition to analyzing the records of past sales, fashion forecasters give thought to the kind and amount of promotion that helps stimulate interest in prophetic styles. They also consider the kind and amount of additional sales promotion they can look forward to. For example, a fiber producer's powerful advertising and publicity efforts may have helped turn slight interest in a product into a much stronger interest during a corresponding period the previous year. The forecaster's problem is to estimate how far the trend might have developed without those promotional activities. The forecaster must also assess how much momentum remains from the previous year's

**FIGURE 4.7** Regional shows and seminars are a reliable source of information for retailers—and provide opportunities for networking and fun!

push to carry the trend forward in the current year, and how much promotional support can be looked for in the future. The promotional effort that a forecaster's own organization plans to expend is only one part of the story; outside efforts, sometimes industrywide, also must be considered in forecasting fashions.

## Canons of Taste

According to Paul H. Nystrom, fashions that are in accord with currently accepted canons (standards) of art, custom, modesty, and utility are most easily accepted.[18] Today's forecasters are careful to take current canons of taste into consideration as they judge the impact of new styles.

**FIGURE 4.8** Fashion shows came to a halt and organizers raised the American flag after the September 11th terrorist attacks on the United States in 2001.

# Then & NOW

## Gucci's Wild Ride
### *Yesterday, Today, and Tomorrow*

The House of Gucci was started in 1906 as a small, family-owned leather saddlery shop. Guccio Gucci quickly built a reputation for quality, and in 1938 Gucci expanded his outreach and opened a boutique in Rome. Guccio was responsible for designing many of the company's most famous products. In 1947, he introduced the bamboo-handle handbag, and during the 1950s, he developed the Gucci trademark, stripped webbing, and the suede moccasin with the metal bit trim.

After Guccio's death in 1953, his son Aldo led the company to a position of international prominence, opening boutiques in London, Paris, and New York. Gucci also targeted the Far East for expansion in the late 1980s, opening stores in Hong Kong, Tokyo, and Korea. During this great growth, the company developed its famous GG logo (Guccio Gucci's initials), the Flora silk scarf, and the Jackie O shoulder bag, Gucci remained one of the top luxury goods companies in the world until the late 1970s, when a series of disastrous business decisions and bitter family fights brought the company to the verge of bankruptcy. In the 1960s and 1970s, writes *Vanity Fair* editor Graydon Carter, "Gucci had been at the pinnacle of chic, thanks to icons such as Audrey Hepburn, Grace Kelly, and Jacqueline Onassis. By the 1980s, Gucci had lost its appeal, becoming a tacky airport brand."

In the mid-1980s, Aldo Gucci was convicted of tax evasion in the United States by the testimony of his own son, and the outrageous headlines of gossip magazines generated as much publicity for Gucci as its designs. However, in 1989, Gucci persuaded Dawn Mello, whose total revival of New York's Bergdorf Goodman made her a star in the retail business, to join the newly formed Gucci Group as the creative director. She put together a creative team consisting of herself, Domenico DeSole, and the designer Tom Ford. But in 1993, Dawn Mello returned to

Bergdorf Goodman and the position of creative director went to Tom Ford, who wanted to take the company's image in a new direction. Domenico DeSole, who had been elevated to CEO, realized that if Gucci was to become a profitable company, it would require a new image, and so he agreed to support Tom Ford's vision.

It was a golden moment for Gucci and all of fashion. The Tom Ford era at Gucci was remarkable. What Ford brought most spectacularly, and most obviously, was sex appeal. He tried to create a new woman who

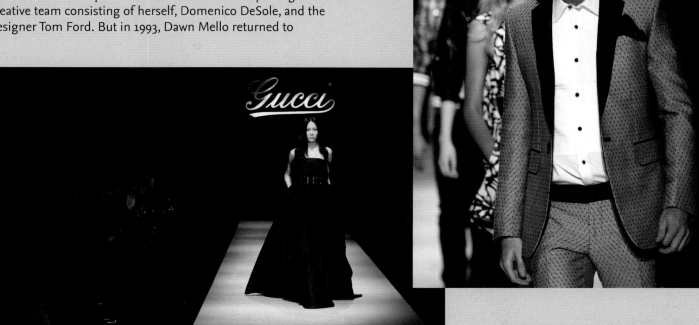

Left page: Gucci Group, 2007 (top); spring/summer collection, 2008 (bottom); right page: during the 1970s, Gucci was the "pinnacle of chic."

lived a modern life of nights out, high-gloss lips, and seriously premeditated chic. The attitude stunned everyone from the start, but he continued to captivate his audience when he depicted a more smoldering, low-key look. After a failed attempt at a contract renewal in 2003, Tom Ford and Domenico DeSole left the Gucci Group. Following Ford's departure, Gucci Group retained three designers—Alessandra Facchinetti, John Ray, and Frida Giannini—who had worked under Ford to continue the success of the company's flagship label. Facchinetti was promoted to creative director of women's wear in 2004 and designed for two seasons before leaving the company. Ray served as creative director of men's wear for three years and resigned in 2006. Frida Giannini, who had been responsible for designing men's and women's accessories, currently serves as creative director for the entire board.

Using the financial capital obtained from PPR, the Gucci Group has expanded beyond just the Gucci brand through a series of takeovers. As of 2004, Gucci Group had 50 to 100 percent financial interests in the following fashion and perfume companies: Gucci, Yves Saint Laurent, Sergio Rossé, Bottega Veneta, Alexander McQueen, Stella McCartney, and Balenciaga in fashion; and Roger & Gallet, Boucheron, Zegna, Oscar de la Renta, Vancleef & Arpels, Fendi, and Armani in perfume.

Because of its iconic status, Gucci is frequently mentioned in popular culture, especially in hip-hop music. In 2003, Gucci was the third-most mentioned brand in Billboard's top twenty single hits, with appearance in forty-seven different songs. Gucci is also constantly mentioned in movies, from *Pretty Woman* to *The Devil Wears Prada*, and is a star mention in the TV series *Ugly Betty*.

The *Guinness Book of World Records* cites the Gucci "Genius Jeans" as the most expensive jeans in the world! A regular pair of Gucci jeans that had been distressed, ripped, and covered with African beads when they debuted in October 1998 in Milan were retail priced at an

## Importance of Timing

Successful merchants must determine what their particular target group of customers is wearing now and what this group is most likely to be wearing one month or three months from now. The data these merchants collect enable them to identify each current fashion, who is wearing it, and what point it has reached in its fashion cycle.

Since merchants know at what point in a fashion's cycle their customers are most likely to be attracted, they can determine whether to stock a current fashion now, one month from now, or three months from now.

## Theories of Fashion Adoption

Fashions are accepted by a few before they are accepted by the majority. An important step in fashion forecasting is isolating and identifying those fashion leaders and keeping track of their preferences. Once these are known, the fashion forecaster is better able to forecast which styles are most likely to succeed as fashions, and how widely and by whom each will be accepted.

Three theories have been advanced to explain the "social contagion" or spread of fashion adoption: the downward-flow theory, the horizontal-flow theory or "mass-market" theory, and the upward-flow theory. Each attempts to explain the course a fashion travels or is likely to travel, and each has its own claim to validity in reference to particular fashions or social environments (see Figure 4.9).

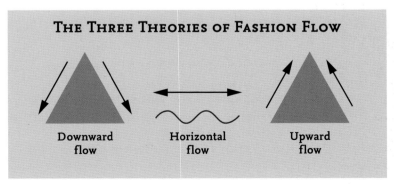

**FIGURE 4.9** The three theories of fashion flow.

## Downward-Flow Theory

The oldest theory of fashion adoption is the **downward-flow theory** (or the "trickle-down" theory). It maintains that in order to be identified as a true fashion, a style must first be adopted by people at the top of the social pyramid. The style then gradually wins acceptance at progressively lower social levels.

This theory assumes the existence of a social hierarchy in which lower-income people seek identification with more affluent people. At the same time, those at the top seek disassociation from those they consider socially inferior. The theory suggests that (1) fashions are accepted by lower classes only if, and after, they are accepted by upper classes, and (2) upper classes will reject a fashion once it has flowed to a lower social level.

Thorstein B. Veblen, an economist at the turn of the 20th century, was among the first to observe this type of social behavior and its effect on fashion. In 1903, French sociologist Gabriel Tarde described the spread of fashion in terms of a social water tower from which a continuous fall of imitation could descend.[19] The German sociologist George Simmel, one of the first of his discipline to undertake a serious study of fashion, wrote in 1904:

> Social forms, apparel, aesthetic judgment, the whole style of human expression, are constantly being transformed by fashion in [a way that] . . . affects only the upper classes. Just as soon as the lower classes begin to copy their styles, thereby crossing the line of demarcation the upper classes have drawn and destroying their coherence, the upper classes turn away from this style and adopt a new one. . . . The same process is at work as between the different sets within the upper classes, although it is not always visible here.[20]

The downward-flow theory has had among its 20th-century proponents such authorities as Robinson, Laver, Edward Sapir, and Flügel. Flügel, in fact, suggested that sumptuary laws originated with the reluctance of upper classes to abandon the sartorial distinctiveness that to them represented superiority.

## Implications for Merchandising

To some extent, the downward-flow theory has validity. Some fashions may appear first among the socially prominent. Eager manufacturers then quickly mass-produce lower-priced copies that many consumers can afford, and the wealthier consumers seek newer styles.

Because our social structure has radically changed, this theory has few adherents today. The downward-flow theory of fashion dissemination can apply only when a society resembles a pyramid, with people of wealth and position at the apex and followers at successively lower levels. Our social structure today, however, is more like a group of rolling hills than a pyramid. There are many social groups and many directions in which fashion can and does travel.

This altered pattern of fashion acceptance is also a result of the speed with which fashion news now travels. All social groups know about fashion innovation at practically the same time. Moreover, accelerated mass production and mass distribution of fashion goods have broadened acceptance of styles. They are available at lower prices and more quickly than ever before.

## Industry Practice

For the reasons given above, those who mass-produce fashion goods today are less likely to wait cautiously for approval of newly introduced styles by affluent consumers. As soon as significant signs of an interesting new style appear, the producers are ready to offer adaptations or even copies to the public.

## Horizontal-Flow Theory

A newer theory is the **horizontal-flow theory** (or mass-market theory) of fashion adoption. This theory claims that fashions move horizontally between groups on similar social levels rather than vertically from one level to another.

One of the chief exponents of this theory was Dr. Charles W. King. He proposed that the social environment, including rapid mass communications and the promotional efforts of manufacturers and retailers, exposes new styles to the fashion leaders of all social groups at approximately the same time. King noted that there is almost no lag between the adoption of a fashion by one social group and another.[21] Paris fashions, for example, are now copied for mass distribution sometimes even before the originals are available to the more affluent markets. The designers themselves are bringing out their ready-to-wear lines at the same time as their more expensive custom designs.

This horizontal flow also has been observed by some modern supporters of the older downward-flow theory. Robinson, for example, said that any given group or cluster of groups takes its cues from contiguous groups within the same social stratum. He claimed fashions therefore radiate from a center of each stratum or class.[22]

## Implications for Merchandising

The theory of horizontal fashion movement has great significance for merchandising. It points out the fallacy of assuming that there is a single, homogeneous fashion public in this country. In reality, a number of distinctly different groups make up the fashion public. Each group has its own characteristics and its own fashion ideas and needs. The horizontal-flow theory recognizes that what wealthy society people are wearing today is not necessarily what middle-class suburbanites, college students, or office workers will either wear tomorrow or wait until tomorrow to accept. This theory acknowledges that there are separate markets in fashion goods as in any other type of merchandise.

Retailers who apply the horizontal-flow theory will watch their own customers closely rather than be guided solely by what more exclusive stores are selling. They will seek to identify the groups into which customers can be divided in terms of income, age, education, and lifestyle. Among their customers, they will look for the innovators and their style choices as well as the influentials and their selections. King defined a **fashion innovator** as a person who is quicker than his or her associates to try out a new style. A **fashion influential** is a person whose advice is sought by associates. A fashion influential's adoption of a new style gives it prestige among a group. The two roles may or may not be played by the same individual within a specific group.

The news that socially prominent women are wearing plunging necklines in exclusive New York restaurants will have less significance for the retailers in a small Midwestern city than the observation that the leader of the country club set in their community is abandoning bright colors for black on formal occasions. If the latter is a fashion influential in the community, she is a more important bellwether for them than the New York socialites.

## Industry Practice

King drew a distinction between the spread of fashion within the industry itself and its adoption by consumers. A vertical flow definitely operates within the industry, he conceded: "Exclusive and famous designers are watched closely and emulated by lesser designers. Major manufacturers are studied and copied by smaller and less expert competitors."[23] And, as any reader of *Women's Wear Daily* knows, the hottest news in the industry concerns what the top designers and the top producers are showing.

King pointed out, moreover, that the innovation process in the industry represents a "great filtering system." From an almost infinite number of possibilities, manufacturers select a finite number of styles. From these, trade buyers select a small sampling. Finally, consumers choose from among retailers' selections, thereby endorsing certain ones as accepted fashions.

This process, King maintained, is quite different from the consumer reaction outlined by Simmel and other proponents of the downward-flow theory. The difference lies in the fact that today the mass market does not await the approval of the "class" market before it adopts a fashion.

## Upward-Flow Theory

The third theory that attempts to explain the process of fashion adoption is relatively new. It reflects the enormous social changes that have occurred in the past five decades. Because the process of fashion dissemination that evolved in the decades of the 1950s through the 2000s was the exact opposite of that which prevailed throughout much of recorded history, this theory has important implications for producers and retailers alike.

This theory of fashion adoption is called the **upward-flow theory**. It holds that the young—particularly those of low-income families and those in higher-income groups who adopt low-income lifestyles—are quicker than any social group to create or adopt new and different fashions. As its name implies, this theory is exactly the opposite of the downward-flow theory. The upward-flow theory holds that fashion adoption begins among the young members of lower-income groups and then moves upward into higher-income groups.

The decades of the fifties through today have outstanding examples of the upward-flow theory. In the 1950s, young people discovered Army/Navy surplus stores and were soon wearing khaki pants, caps, battle jackets, fatigues, and even ammunition belts. In the 1960s, led by the Hell's Angels, the motorcycle clubs introduced the fashion world to black leather—in jackets, vests, and studded arm bands. Soon the jet set was dressed in black leather long coats, skirts, and pants. Meanwhile, other young people were discovering bib overalls, rail-road workers' caps, and all-purpose laborers' coveralls that were soon translated into jumpsuits. Peasant apparel, prairie looks, and styles and designs from various minority groups followed the same pattern. They began as part of a young and lower-income lifestyle and were then quickly adopted among older people with different lifestyles and incomes.

One of the more dramatic illustrations of this pattern has been the T-shirt. In its short-sleeved version, it has long been worn by truckers, laborers, and farm workers. In its long-sleeved version, it was the uniform of local bowling and softball teams. In the 1970s, the T-shirt became a message board and sprouted a brand-new fashion cottage industry. The ultimate T-shirt was the Chanel No. 5; first the perfume, then the T-shirt. Actually, the Chanel T-shirt was a logical application of a tenet long held by the late Coco Chanel, who believed that fashion came from the streets and was then adapted by the couture.

In the 1980s, sources of inspiration for fashion styles representing the upward-flow theory were everywhere, especially in the world of rock music. By following the fashion statements of rock-and-roll idols, America's youth were arrayed in worn denim, metal, leather, lace, bangles, spandex, and glitter. Colors ranged from Cyndi Lauper's peacock looks to Roy Orbison's basic black. Madonna became a style-setter and introduced the country to her underwear worn on the outside.

In the 1990s, rap artists not only composed lyrics that spoke of ghetto life in street language; they also introduced and popularized hip-hop clothing styles.

Today, everything goes, but the new sources of inspiration are the celebrities seen on TV, magazine covers, and any other mode of celebrity status: the Paris Hiltons, Britney Spearses, and others who become part of the reporting of celebrity fashions.

## Implications for Merchandising

For producers and retailers, this new direction of fashion flow implies radical changes in traditional methods of charting and forecasting fashion trends. No longer can producers and retailers look solely to name designers and socially prominent fashion leaders for ideas that will become tomorrow's best-selling fashions. They also must pay considerable attention to what young people favor, for the young have now become a large, independent group that can exert considerable influence on fashion styling.

As a result, today fewer retailers and manufacturers attend European couture showings, once considered fashion's most important source of design inspiration. Now producers and retailers alike are more interested in ready-to-wear (prêt-à-porter) showings. Here they look for styles and design details that reflect trends with more fashion relevance for American youth. Young designers in their twenties and thirties complain that the more established, larger companies are copying their innovations.[24]

## Industry Practice

Apparently, fashion will never again flow in only one direction. Of course, customers will always exist for high fashion and for conservative fashion. But producers and retailers must now accept that they will be doing a considerable proportion of their business in fashions created or adopted first by the lower-income young and by those who choose to be allied with them.

## Fashion Leaders

As different as they may be, the three theories of fashion flow share one common perspective: they recognize that there are both fashion leaders and fashion followers. People of social, political, and economic importance here and abroad are seen as leaders in the downward-flow theory. The horizontal-flow theory recognizes individuals whose personal prestige makes them leaders within their own circles, whether or not they are known elsewhere. Finally, the important fashion role played

by young, lower-income groups in the last half of the 20th century is recognized in the upward-flow theory.

The theories of fashion adoption stress that the fashion leader is not the creator of the fashion; nor does merely wearing the fashion make a person a fashion leader. As Quentin Bell explained: "The leader of fashion does not come into existence until the fashion is itself created . . . a king or person of great eminence may indeed lead the fashion, but he leads only in the general direction which it has already adopted."[25] If a fashion parade is forming, fashion leaders may head it and even quicken its pace. They cannot, however, bring about a procession; nor can they reverse a procession.

## Innovators and Influentials

Famous people are not necessarily fashion leaders, even if they do influence an individual style. Their influence usually is limited to only one striking style, one physical attribute, or one time. The true fashion leader is a person constantly seeking distinction and therefore likely to launch a succession of fashions rather than just one. People like Beau Brummel, who made a career of dressing fashionably, or the Duchess of Windsor, whose wardrobe was front-page fashion news for decades, influence fashion on a much broader scale.

What makes a person a fashion leader? Flügel explained: "Inasmuch as we are aristocratically minded and dare to assert our own individuality by being different, we are leaders of fashion."[26] King, however, made it clear that more than just daring to be different is required. In his analysis, a person eager for the new is merely an innovator or early buyer. To be a leader, one must be influential and sought after for advice within one's coterie. "A fashion influential," said King, "sets the appropriate dress for a specific occasion in a particular circle. Within that circle, an innovator presents current offerings and is the earliest visual communicator of a new style."[27]

### Royalty

In the past, fashion leadership was exclusively the province of royalty. New fashions were introduced in royal courts by such leaders as Empress Eugenie and Marie Antoinette. In the 20th century, the Duchess of Windsor, although an American and a commoner by birth, was a fashion innovator and influential from the 1930s through the 1960s. When the King of England gave up his throne to marry "the woman he loved," style and fashion professionals throughout the world copied her elegance. The Sotheby auction in the late 1980s of the Duchess of Windsor's jewelry sparked new interest in her style, and designers are still showing copies of her jewelry.

Until Princess Diana and Sarah Ferguson married into the British royal family, few royal personages in recent years had qualified as fashion leaders. Despite the belief held by some that kings and queens wear crowns and ermine, the truth is that modern royalty has become a hard-working group whose daily life is packed with so many activities that sensible and conservative dress is necessary for most occasions (see Figure 4.10).

### The Rich

As monarchies were replaced with democracies, members of the wealthy and international sets came into the fashion spotlight. Whether the members of "society" derive their position from vast fortunes and old family names or from recent wealth, they bring to the scene a glamor and excitement that draws attention to everything they do. Today, through the constant eye of television, magazines, and newspapers, the average person is able to find fashion leadership in a whole new stratum of society—the jet set.

What these socialites are doing and what they are wearing are instantly served up to the general pub-

**FIGURE 4.10** Queen Rania of Jordan is recognized as an influential royal and international fashion icon (top). **FIGURE 4.11** Often in the fashion spotlight, socialite Tinsley Mortimer is a well-known trendsetter (bottom).

lic by the media (see Figure 4.11). As far as fashion is concerned, these people are not just in the news; they *are* the news. Any move they make is important enough to be immediately publicized. What they wear is of vital interest to the general public. The media tell us what the social leaders wear to dine in a chic restaurant, to attend a charity ball, or to go shopping. Because they are trendsetters, their choices are of prime interest to designers and to the world at large.

Of course, this inundation of news about what social leaders wear influences the public. The average person is affected because so many manufacturers and retailers of fashion take their cue from these social leaders. Right or wrong, fashion merchants count on the fashion sense of these leaders. They know that the overwhelming exposure of these leaders in the media encourages people of ordinary means to imitate them—consciously or unconsciously.

## The Famous

Fashion today takes its impetus and influence from people in every possible walk of life. These people have one thing in common, however: they are famous. Because of some special talent, charisma, notoriety, or popularity, they are constantly mentioned and shown on television, in fashion magazines, and in newspapers. They may or may not appear in the society pages.

In this group can be found presidents and princesses, movie stars and musicians, sports figures and recording stars, politicians and TV personalities (see Figure 4.12). Because they are seen so frequently, the public has a good sense of their fashions and lifestyles and can imitate them to the extent of the public's means and desires.

Prominent individuals have been responsible for certain fashions that continue to be associated with them. Many times, however, these individuals are not what would be considered fashion leaders. Although the cornrow braiding of hair had been

FIGURE 4.12 Music sensation Justin Timberlake is in the public eye for not only his music but also his role in the fashion world.

practiced among blacks in Africa and America for decades, it was adopted by many young black women only after Cicely Tyson appeared with the hairstyle in the movie *Sounder* in 1972. In 1979, Bo Derek wore cornrows in the film *10* and gave the style new impetus. In the 1930s, a tremendous impact was felt by an entire men's wear industry when Clark Gable appeared without an undershirt in the film *It Happened One Night*. Practically overnight, men from all walks of life shed their undershirts in imitation of Gable. In the late 1930s, women dared to wear slacks after seeing Greta Garbo and Marlene Dietrich wearing them in the movies. In the early 1960s, when First Lady Jacqueline Kennedy appeared in little pillbox hats, both the style and the hat market blossomed under the publicity. Some styles are so closely associated with the famous people who wore them that they bear their names (see Table 4.1).

**TABLE 4.1** *Fashion Styles Named for the Famous*

| TRENDSETTERS | STYLES |
|---|---|
| Amelia Bloomer | Bloomers |
| Earl of Chesterfield | Chesterfield Jacket |
| Dwight D. Eisenhower | Eisenhower Jacket |
| Geraldine Ferraro | "Gerry Cut" (Hairstyle) |
| Mao Tse Tung | Mao Jacket |
| Jawaharlal Nehru | Nehru Jacket |
| Madame de Pompadour | Pompadour (Hairstyle) |
| Nancy Reagan | "Reagan Plastics" (Costume Jewelry), Color Red |
| Duke of Wellington | Wellington Boots |
| Earl of Cardigan | Cardigan Sweater |
| Duke of Windsor | Windsor Knot (Tie) |
| Duke of Norfolk | Norfolk Jacket |
| Nelson Mandela | Madiba Smart (Shirt) |
| The Beatles | Hairstyle |

MADAME DE POMPADOUR

AMELIA BLOOMER

THE BEATLES

DWIGHT D. EISENHOWER

## Athletes

Today, there is strong emphasis on sports. And what prominent sports figures wear is of great importance to the people who seek to imitate them (see Figure 4.13). Television has increased the public acceptance of several sports. For example, people have enjoyed going to baseball, football, or basketball games for years. But sports of a more individual nature, such as tennis and golf, were of minor interest. Now these sports are brought into the living rooms of an increasing number of viewers. As a result, fashions for participating in these sports have grown remarkably in importance. Tennis is now a very popular participation sport and has given rise to an entire specialized fashion industry. Aspiring tennis players have endless fashion styles, colors, and fabrics to choose from. A wide selection of fashion is also available for golf, jogging, running, swimming, skating, cycling, snorkeling, snowboarding, and other sports. The names of Michael Jordan, Tiger Woods, and Venus Williams are known to most Americans.

**FIGURE 4.13** Athletes, such as Thierry Henry, are often used in advertisements and as spokespersons to sell sportswear.

## Fashion Followers

Filling out forms for his daughter's college entrance application, a father wrote of his daughter's leadership qualities: "To tell the truth, my daughter is really not a leader, but rather a loyal and devoted follower." The dean of the college admissions responded: "We are welcoming a freshman class of 100 students this year and are delighted to accept your daughter. You can't imagine how happy we are to have one follower among the ninety-nine leaders!"

Most people want to be thought of as leaders, not followers. But many people are followers, and good ones. In fact, followers are in the majority within any group. Without followers, the fashion industry would certainly collapse. Mass production and mass distribution can be possible and profitable only when large numbers of consumers accept the merchandise. Although they may say otherwise, luckily, more people prefer to follow than to lead. The styles fashion leaders adopt may help manufacturers and retailers in determining what will be demanded by the majority of consumers in the near future. Only accurate predictions can ensure the continued success of the giant ready-to-wear business in this country, which depends for its success on mass production and distribution. While fashion leaders may stimulate and excite the fashion industry, fashion followers are the industry's lifeblood.

## Reasons for Following Fashion

Theories about why people follow rather than lead in fashion are plentiful. Among the explanations are feelings of insecurity, admiration of others, lack of interest, and ambivalence about the new.

### Feelings of Insecurity

Flügel wrote, "Inasmuch as we feel our own inferiority and the need for conformity to the standards set by others, we are followers of fashion."[28] For example, high school boys and girls are at a notably insecure stage of life. They are therefore more susceptible than any other age group to the appeal of fads. A person about to face a difficult interview or attend the first meeting with a new group carefully selects new clothes. Often a feeling of inadequacy can be hidden by wearing a style that others have already approved as appropriate.

## Admiration

Flügel also maintained that it is a fundamental human impulse to imitate those who are admired or envied. A natural and symbolic means of doing this is to copy their clothes, makeup, and hairstyles. Outstanding illustrations of this theory have been provided by movie stars and models—Mary Pickford, "America's Sweetheart" of the 1910s; Clara Bow, the "It" girl of the 1920s; Ginger Rogers, Katharine Hepburn, and Rosalind Russell of the 1930s; Veronica Lake and Ann Sheridan, the "Oomph Girls" of the 1940s; Doris Day and Marilyn Monroe in the 1950s; Twiggy in the 1960s; Farrah Fawcett in the 1970s; Christie Brinkley in the 1980s; Elle McPherson and Cindy Crawford in the 1990s; Reese Witherspoon, Cameron Diaz, and Rachel Bilson (see Figure 4.14) at

**FIGURE 4.14** Rachel Bilson's California style is admired and copied by the public.

the beginning of the 21st century. Their clothes and hairstyles were copied instantly among many different groups throughout this country and in many other parts of the world. On a different level, the young girl who copies the hairstyle of her best friend, older sister, or favorite aunt demonstrates the same principle, as do college students who model their appearance after that of a campus leader.

## Lack of Interest

Edward Sapir suggested that many people are insensitive to fashion and follow it only because "they realize that not to fall in with it would be to declare themselves members of a past generation, or dull people who cannot keep up with their neighbors."[29] Their response to fashion, he said, is a sullen surrender, by no means an eager following of the Pied Piper.

## Ambivalence

Another theory holds that many people are ambivalent in their attitudes toward the new; they both want it and fear it. For most, it is easier to choose what is already familiar. Such individuals need time and exposure to new styles before they can accept them.

## Varying Rates of Response

Individuals vary in the speed with which they respond to a new idea, especially when fashion change is radical and dramatic. Some fashion followers apparently need time to adjust to new ideas. Merchants exploit this point when they buy a few "window pieces" of styles too advanced for their own clientele and expose them in windows and fashion shows to allow customers time to get used to them. Only after a period of exposure to the new styles do the fashion followers accept them.

## Fashion as an Expression of Individuality

In the early part of the 21st century, a strange but understandable trend became apparent across the nation. People were striving, through their mode of dress, to declare individuality in the face of computer-age conformity.

People had watched strings of impersonal numbers become more and more a part of their lives—zip codes, bank and credit card account numbers, employee identification numbers, department store accounts, automobile registrations, social security numbers, and so on. An aversion to joining the masses—to becoming "just another number"—began to be felt. So while most people continued to go along with general fashion trends, some asserted their individuality. This was accomplished by distinctive touches each wearer added to an outfit. A new freedom in dress, color and texture combinations, use of accessories, and hairstyles allowed people to assert their individuality without being out of step with the times. Most social scientists see in this a paradox—an endless conflict between the desire to conform and the desire to remain apart.

We have all known people who at some point in their lives found a fashion that particularly pleased them. It might have been a certain style of dress, a certain shoe, or a hairstyle. Even in the face of continuing changes in fashion, the person continued to wear that style in which she or he felt right and attractive. This is an assertion of individuality in the face of conformity. Although superbly fashion conscious, the actress Joan Crawford never stopped wearing the open-toed, slingback, wedge shoe of the 1940s. When the pointed toe and stiletto heel of the 1950s gave way to the low, chunky heel of the 1960s, she continued to wear the same style. She was perfectly in step with fashion when the wedge shoe finally returned to popularity in the early 1970s. Woody Allen achieved special recognition for wearing—anywhere and everywhere—sneakers! At formal occasions, he conforms by wearing appropriate formal attire. But his feet remain sneakered, and Woody retains his individuality.

Most people prefer to assert their individuality in a less obvious way, and today's ready-to-wear fashions lend themselves to subtle changes that mark each person's uniqueness. No two people put the same costume together in exactly the same way.

Fashion editor Jessica Daves summed up the miracle of modern ready-to-wear fashion. It offers, she said, "the possibility for some women to create a design for themselves . . . to choose the color and shape in clothes that will present them as they would like to see themselves."[30]

## The Paradox of Conformity and Individuality

For decades, experts have tried to explain why people seek both conformity and individuality in fashion. Simmel suggested that two opposing social tendencies are at war: the need for union and the need for isolation. The individual, he reasoned, derives satisfaction from knowing that the way in which he or she expresses a fashion represents something special. At the same time, people gain support from seeing others favor the same style.[31]

Flügel interpreted the paradox in terms of a person's feelings of superiority and inferiority. The individual wants to be like others "insofar as he regards them as superior, but unlike them, in the sense of being more 'fashionable,' insofar as he thinks they are below him."[32]

Sapir tied the conflict to a revolt against custom and a desire to break away from slavish acceptance of fashion. Slight changes from the established form of dress and behavior "seem for the moment to give victory to the individual, while the fact that one's fellows revolt in the same direction gives one a feeling of adventurous safety."[33] He also tied the assertion of individuality to the need to affirm one's self in a powerful society in which the individual has ceased to be the measure.

One example of this conflict may be found in the off-duty dress of people required to wear uniforms of one kind or another during working hours, such as nurses, police officers, and mail carriers. A second example is seen in the clothing worn by many present-day business executives. Far from the days when to be "The Man in the Gray Flannel Suit" meant that a man had arrived in the business world, today executives favor a much more diversified wardrobe. While suits of gray flannel are still worn, so are a wide variety of other fabrics and patterns. And some top executives favor a more relaxed look altogether, preferring to wear appropriately fashioned separate jackets or blazers with their business slacks.

Retailers know that although some people like to lead and some like to follow in fashion, most people buy fashion to express their personality or to identify with a particular group. To belong, they follow fashion; to express their personality, they find ways to individualize fashion.

### Fashion and Self-Expression

Increasing importance is being placed on fashion individuality—on expressing your personality, or refusing to be cast in a mold. Instead of slavishly adopting any one look, today's young person seeks to create an individual effect through the way he or she combines various fashion components (see Figure 4.15). For instance, if a young woman thinks a denim skirt, an ankle-length woolen coat, and a heavy turtle-necked sweater represent her personality, they will be considered acceptable by others in her group.

Forward-looking designers recognize this desire for self-expression. Designers say that basic wardrobe components should be made available, but consumers should be encouraged to combine them as they see fit. For instance, they advise women to wear pants or skirts, long or short, according to how they feel, not according to what past tradition has considered proper for an occasion. They suggest that men make the same choice among tailored suits, leisure wear, and slacks, to find the styles that express their personalities.

Having experienced such fashion freedom, young people may never conform again. Yet despite individual differences in dress, young experimenters have in common a deep-rooted desire to dress differently from older generations.

### Summary and Review

It is the nature of fashion to change, but the speed and direction of its changes are difficult to predict. Some factors that accelerate the pace of change are widespread buying power, increased leisure time, increased education, the improved status of women, technological advances that bring new and improved products to the market, and seasonal changes. However, the pace of change can be slowed by habit and custom, religious restrictions, and sumptuary laws (laws placing limits or requirements on the construction of apparel).

Some types of fashion merchandise change more

**FIGURE 4.15** Musician M.I.A. expresses her personality and style, regardless of social acceptance.

slowly than other types. For example, men's fashions change more slowly than women's. Some fashion historians have tracked the basic shapes of apparel, particularly women's wear, and concluded that three basic silhouettes dominate fashion in turn, each for about 35 years, creating a cycle that lasts about 100 years. Other details of line, such as sleeve shape and skirt length, have similar cycles.

Fashion also focuses on different parts of the body at different times, accentuating the seductive appeal of each part in turn. For fashion merchandisers, success depends on the accuracy of predictions of trends and judging when and to what degree a fashion will be adopted by the producer's or retailer's target market. Inventory and sales records and a careful following of current events, the reception of new styles at the introductory stage of the fashion cycle, sales promotion, and current canons of taste help forecasters make accurate predictions.

Three theories attempt to explain the movement of fashion: the downward-flow, horizontal-flow, and upward-flow theories. The acceptance of a fashion depends on innovators, who are the first to wear it, and influentials, whose personal style is copied by others. On a broad scale, public figures are often innovators and influentials. The buying public watches the fashions of royalty, high society, athletes and other entertainers, and other celebrities. On a smaller scale, individual communities have their own fashion innovators and influentials, but a fashion's acceptance ultimately depends on fashion followers. They are the people who spread a fashion and account for the number of sales. Each person adjusts his or her wardrobe to balance a sense of belonging to a group and being an individual.

## Trade Talk
Define or briefly explain the following terms:

downward-flow theory
fashion influential
horizontal-flow theory
sumptuary law

erogenous
fashion innovator
prophetic styles
upward-flow theory

## For Review
1. Describe the theory of fashion cycles and explain why it accelerated in the 20th century.
2. List the "pieces" of the women's fashion game, according to Madge Garland. What happens to these pieces?
3. According to leading fashion authorities, what are the three basic rules that govern the fashion game?
4. What basic resources are available to the fashion merchant to predict fashion?
5. Explain the term prophetic style.
6. Is the downward-flow theory of fashion adoption as valid today as it was in years past? Explain your answer.
7. How does the horizontal-flow theory of fashion adoption affect fashion merchants today? How are merchants today affected by the upward-flow theory?
8. Explain why (a) rich people, (b) famous people, and (c) athletes are prime candidates for positions of fashion leadership.
9. Give four reasons why most people follow, rather than lead, in regard to fashion. Explain each.
10. How can fashion be used as a means of expressing individuality?

## For Discussion
1. Give at least one current example of each of several factors that are accelerating the forward movement of fashions today.
2. Certain factors tend to retard the development of fashion cycles by discouraging the adoption of newly introduced styles. List these factors and give at least one example of how each factor exerts a braking influence on fashion development.
3. Why do people today seek both conformity and individuality in fashion? How does this affect the fashion designer or manufacturer? The fashion retailer?

chapter five

*Everything you always wanted to know about the levels of the fashion business.*

KEY CONCEPTS
- The four levels of the fashion business
- The three common forms of business ownership
- The role of franchising and licensing
- The role of the designer, the manufacturer, and the retailer in the fashion business

# The Business of Fashion

Fashion is a business, affected by the same technological advances, investment patterns, and economic forces that affect other major businesses in the world. Fashion is not limited just to apparel; it impacts our complete lifestyle as well as the products we buy. Fashion influences the automobile, housing, and entertainment industries, and like these industries, it is shaped by the basic principles of business and economics.

What is business? Business is the activity of creating, producing, and marketing products or services. The primary objective of business is to make a profit. **Profit**, or net income, is the amount of money a business earns in excess of its expenses. Consequently, in the United States, business can be defined as the activity of creating, producing, and marketing products or services for a profit.

## Economic Importance of the Fashion Business

The business of fashion contributes significantly to the economy of the United States through the materials and services it purchases, the wages and taxes it pays, and the goods and services it produces. The fashion business is one of the largest employers in the country. However, employment has declined almost by half since the industry boom in the early 1970s. Now, more than 478,000 people in the United States are employed either in factories that produce apparel for men, women, and children or in textile plants that produce the materials from which garments are made.[1]

More people are employed in apparel production than in the entire printing and publishing business or the automobile manufacturing industry. In addition, more than 133,000 people are employed in producing such fashion items as fur and leather garments and accessories, jewelry and cosmetics; hundreds of thousands more are employed by the retail organizations that distribute these goods. When we add to this number a share of the total number of jobs in finance, transportation, advertising, computers, electronics, and other services that devote part of their efforts to the fashion industry, it becomes obvious that the fashion industry has a tremendous impact on our economy.

The growth and development of mass markets, mass-production methods, and mass distribution have contributed to the creation of new job opportunities in the fashion industry—not only in the production area but in design and marketing as well. Young people are entering the fashion business in greater numbers each year and are having a marked effect on the business. Innovation and change have become increasingly important factors in the economic growth of the fashion business.

## Scope of the Fashion Business

The fashion business is composed of numerous industries all working to keep consumers of fashion satisfied (see Figure 5.1). A special relationship exists among these industries that makes the fashion business different from other businesses. The four levels of the fashion business—known as the primary level, the secondary level, the retail level, and the auxiliary level—are composed of separate entities, but they also work interdependently to provide the market with the fashion merchandise that will satisfy consumers. Because of this unique relationship among the different industries, the fashion business is unusually exciting.

### The Primary Level

The **primary level** is composed of the growers and producers of the raw materials of fashion—the fiber, fabric, leather, and fur producers who function in the raw materials market. The earliest part of the planning function in color and texture takes place on the primary level. It is also the level of the fashion business that works the farthest in advance of the ultimate selling period of the goods. Up to two years' lead time is needed by primary-level companies before the goods will be available to the consumer. Primary-level goods may often be imports from third-world emerging nations, where textiles are usually the earliest form of industrialization.

## The Secondary Level

The **secondary level** is composed of industries—manufacturers and contractors—that produce the semifinished or finished fashion goods from the materials produced on the primary level. On the secondary level are the manufacturers of women's, men's, and children's apparel and also legwear, bodywear, and underwear; accessories; cosmetics and fragrances; and home furnishings.

Manufacturers who function on the secondary level may be based in the United States or overseas. Fashion goods are now produced in the Far East, the Caribbean, South America, and Europe. Secondary-level companies work from six to eighteen

months ahead of the time that goods are available to the consumer.

## The Retail Level

The **retail level** is the ultimate distribution level. On this level are the different types of retailers who buy their goods from the secondary level and then supply them directly to the consumer (see Figure 5.2). In many cases, the retail level works with both the primary and secondary levels to ensure a coordinated approach to consumer wants. The interrelationship among the primary, secondary, and retail levels is vertical. The farther removed a level is from the consumer, the farther in advance it must plan. Retailers make initial purchases for resale to customers from three to six months before the customer buying season.

## The Auxiliary Level

The **auxiliary level** is the only level that functions with all the other levels simultaneously. This level is

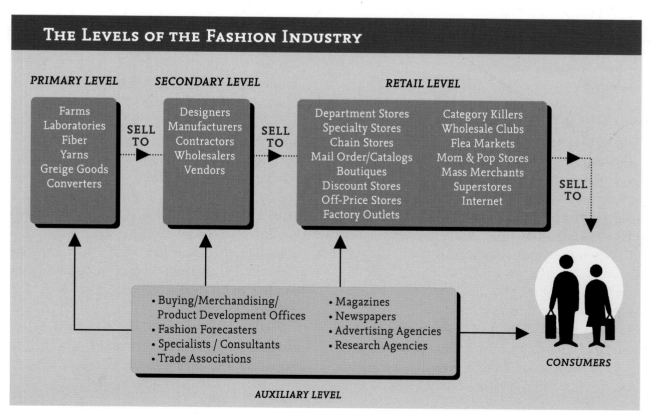

**FIGURE 5.1** The fashion industry operates collaboratively on four levels to serve the customer.

**FIGURE 5.2** The retail level includes nonstore retailers, such as the Home Shopping Network (HSN).

composed of all the support services that are working constantly with primary producers, secondary manufacturers, and retailers to keep consumers aware of the fashion merchandise produced for ultimate consumption. On this level are all the advertising media—print, audio, and visual—and fashion consultants and researchers.

## Diversity and Competition

The enormous variety and diversity that exist in the kinds and sizes of firms that operate on each level of the fashion industry make it a fascinating and competitive business. There are giant firms, both national and international, and small companies with regional or local distribution, doing business side by side as privately or publicly owned corporations, partnerships, or sole proprietorships. Fashion-producing companies may also be part of conglomerates, which also own, for example, entertainment companies, oil wells, professional sports teams, or consumer foods and products divisions.

Whether large or small, the different types of producers have one need in common—the need to understand what their ultimate customer will buy.

Only through complete understanding and cooperation can the four levels of the fashion business be aware of new developments in fashion and apply them to satisfy the wants of their customers. This cooperation allows them to have the right merchandise at the right price, in the right place, at the right time, in the right quantities, and with the right sales promotion for their customers.

However, when you begin to try to sell a product or service in our economic system, chances are that someone else will be trying to sell something similar. No matter what the size of the firm involved, potential customers are free to buy where they please and what they please. Each company must compete with the others for those customers' business. A company can choose to compete in one of three ways: price, quality, or innovation.

## Competition and Price

Selling blue jeans for less than your competition may bring you more business. However, you are taking in less money than your rival does on each pair sold, and you still have to cover the same cost and expenses. The hope is that your lower price will attract more customers, sell more jeans than your competition, and so come out with a good overall profit. Head-to-head competition like this tends to keep prices down, which is good for the buying public. At the same time, it allows a company to look forward to a promise of profits if it can sell more of its product or service than competitors do (see Figure 5.3).

## Competition and Quality

Rather than sell your jeans for less than your competition, you may choose to compete for customers by offering higher-quality goods. Although you may charge more for your jeans, you offer a better fit, more durable fabric, or better styling. This possibility provides a practical incentive for businesses to maintain high standards and increases the choices available to consumers.

**FIGURE 5.3** These three coats are similar in style but different in price: Banana Republic's coat is about $195 (top), the Gap's coat is about $70 (bottom), while Old Navy sells its coat for about $40 (middle).

## Competition and Innovation

Our economic system not only encourages variations in quality and price, it also encourages immense variety in the types of merchandise and services offered to the public. Changes in taste and new technology bring about innovation, so that your jeans could be trimmed or untrimmed, designer made, or French cut. The economy and the competitive environment are constantly creating new business opportunities. The result is an astonishing diversity of businesses.

## Government Regulation of Business

The right of government to regulate business is granted by the U.S. Constitution and by state constitutions. There are two basic categories of federal legislation that affect the fashion industry: (1) laws that regulate competition, and (2) labeling laws designed to protect consumers. Table 5.1 lists the key federal laws that affect and/or regulate the fashion industry.

## Forms of Business Ownership

Ownership of a fashion business—or of any business—may take many different legal forms, each carrying certain privileges and responsibilities. The three most common forms of business ownership are the sole proprietorship, the partnership, and the corporation. Corporations tend to be large-scale operations that account for the greatest share of the profits earned by U.S. business. However, sole proprietorships are more numerous, accounting for more than 70 percent of all business.

Each form of ownership has a characteristic structure, legal status, size, and field to which it is best suited. Each has its own advantages and disadvantages and offers a distinctive working environment with its own risks and rewards (see Table 5.2).

## Business Growth and Expansion

For the past few years, business activity has focused on the change in forms of business growth and expansion. The news media is filled with reports of businesses buying and selling other businesses and seeking new methods to make themselves more efficient and competitive.

One of the most distinct changes in the fashion business has been the rise of corporate giants which grew through mergers, acquisitions, and internal expansion. The growth of these giants has changed the methods of doing business, and has led to the demise of old-time famous-name sole proprietorships, partnerships, and small companies that could no longer compete.

Growth and expansion are fundamental to today's business world. Corporate growth has become a major economic, political, and social issue in recent years. Growth and expansion can occur in a variety of ways—internal growth, mergers, and acquisitions. Many large corporations grow by more than one of these methods. For example, cosmetics giant Estée Lauder developed the Prescriptives brand to expand to a more upscale consumer market. The company also acquired several smaller companies that cater to a younger market, including Bobbi Brown and MAC.

## Internal Growth

A company's ability to grow internally determines its ability to offer more service and broader assortments of merchandise, and to increase profits. This is true because internal growth is real growth in terms of creating new products and new jobs. Internal growth can be accomplished through horizontal means, vertical means, or both. When a company has **horizontal growth**, it expands its capabilities on the level on which it has been performing successfully (see Figure 5.4). An apparel company could add new lines to diversify its product offerings; a retail store could open new branches. When a company has **vertical growth**, it expands its capabilities on levels other than its primary function. An apparel company could begin to produce its own fabric or

## Table 5.1 Key Federal Laws Affecting the Fashion Industry

| Laws Affecting Competition | Purpose and Provisions |
|---|---|
| Sherman Antitrust Act—1890 | Outlawed monopolies. Outlawed restraint of competition. |
| Clayton Act—1914 | Same purpose as Sherman Act but reinforced Sherman Act by defining some specific restraint—for example, price fixing. |
| Federal Trade Commission (FTC) Act—1914 (Wheeler–Lee Act of 1938 amended the FTC Act.) | Established the FTC as a "policing" agency. Developed the mechanics for policing unfair methods of competition—for example, false claims, price discrimination, price fixing. |
| Robinson–Patman Act—1936 | Designed to equalize competition between large and small retailers (i.e., to reduce the advantages that big retailers have over small retailers—outgrowth of 1930 depression and growth of big chain retailers in 1920s.) *Examples of provision of law:*<br>1. Outlawed price discrimination if both small and large retailers buy the same amount of goods.<br>2. Outlawed inequitable and unjustified quantity discounts (e.g., discounts allowable if (a) available to all types of retailers and (b) related to actual savings that vendor could make from quantity cuttings or shipments.)<br>3. Outlawed "phony" advertising allowance monies—that is advertising money must be used for advertising.<br>4. Outlawed discrimination in promotional allowances (monies for advertising, promotional display, etc.)—equal allowances must be given under same conditions to small and large retailers alike. |
| Cellar–Kefauver—1950 | This law made it illegal to eliminate competition by creating a monopoly through the merger of two or more companies. |
| Product and Labeling Laws Designed to Protect Consumers Wool Products Labeling Act—1939; amended in 1984 | Purpose and Provisions Protects consumers from unrevealed presence of substitutes or mixtures. FTC responsible for enforcing law. |
| Fur Products Labeling Act—1951 | Protects consumers and retailers against misbranding, false advertising, and false invoicing. |
| Flammable Fabrics Act—1954; revised in 1972 | Prohibits manufacture or sale of flammable fabrics or apparel. |
| Textile Fiber Identification Act—1960; amended in 1984 | Protects producers and consumers against false identification of fiber content. |
| Fair Packaging and Labeling Act—1966 | Regulates interstate and foreign commerce by prohibiting deceptive methods of packaging or labeling. |
| Care Labeling of Textile Wearing Apparel Ruling—1972; amended in 1984, 1997 | Requires that all apparel have labels attached that clearly inform consumers about care and maintenance of the article. |

## Table 5.2 Advantages and Disadvantages of Each Form of Business Ownership

| Form of Ownership | Advantages | Disadvantages |
|---|---|---|
| Sole proprietorship (single owner) | • Ability to keep all profits<br>• Simple to form and easiest to dissolve<br>• Ownership flexibility | • Unlimited financial liability<br>• Limited capital<br>• Management deficiencies<br>• Lack of continuity |
| Partnership (a few owners) | • Ease of formation<br>• Complementary management skills<br>• Greater financial capacity than sole proprietorship<br>• Less red tape than corporation | • Unlimited financial liability<br>• Interpersonal conflicts<br>• Lack of continuity if partner dies<br>• Harder to dissolve than sole proprietorship |
| Corporation (Inc.) (many owners) | • Limited financial liability<br>• Specialized management skills<br>• Greater financial capacity than other forms of ownership<br>• Economies of larger-scale operation<br>• Easy to transfer ownership | • Difficult and costly form to establish and dissolve ownership<br>• Tax disadvantage<br>• Legal restrictions<br>• Depersonalization |

# Fashion Focus
Fashion Focus

## Young Designers
## Go! Go! Go!—
## But Go Slow!
## Can You Handle it?

Left page: Peter Som plays with proportions during fall 2007 fashion week (top); Derek Lam Design, fall 2007 (bottom left); right page: Hussein Chalayan Collection, spring 2008 (top); Peter Som Design, spring 2008 (bottom).

Those who believe that designers spend all day sketching in their studios should reconsider their choice of career. It takes a mountain of concerns and then some for designers to convey their message. Be media-savvy, aware of global issues, and clever enough to bottle these qualities into a brand identity that speaks to the consumer. Oh, and don't forget to bring along design talent! That's the advice those in the know offer to anyone who aspires to the glamorous title of fashion designers.

In the past, designers spent their days—and their nights—sketching, sewing, and draping, but the role has shifted as fashion has evolved into a billion-dollar global business over the past two decades. As a result, designers have to represent their labels 24/7. Ideally, they should become their brand. And, while they are at it, they shouldn't neglect world events!

Designers must also predict what their customers will want months before they know themselves. In fact, the laundry list of what designers have to do today appears endless.

Now there is the growing competition from celebrity-designers who enter the fashion fray with well-established names and a solid following of fans around the world. Young designers can find other avenues to help them gain recognition. Fashion festivals and scholarships certainly help. Globally, fashion philanthropists are doing more than doling out cash. Nathalie Dufour, who runs France's Andam prize, says, "The idea is to help designers who are starting out to understand what type of business strategy could help them to develop."

The steps to becoming a fashion designer mirror what the Council of Fashion Designers of America (CFDA) is doing with its CFDA/*Vogue* Fashion Fund. The CFDA selects three designers each season for financing of

up to $200,000, as well as mentoring from a senior executive from within the industry. In the United States generally, though, young designers tend to get funding more by doing consultancy work for large companies and assisting on teams of leading designers than by participation in festivals or through scholarships.

France's Chambre Syndicale also is involved in supporting young designers. The biggest hurdle a young designer often faces his naïveté in the ways of the world and the fast-changing nature of today's fashion business. It is not enough to design! Young designers must have a product that is produced in an innovative way.

Today, young designers have a new set of eyes

analyzing their designs: private equity firms and investment bankers. These investors are interested in young designers who have already grown to the $2 million mark and have the potential to grow further. Among recent designers have been Anna Sui, Catherine Malandrino, Hussein Chalayan, and Phoebe Philo. And let's not forget Derek Lam, who as a young designer worked as an assistant to Geoffrey Beene and for Michael Kors; or Peter Som, who was recognized in 1997 by the CFDA as a rising young talent in the scholarship competition and honed his skills in the design rooms of Bill Blass, Michael Kors, and Calvin Klein.

You have to hone your skills and spend time working with and learning from the star designers. As a young designer, your path to star success is Go! Go! Go!—but go slow!

could retail its manufactured goods in stores that the apparel company owns.

## Mergers and Acquisitions

In a **merger** (or acquisition) a sale of one company to another company occurs, with the purchasing company usually remaining dominant. Companies merge to form a larger corporate organization for many reasons. They may wish to take advantage of a large corporation's greater purchasing power, or they may want to sell stock to obtain the financial resources needed for expansion. The desire to constantly increase sales is often able to be fulfilled only by a merger. At the retail level, for example, the acquisition of Macy's by Federated Department Stores extended the conglomerate's market to include Macy's customers.

Operating economies can often be achieved by combining companies. Many times duplicate facilities can be eliminated, and marketing, purchasing, and other operations can be consolidated. **Diversification**, the addition of various lines, products, or services to serve different markets, can also be a motive for a merger. For example, the acquisition of Banana Republic by the Gap broadened the Gap's market to reach customers for clothing at higher

**FIGURE 5.4** An example of internal growth is Donna Karan's expansion of its DKNY line.

price points. Then the Gap started Old Navy to reach to even lower price points. Now the company covers three price points.

### The Franchise

A rapidly growing business arrangement is the **franchise**. This arrangement is a contract that gives an individual (or group of people) the right to own a business while benefiting from the expertise and reputation of an established firm. In return, the individual, known as the franchisee, pays the parent company, known as the franchisor, a set sum to purchase the franchise and royalties on goods or services sold. Franchises may be organized as sole proprietorships, partnerships, or corporations, although the form of business organization that the franchise must use may be designated in the franchise contract.

Franchises generate one-third of all retail sales in the United States today and are steadily growing in volume, according to industry reports. Although the franchise arrangement is most widespread among fast-food restaurants, convenience stores, and automobile dealers, franchises can be found at many levels of the fashion business, especially in retailing.

The growth in the number of manufacturer-franchised shops is phenomenal. Although we learn much more about designer-name franchising when we cover the apparel industries, it is important to note that Ralph Lauren, Donna Karan, and Oscar de la Renta as well as Armani, Benetton Group S.p.A. (see Figure 5.5), BCBG, Hugo Boss, and Juicy Couture are all involved in designer-franchised boutiques and shops in major cities throughout the United States, Europe, and Asia.

### Advantages

Franchising offers advantages to both the franchisee and the franchisor. The franchisee can get into business quickly, use proven operating methods, and benefit from training programs and mass purchasing offered by the franchisor. The franchisee is provided with a ready market that identifies with the store or brand name, thus

UNITED COLORS OF BENETTON.

**FIGURE 5.5** Benetton Group S.p.A. is a popular designer franchise across the globe.

assuring customer traffic. The franchisor has a great deal of control over its distribution network, limited liability, and less need for capital for expansion. Expansion is therefore more rapid than would be possible without the franchising arrangement. Royalty and franchise fees add to the profits of the parent company, and the personal interest and efforts of the franchisees as owner-managers help to assure the success of each venture.

## Disadvantages

Franchising also has drawbacks for both parties. The franchisee may find profits small in relation to the time and work involved, and often has limited flexibility at the local level. In addition, there is the risk of franchise arrangements organized merely to sell franchises rather than for their long-range profitability to all parties involved. The franchisor may find profits so slim that it may want to own stores outright rather than franchise them. Attempts to buy back franchises often lead to troubled relations with the remaining franchises.

## *Licensing*

Licensing is an increasingly popular method of expanding an already existing business. **Licensing** is a legal arrangement whereby firms are given permission to produce and market merchandise in the name of the licensor for a specific period of time. The licensor is then paid a percentage of the sales (usually at the wholesale price) called a **royalty fee**. The royalty fee usually ranges from 2 to 15 percent.

Licensing grew tremendously in the late 1970s and through the 1980s and 1990s. By 2000, retail sales of licensed fashion merchandise in the United States and Canada reached almost $12.7 billion. Of that total, apparel accounted for $4.23 billion, accessories for $1.821 billion, footwear for $88 million, and health and beauty aids for $2.5 billion.[2]

The first designer to license his name to a manufacturer was Christian Dior, who lent his name to

**FIGURE 5.6** Many consumers are not aware that fashion merchandise from Kenneth Cole is not manufactured by the designer.

a line of ties in 1950. Today, many of the best-known women's and men's apparel designers are licensing either the use of their original designs or just their names without a design for a wide variety of goods, from apparel to luggage. Many fashion labels—Ralph Lauren and Betsey Johnson, for example—also extend into home furnishings through licensing. Among the many American designers involved in licensing are BCBG Max Azria, Joe (Joseph Abboud), Michael (Michael Kors), Bill Blass, Calvin Klein, Ralph Lauren, and Oscar de la Renta. Most customers are not aware that some of the fashion merchandise they buy is licensed. For example, to customers every Kenneth Cole product is made by Kenneth Cole. In fact, this licensor manufactures *no* merchandise in house (see Figure 5.6).

## RETAIL SALES OF LICENSED FASHION MERCHANDISE BY PRODUCT CATEGORY U.S. AND CANADA, 2006 *(in millions of dollars)*

| RETAIL SALES | 2000 |
|---|---|
| Accessories | $1.84 |
| Apparel | $4.22 |
| Footwear | $.88 |
| Health/Beauty | $2.55 |

| RETAIL SALES | 2006 |
|---|---|
| Accessories | $6.60 |
| Apparel | $8.90 |
| Footwear | $2.00 |
| Health/Beauty | $4.60 |

| SHARE OF TOTAL (2006) | |
|---|---|
| Accessories | 9% |
| Apparel | 12% |
| Footwear | 6% |
| Health/Beauty | 9% |

**FIGURE 5.7** Retail sales of licensed fashion merchandise has increased over the years.

The licensing phenomenon is not limited to name designers. Manufacturers of athletic shoes expand their business enormously by licensing their logos and names to producers of active sportswear. Nike, Reebok, and Adidas have been particularly successful. Popular movies and TV shows have spawned apparel and other products based on their themes or characters. Disney's sales of licensed merchandise are $7.5 billion to $8 billion annually.[3] Comic or movie characters like Spider-Man, Dora the Explorer, Kidrobot, and Strawberry Shortcake are also frequently licensed, as are most professional sports teams and many players or athletes.[4]

The advantage of a licensing arrangement to a manufacturer is that the merchandise is identified with a highly recognizable name, which also generally connotes high quality and produces sales (see Figure 5.7). Of course, the manufacturer also risks the designer's popularity fading. However, many manufacturers produce licensed goods for several designers.

The recognition factor can be valuable to retailers in presenting their own fashion image. And to consumers, the designer name not only indicates a certain quality of merchandise but symbolizes status or achievement as well. Because of that built-in appeal, stores have stocked up on designer goods from socks to fragrances and jewelry.

### Designers' Retail Programs

A famous designer name is a strong selling point at retail. Licensing spreads a designer's name while giving the financial responsibility—and risk—to licensees who are specialists in their respective product categories. For example, Phillips-Van Heusen (PVH), originally a men's shirt manufacturer, today has a portfolio of licensed brands. From designer labels such as Geoffrey Beene, Kenneth Cole, Calvin Klein, BCBG Max Azria, and Michael Kors to those with celebrity appeal, which include the Sean John and Donald Trump licenses, PVH is currently looking into licensing luggage and watches across all their brands.

PVH consumers can shop for their licensed products in more than ninety different countries, including Australia, the Netherlands, France, Denmark, India, United Kingdom, Portugal, China, and South Africa.[5]

### Birth of a Fashion

But how do fashions generally begin? Who starts them, who sponsors them, and what influences customers to accept them? Answers to these questions are complex and involve designers, manufacturers, retailers—and most of all—customers.

The myth that every change in fashion is caused by a designer seeking a new way to make money is, of course, not true. As we saw in Chapter 1, it is consumers who bring about changes in fashion. The needs and wants of consumers change. Their ideas about what is appropriate and acceptable change, as do their interests in life. These are all reasons that influence fashion designers and manufacturers to produce new and different styles for consumers' consideration. The charting, forecasting, and satisfaction of consumer demand are the fashion industry's main concerns.

Current trends in consumers' purchasing, lifestyles, and attitudes are noted and analyzed. Subsequently, the trends are interpreted and presented to consumers in the form of new styles. Designers and manufacturers influence fashion by providing an unending series of new designs from which consumers choose how best to express their individual lifestyles.

Many precautions are taken to ensure that designers are presenting what customers want. Even so, at least two-thirds of the new designs introduced each season by the fashion industry fail to become fashions. Some designs are introduced too early, before the public is ready to accept them. Other designs fail because they are too extreme for consumer acceptance. Still other designs fail to become fashions because although they are commonly accepted in many places, they meet pockets of resistance in certain areas of the country. What is worn in New York is not necessarily what consumers in less urban areas of the United States are ready to accept (see Figure 5.8). Think about the hot pants, the harem pants, the peasant looks of the 1970s, the punk-rock extremes of the 1980s, and the celebrity nakedness in 2007. Only a trend that reflects a nationwide mood will successfully cross the United States from ocean to ocean and affect the lives and wardrobes of all those in between.

## The Designer's Role

The days when the design world was populated by a few visionaries whose ideas produced all the designs for the public are long gone. Today, there are unlimited opportunities in the field of design

**FIGURE 5.8** What Anna Wintour, editor-in-chief of *Vogue*, is wearing in New York may not yet be seen in less urban areas of the United States.

for those who have the special talents, both artistic and practical, that are needed to shape the consumer's world. Designers are everywhere, and they design everything—fashions, furnishings, housewares, and office equipment. Their tools range from pencil and sketchpad to computer programs.

Designers must continually study the lifestyles of those consumers for whom their designs are intended. Because designers work far in advance of their designs' final production, they must be able to predict future fashion trends. Designers must be aware of the effects of current events, socioeconomic conditions, and psychological attitudes on fashion interest and demand.

In creating designs that not only reflect consumer attitudes and needs but also give expression to artistic ideas, fashion designers are continually influenced and limited by many factors. Of particular importance are practical business considerations. All designs must be produced at a profit and within the firm's predetermined wholesale price range. Consequently, designers must consider the availability and cost of materials, the particular image that the firm wants to maintain, available production techniques, and labor costs. Great designers use their creativity to overcome all these limitations and to produce salable, exciting designs.

## Types of Designers

Most designers can be classified in one of the following three categories:

1. *High-fashion or "name" designers* are responsible for the full range of decisions of a fashion house as well as for establishing the image and creating designs for the company. They design ready-to-wear lines as well as custom designs, and many license the use of their prestigious names to manufacturers of accessories, fragrances and cosmetics, and home fashions. Some, like Ralph Lauren in the United States, run houses that bear their own name. Others take over a design company at the death or retirement of its founder. For example, Karl Lagerfeld took over the designing reins at Chanel, in addition to running his own studio.

2. *Stylist-designers* work for manufacturers and adapt the designs of others, typically of name designers. Usually they create variations in less expensive fabrics to appeal to a market for lower-priced merchandise at the late rise or early culmination stage of the fashion cycle.

3. *Freelance designers* sell sketches of their original designs or adaptations to manufacturers. Freelancers typically work out of design studios. They are not involved in the selection of fabrics and colors or in the business decisions required to manufacture the products based on their designs. Donna Karan, now an internationally recognized name designer, got her start designing for Anne Klein.

## Insight and Intuition

A designer takes a fashion idea and embodies it in new styles. Even the most creative designers, however, disclaim any power to force acceptance of their styles. Few have said so more effectively than Paul Poiret, one of the 20th century's great Parisian couturiers. He once told an American audience:

> I know you think me a king of fashion. . . . It is a reception which cannot but flatter me and of which I cannot complain. All the same, I must undeceive you with regard to the powers of a king of fashion. We are not capricious despots such as wake up one fine day, decide upon a change in habits, abolish a neckline, or puff out a sleeve. We are neither arbiters nor dictators. Rather we are to be thought of as the blindly obedient servants of woman, who for her part is always enamoured of change and a thirst for novelty. It is our role, and our duty, to be on the watch for the moment at which she becomes bored with what she is wearing, that we may suggest at the right instant something else which will meet her taste and needs. It is therefore with a pair of antennae and not a rod of iron that I come before you, and not as a master that I speak, but as a slave . . . who must divine your innermost thoughts.[6]

Insight and intuition always play a large part in a designer's success. Constant experimentation with new ideas is a must. As one fashion reaches the excess that marks its approaching demise, a designer must have new styles ready and waiting for the public.

## Sources of Design Inspiration

Where does the designer get ideas and inspiration for new fashion? The answer, of course, is: everywhere! Through television, the designer experiences all the wonders of the entertainment world. In films, the designer is exposed to the influences of all the arts and lifestyles throughout the world.

**FIGURE 5.9** Museum exhibits, such as the MET Costume Institute's Poiret tribute, often inspire new trends.

Because consumers are exposed to movies through international distribution, films prime their audiences to accept new fashions inspired by the costumes. Museum exhibits, art shows, world happenings, expositions, the theater, music, dance, and world travel are all sources of design inspiration to fashion designers (see Figure 5.9). The fashions of the past are also a rich source of design inspiration.

While always alert to the new and exciting, fashion designers never lose sight of the recent past. They know that consumers need to anticipate something new each season. But they also recognize that whatever new style is introduced will have to take its place with what consumers already have in their wardrobes. No one starts with all new clothes each season. Rarely does a revolutionary new style succeed. Instead, it is the evolutionary new style that so often becomes the best-selling fashion.

## The Manufacturer's Role

Manufacturers would agree with Dwight E. Robinson that "every market into which the consumer's fashion sense has insinuated itself is, by that very token, subject to [the] common, compelling need for unceasing change in the styling of its goods."[7]

Even in such mundane items as writing paper, the need for change has produced rainbows of pastels, brilliant deep shades, and the traditional white with dainty or bold prints. Similarly, in basics such as bedsheets or men's dress shirts, the once traditional white has yielded to a variety of colors, stripes, and prints. There is scarcely an industry serving consumers today in which the manufacturer's success does not depend, in part, on an ability to attune styling to fashion interest and demand. A current trend is to hire merchandisers who do market research for the manufacturer, specializing in identifying the correct customer and his or her needs and wants.

# &Then
# NOW

## Partners
### Wherever We Go, Whatever We Do, We're Gonna Go Through It Together

For years, partnerships have existed in the fashion business. The partner—often part guardian angel and part therapist—quietly served as the foundation from which the designer built his or her success.

*Then,* we had Calvin Klein and Barry Schwartz, Yves St. Laurent and Pierce Bergé, and Oscar de la Renta and Ben Shaw.

*Now,* we have Tom Ford and Domenico DeSole, Marc Jacobs and Robert Duffy, Jimmy Choo and Tamara Mellon, Miuccia Prada and Patrizio Bertelli, and two other very successful partnerships: brand new Proenza Schouler and the Valentino Group, and Nicole Miller and Bud Konheim who have been partners for 25 years.

Bud Konheim, cofounder, partner, and CEO of Nicole Miller, has stayed with the plan that he and Nicole Miller came up with 25 years ago: they did it their way! When they consider their 25 years together, they are proud of the success they are enjoying. Konheim said he told Nicole it would be his job, "no matter how small or big we become," to make the business profitable. While Konheim and Miller have built their firm into an $82 million company and feel they have made their mark, there is a lesson to be learned, according to Konheim: "The biggest companies in our industry are marginal. That's why you always have to be alert and flexible, because you can lose what you have in a very short time."

Since launching with a label based on their mother's maiden name in 2002, Jack McCollough and Lazaro Hernandez, now 26 years old, have developed one of the hottest names—Proenza Schouler—on the New York scene. McCollough and Hernandez were the first recipients of the CFDA/*Vogue* Fashion Fund in 2004, taking home the cash prize of $200,000.

"Throughout our career, we have had a lot of people knocking at the door," Hernandez said. "We never found a partner that felt right." We were waiting for someone who had a similar vision to what we had and experience in developing a brand."

Enter Valentino Fashion Group (VFG), which owns Valentino S.p.A. and holds licensing deals for M Missoni and Marlboro Classics—McCollough and Hernandez thought VFG would make a perfect partner. VFG's global expertise in distribution and logistics would help the boys expand their footprint in leather goods and extend its reach in new markets. Both McCollough and Hernandez agree VFG has "experience in developing fashion brands and luxury brands at

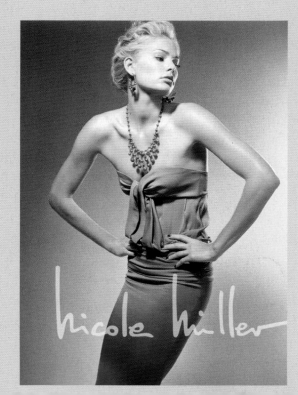

the level we want to be at. At the same time, they don't have an army of brands that compete against each other, so they have the experience, but the vacancy for a brand like ours. It's that mixture that appealed to us."

Partners, whether brand new or celebrating a 25th silver anniversary together, are something special in the fashion business, where there is constant change and businesses go in and out of business—but with the right partner, there is no limit to success!

## Types of Manufacturers

In general, manufacturers of fashion goods can be divided into five groups, differentiated by styling and price.

1. *High-fashion apparel:* This group of designers and firms produce innovative apparel that is very expensive.
2. *Bridge market:* This group bridges the price range between custom designs and high-quality but less expensive merchandise; hence the name **bridge market**. Some high-fashion designers also produce bridge lines.
3. *Better market:* This group is usually identified as the **better market** because its price range is just below that of the bridge lines.
4. *Moderate-priced market:* This group of firms, usually identified as the **moderate-priced market**, sometimes produces originals but usually turns out adaptations of styles that have survived the introduction stage and are in the rise stage of their fashion life cycle.
5. *Budget market:* This group of manufacturers, usually identified as the **budget market**, makes no attempt to offer new or unusual styling. Rather, these firms mass-produce close copies or adaptations of styles that have proved their acceptance in higher-priced markets.

In the field of women's apparel, manufacturers are committed to producing several new lines a year. A line is an assortment of new designs with a designated period for delivery to the retailer. Some of these may be new in every sense of the word and others merely adaptations of currently popular styles. Producers hope that a few of the designs in a given line will prove to be "hot"—so precisely in step with demand that their sales will be profitably large.

For the most part, the fashion industries are made up of manufacturers whose ability to anticipate the public's response to styles is excellent. Those who do badly in this respect, even for a single

**FIGURE 5.10** The different types of retailers include the fashion leaders, such as Nordstrom (top); traditional retailers, such as Macy's (middle); and mass merchants, such as Wal-Mart (bottom).

season, usually reap small sales and large losses. Unless they are unusually well financed, they quickly find themselves out of business. In the fashion industry, the survival of the fittest means the survival of those who give the most able assistance in the birth and growth of fashions that consumers will buy.

## The Retailer's Role

Although retailers do not usually create fashion, they can encourage or retard its progress by the degree of accuracy with which they anticipate the demands of their customers. They seek out from manufacturers styles that they believe are most likely to win acceptance from these target groups.

Some large retailers work directly with manufacturers and firms at the primary level to develop styles for exclusive sale at their stores. Thus, retailers such as the Gap and The Limited can stock only their own labels. Others, such as Federated Department Stores, sell private-label merchandise along with national brands. (We examine the practice of product development by retailers in more detail in Chapter 16.)

## *Types of Retailers*

There are many ways to classify retail firms. However, when firms are evaluated on the basis of their leadership positions, they tend to fall into three main categories.

First, there are firms that are considered *fashion leaders* (see Figure 5.10, top). They feature newly introduced styles that have only limited production and distribution. These styles, called *designer collections*, are usually very expensive. Examples of these firms include Bergdorf Goodman, Neiman Marcus, and Nordstrom.

A second group, called *traditional retailers*—by far the largest in number—features fashions that have captured consumer interest in their introduction stage and are in the late rise or early culmination stage of their life cycles (see Figure 5.10, middle).

These styles are from designers' *bridge collections* or from better or moderate-priced manufacturers. Since these styles are usually widely produced by this time, they are most often offered at more moderate prices. Examples of these firms include Macy's and Dillard's. The distinction between traditional retailers and fashion leaders is somewhat blurred in that the fashion leaders may also carry "traditional" merchandise, and the traditional retailers may have designer departments.

A third group of retailers, often called *mass merchants*, features widely accepted fashions that are well into the culmination phase of their life cycles (see Figure 5.10, bottom). Since fashions at this stage of development are usually mass-produced, mass merchants can and do offer fashions at moderate to low prices. Examples of these firms include JC Penney, Sears, and Kohl's. At the low end of the mass market are the *discounters*, like the off-price Dress Barn, for example, which sold more than $1.3 billion in merchandise in 2006 at discounted prices. Other examples include Wal-Mart, Kmart, and Target.

## Fashion Influence

Sometimes, because of their constant and intimate contact with their customers, retailers are so intuitive or creative that they lead their suppliers in anticipating the styles their customers will accept (see Figure 5.11). Such retailers accelerate the introduction and progress of new fashions by persuading manufacturers to produce styles that answer an upcoming need or demand. Because of this ability, retailers are doing increasingly more product development for their own customers. (This trend is discussed in detail in Chapter 17.)

However, most retailers simply select from what is offered to them by producers with whom they have been successful in the past. There is a constant flow, back and forth, of information about the styles that the customer is buying. The systems that producers and retailers have today for this purpose are

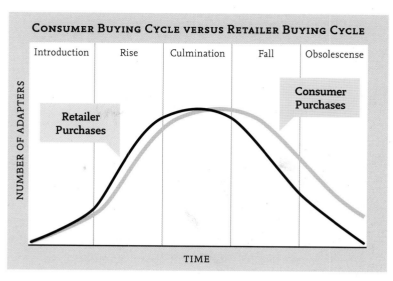

FIGURE 5.11 Retailers have to stay just a step ahead of their target customers. Retailers must have sufficient stock available when customers are ready to buy a new fashion, but they must also avoid being overstocked when customers' interest shifts to a new fashion.

FIGURE 5.12 Retailers can monitor the preferences of their customers based on sales and demand.

rapid and accurate, mainly because of the development of the computer.

Because of these instantly available and accurate records, retailers can monitor sudden or gradual changes in the preferences of their own customers. The variations in what consumers are buying at a particular store are reflected in what the store buys from the manufacturers of fashion merchandise (see Figure 5.12). From these manufacturers come information about customer preferences that flows in several different directions. One flow is back to the retail stores to alert them to trends they may not have noticed themselves.

Retailers can influence fashion by failing to stock styles that consumers are ready to buy if given the opportunity. Conversely, retailers can make the mistake of exposing new styles prematurely. No amount of retail effort can make customers buy styles in which they have not yet developed interest or in which they have lost interest. The more accurately a retailer understands his or her customers' fashion preferences, the more successful the operation will be. And the more successful the operation, the more important the retailer's fashion influence will be.

## Summary and Review

The fashion industry is a major business sector in the United States and around the world. It employs people at four levels: (1) producers of materials, such as natural and manufactured textiles, leather, fur, and materials used in decorative trimmings; (2) manufacturers of apparel, accessories, cosmetics and fragrances, and home fashions; (3) fashion retailers; and (4) auxiliary services to the other three levels, including market research and forecasting and promotional services. Businesses at all four levels collaborate to capture their share of the market.

Companies compete with others at their level by offering advantages of price, quality, and innovation. The federal government regulates the production and sale of fashion goods to ensure safe, functional products for consumers and fair marketing practices among competitors.

Like other businesses, fashion businesses at all levels may be sole proprietorships, partnerships, or corporations. Fashion companies grow horizontally by getting into new markets or vertically by expanding into levels beyond the level of their original business. They may expand internally, acquire or merge with other companies, or franchise or license a part of their business. Continuing into the 21st century, licensing is an important part of virtually every major designer's business strategy, and businesses outside the fashion industry license their names and logos to apparel producers.

At all levels, fashion business executives must be able to predict the tastes of the consumers who wear and use their merchandise. Depending on level, a company must anticipate consumer demand from six months to more than a year in advance of the day a new fashion becomes available at retail.

## Trade Talk

Define or briefly explain the following terms:

| | |
|---|---|
| auxiliary level | better market |
| bridge market | budget market |
| diversification | franchise |
| horizontal growth | licensing |
| line | merger |
| moderate-priced market | primary level |
| profit | retail level |
| royalty fee | secondary level |
| vertical growth | |

## For Review

1. What is the primary objective of all businesses? Explain your answer.
2. Describe the four levels of the fashion business; give examples.

3. How does the auxiliary level differ from the other levels?

4. Compare the advantages and disadvantages of a sole proprietorship and a partnership as a form of business for a fashion retailer.

5. Why do companies seek growth through mergers and acquisitions?

6. What are the practical obstacles that limit fashion designers? What additional factors must be considered in developing each fashion design?

7. List the three types of designers commonly serving the U.S. fashion industry today. Give the responsibilities of each.

8. If you were the president of a national chain of shoe stores, what are five laws and regulations that would affect how you do business? Which

of these laws would not affect a small, privately owned bridal shop?

9. Differentiate between a license agreement and a franchise.

10. How is a licensed designer name an advantage to the manufacturer? To the consumer? To the retailer?

## For Discussion

1. What initial decisions must be made by an individual or group of individuals who plan to form a company with regard to the form of ownership that will be most beneficial to all?

2. What does the statement "You're only as good as your last collection" mean in regard to fashion designers?

unit two

All good stories have a terrific beginning. So it is with fashion—all good fashions have good beginnings. They are the fibers, fabrics, leather, and fur industries known in fashion as the primary markets.

The earliest part of the planning function—in both color and texture—takes place on the primary level. It is also the level of the fashion business that works the farthest in advance of the ultimate selling period for the finished goods.

More fashion apparel and accessories are made of textiles than any other kind of material. Fashion textiles are the product of a network of primary industries, such as the cotton industry, the wool industry, the various industries producing manufactured fibers, and the fabric industry.

Changes in the textile industries have been rapid and important, particularly in recent years. Not only have there been radical new methods of producing and blending fibers, but also advances have been made in the methods of making and finishing fabrics. All of these new and fast-moving advances have contributed to the "green scene" and the sustainability of the products.

The fur and leather industries are also changing at a rapid pace, and giving designers a wider range of products to work with. These changes may be the indicators of the exciting course that fashion in leather and fur may take to satisfy the fashion needs of the future.

# THE PRIMARY LEVEL:
# THE MATERIALS OF FASHION

chapter six

*Everything you always wanted to know about fibers and fabrics.*

KEY CONCEPTS
- The difference between natural fibers and manufactured fibers
- The major steps in the production of most fabrics
- The effect of imports on the U.S. fiber and fabric industries
- The effects of new technology on textiles
- "Going green" with fibers and fabrics

# Textiles: Fibers and Fabrics

Fashion and the materials from which they are made are inseparable. Have you ever bought a fashion product simply because you loved the feel of it? Perhaps it was rough and coarse, or silky and smooth. Maybe it was incredibly soft to the touch. If so, then you, like almost every else, have responded to a fabric rather than to the style or color of a fashion product.

The designer creating a style at the drawing board must consider the material best suited for the particular silhouette and details of design. The manufacturer must then consider the various weights of material currently desired as well as the cost factors.

Finally, the retailer must select fashions made of those materials considered appropriate and desirable by their target customers.

So important is the material or fabric a garment is made of that Christian Dior, the world-famous haute-couture designer, once said of it: "Fabric not only expresses a designer's dream, but also stimulates his own ideas. It can be the beginning of an inspiration. Many a dress of mine is born of the fabric alone."[1]

The enormous appeal of fabric—and the fibers of which it is composed—lies in its many varied textures, finishes, uses, and colors. These are created, as we shall learn, by the fiber and fabric industries that work closely together to produce an end product, which is called fashion textiles.

The production of fiber and fabrics is the first step in the manufacture of clothing, accessories, and home fashions. As a result, textile fiber and textile fabric manufacturers are considered **primary suppliers**. The makers of **trimmings**, such as Criscone, Brooklyn Bow International, and Velcro USA, Inc., are also at the primary level of the fashion business. (Other primary suppliers, who create fur and leather, are explored in Chapter 7.)

## The Fiber Industry

A **fiber**—an extremely fine, hairlike strand almost invisible to the eye—is the smallest element of a fabric. It is also the starting point of a fabric. Fibers can be spun or twisted into continuous threads called **yarn**, and yarns can be knitted, woven, or bonded into **fabrics**. Although tiny, fibers have enormous influence on fashion. They are what gives a fabric its color, weight, texture, and durability.

Fibers are either natural or manufactured. **Natural fibers** are found in nature, that is, they come from plant or animal sources. In contrast, the **manufactured fibers** are made in a chemist's laboratory. They may be made from substances that occur in nature, such as wood pulp, air, petroleum, or natural gas, but these natural substances must be converted into fibers before they can be made into fabric. Manufactured fibers are sometimes called "man-made" or "synthetic fibers." Because manufactured fibers are invented in the laboratory, they are more plentiful than natural fibers. Currently, twenty-six manufactured fibers are available. Some of the manufactured fibers whose names you may recognize are rayon, nylon, acetate, acrylic, spandex, and polyester.

## History and Development

The use of natural fibers is ancient, whereas most of the manufactured fibers have been invented in the past 60 years. Despite their relatively short life span, however, very rapid advances have been made in the use of manufactured fibers. In contrast, the natural fiber industry has developed much more slowly. In fact, many of the recent developments in natural fibers are actually advances made in the manufactured fiber industry that were transferred to the natural fiber industry.

### The Development of Natural Fibers

The use of natural fibers predates written history. Prehistoric humans are known to have gathered

**TABLE 6.1** *Natural Luxury Animal Fibers*

| NAME | SOURCE | CHARACTERISTICS AND USES |
|---|---|---|
| Alpaca | Member of llama family found in Andes Mountains in South America | Fine, hollow-core fleece; annual shearing yields 6–12 lbs of fibers; 22 natural shades; strongest, most resilient wool; scarce |
| Angora | Rabbit hair | Soft fiber; dyes well; sheds easily |
| Camel hair | Camel | Usually left in natural tones; used in coats, jackets, artists' brushes |
| Cashmere | Kashmir goat (60% found in China but also bred in United States) | Rare (1/100 of wool crop); sheared annually; one goat produces enough for one-quarter of a sweater |
| Goose down (often mixed with feathers to cut cost) | Goose | Most compressible insulation; lightweight warmth for jackets, with goose vest, comforters, pillows, sleeping bags, feather beds |
| Llama | Llama found in Andes Mountains of South America, United States, Canada, Australia, and New Zealand | Coarser, stronger than alpaca; used in utilitarian items such as sacks |
| Marabou | African marabou stork or turkey | Soft, fluffy material from feathers |
| Mohair | Angora goat, originally from Turkey, now from South Africa, Texas, and New Zealand | Twice-yearly shearing; $2^1/_2$ times as strong as wool; less allergenic than sheep's wool |
| Ostrich feathers | Ostrich | Used in high-fashion apparel, feather dusters |
| Pashmina | Mountain goats from Himalaya | Softer than cashmere; fiber equivalent to merino |
| Qiviut | Musk ox down from Canada, Alaska | Natural taupe color; soft, light, 8 times warmer than sheep's wool; rare ($20–$25/oz) |
| Vicuna | Rare llama-like animal from Peru | World's finest natural fiber |

flax, the fiber in linen, to make yarns for fabrics. There are four major natural fibers: cotton, silk, flax (linen), and wool. Two other natural fibers are ramie and hemp. In addition, there are many other natural fibers that are in short supply and therefore limited to luxury items (see Table 6.1 and Figure 6.1).

**Cotton**, the most widely used of all the natural fibers, is the substance attached to the seed of a cotton plant (see Figure 6.2). Cotton fibers are composed primarily of cellulose, a carbohydrate that especially lends itself to the manufacture of fibrous and paper products. Cotton fibers absorb moisture quickly, dry quickly, and have a cooling effect that makes cotton a good fiber for hot or warm weather. Usually the fluffy cotton boll is white, but new growing methods have brought about naturally colored cotton. This new cotton can be grown in at least twenty-two colors, thus eliminating the need for dyes. Long and extra long cotton fibers (or staple) produce the finest fabrics. The United States leads the world in the production of long staple Pima cotton, while Egypt is a close second.[2]

**FIGURE 6.1** Ostrich feathers, a natural luxury animal fiber, is used in high-fashion apparel (top). **FIGURE 6.2** A textile worker weaves cotton into cotton fibers on a traditional multiple-harness frame loom (bottom).

**Wool** is the fiber that forms the coat of sheep. Sheep produce one of the few replenishable natural commodities. Shear a sheep's coat time after time, and it quickly grows a new one. An animal fiber, wool is composed mostly of protein. Wool fiber is a natural insulator and is used to make warm clothes. Wool fiber, in fact, has a natural crimp that is ideal for the production of bulky yarns that trap air to form insulating barriers against the cold. Wool absorbs moisture more slowly and dries more slowly than cotton. A lightweight summer wool has been developed to be machine washable.

**Silk** comes from a cocoon formed by a silkworm. The silkworm forces two fine streams of a thick liquid out of tiny openings in its head. These streams harden into filaments, or fibers, upon contact with the air. Silk, best known for its luxurious feel, is a breathable fabric that can be worn year-round. For many years silk required dry cleaning, but much of today's silk is washable.

Silk all but disappeared from the U.S. fashion market during and after World War II. It has made a dramatic comeback! In the late 1970s, a group of U.S. and Hong Kong businesspeople worked with Chinese manufacturers to develop cheaper silk. Within 10 years, the Chinese had a high-quality, washable silk that became a low-cost substitute for polyester.

**Flax**, used to make linen, comes from the stem of a flax plant (see Figure 6.3). Only after the flax fiber is spun into yarn and woven or knit into fabric is the product called **linen** (see Figure 6.4). Flax is the strongest of the vegetable fibers (it is twice as strong as cotton), and like cotton, it absorbs moisture and dries quickly. These features make linen an excellent fabric for warm-weather apparel. However, even with new technology that makes linen less apt to wrinkle, it still has a tendency to wrinkle and is harder to iron than cotton. Most flax is imported from Europe, especially Belgium and Ireland.

**Ramie** comes from a woody-leafed Asian plant grown mostly in China. It has been available in the United States only since 1979, when the United States and China reopened trade with one another.

A linen-like fabric suitable for warm weather apparel, ramie is also inexpensive.

**Hemp** is a fibrous plant with an interesting history in the United States. It was an agricultural staple in America for hundreds of years. In fact, the Declaration of Independence was written on hemp paper. The crop was so important then that three colonies had laws requiring farmers to grow hemp. Today, laws make it illegal to grow hemp in the United States. Raising it in the United States (and most industrialized nations) has been illegal since the 1970s, because lawmakers feared that growers would plant illegal marijuana, which looks very similar to industrial hemp (although industrial hemp lacks hallucinatory power), making the illegal

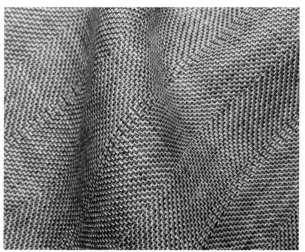

**FIGURE 6.3** The stem of this flax plant is used to make linen (top). **FIGURE 6.4** Flax fiber is spun into yarn and woven or knit to create this lightweight linen look (bottom).

weed harder to find. Imports of finished hemp garments are allowed, however, and demand is soaring. Not only are its ecological, or "green," properties high selling points, but its aesthetic, comfort, and performance have made it a very popular and viable fiber for home furnishings and fashion.[3]

A number of other natural fibers are used in apparel and home furnishings. They are relatively rare and thus expensive. A few are outlined in Table 6.1.

## The Development of Manufactured Fibers

Manufactured or synthetic fibers (see Figure 6.5) have been improving the quality of our lives since rayon, the first synthetic fiber, went into production in 1910. Since then, many other manufactured fibers have been introduced in literally thousands of new apparel, upholstery, and industrial applications (see Table 6.2).

Manufactured fibers offer a variety of characteristics that are mostly unavailable in natural fibers. Each

**TABLE 6.2** *Manufactured Fibers*

| DATE | FIBER | FIRST COMMERCIAL PRODUCTION |
|---|---|---|
| 1910 | Rayon | Rayon fiber was the first manufactured fiber. Its first commercial production of rayon fiber in the United States was in 1910 by the American Viscose Company. By using two different chemicals and manufacturing techniques, two basic types of rayon were developed: viscose rayon and cuprammonium rayon. Today, only viscose rayon is produced in the United States. |
| 1924 | Acetate | The first commercial production of acetate fiber in the United States was in 1924 by the Celanese Corporation. |
| 1938 | Nylon | The first commercial production of nylon in the United States was in 1939 by the E. I. Du Pont de Nemours & Company, Inc. It is the second most used manufactured fiber in this country, behind polyester. |
| 1950 | Acrylic | The first commercial production of acrylic fiber in the United States was in 1950 by E. I. Du Pont de Nemours & Company, Inc. |
| 1953 | Polyester | The first commercial production of polyester fiber in the United States was in 1953 by E. I. Du Pont de Nemours & Company, Inc. Polyester is the most used manufactured fiber in the United States. |
| 1954 | Triacetate | The first commercial production of triacetate fiber in the United States was in 1954 by the Celanese Corporation. Domestic triacetate production was discontinued in 1985. |
| 1959 | Spandex | The first commercial production of spandex fiber in the United States was 1959 by E. I. Du Pont de Nemours & Company, Inc. It is an elastomeric manufactured fiber (able to stretch at least 100 percent and snap back like natural rubber). Spandex is used in filament form. |
| 1961 | Polyolefin/polypropylene | The first commercial production of an olefin fiber manufactured in the United States was by Hercules Incorporated. In 1966, polyolefin was the world's first and only Nobel Prize–winning fiber. |
| 1993 | Lyocell | The first commercial production of lyocell in the United States was in 1993 by Courtaulds Fibers, under the Tencel trade name. Environmentally friendly, lyocell is produced from the wood pulp of trees grown specifically for this purpose. It is specially processed, using a solvent spinning technique in which the dissolving agent is recycled, reducing environmental effluents. |
| 2002 | Polyatide | The first commercial production of PLA in the United States was in 2002 by Cargill Dow Polymers. PLA is a plastic derived from natural plant sugars, bridging the gap between natural fibers and conventional synthetic fibers. |

NYLON · RAYON · POLYESTER

Source: Adapted from Fabric Link/Fabric University, www.fabriclink.com/University/History.cfm, and www.Fibersource.com.

FIGURE 6.5 Lanvin's synthetic polyester dress flows down the runway.

FIGURE 6.6 Manufactured fibers of varying lengths are produced by forcing thick liquids through the tiny holes of a device known as a spinnerette.

year, manufactured fibers find new uses in our wardrobes, homes, hospitals, and workplaces. Designers like Armani, Calvin Klein, and Joseph Abboud all use high-tech, stretch, and classic fabrics to illustrate the constant innovation of their product lines.

All manufactured fibers start life as thick liquids. Fibers of continuous, indefinite lengths are produced by forcing the liquid through the tiny holes of a mechanical device called a **spinnerette** (see Figure 6.6). This is similar to the way pasta dough is pushed through a pasta machine to make spaghetti.

Fibers are then cut into short lengths and spun into yarn, as is the case with natural fibers, or they are chemically processed into yarn directly. In the latter case, the production of fiber and yarn occurs simultaneously.

There are two basic types of manufactured fibers: cellulosic and noncellulosic.

## Cellulosic Fibers

Cellulose, the same fibrous substance found in the natural fibers of plants, is also used to manufacture **cellulosic fibers**. The cellulosic fibers are made with a minimum of chemical steps. They include rayon, acetate, triacetate, and lyocell (Figure 6.7). Triacetate is now produced only in small quantities in Europe. The cellulose used to make these fibers comes mostly from soft woods, such as spruce.

## Noncellulosic Fibers

Petroleum, coal, natural gas, air, and water are used to make **noncellulosic fibers**. They are produced from various combinations of carbon, hydrogen, nitrogen, and oxygen. Fiber chemists working in laboratories link the molecules into long chains called **polymers**. Nylon, acrylic, and polyester are in this category.

## Generic Names for Manufactured Fibers

The Federal Trade Commission has assigned **generic names**, or nontrademarked names, to twenty-six manufactured fibers. Within any of these broad generic categories, fiber producers can modify the composition to produce a new fiber, called a **variant**. The variant is then given a brand name by the producer. There are hundreds of **brand names**, or trademarks, which are registered with the U.S. Patent Office; only the manufacturer of a variant is allowed to use the registered name. For example, polyester is the generic name, and Dacron is the Du Pont trademark for polyester (see Table 6.3).

The properties of these fibers greatly influences the behavior of the finished fabric made from them. Polyester, for example, is strong and wrinkle-resistant, which contributes to its durability and washability. Once scorned as the dull material of inexpensive leisure suits, today's polyester has the subtle sheen of fine silk.

**FIGURE 6.7** Sue Stemp's cotton, Lurex, and Tencel® dress has a flattering drape that is luxurious and breathable.

**TABLE 6.3** *Generic Names and Trade Names of Manufactured Fibers Used in the United States*

| GENERIC NAME | TRADENAMES |
|---|---|
| Acetate | Celanese, Chromspun, Estron, Microsafe |
| Acrylic | Acrilan, Bio Fresh, Bounce-Back, Creslan, Cystar, Cystar AF, Duraspun, Fi-lana, Pil-Trol, Sayelle, So-Lara, Smart Yarns, Wear-Dated, Wintuk |
| Aramid | Kevlar, Nomex |
| Lyocell | Lenzing Lyocell, Tencel |
| Modacrylic | SEF Plus |
| Nylon | A.C.E., Anso, Antron, Assurance, Avantige, Cantrece, Capima, Caplana, Caprolan, Captiva, Cordura, Creme de Captiva, Crepeset, DuraSoft, DyeNAMIX, Eclipse, Hardline, Hydrofil, Hytel, Matinesse, Microsupplex, No Shock, PowerSilk, Resistat, Shimmereen, Silkey Touch, Solution, Sportouch, Stainmaster, Stay Gard, Supplex, Tactel, Tru-Ballistic, Ultra Image, Ultra Touch, Ultron, Wear-Dated, Wellon, Wellstrand, WorryFree, Zefsprot, Zeftron |
| Olefin | Alpha, Essera, Impressa, Inova, Marvess, Patlon III, Polystrand, Spectra, Synera, Trace |
| Polyester | A.C.E., Ceylon, Comfort Fiber, Compet, Coolmax, Corebond, Dacronfi, ESP, Fortrel, Hollofi, Kodaire, Kodel, KodOfill, KodOsoff, Pentron, Premafill Plump, Premafill Soft, Trevira, Trevira Finesse, Trevira Microness, Universe |
| PBI | PBI Logo |
| Rayon | Beau-Grip, Fibro, Galaxy |
| Spandex | Lycra |
| Sulfar | Ryton |

Adapted from www.fibersource.com. Washington, D.C.: American Fiber Manufacturers Association.

# Fashion Focus

Fashion Focus

## Bamboo
### *The Stuff of Floors, Furniture ... and Now Fashion*

**B**amboo is a versatile, ancient plant that shows up in creation myths as well as in gardens and terraces. It comes in clumping varieties and running "timber" types that spread quickly into a grove. But it's that very vigor that has environmentalists hailing bamboo as the new "It" plant for saving the earth.

Bamboo is a workhorse at sequestering carbon dioxide and pumping out oxygen. It is a tough plant that manufactures its own antibacterial compounds and can thrive without pesticides, and its porous fibers make a cloth that breathes and is as soft as silk. Because no bamboo industry exists in the United States, there is a stampede of fabric designers to China and Japan where it is farmed and processed. National Geographic predicted that "this upstart fabric may someday compete with King Cotton."

Yet as the world clamors for more, bamboo is in short supply. A plant that generally flowers only every 60 to 120 years and then dies is hard to propagate from seed. So when Jackie Heinricker and Randy Burr figured out how to make bamboo in test tubes—selling their first 2,000 plants in 2004 to local garden centers in Skagit Valley in Washington state—they made waves in the world of horticulture.

Textile's green giant, bamboo is proving to be a sustainable option of the fashion-friendly sort. The fiber is taking root in diverse categories, from lingerie to denim.

"The first time I saw the fabric was when I was working at Adidas," says Portland, Oregon–based designer Anna Cohen, 28, who did stints at Max Mara before launching her own sportswear line. Cohen's collection is one of a new breed of labels including Form, Racines du Ciel, and Doie—that is incorporating more green fibers into its

clothes. Cohen said she adopted bamboo to give a luxurious edge to her collections. Luxury loungewear designer Sarah Kersner, who formerly worked with cotton, is switching her line, Doie, entirely to bamboo.

"Japan has been using bamboo for four centuries, but it is still an uncommon fiber in clothing today," Elio Tomsini says. Since 1995, his denim line, Kohzu, has been made using Kumazash, a wide-leaf bamboo indigenous to Japan. "Bam-

boo reacts to climates in a similar way to silk: insulating in the winter and cooling in the summer," Tomsini says.

Semi-handwoven on shuttle looms from fine strips cut from bamboo and rice paper pulp, Kohzu jeans retail at $500 and are available in high-end stores worldwide. On the other end of the price scale, French sportswear line Spilan distributes bamboo products, mostly T-shirts and sweaters, in the $20 to $30 range to Europe's mass-market giants Carrefour, Casino, E. Leclerc, and Auchan. The company recently established its own plantations in China and Indonesia. To get the message across, Spilan invested in a $1.3 million television campaign featuring a young T-shirt-clad woman pushing her way through a bamboo forest that eventually opens out into the heart of a bustling city.

The message is simple: a cane the world can lean on.

What goes around—comes around—again. Polyester has gained new famous fans and a hip new lease on life. Once labeled as tacky, scratchy, and even smelly, polyester has become today's designers' favorite "new" fabric. Marc Jacobs says there is plenty to love about polyester, starting with a "radiance to the color."

Made of acids and alcohols derived from petroleum, polyester was greatly welcomed when it was invented in the 1940s. By the 1960s, polyester was the fabric of choice in apparel and consumer products, especially beddings and other home products. It made life easy because it was wrinkle-free and easy to care for.

According to Valerie Steele, director of the Museum at F.I.T. in New York, the hippie counterculture later helped reverse public opinion on all things synthetic, creating a period in fashion history when the thinking become "cotton good, polyester bad." It is true that early polyesters were stifling to wear, reinforcing the belief that natural fibers were purer, more healthy and virtuous, but today's reputation for polyester has changed.

"Cotton may seem natural and virtuous, but the growing and processing can turn out to be more environmentally destructive," says Steele.[4]

## Microfibers

A major technological breakthrough occurred in 1989 with the first commercial production of microfiber in the United States by Du Pont. A **microfiber** is a fiber that is two or three times smaller than a human hair—smaller than wool, cotton, or silk fibers (see Figure 6.8). Microfiber is the thinnest and finest of all manufactured fibers. It has a touch and texture similar to silk or cashmere, but is wrinkle-resistant and can usually be machine washed and dried. Today, microfiber is produced in a number of manufactured fibers—for example, nylon, acrylic, and polyester. Designers use it widely in women's wear, men's wear, activewear, outerwear, and home furnishings (see Figure 6.9).

## MICROFIBER COMPARED TO NATURAL FIBERS

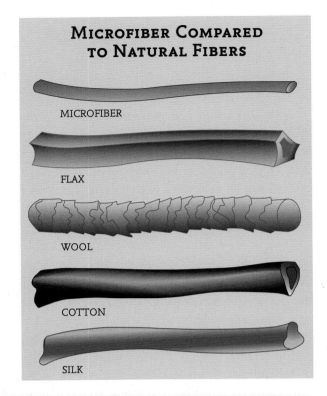

MICROFIBER

FLAX

WOOL

COTTON

SILK

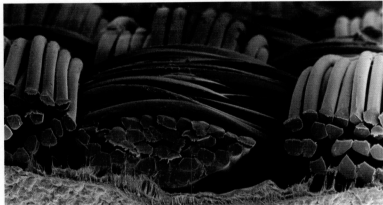

**FIGURE 6.8** A microfiber compared to silk, cotton, wool, and flax (top). **FIGURE 6.9** Gore-Tex fabric is known for extreme weather protection that keeps the wearer dry and comfortable (bottom).

## Organization and Operation

Because of the differences in the origin and characteristics of fibers, each industry—the natural fiber industry and the manufactured fiber industry—is organized along different lines.

### The Natural Fiber Industry

Cotton is produced in four major areas of the United States: the Southeast; the Mississippi Delta; the Texas–Oklahoma panhandle; and New Mexico, Arizona, and California.

Nearly all cotton growers sell their product in local markets, either to mill representatives or, more typically, to wholesalers. The cotton wholesalers bargain at central markets in Memphis, New Orleans, Dallas, Houston, New York, and Chicago.

The wool produced in the United States comes from relatively small sheep ranches in the Western states. Boston is the central marketplace for wool, both domestic and imported.

Linen, silk, and ramie are not produced in any great quantities in the United States. Like hemp, these fibers are imported from foreign sources.

The natural fiber industry in the United States has been greatly affected by the advent of manufactured fibers. The ability to tailor the manufactured fibers to the demands of the ever-changing marketplace has forced the natural fiber industries to become more attuned to the needs of their customers. To compete, the natural fiber industries have become more aggressive about developing new uses for their products and have aggressively promoted themselves. Cotton, usually a warm-weather fiber, is now promoted as a year-round fiber, largely through the use of heavier cotton fibers used to make cotton sweaters. And wool, usually designed for cold-weather wear, is now being treated to make new, lightweight fibers suitable for year-round wear. Through advanced technology and innovative chemical processing, many natural fibers are treated with special finishes to give them care-and-wear properties equal to those of manufactured fibers.

### The Manufactured Fiber Industry

Obviously, climate and terrain have nothing to do with the production of a manufactured fiber. Indeed, chemical plants are extremely adaptable, requiring only supplies of raw chemicals, power, and labor. Chemical companies have thus erected their plants in every part of the United States—up and down the East Coast, in the South, the Midwest, and increasingly on the West Coast. Operations are located wherever companies have found raw materials or railroads and waterways for convenient shipment of those materials. Most of these plants are huge.

With manufactured fibers, it is also possible for the producing plant to serve as its own market. It purchases fibers from chemical companies, spins them into yarn, and then knits or weaves the yarn into fabric. Burlington Industries and Galey & Lord, Inc. are two of the giants that consolidate all operations, from spun yarn manufacture to finished fabric.

## Fiber Development

Limited quantities of a new or modified manufactured fiber are usually first produced in a pilot plant on an experimental basis. If research indicates that both industry and consumers will accept the new product, mass production begins. New applications of the fiber are then explored and new industries are consulted and encouraged to use it.

While this procedure is going on in one chemical company, there is always the possibility that another company may be working along similar lines to develop a competitive fiber. The company that is first to develop a new fiber has no assurance that it will have the field to itself for long. There are many brands of such manufactured fibers as nylon, rayon, and acetate on the market and a roster of companies producing various acrylics and polyesters (see Table 6.2).

The fierce competition among various producers of manufactured fibers is tied to the fact that in one season, a need may arise for fiber that is stretchable, offers warmth without weight, and is also wrinkle-resistant. Armed with a list of customer preferences, competing laboratories go to work to develop new products. It is no wonder that several of them come up with the same answer at the same time.

Under the Textile Fibers Products Identification Act of 1960, consumer products that use textile fibers are required to label their products by the country where processed or manufactured and by the generic names and percentages of each fiber that is used, assuming that it is more than 5 percent, in order, by weight (see Figure 6.10). Brand names or trademarks may also be used on the label, but they are not required by law.

## Fiber Distribution

Producers of manufactured fibers sell their fibers to fabric manufacturers in one of three ways:

1. As unbranded products, with no restrictions placed on their end use and no implied or required standards of performance claimed
2. As branded or trademarked fibers, with assurance to consumers that the quality of the fiber has been controlled by its producer, but not necessarily with assurance as to either implied or required standards of performance in the end product
3. Under a licensing agreement, whereby the use of the fiber trademark is permitted only to those manufacturers whose fabrics or other

**FIGURE 6.10** Even unbranded fibers must be carefully identified on labels, along with International Care Symbols, bar codes, and, of course, the manufacturer's name and logo.

**TABLE 6.4** *Natural Fiber Trade Associations*

| FIBER | ORGANIZATION |
|---|---|
| Cotton | Cotton Incorporated<br>National Cotton Council, Supima Association of America |
| Linen | Masters of Linen (European) |
| Mohair | The Mohair Council of America |
| Silk | International Silk Association |
| Wool | America Wool Council<br>The Woolmark Company |

Source: Hemp Industries Association, 1999. Available at www.thehia.org.

end products pass tests set up by the fiber producer for their specific end uses or applications

Licensing programs set up by different fiber producers and by processors of yarn vary considerably in scope. The more comprehensive programs entail extensive wear testing to back up the licensing agreement. The fiber and yarn producers exercise considerable control over fabric products that have been licensed, sometimes specifying blend levels, and offer technical services to help correct a fabric that fails to pass a qualifying test. The trademarks used under such licensing agreements are referred to as **licensed trademarks**. Fiber Industries' Fortrel is an example of a licensed trademark.

## Merchandising and Marketing

No matter how familiar producers and consumers may be with the qualities of each fiber, there is always the need to disseminate information about the newest modifications and their application to fashion merchandise. To do this, producers of both natural and manufactured fibers make extensive use of advertising, publicity, and market research. They also extend various customer services to manufacturers, retailers, and consumers.

The American Fiber Manufacturers Association, Inc. (AFMA) is the trade association for U.S. companies that manufacture synthetic and cellulosic fibers. The industry employs thirty thousand people and produces more than 9 billion pounds of fiber in the United States. AFMA member compa-

nies produce more than 90 percent of the total U.S. output of these fibers. The membership is limited to U.S. producers that sell manufactured synthetic fiber in the open market. The association maintains close ties to other manufactured fiber trade associations worldwide.[5]

So that they can better promote their new products (and themselves), the natural fiber industries also have organized trade associations that carry their messages to the textile industry as well as to the customer (see Table 6.4).

## Advertising and Publicity

As you might suspect, given their greater potential for competition, the manufactured fiber industries spend considerably more money on advertising than do the natural fiber industries (see Figure 6.11). They maintain a steady flow of advertising and publicity directed at both the trade and consumer markets. Sometimes an advertising campaign promotes an entire range of textile fibers; at other times, it concentrates on only a single fiber. Fiber companies give most of their advertising dollars to support the manufacturers who use their fibers.

Some natural fiber groups are putting more effort and money into campaigns to combat the growing domination of manufactured fibers. Because these campaigns are mainly handled by trade associations, they promote the fiber itself, not the products of an individual natural fiber producer. One of the most eye-catching campaigns is that of Cotton Incorporated (see Figure

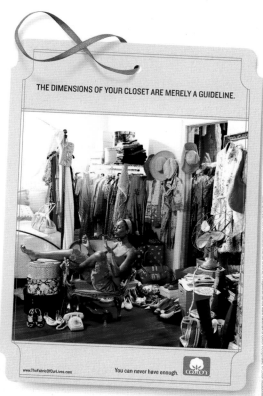

FIGURE 6.11 DuPont uses advertising to promote their swimwear products that have Lycra (top). FIGURE 6.12 This eye-catching campaign from Cotton Incorporated focuses on its products and its importance in the economy (bottom).

6.12). The ads and posters not only emphasize cotton's advantages as a fiber but also point to the cotton industry's importance in the economy and to cotton's ecological appeal. Cotton Incorporated started a campaign to improve its environmental image and market cotton as a natural fiber. It signed up six companies to use its latest "natural" trademark in 2008.[6]

Fiber sources also provide garment producers and retailers with various aids that facilitate mention of their fibers in consumer advertising, adding to the recognition already achieved by the fiber producer's name, trademark, slogan, or logo. For example, the Wool Bureau encourages the use of its ball-of-yarn logo in producer and retailer advertising of all wool merchandise as well as in displays.

Fiber industry producers and trade associations continually provide the press with new information, background material, and photographs for editorial features. Some of this publicity effort is accomplished by direct contact with the press; some of it is done by supplying garment producers and retailers with materials they can use for promotion.

Advertising undertaken by fiber producers in cooperation with fabric and garment manufacturers and retailers benefits the fiber industry in two ways. First, consumers begin to associate the fiber name with other names that are already familiar, such as the name of the fiber source or the name of the retail store selling the garment. This is particularly important in introducing a new manufactured fiber. Second, fabric and garment producers, as well as retailers, are encouraged to use and promote the fiber because the fiber producer's share of advertising costs subsidizes its local or national advertising.

## Research and Development

Both natural fiber producers and manufactured fiber producers are constantly seeking ways to improve their products. Individual large manufactured fiber producers conduct research and devel-

# &Then
# NOW

## Hemp
### *From High—*
### *To*
### *Low*

Left page: Hayley Starr's organic hemp dress (top center); Hemp twine (middle); Japanese hemp weaver Chiba Anyano (bottom center); Right page: Dressing hemp crop for weaving into linen, 1958.

In 1942, the Department of Agriculture made a movie called *Hemp for Victory*, which urged farmers to rally to the wartime cause: "Hemp for mooring ships! Hemp for tow lines! Hemp for tackle and gear!" The plant's long, strong fibers twist easily into rope, which made it useful for parachute webbing. However, with the seizure of the Philippines by the Japanese, our hemp supply was cut off.

But despite the enthusiasm of the wartime planners, hemp never became used because taxes and regulations, introduced in 1939 but minimally enforced during the war, kicked in again during the 1950s. Hemp is a variety of the cannabis plant, which also produces marijuana—although industrial hemp has a much smaller concentration of the compound tetrahydrocannabinol, or THC. There was great pressure to shut down hemp production.

Today, farmers are banned from growing hemp without a permit from the Drug Enforcement Administration (DEA). Therefore, many hemp products in America—food, lotions, clothing, paper, and more—are imported from China and Canada, where farmers have been allowed to grow hemp commercially since 1998.

Hemp has been grown for at least 12,000 years for use in fiber and food. It has a proud American heritage: George Washington and Thomas Jefferson both grew hemp, and in fact, Jefferson drafted the Declaration of Independence on hemp paper.

Is hemp making a comeback? Hemp grows so easily that few pesticides or even fertilizers are needed. "Feral" hemp grows by the roadsides in Iowa and Nebraska. American farmers would love to grow hemp. North Dakota, in 1999, was the first state to allow industrial hemp farming.

Barbara Filippone, owner of a hemp fabric company called Enviro Textiles, says demand has skyrocketed—sales are growing by 35 percent a year. Nutiva, a California-based hemp company that sells hemp bars, shakes, and oils, saw sales rise from under $1 million to $4.5 million in three years. "Hemp is the next soy," predicts John Roulac, Nutiva's founder.

Since hemp grows so easily, there is interest in using the crop as a biofuel. A Mercedes-Benz "hemp car" made its way across America in 2001, and in an MTV show, a 1963 Chevy Impala runs on biodiesel and has hemp upholstery.

opment. The natural fiber producers, which tend to be small in size, often work through the trade group for a particular fiber.

### Customer Services

All major producers of manufactured fibers and many smaller firms offer a number of services to direct and secondary users of their products. Producers of natural fibers, working through their associations, also offer many such services. These include:

- Technical advice as well as technical know-how on weaving and knitting techniques
- Assistance to textile and garment producers and retailers in locating supplies
- Fabric libraries that include information about sources, prices, and delivery schedules (research in a fabric library saves precious time spent shopping the market for trend information)
- Fashion presentations and exhibits for the textile industry, retailers, garment manufacturers, the fashion press, and occasionally, the public
- Extensive literature for manufacturers, retailers, educators, and consumers about fiber properties, use, and care
- Fashion experts who address groups of manufacturers, retailers, or consumers, staging fashion shows and demonstrations
- Educational films and audiovisual aids for use by the trade, schools, and consumer groups

## Trends in the Fiber Industry

The most dramatic trend in the fiber industry is the increasing use of blends of natural and manufactured fibers. This trend is discussed in more detail in the next section of this chapter, as is the second most widespread trend, the use of microfibers.

The fiber industry is fighting hard to overcome a major problem: the encroachment of imports into its domestic markets. Since manufactured fibers account for over 75 percent of fiber usage annually in the United States, it is obvious that this will be a continuing problem. The U.S. fiber industry will have to fight harder than ever for its share of the international and even the domestic market. Added to this challenge is consumers' tremendous interest in "going green" (see the section "Synthetic Fabrics Going Green" later in this chapter).

Computers are also playing an important role in the fiber industries' abilities to service their customers more quickly and efficiently. In addition to facilitating communications, computers offer important linkages between the various industries and enable them to do such things as coordinate delivery schedules and provide bar coding.

To many observers, the manufactured fiber story is just beginning, and the next half-century promises to be even more exciting than the previous one. Productivity rises by 3.4 percent per year with fascinating new products emerging from the laboratories. With approximately $2 billion spent annually on automated technology in the past decade, today's looms require less workers, raising the competition among plants.

## The Textile Fabric Industry

Midway between the fiber and the finished apparel, accessory, or home furnishing product is the fabric. **Textile fabric** is any material that is made by weaving, knitting, braiding, knotting, laminating, felting, or chemical bonding. It is the basic material from which most articles of apparel, accessories, and home fashions are made (see Figure 6.13).

Americans use a lot of textile fabric. Each person consumes nearly eighty-six pounds of textile fabric annually. We use fabric for clothing and home furnishings; in transportation, industry, defense, recreation, and health care; and for space exploration.

The production of most fabrics begins with the creation of yarn from fibers. With the exception of felted fabric and a few other nonwoven fabrics,

fibers cannot be made into fabrics without first spinning or twisting them into yarn. Yarns are then woven or knit into greige (pronounced—and sometimes spelled—"gray") goods, or unfinished fabrics. **Greige goods** are converted into finished fabrics for consumer or industrial use.

## History and Development

The earliest step toward the mechanization of the textile fabric industry was the introduction of the spinning wheel. It was brought to Europe from India in the sixth century. Even with the spinning wheel, yarn-making remained tedious work that was mostly done in the home. Not until the 18th century did the British develop mechanical methods of spinning cotton fibers into yarn.

The result of mechanized spinning—large quantities of yarn—increased the need for better looms to weave the yarn into fabric. The first power loom was invented by an English clergyman, Dr. Edward

**FIGURE 6.13** A hand-shuttle loom is used by many designers to create unique fabrics.

Cartwright, and patented in 1785. It used water as a source of energy.

The new mechanization soon spread to America. In 1790, Samuel Slater established a yarn mill in Pawtucket, Rhode Island. The present-day giant in the textile fabric field, J. P. Stevens and Company, is descended from Slater's mill. For decades, though, fabric production remained both a hand operation and a home industry, totally inadequate to meet the demand. Then Francis Cabot Lowell, a New Englander, visited a textile factory in England and memorized the detailed specifications of its power-operated machinery. In 1814, Lowell built the first successful power loom and the first textile fabric mill in the United States. The demands of a rapidly growing country provided an eager market for the output of American textile mills, and the young industry flourished. Even more automation and mechanization followed (see Figure 6.14).

One of the biggest changes in the U.S. textile industry has been the massive shift to shuttleless looms. These looms are much faster and quieter. They are also wider and less likely to break the yarns. While the initial cost is high, they are usually cheaper to operate. In 1972, only 3 percent of the looms in the United States were shuttleless. By 2000, 95 percent of looms were shuttleless.[7]

Today it is possible for a single operator to oversee as many as a hundred weaving machines, if the fabric is not too detailed. Similarly, today's dyeing and finishing plants can produce more than 1 million square yards of finished textiles per week.

## Organization and Operation

For decades, there was no pattern of organization in the textile fabric industry. Some textile fabric companies were large corporations employing thousands of people, but many remained small operations with only a few dozen employees.

Many companies have adopted a strategy of economies of scale; they see "big" as vulnerable and seek to be "giants." Other companies aim to fill in

**FIGURE 6.14** Early cotton textile mill.

gaps in their product offerings quickly through acquisitions rather than developing new products more slowly themselves.

Industry mergers generally assume one of two forms. The first strategy is for a company to buy all or part of a competitor in order to dominate a segment of the market. The second and less popular strategy is for a company to diversify by buying an apparel company that manufactures clothes out of imported apparel fabric.

Textile mills are widely dispersed throughout the country. The industry has tended to seek areas where labor and land costs are low. There has also been little advantage in concentrating production in any one area through the construction of giant mills or complexes. Textile mills used to be concentrated in the northeastern states, but in recent years the southeastern part of the country has offered cheaper labor and land.

Because commitments to specific weaves, colors, and finishes must be made 6 to 18 months in advance, the textile fabric industry is extremely well-informed about fashion and alert to new trends (see Figure 6.15). Information about these trends comes from fashion designers, predictive services, fashion directors for fiber or yarn companies, and advance textile shows throughout the world. But because they are geared to mass-production methods, most mills were reluctant to produce short experimental runs for individual designers. This is changing as new technology comes online.

The market centers for textile fabrics are not at the mills but in the fashion capital of the country, New York City. There, on the doorstep of the garment industry, every mill of importance has a salesroom. A fabric buyer or designer for a garment maker, or a retail store apparel buyer or fashion coordinator, has only to walk a block or two to obtain firsthand information on what the fabric market offers.

## Types of Mills

Some mills sort and select the fibers to be used, spin them into yarn, then weave or knit them and finish the fabric. Finishing may include dyeing, napping, adding fire retardants, glazing, waterproofing, and pressing. It may also include treating the fabric to ensure such attributes as nonshrinkage and permanent press. Fashion influences decisions every step of the way.

**FIGURE 6.15** Fabrics come in a wide variety of weaves, colors, and finishes and follow the latest fashion trends.

Some mills produce only the yarn. Others weave or knit fabric from purchased yarn but do not carry the process beyond the greige state. There are also plants that bleach, dye, preshrink, print, or in other ways impart desired characteristics to fabrics produced by other mills. The plants that handle the various stages may or may not be under common ownership, and may or may not be geographically close to one another.

For richer and deeper color, yarns may be dyed before being woven or knitted. This process is known as **yarn-dyed**. However, most fabrics are knitted or woven first and then dyed. This process is known as **piece-dyed**. The piece-dyed process gives manufacturers maximum flexibility.

Many mills no longer limit themselves to working with yarns made of a single fiber. Fibers may be used alone or with other fibers, as demand dictates. Any of the types of mills described above may combine a natural fiber with another natural fiber, or, more commonly, a natural fiber with a manufactured fiber, to achieve a desired effect. For example, polyester is the most blended manufactured fiber. It is strong and resists shrinking, stretching, and wrinkling. Best of all, it is easily washed and machine dried. A blend of sixty-five percent polyester with thirty-five percent cotton yields an easy-care fabric widely used for shirts, blouses, and sheets.

## The Converter

It is probably correct to say that the textile converter is the real middleman of the textile industry. **Textile converters** buy greige goods from the mills, have the goods processed to order by the finishing plants, and then sell the finished goods to garment makers. Therefore, textile converters must be on top of trends in colors, patterns, and finishes. They must fully understand fashion and must be able to anticipate demand. Converters work very quickly because they come on the production scene toward the end of the operation and are primarily interested in the finish and texture applied to the greige goods.

In recent years, converters' know-how has helped U.S. textile producers meet the competition from foreign textile producers who offer more fashion-oriented goods in small yardages. Converters can supply apparel producers with fewer yards of selected fabrics than can larger fabric mills. The latter must produce tremendous yardages of a designated pattern or design in order to maintain a profitable operation. While many converters are small operators, others, such as Springs Industries, are large. As the industry continues to consolidate, the converter function is still important, but it is done within the corporation rather than by an outside firm.

## Merchandising and Marketing

Many designers let the fabric act as the creative impetus for their designs. Good designers respond to new fabrics and search for that special fabric that will drape in the way they want or has just the color or texture they need. It is the job of the fabric industry to introduce designers to the particular fabric needed.

The textile industry works several seasons ahead. Fiber producers usually work 2 years ahead of a season. They must present their products this early to textile mills and converters so they will have enough lead time to plan their color and fabric lines. The fabric market presents its products a year ahead of a season. Their first presentation is to the manufacturers of apparel and accessories, after which they present their finished products to retail stores and the press—all ahead of season—so they can publicize upcoming trends.

Because the textile industry must work several seasons ahead of consumer demand, it must also take the lead in recognizing new fashion directions.

### The Industry's Fashion Experts

To guide them in future planning, textile firms employ staffs of fashion experts. These experts work with textile designers to create fabrics in the weights, textures, colors, and patterns that they anticipate consumers will want. Since most of the early decisions in both the fiber and the fabric market are based on color, the industry's fashion experts also work closely with specialized associations within the fashion industry that provide advance research and trend information.

Most prominent among these groups are the ones that work exclusively with color, such as the Color Association of the United States, the International Color Authority (ICA), the Color Box, and Pantone (see Figure 6.16). Pantone revamped its 19-year-old textile color system. It is now called Pantone for fashion and home and is chromatic.

Color forecasting services provide their clients with reports and newsletters, color swatches, palette predictions, and color-matching services—all geared to each of the apparel markets (men's, women's, children's).

In addition to making decisions about color, the fabric industry must also consider fabrication and texture. If the trend is toward structured clothing, firm fabrication will be necessary, but when a soft, layered look is in, fabrication can be lightweight and soft.

Since trends must be spotted so far in the future, the fashion experts play an important role as they work with fiber and fabric mills as well as designers and buyers.

### Textile Trade Shows and Fairs

New trends are also introduced at trade shows and fairs held throughout the world. Usually semiannual events, these shows are attended by designers, manufacturers, and retailers. The most important of these shows are:

- Interstoff Textile Fair in Asia
- Premiere Vision (First Look) in Paris, France
- Ideacomo (Ideas from Como) in Como, Italy
- Pitti Filati (Pitti Yarns) in Florence, Italy
- Canton Fair in Guangzhou, China
- Yarn Fair International in New York City

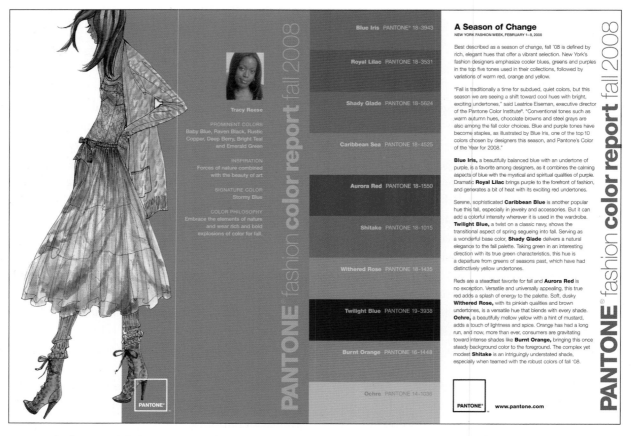

**FIGURE 6.16** Pantone's fashion color report for fall 2008.

- International Fashion Fabric Exhibition (IFFE) in New York City

The failure to identify and act on a trend seen at a major textile show, for example, would mean that retailers and apparel manufacturers would be unable to supply the fashions that consumers want.

### Advertising and Publicity

Unlike fiber producers, fabric manufacturers rarely advertise these days. But when they do, their advertising usually features the brand names of their products and frequently the names of specific apparel manufacturers that use their goods. Either with the cooperation of fiber sources or on their own, these fabric houses run advertisements in a wide variety of mass-circulation magazines and newspapers and share the cost of brand advertising run by retail stores. Their advertising generally makes consumers aware of new apparel styles, the fabrics of which they are made, and often the names of retail stores where they may be purchased.

Fabric producers compete among themselves for the business of apparel producers. They also compete for recognition among retail store buyers and for consumer acceptance of products made of their goods. They publicize brand names and fabric developments, and stage seasonal fashion shows in market areas for retailers and the fashion press. They provide hang-tags for the use of garment manufacturers. These tags may bear not only the fabric's brand name but also instructions relating to its care. In accordance with federal regulation, fabric producers also supply manufacturers with the required care labels that must be permanently sewn into all garments. Many fabric firms supply information to consumers and the trade press and make educational materials available to schools, consumer groups, and retail sales personnel.

### Research and Development

Fabric producers, like fiber producers, now devote attention to exploring the market potential of their products and anticipating the needs of their customers. Success in the fashion industry depends on supplying customers with what they want. Swift changes are the rule in fashion. Anticipation of such changes requires close attention to the market and a scientific study of trends. Market research is used to identify changing lifestyles as well as geographic demands.

Many of the large fabric producers maintain product- and market-research divisions. Their experts work closely with both the trade and consumer markets in studying fabric performance characteristics. Many fabric producers provide garment manufacturers with sample runs of new fabrics for experimental purposes. The market researchers conduct consumer studies relating to the demand for or acceptance of finishes, blends, and other desired characteristics. Such studies also help fabric and garment producers to determine what consumers will want in the future, where and when they will want it, and in what quantities.

## The Green Scene

Being eco-friendly in the production of fibers and fabrics is at the forefront of customer concerns. Textile manufacturers are collecting plastic bottles, used clothing, and cotton and wool scraps, then turning them into first-quality fleece fabrics.

The public is being asked to recycle waste, fly less frequently, and drive smaller cars. A report on the environmental impact of clothing and textiles industries in 2006 took a dim view of both global manufacturing practices and consumer habits. The report, entitled "Well-Dressed?" says that if the textile industry switched to organic cotton (see Figure 6.17), it would reduce its usage of toxic chemicals—such as insecticides, chemical defoliators, and nonorganic dyes—by 92 percent.

Encouraging consumers to buy fewer clothes, choose eco-friendly materials like organic cotton or hemp, wash them less often, keep them longer, and

FIGURE 6.17 Gary Harvey's green design worn by Alicia Silverstone is made of 100 percent recycled cotton, polyester, silk, and nylon.

recycle them could dramatically reduce the industry's environmental impact, says Julian Allwood, who wrote the report with Soren Larrson, both at the Institute for Manufacturing at Cambridge University in England.[8]

Wellman, one of the handful of companies that make recycled fibers, estimates that it recycles 2.5 billion bottles annually. That saves enough petroleum to power the city of Atlanta for a year! Wellman developed Fortrel EcoSpun from recycled soda bottles; it is being used in backpacks, ski hats, and work gloves. The French company Rhovyl produces an apparel textile fiber called Rhovyl'Eco from recycled mineral water and cooking oil bottles. It takes twenty-seven recycled water bottles to make enough fabric for a sweater.

The U.S. floorcovering industry has responded to the issue of decreasing space in existing landfills by collecting used carpets and researching new ways to recycle them. Hoechst Celanese has created a new polyester carpet without a latex backing; this carpet can be easily reprocessed.

The American Textile Manufacturers Institute (ATMI) launched an environmental protection program called E3 (Encouraging Environmental Excellence) in 1992. It has ten guidelines for member companies to follow, including environment audits and developing spill prevention and control plans.

Unfortunately, the United States is not in the forefront of the environmental movement. In 1988, German companies voluntarily stopped the production of some azo dyes that were thought to cause cancer in textile workers. By 1996, Germany had banned the import of 150 azo dyes and any textiles made using these dyes. The search continues for new dyes that do not cause cancer or pollute.

## Synthetic Fabrics Going Green
During the 1930s, 1940s and 1950s, nylon's durability, polyester's UV protection, and spandex's stretch were developed. Activewear textiles have been characterized by their performance capabilities—and their extremely negative impact on the environment—ever since.

Synthetic or man-made fibers are derived from petroleum, one of the earth's finite and most environmentally problematic resources. A new fiber, Ingeo, offers the best properties of natural and synthetic fibers without the use of petroleum. One of Ingeo's remarkable characteristics is that it is completely biodegradable and compostable. Ingeo com-

pletes the cycle of production, consumption, disposal and reuse.[9]

Today, there is a new crop of textiles with exceptional properties. Along with a promise to work hand-in-hand with Mother Nature, mills are developing some of the most comfortable, sanitary performance materials ever, including the following:

- Hemp is known for moisture absorption, antibacterial properties, and reutilization.
- Soy clothing has excellent moisture absorption and transmission, making it more sanitary than cotton, but the fiber is versatile enough to make everything from cashmere-like sweaters to faux fur.
- Bamboo is a fiber that comes from refined bamboo pulp made of the plant's stems and leaves. Bamboo fabrics, which are soft and inhibit the growth of bacteria, are perfect for yoga, aerobics, and activewear.[10]

## Customer Services
Today's well-integrated and diversified fabric companies speak with great fashion authority. They also employ merchandising and marketing staffs whose expertise in fashion trends is available to apparel manufacturers, retailers, the fashion press, and frequently to consumers. Fashion staffs attend fashion forecasts. They conduct in-store sales training programs, address consumer groups, and stage fashion shows for the trade and press. They help retail stores arrange fashion shows and storewide promotions featuring their products, and they assist buyers in locating merchandise made from their fabrics.

## Trends in the Textile Fabric Industry
A dramatic change in the mindset of the textile producers and marketing managers has broadened the product mix, quickened the response time required

to meet customer demand, and made possible shorter runs of more innovative and fashionable fabrics. Currently, retailers, apparel manufacturers, and the fiber and fabric industries are working together to explore new and innovative ways to move textile products through the pipeline to the ultimate consumer more quickly and efficiently (see Figure 6.18).

Fortunately, the consumption rate of textiles increases every year. Economists forecast that this trend will continue and even accelerate in the 2000s. The role of the textile fiber and fabric industries in the U.S. economy is an important one. These industries employ 1.4 million people from all fifty states, making this the largest U.S. manufacturing sector. However, from 1997 to 1998, the Asian currency began to fall, making their extremely low-priced textile and apparel products very attractive to U.S. buyers. As a result of a continued fall in currency, more than one hundred textile plants in the United States closed in 2001, making for the worst industry downturn in 50 years. In spite of industry problems, the textile business is still one of the nation's essential industries.[11]

Some of the major trends that affect both the fiber and fabric industries are:

- Environmental concerns
- Growing global competition
- Increasing exports
- Greater diversification of products
- Increased government regulations
- New technology in equipment

## Production of High-Tech Fabrics

We live in a high-tech age, when almost every new product is a result of combined effort and sophistication in research and development. Fabric is no exception, as evidenced by the frequent introduction of new textiles endowed with some novel and valuable property, characteristic, or performance.

A fabric that has been constructed, finished, or processed in a way that gives it certain innovative, unusual, or hard-to-achieve qualities not normally available can be defined as **high-tech fabric.**

### Protective Uses of High-Tech Fabrics

Many common fabrics have been transformed into high-tech fabrics by coating or laminating them, or by making them with innovative yarns such as Kevlar (see Figure 6.19), Nomex, Spectra, and so on. These fabrics are engineered to resist extreme temperature changes, or to have superior strength, or to

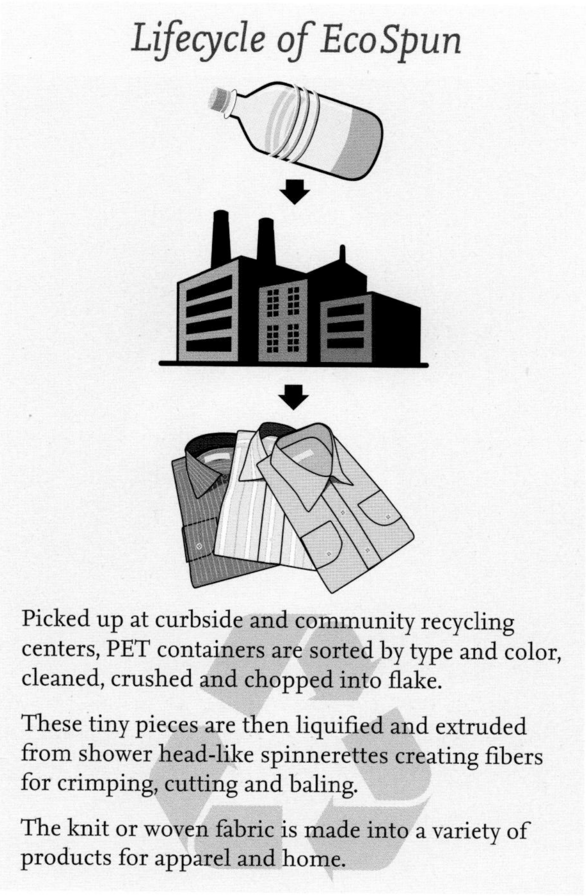

## Lifecycle of EcoSpun

Picked up at curbside and community recycling centers, PET containers are sorted by type and color, cleaned, crushed and chopped into flake.

These tiny pieces are then liquified and extruded from shower head-like spinnerettes creating fibers for crimping, cutting and baling.

The knit or woven fabric is made into a variety of products for apparel and home.

**FIGURE 6.18** From garbage to garments: This diagram demonstrates how attractive sweaters have been made from EcoPile, which is produced from recycled plastic bottles.

**FIGURE 6.19** The company Blade Runner produces this Kevlar slash-proof hooded top, which is specially made for security employees.

have resistance to radiation, corrosive chemicals, and other stresses.

A bright future is forecast for these specialized fabrics in a variety of situations:

- *Activewear*—Apparel for jogging, golfing, cycling, skating, sailing
- *Rainwear*—Raincoats, capes, hats
- *All-weather wear*—Apparel for hunting, fishing, skiing, mountaineering, and so forth
- *Swimwear*—Bathing suits, bodysuits for diving, life vests
- *Protective clothing*—Garments to protect the wearer from hazardous waste; medical contamination; bullets or shrapnel; radiation; cutting or abrasion; electronic, computer, and pharmaceutical manufacture
- *Heat and fire protection clothing*—Occupational clothing for firefighters, blast furnace workers, car racers, tank crews
- *Chemical protection clothing*—Occupational clothing for chemical workers, workers at toxic waste sites and spills

## Designers' Use of High-Tech Fabrics for Apparel

Designers at all price points are incorporating a range of materials besides natural fibers—metallic threads, plastic, vinyl, rubber, and reflective material. In one of his early collections, Alexander McQueen attracted a lot of attention when he cut out pieces of lace, backed them with latex, and splattered them on nude chiffon. The late Gianni Versace used clear vinyl extensively, as well as a chain-mail fabric that drapes easily (see Figure 6.20). "I have always been in love with antique armors," Versace said. "I wanted to use metal in a dress as though it were fabric." Helmut Lang adopted the reflecting strips commonly found on backpacks, running shoes, and firefighters' uniforms, into reflective jeans. Fredric Molenac, designing for the Madame Grès collection, used Lycra with neoprene, a rubberlike fabric. Cynthia Rowley incorpo-

rated stainless steel organza into some of her designs. Miuccia Prada uses mostly synthetics in her Miu Miu line; some of her jackets have Velcro fastenings. As the expanding field of new fabrics grows, more and more designers are finding inspiration and esthetic value in high-tech fabrics.

## Growing Global Competition

The major concern of the U.S. textile industry is the growth of a global competition that shows every promise of being permanent. Although the domestic fiber and fabric industries produce a huge amount of goods, the United States still imports vast quantities of fiber, yarn, and fabric from around the world. From 1980 to 1986, imports of apparel and apparel textiles doubled! Since the WTO went into effect in 1995, U.S. imports of textiles and apparel have increased 90 percent. A study by Kurt Salmon Associates (KSA), a leading textile and apparel consulting firm, stated that imports control 90 percent of the U.S. apparel market.

**FIGURE 6.20** Versace's dress design from his fall/winter couture show, 1995.

Like other American industries, the fiber and fabric mills have been adversely affected by overseas competition. Wages are so much cheaper in those markets that U.S. apparel makers have turned to such countries as Korea and China for fabrics. As a result, most domestic textile companies have restricted their production of apparel fabrics and gone into the production of industrial and household goods.

The United States is still the world's leading exporter of raw cotton. Sluggish world economic growth has kept the world's consumption of cotton relatively even from 1990 to 2000. But the even world numbers mask the changes that have occurred in the spinning of cotton and its distribution since 1995. Cotton consumption in China and Pakistan has had the largest increase, while the United States experienced the greatest decrease. Consumption of raw cotton is forecast to rise in China, while declining in the United States, Mexico, and India.

Not surprisingly, another trend, limited to fabric producers, is toward the acquisition or establishment of mills abroad. Such foreign-based mills may be wholly owned by a U.S. firm or jointly owned by a U.S. firm and a host-country firm. Most mills are located close to the fiber sources. The engineers may be American or American-trained, but the rest of the staff are local workers who are paid according to local wage scales. Advantages to the host-country firm are the availability of the facilities, the fashion knowledge gained, the technical skill of the U.S. owners or part owners, and increased employment opportunities for its citizens. By producing some goods abroad, domestic manufacturers are able to defend themselves against the competition of foreign-made fabrics.

Another trend involves foreign business firms buying into fabric or finishing plants here. Some of these firms are becoming partners in, or sole owners of, new facilities being built in the United States. An example is Hoechst, a West German company that bought Celanese, a major U.S. producer.

Despite these trends, domestic producers, particularly given their closeness to their customers, still have a number of important advantages over importers. They can react more quickly, provide shorter lead time, structure shorter production runs, and in general, remove much of the guesswork that used to hinder the industry.

### Increasing Exports

The industry has nearly tripled its exports over the past decade, exporting 20 percent of its output—roughly $16 billion a year. The textile industry is now directing more of its efforts toward capturing a share of the global market. A number of corporate strategies for the years ahead include:

- Increasing the focus on foreign markets and operations for apparel fabrics, since most studies indicate that the major growth in apparel markets will be outside the United States
- Developing overseas manufacturing operations, or exploring licensing in conjunction with foreign mills, to attain a stronger foothold on the international scene
- Devoting increased resources to market research
- Continuing technological advances

For example, the United States is currently a world leader in home-furnishing textiles, offering more diversified products than any other country. In an attempt to expand this trade, the U.S. textile industry is focusing more of its manufacturing and marketing activities abroad on fabrics for home furnishing and industrial end uses, which are projected to gain larger market shares in the future.

Another relatively new concern for U.S. companies that want to export to European countries are the ISO 9000 standards. These are a set of international standards that companies must meet to be "ISO certified." These standards are generic and apply to any industry. Basically, in order to be certi-

fied, companies must have systems in place to judge quality. Many European companies will not buy from a company that is not ISO certified.

The ISO 14000 was a set of standards that was developed after the success of the ISO 9000. It was designed to assess the need for international environment management standards.

## Greater Diversification of Products

Today, the textile industry produces a more diversified range of fibers and fabrics than ever before. The specialization that once divided the industry into separate segments, each producing fabrics from a single type of fiber, has all but faded. To meet the needs of consumers, it is often necessary to blend two or more fibers into a yarn or to combine yarns of two fibers. Mills are learning to adjust their operations to any new fiber or combination of fibers.

One of the largest firms in the field illustrates how the industry is moving toward greater product diversification. Burlington, originally a rayon mill specializing in bedspreads, now produces and sells spun and textured yarns of both natural and manufactured fibers. Its new products include a variety of finished woven and knitted fabrics, some unfinished fabrics, and hosiery for men, women, and children. It also produces domestic and home furnishings ranging from bed linens to rugs and furniture.

Another bright spot for the domestic textile market is **geotextiles**, or manufactured permeable textiles that are currently used in reinforcing or stabilizing civil engineering projects. Two examples of industrial fabrics are Kevlar and Tyvek, which are used for diverse applications such as book covers and wrapping houses to prevent moisture penetration.

An example of an industrial protective coating is Teflon® (see Figure 6.21)—yes, the coating used on nonstick frying pans—which is now being used to protect delicate fabrics. With fashion designers

**FIGURE 6.21** Zac Posen uses Teflon® for this white coat and stretch satin dress.

searching for new fabrics every day, can apparel applications for industrial and geotextiles be far behind?

## Increased Government Regulation

One of the biggest impacts on the textile industry in the past decade has been the intervention of the federal government in every aspect of the industry: health and safety, noise levels and chemical pollution, consumer product liability, environmental impact, and hiring practices.

Until recently, federal regulation of the textile industry was mainly concerned with the fiber content labeling of fabrics and products made of those fabrics. In 1953, the Flammable Fabrics Act was passed, but it served to ban from the market only a few very ignitable fabrics and apparel made from them. The increasing strength and direction of the consumerism movement, however, resulted in more government regulation of the textile industry on both the federal and state levels.

In July 1972, two important changes in federal textile regulations took effect: the Federal Trade Commission's (FTC's) rule on Care Labeling of Textile Wearing Apparel and the revision of the Flammable Fabrics Act. The FTC's care-labeling rule requires that all fabrics—piece goods as well as apparel and accessories made of fabric—be labeled to show the type of care they require. In 1997, the FTC again changed the rules by introducing new care label symbols. They indicate whether the fabric can be hand washed or machine washed or should be dry-cleaned. The symbols also indicate whether ironing is required, and if so, at what temperature. The manufacturer must sew a permanent label with these care symbols into each garment.

Other trends in the textile industry that are a result of government environmental and consumer regulations include:

- Fibers and textile products will be made by larger producers with a resulting decrease in

the number of small concerns and marginal operations. This will result primarily from the higher production costs related to complying with the new government regulations and the greater capital investment required to stay competitive in a period of continually rising costs.
- Manufacturing operations will function at higher efficiencies, recycling as much material as possible and converting waste to energy.
- New chemical processes will be developed to recover, recycle, and reuse fibers, dyes, and other chemicals.
- Fibers with built-in environmental disadvantages will slowly give way to more suitable replacements, or new processing techniques will be devised to allow their continued use.
- Transfer printing may be an important way to reduce some of the dye-house stream-pollution problems.
- Consumers will be increasingly protected, with particular emphasis on children's apparel and home furnishings.
- Consumers will be better advised on the characteristics of their purchases.

## New Technology in Equipment

"New technology is totally revolutionizing the textile industry," says Jack Lenor Larsen, an eminent textiles designer in the home furnishings industry. The trend toward increased mechanization and automation is clearly apparent throughout the industry as it has changed from one that is labor-intensive to one that is equipment-intensive.

In recent decades, the textile industry has experienced a number of technological developments, such as the shuttleless loom and computer design of fabrics. In the mills, new machines combine higher production speeds with lower energy consumption. Automated weaving and knitting machines produce more with fewer operators.

The industry is also experimenting with new printing techniques. Rotary-screen printing is truly

**FIGURE 6.22** A textile manufacturing plant.

the technology of the 21st century and will replace flat-screen and roller printing techniques. Powerful computers will enable the industry to set the cost and price of fabrics before they are knitted or woven. These elements are needed to be competitive in the global textile market.

Computer technology is playing a key role in Quick Response programs that improve communications among fiber, fabric, apparel, and retail businesses. Quick Response shortens the time between the placement of orders by retailers and the delivery of goods. Bar codes have been established by the Fabric and Supplier Linkage Council so that vendors can label shipments with standard bar codes that purchasers can enter immediately into inventory records. This reduces inventory costs, warehouse time, forced markdowns, and stock outs.

The industry experimented widely with robots in the 1980s and will probably employ them with increasing frequency into the next century.

Although the new technology has created job losses, it will ultimately help the industry by attracting bright, ambitious young workers and leaders who want to work in a progressive environment (see Figure 6.22).

Today, U.S. textile plants are characterized by computer-run looms that feed a mile of yarn per minute, as well as completely automated yarn spinning plants that can run 24 hours a day, 7 days a week. Technological advances have long been introduced at the Bobbin Show, a 3-day event held annually in the United States. In 1998, the Bobbin Show became Bobbin World, a triennial international show, which alternates with the Bobbin Show. Other major shows are the International Machinery Show in Germany and the Japanese International Apparel Machinery Show.

## Summary and Review

Textiles begin with fibers, which may be natural (cotton, wool, flax, and silk) or manufactured. Manufactured fibers are either cellulosic (made of cellulose, which is also the substance of natural plant fibers) or noncellulosic (combining chemicals in a laboratory). Variants of generic manufactured fibers bear the trade name of the manufacturer. For example, Dacron is Du Pont's brand of polyester.

The main market for fibers is the textile fabric industry, which weaves, knits, or otherwise turns fibers into greige goods. These goods are then finished by either the textile mill or converters, who add such treatments as dye, waterproofing, and fire-retarding and permanent-press finishes. Finishes added to natural fibers allow them to compete more effectively with manufactured fibers by taking on some of the properties that consumers demand in apparel and other textile products.

Textiles are sold primarily to manufacturers of apparel and home fashions, but marketing of fibers and textiles is directed at retailers and consumers, too, to build demand. U.S. textile manufacturers compete with foreign imports through technological advances that speed production, minimize pollution, and improve the performance of fabrics in terms of colorfastness, insulation, and other desirable features. Computerized systems expedite order fulfillment.

## Trade Talk

Define or briefly explain the following terms:

| | |
|---|---|
| brand names | cellulosic fibers |
| cotton | fabrics |
| fashion textiles | fiber |
| flax | generic names |
| geotextiles | greige goods |
| hemp | high-tech fabric |
| licensed trademarks | linen |
| manufactured fibers | microfiber |
| natural fibers | noncellulosic fibers |
| piece-dyed | polymers |
| primary suppliers | ramie |
| silk | spinnerette |
| textile converters | textile fabric |
| trimmings | variant |
| wool | yarn |
| yarn-dyed | |

## For Review

1. What is the difference between a natural and a manufactured fiber? Give five examples of each, and indicate the source of each natural fiber you name.

2. What has the natural fiber industry done to counteract the effects of manufactured fibers in the marketplace?

3. Trace the steps through which a new or newly modified manufactured fiber passes as it goes from conception to general availability.

4. Name and explain the three ways in which producers of manufactured fibers usually sell their products to fabric manufacturers.

5. Describe the three major merchandising and marketing activities of natural and manufactured fiber producers.

6. Describe the major steps in the production of most fabrics.

7. What is the function of the textile converter? What are the advantages of dealing with a converter for (a) a fabric mill, and (b) an apparel producer?

8. How do textile fabric producers keep informed about new fashion trends?

9. How have increased fiber, yarn, and fabric imports affected the American textile industry?

10. What are the provisions of the Flammable Fabrics Act of 1953 and the FTC's rule on Care Labeling of Textile Wearing Apparel of 1972?

## For Discussion

1. What is the role of trade associations in the marketing of fibers and textile fabrics?

2. When a major designer designed his collection for a mass merchandiser, he went directly to the textile mills with specifications for his fabrics in regard to width, pattern repeats, and so on. Can most designers do this? Why or why not?

3. Discuss the relationship of environmentally green fibers/fabrics and manufactured fibers/fabrics by a manufacturer and retail customer.

# chapter seven

*Everything you always wanted to know*

*about the leather and fur industry.*

**KEY CONCEPTS**

- The three major types of companies in the leather industry and their functions
- The nine different categories of leather and the special finishes used on leather
- The history and development of the fur industry in the United States
- The functions of the three major groups in the fur industry
- The steps in transforming fur pelts into finished garments

# Leather and Fur

The most glamorous and sought-after textiles—leather and fur—are also the two oldest. Prehistoric people discovered that the animals they killed for food could serve another purpose, that of providing them with warmth and protection from the elements. One side of an animal skin could be worked into leather; the other furnished fur. Today leather and fur are vital to the apparel, home furnishings, and automotive industries, contributing the raw materials for coats and jackets, handbags, shoes, gloves, and an ever-widening range of fashion products.

The leather industry is currently in the process of expanding its markets in ways that no one even dreamed of 10 years ago. New processing methods have created leathers so thin and supple that designers can use them for everything from bikinis to shirts to evening wear—all available in an incredible array of colors.

After several years of decline because of environmental concerns over the use of scarce or rare animal skins, furs are making a comeback, especially with the young, first-time customer. The demand for furs has never been greater, at the very time when the fur industry is experimenting with new colors and styles.

## The Leather Industry

Leather-making is a highly specialized and time-consuming operation. Because of the time involved, the leather industry must anticipate and predict trends far in advance of other textile suppliers. Leather producers typically decide what production method, textures, finishes, and colors they will use 8 to 16 months before a leather reaches apparel and accessory manufacturers. As a result, those in other fashion industries often look to the leather industry for leadership, particularly in terms of color and texture.

Since leather is a by-product of the meatpacking industry, it is not the target of environmentalists as is the fur industry. Few animals are raised specifically for their hides. Most animals are raised to feed people, and their skins and hides, which have no food value, are then sold to the leather trade.

## History and Development

Archaeologists have found leather thong sandals in the tombs of ancient Egypt. They were the prized possessions of priests and pharaohs more than 5,000 years ago (see Figure 7.1). From the earliest times, leather was valued as clothing, but as tanning methods improved, leather became important for armor, helmets, and saddles. In Europe in the Middle Ages, leather was considered a luxury product within the reach of the rich and noble only.

In the many years that Indian tribes roamed the North American continent, long before the arrival of the first European colonists, the tanning of leather was an important part of tribal life. Indians used deerskins to make clothing, soft yet sturdy moccasins, and tepee homes. By today's tanning standards, their methods would be considered limited and primitive, yet the techniques they used to transform raw animal hides into a variety of products certainly served them well.

In 1623, not long after the arrival of the Pilgrims in Massachusetts, the first commercial tannery in the American colonies was established in Plymouth by an Englishman with the fitting name of Experience Miller. Later, Peter Minuet, Governor of New Amsterdam, invented the first machinery used for tanning in the colonies. His invention was a horse driven stone mill that ground the oak bark then used to convert animal skins into leather.

Many years passed before more important mechanization of the leather industry occurred. But in 1809, a giant step was taken. Samuel Parker invented a machine that could split heavy steer hides twenty-five times faster than people could do it by hand. The machine also produced a lighter and more supple leather; just what people wanted for their shoes, boots, and other clothing.

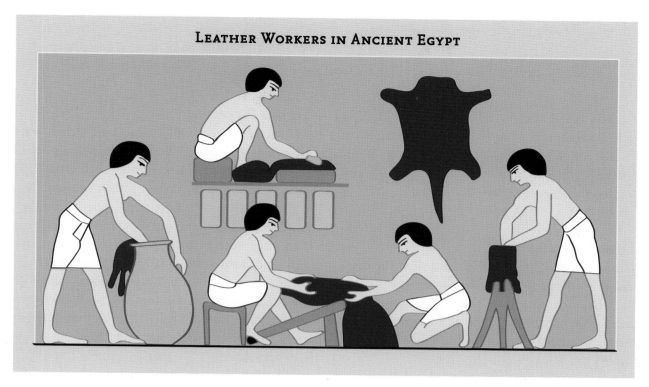

**FIGURE 7.1** Working with leather dates back to 1550 B.C. in Ancient Egypt. The figure on the left is soaking the hide in a large jar; the figure on the right is stretching and kneading a skin on a trestle to soften it. The figures at the center bottom are cutting a skin with a knife. At the top right is the completed skin of an animal.

Today, new machines do much of the manual work formerly required to stir hides and skins as they soaked. Other machines dehair and deflesh them. Still others split the skins and emboss patterns on them. Machinery has taken much of the human labor out of the processing of leather. In addition, chemistry has provided new tanning agents that reduce the time required to transform hides and skins into leather. These new tanning agents also help achieve a greater variety of finishes. This variety is possible in spite of restrictions on the commercial use of the skins of some animals that have been placed on endangered-species lists.

## Organization and Operation

Although tanning was once a cottage industry in the United States, it quickly became, relatively speaking, big business. By 1870, there were over 6,600 small tanneries in the United States. By 1979, only 4,500 tanneries operated in the United States. Like the textile industry, the leather business has been subjected to its share of mergers since the late 1970s. A combination of factors hit the American

tanning industry then: overwhelming shoe imports, stronger environmental regulations, and sharply increased exports of hides. Today, there are only about 340 tanneries in the United States, but they are large plants that produce tens of millions of square feet of leather. The Northeast dominates the industry with 146 establishments, 66 that are located in New York City. Most of the other tanneries are located in Massachusetts, Texas, California, and Wisconsin.[1]

The American leather industry is divided into three major types of companies: regular tanneries, contract tanneries, and converters. **Regular tanneries** purchase and process skins and hides and sell the leather as their finished product. **Contract tanneries** process the hides and skins to the specifications of other firms (mainly converters) but are not involved in the final sale of the leather. **Converters** buy the hides and skins from the meatpackers, commission the tanning to the contract tanneries, and then sell the finished leather. In recent years, converters have been buying finished leather from both regular and contract tanneries.

The leather industry has remained specialized.

Calfskin tanners do not normally tan kidskin, and gloveskin tanners do not work with sole leather.

Like textile producers, most leather firms maintain sales offices or representatives in New York City for the convenience of their customers.

## Categories of Leather

Almost all leather comes from cattle. But the hides and skins of many other animals from all parts of the world are also used in fashion apparel and accessories. There are nine major categories of leather (see Table 7.1).

### The Equine Group

Horses provide a rugged leather. Some horsehide is tanned into cordovan leather, which makes extremely durable and sturdy shoe uppers. The hide is also used for leather jackets. But it is important to know that most of what is called "pony skin" is really stenciled calfskin, which is used because it is more pliable than real pony skin. Real top-quality pony skin comes from wild horses in Poland and Russia.

### The Exotic Leathers

Supplies of the so-called "exotic leathers" are diminishing worldwide, driving prices up sharply. There is some good news, however. From 1967 to 1987, the American alligator was listed as an endangered species. Today, the alligator is out of danger because of a policy called **sustainable use**, an environmental program that encourages landowners to preserve alligator eggs and habitats in return for the right to use a percentage of the grown animals.

In a related development, Native American Indian tribes are raising bison (American buffalo) and have opened a tannery in Billings, Montana, to tan the hides with the hair on them to make them into buffalo robes. They use an environmentally friendly process known as brain tanning, which leaves the hides softer than chemical tanning and easier to sew.[2]

## Leather Processing

Animal pelts are divided into three classes, each based on weight. Those that weigh 15 pounds or less when shipped to the tannery are called **skins.** This class consists mostly of calves, goats, pigs, sheep, and deer. Those weighing from 15 to 25 pounds, mostly from young horses and cattle, are called **kips.** Those weighing more than 25 pounds, primarily cattle, oxen, buffalo, and horse skins, are called **hides.**

The process of transforming animal pelts into leather is known as **tanning.** The word is derived from a Latin word for oak bark, which was used in early treatments of animal skins. Tanning is the oldest known craft.

Three to six months are needed to tan hides for sole leather and saddlery. Less time is required for tanning kips and skins, but the processes are more numerous and require more expensive equipment and highly trained labor. The tanning process involves minerals, vegetable materials, oils, and chemicals, used alone or in combination. The choice of a tanning agent depends on the end use for which the leather is being prepared.

### Minerals

Two tanning methods use minerals. One uses alum; the other uses chrome salts. Alum, used by the ancient Egyptians to make writing paper, is rarely used today. Chrome tanning, introduced in 1893, is now used to process nearly two-thirds of all leather produced in the United States. This is a fast method that takes hours rather than weeks. It produces leather for shoe uppers, garments, gloves, handbags, and other products. Chrome-tanned leather can be identified by the pale, blue-gray color in the center of the cut edge. It is slippery when wet. It is usually washable and can be cleaned by gentle sponging.

### Vegetable Materials

Vegetable tanning, which is also an ancient method, uses the tannic acids that naturally occur in the bark, wood, or nuts of various trees and shrubs and in tea leaves. Vegetable tanning is used on cow,

## TABLE 7.1 *Nine Major Categories of Leather*

| CATEGORIES | HIDES FROM | PRODUCING LEATHER FOR: | |
|---|---|---|---|
| **Cattle** | **Steer**<br>**Cow**<br>**Bull** | • Shoe and slipper outsoles, insoles, uppers, linings, counters, welts, heels, etc.<br>• Traveling bags, suitcases, briefcases, luggage straps, etc.<br>• Gloves and garments<br>• Upholstery for automobiles, furniture, airplanes, buses, decoration<br>• Handbags, purses, wallets, waist belts, other personal leather goods | • Harnesses, saddles, bridles, skirting (for saddles), etc.<br>• Machinery belting, packings, washers, aprons, carders, combers, pickers, etc.<br>• Footballs, basketballs, volleyballs, and other sporting goods<br>• Laces, scabbards, holsters, etc. |
| | **Kips or kipskins**<br>(from large calves or undersized cattle) | • Shoe and slipper uppers and linings<br>• Handbags and other personal leather goods<br>• Gloves and garments<br>• Sweat bands for hats | • Rawhide and parchment<br>• Athletic helmets<br>• Bookbindings<br>• Handicrafts, etc. |
| **Sheep and Lamb** | **Wooled Skins, Hair Skins**<br>**(cabrettas), Shearlings** | • Shoe and slipper uppers and linings<br>• Gloves and garments<br>• Chamois<br>• Handbags and other personal leather goods<br>• Moutons and shearlings (skins with wool on)<br>• Parchment | • Textile rollers<br>• Hats, hat sweat bands, millinery, and caps<br>• Bookbindings<br>• Piano actions<br>• Sporting goods (balls, gloves, etc.) |
| **Goat and Kid** | **Goat and Kid** | • Shoe and fancy uppers, linings<br>• Gloves and garments | • Fancy leather goods, handbags<br>• Bookbindings |
| **Equine** | **Horse, Colt, Ass, Mule, and Zebra** | • Shoe soles and uppers<br>• Luggage<br>• Gloves and garments<br>• Belts | • Aviator's clothing<br>• Sporting goods (baseball covers and mitts, etc.) |
| **Buffalo** | **Domesticated Land and Water Buffalo** (not American Bison, whose hide is not tanned for their leather) | • Shoe soles and uppers<br>• Handbags<br>• Fancy leather goods, luggage<br>• Buffing wheels | |
| **Pig and Hog** | **Pig, Hog, Boar,**<br>**Peccary, Carpincho**<br>(a brazilian rodent) | • Gloves<br>• Innersoles, contours, etc.<br>• Fancy leather goods, luggage<br>• Saddlery and harnesses | • Shoe uppers<br>• Upholstery |
| **Deer** | **Fallow Deer, Reindeer, Elk and Caribou skins** | • Shoe uppers<br>• Gloves<br>• Clothing<br>• Piano actions | • Moccasins<br>• Mukluks<br>• Fancy leather goods |
| **Kangaroo and Wallaby** | **Skins producing very strong leather** | • Shoe uppers, including track and basketball shoes | |
| **Exotic Leathers**<br> Aquatic<br><br> Land<br><br> Reptile | • **Frog, Seal, Shark, Walrus, and Turtle**<br>• **Camel, Elephant, Ostrich, and Pangolin**<br>• **Alligator, Crocodile, Lizard, and Snake** | | |

CATTLE  GOAT  KANGAROO

Source: Leather Industries of America, *Dictionary of Leather Terminology*, 8th ed. (Washington, D.C.: Leather Industries of America).

steer, horse, and buffalo hides. The product is a heavy, often relatively stiff leather used for the soles of shoes, some shoe uppers, some handbags and belts, and saddlery. Vegetable-tanned leather can be identified by a dark center streak in the cut edge. It is resistant to moisture and can be cleaned by sponging. Vegetable tanning is the slowest tanning method and takes months to complete. Because it is so labor intensive, relatively little vegetable tanning is done in the United States.

## Oil

Processing with oil is one of the oldest methods of turning raw animal skins into leather. A fish oil—usually codfish—is used. Today, oil tanning is used to produce chamois, doeskin, and buckskin—relatively soft and pliable leathers used in making gloves and jackets.

## Chemicals

The most widely used and quickest method of tanning relies primarily on formaldehyde. Because the processing turns the leather white, it can easily be dyed. Formaldehyde-tanned leather is washable. It is often used for gloves and children's shoe uppers.

## Combinations

It is possible to combine tanning agents. A vegetable and mineral combination is used to "retan" work shoes and boots. Combinations of alum and formaldehyde or oil and chrome are common.

## Finishing

The finishing process gives leather the desired thickness, moisture, color, and aesthetic appeal (see Figure 7.2). Leather can now be dyed in nearly five hundred different colors. Dyed leather is also sometimes finished with oils and fats to ensure softness, strength, or to waterproof it. Special color effects include sponging, stenciling, spraying, or tie dyeing. Other finishes include matte, luster or pearl, suede, patent, or metallic. It is important to note that suede is a finish, not a kind of leather. Table 7.2 describes the characteristics of different leather finishes.

### Merchandising and Marketing

Because of the lead-time needed to produce leather, the leather industry not only must stay abreast of fashion, it must be several steps ahead of it. Months before other fashion industries commit themselves to colors and textures, leather producers have already made their decisions. They have started the search for the right dyes and treatments to meet expected future demand. As a result, the leather industry's forecasters are considered the best and most experienced in the fashion industry.

### *Fashion Information Services*

Because they make their assessments of fashion trends so far in advance, others in the industry look

**FIGURE 7.2** The drying out (top) and finishing processes (bottom) give leather the desired thickness, moisture, color, and aesthetic appeal.

**TABLE 7.2** *Special Finishes for Leather*

| FINISHES | CHARACTERISTICS |
|---|---|
| Aniline | Polished surface achieved with aniline dyes |
| Matte (mat) | Flat eggshell-surface look |
| Luster or pearl | Soft, opaque finish with a transparent glow |
| Antiqued | Subtle two-toned effect like polished antique wood |
| Burnished | Similar to antiqued but with less shadowing |
| Metallic | Surface look of various metals—copper, gold, silver, bronze |
| Waxy | Dulled, rustic look, as in waxy glove leathers |
| Patent | Glossy, high-shine finish |
| Napped | Buffed surface such as in suede or brushed leather |
| Suede | Leather finish that can be applied to a wide variety of leather |
| Washable | Waterproof finish that can be applied to some leathers |

PATENT

METALLIC

WAXY

SUEDE

Source: William A. Rossi, "What You Should Know about Leathers," *Footwear News Magazine*, June 1982, p. 16; and Rohm-Hass, Leather Technicians Handbook of Furnishings, 1994.

to the leather industry for information. Like other fashion industries, the leather industry retains experts to disseminate information about trends and new products in the leather industry. They often produce booklets that forecast trends, describe new colors and textures, and generally promote the leather industry. Samples of important textures and looks are included.

Fashion experts also work directly with retailers, manufacturers, and the press to help crystallize their thinking about leather products. One-on-one meetings, seminars, and fashion presentations are used to educate the fashion industry and consumers about leather.

Despite all this activity, individual tanners are not known by name to the public. Nor is a fashion editor, in describing a leather garment, likely to mention its manufacturer. Leather producers are not named in retail stores or in leather manufacturers' advertising. Consumers who can name several fabric and fiber producers would have a difficult time naming any leather tanners.

## Trade Associations and Trade Shows

Much of the information collected and disseminated by the leather industry comes through its strong trade association, Leather Industries of America (LIA). LIA has worked hard to broaden the market for all types of leathers, often in the face of serious competition. For example, shoe manufacturers, who were important leather users a few years ago, have now turned to other products as well. This has compelled the leather industry to promote and defend its products, and LIA has taken the lead in this activity.

LIA sponsors semiannual color seminars and sells a packet of each season's color swatches to industry members. It supports a Hide Training School and sponsors a student design award. LIA's weekly newspaper, *Council News*, covers the leather industry.

Trade shows are another important source of information within the leather industry. Two years before the ultimate consumer sees finished leather products in retail stores, the leathers are introduced in several industry trade shows (see Figure 7.3). The oldest and most established show, the Semaine du

Cuir, is held in Paris in the fall, usually September. The Hong Kong International Leather Fair is held in June, and the Tanners' Apparel and Garment Show (TAG) is held in New York City in October.

### Research and Development

The leather industry retains and expands its markets by adapting its products to fashion's changing requirements. Before World War II, relatively few colors and types of leather were available in any one season, and each usually had a fashion life of several years. Today, a major tannery may turn out hundreds of leather colors and types each season, meanwhile preparing to produce more new colors and textures for the next season.

To protect and expand their markets, leather producers constantly broaden their range of colors, weights, and textures. They also introduce improvements that make leather an acceptable material where it formerly had either limited use or no use at all.

Leather has the weight of tradition behind it; people have regarded fine leather as a symbol of luxury for centuries. But today, leather shares its hold on the fashion field with other and newer materials. Through product research and development, producers are attempting to meet the competition not only among leathers but also from other materials.

### Trends in the Leather Industry

Until just a few decades ago, the leather industry concerned itself primarily with meeting consumer needs in relatively few fashion areas—mainly shoes, gloves, belts, handbags, luggage, and small leather goods. The use of leather for apparel was restricted largely to a few items of outerwear, such as jackets and coats. These were stiff, bulky, and primarily functional in appeal. Now designers offer colorful, supple leather vests, jeans, pants, blazers, anoraks, skirts, and suits of every description, in addition to jackets and coats (see Figure 7.4).

Today, the leather industry has changed as a result of three trends: enlarging market opportunities, increased competition from synthetics, and increased foreign trade.

### Enlarging Markets

Improved methods of tanning are turning out better, more versatile leathers with improved fashion characteristics. In general, these improvements include the following:

- The new leathers are softer and more pliable. Tanners' ability to split full-grain leather thinner and thinner creates this new suppleness.
- The new leathers can be dyed more successfully in a greater number of fashion colors.
- Washable leather finishes and improved cleaning techniques have made it easier for consumers to care for leather garments.

In cowhide leathers, the demand is high for the lighter-weight, mellow, natural-looking, full-grain leathers. Especially desirable are the glazed, rich-colored, aniline-dyed types that accentuate the natural beauty of the grain. These leathers are used predominantly in luggage, portfolios, and furniture.

Sheep and lamb tanners are encouraged by the sustained demand for glazed and suede leathers in the leather apparel market. They are also very pleased by customers' enthusiastic response to the new lighter-weight shearling used in coats, jackets, and vests. Some new shearling styles are also

**FIGURE 7.3** Different materials, garments, accessories, and patterns showcased at the China Fur & Leather Products Fair in Beijing.

FIGURE 7.4 The beauty and versatility of soft leather is a hit on the runway. John Bartlett's fall/winter collection, 2006 (top), and Yohji Yamamoto's fall/winter look, 2008 (bottom).

FIGURE 7.5 An exotic, snakeskin leather jacket by Gucci.

reversible. The nonwool side is traditionally finished as suede, but it can also have a napped finish.

Prada and Gucci (see Figure 7.5) are two upscale fashion companies built on leather. They continue to expand their offerings season after season. Other designers working with leather include Vakko, Donna Karan, Ralph Lauren, Escada, and more recently Michael Kors and Calvin Klein.[3]

## Increased Competition from Synthetics

In the past few decades, the leather market has been eroded by synthetics. Leather heel lifts, which used to be commonplace, are now more often than not replaced with plastic. Synthetics that look and feel

# Fashion Focus

Fashion Focus

## Fur Frenzy
### *For the Love of Fur*

Left page: Fashionable furs come in all styles and colors: Giorgio Armani's design, 2008 (top); Christian Dior's flared fur coat, 2008 (bottom); Right page: Viktor & Rolf's luxurious fur coat screams, "Wow!" in 2008.

On both sides of the Atlantic, designer shows demonstrated that fur is the essential must have for the stylish women's—or men's—wardrobe.

No matter what specific directions are in store for fur in upcoming seasons, one thing is certain—today, consumers are looking for versatility. Reflecting busier, more varied lifestyles, women look for fur fashions that can add a dash of elegance and drama to jeans, slacks, or skirts; bring casual sophistication to the soccer mom's weekend wardrobe; or complement the elegance of an evening gown or cocktail suit. From sidewalk cafés to the opera house, from downtown to uptown, she wants to wear fur.

While fur continues to be the choice of the affluent and fashion savvy, almost anyone can freshen up his or her wardrobe and add a touch of luxury without spending a fortune. The wide range of products, from full-length fur coats to innovative fur trims and bold fur accessories, means there is something in fur for everyone. Today, over four hundred international designers are working in fur. Fur is the fabric of choice! The tremendous creative possibilities provided by new techniques in manufacturing, shearing, and dyeing have made fur one of the most versatile fabrics. Fur has a unique quality that enhances the design element, bringing a kind of drama and richness to the runways that no other fabric can match.

Leading designers, including Oscar de la Renta, Carolina Herrera, Michael Kors, Chado Ralph Rucci, Carmen Marc Valvo, and Badgley Mischka, have interpreted fur in ways that are heart-stopping and luxurious yet completely wearable. Fur has been used by Zang Toi, Derek Lam, Jeremy Scott, and Peter Som in innovative and bold new ways to add depth and excitement to their collections. For J. Mendel and Dennis Basso, fur has been the core of their creative inspiration, and they have expanded their artistry to create sexy, sophisticated, elegant ready-to-wear collections.

Fur, once the ultimate luxury reserved for only special occasions, is bursting out of consumers' closets. And for now—it's all about fur!

like leather but are less susceptible to scratches and easier to maintain are used to make handbags and other small leather goods.

Since most synthetic leather products were not as attractive as leather, synthetics did not offer leather any real competition for a long time. Over a decade ago, however, imitation leathers and suedes that were true substitutes began to be marketed. The most important one, Ultrasuede, quickly became a fashion classic. Although a washable synthetic, Ultrasuede does not have an image of being fake or cheap, and it is used by high-fashion designers. Another more recent artificial suede, called Facile, has improved suppleness. It is also widely used by high-fashion designers. Vinyl is widely used for shoes, handbags, and other accessories, and its appearance has improved over the years.

### Increased Foreign Trade

An increased worldwide demand for leather has enabled American hide dealers to obtain higher prices for their products in countries where demand outstrips supply. This, in turn, has led to sharp increases in the export of hides because foreign tanners are able to produce leather more cheaply than their U.S. counterparts.

While the United States has been inundated with cheap leather products in the past few years, its own tanners have turned to exporting their own products. American tanners, known for the high quality of their tanning process and their excellent finishing techniques, have had no trouble expanding into foreign markets.

### Industry Growth Factors

Several factors point to overall industry growth. Foremost among these is the trend toward a classic and elegant fashion look with an emphasis on quality. When quality is desired, consumers want real leather with all its mystique and will not settle for substitutes. Another hopeful sign is that the supply of raw hides is large enough to allow for growth in production.

Actively supported by a federal export program, the industry's aggressive efforts to develop foreign markets ensures future growth for the industry, as does the industry's expanded research programs.

## The Fur Industry

Long before prehistoric people learned how to plant crops, weave cloth, or build shelters, they figured out how to use fur. They spread it on the floor and used it as rugs. They used it to cover and create walls, thus bringing some warmth into an otherwise cold and drafty cave (see Figure 7.6).

By the Middle Ages, the wearing of fur announced one's wealth and status. Sable, marten, ermine, and fox were the favored furs of nobility (see Figure 7.7). Italian cardinals wore ermine as a symbol of purity; English nobles wore it as a sign of power. Fur was also a valued commodity used in trading. For centuries in Northern Europe, furs were valued more than gold and silver. Fur was still as good as gold in 1900 when Chile banked chinchilla skins as security for a loan.

Fur is still big business in America. "Fur sales continue their upward trend, reflecting fur's importance in today's fashion," explains Keith Kaplan, executive

**FIGURE 7.7** Louise Cromwell poses in fox furs, c. 1911.

director of Fur Information Council of America (FICA). In 1985, only forty-two fashion designers were using fur in their collections. Today, more than four hundred renowned fashion designers show fur fashions, coats, and fur-trimmed merchandise appealing to a broad cross section of consumers. Men and women of all ages are buying fur today, and fur can be found in designer boutiques, specialty retailers, sporting goods stores, accessories shops, and boutiques for men and women, as well as at the more traditional fur salons and department stores.[4]

## History and Development

The search for a northwest passage that would shorten the route between Europe and the Orient led to the establishment of the fur trade in North America. When French explorer Jacques Cartier arrived at the mouth of the St. Lawrence River in 1534, he traded furs with the Indians. The next year, when he sailed even farther up the river, he realized what a vast wealth of fur-bearing animals existed on the conti-

**FIGURE 7.6** Eskimos have been wearing fur for years as a source of warmth.

nent. English and Dutch explorers soon joined the French in setting up trading posts. The first posts were situated along the St. Lawrence and Hudson rivers, but they soon dotted the continent. Early fur-trading posts played a role in establishing such cities as St. Louis, Chicago, Detroit, St. Paul, and Spokane.

The plentiful supply of furs helped the colonists in other ways. They were able to export furs and use the money to bring European necessities—and even some luxuries—to the New World. Furs were an important source of clothing and furnishings. For a while in the mid-18th century, furs were virtually the currency of North America.

It is the beaver, however, that truly deserves a special place in North American history. The discovery of this fur led to a "fur rush" that rivaled the Gold Rush. Beaver was used mostly to make men's hats, but in Canada in 1733, one beaver pelt could also buy a pound of sugar or two combs or six thimbles or eight knives. Settlers pushed west in search of beaver, leaving behind communities with names like Beaver Creek, Beaver Falls, and Beaver Lake. Fortunes were made. John Jacob Astor was among the first to become a millionaire in the beaver trade. He dreamed of a beaver-fur empire stretching from New York to the Northwest Territory.

Ironically, just as beavers were becoming scarce, the fashion changed. Abraham Lincoln wore a silk top hat to his inauguration, and men stopped wearing beaver hats and began to buy hats made of silk and felt. The demand for beaver ceased overnight.

The interest in women's furs remained strong, however, and during the Civil War, the first mink ranch was established by T. D. Phillips and W. Woodstock. In 1880, silver fox fur farming began on Prince Edward Island, off the eastern coast of Canada. Fur farming and ranching have undergone renewed expansion in the past half century.

Fashions in furs (see Figure 7.8) do change, although they change less quickly than do other apparel styles because furs are expensive. While mink coats account for half of all furs sold today, 50 years ago, a woman who wanted to look glamorous

**FIGURE 7.8** Luxurious and eye-catching furs find themselves in the fashion spotlight throughout changes in seasons and trends.

chose an ermine cape. Today, an ermine cape would be valuable only as a theatrical prop—and it could be picked up fairly cheaply in a secondhand store.

More than at any other time in the history of fur fashion, the current list of furs is long and varied. Mink is the overwhelming favorite among consumers. Sable is a distant second, followed by fox and beaver. A new category, called sport or contemporary, includes such furs as raccoon, fox, beaver, coyote, muskrat, tanuki (Japanese raccoon), and nutria (a South American beaverlike animal). Table 7.3 lists furs and their characteristics.

In addition to the use of newer furs such as tanuki and nutria, fur manufacturers often reintroduce

### TABLE 7.3 *Selected Popular Furs and Their Characteristics*

| Fur | Characteristics | Look For | Fur | Characteristics | Look For |
|---|---|---|---|---|---|
| **Beaver**<br>Sheared | Soft, plushy texture. | Silky texture. Well-matched pelts, evenly sheared. | **Lynx** | Russian lynx is the softest and whitest of these long-haired furs, with the most subtle beige markings. Canadian lynx is next, while Montana lynx has stronger markings. Lynx cat or bobcat is reddish black fading to spotted white on longer belly hairs. | Creamy white tones and subtle markings. |
| Natural | Long, lustrous guard hairs over thick underfur. | Lustrous sheen of guard hairs and thickness of underfur. | | | |
| **Calf** | Short, sleek, flat hairs. Comes in many natural colors and patterns and may be dyed. | Lustrous, supple pelt with bright luster. Marking should be attractive. | **Marten**<br>American | See also sable.<br>Long, silky guard hairs and dense underfur. Color ranges from blue-brown to dark brown. | Texture and clarity of color. |
| **Chinchilla** | A short, dense, very silky fur. Originally from South America but now wholly ranch raised. | Lustrous slate-blue top hair and dark underfur, although mutation colors are now available. | Baum<br><br>Stone | Softer, silkier, and shinier than American marten.<br>The finest marten has soft, thick guard hairs and a bluish-brown cast with pale underfur. | |
| **Coyote** | A long-haired fur, often pale gray or tan in color. Durable and warm. | Long guard hair and thick, soft underfur. | **Mink**<br><br>Mutation | Soft and lightweight, with lustrous guard hairs and dense underfur.<br>Most colors of any natural ranched fur, from white to grays, blues, and beiges. | Natural luster and clarity of color. Fur should be full and dense. |
| **Ermine** | A fur with very silky white guard hairs and dense underfur. | Clear white color. | Ranch<br><br>Wild<br>Pieced* | Color ranges from a true, rich brown to a deep brownish black.<br>Generally brown in color. Color and pattern depend on pieces used. This is the least expensive mink. | Pattern and well-made seams. |
| **Fox** | The widest range of natural mutation colors of any fur except mink; silver, blue, white, red, cross, beige, gray, and brown. Can also be dyed in a wide variety of colors. | Long, glossy guard hairs and thick soft underfur; clarity of color. | **Nutria** | Similar to beaver, often sheared for a sporty, more lightweight feel. Popular for linings and trims. Often dyed in a variety of colors. | Clarity of color. |
| **Lamb**<br>American<br>processed | Pelts of fine wool sheep sheared to show the pattern near the skin. Naturally white but may be dyed. | Silky, lustrous moire pattern, not too curly. | **Rabbit** | Generally long hair in a variety of natural colors, including 14 natural mutation colors in ranch rabbit. May be sheared and grooved. Not very durable, shed easily. | Silky texture and uniformity of colors. |
| Broadtail | A natural (unsheared) flat moire pattern. Color may be natural browns, gray, black, or dyed in more exotic colors. | Silky texture and uniformity of pattern. | | | |
| Mongolian | Long, wavy, silky guard hair. May be natural off-white, bleached, or dyed in more exotic colors. | Silky texture, with wavy—not frizzy—hair. | **Raccoon** | Long silver, black-tipped guard hairs over wooly underfur. May also be plucked and sheared and dyed. | Silvery cast. Plenty of guard hair with heavy underfur. |
| Mouton | Pelts are sheared; hairs are straightened for soft, water-repellent fur, generally dyed brown. | Uniformity of shearing. | **Sable** | Member of marten family. Russian sable has a silver cast, the most expensive. Crown sable is brown with a blue coat. Canadian golden sable, an amber tone, is less expensive. | Soft, deep fur in dark, lustrous brown, with silky guard hairs. |
| Shearling | Natural sheepskin (lamb pelt), with the leather side sueded and worn outside. The fur side (or inside) is often sheared. | Softness of leather side and even shearing. | | | |
| Persian<br>lamb | From karakul sheep raised in Southwest Africa or central Asia. Traditionally black, brown, and gray, new mutation colors available; also dyed. | Silky curls or ripples of fur and soft, light, pliable leather. | **Tanuki** | Also called Japanese raccoon. Color is light amber brown with distinctive cross markings. | Clarity of color and dense, full texture. |

LAMBSWOOL    FOX    LYNX    MINK

*The same piecing technique can be used for almost any fur. The most common pieced furs are mink, sable, marten, fox, Persian lamb, raccoon, and beaver.

Adapted from a number of sources, including the booklet *Choosing Fur* published jointly by the Fur Council of Canada and the Fur Information Council of America, Herndon, Virginia, pp. 4–5.

older ones. Persian lamb, shunned by fur buyers for over two generations, has now made a comeback. Remembered as a fur that was used for grandmother's conservative coat, Persian lamb, which is flat enough to be cut almost like cloth, is now being put to new uses. It is a prime choice in new fur garments such as scarfs, sweaters, and jackets.

Sometimes an interest in a fur comes about because fur manufacturers invent a finishing technique that makes a fur seem new. A renewed interest in raccoon can be traced to a technique that eliminated much of its bulkiness. In the 1940s, beaver was invariably sheared to look like a short fur; today it is sometimes left unplucked, giving it a totally new look. Or beaver may be sheared and have multicolored insets.

## Animal Rights Groups

Over the past 30 years, animal rights groups have protested the wearing of animal fur as cruel and inhumane. Some groups are opposed to trapping fur-bearing animals in the wild. Others also protest fur farming. Some groups, such as PETA (People for the Ethical Treatment of Animals) and the Friends of Animals, have staged confrontations and demonstrations to get media attention (see Figure 7.9). Longstanding activists Carnie Wilson, Pamela Anderson, Kim Basinger, Tyra Banks, and Joaquin Phoenix were all used as endorsements in PETA antifur campaigns that coincided with the New York Fashion Week. Some activists have thrown paint at women wearing furs. Others have picketed fur stores and industry trade fairs. Still other groups, such as the Animal Liberation Front, have raided mink and fox farms and let the animals loose. They also destroyed pedigree cards containing irreplaceable genetic data.[5]

The industry response has been strong on a number of fronts. It is working with the U.S. and Canadian governments and the International Standards Organization to develop global humane trapping standards. Fur farmers are proposing legislation to make the crime of releasing fur-bearing animals a felony. Associations of American and

FIGURE 7.9  PETA's demonstrations and antifur campaigns atract media attention.

Canadian fur farmers have also offered rewards for information leading to the arrest of fur raiders. Fur auction houses are offering farmers vandalism insurance. The industry has done a great deal of consumer education to stress that today's farmed furs come from only nonendangered species. They also stress that:

- Fur farms do not remove animals from the wild.
- Ninety-five percent of U.S. mink production comes from farms certified as humane.
- Unlike manufactured (fake) fur, real fur does not use nonrenewable petroleum by-products.

## Manufactured Furs

Manufactured, synthetic, or "fake" furs were long regarded as beneath the notice of serious designers and were limited to inexpensive garments. Technological developments and animal rights activism changed that view. The new manufactured furs look so good that fashion writers have dropped the word *fake* and began calling them *faux* furs. (*Faux* is the French word for false.)

The improved synthetic furs are used by a wide range of designers for higher-priced garments that still cost less than real fur. In 1999, Oleg Cassini unveiled a 100-piece fake fur line in a show sponsored by the Humane Society. The event was videotaped so that many people could view the show. Named the "Evolutionary Fur," the fake fur line retailed from $500 to $1,000 and was carried in major department stores. Since then, some designers, such as Calvin Klein, Betsey Johnson, and Stella McCartney, still shun real fur as a matter of principle and use fakes instead. However, many industry observers feel that the fur industry has profited from the popularity of both real and manufactured fur.

## Real Fur versus Fake Fur

Imitation is the greatest form of flattery. The proliferation of fake or faux fur only proves that fur is in! But, no matter how good the fake (see Figure 7.10, top), it will never have the warmth, the feel, or the durability of real fur (see Figure 7.10, bottom).

A strong argument against faux fur, from an

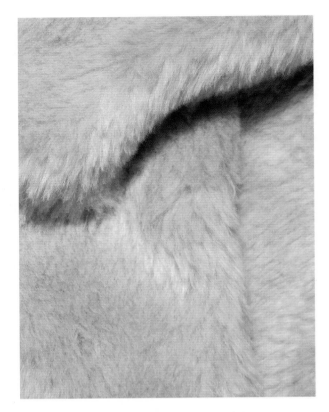

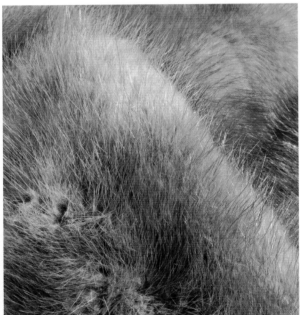

**FIGURE 7.10** No matter how good the fake fur looks (top), it will never have the warmth, the feel, or the durability of real fur (bottom).

environmental standpoint, is that most of it is made from natural resources (such as oil) that are limited in availability, while fur is a renewable resource. The manufacture of fake fur also releases harmful chemicals into the atmosphere.

In the Environmental Consequences of Textile

Marketing study undertaken by Oregon State University, a broad range of textiles, including wool, leather, fur, cotton, silk, linen, rayon, polyester, nylon, and acrylic, were evaluated across a number of environmental variables. For a textile to be considered compatible with the environment, it had to be nonpolluting to obtain, process, fabricate, maintain, and dispose; 100 percent biodegradable; longlasting; renewable; reusable; natural/nontoxic; energy efficient to obtain and produce; and its production had to produce minimal waste. In composite scoring across all environmental criteria, the farmed and wild fur outperformed all other textiles.

## Organization and Operation

The fur industry in the United States is divided into three groups, which also represent the three stages of fur production: (1) the trappers, farmers, and ranchers who produce the pelts and sell them at auction; (2) the fur-processing companies; and (3) the manufacturers of fur products.

### Pelt Production

The first step in the production of fur is to obtain the necessary pelts. A **pelt** is the skin of a fur-bearing animal.

Trappers are the primary source of wild-animal pelts, which must be taken only during the coldest season of the year in order to be of prime quality. Trappers sell pelts to nearby country stores or directly to itinerant buyers. In some areas, collectors or receiving houses accept pelts for sale on consignment from trappers or local merchants. When enough pelts have been gathered, a fur merchant exports them or sends them to an auction house, or they are sold at a private sale through a broker.

Most furs come from farms or ranches, where fur-bearing animals are bred and raised strictly for their fur. Almost all mink, rabbit, fox, and more recently, chinchilla, Persian lamb, and broadtail are ranched. Fur farming offers two important advantages. First, animals can be raised under controlled conditions. Second, they can be bred selectively. When wild mink roamed North America, they came in one color, a dark brown with reddish highlights. Today, many beautiful colors, some of which are trademarked and denote a manufacturer's private label, are available. Among the better-known names are Azurene, Lunaraine, Rovalia, Lutetia, Jasmin, Tourmaline, Cerulean, and the most recognizable name of all, Blackgama.[6]

### Fur Auctions

Fur pelts are sold at auctions today, much as they were in the 13th century. Fur buyers and manufacturers bid on the pelts, which are sold in bundles. Buyers look for bundles that are matched in quality and color (see Figure 7.11). This enables a manufacturer to make up a garment of uniform beauty.

Recently, competition has increased among buyers to purchase a "top bundle"—that is, an unusually beautiful bundle that goes for an unusually high price. This, in turn, results in a much-touted coat—often costing $100,000 or more—that is made from the top bundle.

The auction trail is an international one, although except for England, Tokyo, and more recently, Beijing, each market sells indigenous furs. Fur buyers from the United States travel to Canada, Scandinavia, China, and Russia. To buy North American furs, fur buyers travel to auction houses in New York, Seattle, Toronto, and North Bay, Canada.

**FIGURE 7.11** When buyers purchase pelts, they look for bundles that are matched in quality and color.

# Then & NOW

## From Hermès to Eternity
### *From Harnesses and Saddles to Handbags and Scarfs*

It all began with Thierry Hermès, the sixth child of an innkeeper, born a French citizen in Germany. Hermès went to Paris when he became an orphan. He found he was a gifted leather worker and opened a shop in 1837. Hermès specialized in horse harnesses! As Robert B. Chavey, president and CEO of Hermès USA, said, "We never forget that the horse was our first customer." It was a business built on the strength of a stitch that can only be done by hand: the saddle stitch. The saddle stitch requires two needles working two waxed linen threads in tensile opposition. It is a handsome, graphic stitch, and done properly, it will never came loose.

In 1850, Hermès added custom saddlery to his shop's services, a process that required measurements from both horse and rider. In the 19th century another Hermès institution was added: the wait. It got its name because hand-stitched perfection cannot be rushed. royal coronations were sometimes delayed until Hermès fittings for the carriage and the guard had arrived. Now, in the 21st century, the "wait" for items such as the Kelly and Birkin bags can be up to 5 years!

In the early 1920s, Hermès understood that the demand for saddlery was bound to dwindle, so he turned Hermès' leather-working expertise to the making of "saddle-stitched" leather goods and trunks for the growing number

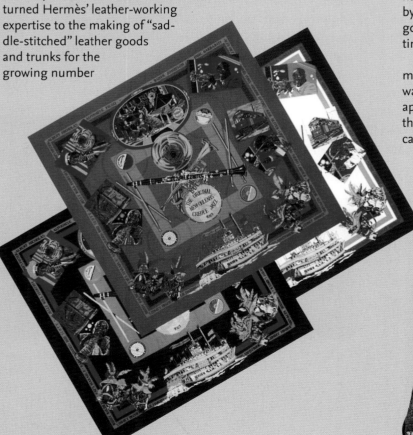

of customers traveling by car, train, ship, and eventually airplane.

Today, Hermès' flagship products are leather handbags, clutches, briefcases, and luggage, crafted by more than a thousand saddlery and leather goods craftspeople in its production facility in Pantin, outside of Paris. That was then; this is now.

Celebrating its 170th anniversary in 2007, Hermès is now a "luxury" brand, and when customers want incomparable leather goods, scarfs, ties, apparel, and iconic jewelry and watches, they go to the 283 stores worldwide that carry the name Hermès.

### Fur Processing

After manufacturers of fur goods buy the pelts, they contract with fur-dressing and fur-dyeing firms to process them.

The job of fur dressers is to make the pelts suitable for use in consumer products. The pelts are first softened by soaking and mechanical means. Then a flesher removes any unwanted substances from the inner surface of the skin. For less expensive furs, this is done by roller-type machines. At this point, the pelts are treated with solutions that tan the skin side into pliable leather. The fur side may be processed at the same time. This involves either plucking unwanted guard hairs or shearing the underfur to make the fur more lightweight. Although fur dressing has traditionally been a handcraft industry, modern technology is turning it into a more mechanical process.

After dressing, the pelts may go to a dyer. Fur dyes were once made from vegetable matter but are now mostly derived from chemical compounds. New dyes are constantly being developed, making it possible to dye fur more successfully and in more shades than ever before.

### Fur Manufacturing

Most fur manufacturers are small, independently owned and operated shops, although a few large companies have emerged largely as a result of the explosion in the number of fur products. New York City's fur district on Seventh Avenue between 23rd and 30th Streets is the main center for fur manufacturing.

The production of fur garments lends itself neither to mass production nor to large-scale operations. Skill and judgment are required at every stage of manufacturing. Doing each step by hand lets a worker deal with each pelt's color, quality, and peculiarities.

The following steps transform pelts into finished garments:

1. A design of the garment is sketched.
2. A paper pattern is made of the garment.

3. A canvas pattern is made.
4. The skins are cut to conform to the designer's sketch, exhibit the fur to its best advantage, and minimize waste.
5. The cut skins are sewn together.
6. The skins are wetted and then stapled to a board to dry, a process that sets them permanently.
7. The garment sections are sewn together.
8. The garment is lined and finished.
9. The garment is inspected.

For some luxurious furs, the cutting operation becomes extremely complex. Short skins must be **let out** to a suitable length for garments (see Figure 7.12). Letting out mink, for example, involves cutting each skin down the center of a dark vertical line of fur (the grotzen stripe). Each half skin must then be cut at an angle into diagonal strips one-eighth to three-sixteenths of an inch wide. Then each tiny strip is resewn at an angle to the strips above and below it to make a long, narrow skin. The other half-skin is sewn in a similar manner.

The two halves are then joined, resulting in a longer, slimmer pelt that is more beautiful than the original. Considerable hand labor is required to do all of these operations. Ten miles of thread and over 1,200 staples may be used in a single coat.

In an industry that for generations has produced furs in much the same way as in ancient times, a revolutionary process was developed through technology in 1989. The famous Fendi sisters of Italy showed an entire collection of furs based on a new process that made them all, from sables to squirrels, reversible. Interfacing, lining, and construction are all eliminated, and the result is fur coats of incredible lightness and minimal bulk. These coats are so light, in fact, that a full-length fur coat can be folded up and put into a knapsack. Changing from the fur side to the leather side can be done in a minute, and there is no bulky look—no matter which side is outside. The fact that all inner construction was eliminated changed the look of the coats themselves. Eliminating the shoulder pads makes everything fit naturally, and the lightness of the fur makes them swing and swirl as if made of chiffon.

## Retail Distribution of Furs

There are more than fifteen hundred retail stores across the United States that specialize in furs. While some are chain operations, 85 percent of fur retailers are small, family-owned businesses. That said, the line between manufacturing and retailing is less clear in the fur industry than in most other industries. Retail fur merchants, for example, typically make up an assortment of garments to sell off the rack to customers, but they also maintain a supply of skins in their workroom for custom work.

In retail stores, fur departments are either leased or consignment departments. Both operations permit a retail store to offer its customers a large selection without tying up a lot of capital in inventory.

A **leased department** is situated in the store but run by an independent merchant (such as Maximillian at Bloomingdale's), who pays a percentage of sales to the store as rent. The operator either owns or leases the stock. Lessees often run several similar departments in many stores and can, if necessary, move garments and skins from one location to another. Lessees, who are a unique kind of retailer, are usually well capitalized and have expert knowledge in both furs and retailing.

**FIGURE 7.12** This worker is letting out this short-skin fur to make a longer garment.

In **consignment selling**, a fur manufacturer supplies merchandise to a retail store, which has the option of returning unsold items. In effect, the manufacturer lends stock to a store. Consignment selling is influenced by the state of the economy. When interest rates are high, stores tend to buy less stock.

## Merchandising and Marketing

Fur traders, dressers, producers, and their labor unions all work through their various trade associations to encourage the demand for fur.

### Trade Associations

Trade associations mount their own campaigns to promote furs, and they also work with retailers. The leading trade association is the Fur Information Council of America (FICA) (see Figure 7.13), which represents fur retailers and manufacturers. It has placed ads in various fashion magazines to counter some of the animal-rights arguments.

The ranch mink association, American Legend, is a nonprofit cooperative formed through the combination of two major mink-producing groups: Emba Mink Breeders Association (EMBA) and Great Lakes Mink Association (GLMA). With more than a thousand members, American Legend now markets about 70 percent of the total American mink production at the Seattle Fur Exchange.[7] It has a program to protect its trademarks from infringement. The association supplies labels and other point-of-purchase materials only to retailers and manufacturers who can prove they purchased the group's pelts at an American Legend auction.

Trade associations not only monitor the industry but also help to educate consumers. Fur is a product that is most successfully purchased when the consumer has some specialized knowledge about what he or she is buying. Consumers need to know, for example, that the rarer the breed, the more expensive the fur. Mink is sold at a wide variety of

**FIGURE 7.13** The "Runway Report" from the Fur Information Council of America (FICA) features the latest fur fashions and trends.

price points, with the commercial mink coat in the early 2000s priced anywhere from $2,499 to $5,999. The moderate mink can be purchased for $6,000 to $9,999, while on the upper end, one can expect to spend as much as $50,000.[8]

Another important factor in the quality of fur is whether the pelts are female or male. Most female skins are softer and lighter. Although there are exceptions, such as fitch, for which the male skins are preferred, a coat of female mink costs more than one of male skins.

### International Fur Fairs

As the demand for fur increases, and the world supply of fur pelts decreases, people are traveling far-

**TABLE 7.4** *Leading International Fur Fairs*

| SITE | NAME OF FAIR | MONTH HELD |
|------|--------------|------------|
| Tokyo | Japan International Fashion Fair Outerwear | February |
| Hong Kong | Hong Kong International Fur & Fashion Fair | February |
| Milan | Mifur Fur & Leather Exhibition | March |
| Lausanne | Comispiel | March |
| Moscow | Moda Spring & Mexa Fall | March, October |
| Frankfurt | Frankfurt International Outerwear Fair | March, October |
| Montreal | North American Fur & Fashion Outerwear Expo | May |

ther than ever before to get the best buys. Designers, manufacturers, retailers, importers and exporters, wholesalers, and the media all attend one or more of the leading international fur fairs listed in Table 7.4.

## Labeling

The Fur Products Labeling Act of 1952 requires that all furs be labeled according to:

1. The English name of the animal
2. Its country of origin
3. The type of processing, including dyeing, to which the pelts have been subjected
4. Whether or not parts have been cut from a used garment or from the less desirable paw or tail sections

Years ago, such labeling would have been helpful, for example, to prevent a customer from buying a less expensive, dyed muskrat that was touted as the much rarer and more expensive Hudson seal. Today, such labeling is helpful in distinguishing one fur from another in an industry that, without intending to defraud, has learned to capitalize on fashion trends by treating less expensive furs to look like more expensive ones.

## Trends in the Fur Industry

As a general rule, the demand for furs is related to the economy. During the Depression, fur sales dropped off dramatically. After World War II, when the economy was expanding, fur sales boomed. In the early 1970s, conservationists' concerns about the diminishing wildlife species put a temporary damper on fur sales, but the industry rebounded in the 1980s. Mid-1987 saw the highest point, the $2 billion mark. But in the early 1990s, a combination of antifur activism and mild winters brought a rapid downturn in fur sales. Synthetic fur sales rose rapidly. But then the record-breaking bad weather in the mid-1990s saw a renewed interest in real fur. Sales in 2000 increased 21 percent over 1999, to $1.69 billion.[9] Industry experts say the outlook for the fur industry continues to be good.

Growth will be affected by the following four major trends:

- Renewed fashion interest in furs
- Increased foreign trade
- Restrictive legislation that actually helps the industry
- New channels of retail distribution

### Renewed Fashion Interest

Once worn only by the rich or for formal occasions, furs are now bought and worn by many kinds of consumers for many occasions. The average customer no longer buys one conservatively cut coat, either. Furs are now sporty and casual, elegant and classic, or faddish and trendy (see Figure 7.14)—and with such choices, many customers have been persuaded to buy more than one.

Not only have older women—the traditional market—continued to buy furs, but the market has expanded to young and working women as well. In the 1970s and 1980s, a new market opened up for fur—namely, women themselves. For many years, women received fur coats only as gifts. They seldom bought this luxury item for themselves. But in the 1970s and 1980s, when more women started working and also began to get paid more for their work, they started buying furs for themselves, thus creating, in effect, a new market—one that the fur industry has been quick to recognize and expand upon.

Odd as it seems today, fur advertising had always been directed at men buying fur coats as gifts for women.

Fur manufacturers are exploring other new markets as well. For most of history, men as well as women wore furs, but in the past 100 years, the fur coat became almost exclusively a woman's garment. In the early 1980s, men once again began wearing fur coats. The fur industry is also expanding into new products, using fur to make garments, such as vests, sweaters, and dresses that have not traditionally been made of fur.

Finally, the growing excitement and sales of fur have led to big-name designers entering the field or expanding their fur collections. In 1985, only 42 fashion designers created fur garments. By 2007, more than 400 designers were working with fur.[10] French designers—among them Christian Dior, Yves Saint Laurent, Karl Lagerfeld, and Jean-Paul Gaultier (see Figure 7.15)—are also presenting furs. Italian designers such as Fendi, Valentino, and Soldano are known for their innovative techniques.

The fur industry—from breeder to manufacturers, to retailers, to customers—has changed drastically in the first decade of the 21st century. This is most evident from a style and design standpoint, where more youth-oriented styles are being paraded down the runways.

Some American designers, such as Oscar de la Renta and Jerry Sorbara, have produced fur collections for years. A trio of designers—Marc Jacobs, Byron Lars, and Michael Kors—have developed signature looks over the past few seasons and have already established a following of fashion insiders. An important addition to this group is Dennis Basso, who retails his fur designs.

Canadian designers have traditionally worked with fur. D'Arcy Moses presents themes of Canada's indigenous peoples in furs inset with patterns of

**FIGURE 7.14** Elegant or casual, furs come in all colors and shapes (left). **FIGURE 7.15** Jean Paul Gaultier sends these models down the runway wearing pelts (right) and a beaver hat (middle).

forest and eagle feathers. Fellow Canadian Paula Lishman is famous for her knit fur and washable fur-with-cotton knits. And Zuki made waves with his eye-popping "op-art" sheared beaver coats.

### Increased Foreign Trade

The export market is strong for the American fur industry, not only because of the variety of furs that are available but also because of the reputation for quality in U.S. pelt dressing. The United States produces innovative, high-style furs that are in great demand around the world.

### New Legislation

The Federal Trade Commission and the fur industry are constantly engaged in talks about fur labeling. Ironically, the most important recent legislation, which was intended to restrict the fur industry, has actually been a boom to sales. The Endangered Species Act of 1973 forbade the sale of furs made from endangered species such as leopard, tiger, ocelot, cheetah, jaguar, vicuna, and a few types of wolf. Since women no longer have to worry about wearing an endangered species, many have returned to the fur market.

### New Channels of Retail Distribution

Fur manufacturers have sought other distribution channels in addition to the retail outlets that they have opened.

Hotel, armory, and arena fur sales are held almost every fall and winter weekend in New York City and other large cities. Fur manufacturers can conduct these sales for a fraction of the cost in wages and rent that would be required if they were to maintain comparable facilities year round. Even better, the average hotel ballroom, armory, or arena showroom is suitable for displaying thousands of coats, far more than the average fur salon can attractively exhibit. The sales appeal to customers, who like the hands-on approach and lower prices. The same customers who frequent weekend sales also can shop in manufacturer-leased discount and off-price stores such as Filene's, Syms, and Loehmanns'.

### Summary and Review

In America, the tanning of leather for clothing and footwear dates back to the precolonial Native American populations. Today, the industry consists of three major types of businesses: regular tanneries, contract tanneries, and converters.

Most leather comes from cattle as an offshoot of the meatpacking industry, but leather is also produced from the pelts of eight other animal groups. Tanneries tend to specialize according to the end use of the leather. Tanning may involve one or more processes using minerals, vegetable materials, oils, and chemicals, alone or in combination, to achieve the desired color and textural finish.

Leather Industries of America (LIA), the industry's trade association, advises its members on fashion and technical issues and promotes the industry to its markets.

Fur has been used for warmth in clothing and shelter since prehistoric times. Fur trading, especially in beaver skins, was a major industry in the European colonization of America, and it remained so well into the 19th century. For much of the 20th century, fur was considered a luxury fashion item for women, but in recent years, fur has been used as a trim for various types of apparel, and men's furs have become a growing market. The efforts of animal rights activists, periods of economic downturn, and competition from imports and from faux furs have challenged the industry, but most recently, economic prosperity and industry campaigns to educate the public about humane industry practices have had a positive effect on sales.

The fur industry is made up of three groups: (1) trappers, farmers, and ranchers, (2) fur-processing companies, who buy furs at auctions, and (3) manufacturers of fur products. Processing pelts and turning them into fashion products require skilled labor, although some mechanization has been introduced into processing. The distinction between levels in the fur industry is less precise than in other segments of the fashion industry. Because of the specialized knowledge and the financial investment required, furs are often sold to consumers by consignment or leased departments in retail stores, by mail order, or in manufacturers' shows in hotels or other large spaces.

## Trade Talk

Define or briefly explain the following terms:

| | |
|---|---|
| consignment selling | contract tanneries |
| converters | let out |
| fur farming | hide |
| kips | leased department |
| pelt | PETA |
| regular tanneries | skins |
| sustainable use | tanning |

## For Review

1. In what ways have technological advances in machinery and chemistry benefited the leather industry?
2. Name and describe the three major types of companies in the leather industry.
3. What are the nine major groups of fur-bearing animals?
4. What has Leather Industries of America done to broaden the leather market and soften the impact of competition from synthetics?

5. What factors point to growth for the leather industry?
6. Describe the history and development of the fur industry in the United States.
7. Into what three groups is the fur industry divided? Briefly describe the function of each.
8. What are the advantages of fur farming over trapping?
9. Outline the steps in transforming processed fur pelts into finished garments.
10. Differentiate between leased departments and consignment selling as these terms apply to retail distribution of fur garments. What major advantages does each have for retail merchants?

## For Discussion

1. Discuss the following statement from the text and its implications for leather merchandising: "The leather industry not only must stay abreast of fashion, it must be several steps ahead of it."
2. Discuss current trends in the leather industry that relate to (a) enlarging markets, (b) competition from synthetics, (c) increased foreign trade.
3. Discuss the pros and cons of trapping and raising animals for their fur. Explain your support or rejection of the arguments advanced by animal rights activists and by the fur industry.
4. Discuss current trends in the fur industry as they relate to (a) fashion interest, (b) increased foreign trade, (c) new channels of retail distribution, (d) low-cost imports, (e) rising overhead, and (f) lack of skilled workers and managers.

# unit three

Fashion has many faces—different faces for different places, different looks for different years. Fashion is also products, and products have a past. The history of a product includes all the designers and manufacturers who have watched their customers and are always trying to give them what they want.

Fashion fascinates, it holds our interest, and it even appears in our dreams. This is quite an extraordinary challenge for the producers of fashion.

In the past few decades, the fashion apparel manufacturing business has changed from an industry composed of many small companies into a much larger one dominated by a growing group of giants. This has changed the way apparel is designed, manufactured, and merchandised. Large companies can afford to invest in the newest technology. Technology, in turn, has helped make high style and quality accessible to everyone. This unit explores several aspects of apparel production.

# THE SECONDARY LEVEL: THE PRODUCERS OF APPAREL

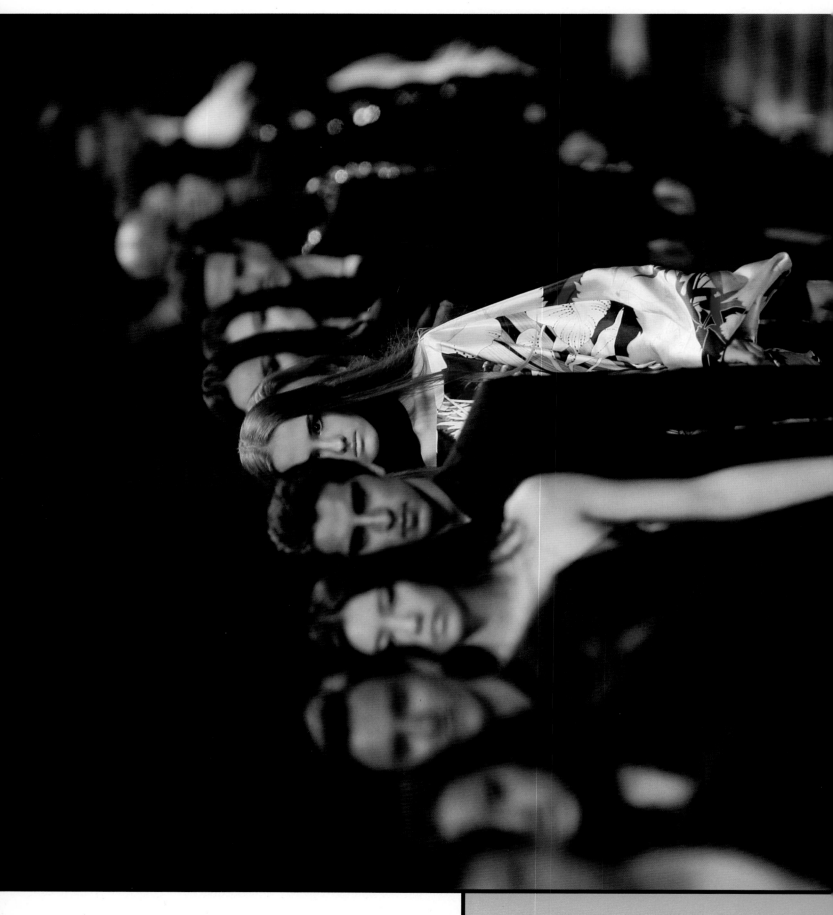

chapter eight

KEY CONCEPTS

• The major advantages and disadvantages of the contractor system

• The six-stage process of developing and producing a line

• The major industry practices of licensing, private-label and specification buying, offshore production, CAD/CAM use of factors, and chargebacks

• Industry trends, such as brand extensions, globalization, and industry cooperation

• The Quick Response movement and the mass customization theory and their effects on the product development chain

• The new SIC/NAICS codes and how manufacturers and retailers can use them

*Everything you always wanted to know*

*about the product development process*

*in the apparel and fashion related industries.*

# Product Development

The level of activity in textile and apparel product development has been steadily increasing. This increase in activity, together with the global manufacturing and assembly practices, has integrated product development into the mainstream business-decision structure of all fashion industry firms, from manufacturers to retailers.

If new apparel and fashion-related products are not developed, sales and profits decline, technology and markets change, or innovation by other firms makes the original product obsolete. All of this points to the importance of product development for the continued success of a company.

**Product development** is the teaming of market and trend research with the merchandising, design, and technical processes that develop a final product. Product development is used by both wholesale manufacturers, who develop products for a signature brand, and retailers who use it for private-label development for their own stores.

Whether making plain T-shirts or elaborate evening gowns, the men's, women's, and children's apparel industries in the United States have managed to settle into a basic cycle of design and production that repeats itself more or less unchanged from season to season. However, before an article of

clothing reaches the retail store racks, a great deal of work and planning are involved. (There are similar cycles for accessories, cosmetics and fragrances, and home fashions; they are discussed in Unit Four.) This chapter focuses on the design and production of apparel for men, women, and children; subsequent chapters examine each area in detail.

## What Is a Product Line, and Who Develops It?

Product lines of apparel are created and styled for wholesale presentation several times, or seasons, per year. In the fashion industries, a product line is simply called a *line*. A line not only encompasses the individual item of apparel or accessories but the entire season's production from that manufacturer as well. The term line is used for moderate- and popular-priced apparel. The term **collection** describes an expensive line in the United States or in Europe. Lines are divided into **groups** of garments, linked by a common theme like color, fabric, or style (see Figure 8.1). Each garment is known by a style number or "number," such as 401 or 57.

It is important to note here that in the United States, designs cannot be copyrighted, as they are in France. Copying from creative designers is common throughout the fashion industry; it is not considered piracy. At some firms, few if any designs are original; rather they are copied **line-for-line** in a similar fabric, or adapted from another designer in a cheaper fabric (knockoffs), or reworked from a previous season in a different color or fabric (**anchors**).

Designers typically work on three seasonal lines at a time. They monitor the sales of the *current* season's line, put the finishing touches on *next* season's line, while they begin to develop the new line for the *following* season. Clearly, this is a challenging balancing act!

Clothing manufacturers produce between four and six lines every year. For women's wear, these are spring, summer, transitional or fall I, fall or fall II, resort, and holiday (see Table 8.1).

Many firms, however, add new styles to lines

**FIGURE 8.1** Christian Dior's fall/winter collection, 2007.

**TABLE 8.1** *Seasonal Lines*

| NAME OF LINE | WHEN SHOWN |
|---|---|
| Spring | September (New York), October (Los Angeles and Dallas) |
| Summer | Early January |
| Transitional or fall I | February |
| Fall or fall II | February |
| Resort | June (New York), July (Miami), August (Dallas) |
| Holiday | July (New York), August (Dallas) |

throughout the year to keep buyers "shopping" their lines to see what is new. Or, at a minimum, they update styles or change the fabrics used in the line (see Figure 8.2). Conversely, as new styles are added, old ones are dropped.

Manufacturers start work on their new lines anywhere between 3 and 12 months before presentation to retail buyers. This means clothes are planned and designed as much as a year before customers see them in the stores.

**FIGURE 8.2** Chanel's couture and ready-to-wear (RTW) for 2007 and 2008 (top left to right): spring/summer RTW, spring/summer couture, fall/winter RTW; (bottom, left to right): fall/winter couture, resort collection, spring/summer RTW.

Now we examine the roles played by the merchandiser, the designer, and the producer.

## Role of the Merchandiser

The merchandiser is the person who channels the creativity of the designer and design staff so that the six "rights" of merchandising can be successfully accomplished. These rights are the right merchandise, at the right price, at the right time, in the right place, in the right quantity, with the right promotion. To these rights must be added another one—the right customer! Because this customer is so important, the merchandiser is given the responsibility to research who the "right" customer is.

Some people in the industry have described the merchandiser as the "glue" that holds the whole product development concept together. In fact, the merchandiser is the liaison among the design staff, the production facilities, and the sales staff. The merchandiser has to view the line from the design point of view and also has to be knowledgeable about production and sales efforts.

## Role of the Designer

Designers can create by sketching (croquis), by drawing on a computer (computer-aided design [CAD]), or by draping cloth on a model. In addition to looking for artistic excellence, designers must keep practical business considerations in mind. All designs must be produced at a profit and within the firm's wholesale price range. Consequently, designers must keep in mind the availability and cost of materials, the cost of cutting and sewing the garment, and labor costs.

Most U.S. designers who use their artistic and innovative talents to design fashion-oriented merchandise fall into one of three categories:

- High-fashion or "name" designers
- Stylist-designers
- Freelance artist-designers

**High-fashion designers** are usually referred to in this country as "name" designers. Because of the success and originality of their designs, name designers are well known to fashion-conscious customers. High-fashion designers are responsible not only for creating the designs but also for the choice of fabric, texture, and color in which each design is to be executed. They may often be involved in development of the production model as well as in plans for the promotion of a firm's line. Some name designers work for fashion houses, as does John Galliano for Dior. Others, like Oscar de la Renta and Anna Sui, own their own firms or are financed by a "silent partner" outside the firm. Still others, like Ralph Lauren and Donna Karan, are publicly owned corporations that are listed on a stock exchange.

Designer names were once associated only with original, expensive designs in apparel. Then, beginning in 1922 with Chanel, many designers licensed their names to fragrances. Today, most name designers also license their names to manufacturers of accessories and home furnishings.

**Stylist-designers** use their creative talents to adapt or change the successful designs of others. A stylist-designer must understand fabric and garment construction as well as the manufacturing process, because designs are usually adapted at lower prices. Stylist-designers usually create designs at the late rise or early culmination stages of the fashion cycle. They are usually not involved in details relating to the production of the firm's line or in the planning of its promotional activities. Rather, their focus is on designing within the limits of the firm's production capacity and capability. Stylist-designers who work in a firm that sells to major retail store chains often accompany the firm's salespeople to define the look or to learn firsthand what the retail store buyer wants.

Freelance artist-designers sell their sketches to manufacturers. They may work independently at home or from a design studio. These sketches may be original designs by the freelancer or adaptations of a design furnished by the manufacturer. The sketches may reflect the freelancer's own ideas or the manufacturer's detailed specifications. With the delivery of a sketch to the manufacturer, a freelancer's job ends, and he or she goes on to another project.

### Role of the Producer

The fashion apparel industry consists of three types of producers: manufacturers, jobbers, and contractors. An **apparel manufacturer** is one who performs all the operations required to produce apparel, from buying the fabric to selling and shipping the finished garments. An **apparel jobber** handles the designing, the planning, the purchasing, usually the cutting, the selling, and the shipping, but not the actual sewing operation. An **apparel contractor** is a producer whose sole function is to supply sewing services to the industry, where it is sometimes called an **outside shop**. Contractors that specialize in the production of one product are sometimes called **item houses**. Increasingly, the term manufacturer is being used more loosely to describe any firm that handles any part of the cutting or sewing process, and the terms jobber and contractor are used less often.

### Manufacturers

A manufacturer, by definition, is a producer who handles all phases of a garment's production. The staff produces the original design or buys an acceptable design from a freelance designer. Each line is planned by the company executives. The company purchases the fabric and trimmings needed. The cutting and sewing are usually done in the company's factories. On certain occasions, however, a manufacturer may use the services of a contractor if sales of an item exceed the capacity of the firm's sewing facilities and if shipping deadlines cannot otherwise be met. The company's sales force and traffic department handle the selling and shipping of the finished goods. One great advantage of this type of operation is that close quality control can be maintained. When producers contract out some part of their work, they cannot as effectively monitor its quality.

### Apparel Jobbers

Apparel jobbers handle all phases of the production of a garment except for the actual sewing and sometimes the cutting. A jobber firm may employ a design staff to create various seasonal lines or may buy sketches from freelance designers. The jobber's staff buys the fabric and trimmings necessary to produce the styles in each line, makes up samples, and grades the patterns. In most cases, the staff also cuts the fabric for the various parts of each garment. Jobbers, however, do not actually sew and finish garments. Instead, they arrange with outside factories run by contractors to perform these manufacturing operations. The sales staff takes orders for garments in each line, and the shipping department fills store orders from the finished garments returned by the contractor. (Note that apparel jobbers are involved in manufacturing, whereas most other "jobbers" buy finished goods and sell them to small users who are not able to place large orders.)

### Contractors

Contractors usually specialize in just one phase of the production of a garment: sewing. In some cases contractors also perform the cutting operation from patterns submitted by a jobber or a manufacturer. Contractors developed early in the history of the fashion industry, with the beginning of mass-production techniques. Contractors serve those producers who have little or no sewing capability of their own as well as those whose current business exceeds their own capacity. Sometimes a subcontractor is used by the initial contractor to perform specialized work that the initial contractor is not equipped to perform, such as beading or embroidery. When there is a very large order, a subcontractor may be used to produce the overbooked production.

If a contractor is used, cut pieces of the garment are provided by the manufacturer. For an agreed price per garment, the article is sewn, finished, inspected, pressed, hung, or packaged, and returned to the manufacturer for shipment to retail stores.

In the mass production of ready-to-wear apparel, a single sewing-machine operator rarely makes a complete garment. Each operator sews only a certain section of the garment, such as a sleeve or a hem. This division of labor, called **section work** or **piecework**, makes it unnecessary for an operator to switch from one highly specialized machine to another or to make adjustments on the machine. Any change or adjustment in equipment takes time and increases labor costs. In the fashion trade, time lost in making such changes also causes delays in getting a style to consumers. Delays in production could mean the loss of timeliness and sales appeal before an article reaches market.

A contractor may arrange to work exclusively with one or more jobbers or manufacturers, reserving the right to work for others whenever the contractor's facilities are not fully employed. Such agreements are necessarily reciprocal. If a contractor agrees to give preference to a particular jobber's or manufacturer's work, the jobber or manufacturer gives preference to that contractor when placing sewing orders.

The advantages and disadvantages of the contractor system for the manufacturer are as follows:

Advantages:
- Large amounts of capital are not required for investment in sewing equipment that may soon become obsolete.
- Difficulties in the hiring and training of suitable workers are minimized.
- The amount of capital necessary to meet regular payrolls is greatly reduced.
- By providing additional manufacturing facilities in periods of peak demand, contractors help speed up delivery of orders.
- It is unnecessary to keep one factory busy year round.

Disadvantages:
- No individual has full responsibility for the finished product.

- Other "manufacturers" (jobbers) may use the same facilities and get preferential treatment, because they place larger orders, or offer repeat business, or even guarantee future business.
- The quality of workmanship and inspection tends to be uneven.

## The Product Development Process

In a recent study published in the *Journal of Textile and Apparel Technology and Management*, the authors listed the following functions for an effective integrated system of product development:[1]

- Marketing
- Forecasting
- Merchandising
- Product line development
- Product design and specifications
- Material requisition planning
- Inventory control
- Costing
- Production planning and scheduling
- Sourcing and manufacturing
- Quality control
- Human resources
- Purchasing
- Logistics
- Warehouse inventory movement systems
- Finance
- Sales
- Field sales support
- Performance measurement
- External communication

Currently there are many variations in the product development process. We discuss a simple six-stage process that covers the functions performed at every firm, regardless of size (see Figure 8.3). The major differences are the number of people involved and how they communicate and interact.

The six-stage product development process is outlined in the following pages (see Figure 8.4)

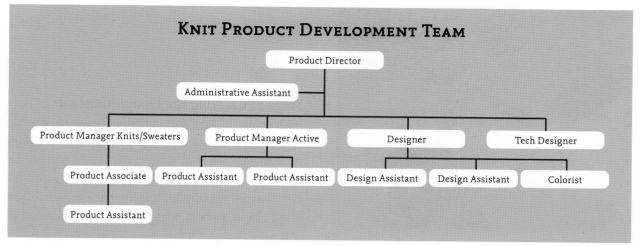

FIGURE 8.3 This organizational chart outlines the hierarchy of a product development team.

- Stage 1. Planning the line
- Stage 2. Creating the design concept
- Stage 3. Developing the designs
- Stage 4. Planning production
- Stage 5. Production
- Stage 6. Distributing the line

## Stage 1: Planning a Line

The first step of the product development process involves the work of a designer or a product development team, working under the direction of a merchandiser. These people are charged with creating a line. Their first task is research. They review information on trends, colors, fabrics, and other materials, often using fashion forecasting services, such as Doneger Group, Stylesight, Promostyl, or Color Box. Of course, team members must keep in mind previous fashion successes or failures, so past sales records as well as markdown reports are reviewed. Some firms develop "trend boards" that contain visual or graphic representations of developments that are affecting their target customer. All of this research helps designers or product development teams formulate some idea of what the new line will contain.

Using all their merchandising and marketing skills, merchandisers or designers help to form and maintain a positive image in the marketplace for the manufacturer. It is this image that influences a specific consumer group to buy a particular line at the retail level.

In most cases, design has to be disciplined and directed so that the particular image of the manufacturer and the merchandise that is produced will continue to fit the needs and wants of a specific consumer group.

There are three major types of firms that develop a line of apparel:

1. *Large Manufacturers.* In a large apparel firm, such as Liz Claiborne, Vanity Fair, and Levi Strauss, merchandisers are responsible for developing new lines. Merchandisers plan the overall fashion direction for the coming season and direct a design staff about the kinds of garments to be designed. They may also determine color choices. The design staff is generally not known to the public. Together with the marketing and sales departments, the merchandiser and designer form a **product development team**, which is responsible for a particular product line or brand.

2. *Designer-Owned Firms.* In firms at which the designer is also the owner (or part owner), the designer may design all or part of a line, using other designers to fill out the line. Examples of this kind of firm are Donna Karan, Ralph Lauren, Vera Wang, and Oscar de la Renta.

3. *Small Manufacturers.* In small firms, all the activities in the product development process may be done by the owner, with one or more assistants.

**FIGURE 8.4** The product development process. From top to bottom: planning a line, creating the design concept, developing the design, planning production, production, and distributing the line.

### Stage 2: Creating the Design Concept

Next come designs for individual garments. Each one is sketched or developed in muslin. At this stage, the designer or design staff considers his or her work and weighs it on two points: first, on its own individual merit and, second, for its suitability in the line as a whole. Many designs are discarded at this point.

Price is also a critical factor in determining whether or not a design is deleted from a line. A cost analysis is often done at this stage, and designs that are too expensive to produce profitably at the desired price point are rejected.

### Stage 3: Developing the Designs

Those designs that seem most likely to succeed are made up as finished sample garments. A pattern-maker creates a production pattern in the garment size the company uses to produce its samples. From this pattern, one or more samples are cut. Finally, the garment is sewn by a designer's assistant, who is also a seamstress. This person is called a **sample hand**.

Now the design is presented to various executives and managers of the company—people in sales, purchasing, production, and cost accounting. Both the cost of the fabric and the cost of producing the garment are carefully analyzed. Many designs are discarded at this point, while others are sent back to the design department for modification. A few are accepted. The accepted design is assigned a style number. At this point, it is officially part of a manufacturer's line.

#### Computer-Aided Design

Although the day has not yet arrived when designers will throw away their sketch pads and pencils, the advent of **computer-aided design (CAD)** is giving designers new freedom to explore and manipulate their designs in relatively easy, quick, and inexpensive ways. A designer no longer has to take a chance that he or she is having a sample made up in the best color. Now CAD is used to test various colors and color combinations, fabrics, and styles. CAD allows three-dimensional (3-D) contouring of objects on screen (see Figure 8.5). Folds, creases, and textures are simulated so that CAD-generated garments drape and hang accurately. Once the design is set on the computer, the computer image is used to create a pattern complete with darts, seams, and tailor's markings. Because the computer can create the design in 3-D, the computer image can be rotated to see all sides of the garment. Many companies are thus reducing the number of costly sample garments that they produce. Instead of a physical sample, they use the computer image in merchandising and sales presentations.

## Linked CAD/CAM/CIM

But that is no longer the end of the road for CAD systems. Instead, CAD is now being linked to **CAM (computer-aided manufacturing)**, and **CIM (computer-integrated manufacturing)** systems to provide information internally and to suppliers and even to retailers across the country and around the world.[2] Linked CAD/CAM/CIM technology is discussed in more detail later in this chapter.

## *Stage 4: Planning Production*

This stage of the product development process begins with sourcing, or determining where the components of a garment (fabric, thread, linings, facings, buttons, trim, etc.) will be purchased and, in some cases, where the garments will be cut and sewn. It is now that the vital question of domestic or foreign manufacture must be decided. (The role of Quick Response in this decision is discussed later in this chapter.) Reservations for production must be made so that the garments will be available when needed. The fabric must be ordered, along with orders for the other components of the garment. Finally, each garment must be costed out so that the exact cost and selling price can be set. See Figure 8.6 for an illustration of how a typical gar-

ment is costed. The samples are used to determine the cost of producing the garment. The money needed to finance production must be obtained. Only when all of these steps have been completed can actual production begin.

The samples, each with its style number, are then presented to retail buyers at the manufacturers' seasonal shows. The retail buyers either accept or reject parts of the line, or more rarely, the entire line. The buyers usually place orders for some of the individual designs. Sometimes they test a line by buying a small number of styles in small quantities. If these styles sell, they reorder them. Most manufacturers have set **minimum orders** for the quantity, number of styles, and/or dollar amount required to accept the retail buyer's order.

Because the manufacturer usually has not yet begun production when a line is shown to the buyers, it may be possible to fine-tune production to the buyers' orders. When a particular style receives a lot of attention from buyers, it is then scheduled for production. Items that generate little or no enthusiasm are dropped from the line.

Production contracts are often being finalized while the manufacturer's representatives are selling the line to retail accounts. If these two things can be done simultaneously, the manufacturer has a better chance of moving to the next step or "cutting as close to paper as possible," which means limiting the risk of investing in fabric, trim, and production costs while negotiating quantity discounts.

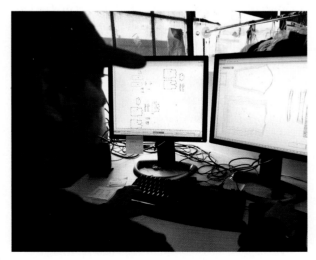

**FIGURE 8.5** Many designers use CAD systems to change, clarify, and perfect their designs.

## BEHIND THE PRICE TAG OF A $118.00 SKIRT

### MANUFACTURER'S COSTS

| | |
|---|---|
| Materials | |
| Wool-blend fabric | $14.60 |
| Lining | 1.90 |
| Thread | .20 |
| Zipper | .20 |
| Button | .40 |
| Total Materials 17.30 | |
| Labor | |
| Direct: cut/sew/finish | 5.00 |
| Factory burden | 6.25 |
| FG warehousing, | |
| & distribution | 2.60 |
| Total Labor 13.85 | |
| Packing costs | 1.95 |
| (tags, labels, hangers, | |
| pins, bags) | |
| Overhead | |
| Sewing expense | 2.54 |
| Administrative expense | 5.62 |
| Financing (interest) | .60 |
| Returns & allowances | 2.62 |
| Total Overhead 11.38 | |
| Trade discount | 3.40 |
| (8% off for prompt payment) | |
| Taxes | 2.20 |
| Net profit | 2.87 |
| **Wholesale** | **$52.95** |

**WOOL-BLEND SKIRT:**

| | |
|---|---|
| Wholesale price | $52.95 |
| Retail price | $118.00 |

### RETAILER'S COSTS

| | |
|---|---|
| Initial cost | $52.95 |
| $56.35 less discount | |
| for prompt payment | |
| Markdowns | 13.50 |
| (10.6% average over | |
| all sportswear) | |
| Shortage | 2.36 |
| (2% of retail price) | |
| Store/retailing expense | 42.48 |
| (36% of retail price) | |
| Salaries, sales, | |
| promotions, rent, | |
| utilities, receiving, | |
| marking, administrative | |
| costs, insurance. | |
| Taxes | 2.80 |
| Net profit | 3.91 |
| **Retail Sales Price** | **$118.00** |

**FIGURE 8.6** A costing sheet for a garment includes each component and its cost.

### Stage 5: Production

#### Cutting

One of the most important steps in the mass production of apparel is the cutting of the garment pieces (see Figure 8.7). Once a garment is slated for production, it is **graded**, or sloped, to each of the various sizes in which it will be made. After a pattern has been graded into the various sizes, the pieces are laid out on a long piece of paper called a **marker**. The success of cutting depends on the accuracy with which each of the many layers of material are placed on top of one another. A **spreader**, or laying-up machine, carries the material along a guide on either side of the cutting table, spreading the material evenly from end to end. The marker is laid on top of these layers.

For many years, material was cut by hand, but today, the cutting process is either computer-assist-ed or totally computerized. Computers are programmed to feed instructions to laser, blade, or high-speed water jet machines that do the actual cutting.

Once the cutting is completed, the pieces of each pattern—the sleeves, collars, fronts, and backs—are tied into bundles according to their sizes. This

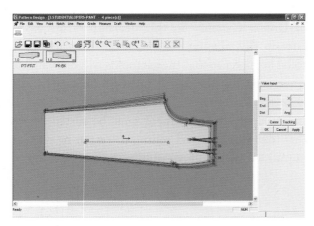

**FIGURE 8.7** Laying out and grading a garment in a factory require both great care and skill.

process is called **bundling**; it must be done by hand. The bundles are then moved to the manufacturers' sewing operators, who may be on the premises or in contractors' shops.

## Sewing

Technology has dramatically changed the sewing stage of production. The industrial sewing machine sews much faster than a home sewing machine because it has an engine with a clutch and brake rather than a motor. Home sewing machines perform many functions, while industrial machines perform specialized functions. Some sew only seams, while others sew blind hems. Button machines sew on buttons. Computerized sewing machines that do embroidery can be set up to stitch whole patterns without a machine operator. Robotic sewing equipment is being developed. A completely automated sewing assembly line is under development in Japan. The only thing humans will do in this new system is supervise.

Meanwhile, **single-hand operations** still exist, in which one operator sews the entire garment. These are used for very high-priced garments that are produced in very small quantities. Today, most manufacturers use a combination of mass-production systems, including the popular **modular manufacturing system**, in which teams of seven to nine workers produce entire garments, passing them on to each other, until the garment is complete. This system requires extensive cross-training, so each team member can learn all the tasks involved and do them as the flow of work demands.

## Finishing the Product

The sewn garment is still far from ready for the retail floor. Pants, for example, are sewn with the legs inside out. They must be turned right side out. A label must be sewn in. Buttons and buttonholes may be added at this stage.

Some fabrics are washed at this stage to prevent shrinkage. Others have a wrinkle-resistant finish applied. Still others are dyed at this point, called garment-dyeing, which gives the manufacturer last-minute control of color.

The garment is then pressed and folded or hung on a hanger with a plastic bag over it. Some manufacturers also offer services that make their apparel **floor ready**—that is, with bar-coded price tickets attached, cartons labeled, and shipping documents attached. Of course, this service adds to the cost, but many retailers find that this portion of the Quick Response strategy makes up in speed for the cost. See "Stage 6: Distributing the Line."

## Inspecting the Product

Garments are inspected many times during the production process. First the fabric and the dye quality are checked. Cutting is checked for pattern matching and size specs, among other things. Sewing is also checked repeatedly along the way, for stitch length, seam type, buttonhole stitching, and hem stitching. **Quality assurance**, or **QA**, which refers to the product meeting the standards established for it, includes the inspection of each ingredient of the garment: fabric, thread, buttons, snaps, or zippers, hem tape, linings, shoulder pads, and so forth.

## Stage 6: Distributing the Line

Once the line is completed, it still requires more work before the retailer can sell it. Sales tickets and bar codes must be added; these time-consuming tasks are frequently done by the manufacturer, except for the smallest stores. Then shipments must be consolidated and finally sent to retailers by truck, rail, or air.

As the season progresses, manufacturers remain sensitive to retail sales. For example, when reorders come in, they recut only the garments that are most in demand—and therefore, the most profitable. Manufacturers may also recut "hot sellers" in different fabrics and colors to maximize the sales generated by high customer demand.

# Fashion Focus

## Form and Function
### Product Lifecycle Management
## *PLM to the Rescue*

O nly a few years ago, product lifecycle management (PLM) software, designed especially for the apparel industry, was in its infancy. Today it is an important part of the product development of many large apparel companies.

PLM software helps apparel companies coordinate the departments and details that go into making any item of clothing. Design, sourcing, sample making, and shipping departments, as well as overseas factories, can view the same electronic files and see the status of any garment and its components at a moment's notice.

Historically, the apparel industry has utilized a wide variety of systems, methods, and controls to develop new products, track the manufacturing process, and deliver finished products to the customers. Often, designers, merchants, buyers, technical design, and production associates perform their tasks independently. Fast fashion initiatives are forcing manufacturers and retailers to shorten product development cycle times. Because design and development account for a major portion of a product's lifecycle, entering the supply

**Transforming your business with product lifecycle management**

Siemens PLM Software    www.siemens.com/plm

Your products hold the key to innovation, leadership and top-line financial growth. Unite your enterprise around product and process innovation. Unleash the hidden power in your product lifecycle – from concept design to product development, launch and retirement.

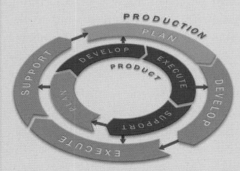

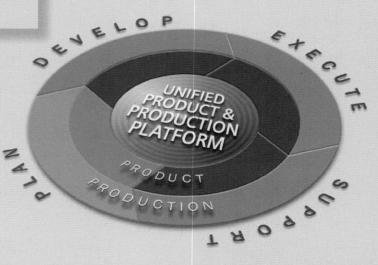

## Specializing by Product

Apparel producers have typically been specialists, producing apparel for a particular gender and age, a particular size range, and a specific price range. A women's blouse manufacturer, for example, seldom makes dresses, and a dress manufacturer usually does not turn out dresses in both women's and junior sizes. A coat and suit manufacturer does not usually produce both expensive and popular-priced lines.

### *By Gender, Age, and Size Categories, and by Classification*

Historically, the U.S. apparel industry has been divided into three major categories: women's, men's, and children's. These three categories are discussed in detail in Chapters 9, 10, and 11. Within these three categories are smaller subcategories, divided by age. For example, children's wear is subdivided into infants', toddlers', girls' and boys', preteen (girls), and young men's. Within infants' wear, sizes include 0 to 3 months, 6 months, 12 months, 18 months, and 24 months.

Another way that apparel is organized is by the type of garment produced, or classification. Examples for girls' wear include the following:

- Outerwear—coats, jackets, and raincoats
- Dresses
- Blouses
- Sportswear—pants, sweaters, shirts
- Active sportswear—swimsuits, skiwear, bike shorts
- Underwear
- Sleepwear
- Socks
- Tights
- School uniforms

Despite a move toward greater diversification, producers and retailers still have to think and work like specialists. For instance, a producer must of

chain early in the process is key to cutting lead time and improving efficiency in global product development.

Global product development, fast fashion, and increased distribution channels have made the process of creating and managing a line more complex. Before a merchandiser begins creating a new line plan, analysis is required on line performance, market trends, product assortment, and financial goals. This information then guides the look of the future product, including product attributes such as fabric type, silhouette, color, and "fashion trend." Only in a PLM system will this quantity of information coherently integrate so that merchandisers, planners, and designers can collaborate at the same time.

Today, more and more apparel companies, including Liz Claiborne, Marc Jacobs, Tommy Hilfiger, Sean John, Brooks Brothers, Diane von Furstenberg, and well over 100 others, are using PLM software to streamline and integrate their operations and supply chains.

necessity choose an inexpensive fabric for a popular-priced line and a more expensive fabric for a better-priced line. Retail buyers still shop one group of producers for sportswear, another for coats, and still another for bridal wear—and this practice is not likely to change in the near future.

### Brands and Labels

A special supplement to *Women's Wear Daily* listed five distinct kinds of brands or labels used by apparel industry insiders:[3]

1. National/designer brand
2. Private label
3. Retail store brand
4. All other brands
5. Nonbrands

Customers, of course, realize few of these distinctions; they think of them all as "brands" or "nonbrands." But to retailers and manufacturers, these distinctions are vital, impacting heavily on their profits and offering differentiation in an era when customers complain of the "sameness" of many stores and the goods they offer (see Figure 8.8).

### National/Designer Brands

National brands are those that are owned by a manufacturer who advertises them nationally. Some of the first apparel brands to gain national recognition were the Arrow Shirt Company and the BVD Company, a maker of men's underwear, in the 1930s. National brands continued to grow in number over the next five decades, but the 1980s and 1990s saw a tremendous leap in sales for national brands. In part, this growth resulted from a huge increase in the number of national advertising campaigns directed at consumers. National brands are expected to continue to predominate in the industry, while private labels "fill in the cracks."[4] Examples of national brands include Pendleton, Fruit of the Loom, Levi's, Carter's, Liz Claiborne, Reebok, Hanes, Revlon, and Juicy Couture.

Designer labels carry the name of a designer; they have grown enormously in number and importance since the 1940s. As mentioned previously, the four U.S. mega-designers are Ralph Lauren, Calvin Klein, Donna Karan, and Tommy Hilfiger. Hundreds more are working in the United States today. Many other designer names continue to be featured, although the original designer has retired or died; examples include Anne Klein, Liz Claiborne, and Halston.

Designer labels are no longer limited to apparel; they are frequently found on accessories of every kind, on fragrances and cosmetics, and on home furnishings.

### Private Labels

A **private label** is one that is owned by a retailer and found only in its stores. For decades, private label occupied a comfortable but unspectacular niche in U.S. apparel retailing. Starting 20 years ago, things began to happen. Specialty chains, most notably the Gap, began to put their names on the clothes, to the exclusion of national brands.

Examples of private-label apparel are the Kathie Lee Gifford line sold by Wal-Mart, the Jaclyn Smith line sold by Kmart, I.N.C. sold by Macy's (see Figure 8.9), and the Original Arizona Jeans Company line sold by JCPenney. Today, it is standard practice for specialty chains to sell merchandise only under their own brands programs. "Everyone is trying to

**FIGURE 8.8** Nordstrom uses private designer labels to convey the store's image.

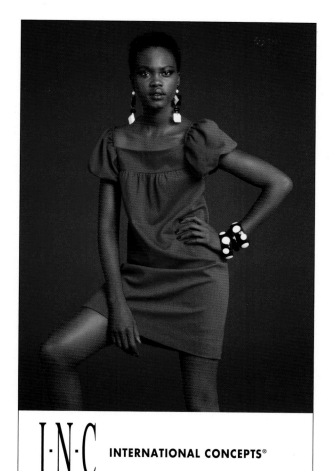

I·N·C INTERNATIONAL CONCEPTS®

**FIGURE 8.9** I.N.C. sold by Macy's is an example of a private label.

get directly to the consumer with as few middlemen as possible," says Tom Burns, senior vice president of the Doneger Group, the trend analysts and forecasters who work with dozens of stores in the United States and abroad. "Retailers feel they understand consumers and their lifestyles better than anyone and feel that by creating lifestyle brands, whether created, licensed, or bought, they can better control the product and the direction of the product."[5]

Private-label brands such as Worthington, Arizona, and a.n.a, designed and made by JCPenney, now make up nearly 50 percent of its total sales. At Macy's, private-label lines have been growing three times as fast as wholesale lines—making private-label clothes the fastest growing product category in American department stores.[6]

## Retail Store Brand

A **retail store brand** is the name of a chain that is used as the exclusive label on most of the items in the store or catalog. Examples of retail store brands for apparel and accessories include the Gap, The Limited, Ann Taylor, Victoria's Secret, Talbots, L.L. Bean, J. Crew (see Figure 8.10), and Lands' End. Examples of store brands for home furnishings include Pier 1, Crate & Barrel, and Williams-Sonoma. Few, if any, national or designer brands are carried by these stores or catalogs.

## Other Brands

This catchall category includes labels not in the preceding three categories; for example, cartoon characters, like Disney's Mickey & Co. and Warner Brothers' Looney Tunes; sports teams, like the Chicago Bulls; colleges, like the University of California at Berkeley; and museums, like the Museum of Fine Arts–Chicago. These brands are often licensed.

## Nonbrands

This is a label to which customers attach little or no importance. These labels are usually used by firms that manufacture low-priced goods and do little or no advertising to consumers. These labels are found in discount and off-price stores.

**FIGURE 8.10** The retail store J. Crew uses its own label on merchandise sold in the store and catalog.

## Industry Practices

Every industry has its own particular way of conducting business; the apparel industry is no exception. Some of the practices discussed in this section grew as responses to specific industry problems. These practices were once considered "trends" but are so established now that they are no longer trends but business as usual. The six major industry practices that we discuss are manufacturers acting as retailers, licensing, private-label and specification buying, offshore production, the use of factors, and chargebacks.

## *Manufacturers Acting as Retailers*

An increasing number of clothing manufacturers are opening their own stores. Disappointed by the sales, service, and space allotted to them in retail stores and wanting to create the "right" atmosphere for this clothing, they are choosing to enter the retail business themselves. Of course, larger profits are also part of the attraction. The manufacturer can sell the product to consumers at full retail price rather than at the wholesale price required by retail customers.

Designer Ralph Lauren was the first to take this step. Frustrated by the way department and special-

ty stores were selling his clothes, he opened the first Polo/Ralph Lauren shop on Rodeo Drive in Beverly Hills in 1971. Since then, he has built an empire of Polo/Ralph Lauren shops that stretches coast to coast in the United States and across the oceans to Europe and Asia.

Calvin Klein, Donna Karan, Adrienne Vittadini, Marc Jacobs, and Vivienne Tam have also opened their own retail outlets. Besides designer stores, manufacturing giants VF Corporation, Liz Claiborne, Inc., Jones Apparel Group, and Kellwood Company are mutating into multiheaded beasts, with direct-to-consumer sides becoming an increasingly large part of their businesses.

The distinction between wholesalers and retailers is blurring as the manufacturers find the best way to connect with their consumers as they integrate their brands. The Internet, retail consolidation, and private label all have changed the landscape to make it advantageous for them to be a retailer.[7]

But whether all manufacturers and designers will be successful retailers remains to be seen. A producer first has to compete for good retail talent, as well as retail space in a prime location, both of which can be expensive. The risks escalate if the manufacturer franchises, which many must do when they cannot personally oversee their retail empire.

Another problem is the reaction of the department and specialty stores that carry the manufacturers' lines. They feel such competition is unfair, and many have decided to stop carrying lines that are sold in manufacturers' own outlets. Other stores have learned to live with the new outlets.

Manufacturers' outlet stores, called "factory outlets," have also grown at a rapid rate (see Figure 8.11). They allow manufacturers to dispose of poor sellers, overstocks, and "seconds" and still make more money on them than they could by selling them to discount retailers as "closeouts."

The opposite of manufacturers acting as retailers is retailers acting as manufacturers, through the

**FIGURE 8.11** Outlet malls, like Woodbury Common Premium Outlets, feature factory outlets for stores such as the Gap, Banana Republic, and Polo Ralph Lauren.

**FIGURE 8.12** The great appeal of licensing is that merchandise is identified with a highly recognizable name, like Vera Wang's licensed jewelry line.

private-label programs of department stores and discounters, and through the retail store brands of specialty chains like the Gap and Talbots. These strategies are discussed in depth in Chapter 19.

## Licensing

Licensing, which was described in Chapter 5, experienced a boom in the United States in the 1980s and 1990s, largely because of the emergence of an important new market segment—working women. As a group, they are not quite in the income bracket to buy designer clothes, but designers have learned that they can capitalize on the market these women represent through licensing ventures.

The great appeal of licensing is that merchandise is identified with a highly recognizable name (see Figure 8.12). Licensed products are estimated at $71.25 billion annually.[8] The advantages for designers include the royalties they receive on the sale of

each product (usually from 2 to 15 percent), greater exposure of their name, and little investment in product development and manufacturing.

The disadvantages in licensing are few. When designers turn over control to a manufacturer, as they do when they license a product, they may lose some quality control. A bigger problem is that a designer will move too far afield for his or her more exclusive customers, but considering the potential profits in licensing, this is unlikely to worry many designers.

Christian Dior was a pioneer in licensing, having granted his first license in 1949. Even though Dior died in 1957, his name still appears on many products. Beside the Christian Dior shoe, jewelry, perfume, and cosmetic products that are owned and produced under the umbrella of Dior's parent company LVMH, the brand also has a license with Sanofi Eyewear.[9] Pierre Cardin used licenses to create a fashion empire—the largest of its kind—with over 800 products, from perfumes to pencil holders!

The first landmark deal in licensing in the United States occurred in the 1930s when Mickey Mouse products flooded the market. Later in the 1930s, Shirley Temple was the first human to find a windfall in selling her name for use on dresses, dolls, and an assortment of other products.

One of the pioneers of designer apparel licensing in the United States was Bill Blass, who had forty-two licenses for men's and women's apparel and accessories and home fashions. Anne Klein has many licenses for accessories, such as with Swank for jewelry and other manufacturers for eyeglasses, watches, and coats.

Valentino, another fashion pioneer, was among the first to enter into product extension licensing, and explains it as this: "Licenses allowed us to expand our business, maintain the couture collection, open boutiques, but in hindsight, a number of those licenses backfired because there was not enough couture. Licenses work if they are under a partnership format." Stefano Sassi, Valentino's cur-

# &Then NOW

## The WWD 100
### Top Names in the Apparel and Accessories Markets

THE WWD 100
A WOMEN'S WEAR DAILY SPECIAL REPORT • JULY 2007
The 25th annual survey of the apparel and accessories brands American women know best.

### Hanes

Product: Underwear, bras, daywear, casual-wear, sleepwear, hosiery, socks.
Volume: $2.4 billion (est.)
Owner: Hanesbrands Inc., Winston-Salem, N.C.

Hanesbrands celebrates its first anniversary as a separate, public company in September, following its $4.7 billion spin-off from Sara Lee Branded Apparel. The Hanes super brand has not budged from its number-one spot in the WWD 100 for five consecutive years. The worldwide recognition and an estimated ad budget in excess of $90 million for TV ads featuring celebs like Jennifer Love Hewitt and Kevin Bacon, Hanes has stayed the course with new products such as the Hanes All-Over Comfort Bra and Hanes ComfortSoft Waistband underwear.

### Timex

Product: Watches
Volume: $700 million
Owner: Timex Corp., Middlebury, Conn.

This year, Timex launched its "Keep On" campaign, a throwback to the original tag line, "It Takes a Lickin' and Keeps on Tickin.'" But this message applies to the wearer, not the watch. According to the brand, Keep On seeks to recognize and encourage the wearer's own values of design, durability, and performance. The campaign premiered this spring with the launch of the T Series Collection, a drive to elevate the Timex brand. Timex is also gearing its brand toward women. Two new collections for fall represent the fusion of fashion and sport. Hi-Ti uses lightweight titanium on resin straps with pared-down digital faces for a more modern look, in vibrant two-tone combinations and neutrals, while the Timex Diamond Collection will offer affordable, everyday luxury for women.

### L'eggs

Product: Hosiery, enhancewear.
Volume: $235 millions (est., retail)
Owner: Hanesbrands Inc., Winston-Salem, N.C.

While it may be the leading brand for the budget conscious, L'eggs is not short on innovation. Among its product extensions are Sheer Vitality Benefits Fresh Feet Knee High, designed to neutralize odor to keep feet fresh; Brown Sugar Luxury, a feminine collection for women of color, featuring lace details and a silky sheer leg; and Casual Comfort Solutions, semi-sheer and opaque trouser socks with cushion sole padding and soft microfiber yarns. The brand also offers comfortable waistband-free styles in its Silken Mist and Sheer Energy lines, as well as a moisturizing and anticellulite component in Sheer Vitality. L'eggs continues to promote itself through online coupons and giveaways and inserts in major newspapers. It has an ongoing multicultural campaign to target African-American and Hispanic women.

### Fruit of the Loom

Product: Underwear, bras, T-shirts, daywear, casualwear.
Volume: $1.8 billion (est., including licensing)
Owner: Berkshire Hathaway Inc., Omaha

Big changes have taken place since billionaire Warren Buffet's company acquired the 151-year-old Fruit of the Loom brand in 2002. The deal to acquire VF Corp.'s Intimate Apparel Business by FTL was completed in April, and is expected to bolster market share and synergies among varying product categories. FTL's annual TV and national print ad budget was pumped up to an estimated $75 million, with humorous, edgy ads aimed at a young, hip consumer. FTL is also expanding its licensed bra business with a contemporary spin for mass channels, and the brand is building a global presence with its first line of women's underwear in Europe.

### Levi Strauss

Product: Jeanswear
Volume: $2.87 billion (Levi's brand)
Owner: Levi Strauss & Co., San Francisco

Growth has been difficult for Levi Strauss & Co and its core Levi's brand. The venerable denim giant, which also owns the Levi Strauss Signature and Dockers brands, managed to reverse eight years of sales declines in 2005, but that trend was short-lived. Sales and revenue fell again in 2006 and results so far in 2007 have been mixed. The Levi's brand has consistently accounted for approximately 70 percent of the firm's sales, and future expansion hinges on the company's ability to grow in places like Asia and India. John Anderson took over as president and chief executive from Phil Marineau last November.

### Nike

Product: Activewear, athletic footwear, accessories sports equipment, personal electronics, retail.

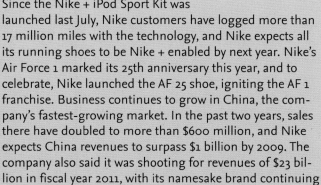

Volume: $14.1 billion, Nike brand; $16.3 billion, entire company

Owner: Nike Inc., Beaverton, Ore.

Since the Nike + iPod Sport Kit was launched last July, Nike customers have logged more than 17 million miles with the technology, and Nike expects all its running shoes to be Nike + enabled by next year. Nike's Air Force 1 marked its 25th anniversary this year, and to celebrate, Nike launched the AF 25 shoe, igniting the AF 1 franchise. Business continues to grow in China, the company's fastest-growing market. In the past two years, sales there have doubled to more than $600 million, and Nike expects China revenues to surpass $1 billion by 2009. The company also said it was shooting for revenues of $23 billion in fiscal year 2011, with its namesake brand continuing to lead growth.

### Victoria's Secret

Product: Bras; underwear; daywear, at-homewear, casualwear and sleepwear; robes, shoes, dresses, fragrance, body care.

Volume: $5.1 billion ($3.7 billion at retail; $1.42 billion catalogue and e-commerce; $23 million La Senza)

Owner: Limited Brands Inc., Columbus, Ohio

Victoria's Secret, the most powerful lingerie specialty retailer in the U.S., appeals to women who aspire to be sexy, sophisticated and forever young, and who appreciate fashion-forward lingerie. In 2006, VS continued to revolutionize the bra with Secret Embrace technology. VS operates 1,003 stores nationwide and 323 La Senza stores worldwide. Acquired by Limited Brands in 1982, VS stores average sales of $731 a square foot. Overall, 2006 sales rose 16 percent, and operating income jumped 8 percent. Leslie H. Wexner, chairman and CEO of parent company Limited, noted in its 2006 annual report that VS's catalog and e-commerce businesses had a "phenomenal year" in 2006, with sales growth of 16 percent, and a significant increase in operating income.

rent CEO, added that licenses are "key for anyone with goals to develop new projects, expand one's visibility, and complete the brand's perception," and that "it's fundamental to create the right balance between licenses, accessories, and clothing, which should remain Valentino's core business."[10]

A final note on the importance of a company's brand name: **corporate licensing**, or the use of a company's name on related merchandise, is the fastest growing segment of licensing today. Overall, corporate licensing reached $108.6 million in sales in 2005, according to the International Licensing Industry Merchandisers' Association.[11] The Nike "swoosh" is seen worldwide. Harley Davidson has licensed its name for T-shirts and children's wear, Dr. Scholl's has expanded from foot care to pillows, and Jeep now has a line of sunglasses.

## Private Label and Specification Buying

The terms *private label* and *specification buying* may be used to describe the same items of merchandise, but the meanings are slightly different. If the retailer agrees, the manufacturer may design private-label merchandise for the retailer. Macy's private labels include Jennifer Moore, Charter Club, and Badge. On the other hand, **specification buying** is a type of purchasing that is done to the store's, rather than the manufacturer's standards. JCPenney and the Gap are two examples of stores that make extensive use of specification buying. These retailers provide the standards and guidelines for the manufacture of clothes they order. Standards cover everything from the quality of materials and workmanship to styling and cost.

Specification buying has become so specialized that many stores now employ a **specification manager** or **product manager** who is trained in specification buying. While keeping an eye on industry and government standards, specification managers work closely with manufacturers to ensure that their products will be economically successful for both the retailer and the manufacturer.

As they grow more successful with specification buying, stores have begun to use it for their private-label lines. Initially intended as a way to keep production at home, a growing amount of private label is now purchased offshore. (See the following section and Chapter 2).

Because retailers often place large orders for a few related lines, the private labels are a growth area for the manufacturers and may account for 20 to 45 percent of the manufacturer's output. According to the individual agreement between retailer and manufacturer, product development can be in the hands of either party. To maintain the separate, distinctive images of their retailer clients' private brands and their own national brands, some manufacturers have separate teams of designers. The manufacturer can achieve economies of scale by sourcing both their national brand and their retailer clients' brands from the same offshore supplier.

## Offshore Production

American manufacturers are increasingly turning to **offshore production**, that is, the manufacture of American goods in cheap-labor foreign countries. Offshore production is seen as a way to generally lower costs and therefore compete more effectively with low-cost imports. Some industry insiders view this practice as a threat to the health of American labor; others regard it as a necessity in order for U.S. manufacturers to remain competitive.

Offshore production is appealing under certain conditions because the federal government gives domestic producers a special tariff advantage, provided only part of the production is done offshore. Under Section 807 of the Tariff Classification Act, for example, manufacturers can cut and design their own garments and finish them domestically, sending only the sewing to a labor-cheap offshore country. Duty is paid only on the value added to the garment by the work done abroad. Under the North American Free Trade Agreement (NAFTA), a substantial amount of offshore production has shifted from Asian countries to Mexico, where wages are low and shipping costs less.

## Use of Factors

Apparel manufacturers and contractors need cash or credit to produce garments the season before they are sold. Some banks have been reluctant to lend money to apparel companies because of the high risks involved. So an alternate system of financing has developed for the apparel industry. Called **factors**, these companies either purchase a manufacturer's accounts receivable or advance cash on the basis of the accounts receivable. Their interest rates are generally higher than those of a bank.

Another more recent development is the use of credit insurance by firms that do not use factors. Credit insurance, used for decades in Europe, protects the insured company from losses as a result of a customer's bankruptcy or very late payment. Credit insurance is also useful for a U.S. manufacturer with international business, since it is cheaper than international letters of credit.[12]

## Chargebacks

As retail chains have grown in size, their power over their suppliers has also increased. Apparel manufacturers are increasingly hit with demands for **chargebacks**, which are financial penalties imposed on manufacturers by retailers. The reasons for chargebacks include errors like mistakes in purchase orders or ticketing. Sometimes retailers request chargebacks for partial or late shipments, or even for poor-selling products. Chargebacks are also used for cooperative advertising. Naturally, chargebacks can cause financial problems for designers and manufacturers, especially small ones.

## Advanced Technologies and Strategies

A number of advanced technologies and the strategies used to harness them have been implemented

**CHAPTER EIGHT**
**PRODUCT DEVELOPMENT**

**221**

by the U.S. apparel industry. These technologies have already had a profound impact on the profitability of the business. They include the use of computer-integrated manufacturing, Quick Response, bar codes and scanners, electronic data interchange (EDI), mass customization, and body scanning.

## Computer-Integrated Manufacturing

Standalone computerized equipment is now common in most manufacturers' plants. Known as computer-aided manufacturing (CAM), it includes such things as programmable sewing machines, pattern-making machines, and cutting machines.

But the enormous power of the computer lies in its ability to be linked to other computers, so that the computers can direct the entire production process from design to finished garment. In computer-integrated manufacturing (CIM), data from many computers within a manufacturing company is linked from design through production stages. The potential for cost savings is tremendous, since repeated data entry is eliminated, along with entry errors.

In the apparel industry, CAD and CAM are linked into a CIM system so that a design, pattern-making, and grading are linked to cutting equipment as well as to computers that prepare costing reports and specification sheets. In some plants, these computers are even linked to stitching machines.

One example of a software product that helps manufacturers harness CIM to quickly search for information is called ConceptManager97. It allows users to search for, display on screen, and print any visual element. For example, a manufacturer can search for all fabrics priced below $10 a yard, a primary color of blue, and sourced in Hong Kong.[13]

The specialty retailer/cataloger Talbots is using a groupware computer program combined with the Internet to share critical information among members of its product development team: the product manager, who is responsible for developing new clothing lines; a source, who is responsible for getting an item manufactured once it has been designed; and a buyer, who decides on quality and price.

## Quick Response

Quick Response—the industry buzzword is bandied about at trade conferences, seminars, boardrooms, and back rooms. Many say this is where all textile, apparel, and retail industries are headed. Simply put, it aims at delivering the right product at the right time!

**Quick Response**, or **QR**, is a business strategy that shortens the time from raw materials to design to production to finished product to the consumer. It was developed to give U.S. manufacturers a potent weapon against imports and foreign competitors. The necessary partnerships and electronic high-tech mechanisms are in place to link all parts of the supply pipeline directly to the nation's retailers.

What QR really means is a far closer association between manufacturer, supplier, retailer, and customer. QR requires the development of trust and communication, and that goes all the way from the cash register to the apparel people and the textile suppliers.

As Kurt Salmon Associates, a prestigious consulting firm that was in on the birth of Quick Response in 1985, put it:

> From a manufacturer's point of view, QR can be defined as having in place an operating strategy which has been designed to enable the company to profitably supply its chosen markets with the right product at a competitive price, in the right quantities, at the right time, and with minimum commitment to inventory. Certainly there is nothing new about such a formula. What is new is the change of emphasis and timing, plus the fact that for many companies survival is at stake.[14]

QR had evolved from a theoretical concept in 1985 to a comprehensive integrated system by 1995, one that has shortened total cycle time and improved service. But there is more to QR than moving goods more quickly to a retailer's shelf and ultimately more quickly into the consumer's hand. Once belittled as the pipedream of a few idealistic textile and apparel executives, QR has proved effective. In a study conducted by North Carolina State University, domestic QR resulted in better overall retail performance than did a strategy of importing apparel. The key advantage of QR was that it allowed retailers to reorder during the season, as customer demand was being revealed to them. The retailers could look at their point-of-sale data and make small, frequent reorders, preventing both big oversupply of inventory and stockouts (being out of stock).[15]

The growing segment of companies that has tried QR is gleeful about the payoffs. The point of QR is not only to restock but also to let both the retailer and manufacturer see what the customers like and what sizes they wear—tools for planning and implementing the next season's line. Thus QR is a change from the "push" system strategy of the past, in which products were produced and then "pushed" on the consumer. Instead, QR is a "pull" system strategy, because information about what consumers want flows from the consumers to the producers.

### Bar Codes and Scanners

Bar coding, scanning, and computer-to-computer communications have become integral parts of QR. Bar coding makes tracking merchandise—from fabric rolls to designer dresses—easier, faster, and more accurate (see Figure 8.13).

The **universal product code (UPC)** is one of a number of bar codes used for automatic identification of items scanned at retail cash registers. UPC is the symbol that has been most widely accepted by retailers and manufacturers.

*The Role of Technology in Getting the Right Product to the Right Place at the Right Time*

1. SCANNING AT THE POINT OF PURCHASE
   Instant inventory monitoring
2. USING LOCATOR COMPUTER PROGRAM
   Find nearest supply when product runs low
3. TRANSMITTING DATA BY SATELLITE
   Stores can track and order changes
4. USING SUPPLIER/RETAILER COMPUTER LINKS
   Sales history is available to supplier
5. FORECASTING BY COMPUTER
   Improves coordination between retailers and suppliers.

**FIGURE 8.13** Bar codes give vital product information.

Bar codes are made up of a pattern of dark bars and white spaces of varying widths. A group of bars and spaces represents one character. Scanners "read" the bar code. The UPC symbol does not contain the price of the merchandise; that information is added by the retailer to the store's computerized cash registers. It can be easily changed.

### Electronic Data Interchange (EDI)

**Electronic Data Interchange (EDI)** is the electronic exchange of machine-readable data in standard formats between one company's computers and another company's computers. It replaces a large number of paper forms that were the primary link between manufacturers and their retailer customers. These included forms like purchase orders, invoices, packing slips, shipping documents, and inventory forms.

EDI is faster than mail, messenger, or air delivery services. By eliminating paper-based transactions, large companies can save clerical time, paper, and postage. EDI goes beyond bar code scanning to include handheld laser scanners, satellite links, and wireless systems. This technology results in both increased productivity and improved customer service. Using EDI, Federal Express and UPS, for example, can trace any of the millions of packages they ship anywhere in the world. EDI also offers shops an avenue to e-commerce. The EDI system supplies a business with the infrastructure necessary to take the business on to the Internet. However, since the configuration process is complicated, fewer than 30,000 shops have actually implemented the technology.[16]

## Mass Customization

For the past 80 years, we have lived in a world where mass production was the model for products and services, because standardized products meant lower costs. Every time a customer takes home an attribute that he or she really does not want in the product, it is a form of waste. In **mass customization**, the idea is to tailor the product to fit one particular customer—not one size fits all—and to supply thousands of individuals, at mass prices, not custom-made prices.

Women have a harder time than men finding clothes that fit. Today, mass customization is not technically true customization but rather an automated form of made-to-measure apparel.[17]

Since Levi's introduced its now-discontinued Personal Pair Jeans in 1995, more than a dozen fashion companies have tried mass customization, so named because it combines advanced technology with factory production, instead of old-fashioned craftsmanship, to make something unique yet affordable. Among the companies who are using mass customization are Lands' End, Tommy Hilfiger, Target, Ralph Lauren, JCPenney, Nike, Timberland, Atelier, and Brooks Brothers.[18]

## Body Scanning

Currently, more than one-third of the apparel returned by American women is brought back to stores because it doesn't fit well. Body shapes tend to change significantly three times in a woman's life—around ages 20, 35, and 55—and those variations, along with the 60-year-old sizing system that hasn't evolved with women's changing body type, has made a good fit harder to find.

Body scanning technology has evolved today to help manufactures, retailers, and customer to get a better fit![19] Among the 3-D body scanner systems in use today are Fit Logic and Intellifit (see Figure 8.14). Recently, Lectra has announced 3D Fit, a new program for virtual prototyping.[20]

As technology continues to improve and to become less costly, scanning of the entire body will become common, resulting in a better fit for all customers (see Figure 8.15).

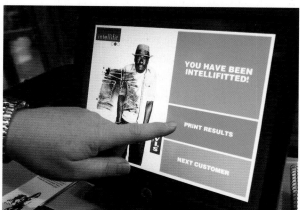

**FIGURE 8.14** Intellifit allows shoppers to get better fitting clothing, without having to waste too much time in the dressing room.

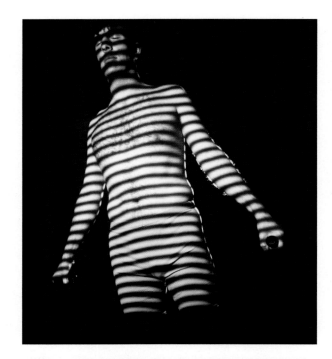

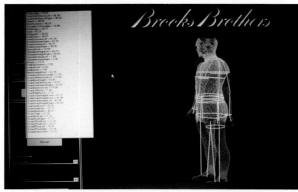

**FIGURE 8.15** Advances in technology are improving body scanners, giving everyone better fitting clothing.

can diversify its product line. This is a common strategy of packaged goods manufacturers; for example, the Dial brand of the Armour conglomerate was used on a variety of products beyond the original bar soap. One fashion company that extended its line is Fossil, which was successful with watches and then branched out into handbags and belts.

In the apparel industries, a move into a related category of apparel is the easiest and cheapest way to diversify. A company that makes T-shirts may add

## Industry Trends

The fashion industry is moving closer to traditional marketing models for consumer goods. We focus on three trends that prove this point: brand extensions, industry cooperation, and globalization.

### Brand Extensions

A common technique in consumer goods marketing is **brand extension**, a strategy in which a company uses a successful brand name to launch new or modified products. Brand extension saves the company the high cost of promoting a new name and creates instant brand recognition of the new product line (see Figure 8.16). It is one way in which a company

**FIGURE 8.16** Coach, originally known for its handbags (top), extended its brand by adding a perfume line (bottom).

a line of cotton sweatshirts, which are also sized small, medium, large, and extra-large. A designer of men's suits may add coats. A children's wear manufacturer may add an infants' line. A woman's shoe manufacturer may add matching handbags.

The move to an unrelated line has traditionally been more difficult—and more costly. One of the first brand extensions by designers was expanding into fragrances and cosmetics.

## Fragrances and Cosmetics
Chanel and Schiaparelli had paved the way into fragrances in the 1920s and 1930s. After World War II, Pierre Cardin and Christian Dior launched new perfumes. In the United States, what was once a trickle of designer fragrances has become a torrent—with many introductions each season. The move into color cosmetics, however, has been much slower because of the high cost of entry into this line and the established competition (see Chapter 14).

## Accessories
The next natural product extension for many designers was accessories. Scarves, ties, jewelry and watches, leather shoes, belts, handbags, furs, hosiery and socks—it sometimes seems that every name designer does it all. This extension into accessories helps them create a "total concept" or look that distinguishes their merchandise. It also ties into the licensing trend, which is the low-cost, low-risk way that most designers choose to move into specialized areas, like leather apparel or shoes, or fur.

## Men's and Women's Wear
Designers who have been successful in either men's or women's wear now regularly turn to designing for the opposite sex. This practice has become so routine that it is difficult for newcomers to the fashion industries to appreciate what a dramatic change this is from the practice of the past.

For many years (1930s to the mid-1950s), women wore men's jeans because manufacturers did not make jeans in women's sizes. Adding women's sizes to a jeans line was a bold, unprecedented move at the time—but it succeeded. Today, manufacturers and designers both move easily into unisex wear. The move from men's wear to women's wear was made first; only in 1991 did a women's wear designer (Donna Karan) dare to move into men's wear.

## Children's Wear
While expanding into children's wear is still done less frequently than the expansions discussed previously, it is becoming more common. Children's lines such as Italy's Moschino, with both Moschino Bambino for infants and toddlers and Moschino Junior for 2 to 15 year olds, are well known. American and European designers are aiming to differentiate themselves from the frilly, fussy dress clothes available from established children's wear firms, as well as from the casual basics offered by Polo Ralph Lauren, Tommy Hilfiger, and CK Calvin Klein.

Many retailers of adult apparel have also expanded into children's wear; examples include Baby Gap, Talbots Kids, and The Limited Too.

## Home Furnishings
Once limited to Bill Blass in the United States, this extension exploded in the 1990s because of a downturn in women's wear and growing sales of home furnishings. Ralph Lauren is perhaps the most successful designer in this field, but he is getting lots of company as many name designers make licensing agreements with established manufacturers. In fact, the largest dollar growth area for designer licensing is in home fashions. Designers such as Calvin Klein, Alexander Julian, and Liz Claiborne have had great success in home fashions. Interior designers such as Christopher Lowell and Lynette Jennings are also entering the field via licensing. Martha Stewart, also known for her domesticity, has licensed a line of sheets and towels with Kmart.

## Adding Different Price Lines

The practice of moving into different price levels is now widely accepted by both manufacturers and name designers. As price lines blur, the distinctions of yesteryear are blurring too. Most name designers now have several price levels, none of which is perceived by customers as cheapening the image of the others. Examples abound: one is Donna Karan's signature collection. Its sales have not been adversely affected by the huge sales of her lower-priced DKNY line.

## *Industry Cooperation*

It is necessary for companies in the fashion industry to harness technology as they strive to push costs out of the entire product distribution pipeline rather than to just push costs onto their trading partners.

Industry cooperation, already at an all-time high, continues to grow. The issue of partnerships, or strategic alliances, between textile producers, apparel and accessories manufacturers, and retailers is discussed in more detail in Chapter 19. Two current examples of industry cooperation are VICS and ANSI X.12.

### VICS

Voluntary Inter-Industry Communications Standards Committee (VICS) was formed in 1986 by retailers and producers to establish common standards of communication, including the current UPC system. This group grew out of the Crafted With Pride program and has members from Wal-Mart, Kmart, Dayton Hudson, Sears, Levi Strauss, and VF Corporation. This group also developed a retail-specific version of ANSI X.12, the standards for electronic documents.

### ANSI X.12

ANSI X.12 is the backbone of the Quick Response movement, because it is the set of standards that govern creating an electronic document. Since all the documents use the same format, the entire apparel industry can use the ANSI standards, whether they are sending or receiving documents, whether the company is small or huge. For example, the first three-digit number describes the type of document being sent (like a purchase order), the next ten numbers give the sender's name, and on and on through every line of the document.

## *Globalization*

Globalization of the marketplace—finding both foreign competitors and foreign customers—has happened to a wide range of U.S. heavy manufacturing industries; for example, cars, televisions, electronics, steel, and computers. Starting in the 1970s and through the 2000s, globalization occurred in the apparel industries. In this chapter, we have explored several high-tech responses to protect U.S. manufacturers: CAD/CAM/CIM, EDI, QR, and mass customization, among others. In Unit Five, we explore the opportunities presented by global markets.

The globalization of the fashion business has made it necessary for companies both large and small to have a worldview, a global perspective that helps them to see the possibilities for their business. It is particularly essential for manufacturers whose markets demand that they source overseas.

Today, a U.S. apparel company might source fabric from China, manufacture garments in Vietnam, send them to Italy for custom design work, and ship the final product to a U.S. warehouse for retail delivery. There is no way this can be done without a worldview and some sophisticated logistics technology. The need for advanced IT solutions is growing, and research from the Aberdeen Group suggests that a large number of companies still have a long way to go to having the kind of sophisticated global supply-chain technology that can help them make crucial and timely financial decisions.[21]

### SIC/NAICS Codes

Another reflection of globalization is the change from the Standard Industrial Classification (SIC) codes to North American Industry Classification System (NAICS). SIC was originally developed in the 1930s to classify U.S. establishments by the type of activity in which they primarily engage and to create a database of comparable information that would describe the parts of the U.S. economy.

Over the years, the SIC was revised periodically to reflect the changes in the businesses that make up the U.S. economy. The last major revision of the SIC was in 1987. In 1997, the SIC was replaced by the NAICS, which is also being used by Canada and Mexico.[22] The NAICS provides industrial sta-

**TABLE 8.2** *Comparison of Selected NAICS and SIC Codes*

| NAICS CODES | | SIC CODES | |
|---|---|---|---|
| 315 | Apparel Manufacturing | | |
| 3152 | Cut and Sew Apparel Manufacturing | | |
| 31521 | Cut and Sew Apparel Contractors | | |
| 315211 | Men's and Boys' Cut and Sew Apparel Contractors | 2311 | Men's and Boys' Suits, Coats, and Overcoats (contractors) |
| | | 2321 | Men's and Boys' Shirts, Except Work Shirts (contractors) |
| | | 2322 | Men's and Boys' Underwear and Nightwear (contractors) |
| | | 2325 | Men's and Boys' Trousers and Slacks (contractors) |
| | | 2326 | Men's and Boys' Work Clothing (contractors) |
| | | 2329 | Men's and Boys' Clothing, NEC (contractors) |
| | | 2341 | Women's, Misses', Children's, and Infants' Underwear and Nightwear (boys' contractors) |
| | | 2361 | Girl's, Children's, and Infants' Dresses, Blouses, and Shirts (boys' contractors) |
| | | 2369 | Girl's, Children's, and Infants' Outerwear, NEC (boys' contractors) |
| | | 2384 | Robes and Dressing Gowns (men's and boys' contractors) |
| | | 2385 | Waterproof Outerwear (men's and boys' contractors) |
| | | 2389 | Apparel and Accessories, NEC (contractors) |
| | | 2395 | Pleating, Decorative and Novelty Stitching, and Tucking for the Trade (men's and boys' apparel contractors) |
| 315212 | Women's, Girls', and Infants' Cut and Sew Apparel Contractors | 2331 | Women's, Misses', and Juniors' Blouses and Shirts (contractors) |
| | | 2335 | Women's, Misses', and Juniors' Dresses (contractors) |
| | | 2337 | Women's, Misses', and Juniors' Suits, Skirts, and Coats (contractors) |
| | | 2339 | Women's, Misses', and Juniors' Outerwear, NEC (contractors) |
| | | 2341 | Women's, Misses', Children's, and Infants' Underwear and Nightwear (contractors) |
| | | 2342 | Brassieres, Girdles, and Allied Garments (contractors) |
| | | 2361 | Girls', Children's, and Infants' Dresses, Blouses, and Shirts (girls' and infants' contractors) |
| | | 2369 | Girls', Children's, and Infants' Outerwear, NEC (girls' and infants' contractors) |
| | | 2384 | Robes and Dressing Gowns (women's, girls', and infants' contractors) |
| | | 2385 | Waterproof Outerwear (women's, girls', and infants' contractors) |
| | | 2389 | Apparel and Accessories, NEC (contractors) |
| | | 2395 | Pleating, Decorative and Novelty Stitching, and Tucking for the Trade (women's, girls' and infants' apparel contractors) |

tistics produced in the three countries that are comparable for the first time, reflecting the interrelated nature of these economies. This data is extremely useful for businesses, and the fashion industry is at the forefront of those using the information to aid in decision making. Table 8.2 shows one section of the old SIC and the comparable new NAICS codes. The new codes are much simpler.

## Summary and Review

The men's, women's, and children's apparel industries develop and produce lines of apparel following a standard cycle. The six-stage process of developing and producing a line involves (1) planning a line, (2) creating the design concept, (3) developing the designs, (4) planning production, (5) production, and (6) distributing the line.

Types of producers include manufacturers, apparel jobbers, and contractors. Producers specialize by gender, age, and size categories, as well as by classification. While consumers generally do not know the differences, industry insiders distinguish between five major types of brands and labels: (1) national/designer brands, (2) private labels, (3) retail store brands, (4) other types of brands, and (5) nonbrands.

Major industry practices that directly affect profitability include licensing, private label and specification buying, offshore production, the use of factors, and chargebacks.

Advanced technologies affecting product development of apparel include computer-integrated manufacturing, Quick Response, the use of bar codes and scanners, electronic data interchange, mass customization, and body scanning computers.

Product development is also affected by the major industry trends of brand extensions, globalization, and industry cooperation. A reflection of globalization is the new NAICS codes used by Canada, the United States, and Mexico, which replace the SIC codes that classified industries and made company comparisons possible.

## Trade Talk
Define or briefly explain the following terms:

anchor

brand extension

chargeback

computer-aided manufacturing (CAM)

contractor (apparel)

corporate licensing

factor

freelance artist-designer

group

item house

manufacturer (apparel)

mass customization

modular manufacturing

outside shop

private label

product manager

quality assurance

retail store brand

section work

sourcing

specification manager

stylist-designer

universal product code (UPC)

apparel jobber

bundling

computer-aided design (CAD)

computer-integrated manufacturing (CIM)

collection

electronic data interchange (EDI)

floor ready

graded

high-fashion or name designer

line-for-line copy

marker

minimum order

offshore

piecework

product development

production system

Quick Response (QR)

sample hand

single-hand operation

specification buying

spreader

team

## For Review
1. How does EDI differ from CIM?
2. How does a jobber differ from a manufacturer?
3. What are the major advantages of the contractor system? What is the key disadvantage?

4. What are the six stages of the product development process?
5. What is a chargeback?
6. What is the goal of Quick Response?
7. Why do most fashion producers sell directly to retail stores rather than through wholesalers?
8. What is the difference between a national brand and a private label?
9. What role do factors play in the fashion industry?
10. Discuss the major problems facing a manufacturer who is also a retailer.

## For Discussion

1. Compare and contrast the roles of the designer, the merchandiser, and the product manager in developing a line.
2. Give current examples of brand extensions in apparel, accessories, fragrances and cosmetics, and home furnishings.

chapter nine

*Everything you always wanted to know*

*about the history, organization, and operation*

*of women's apparel.*

# Women's Apparel

Located in the heart of midtown Manhattan, the fashion district is the capital of American fashion. It is a vibrant and diverse community where more than 80,000 people work at over 5,000 companies in the 450 properties that make up the neighborhood. To celebrate the fashion designers whose innovative and distinctive styles helped shape the course of American fashion, the Fashion Walk of Fame was created in 2000. The series of twenty-four commemorative sidewalk plaques run the length of "Fashion Avenue" between 35th and 41st Streets, highlighting the names and designs of these national fashion treasures.[1]

The manufacturing and merchandising of women's apparel is a giant multibillion dollar industry employing hundreds of thousands of people. Its influence on the economy is so strong that retail sales figures are one indicator of the health of the nation's economy.

Of necessity, the industry exists in a constant state of change, reacting on an ongoing basis to women's tastes and styles, to an increasingly global economy, and to new technology (see Figure 9.1). It is an industry that truly thrives on change and novelty.

## History of the Women's Apparel Industry

For thousands of years, people made their own clothes, often producing their own raw materials and converting them into textiles with which they could sew. A farmer might grow cotton, for example, and his wife would spin and weave it into cotton fabric, which she then used to make the family's clothes. Until the mass manufacturing of clothing began, sewing was considered women's work, except for the wealthy man, who "bespoke" handmade garments from a male tailor, who specialized in men's high-fashion apparel.

The first step in moving the manufacture of clothes out of the home came around 1800, when professional male tailors began to make more men's clothing. These clothes were still **custom-made**, that is, fitted to the individual who would wear them, and then sewn by hand. A few professional dressmakers began to make women's clothes, but only rich women could afford these custom-made designs. Most women still sewed their own clothes at home.

### Growth of Ready-to-Wear

The mass production of clothing did not begin until the mid-19th century. After the Civil War, some manufacturers began to mass-produce cloaks and mantles for women. These garments were not fitted, so they could be made in standard sizes and produced in large numbers.

By the turn of the century, limited quantities of women's suits, skirts, and blouses were being made in factories. Around 1910, someone had the idea of sewing a blouse and skirt together in what was called a shirtwaist, and the women's ready-to-wear dress business was born. In contrast to custom-made clothes produced by professional dressmakers or tailors or made by home sewers, **ready-to-wear (RTW)** refers to clothing produced in factories to standardized measurements. In the first decade of the 20th century, growing numbers of women began to substitute store-bought clothes for home-sewn ones.

### Acceptance of Ready-to-Wear in the 20th Century

By the 1920s, most women shopped for their wardrobes in department and women's specialty stores. Mass production and distribution through retail outlets accelerated the fashion cycle of styles produced in the following three decades and made the latest fashions available to the vast middle and working classes. With technological improvements in machinery and the development of synthetic fabrics, fashion producers were able to respond quickly to the changing needs of women for clothing that suited changing social, economic, and political conditions.

## Growth of the Fashion District

Crucial in the evolution and success of the American ready-to-wear business is New York's fashion district. This fashion center was created early in the 20th century by a committee of clothing manufacturers working with investors and a major real estate developer. The manufacturers had outgrown their small shops and factories on the Lower East Side and needed to expand. They wanted to move into a new, mostly undeveloped area of the burgeoning city. Between 1918 and 1921, fifty to sixty manufacturers moved uptown to Seventh Avenue along the west side of Manhattan. With more room for expansion in the new area, these entrepreneurs were able to parlay a baby business into a mature industry.

New York City, already a major industrial center, was well positioned to capitalize on the ready-to-wear boom. A large pool of cheap, immigrant labor was available. In addition, New York was ideally located near the textile producers in New England and the South. It was also a port city, so imported textiles could be brought in when needed. By 1923, the city was producing 80 percent of all women's apparel, with 20 percent still being done by home sewers and custom tailors. The 1920s and 1930s saw the emergence of several large clothing manufacturers.

Although New York remains the fashion capital of the United States and an international fashion center, sportswear and activewear manufacturers are booming in California, especially in Los Angeles.

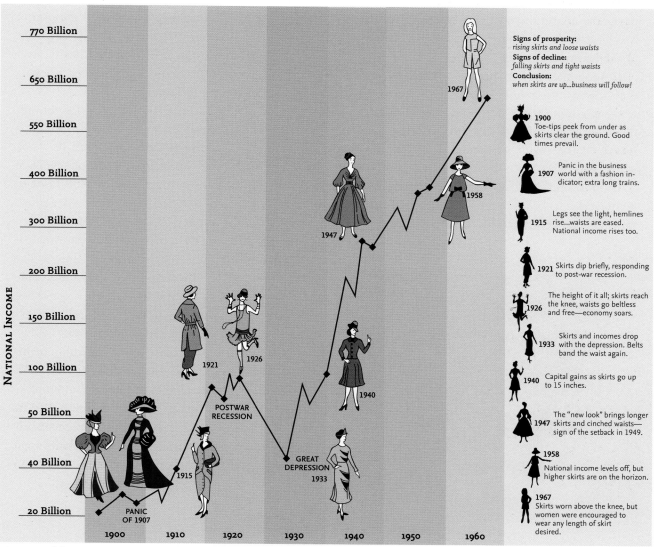

Courtesy of the H.W. Gossard Co.

**FIGURE 9.1** The ups and downs of fashion: in the free-wheeling decade of the 1960s, women were for the first time encouraged to wear any length of skirt they desired—not what the "pundits" of fashion decreed.

## Unionization

The history of the women's apparel business cannot be told without also describing the growth and influence of the clothing unions. The success of the industry in the early 20th century came about largely because the manufacturers were able to draw upon a substantial supply of immigrant labor. The industry was dominated by Jewish and Italian workers. In 1910, 55 percent of garment workers were Jewish, 35 percent were Italian, and 10 percent were from other groups. Many of the immigrants had no skills, but a sizable number had trained as dressmakers or tailors in their homelands. Skilled and unskilled labor was needed in the garment industry, which seemed to have gotten big overnight. The opportunity to turn a large and quick profit was enormous, at least for the owners.

At the other end of the scale, unfortunately, were the workers, who worked long hours for very little pay under conditions that were totally unregulated. A typical garment factory was dark, overcrowded, unsanitary, and unsafe.

In 1900, the workers began to unionize, a move they saw as their only chance to improve their working conditions. The International Ladies Garment Workers Union (ILGWU) was formed, and it remained the major garment industry union for many years.

Unionization did not happen overnight, and employers resisted the new union's demands as much as they could. Strikes in 1909 and 1910 paved the way for collective bargaining (see Figure 9.2), but public sympathy for the ladies' garment workers was not aroused until the devastating Triangle Shirtwaist Factory fire in 1911. One hundred forty-six workers, most of them young women, were killed. A tragedy of massive proportions, it nonetheless lent strength to the union movement.

At last people began to realize that the union stood for more than collective bargaining, that indeed many of its demands revolved around matters of life and death. The union's new strength opened the door to many concessions that helped the workers, such as strict building codes and protective labor laws. Child labor was outlawed.

The ILGWU managed to survive the Depression years. Under the guidance of David Dubinsky, who took the helm in 1932 and held it for 34 years, the ILGWU enjoyed a period of expansion, and the garment industry underwent a period of innovative growth. ILGWU negotiated a 35-hour, 5-day work week and paid vacations. It instituted health, welfare, and pension programs and financed housing projects and recreation centers.

From 1975 until 1995, the ILGWU fought imports—the first real threat to the American women's apparel industry in several decades—with its "Look for the Union Label" campaign. As part of UNITE, it actively supports the current "Crafted With Pride in U.S.A." campaign and the movement to abolish sweatshops at home and abroad (see Chapter 17).

In 1995, the ILGWU merged with the Amalgamated Clothing and Textile Workers Union. The new Union of Needletrade, Industrial, and Textile Employees, or UNITE, as it was known, represented the majority of workers in basic apparel and textiles, as well as millinery, shoes, and gloves.

However, in 2004, because of waning union membership in the apparel and textile industries, UNITE and HERE (Hotel Employees and Restaurant Employees International Union) merged, forming UNITE HERE. UNITE HERE has a diverse membership, largely composed of immigrants, and includes high percentages of African American, Latino, and Asian

**FIGURE 9.2** Women picketed in the early 1900s to improve their unsatisfactory working conditions.

American workers. UNITE HERE represents workers in apparel and textile manufacturing, apparel retail stores and distribution centers, hotels, casinos, food-service, airport concessions, and restaurants.

## Organization and Operation of the Women's Apparel Industry

For many decades, the typical women's apparel company was a small, independently owned, and often family-run business. Unlike the automobile industry, no Ford or General Motors dominated the women's apparel industry. In the early 1970s, about 5,000 firms made women's dresses. The industry's power came from its collective size. Its 5,000 firms did $3 billion in business every year.

All this changed in the 1970s. An expanding economy led to increased demand for everything, including clothing. Many of the textile companies had grown into huge businesses, as had several major retailers. Pushed from both directions, the clothing manufacturers responded by merging to create large publicly owned corporations.

Within a few years, it became obvious that many of the large corporations and conglomerates were not as successful as the smaller companies had been. The major problem was that the giants lacked the ability to respond quickly, a necessity in the fashion industry. Those that have survived and prospered have combined the advantages of large and small size by having divisions and subsidiaries function independently within the larger structure.

Regardless of whether a company is part of a conglomerate or a family-owned shop, the way in which clothes are produced does not vary. The operation of the apparel industry remains remarkably similar from business to business. The organization of the industry is currently undergoing changes, however. After years of specialization, the emergence of giant apparel producers has brought diversification. A number of the giants have divisions manufacturing men's wear, children's wear, home fashions, and accessories. Some began by

serving a discreet segment of the women's apparel market. For example, Liz Claiborne started with fashionable but affordable business dresses and branched out into Liz Sport, Liz Wear, Elisabeth (for plus-size apparel), shoes, accessories, and even men's wear. Other fashion businesses branched *into* women's wear. Ralph Lauren, who began his career designing neckties, subsequently began a women's line to parallel his men's wear designs. Nike and Reebok expanded from manufacturing athletic footwear to producing men's and women's activewear to go with their lines of shoes.

### Size of Producers

The legacy of the mergers and acquisitions of the 1980s is a bottom line mentality. The trend toward giantism shows no signs of letting up. It will continue if for no other reason than that the economy demands it. This means that as some firms strive to become giants, many small- and medium-sized firms will be swallowed up or will go out of business because they cannot compete. But those giants that give their subsidiaries and divisions the autonomy needed to serve their markets and thereby get to the bottom line can expect to continue to prosper. One example of a giant apparel firm that is growing is the VF Corporation, which designs, manufactures, and markets apparel for women, men, and children, with the following brand names: Lee, Wrangler, Riders, Rustler, Chic, Gitano, Vanity Fair, Vassarette, Bolero, Healthtex, North Face, Jantzen, and Jansport, among others.

### Specialization by Product

Apparel producers have typically been specialists, producing apparel for a particular lifestyle, a particular size range, and a specific price range. Nowhere in the industry is this more true than in women's wear, the segment with the largest, most varied, and fastest changing market. A woman's coat manufacturer, for example, seldom makes dresses, and a dress manufacturer does not turn out bathing suits. This is completely hidden from the customer by the growing practice of putting national brands and licensed designer names on a wide variety of merchandise—from evening gowns to bathing suits to shoes to perfume to sheets.

Despite a move toward greater diversification, producers and retailers still have to think and work like specialists. For instance, retail buyers still shop one group of producers for formals, another for rainwear, and still another for maternity wear—and this is not likely to change in the future.

### The Role of Designers

Designers, too, must balance diversification with specialization. From superstars to the new generation struggling to be recognized, all designers specialize to the extent that they are marketing their own artistic identity to a segment of the population that shares their vision (see Figure 9.3).

Today, as designers from the United States show in Paris and Milan, and European and Japanese designers show in New York, fashion-conscious consumers have a virtually limitless choice of looks they can adopt. There is the street-smart hip-hop style of Sean John; the casual, gentrified elegance of Ralph Lauren; the spare, clean look of Jil Sander;

**FIGURE 9.3** At the end of another successful show, Oscar de la Renta receives applause for his unique designs in women's apparel.

the meeting of Asian and Western sensibilities in the designs of Issey Miyake; and the luxury and sumptuousness of Giorgio Armani. The established designers of upscale lines not only cater to the people who can afford their clothing but also lead the way for producers of more moderately priced fashion in interpreting trends in fashion and popular culture.

### Categories in Women's Apparel

The following are the basic categories in women's apparel, and the types of garments generally included in each are organized in Table 9.1.

The categories of outerwear, suits, dresses, and blouses, have been fixtures in the women's ready-to-wear industry from the beginning, and sportswear and separates has been an important category since the 1930s. Jeans are considered a separate category by many manufacturers and retailers because of their unique position in Americans' wardrobes. The uniforms and aprons category fills a consumer need but does not set fashion trends. The same is true of the category for special needs.

Increasing attention to the categories of activewear, formal or after-5 wear, bridal wear, and maternity deserve further discussion. Along with apparel for the physically challenged, these categories may be thought of as small market segments or "niche" markets, that can be grouped by lifestyle and interests.

#### Activewear

Two-thirds of women dedicate a least half of their closets to activewear. According to a survey by Kelton Research in 2006, women are not saving workout clothes for the gym. They are trading traditional sportswear for activewear as their casual apparel of choice. The survey found that half of women dress in activewear regularly, even when they have no intention of working out, and a third of women choose activewear to run weekend errands because

**TABLE 9.1** *Basic Categories in Women's Apparel and the Types of Garments Included in Each Category*

| Category | Types of Garments | Category | Types of Garments |
|---|---|---|---|
| Outerwear | Coats, rainwear, jackets | Activewear | Clothing for participatory sports and athletic activities such as swimwear, tennis dresses, running suits, cycling shorts, exercise apparel, and skiwear |
| Dresses | One- or two-piece designs and ensembles (a dress with a jacket or coat) | | |
| Blouses | Dress and tailored | Uniforms and aprons | Aprons, smocks, housedresses, and a variety of uniforms |
| Suits | Jacket/skirt and jacket/pants combinations | Maternity | Dresses, sportswear, evening clothes, suits, and blouses designed to accommodate the special needs of pregnant women |
| After-5 and evening clothes | Formal and prom gowns, and other dressy apparel; this is often called "special occasion" | | |
| Bridal wear | Gowns and dresses for brides, attendants, and mothers of the bride and groom | Innerwear | Brassieres, panties, shapewear, bodywear, sleepwear, and other intimate apparel (see Chapter 12) |
| Sportswear and separates | Town-and-country and spectator sportswear, such as pants, shorts, tops, sweaters, skirts, shirts jackets, casual dresses, and jumpsuits | Special needs | Dresses, slops, nightgowns, hosiery, and other intimate apparel designed with snaps or Velcro for ease of use by elderly or physically challenged women |

**OUTERWEAR**     **DRESSES**     **AFTER-5 AND EVENING**     **UNIFORMS**

the fitness apparel is more comfortable and easier to care for than other clothing options.[2]

Demand for high-tech performance apparel, from weekend warriors and world-class athletes alike, helped drive up sales of sports apparel. Although prices have been steadily rising in the active apparel area, they have not deterred customers because the performance products today deliver more than is traditionally expected of fashion, such as moisture management and temperature control. Still, fashion and lifestyle play a big part. NPD Research shows that only about 30 percent of the money spent on sports apparel is for clothing that will actually be worn for exercise.[3]

As the country becomes more casual and the gymrats become more fashionable, the lines between sportswear and activewear are blurring. As sportswear companies enter the athletic area and customers look to active companies to dress them outside the gym, athletic apparel companies are examining the balance between performance and fashion (see Figure 9.4). "It would be foolish to think

**FIGURE 9.4** Nike understands that its activewear needs to be both functional and fashionable.

that performance gear can't be fashion-forward and that fashionable prices can't be functionable," said a Nike spokeswoman. One way is enlisting big-name designers from the fashion world. Fashion-focused lines, particularly big-name collaborations like Adidas with Stella McCartney (see Figure 9.5) and Reeboks with Scarlett Johansson, can have positive effects on the whole brand.

Swimwear has been an important segment of the women's apparel industry for decades, and the business has evolved somewhat differently from other activewear. Stodgy swimsuits just won't cut it anymore. Newer brands are among those companies picking up the slack. However, manufacturers jumping into the swimwear market beware: adjusting to rapid fashion trends that have kept contemporary apparel whirling has become critical for success in swimwear as well.

Old and young women are getting bigger in one area: cup size. Some brands are cutting cups up to DD and E, and Lauren by Ralph Lauren is increasing the number of swimsuit groups that feature D cups.

Some of the fabrics that are used in other activewear are also used in swimsuits, but for a different purpose. Lycra, for example, provides control that improves the appearance of the fit. The biggest U.S. manufacturers of swimwear continue to be such specialists as Cole of California, Jantzen, and Catalina, which produce designer brands through licensing agreements and also produce their own lines.

The ski industry has been slow to adapt to wider fashion trends over the years. But now, ski looks have been getting more fashionable as ski companies are teaming with big-name designers to create special collections.

Ski companies, similar to activewear collaborations such as Adidas with Stella McCartney and Puma with Neil Barrett, are getting fresh ideas from top fashion designers. Burton Snowboards is collaborating with British designer Sir Paul Smith, Moncler has worked with Balenciaga's Nicolas Ghesquière, and Ski Rossignol has joined with the design house Emilio Pucci for its newest line. Although Pucci is best known for colorful prints, the move to designing skiwear takes the firm full circle. The late designer Emilio Pucci got his start designing ski clothes and was a member of the 1934 Olympic ski team.[4]

## Formal Wear

Despite the growing casualness of everyday apparel, people all over the world still like to mark special

**FIGURE 9.5** Stella McCartney and Adidas joined together to form a fashion-focused line of activewear and yogawear.

occasions by wearing formal clothing. Elegant fabrics, trim, and silhouettes—worn with more elaborate jewelry, watches, and other accessories—mark most formal wear. This category is often called "after-5" or "special occasion."

Designers like Bob Mackie and Roberto Cavalli specialize in dressing Hollywood stars for opening nights and awards ceremonies; thousands of women across the country want similar looks for weddings, dances, and formal dinners.

It is interesting to note that evening wear gets more media coverage than any other category, especially at the Oscars, the Tony Awards, the VH1 awards, and similar events.

Picking out a prom dress has become a coming-of-age ritual in many parts of the United States, not unlike the formal "coming out" party ritual for debutantes—as well as a solid source of income for many manufacturers and retailers.

## Bridal Wear

Bridal wear has always been a category for a personal fashion statement, both for brides and designers. The tradition of the haute couture runway shows in Paris is to conclude with the modeling of a bridal gown, and some designers are known primarily for their work in this category. Weddings of movie stars, royalty, and other celebrities often inspire trends in bridal fashions, but the range of available styles runs from modern interpretations of Victorian designs to unadorned slip dresses. Hemlines range from the traditional floor length to street length to mini, and variety appears even in color. The rising age of first-time brides and the increase in the number of second weddings in recent years has contributed to the popularity of sophisticated styles.

In 2007, more than 2.4 million couples were married in the United States—and spent more than ever: an estimated $27,490 each. Theweddingreport.com, an online wedding statistical service, provides the year's average of top wedding experiences—and it's mostly all about the party. The wedding reception with food, liquor, music, photographs, and so on, costs most of the money. But what about the wedding dress? For many brides, the wedding dress is really the top priority, and she spends $1,500 or more for her gown. Designers like Vera Wang, Carolina Herrera, Reem Acra, Badgley Mischka, and Nicole Miller cater to these brides each year (see Figure 9.6). Shrugs, jackets, and shorter dresses are all trends that have been seen on the bridal runways. Are there ways to cut the dress

**FIGURE 9.6** Fashion designers offer a wide range of fashionable gowns for the modern bride. From left to right: Dresses from Vineyard, Vera Wang, and Platinum Collections.

# Fashion Focus

Fashion Focus

## Birth of a Notion
### *It's the Thought That Counts*

**DIANE VON FURSTENBERG SPRING 2008**
"'Under the Volcano' is every woman's fantasy to escape daily life for the exotic adventures of faraway shores..."

Designers say there is no rhyme or reason to when and how inspiration will strike—and that's half the fun! Here are some sketches by famous designers for their designs and what each felt inspired them.

**DONNA KARAN SPRING 2008**
"Chez Nueva York."

**BENJAMIN CHO FALL 2008**
"A fixation on beauty ignores an entire other half of life! Needless to say, I unfixated on beauty and the collection is turning ugly."

costs? Mainstream retailers such as J. Crew and Ann Taylor are bringing bridal gowns into their stores at lower prices. And of course there's always eBay. More than 5,000 dresses in a 6-month period were sold on the auction site, with winning prices ranging from $50 to $5,200. There is also the option of borrowing a dress from a friend—which is widely accepted today. Besides, each bride needs "something borrowed," doesn't she?[5]

## Maternity

Providing quality, comfort and fit, maternity wear is so popular, some moms admit they were better dressed when they were pregnant than after their babies were born. The influx of ready-to-wear designs joining the maternity sector has changed the image of maternity wear. The designers are translating current trends and bringing them into the maternity industry faster than they did in the past (see Figure 9.7).

In the last few years, there has been a new image on the state of pregnancy, and many retailers credit Hollywood for the change. Celebrities have been influencing fashion through celebrity clothing lines, and what they wear becomes very popular.

Mothers Work is the leading designer, manufacturer, and marketer of maternity fashion in the United States, with over 1,500 locations nationwide and growing. It owns leading brands Motherhood Maternity, Mimi Maternity, Mimi Essentials for Maternity, A Pea in the Pod, and Motherhood Outlets. Mothers Work offers online Internet retailing at www.destinationmaternity.com.

## *Size Ranges*

Women's apparel is divided into several size ranges. Unfortunately, the industry has not yet developed standard industry-wide size measurements for each of these ranges, although exploratory work has been undertaken in this direction. In many cases, the manufacturer has the pattern made to fit its target-

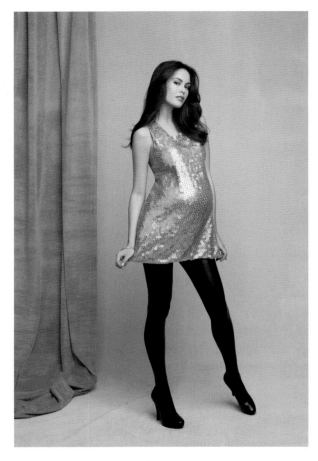

**FIGURE 9.7** Customers can find comfort, sophistication, and style in today's maternity wear.

ed customer's approximate size measurement. This is why one manufacturer's misses' size 12 is likely to fit quite differently from another manufacturer's misses' size 12. With licensing agreements and off-shore production playing an increasing role in apparel manufacturing, even two different styles bearing the same label in the same size may fit differently.

Women's wear is produced in the following size ranges:

- *Misses*—Includes regular even-numbered sizes 4 to 20, tall sizes 12 to 20, and sometimes sizes as small as 0 to 2.
- *Juniors*—Includes regular sizes 5 to 17 and petite sizes 1 to 15.
- *Petites*—Includes misses' even-numbered sizes 2P to 16P and junior sizes 1P to 15P.
- *Women's and Women's Petites*—Includes even-numbered sizes 12WP to 26WP, straight sizes 26 to 52, and XL to 5X.

## Misses

Misses' sizes are cut to fit the average adult woman's figure. Most women who are between 5 feet, 5 inches and 5 feet, 9 inches tall and of average weight can find suitably proportioned sizes in this range. You may hear the term "missy" used to describe this size range.

## Juniors

The juniors' range was introduced in the 1950s by Anne Fogarty, whose Anne Fogarty Five was designed to fit a slimmer, shorter-waisted figure than the misses' size 6, which was the smallest readily available size at the time. Because the junior figure is more common among teenagers than fully developed women, much of the apparel in this range has youthful styling, and many of the customers in junior departments and stores are teenagers.

Because many of the first baby boomers had their children at a relatively late age, the teen population is slated to be the strongest sector in terms of purchasing power. Teens make up 7 percent of the U.S. population but contribute 11 percent in spending power. According to a survey conducted by Market Research.com, the teen population has a total income of $80 billion, and their parents spend an additional $110 billion annually on their teen children.[6] Companies like Wet Seal/Contempo, Rampage, and XOXO are responding to the growth of the junior market, as is the specialized junior's catalog and store dELiA's. Clearly, this segment of market promises great opportunities for producers and retailers.

## Petites

Forty-seven million women are estimated to be under five feet four inches tall and thus in need of small sizes—a statistic that has caused rapid growth in market for this size range.

Proportioned for short, small-boned women who wear sizes 0 to 8, petite sizes are worn by both junior and misses' customers. Not only are the skirts and pants legs shorter than in regular-sized apparel; the sleeves are shorter, and details such as collars and pockets are scaled down.

As some department stores scale back their petite size offerings, Charming Shoppes, which caters to plus-size customers, has reintroduced the Petite Sophisticate stores. Believing that the petite size range is a $10 billion market, it is expected that these stores are looking toward a strong future.[7]

## Women's and Women's Petites

Approximately one-third of all women in the United States wears women's sizes 16 through 20, 26 to 52, XL to 5X, and women's petites sizes 12WP to 26WP, which are designed to fit shorter women with a fuller bust and shorter waistline. Until recently, however, apparel in these sizes made up a small percentage of production and were notable for their lack of style. This has all changed! Designers and manufacturers got on the bandwagon, and labels like Liz Claiborne, Dana Buchman, and Eileen Fisher began making stylish clothes for larger-sized women.

Today, the large-size or plus-size market, as it is now known, does $35 billion annually. Industry watchers say the plus-size apparel market for women is one of the fastest growing sectors in retail (see Figure 9.8). Department stores took the lead, moving larger sizes to their main apparel shopping floors. It is estimated that 30 percent of clothes in larger sizes are private-label or store brands.

Many specialty retailers have also begun to woo this customer. Talbots started "Talbots Woman" as a store dedicated to larger sizes, and the Gap and Old Navy are offering clothing through size 20. Lands' End and L. L. Bean, leading catalog companies, have devoted special catalogs to these customers, and their business has been overwhelming. Both Catherine's and Lane Bryant, part of the Charming Shoppes Company, have had a staggering increase in their plus-size business.

With celebrities like Mo'Nique; Queen Latifah; Cherese Lewis, who was the first woman crowned Miss Plus America; and Toccara Jones, the first plus-size supermodel appearing on television regularly, the new look of the stylish and sophisticated

**FIGURE 9.8** Lane Bryant's Limited Edition Crystal Seven7 jeans embellished with real Swarovski crystals provide stylish apparel for the plus-size consumer.

plus-size woman has been reinforced. Mass and mid-tier stores are the top destinations for plus-size fashions. Kmart, Sears, Fashion Bug, and Dress Barn are some of the top destinations, but retailers like Wal-Mart and Kohl's are taking their trendy lines, such as Metro7, Daisy Fuentes, and apt. 9, into plus sizes.

Adding to the availability of stylish plus-size fashions is the one-stop shopping offered on the Internet. Among the most popular is Pasazz.net, which features many plus-size merchants and offers fashion-conscious, plus-size women around the world a welcoming community where they can share their joys and frustrations about being full figured in a "thin is in" world.

## Wholesale Price Points

Women's apparel is produced and marketed at a wide range of wholesale prices. Major factors contributing to the wholesale price of a garment are

- The quality of materials
- The quality of workmanship
- The amount and type of labor required in the production process

- The executive and sales position structure of the organization
- Showroom rent and business overhead

## Major Price Zones

Within the wide range of prices, however, there are certain traditional **price zones**, or series of somewhat contiguous price lines that appeal to specific target groups of customers (see Figure 9.9). The women's ready-to-wear market has six major price zones. In order from the most to least expensive, they are as follows:

1. *Designer Signature.* The highest price zone includes lines by such name designers as Ralph Lauren, Oscar de la Renta, Calvin Klein, Donna Karan, Jean-Paul Gaultier, and John Galliano. A jacket alone costs more than $1,500.
2. *Bridge.* This zone is so named because it bridges the price ranges between designer and better prices. Bridge merchandise usually costs one-third to one-half of designer prices, or $800 to $1,000 for a three-piece outfit. A jacket alone costs about $300. Some designers who produce lines at the designer signature zone or at lower zones also have bridge lines. Examples include

**FIGURE 9.9**  Price determines which customers are buying what products. From left to right:  Vera Wang (designer signature price point), Vera Wang Lavender Label (contemporary price point), and Simply Vera Wang for Kohl's (moderate price point).

Tommy by Tommy Hilfiger, Donna Karan's DKNY, Calvin Klein's CK, and Theory's Premise.[8] Ellen Tracy, Tahari, Dana Buchman, Eileen Fisher, and Andrea Jovine are positioned as bridge companies.

3. *Contemporary.* This new zone is favored by young designers who want to enter the market with innovative, designer-quality lines but, at the same time, seek a broader market than that of the designer signature zone. By using less expensive fabrics and locating in lower-rent spaces, they can offer their lines at lower prices. Jackets wholesale from $90 to $120. Labels in this zone include Laundry by Shelli Segal, Vivienne Tam, Cynthia Rowley, Geronimo, Susan Lazar, Catalyst, and Misc.

4. *Better.* Apparel in this zone is usually medium to high in price. New labels in the better category include the O Oscar, an Oscar de la Renta line, which is sold exclusively at Macy's. O Oscar retails from $199 to $229 for jackets.[9] A new better collection by Calvin Klein will retail jackets at $198.[10] Other labels found in better departments include Liz Claiborne, Jones New York, Nautica, and Chaus.

5. *Moderate.* As the name suggests, this zone includes lines of nationally advertised makers, such as GUESS, Esprit, Levi Strauss, Jantzen, Alfred Dunner, and J.G. Hook, which have less prestige than lines with designer names but still appeal to middle-class consumers. However, more designer firms are moving into this price zone. Notably among them are Vera Wang with her new line. Simply Vera Wang, made exclusively for Kohl's Department Stores. Moderate merchandise is sold mostly in chain stores or in main-floor departments in department stores.

6. *Budget.* The lowest price zone is sometimes referred to as the "promotional" or "mass" market. It includes some national brand names such as Wrangler, Donnkenny, and Judy Bond Blouses but is primarily a mass-market retailer

private label, such as JCPenney's Arizona line of jeans or Sears's Canyon River Blues line of jeans, or Kmart's Jaclyn Smith line.

A recent development is the emergence of a seventh price zone, the new high end, for the super-rich. Some designers are trading up, offering special pieces in very limited quantities, at astronomical prices. This range is aimed at people who crave exclusivity and have the means to afford it. Ralph Lauren calls his line of hand-tailored women's classic suits and sportswear in luxury fabrics the Purple Label Custom Collection. Donna Karan offers a Limited Edition label with her signature on dresses costing $5,000 to $6,000. Carolina Herrera, Bill Blass, and Oscar de la Renta are also known for developing exclusive designs for special customers.

## Multiple Price Zones

Some producers offer merchandise in several price zones to capture a share of the business in each of several market segments. Manufacturer/retailer firms such as The Limited and the Gap cater to different price zone markets in each of their member store chains. Merchandise at The Limited stores appeals to a higher income customer than that at Lerner's. The Gap's stores have a somewhat overlapping price zone structure with Banana Republic merchandise at its highest zones, the Gap catering to the middle of its market, and Old Navy at its low end.

Designers also produce lines segmented by price zone. For example, DKNY is the label of Donna Karan's bridge collection; the Donna Karan label is reserved for her lines in the designer price zone, and the Limited Edition label for her custom-made collection. Ralph Lauren is another designer with lines in several different price zones. In descending order, a partial list of his lines are Ralph Lauren Purple Label Collection, Ralph Lauren, RL, Polo Sport, Black Label, and Polo.

Off-price apparel stores, which sell name-brand and designer merchandise at prices well below tra-

# Then & NOW

## The Celebrity Turned Fashion Designer
### *Does It Have a Future?*

Whereas past celebrity lines by Jaclyn Smith, Kathie Lee Gifford, and Cheryl Tiegs targeted customers who shop in retail chains such as Kmart, Wal-Mart, and Sears, the newest generation of stars turned designers aims to compete directly with Donna Karan, Ralph Lauren, Calvin Klein, and Marc Jacobs, bringing their star power to the fashion industry and targeting more upscale store sales.

Some celebrities become partners in newly created business, while others establish brand names that they license for sportswear, ready-to-wear, fragrances, and accessories.

Do you wonder why so many celebrities are rushing into the fashion world now? The answer is simple—the money! In fact, if a celebrity designer has any success, it could provide an income that far exceeds what a CD or movie role might provide them.

Gwen Stefani says this about her fashion designing venture: "It's something that is going to be what I do to express myself creatively, that is a lot less draining than writing music or performing." Designing clothes, in her view, has a whole different staying power.

Celebrities come to fashion with a clear advantage over young, unknown designers. They have instantly recognizable profiles, often

**AUGUST 20, 1984**     $1.75

**TIME**

SPECIAL REPORT
A Memorable Olympics

**SASSY SEARS**
**Toasters And Tires ...and Cheryl Tiegs**

SEARS

established through reams of press coverage, music videos, and red-carpet appearances. Celebrities are real people, and we know every intimate detail about their lives. There is a feeling that by knowing them, we have a connection, a true friendship that brings something to our lives.

Just how much longevity do these celebrity brands have? Some stars got into the fashion game early and reaped the rewards. Jaclyn Smith, of television's *Charlie's Angels* fame (now being rerun on cable every night), teamed with Kmart over two decades ago, and her clothes are still flying off the shelves.

The new crop of celebrity designers who want to enter the fashion space must have that fashion personality, style, real point of view, and a true vision of who their customer is. What brands do succeed?

"The ones that are modeled on the celebrity's own unique style," says Danielle De Marne fashion director of Scoop, an upscale clothing chain.

Among the most successful of the celebrity designers have been Sean John, Jennifer Lopez, Gwen Stefani, Beyoncé Knowles, Jessica Simpson, and the original "hip-hop boys" Jay-Z, Damon Dash, Snoop Dogg, Ice-T, and Nelly. Today they are joined by Kimora Lee Simmons, Justin Timberlake, Victoria Beckham, Sienna Miller, Sarah Jessica Parker, Usher, and Mary-Kate and Ashley Olsen.

ditional department store levels, are putting increasing pressure on all the traditional price zones, especially moderate to better. These outlets, such as Marshalls, T. J. Maxx, Filene's Basement, and Loehmann's, are thriving because customers are aware of the price zones associated with the labels and realize they are getting a bargain, though perhaps not this season's look. Factory outlets offer prices similar to those found in off-price stores, but the merchandise is limited to the goods of a single producer.

Perhaps the most compelling reason a consumer would be willing to pay full retail price at a traditional department or specialty store is the availability of a broad assortment of styles, sizes, and colors from the beginning of each season. Generally, the stock in off-price and factory outlets is limited to merchandise that was not ordered earlier by stores charging full retail price.

## Private Labels

Traditional department and specialty stores can also compete in pricing by developing their own private labels. Much of this merchandise is priced in the better price zone, but the quality is comparable to that of designer signature or bridge apparel. Some of the same manufacturers who produce the name-brand merchandise that a store is selling at higher prices also make the store's private label goods. Private label merchandise is vigorously promoted to develop brand recognition, and some customers do not distinguish between private and national brands when they shop.

## *Seasonal Classifications*

In addition to classifying women's apparel by function, size, and price zone, retailers and producers also pay attention to season. This classification is different from the others, however, in that few businesses specialize in just one season. Even swimwear is sold in the winter resort season as well as the summer.

The major apparel seasons correspond to the calendar, with the semiannual designer runway shows introducing fall/winter and spring/summer collections (see Figure 9.10, bottom), each a half-year in advance of the time when the new fashions appear on the retail selling floor. Within the fall season are the holiday season, which features evening wear for New Year's Eve, and the resort season (see Figure 9.10, top), when cruise wear and swimsuits are the focus of attention. The spring/summer season has its emphasis on summer. In temperate climates with seasonal temperature changes, spring weather does not last long. Therefore, lightweight topcoats and linen suits in dark colors have less of a market than apparel designed for warmer weather.

## Merchandising and Marketing

Most fashion producers sell directly to retail stores rather than through intermediaries. The pace of fashion in all but a few staple items is much too fast to allow for the selling, reselling, or warehousing activities of wholesale distributors or jobbers.

As a result, women's apparel producers aim their sales promotion efforts at both retailers and consumers. Such efforts take the form of advertising, publicity, and sales promotion. (Chapter 19 discusses the collaborative marketing efforts of producers and retailers from the retailers' perspective.)

### Advertising

Today most retail advertising of women's fashion apparel carries the name of the manufacturer. But this was not always the case. Until the 1930s, many retailers refused to let manufacturers put any tags or labels on the clothes they made. Merchandise shortages during World War II, coupled with government regulations, helped to reverse this situation. Most merchants are now happy to capitalize on the producers' labels that are attached to clothes. They feature manufacturers' names in their own advertising and displays and set up special sections within stores that are exclusively devoted to individual producers' lines.

The apparel manufacturing industry spends less than 1 percent of its annual sales on advertising, but the exposure given to its products is impressive (see Figure 9.11). After all, that 1 percent is usually based on very healthy sales figures.

The 1980s saw a tremendous growth in sales for national brands and nationally known designer labels. In part, this growth resulted from national advertising campaigns directed at consumers.

**FIGURE 9.10** Gucci fall/winter, 2008 (bottom), and Gucci Resort, 2007 (top) collections.

National brands and designer labels continued with no signs of a change in this trend.

## Print Advertising

Fashion and general-interest magazines and newspapers are prime outlets for apparel advertising (see Figure 9.12), as are trade publications such as *Women's Wear Daily*, with its large circulation among retailers. Fashion magazines provide another forum for exposure, largely directed to the customer, with editorial reports about clothes and fashion trends of the season and with both United States and international coverage.

Considering the amount of money that goes into advertising, and the use that retailers are now willing to make of manufacturer's names, it is not surprising that cooperative advertising appears both in magazines and newspapers and now also in store catalogs, such as those from Federated Department Stores.

## Broadcast Advertising

Because radio is dominated by local stations and because it lacks the visual element, it is not the medium of choice for product advertising of apparel. Mention of brand names or categories of clothing usually take the form of retailers' spot commercials advertising a sale or the arrival of new seasonal merchandise.

Television advertising of women's wear is dominated by large producers, such as Levi Strauss, and national retail chains, such as Sears and JCPenney, which can afford the expense of producing the commercials and purchasing network air time. Locally broadcast spot announcements are sometimes paid for with cooperative advertising dollars. The commercial is produced for the manufacturer with a voice track that can be changed to name the retail outlet that is advertising as a source of the brand.

Cable TV advertising is less expensive than network TV and is used by smaller manufacturers and retailers of women's wear, especially on cable chan-

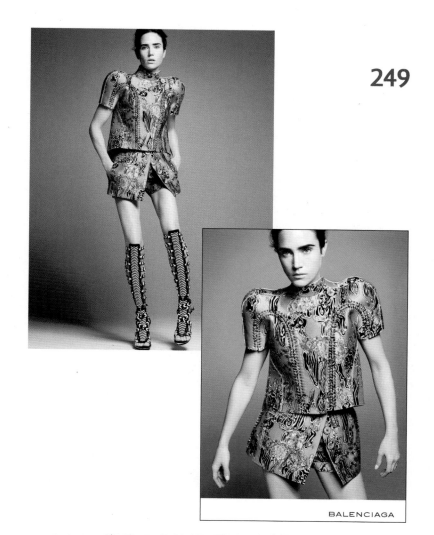

BALENCIAGA

**FIGURE 9.11** Advertisements, such as these for Balenciaga (top) and Diane von Furstenberg (bottom), bring in publicity and sales for designers.

**FIGURE 9.12** Fashion magazines, such as *Allure* (left), *W* (middle), and *Lucky* (right), report the latest fashion trends.

nels with programming directed to women, such as Lifetime Cable.

Large producers are also showing ads that look like movie trailers in movie theaters across the country.

## Other Electronic Advertising

The Internet is exploding with advertising for apparel of all kinds, as even very small manufacturers and retailers develop their own sites. Designers are offering their fans more detailed information on their collections and pushing their lifestyle visions. See the discussion under "Industry Trends" at the end of this chapter.

## *Publicity*

In addition to the enormous amount of money spent on advertising, apparel producers use publicity to promote their names. Many manufacturers, especially in the designer area, retain the services of a public relations firm, whose primary job is to ensure coverage in the editorial pages of magazines and newspapers. Cable television is another source

of editorial coverage for designers; C-Span, MTV, and VH1 broadcast fashion programs that feature designers who cater to their audiences' tastes. VH1 gives annual Fashion Awards that are extremely influential.

Manufacturers also supply sports personalities and other celebrities with clothes in an attempt to attract public attention. One rarely watches a sports event these days without seeing and hearing mention of the brand names not only of the equipment being used but also of the apparel that is worn, along with endorsements from leading athletes.

## *Fashion Shows, Press Weeks, and Trade Shows*

The major public relations effort in women's wear goes into the presentations and fashion shows at which designers show their new collections for retailers and the fashion reporters for the press, and the broadcast and Internet media.

The shows provide the country's newspaper, magazine, radio, television, and Internet fashion editors and reporters an opportunity to examine the newest American designer collections as well as those of leading European manufacturers. Editors are deluged with press releases and photo and interview opportunities that will help them tell the fashion stories to their readers. Initially, there were "press weeks" that followed the formal line openings at which designers exhibited merchandise lines in all price categories specially to the press rather than to buyers. Gradually, however, the lower-priced merchandise was eliminated. Press weeks as exclusive showcases for high-priced fashion continued; then, as a result of cost and timing factors, they were eliminated. Now the press sees the collections at the same time as the retailers do.

To coordinate shows of their new lines during market weeks, the manufacturers who lease permanent or temporary showroom space at the major regional markets in Los Angeles, Dallas, Miami, Atlanta, and Seattle depend on the services of the management of their market buildings. New York designers (including foreign designers with New York showrooms) are not housed in a single site, so they have joined together to form 7th on Sixth, an organization that manages the fashion week shows that are staged in Bryant Park in New York City. IMG sponsors an annual award show that attracts international press and broadcast coverage. The giant MAGIC show for women's wear is held semi-annually in Las Vegas. The B.A.T. Woman Show for plus and tall sizes has become an international hit. Other major international women's wear shows include those held semianually in Paris, London, Milan, Tokyo, and Hong Kong. These shows are discussed in more detail in Chapter 16.

### Trunk Shows

Trunk shows are another excellent form of publicity for the women's apparel industry. **Trunk shows** present a manufacturer's line to a retail store's sales staff and its customers (see Figure 9.13). A representative of the company, sometimes a designer, typically mounts a fashion show of sample garments. After the show, he or she meets with customers to discuss the styles and their fashion relevance. The retail store's customers may review items they have seen and order them.

Everyone benefits from trunk shows. Customers see clothes as the designer planned them and coordinated them, and they experience some of the glamour of the fashion industry. The retailer enjoys the dramatic influx of customers who come to such personal appearances and shows and any profits that result as clothes are ordered. The manufacturer tests the line on real customers in order to understand real consumers' needs *firsthand*! If customer response is enthusiastic, the designer achieves new status—and bigger orders—from the retailer than otherwise expected.

Although trunk shows may mean headaches for designers, they still pack a punch when it comes to selling high-priced clothes. Designers say that

**FIGURE 9.13** This trunk show by designer Charlotte Ronson features the designer herself describing her latest line.

trunk shows account for anywhere from 20 to 43 percent of a line's business. They also give the designer an opportunity to make a personal statement directly to the consumer. Oscar de la Renta says that trunk shows are very important because of the promotional impact, especially if the designer is working with licensees.

Donna Karan joined the trunk show circuit when she began designing under her own name. Besides being good for profits, trunk shows seem to have a great effect on the designer's designs. Being able to see their clothes on the women who wear them, in the part of the country where they live, helps the designer find out what works and what does not.

Most of these clothes retail for over $500, making them investment dressing. Many designers say that store buyers have a limit on how much they may purchase from any one designer. At a trunk show, the consumer can see almost everything that the designer has created and is given a much larger choice and selection.

### DVDs and CD-ROMs

DVDs and CD-ROMs that show off a manufacturer's line are another promotional tool. The manufacturers' and designers' seasonal premiers are videotaped with live models; a running commentary is then added by the manufacturer or designer. DVDs are primarily shown to retailers' sales staffs to explain the fashion importance of items and to give tips on selling, but they are also sometimes shown on the selling floor.

Unfortunately, in-store showings of DVDs have not been the potential goldmine that manufacturers had hoped, perhaps because women who are already in the store to shop do not want to stand around and look at a videotape. DVD producers have begun to zero in on their market, though, and fashion DVDs are now showing up in restaurants, hospitals, airports, doctors' and dentists' offices, and discos—all places that seem to be more conducive than the store to this form of entertainment. There is no charge to the apparel producer (the video user on location pays a use fee), so this amounts to another form of publicity for the fashion industry. But apparel manufacturers have not given up entirely on the idea of fashion DVDs.

## Promotion Aids

Manufacturers also provide retailers with an assortment of other promotional aids designed to assist them and speed the sale of merchandise. A firm may offer any or all of the following:

- Display ideas
- Display and stock fixtures
- Advertising aids
- Reorder forms and assistance in checking stock for reordering purposes
- Educational and sales training assistance for salespersons and customers
- Promotional talks by producers' representatives
- Assistance in giving in-store fashion shows
- Statement enclosures or other ads designed to reach customers by mail
- Special retail promotions to tie in with national advertising campaigns
- Advertising mats for smaller stores
- Cooperative advertising funds from the manufacturer or the fiber association

## Industry Trends

Throughout the coming decades, the U.S. women's apparel industry and the U.S. apparel industry overall will face dramatic changes. American designers have finally succeeded in rivaling designers from Paris and Milan as definers of high fashion. However, the American manufacturing industry faces what may be its toughest competitive challenge ever: the growth of a global clothing market out of which U.S. manufacturers must carve their market share, since a rise in imports has threatened the market they had enjoyed within the United States.

After decades of domination at home, the American wholesale market has been inundated with imports from countries with cheap labor. More and more U.S. manufacturers are using foreign labor, a process called global sourcing, in factories they own or lease in low-wage countries around the world. The U.S. apparel industry is taking steps, however, to enable it to compete more effectively in an increasingly global marketplace. Some of its tactics include:

- Emergence of manufacturers as retailers (see Figure 9.14)
- Greater emphasis on licensing
- Increased offshore production
- Increased emphasis on Quick Response
- Use of computers and the Internet

## Manufacturers as Retailers

As discussed in Chapter 8, designer Ralph Lauren was the first designer to open his own retail store. Frustrated by the way department and specialty stores were selling his clothes, he opened the first Polo/Ralph Lauren shop in 1971. Since then, his empire has grown to shops throughout the United States, Europe, and Asia. Because of his investment in the design and interior decoration of his stores, particularly the Madison Avenue store, Ralph Lauren's foray into retailing has benefited his business more as a promotional tool for his fashion collec-

**FIGURE 9.14** Coach both manufactures and retails—a prime example of vertical integration.

tions than as a source of income. He still exercises tight control over the sale of his collections in stores-within-stores in the major department store chains. Today, dozens of designers have followed Ralph Lauren's example.

Other producer/retailers sell at retail exclusively through their own outlets. Benetton is one example; Talbots is another.

Which manufacturers will succeed as retailers remains to be seen. A producer first has to compete for good retail talent, which can be expensive, as well as retail space in a prime location. The risks escalate if the manufacturer franchises, which many must do because they cannot personally oversee their retail empire.

## Licensing

As was discussed in Chapter 5, licensing, selling the right to produce merchandise bearing a designer's name, is a strategy of virtually every major American designer. In women's wear, some designers, like Donna Karan, have relatively few licensed products,

while others, like J.G. Hook, are full-time licensors that produce nothing in house. Still others offer an extensive range of licensed accessories and home furnishings, while producing most apparel in house. Sometimes the revenue from licensed products exceeds that of the main business; it is rumored that some designer fragrances bring in far more than their signature apparel lines! Some manufacturers see licensing as a way to test market a new product category in a relatively low-risk way. If the new category succeeds and proves it will sell, it may be brought in house for manufacture.

## Offshore Production

With their promise of delivering low cost, imports have made inroads into women's wear. Producers' associations such as the Crafted With Pride Council and labor unions such as UNITE HERE have been diligently applying the same anti-import pressure on behalf of the women's wear industry that they have applied on behalf of the textile, men's, and children's wear industries. Imports—particularly those involving textile and apparel—are seen as a major threat to the survival of the U.S. clothing industry.

The federal government is reluctant to impose any curbs on offshore production that might interfere with its role in keeping clothing prices (and inflation) down, and U.S.-owned manufacturers that benefit from the lower labor costs of overseas assembly naturally support policies that favor their operations. As good corporate citizens, however, many apparel manufacturers were quick to recognize the need for self-regulation when sweatshop conditions in third-world countries—and even in some domestic factories employing illegal aliens—came to light in the mid-1990s.

Buying foreign-made women's wear has many limitations. Very early commitment—as much as eight to nine months lead time, for example—is necessary. Usually there is no opportunity for reorders. These limitations have been seized upon by U.S. manufacturers anxious to stem the tide of imports.

### Increased Emphasis on Quick Response

American manufacturers who rely on domestic production facilities have several advantages over those who use global sourcing. Some of the cost savings of manufacturing in countries where labor is cheaper are reduced by import duties, so American manufacturers have learned to have the less labor-intensive operations performed at home. American garment workers trained to operate computerized equipment are skilled employees, and the difference between their wages and those of factory workers in low-income countries represents a difference in the job performed. Furthermore, the automation of production processes means that they can be completed more quickly. Add the speed of production to the time saved by not having to ship goods overseas, and the producer can offer retail customers Quick Response, a crucial consideration in the fashion business.

### Use of Computers and the Internet

Another way U.S. fashion manufacturers attract business is through their use of computers, especially the Internet (see Figure 9.15). As we discussed in Chapter 8, computerization is now an integral part of the production process, starting with designing. The Internet is a very popular shopping

**FIGURE 9.15** Manufacturers and designers often use Internet promotion in the form of lookbooks to attract customers (top).
**FIGURE 9.16** Online sales makes shopping quick and easy for customers (middle and bottom).

destination. Adult Americans surveyed estimate that about one-quarter of their clothing was bought online.[11] Online sales (see Figure 9.16) in the apparel category was over $13.8 billion in 2006 and is the fastest growing form of shopping for apparel.[12] Today, not only retailers have Web sites, manufacturers and designers also have Web sites that keep their names and brands in front of the consumer.

## Summary and Review

Women's wear is the largest segment of the fashion industry, and it sets the trends for other segments. In the 20th century, merchandising of ready-to-wear apparel has in the United States has been centered in the fashion district of New York City, with other major markets in Los Angeles, Dallas, and Atlanta. Mass production has depended on a unionized labor force, represented by UNITE HERE.

The production of women's wear is segmented in several ways, and companies may specialize according to use categories, such as activewear or bridal wear; sizes, including misses', junior, petite, women's, and half sizes; price zones, ranging from designer signature to bridge to better and contemporary to moderate and budget. Manufacturers and designers change their goods by selling season.

Merchandising and marketing activities include advertising; publicity; fashion shows, press weeks, and trade shows; trunk shows; DVDs; and other promotion aids.

Five major industry trends include manufacturers acting as retailers, more and more licensing, increasing offshore production and imports, increased emphasis on the Quick Response strategy in the United States, and the widespread use of computers and the Internet.

## Trade Talk

Define or briefly explain the following terms:

custom-made                price zones
ready-to-wear (RTW)        trunk show

## For Review

1. Why did New York City become the center of the garment industry in the United States?
2. Discuss the growth and contributions of UNITE to the apparel industry.
3. Name some specialized market segments served by apparel manufacturers.
4. List the traditional basic categories of women's apparel, giving types of garments in each category.
5. Into what size ranges is women's apparel traditionally divided?
6. List and describe the six major price zones into which women's apparel is divided. What are the major factors contributing to the wholesale price of garments?
7. Why do most fashion producers sell directly to retail stores rather than through wholesalers?
8. Discuss the merchandising activities of women's fashion producers today.
9. How does a manufacturer or designer benefit from attending a trunk show in a retail store?
10. Discuss the major problems facing a manufacturer who is also a retailer.

## For Discussion

1. Discuss the advantages and disadvantages of standardization of women's apparel sizes.
2. What are the repercussions of a name-brand or designer manufacturer selling current-season apparel to off-price outlets as well as to department and specialty shops?

chapter ten

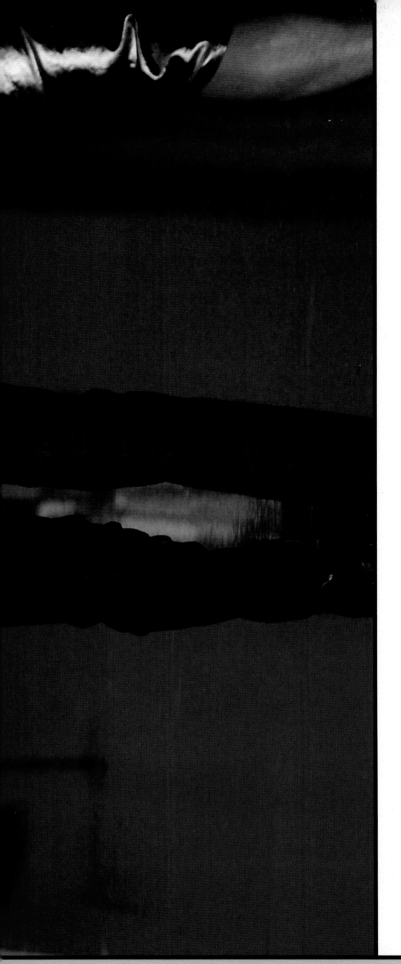

*Everything you always wanted to know*

*about trends in the men's apparel industry.*

**KEY CONCEPTS**

• The history of the men's wear industry

• Categories of men's apparel

• Roles of brand names and designer names in the marketing of men's wear

• Advertising and promotional activities in the marketing of men's apparel

# Men's Apparel

Clothes have been part of the story of man—yes, "man"—because most of the world's great clothes have been worn by men to express power, wealth, and glory. Such male clothes are shown in museums around the world. These clothes represented the tribal chief, the warrior, the cleric, and the monarch—in a word, the male (see Figure 10.1).

In fact, the men's business outfit in the 21st century has retained a basically conservative style that evolved in the late 1700s. Over the years, neutral colors have prevailed, and changes in style have occurred mostly in the details. Jackets are longer or shorter, with wider or narrower lapels; jacket vents and trouser cuffs come and go. Shirt collars mutate into various shapes, and ties are invented and reinvented. But overall, men's clothing has changed very little (see Figure 10.2).

## History of the Men's Apparel Industry

The oldest of the domestic apparel industries, the men's wear industry gave birth to the women's and children's wear industries. It got its start in the late 1700s. Prior to that, the rich patronized tailor shops, where their clothing was custom-made or fitted to them. Everyone else wore homemade clothing.

### Birth of Ready-to-Wear

The first ready-to-wear men's clothing was made by tailors in port cities along the Atlantic Coast. Seamen arrived in these cities in need of clothes to wear on land but without the time to have them tailor-made. To meet their needs, a few astute tailors began anticipating the ships' arrivals by making up batches of suits in rough size groupings. Sailors, who could put on the new clothes and walk away in them, liked the idea. These early ready-to-wear stores were called **slop shops**, a name that was appropriate to what they sold. Ready-to-wear clothing offered none of the careful fit or detail of custom-tailored clothes. But the price was right and the convenience was important, so ready-to-wear clothing gradually gained acceptance in ever-widening circles.

Although never considered slop shops, some distinguished men's wear retail operations got their start on waterfronts. Brooks Brothers' first store opened in 1818 in downtown New York, and Jacob Reed's Sons' first store opened in 1824 near the Philadelphia waterfront.

### Role of the Industrial Revolution

The market for ready-to-wear clothing was further increased by the industrial revolution. Ironically, though, the industrial revolution also helped to create the new conservative look that prevailed for so long. The industrial revolution led to the introduction of machinery in all areas of production and replaced the absolute dependence on human hands in the making of goods. Clothing, like much else, could be mass produced. This, in part, led to standardization in people's tastes. Mass-produced clothes were made for the lowest common denominator, which in men's wear led to a conservatively cut, dark-colored suit.

The look, however, was not entirely the result of mass production. The idea of conservative men's suits also had its origins in a new role model that emerged during the industrial revolution—the industrialist. On the one hand, these newly rich tycoons had working-class roots and were not about to dress like the rich peacocks. On the other hand, they had finally gained access to something long denied them—power and money—and they wanted this distinction to show in their dress. Sober and conservative themselves, they chose to wear clothes that were sober and conservative.

The industrial revolution also helped to create a managerial class made entirely of men who were happy to emulate the look of the rich industrialists.

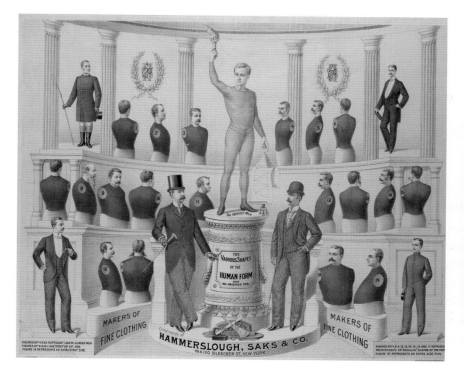

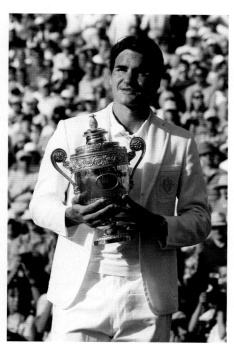

**FIGURE 10.1** The various shapes of the male form (top left). **FIGURE 10.2** Over the years, there have been minimal changes in men's apparel. From top right to bottom right: men's sportswear looks from 1880, 1955, 1982, and 2007.

Soon all men who worked in offices wore the look, and the tailored, dark-colored work suit that men would wear for the next 150 years was born.

The industrial revolution helped to move the production of clothing out of the home. The demand for people to operate the new machines was so great that entire families often went to work.

This left no one at home to sew and further boosted the demand for ready-to-wear clothing.

### Mid- to Late 1800s

As late as the mid-1800s, rich people still did not consider buying their clothes off the rack in shops that had been slop shops but had become respectable. The middle class, usually the most important element in making a style acceptable, patronized the stores.

## Advances in Production Techniques

The introduction of the sewing machine in 1846 was another important advance in men's apparel; it sped up production. During the Civil War, when manufacturers scrambled to make uniforms according to specification, standardized sizes for a variety of figure types developed. The invention of paper patterns by Ebenezer Butterick and his wife in 1863 improved the consistency of the sizing, assuring a better fit in ready-to-wear clothing—the last thing that was necessary to make them popular with all classes.

## Use of Contractors

As the men's ready-to-wear business grew, so did its attractiveness as a profitable investment. But going into business as a men's wear manufacturer required considerable capital in terms of factory construction, equipment, and labor costs. This situation led to the birth of the contractor business, described in Chapter 8. By hiring a contractor to do the sewing and sometimes the cutting as well, manufacturers eliminated the need for their own factories, sewing machines, or labor force. They could function with just a showroom or space for shipping.

Early contractors of men's wear operated in one of two ways. Usually, they set up their own factories where the manufacturing was done. But sometimes they distributed work to operators who would work at home, either on their own machines or on machines rented from the contractors. These workers were paid on a piecework basis.

Right after the Civil War and for the next two decades or so, men's wear was manufactured in three different ways:

1. In inside shops, or garment factories, owned and operated by manufacturers

2. In contract shops, or contractors' factories, where garments were produced for manufacturers
3. In homes, where garments were made usually for contractors but sometimes for manufacturers

## The Rise of Unions

As the men's wear market and industry grew, so did competition among manufacturers. To produce ready-to-wear clothing at competitive prices, manufacturers and contractors demanded long hours from workers and yet paid low wages. In addition, factory working conditions, which had never been good, deteriorated further. Contractors were particularly guilty, and their factories deserved the names sweatshops or "sweaters" that were given to them. According to an official New York State inspection report of 1887:

> The workshops occupied by these contracting manufacturers of clothing, or "sweaters" as they are commonly called, are foul in the extreme. Noxious gases emanate from all corners. The buildings are ill smelling from cellar to garret. The water-closets are used by males and females, and usually stand in the room where the work is done. The people are huddled together too closely for comfort, even if all other conditions were excellent.[1]

What happened next was inevitable. Workers finally rebelled against working conditions, hours, and pay. Local employee unions had existed in the industry since the early 1800s, but none had lasted long or wielded much power. The Journeymen Tailors' National Union, formed in 1883, functioned mainly as a craft union. A union representing all apparel industry workers, the United Garment Workers of America, was organized in 1891, but it had little power and soon collapsed. Finally, in 1914, the Amalgamated Clothing Workers of America (ACWA) was formed. It remained the major union of the men's wear industry until the 1970s, when it merged with the Textile Workers of America and the United Shoe Workers of America to form the Amalgamated Clothing and Textile Workers Union (ACTWU). Then, in 1995, the ACTWU joined with the International Ladies Garment Workers Union (ILGWU) to form UNITE, the Union of Needletrade, Industrial, and Textile Employees, and in 2004 its name changed to UNITE HERE.

UNITE represents the workers in virtually all domestic plants in the tailored-clothing segment of men's wear manufacturing. The common beginnings of both the union and the factories in the Northeast may account for this strong presence. However, its influence in factories producing men's work clothes, furnishings, and sportswear in other parts of the country was almost nonexistent until the famous strike during the early 1970s at the El Paso, Texas, factory of the Farah Company, one of the largest manufacturers of men's pants and work clothes. The company had resisted the attempt of the ACTWU to organize the Farah workers for many years, and only after a long court battle were the plant and its workers unionized. However, the influence of UNITE is still not as strong in other segments and regions as it is in tailored clothing in the Northeast.

### Acceptance of Ready-to-Wear in the 20th Century

Store-bought clothes finally broke the class barrier during the last half of the 19th century. Financial crises such as the panics of 1869, 1873, and 1907 sent men who had formerly worn only custom-tailored clothes into the ready-to-wear clothing stores. Even though custom-tailoring remained a vital part of the men's wear industry far longer than it lasted in women's wear, it was dealt a final blow during the Great Depression. Today, it represents only a small segment of the industry.

### World War II

The Great Depression of 1929 brought about a decline in demand for all consumer products, and the economy did not get back on its feet again until World War II.

During the war, of course, the entire apparel industry was given over to the war effort. The men's wear industry ground to a halt and turned its attention to making uniforms. Restrictions were placed on the design and use of fabric. Trouser cuffs, which required extra fabric, disappeared. Once the war ended, however, the restrictions were lifted, and even more important, a long era of postwar prosperity began.

The returning servicemen were eager to get out of their uniforms. The demand for "civvies," or civilian clothes, was so great that for a few years clothing manufacturers worked—with little thought for changing styles—simply to keep up with the demand. By the late 1940s, manufacturers were meeting demand and could even stand back and consider style.

### The Postwar Era

The major change in the men's wear industry in the postwar period was the emergence of a new class of clothes called sportswear. It originated in Southern California in the late 1940s, where suburban living and a climate conducive to leisure created a demand for clothes to be worn outside work.

For a while, the demand for sportswear was filled by a group of former New York manufacturers who had gravitated to the West Coast. They gave sportswear not only to California but to the entire nation. The California market, as sportswear came to be known in the business, gained further momentum when buyers from major department stores such as Marshall Field, Hudson's, Macy's, and Lord & Taylor traveled to the West Coast to attend the spring sportswear show held every October in Palm Springs. New York clothing manufacturers wasted no time cashing in on the trend. By the mid-1960s, men's sportswear was as much a part of the East Coast market as tailored clothing.

What later become known as "designer clothes"

**FIGURE 10.3** Both the Edwardian look (top) and the hippie look (bottom) were popular looks for men in the 60s and 70s.

also got their start in California in the 1940s. Hollywood motion-picture costume designers such as Don Loper, Orry-Kelly, Howard Greer, and Milo Anderson created lines for California sportswear manufacturers. Oleg Cassini and Adrian began licensing agreements with New York neckwear producers.

Designer clothes, à la California, proved to be an idea born before its time, a rare occurrence in the trendy fashion world. The designer sportswear could not compete with the new Ivy League or continental look that emerged on the East Coast. Designer clothes faded away and did not reemerge until the 1960s when designers like Pierre Cardin and John Weitz would try again, with much greater success.

## Fashions of the 1960s and 1970s

Little happened in men's fashion until the 1960s, when suddenly men's wear blossomed, cultivated by the costuming of such British rock groups as the Beatles and the Rolling Stones. The "Mod look" brought color to men's wear after a 150-year absence. It was followed by the "Edwardian look," which changed the shape of men's wear for the first time in decades (see Figure 10.3, top). Other styles, such as the Nehru jacket, were little more than fads.

**Revolutionary Fashion.** The social revolution of the 1960s was reflected in the hippies' all-occasion dress code. For men, it prescribed long hair and beard; jeans; a choice of tie-dyed T-shirt, denim work shirt, or a colorfully flower-powered shirt with no tie; love beads; and, weather permitting, sandals (see Figure 10.3, bottom). The civil rights movement was expressed in fashion by the adoption of African clothing, especially the *dashiki*, a colorfully printed, loose-fitting, collarless woven shirt.

In Europe, Pierre Cardin's "Peacock look," with its peaked shoulders, fitted waist, and flared pants, transformed the male uniform and blazed the trail for current men's fashions.

**Revolutionary Fabrics.** For the first time since

the development of the sewing machine, technology influenced men's wear fashions. Knits, made from synthetic fibers, enjoyed a boom in the 1970s. Suddenly a man could outfit himself entirely in knit clothes—a double-knit suit, circular knit shirt, interlock knit underwear, a knit tie, and jersey knit socks.

The overexposure of knits, often in poorly designed and constructed clothing, gave polyester a bad image. Its use fell off in the women's apparel industry, but men's wear manufacturers continued to use it in a low-key way in woven fabrics. Today, 95 percent of men's tailored clothing is made with polyester, most typically blends combining polyester with wool or cotton. Sixty-five percent of men's finer quality suits are made of 55/45 polyester/wool blend; it is the most popular suiting fabric in the United States.

Another technological development of the period that has had staying power is the permanent press finish of cotton. Home laundering of no-iron shirts has made a difference in the maintenance of men's wardrobes.

## The Last Decades of the 20th Century

In the 1980s, men's fashion took on new life once again, as it had in the 1960s. For the first time, magazines devoted exclusively to men's fashion appeared. Men's fashion types emerged, and a variety of styles became acceptable. A man could be the continental type or the Ivy League type; he could be Edwardian, if he chose.

For those who did not trust their own judgment, scientifically confirmed "dress for success" guidelines were suggested in John Malloy's book of the same name. The book prescribed style and color details to create the right combination of authority and friendliness for a variety of business negotiations. Intentionally conservative in its advice, it promoted what came to be known in the 1980s as the "power suit" and "power tie" for "power lunches" (see Figure 10.4).

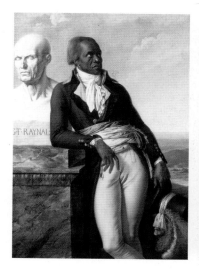

**FIGURE 10.4** From top left to bottom: Power suits from 1797, 1897, 1997, and the future.

# Fashion Focus

Fashion Focus

## Tom Ford
### It's a Man's, Man's, Man's World—For Now!

When designer Tom Ford exited the Gucci empire and the fashion world in 2004, shockwaves ensued. How could he leave an industry in which he was such a force? He will tell you himself that the Gucci–Tom Ford moment was then—and now he has become an exciting, multifaceted designer of all things luxe and directed mostly to men!

Tom Ford doesn't do small. Two months after the debut of his men's line and standalone flagship store in Manhattan, the entrepreneurial designer was ready to take his brand global.

After a year of exclusivity of the Ford Men's Line in his store on Madison Avenue in New York City, the designer label embarked on a focused rollout in the United States and abroad. Set within a 10-year timeframe, the plan, when completed, will create 100 freestanding Tom Ford stores and many shop-in-shops.

Explaining why he chose to move into men's wear, Ford said, "I love designing the men's collection because in the men's business, people respond to fabric, cut, and the shoulder. In women's, the overall image is more important than the actual clothes. With men's wear, I'm very comfortable doing it myself because I am the men's customer. Men are really weird: if you change a pocket a little bit, they can go crazy, something a woman wouldn't be conscious of."

Tom Ford has approached his new venture as a sartorial architect for men who want the surface perfection of "Old School" haberdashery meets "New School."

Tennis shorts, pinwale corduroy jeans, walking sticks, and onyx and diamond shirt studs and cuff links are just some of the wonderful wares for sale. The fabulous Ford sunglasses are Ford's personal passion. "For a man, it's almost the only fashion accessory you can have" he said. The designer has also created a dozen new men's fragrances in deep ombré apothecary-like bottles, with names like Noir de Noir, Velvet Gardenia, and Moss Breeches.

Dressing gowns in extravagant silk brocade are destined to become favorites of women who want an incredible gift. Ford's velvet evening slippers will become a must for women who like that kind of le smoking androgyne chic. As the late Godfather of Soul, James Brown, sang, "It's a man's world—but it wouldn't be nothing without a woman or a girl."

Left page: Tom Ford on the runway, 2004 (top center); Ford's Gucci store in New York City (bottom left); Right page: Ford's ready-to-wear creations for Yves Saint Laurent, 2004.

As for that perennial question—whether he will add women's wear—Ford said, "Right now, I'm concentrating on men's wear because I feel I'm making a new statement. If and when I find the same statement for women, I'll think about it. Right now, I have several years of work with the men's alone because we've done a lot—but there's still a lot to be done."

## The Casual Look

The look that really took off among more self-confident dressers was one of casual elegance, personified by the stars of the popular television show *Miami Vice*. The clothes were designed by big designer names, which ensured their elegance, and they were casual, which basically added up to T-shirts worn under Italian sports jackets, classic loafers with no socks, and ever-present designer sunglasses. For the first time, the American men's wear market was segmented as the women's market always had been by age, education, and income.

## Dress-Down Fridays

In the 1990s, the casual look was officially welcomed to the corporate office, sometimes without the elegance. It began with "dress-down Fridays" in the summer, when companies made allowance for the quick weekend getaway to the beach. Gradually, the trend expanded to the cooler months and to other days of the week. Each firm that followed the trend had to make up its own rules—or decide not to.

Men's buying patterns are changing. "Men aren't shopping just out of need anymore," says Tom Kalenderian, executive vice president and GMM of men's wear at Barney's New York. "The shopping experience has become one of entertainment, and that creates a naturally fertile ground for more impulse buying."[2]

In the 21st century, male executives are thinking and talking more about fashion because greater numbers of men are buying their clothes themselves. This trend represents a huge change from years ago, when women purchased 75 percent of men's clothing. Today, almost 70 percent of men are taking the reins to outfit themselves.[3]

The men's fashion market is expected to grow by more the 10 percent by 2010, boosted by men buying dressier styles and purchasing more suits and tailored clothes. "Suits are making a comeback," said Erin Fowler, analyst for Mintel Reports. "After a decade of substituting khakis for suits on casual

Fridays, men are now investing in more tailored clothing."[4]

## Demographic Influences

The popularity of casual business wardrobes may be attributable to the coming of age of the baby boomers. The young adults and teenagers of the 1960s have reached middle age and the height of their earning power. Many male baby boomers have been worrying more about aging and are doing something about it. The baby boomer generation is not only the most celebrated of generations but also presents a lucrative opportunity for the grooming market, as aging men become obsessed with retaining a youthful and distinguished appearance. As David Wolfe, creative director at the Doneger Group stated, "We expect to feel good, look good, and stay young and sexy forever, and that makes us the perfect customer."[5]

The young adults of the 1990s are the children of these baby boomers. For both age groups, alternative lifestyles with untraditional wardrobes are not news. Urban "hip-hop" styles popularized by rap stars exploded into dozens of new manufacturers like Phat Farm, Fubu, Karl Kani, Shabazz Brothers, and Third Rail. Inevitably, some of their merchandise found its way into the newly informal office, along with earrings and nose studs. Currently there is as much room for the conservatively casual dresser as for the man who wants to express a uniquely personal style. What is news is the expanded range of choices that comes with the relaxing of the rules. And with freedom to choose comes responsibility for evaluating the options and making decisions.

Style is expected to remain an important factor in men's wear. It should be noted, however, that in the midst of the interest in new styles, the classic look, popularized in the 1980s by designers such as Ralph Lauren and Giorgio Armani, continues to be strong. The conservative men's suit remains the outfit of choice for formal business and social occasions, and not only for the president.

## Organization and Operation of the Industry

The men's wear industry traditionally has been divided into firms making different kinds of clothing (see Figure 10.5):

1. *Tailored clothing*—Suits, overcoats, topcoats, sports coats, formal wear, and separate trousers
2. *Furnishings*—Dress shirts, neckwear, sweaters, headwear, underwear, socks, suspenders, robes, and pajamas
3. *Outerwear*—Raincoats, coats, jackets, and active sportswear
4. *Work clothing*—Work shirts, work pants, overalls, and related items

**FIGURE 10.5** The popular television show *The Sopranos* reflects the different ways the 21st-century man defines himself, based on individual styles and ages.

5. *Other*—Uniforms and miscellaneous items

The federal government uses these five classifications. Although it is not an official classification, sportswear (including active sportswear) has become a vital portion of the business, and should be considered a men's wear category.

## Size and Location of Manufacturers

According to estimates from the NPD Group, men's wear sales rose to $52.78 billion in 2005. However, the value of the U.S. men's wear market is forecasted to have a value of $112.0 billion by 2009.[6]

Key players in the U.S. menswear manufacturing sector include Levi Strauss, V.F., Phillips-Van Heusen (PVH), and Sara Lee. One of the largest producers of men's tailored and luxury garments is Hartmarx Corporation. Originally known as Hart Schaffner Marx brand, today Hartmarx is the largest premier clothing manufacturer and possesses the men's wear industry's broadest distribution. Labels such as Austin Reed, Tommy Hilfiger, Perry Ellis, and Pierre Cardin are all part of the HMX Tailored brand group. In the Luxury Group, they produce Hickey-Freeman, Bobby Jones, and Burberry. The Luxury Group has a large, vertically integrated structure that encompasses owned stores and e-commerce and catalog operations. The strategy for HMX sportswear has been to create and market national and dedicated store brands, including Jack Nicklaus, Ted Baker, and Lyle & Scott.[7]

Although there are men's wear manufacturers in almost every section of the country, the greatest numbers of plants are in the mid-Atlantic states. New York, New Jersey, and Pennsylvania form the center of the tailored-clothing industry (see Figure 10.6). More than 40 percent of all men's wear manufacturers are located in this area.

However, the industry's center is gradually moving. A number of northeastern manufacturers have set up plant facilities in the South, where both land and labor are less expensive. These include not only

**FIGURE 10.6** Tailored clothing is a popular part of the men's wear industry, with the number of manufacturing plants continuing to grow.

apparel manufacturers from the mid-Atlantic states but also some men's shoe manufacturers, who were once found almost exclusively in New England. Some men's wear manufacturers have always been located in the South, which has long been a center for manufacturers of men's shirts, underwear, and work clothes.

The number of firms located in the West is also steadily growing. For instance, two of the largest firms manufacturing separate trousers—a segment of the tailored clothing industry—are located in Texas: Farah in El Paso and Haggar in Dallas. Other areas of the West are also popular; for example, Guess? and L.A. Gear are located in Los Angeles, and Levi Strauss, Nautica, and Patagonia are head-quartered in San Francisco. In the Pacific Northwest, Portland, Oregon, is the home of White Stag and Pendelton, while Eddie Bauer and R.E.I. are located in Seattle, Washington. Most of these companies produce sportswear or casual attire. The upper Midwest (Lands' End in Wisconsin) is also important for sports outerwear and activewear such as parkas, skiwear, and hunting and fishing gear (see Figure 10.7).

New York City is the capital of manufacturers' showrooms. Many are located at 1290 Sixth Avenue, and others are situated on 51st, 52nd, and 53rd Streets between Fifth and Seventh Avenues. The showrooms for men's furnishings are concentrated in the Empire State Building at Fifth Avenue and 34th Street.

## Dual Distribution

It is far more common in the men's wear industry than in women's apparel for clothes to be distributed on a two-tier system called dual distribution. In **dual distribution**, apparel is made available through both wholesale and retail channels; that is, the manufacturer sells it in its own retail stores as

**FIGURE 10.7** Activewear and outerwear is a major part of the men's wear industry.

well as to retail stores owned by others. The practice got its start in the first half of the 19th century when the ready-to-wear business, along with the country's population, was expanding. Its popularity has proven to be cyclical. Interest last peaked in the 1960s and 1970s but subsided when the industry was threatened with antitrust suits. Federal law forbids the domination by any one company of a segment of any industry.

## Designing a Line

For generations, tailored clothing manufacturers in the United States were known as slow but painstakingly careful followers, rather than leaders, in men's wear styling. The typical tailored clothing manufacturer had a staff of tailors to execute existing designs or bought freelance designs. Designers' names were known only within the trade and were seldom considered important by consumers.

Traditionally, the leading fashion influence was English styling. Designers in this country would study the styles currently popular in England (specifically Savile Row), decide which might be acceptable here, and gradually develop a line based on those styles. Production was a slow process because of the amount of handwork involved in making tailored clothing. Usually, a full year passed from the time a style was developed until a finished product was delivered to a retail store.

The first signs of male rebellion against traditional styling came during the late 1940s and early 1950s. As described earlier, year after year manufacturers had been turning out versions of a style that had long been popular on Savile Row—a draped suit with padded shoulders, based originally on the broad-chested uniform of the Brigade of Guards. A number of young men attending well-known northeastern colleges became tired of the traditional look. They took their objections to New Haven clothing manufacturers, and the result was the natural-shoulder, Ivy League suit.

A radical shift in attitudes in the 1960s finally

made men willing to wear suits as fashion. The anti-war protests, student activism, black power, and other political movements encouraged American men to express themselves in a nonmainstream manner. They led to the era of the "Peacock revolution," when men once again took great pride in their appearance, as in days long ago. Some favored long hair, bold plaid suits, brightly colored shirts, wide multicolored ties, and shiny boots. Others dressed, even for work, in Nehru and Mao jackets, leisure suits, white loafers, polyester double knits, and the "Las Vegas look"—shirts unbuttoned to the waist and gold necklaces in abundance around their necks.

## Importance of Name Designers

By the late 1960s, designer names in the men's wear industry mushroomed. Most of them were women's wear designers, often from Europe, who decided to exploit their renown by trying out their creativity in the men's field. So popular was the European designer image that even an American designer like Bill Kaiserman gave his firm an Italian name, Raphael.

Among the first American designers who made no bones about being American were Oleg Cassini, John Weitz, Bill Blass, and Ralph Lauren. In fact, Bill Blass won the first Coty Award ever given for men's wear design, in 1968.

Since most of these designers were famous as designers of women's apparel, there was a question about whether men would buy their designs. The movement of men into fashion during the 1960s and 1970s dispelled that doubt. As reported in the *New York Times*:

> The idea that men would wear clothes designed by a woman's apparel designer was never considered seriously, and one thing that men have arrived at today is that being interested in clothes does not carry a stigma.[8]

The fact that much men's wear, particularly furnishings and sportswear, was bought by women for men also aided in the acceptance of name designer styles. Women were familiar with the names and had confidence in the designer's taste.

Although the first foreign country that influenced the design of men's wear was England, French and Italian designers became as important in men's wear as the traditional English. Pierre Cardin signed his first contract for men's shirts and ties in 1959 and did his first ready-to-wear men's designs in 1961. Christian Dior, Yves Saint Laurent, and other famous women's designers followed his example. One important men's wear designer who did not come from the ranks of women's wear is Ralph Lauren. He began his career in men's wear, designing for women only after he became successful and famous designing for men (see Figure 10.8).

## Designer Names Today

Currently, an entirely new world of men's wear has emerged in which designer labels are promoted as heavily as well-established brand names used to be. A designer who licenses his or her name in suits may also license men's jeans, shirts, jackets, sportswear, activewear, or ties. The manufacturer pays for the design or name of the designer in royalties based on gross sales. Royalties average from 5 to 7 percent on men's suits and 5 percent on men's sportswear, according to industry sources.

Manufacturing companies that license name designers usually establish separate divisions and in many cases allocate separate manufacturing

**FIGURE 10.8** Ralph Lauren redefines tailored American style with his fashionable men's wear designs.

# Then & NOW

## Matinee Idols
### Before You Lose Your Hair, Do Your Hair—In Fashion

Left page: Hugh Jackman/Clint Eastwood (top left); Bruce Lee/John Cho (top right); Brad Pitt/Robert Redford (bottom left); Paul Newman/Matthew McConaughey (bottom left); Right page: Sidney Poitier/Denzel Washington.

Something strange is going on with men's hair. What was once neatly parted and combed down with a little water is now being moussed, gelled, and otherwise coiffed into bed-of-nails spikes, new-fangled pompadours, and forward twists into a swoop forelock.

Perhaps because of the possibility that they will lose it all someday, men develop emotional ties to their hair. They equate a full head of hair with youth and virility, and as the saying goes, they want to flaunt it while they've got it.

Of course, this certainly isn't the first time men have fallen under the sway of styling products and scissors. In the 1930s and 1940s, Hollywood stars like Clark Gable and Cary Grant slicked their hair back with Brylcreem, and their audiences copied them. The 1960s brought the Beatles' bowl cut. The 1970s saw David Cassidy's feathers and John Travolta's wings. And in the 1980s, Michael Douglas, as Gordon Gekko in *Wall Street*, inspired a fresh group of power players to go slick again. What is different now in the 2000s is that older and older men are imitating younger and younger stars. Today we have fathers of four copying Ashton Kutcher's man shag and Nick Lachey's crispy waves.

The wacky 'do of choice varies slightly in today's geography. In France, "the Jerry Lewis hair" is popular (short, jet black, and sticky). In Los Angeles, long hair like the guys in the Strokes is the thing. L.A. guys, even with those longer locks, are less likely to overdo it with hair products, while in New York they're really into gel and the grooming cream. They definitely take care of their hair.

So who do we have to blame for this long list of hair offenses? The ladies! Girls pick the men they want their men to look like. She may be smitten with an actor, a musician, a famous chef, or even her boss—so she will steer her man to the hair salon for the inevitable makeover.

Shags, spikes, pompadours, feathers, flips—an epidemic of new haircuts is afflicting modern man—all so they can be in fashion.

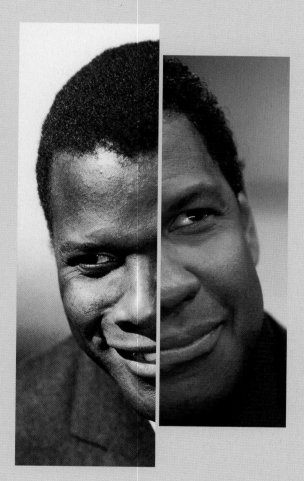

facilities for them. In licensing agreements, the extent of designer involvement varies; designers are not necessarily responsible for all the designs that bear their name. Some licensing agreements simply pay for the use of the designer's name, and the name designer has no design input at all.

Today the "name game" is big business in all segments of the men's wear industry. While there are no hard figures on the amount of designer business alone at the wholesale level, the best market estimates for retail sales are over $1 billion for all categories combined.

One reason for the continuing popularity of designer names is that they are so easily promoted. Consumers associate them with prestige and fashion and recognize them when they see them. Designers have helped by becoming highly visible. Their names are household words, and their faces frequently appear in newspapers and magazines. They lend themselves to the fantasy of the customer who longs for wealth and excitement.

Leading Italian designers of men's wear include Armani, Brioni, Donatella Versace, Dolce & Gabbana, Romeo Gigli, Kiton, and Ermenegildo Zegna, not to mention Stephen Fairchild of Valentino. Four Belgian designers achieved widespread popularity in the late 1990s; Raf Simons, Wim Neels, Dries Van Noten, and Walter van Beirendonck. Other influential European designers include Helmut Lang, Paul Smith, Hedi Slimane, Comme des Garçons, Yohji Yamamoto, and Jean-Paul Gaultier (see Figure 10.9).

**FIGURE 10.9** A fashion-forward design from Jean-Paul Gaultier's fall 2008 collection.

American designers of men's wear include, of course, the "Big Four": Ralph Lauren, Calvin Klein, Donna Karan, and Tommy Hilfiger. Other popular designers include Mossimo, Gene Meyer, John Bartlett, Alexander Julian, Richard Edwards, and Jhane Barnes. A recent entry into men's sportswear is Nicole Miller, already well known for her ties.

High-end fashion designers are edging into the booming market for specially made men's suits. Retailers including Brooks Brothers are getting customers to pay more for so-called made-to-measure suits. Now luxury labels, including Tom Ford, Versace, and Jil Sander, are producing their own options that start at 20 to 30 percent higher than their off-the-rack lines. In the United States, the custom and made-to-measure market accounts for more than 20 percent of suits costing more than $1,200. "One of a kind is the ultimate luxury," says Milton Pedraza, chief executive of consultant Luxury Institute.[9]

### Market Segments

Most market segments are based on style differences, but some exist because they involve different production methods. The five main market segments in men's wear are (1) tailored clothing, (2) sportswear, (3) activewear, (4) contemporary apparel, and (5) bridge apparel.

### Tailored Clothing

**Tailored-clothing firms** produce structured or semistructured suits, overcoats, topcoats, sports coats, formal wear, and separate slacks that involve hand-tailoring operations. This kind of clothing once dominated the market, but in recent years, the demand for tailored clothing has steadily declined. The higher price of tailored clothing makes the difference all the more striking. Despite the decline, tailored suits have long been—and still are—considered the backbone of the men's wear industry.

A tailored suit is structured, or three-dimensional, which gives it a shape even when it is not worn. Until very recently, tailored clothing was graded according to the number of hand-tailoring operations required to make it. The grades were 1, 2, 4, 41, 6, and 61, with a grade 1 suit representing the lowest quality.

At the top of the quality scale, the number of hand-tailoring operations has been reduced by machinery that can produce stitching of a similar caliber. However, the finest suits still have hand-sewn details representing hours of work by skilled tailors.

**Designer Suits.** Another difference between an inexpensive, low-grade suit and an expensive designer suit is the way each is cut. Designer suits are typically sized on a "7-inch drop." **Drop** refers to the difference between the chest and waist measurements of a jacket. Some jackets designed for young men and other customers who keep in shape may have an even greater drop. Nondesigner suits, in contrast, have a 6-inch drop, which gives a suit jacket an entirely different look and fit.

Differences also exist between traditional suits, which have a natural shoulder, and suits with **European styling**, which feature a more fitted jacket, built-up shoulders, and a higher armhole.

**Production.** The production of tailored clothing, as you have probably guessed, is a long, complicated process, although it does parallel the production process for women's apparel. Styles are selected for a new line, after which a manufacturer orders fabrics for the line. Delivery of the fabric may take up to 9 months, so it must be ordered far in advance of when it will be used. Next, the line is presented to buyers. Manufacturers do not start to cut suits until enough orders have accumulated to make production of a style worthwhile.

Men's tailored clothing is produced in the following proportioned sizes, with the number ranges representing chest measurements:

- Short (36–44)
- Regular (35–46)
- Long (37–48)
- Extra long (38–50)
- Portly short (39–48)
- Large (46, 48, 50)

Not every style is cut in every size range, but the most popular styles are made up in at least half the size ranges.

**Suit Separates.** The steady decline in structured and semistructured tailored men's wear has been offset by an increased demand for **suit separates**—sports jackets and trousers that are worn much as the tailored suit used to be (see Figure 10.10). Tailored suits are now the business uniform only in large, sophisticated cities, and even there, only in some firms and industries and for some levels of management. Elsewhere, suit separates are often worn to work—or for almost any occasion except where formal wear is required.

Although an attempt was made in the 1960s to sell men's wear consumers on the idea of coordinated sportswear, that is, jackets, vests, and pants that could be mixed and matched with one another, the idea never took hold. Today, suit separates refers to sports jackets and trousers.

Suit separates are usually machine-made and, as a result, can be significantly lower-priced than tailored garments. When they are made for better-priced lines, they can also be expensive. Because each item is bought separately, the expensive alterations that manufacturers and retailers must often make on tailored clothes are avoided. One industry expert believes that men who buy separates are more fashion-aware than those who need the reassurance of a preassembled look.

## Sportswear

Sportswear, or casual wear, which runs the gamut from unconstructed jackets, knits and woven sports shirts, slacks, and leisure shorts to coordinated tops and bottoms, has been the fastest growing segment of the men's wear industry since the 1970s. Changes in lifestyle, plus men's growing interest in having more variety and fashion in their wardrobes, have created a demand for leisure clothes.

A generation ago, tailored clothing was office or formal wear, and sportswear was strictly weekend or vacation wear. Today, the real difference between

**FIGURE 10.10** Patrick Dempsey wearing a suit separate by Versace.

the two lies in the construction rather than the occasion or the styling, colors, or fabrics of the garments.

Sportswear is unstructured, or at minimum, less structured than tailored clothing. Few if any hand-tailoring operations, for example, are required to make a sports jacket. Sportswear lacks padding, binding, and lining and takes its shape (if indeed it has any shape these days) from the person who is wearing it.

Sportswear production also differs from that of tailored wear. Unlike tailored-wear manufacturers, who want staying power for their styles and a lot of lead time, sportswear manufacturers are interested in short runs and a quick response to customer demand. A **short run** is the production of a limited number of units of a particular item, fewer than would normally be considered an average number to produce. Producers of men's sportswear some-times rely on contractors to keep up with the fast-moving fashion cycles of this market segment. The quality of workmanship is much less important than the quick production of the styles, colors, and fabrics that customers want.

In addition, unstructured sportswear, regardless of the kind of firm producing it, is likely to be made up in a much narrower size range than tailored clothing. For instance, a sport shirt is not produced in the wide variety of neck sizes, sleeve lengths, and collar and cuff styles in which a dress shirt is made. Instead, a sport shirt is usually produced in four basic sizes (small, medium, large, and extra large), with a choice between short and long sleeves.

This is the kind of production work that contractors handle most successfully. When contractors are used, the sportswear manufacturer may be the designer, a designer may be hired, or a design may be bought from a freelancer. The manufacturer buys the needed fabric. Then sometimes the cutting and all of the sewing are done by the contractor, as in the women's apparel field. Finally, the finished goods are returned to the manufacturer, who handles the distribution.

## Activewear

Another phenomenon that emerged in the 1980s and continued into the 2000s is the rapid growth of the **activewear** market, which consists of clothing worn during active sports participation as well as during leisure time (see Figure 10.11). In fact, the larger segment of this market is men who want to look as if they are doing something athletic, even when they are ambling to the store for the Sunday paper or flopping down in front of the television set to watch a ball game. As a result, the active sportswear producers make running suits for men who run and for men who do not but want to look as if they do. Sportswear was also responsible for making color a permanent part of men's wardrobes. Colorful skiwear dominates the slopes. Golf wear has become popular on and off the links, with

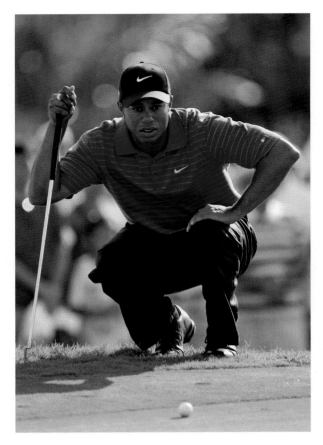

**FIGURE 10.11** Athletes are often seen marketing activewear brands, such as Tiger Woods for Nike (top) and David Beckham for Adidas (bottom).

licensed apparel and accessories by players like Tiger Woods (for Nike) and Greg Norman (for Reebok). These major brand names in athletic shoes have become big names in activewear as well.

## Contemporary Apparel

**Contemporary men's wear** refers to a special type of styling that provides high quality and fashion. Contemporary men's wear, which produces clothing in all categories, can often be distinguished by its use of bright colors.

Initially, the typical consumer was a young, educated man with the verve to look fashionable. Today, contemporary men's wear no longer belongs exclusively to the young but is worn by elegant, style-conscious men of all age groups.

Contemporary merchandise is produced by both tailored-clothing and sportswear firms. It is usually produced under a name designer's licensing agreement rather than styled by a manufacturer's in-house or freelance designer. When this type of merchandise is produced by a firm already making other types of apparel and furnishings, new operating divisions are usually created to handle the product, give it identity, and enhance its marketability.

## Bridge Apparel

The term **bridge apparel** came into play in the men's wear industry to define clothing that spanned the style gap between young men's and men's collections, and the price gap between contemporary and designer apparel. In broad terms, the bridge customer is an aging baby boomer who has grown out of young men's clothing but can't yet afford designer clothes. Bridge customers are between 25 and 40 and have sophistication and style.

Unlike the bridge concept in women's sportswear, for which certain manufacturers and designers have developed collections specifically created as bridge lines, men's bridge apparel is defined much more by retailers than by manufacturers. Each retailer may interpret bridge differently in order to fit its own customer profile. Therefore, one store might have bridge lines while another might call them contemporary. Whatever their definition of bridge apparel, retailers that identify a portion of their men's wear assortment as bridge apparel are seeking to balance fashion with price.

## Merchandising and Marketing

Like the women's wear producers, men's wear producers back their lines with advertising and publicity. Men's wear fiber and textile producers sometimes promote their products. The largest percentage of promotion is done, however, by the men's wear producers, who rely on agencies, freelancers, and less often, on an in-house department for advertising and publicity.

### Advertising

Men's apparel producers began advertising in the late 1800s. Initially, they used trade advertising to establish contact with retailers. Strong, stable relationships were built, and in many large towns and small cities, major manufacturers maintain an exclusive arrangement with one retailer. Not surprisingly, the producers tend to put a lot of their advertising money into cooperative advertising for their long-term retail accounts. Brand-name and designer name producers also sponsor national advertising campaigns.

Sportswear houses, relative newcomers to the marketplace, do not have long-established or exclusive ties with retailers, so they compensate with large national advertising campaigns as well as cooperative advertising with retailers.

### Publicity in Newspapers and Magazines

The only trade newspaper devoted to men's wear is the *Daily News Record*, published by Fairchild Publications, Inc. Consumer magazines devoted to men's fashions also provide an interesting forum for pub-

**FIGURE 10.12** Consumer magazines devoted to men's fashions include *Men's Vogue* (left), *GQ* (middle), and *Menswear* (right).

licity for men's wear products (see Figure 10.12). They include *Gentlemen's Quarterly (GQ)*, a recognized leader in the field; *Esquire*, once the leader in men's fashion and now reasserting itself; *Details*; and an assortment of ethnically oriented publications. Producers make excellent use of the editorial pages of these various publications, and also supply clothes to be modeled.

## Trade Associations

The major publicity efforts, however, are still undertaken by the trade associations, which sponsor market weeks, trade shows, and other promotions designed to publicize individual producers and the industry as a whole (see Figure 10.13). New York is the largest U.S. market center for all kinds of men's wear, including tailored clothing, sportswear, contemporary lines, and furnishings. Regional markets in other parts of the country—Chicago, Los Angeles, and Dallas, for example—are growing in importance, but the largest number of permanent showrooms are still located in New York.

A number of trade associations support the men's wear industry. The following have a major role:

- National Association of Men's Sportswear Buyers (NAMSB). As the name suggests, this is an organization of men's wear retailers. Since its 1953 founding, it has expanded beyond sportswear to other men's apparel. Its market week

**FIGURE 10.13** The ISPO (International Trade Fair for Sports Equipment and Fashion) trade show displays the newest skiwear available, while promoting individual producers and the industry.

trade shows give members access to more than a thousand producers exhibiting at each show. NAMSB also provides seasonal fashion-trend slide kits for members' use in merchandising and marketing. It has a scholarship program for children of members and their employees.

- Men's Apparel Guild of California (MAGIC). This group was founded in the late 1930s as the Los Angeles Men's Wear Manufacturers Association to promote California-style men's sportswear. It has since expanded beyond California to an international show and to other segments of the men's wear industry. Currently it includes women's and children's trade shows in addition to its semiannual extravaganzas in Las Vegas.
- Big and Tall Associates. Founded in 1971 for manufacturers and retailers who cater to men over 5 feet, 11 inches tall and/or with chest measurements over 48 inches, this organization conducts semiannual market weeks.

Table 10.1 lists the major men's wear trade shows in the United States. As the market for imports and exports has grown in size and importance, more and more domestic manufacturers now attend the important international shows, most notably Pitti Uomo in Italy, IMBEX in London, and SEHM in France.

## Industry Trends

The dynamics of population growth as well as lifestyle changes and developments in the economy are bringing about changes in all segments of the men's wear industry. Some of the most noteworthy trends include a diversification of products on the part of producers, the automation of production processes, an increase in foreign production and sales, and a proliferation of specialty stores. Consumers are showing greater interest in style and are demanding quality in fabric and construction. All of these trends relate to the growing informality of American culture.

### Trends in Production

The manufacturing side of the men's wear industry has grown increasingly complex as individual firms find new ways to compete. The major producers that dominate the tailored clothing, sportswear, and activewear segments are expanding through mergers and acquisitions in each other's markets. Technological advances are speeding production, and offshore contracting is being used to control costs.

### Diversification of Product

In addition to mergers and acquisitions, diversification is occurring through expanded product lines. Producers that for years were highly specialized, often producing only a single type of garment in one grade, are now expanding into other grades and product lines.

Some of the biggest changes have taken place in an area that was one of the most specialized, that of work clothes. Firms like H. D. Lee and Levi Strauss, which for years never varied their products, began to expand when the casual market took off. In addi-

**TABLE 10.1** *Major U.S. Trade Shows for Men's Wear*

| WHO | WHERE | WHEN |
|---|---|---|
| The Collective | Pier 94, NYC | January & July |
| ENK International/ Blue | Pier 92, NYC | January & July |
| Chicago Collective | The Merchandise Mart, Chicago | February & August |
| The Atlanta Apparel Men's Market | Cobb Galleria, Atlanta | January & July |
| MAGIC Project Show | Sands Expo Center, Las Vegas | February & August |

tion to designer jeans, which had saturated the market by the mid-1970s, Lee, Levi Strauss, and similar manufacturers moved into slacks, casual pants, and jackets—and even tailored clothing.

### Increased Automation

New equipment and computer systems are helping manufacturers combat one of the more serious problems faced by apparel producers: labor. The rising cost of labor is pitted against a dwindling skilled labor force. The men's wear industry has also experienced a turnover rate of between 60 and 70 percent for the past few years. Good tailors and sewers take time to train, and supply has not kept up with demand.

Automation has also invaded the labor-intensive, better-tailored-clothing industry (see Figure 10.14). In the past, 1 to 1$\frac{1}{2}$ hours were required to

**FIGURE 10.14** Before advances in technology, hand tailoring was the only option.

hand-press a man's grade 6 or 61 suit. Today that time is reduced to a matter of minutes by means of a computer-controlled, automated system that steam-presses each part of the suit. In fact, with computer-assisted machines to mark and cut cloth, manufacturers of tailored clothing can, and sometimes do, turn out a garment entirely by machine.

In general, the industry is gradually becoming more machine oriented than operator oriented. This is a vast change for an industry that, throughout most of its history, prided itself on the individual workmanship that went into many of its products.

## Foreign Production and Imports

Price competition is extreme in the men's wear market. An important factor in setting prices at wholesale is the cost of labor. Because of high labor costs, an increasing number of men's wear producers, particularly sportswear firms, are building plants or contracting to have work done in areas outside the country, where land and labor costs are lower.

Traditional men's wear manufacturers had turned away from contractors and stayed away until recently for several reasons.

1. The men's wear industry had a pattern of very slow style change, and contracting was not as economical as inside-shop production.
2. Improved equipment and cheaper electric power helped make production in inside shops more practical and efficient.
3. As quality became increasingly important, men's wear manufacturers found it easier to control work within their own factories than in the contractors' factories.

Imports have also made inroads in the U.S. men's wear market. Their promise of lower production prices and solid quality, plus a demand for exclusivity, have led more retailers to build up their direct-import programs and buy indirect imports (clothing made abroad for U.S. manufacturers).

## Specialty Trends in Retailing

From the very beginning, independent specialty stores such as Brooks Brothers were important to the growth and impact of fashionable men's wear. Although many small retailers have closed over the years, others such as Mitchells/Richards in Connecticut; Mario's in Portland, Oregon; and Coffman's in Greenville, North Carolina, have found a formula that has allowed them to survive. They all attribute their success to an unwavering devotion to the customer. In fact, Mitchells/Richards CEO Jack Mitchell has written a book called *Hugging Your Customers* that details to what lengths retailers need to go to the take care of their loyal customers.

One of the country's largest men's wear retailers is The Men's Wearhouse. Opened in 1973, the company continued to grow, and today CEO George Zimmer is known for his now-famous tagline, "You're going to like the way you look. I guarantee it," on radio and TV. Today, Zimmer boasts the flagship Men's Wearhouse chain, Moores in Canada and K&G Superstores in the United States. Today, Men's Wearhouse has annual sales of over $1.7 billion and operates more than 700 stores in the United States and Canada.[10]

Catalog sales are another specialty trend. Major retailers, as well as specialty stores, have begun to send out catalogs geared exclusively to men, and stores such as L.L. Bean, which always sold by catalog, report an increase in business. Catalogs are typically slated for a specific market; that is, they specialize in low prices; certain styles or fashions, such as golf or western; a certain size range, such as big and tall; or exclusivity. Those specialty catalogs that have done thorough market research and have offered their customers exactly what they want have been quite successful.

## *Style and Lifestyle*

In 1987, a vice president and director of men's clothing at Neiman Marcus summed up the men's market, saying: "The clothing business hasn't changed, but the lifestyle has."[11] At least the second half of that observation remains true more than two decades later. The first half is debatable: many of the major players remain the same, but their continuing success has been correlated with their ability to adapt to the changes in the buying behavior of the ultimate consumer. Because men are now interested in fashion, they are buying different kinds of clothes. Most men's wardrobes today can be divided into three categories according to use: suits for formal business and social occasions, activewear for sports (spectator as well as participatory) and for the most casual situations, and slacks and sports coats for everyday office wear and after-work socializing. Matching the category to the occasion is not always a clear-cut, easy decision, however. Separates may be acceptable for client meetings, depending on the firm and the client, for example. And at some social events, men dressed in the three categories may mingle comfortably.

The daily decision about what to wear to work is probably the most important wardrobe choice because of its relationship to career success. The question plagues employers as much as employees. When dress codes began to be relaxed, the certainty about image that was associated with the business suit faded. Deliberately or by chance, new dress codes are being created. Savvy men's wear marketers among both producers and retailers are coming to the rescue with seminars and brochures.

When men do wear traditional tailored clothing these days, they favor quality in fabric and workmanship and styling that flatters their build and expresses their taste. Spending $700 to $1,200 for a tailored suit is not unusual. Since many men no longer need an assortment of suits for business wear, they can afford to invest more in each suit they do buy. And they want value for their money.

## Separates

Although the popular-priced blazers, vests, and slacks produced by such companies as Levi Strauss and Haggar have found a permanent place in the men's wear market, with the renewed emphasis on quality, better-priced tailored clothes are once again selling well. They are unlikely, however, to edge out separates. Even Hartmarx, the giant maker of men's suits, introduced sportswear lines under the Hickey-Freeman and Hart Schaffner & Marx names. Colors are lighter and brighter in these new lines, and the items are meant to be mixed and matched, as women have done for decades with separates.

## Shirt Styles

Producers have recently made some changes in shirt sleeve sizes. Men's long-sleeved dress shirts are made in neck sizes 14 to 17 inches, graduated in half inches. In each size, the sleeve length has, until recently, also been graduated from 32 to 35 inches. In an effort to reduce inventories and increase stock turnover, however, producers have begun making dress shirts in two sleeve lengths. The lengths include both regular (32–34 inches) and long (34–35 inches). Over 50 percent of all men's dress shirts are now produced only in regular and long-sleeve lengths.

Whether this trend will prevail is unclear. Not all shirtmakers have converted to the new sizing, and with the renewed interest in quality, there has also been a reverse trend among some producers toward making exact sleeve sizes again.

Fitted dress shirts, tapered through the torso, or with darts to make them fit close to the body, resurfaced in the late 1990s after an absence of more than a decade. They were widely supported by designers, led by Ralph Lauren and including Perry Ellis and Tommy Hilfiger.

At the opposite end of the fashion spectrum, interest in short-sleeved dress shirts blossomed, with the cartoon character Dilbert leading the way.

## Designer and Brand-Name Labels

When Michael Bastian announced in 2006 that he was leaving his post as men's fashion director at New York's Bergdorf Goodman to design a line of men's clothing, he said he saw a niche in American men's wear no one was filling—upscale versions of classic styles.

A number of other designers had the same idea. Among them, Tim Hamilton, an alumnus of Polo Ralph Lauren and J. Crew; Gurgen Oeltjenbruns, previously of Versace and DKNY; and Tony Melillo, a former *Esquire* magazine style director, launched lines that are updates of classic American men's wear. So have Isaac Mizrahi, Narciso Rodriguez, Elie Tahari, designers known for their women's wear. Now, for the first time in years, shopping for men's clothing is no longer as simple as choosing among Ralph Lauren, Calvin Klein, and Tommy Bahama. Shoppers now face a large choice of brands, some from designers whose names are familiar only to the fashion-oriented consumer.

The proliferation of new labels is a big change in the traditionally slow-moving men's category and is seen as an attempt by designers and retailers to use strategies that have worked successfully in the women's apparel department. By pushing new lines and fresh looks more often, they hope to generate excitement and increase sales.[12]

Joining the push for fashion-forward men's wear in the luxury market, traditional American men's wear brands are going after younger customers, taking lessons from designers like Ermenegildo Zegna, Giorgio Armani, and Hugo Boss, who have successfully reached younger customers by producing junior lines with slimmer-fitting jackets and pants. The Joseph Abboud brand launched Joe Joseph Abboud, a line aimed at 22- to 30-years-olds. Jos. A. Bank Clothiers, Inc., introduced Joseph. Hartmarx's Hickey Freeman started selling Hickey. Hartmarx's Hart Schaffner Marx and Oxford clothes have lines aimed at young men who don't want to look like their dads or grandfathers. By launching these new labels, the companies hope to build brand loyalty among men who will eventually trade up to their pricier lines, where similar items can cost hundreds of dollars more.[13]

National brands, which have already had considerable impact, are expected to remain strong in the foreseeable future. In tailored men's wear, brand names are seen as a sign of quality. Private-label merchandise is also making inroads. As is the case with women's private labels, they provide men's wear retailers with exclusivity and higher profit margins (see Figure 10.15).

Retail operations strive to provide their customers with a mix of designer names, brand names, and private labels. For manufacturers, representation in the men's department of a department store may mean supplying fixtures and promotional videos for their own store-within-a-store or for sections within such areas as activewear or sportswear.

## Summary and Review

Designer and brand names are part of the push to provide men with up-to-date fashion. And while there will always be a market for classic or tradi-

**FIGURE 10.15** J.Crew offers updated American classics to its men and women customers. The apparel company looks to expand into the luxury male market.

tional men's clothes, industry forecasters predict that men's wear will continue to be ever more fashion oriented. The Europeanization of the American tailored clothing market has brought an appreciation of quality and fit. Comfort and convenience remain important to the average man, especially in casual wear and active wear.

While men's wear changes more slowly than women's wear, the industry saw dramatic change and growth in the 1990s, as dress-down Fridays were adopted by most businesses in the United States. The activewear category also saw dramatic growth as firm, toned bodies became the goal of tens of thousands of men. As the baby boomers aged, more and more men turned to plastic surgery and cosmetics to hide the signs of aging.

The industry was quick to capitalize on the new interest in men's wear, offering increasingly diverse products by using increased automation. Meanwhile, foreign production and imports continued to climb. Retailers jumped on the bandwagon, offering improved visual merchandising, and increased advertising in newspapers, magazines, and on the Internet.

## Trade Talk

Define or briefly explain the following terms:

| | |
|---|---|
| activewear | bridge apparel |
| contemporary men's wear | drop |
| dual distribution | European styling |
| short run | slop shop |
| suit separates | tailored-clothing firm |

## For Review

1. What effect did the industrial revolution have on male apparel? What socioeconomic factors were responsible for the drastic changes that occurred?

2. What three developments in the mid-19th century were largely responsible for the development of the men's ready-to-wear industry in this country? How did each help to accelerate those developments?

3. Discuss the development of sportswear and casual wear in the men's market and the influence they have had on the men's wear industry as a whole.

4. For what three reasons did early manufacturers of men's tailored clothing give up the use of contractors?

5. What role have unions played in the production of men's wear? Why were unions formed in the 19th and early 20th centuries? What role do they play in the industry today?

6. Name the different segments into which the men's wear industry is subdivided on the basis of the type of product lines each produces. What specific products are produced by each segment?

7. How has the sizing of men's suits and dress shirts been simplified in recent years?

8. What is the role of trade shows in promoting men's fashions? Name and describe five trade shows that command national attention.

9. How have men's wear producers tried to compensate for the rising cost of labor and the shortage of skilled workers in the United States?

10. Describe two men's wear style trends that are likely to continue.

## For Discussion

1. Is the conservative men's suit dying out, or is it taking on a new life in the wake of more casual business dress codes? In what situations are tailored suits commonly worn in your community? What local trends do you see?

2. What is the role of designer names in men's wear? Which men's designer fashions are currently popular?

3. Discuss the influence of modern production techniques on the manufacturing of men's wear. What are the effects on costs and pricing?

# chapter eleven

*Everything you always wanted to know*

*about the influence of fashion on the children's*

*and teens' apparel industry.*

KEY CONCEPTS
- The impact of demographics on the children's apparel industry
- The history of the children's apparel industry
- Size categories of children's wear
- Unique features of infants' and toddlers' wear
- Merchandising and marketing of children's apparel
- Licensing in the children's apparel industry
- Industry trends and responses to social issues

# Children's and Teens' Apparel

We are all familiar with the phrase "Out of the mouth of babes." Today, as media bombards children with grown-up images, new demands are heard out of the mouths of babes—demands for all things that are presented to them on television, in movies, and in books. Gone are the days when children were seen and not heard—producers of products such as soft drinks, candy, food, music, movies, and apparel heed the newly acquired sophistication of children. Everything presented to children is entertainment, and children want it all! This presents a wonderful opportunity for designers and producers of children's apparel to adapt to the wants of these savvy new customers. A classic example of this is the way that Burberry, the famous London fashion house, decided to continue its brand extension. Burberry produced two new products featuring its famous signature plaid—a luxury children's line featuring shearling coats, plaid duffle bags, and a Burberry Barbie. Burberry outfitted this legendary doll icon with a plaid skirt and classic trench coat, plus a plaid messenger bag. Ah, to be young, fashionable, and in love with Barbie![1] (See Figure 11.1.)

Making clothing fun for pint-sized consumers and the adults who pay for their wardrobes is a serious business, generating more than $30 billion annually in U.S. retailing.[2]

## Psychological Importance of Children's, Tweens', and Teens' Clothes

The apparel industry is not the only beneficiary of the growing interest in dressing children well. Psychologists believe that clothes play an important role in shaping and guiding a child's self-image (see Figure 11.2). As parents understand the role that clothes play at various stages of a child's growth, they can help to ensure that a child's appearance will enhance his or her striving to become a mature, self-confident adult.[3] As California designer Maline Gerber said:

A customer who had dressed her daughter in my line throughout the girl's childhood recently thanked me for the influence that my clothes had on her child's development. The girl received consistent positive attention, which contributed significantly to her confidence. This comment made me realize that my work really has an impact on the development of children's personalities.[4]

Proponents of the idea of school uniforms argue that uniforms foster a sense of belonging to a group and encourage neatness. Their opponents point out that selecting one's own attire is a form of self-expression. Both views recognize the importance of clothing to a child's self-identity.

## Demographics and the Children's, Tweens', and Teens' Apparel Industry

This apparel industry is unusual in the extent to which it has been shaped by demographics. Patterns of childbearing tend to be cyclical. Although the birth rate had been steadily declining since the end of the 19th century, the aftermath of World War II brought about a baby boom. Women who had been working to support the war effort turned over their jobs to the returning soldiers and went home to become full-time housewives—and mothers. The birth rate soared. Three to four children per family was not unusual. Between 1953 and 1964, a whopping 4 million births occurred every year.

In the 1970s, many people became concerned that the world population was growing too rapidly and advocated that families have fewer children. More women began to work outside the home again. The birth rate declined, and the average number of children per family sank to fewer than two.

FIGURE 11.1 Barbie, the famous fashion doll, has a wide variety of clothing and style—much like today's teen fashion (left)! **FIGURE 11.2** Indonesian women dress and assemble packaging of "Arrosa" dolls in Muslim headscarfs and clothing. Muslim headscarfs are popular in Indonesia among women, where nearly 90 percent of its 235 million people are Muslims. Within 8 months of production, 800 dolls were sold out (right).

The 1980s did not bring about another baby boom, with three to four children per family, but because the baby boom babies had themselves reached childbearing age, the number of babies born increased for the first time since the 1960s. This increase occurred even though women continued to have a statistical average of 1.5 children, and many postponed motherhood to continue their careers. Over 3.5 million babies were born in 1987, and almost 3.9 million were born in 1988. Besides the increasing number of children, the culture of spending in the 1980s contributed to the success of the children's apparel industry. The number of mothers who worked soared, and two-income families generally had more discretionary income. People not only bought more for each child, but they purchased more expensive goods than in the past.

In the 1990s, parents reined in their family clothing budgets. For single mothers and for couples whose sense of job security was diminished by mergers and downsizing, the mother's income came to be viewed as essential to the family's financial well-being rather than "extra" money. But par-

ents' more cautious spending behavior has not caused a downturn in the children's apparel industry. What has happened instead is that new markets for children's wear have emerged. In 1996, the first wave of baby boom babies turned 50, and the population of their elders was growing, thanks to life-prolonging improvements in health care. All those doting grandparents have made the over-50 age group the top spenders on children's retail clothing. Toward the other end of the age spectrum, children themselves, especially those over age 12, have become a formidable group of shoppers. They spent more than $124.2 billion in 2001, much of it on clothing, and their style- and brand-consciousness contributes significantly to the success of such brands as Tommy Hilfiger, Calvin Klein, GUESS, Levi's, and Gap.

The teen market is steadily growing and has been successfully impacted by fashion apparel and accessories. A growing number of well-known designers and retailers are cashing in on the trend by getting into the teen and tween business, which is constantly growing. Teens spend about $160 billion annually with a large percentage spent on clothing, so this market is a potential growth area for the fashion industry.[5]

A baby boom birth rate has been occurring for the past few years in the 21st century. Given the number of women in their prime childbearing years, it's a trend that is likely to continue; and more good news for the industry is that birth rates are rising for older and better-educated women. This means that women who have more money to spend on fashions for their little ones are entering the market.

Between 2001 and 2010, the number of women between the ages of 20 and 35, who account for about three-fourths of all births in the United States, is projected to increase by 7 percent.

## History of the Children's Apparel Industry

Although boy's wear is considered part of the men's apparel industry, for our purposes, it is considered as part of children's wear and described in this chapter.

As a commercial activity, the children's wear industry is a phenomenon of the 20th century. For most of history, children were dressed like miniature adults. Study a portrait from the Renaissance or the American colonial era, and you will see children wearing the same low necklines, bustles, and pantaloons that were currently stylish with adults.

When children's clothes finally began to look different from those that adults wore toward the end of the 1800s, they took on the look of uniforms. All little girls, for example, dressed in a similar drab outfit—dark, high-button shoes; a mid-calf-length skirt; and dark stockings.

Clothes were made extra large so children could grow into them. Their construction was sturdy so they could be handed down to younger children. Many children's clothes were hand-sewn or made by a few apparel manufacturers who seldom offered any variations on the clothes or, for that matter, experienced any growth in their businesses. It did not matter that children's clothes were dull and unattractive because no child would dare to protest what parents wanted him or her to wear. One 1800s success story was the William Carter Company, which began in 1865 and became one of the largest children's underwear companies. It is still in business today.

Although a few designers specialized in high-priced children's wear in the early 1900s, it was not until after World War I that the commercial production and distribution of stylish children's wear began. Not surprisingly, the growth of the children's wear industry followed in the wake of the developing women's wear industry. When women stopped making their own clothes, they also stopped making their children's clothes.

---

### FIGURE 11.3 TIME LINE FOR CHILDREN'S WEAR 1900—2008    *Events and their Effects on Apparel*

**1900-1910**

- **1902** JCPenney opens his first store.
- **1904** Buster Brown, a popular comic strip character, is licensed for use with over 100 products at the St. Louis World's Fair.
- **1905** The Teddy Bear is invented and becomes a popular emblem on children's wear.
- **1906** Sears, Roebuck and Co. opens its first store. The catalog started earlier.
- **1907** Child labor laws were enacted. They kept children from working more than 66 hours a week and at night.
- **1909** Dr. Denton's Sleeping Garment Mills is established; it is the first company to manufacture only children's wear.

CHILD LABOR LAWS

- **1910** Rubber pants are manufactured. They caused a revolution in how baby boys were dressed, since the pants allowed them to wear trousers instead of skirts before they were potty trained.
- **1910** OshKosh B'Gosh introduces overalls for boys.

**1910-1920**

- **1910** *Women's Wear Daily*, which also covers girl's wear, begins publication.
- **1913** L.L. Bean is founded. Mary Pickford, "America's Sweetheart," appears in feature-length silent films.
- **1911** The Triangle Shirtwaist fire leads to the movement to end sweatshops.
- **1916** The athletic shoe is invented.
- **1917–1918** The United States enters World War I. Little boys' fashions feature "military look," with epaulets and brass buttons.
- **1917** The first issue of *The Infant's Department*, which became *Earnshaw's Infants', Girls' and Boys' Wear Review*, was published.
- **1919** The Stride Rite Corp. is founded to make children's shoes.

MARY PICKFORD

The children's wear industry also grew because manufacturers found ways to make factory-produced clothing sturdier than homemade clothes. The development of snaps, zippers, and more durable sewing methods were important contributions.

Another important step in the manufacture of children's clothes occurred after World War I, when manufacturers began to standardize children's wear sizes. What began as a very primitive method of sizing children's clothing has since turned into a highly sophisticated sizing operation, with many categories and subdivisions.

The next major change in the children's wear industry was the introduction of radio and movies into Americans' lives in the 1920s, 1930s, and 1940s. All across the country, mothers dressed their little girls like Shirley Temple and their boys like cowboy western heroes. Teens wanted to dress like Judy Garland and Mickey Rooney, stars of countless teen musicals.

In the 1950s, another change—really a revolution—was brought about by the introduction of television into Americans' homes. It did not take advertisers long to discover that children, among the largest group of consumers of television, could be targeted directly. From *Howdy Doody* to the *Mick-*

*ey Mouse Club*—and the innumerable shows that have followed—kids loved television, shows and commercials alike. Then it was a short step to gear the advertising in other media—radio as well as magazines and newspapers—toward children. See Figure 11.3 for a time line of children's wear in the 20th century.

Television programs geared to audiences of different ages help to establish the popularity of clothing styles for each age group, from the preschoolers playing on *Sesame Street* to the high school students on *Dawson's Creek* and *Buffy the Vampire Slayer*. Interestingly, it is the Los Angeles area manufacturers and retailers who are taking the lead in providing teen fashions tailored to the less developed proportions of preteen girls.[6]

## Organization and Operation of the Children's, Tweens', and Teens' Apparel Industry

There are close to one thousand companies that make children's apparel. Despite the prominence of such giant companies as Carter's, OshKosh B'Gosh, Bugle Boy, Gerber Children's Wear, and Health-tex, most children's clothes are still made by small, fam-

**1920-1930**

- **1921** The first Miss America is crowned. Thousands of girls aspire to become beauty queens.
- **1921** The Health-tex Company is founded.
- **1922** The first commercial radio broadcast is made.

MISS AMERICA

- **1923** The romper is invented.
- **1924** The first Macy's Thanksgiving Day parade is held.
- **1926** *Winnie-the-Pooh* by A.A. Milne is published.
- **1926** The Lee Company invents the zipper jean.
- **1927** The sunsuit is invented to provide children with maximum exposure to sunlight, which was thought to be healthful.
- **1927** The first "talking" motion picture is made.
- **1928** Walt Disney introduces Mickey Mouse.
- **1929** The stock market crashes, ushering in the Great Depression. As a result, millions of children wear hand-me-down adult cast-off clothing, and patched garments.

**1930-1940**

- **1934** Shirley Temple, age 6, makes her first movie, and her long licensing career begins. Little girls want to look just like her—from her fifty-two bouncy curls to her short, frilly dresses.
- **1934** The Dionne Quintuplets are born and everything is licensed in their name.
- **1938** Walt Disney makes *Snow White and the Seven Dwarfs*, which becomes the top-grossing movie of the year and a licensing bonanza.
- **1938** Judy Garland and Mickey Rooney star in *Love Finds Andy Hardy*, the first of their many teenage films together.
- **1938** Superman and Batman comics are published.
- **1934** Nylon is invented by DuPont, and nylon stockings are introduced.

SHIRLEY TEMPLE

ily-owned businesses. Notable among them are the following multigenerational firms: Quiltex, Celebrity International, Will'Beth, Raj Manufacturing, and Spencer's of Mount Airy.

Many adult apparel producers, including Levi Strauss, Patagonia, Old Navy, Gap, and Reebok, also operate children's apparel divisions. Many adult apparel designers have also begun children's divisions.

Like adult clothing, children's wear is divided into categories based on price, size, and type of merchandise. Children's clothes are produced in budget, moderate, better-priced, and designer price ranges. Most children's clothes bought by parents are in the budget and moderate price ranges, while better-priced and designer merchandise is a common gift purchase by grandparents and other adults.

## Size Categories

A super-sophisticated marketplace makes sizing little customers more challenging than ever before. The industry debates whether the traditional size categories really reflect a child's age and maturity level—particularly in the sophisticated state of today's market. Across the country, retailers and

manufacturers are questioning and re-imaging the size standards, each with their own idea of what would constitute the ideal size categories.[7]

According to the American Obesity Association, about 30 percent of children ages 6–11 are overweight and 15.5 percent are obese. The latest data from the Centers for Disease Control show that the number of children considered overweight has tripled since 1980.

Some retailers and vendors do offer plus-size clothing selections, but the availability of attractive, flattering plus-size is scarce. JCPenney has carried extended sizes for children for more than 10 years.

Although the actual size range is the same, the **preteen sizes** for girls offer more sophisticated styling than the **girls' sizes**. Similarly, the **young men's** category (also called **prep**, **student**, or **teen**) stresses sophisticated styling more than boys' sized apparel does.

## Special Features of Infants' and Toddlers' Wear

Clothing in infants' and **toddlers' sizes** is designed to meet needs that are unique to the youngest children. For example, pants are available with snaps along the

---

**TIME LINE FOR CHILDREN'S WEAR 1900—2008**    *Events and their Effects on Apparel*

**1940–1950**

- **1940** The Child Labor Law restricts employment for those under 16.
- **1940** An embargo is placed on Japanese silk.

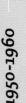

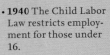
SADDLE SHOES

- **1940–1946** The United States enters World War II, and there is a new austerity in children's wear. Clothes and shoes are rationed. The short Eisenhower jacket becomes popular in boy's wear.
- **1945** Florence Eiseman Inc. founded; influential designer of children's wear.
- **1946** *Baby and Child Care* by Dr. Benjamin Spock is published.
- **1946** Teen girls wear saddle shoes, sweater sets, and pageboy hairdos. They swoon over "crooners" like Frank Sinatra. Teen boys wear "zoot suits" after the war.
- **1947** *Howdy Doody* is an early TV show for kids; its popularity licensed playwear.
- **1949** *Hopalong Cassidy* is the first western shown on a new invention called "television." It's only in black and white, but a bright new era in licensing has dawned.

**1950–1960**

- **1950** Acrylic fibers introduced; Orlon sweaters quickly become popular.
- **1950** Color TV is introduced. It is very expensive at first.
- **1952** *Charlotte's Web* by E.B. White is published.
- **1957** *The Cat In The Hat* by Dr. Seuss is published. (1957)
- **1950–1953** The United States enters the Korean War.
- **1953** Girls wear short "poodle-cut" hairdos, and circle skirts with crinoline petticoats. Saddle shoes are "out" and "ballerina" flats are "in."
- **1953** Polyester fibers introduced.
- **1954** *Davy Crockett* becomes a hit song, movie, and TV show; kids all over America wear coonskin caps.
- **1955** Polio vaccine developed by Dr. Jonas Salk.
- **1955** *The Mickey Mouse Club* starts on TV and Disneyland, in California, opens.

- **1955** *Rebel Without A Cause* raises James Dean to stardom; he becomes a symbol of rebellion to the young.
- **1956** Elvis Presley appears (from the waist up) on *The Ed Sullivan Show*, becomes "The King of Rock and Roll"
- **1958** Spandex fiber is introduced by DuPont; it is widely used in swimwear, hosiery, and intimate apparel.
- **1958** The Hush Puppies Company opens.
- **1959** The first Barbie doll is introduced by Mattel.
- **1959** *Peanuts* and Snoopy become national icons.

HOPALONG CASSIDY

inseams to facilitate diaper changes. Undershirts may have snaps to open at the front so that they don't have to be pulled over the baby's head. Elasticized waistbands—rather than buttons or zippers—make changing pants or skirts easier for adults and for toddlers who are learning to dress themselves. Stretchy suits and snowsuits for infants and sleepwear for infants and toddlers may be fitted with soft-soled "feet" to offer extra warmth and protection. Mitten-like flaps on newborns' sleepwear help to prevent babies from scratching themselves with their fast-growing fingernails. Bonnets and caps tie under the chin, and bootees have elastic around the ankles to keep these clothing items on the baby.

Layettes—collections of crib and bath linens, sleepwear, and underwear for infants—include some unique items, such as sleeping sacs with drawstrings at the bottom. A one-piece undergarment, known as a "onesie," consisting of a shirt with a long tail that extends under a diaper and snaps to the front of the shirt, is another item designed specifically for infants.

## Product Specialization

Children's wear manufacturers typically specialize by product. One producer will make only girls' knits, while another makes only girls' dresses, and another makes only preteen sportswear. But unlike the producers of adult wear, children's wear producers often make a single type of clothing in several size ranges. For example, a producer may make boys' sportswear in sizes 8 through 20, while a producer of girls' dresses may make a product in toddlers through girls sizes.

A few observations about the fabrics used in children's wear are worth keeping in mind. One is the enduring popularity of knits for infants' wear and for tops in the everyday wardrobes of girls and boys through the larger size ranges. Another is the demand for natural fibers, especially cotton. Anyone interested in the children's apparel industry should be aware of the Flammable Fabrics Act of 1972 and its subsequent modifications, which require that sleepwear for children be treated with flame-retardant finishes.

The same design and production methods that are used in the manufacturing of adult apparel are used in children's wear, although these methods are often simplified. While children's garments require less fabric, they are usually more expensive to make because they require more labor.

**1960–1970**

- **1961** Communists erect the Berlin Wall.
- **1961** The disposable diaper is invented.
- **1962** The first Wal-Mart and the first KMart open.
- **1965–1975** The United States Enters the Vietnam War.
- **1964** Spandex yarns are introduced.
- **1969** The Gap opens its first store in San Francisco.
- **1966** *Star Trek* begins on TV.
- **1964** The Beatles conquer the music world.
- **1969** *Sesame Street* begins on TV.
- **1969** *The Brady Bunch* begins on TV.
- **1970** The first Earth Day is held; environmental awareness grows; issue fascinates children. "Flower children" protest war, wear jeans, tie-dye T-shirts, long hair, beads. Unisex look trickles down to kids.

THE BRADY BUNCH

**1970–1980**

- **1971** Disney World opens in Orlando.
- **1976** *The Muppet Show* premieres.
- **1977** *Star Wars* opens and The Empire begins.
- **1977** Soccer becomes the fastest growing sport in the United States
- **1977** Skateboards introduced.
- **1977** The *Annie Hall* men's wear look for women and girls.
- **1977** *Saturday Night Fever* starts disco craze. Teen boys wear white polyester leisure suits and black shirts.
- **1978** Fruit of the Loom introduces Underoos, decorated boys underwear; girl's Undaroos follow.
- **1978** *Superman: The Movie* and *Superman II* (**1980**) are mega-hits, and little boys begin wearing caped pajamas and undershorts like Superman's.
- **1979** Sony introduces the Walkman.
- **1979** Hip-huggers, bell-bottoms, granny gowns, tube tops, vests. Designer jeans with back pocket logos sweep the world.

STREET FASHION

## The Role of Fashion in Children's Wear

Even the most basic lines of children's clothing reflect attempts to make the clothes fashionable, and the demand for style, once primarily an urban phenomenon, is now felt in every area (see Figure 11.4).

The demand for stylish children's clothes, which has escalated every year, has most recently culminated in designer clothing for children. Children's wear, however, must still be viewed as a business that is a *fashionable* rather than a *fashion* business. The difference is that while the children's wear industry produces fashionable clothing, the styles adapt men's and women's styles. They are not in and of themselves innovative, nor does new fashion start in children's wear lines. The backpack is one recent exception.

The children's wear industry also does not operate with the intensity of the adult clothing industry. Children's clothes, for example, do not follow a ready-to-wear production and design schedule.

Producers of children's clothing have typically operated on a one-line-per-season production schedule, and four lines—spring, summer, winter, and fall—are typical. Lines are not updated during a

**FIGURE 11.4** Fashion consciousness starts with the very youngest (above and opposite).

season. Once a line has been shown and accepted, that is all the manufacturer produces. An exciting and very hot new look might appear at midseason, but only rarely. Most manufacturers could not produce a new look until the following season, at which point demand may even have begun to decline.

---

### TIME LINE FOR CHILDREN'S WEAR 1900—2008  *Events and their Effects on Apparel*

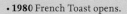

**1980–1990**

- **1980** French Toast opens.
- **1982** Michael Jackson's *Thriller* album is bestseller ever.
- **1982** VCRs and home videos are popular.
- **1982** Roller blades, bike shorts—active wear takes off.
- **1982** Yuppies and the "baby boomlet"
- **1982** California surf wear with bold colors and graphics.
- **1982** *ET: The Extra-Terrestrial* is a hit with kids all over the world, and another licensing frenzy begins.
- **1983** Cabbage Patch Kids introduced.
- **1983** The "ribbon dress" for girls.
- **1984** *Miami Vice* on TV has huge impact—unconstructed jackets with T-shirts and sunglasses.
- **1985** Baby Guess/Guess Girls begin.
- **1985** Cotton Caboodle, Flapdoodles, and Joe Boxer Corp. open.

ET: THE EXTRA-TERRESTRIAL

- **1986** L.A. Gear opens.
- **1987** The Limited Too opens.
- **1987** Natural fibers preferred; polyester scorned.
- **1987** Catalog shopping increases dramatically.
- **1987** Backpacks appear on kids; adults want them, too.
- **1989** Tommy Hilfiger opens.
- **1989** *The Little Mermaid*, Disney's film, opens.

**1990–2000**

- **1990** Cow & Lizard opens.
- **1990** *Home Alone* opens and spawns sequels.
- **1992** *Barney* starts on TV and toddlers love him.
- **1992** Home computers proliferate and surfing the Internet is "in." Fleece and shearling newly popular as cold winters occur. "Grunge" music and look sweep the country.
- **1993** *Jurassic Park* and dinosaurs everywhere.
- **1994** *The Lion King* is a blockbuster hit for Disney.
- **1994** *All That* premieres as Nickelodeon's PG-version of NBC's *Saturday Night Live* .
- **1995** Nicole Miller for Kids opens.
- **1995–1997** School uniform legislation.
- **1996** *Toy Story* opens.
- **1996** Manufactured fibers blended with natural fibers. Spandex is blended with almost every fiber!
- **1996** Michael Jordan and Air Jordans super popular.
- **1997–2000** The *Star Wars* Trilogy returns.

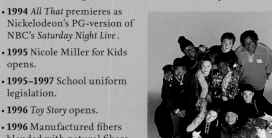

ALL THAT

and to the group just ahead of them, young adults, for pace-setting styles and trends. Successful children's wear producers have learned that they too must look to the young adult fashion world for inspiration. This means watching fads as well as trends. Popular young adult fads and styles are increasingly being translated into children's wear lines (see Figure 11.5).

The industry has also begun to use fashion-forecasting specialists to enable manufacturers to incorporate new styles into their lines as soon as a trend is spotted. At this point, the smaller (and trendier) manufacturers are still quicker to incorporate new styles and fashion than are the larger companies. The leading designers of adult fashion who have developed lines of children's apparel and the retailers whose store brands extend to the children's market—Talbots Baby and Talbots Kids, for example—can bring out corresponding lines of adults' and children's fashion concurrently.

The children's wear business has begun to make the kinds of operational changes necessary to permit it to stay more on top of changing fashion. Styles in children's wear used to trickle down from the adult fashion world, and typically lagged a year or more behind adult fashions. Today, however, the lag is shrinking.

Increasingly, children look to their own peers

## The Role of Fashion in Teens' and Tweens' Wear

Today's teens and tweens are the first age groups for which television has not been the primary enter-

**2000-2008**

- **2000s** Disney tries to go back to its roots when returning to the classics. Making sequels to these classic Disney favorites was a huge hit with children.
- **2001–2003** *SpongeBob SquarePants* became one of the most watched TV shows, and from **2005–2007** it is one of the top children's shows.
- **2004** Polo Ralph Lauren Corporation acquired RL Childrenswear. In **2008**, the company sells infant and children's apparel.
- **2001** *The Little Mermaid II: Return to the Sea*
- **2001** The first *Harry Potter* movie comes out and takes off with sequels. Books and merchandise are seen everywhere.
- **2006** *High School Musical* and *High School Musical 2* (**2007**). Toys, apparel, and accessories quickly become available.
- **2006** Miley Cyrus becomes a musical influence for children and teens with the start of her TV show *Hannah Montana*.
- **2006** J.Crew's children collection, Crewcuts, makes a comeback and hits store shelves.

HANNAH MONTANA

**FIGURE 11.5** Harajuku clothing by Gwen Stefani is available for kids, as well as women.

tainment; it is but one technology of many at which they spend their leisure hours. Their top leisure activity: surfing the web.

There are distinct differences between teens and tweens in attitudes, buying habits, and other consumer behaviors, as reported in *Marketing to Teens & Tweens*, published by EPM Communications, owner of *The Licensing Letter*.[8] The report looks at the trends shaping these consumers with an eye toward where these trends will lead in the future. Teens and tweens both like to be defined as individuals yet still fit in with peers. But teens in general show more individualistic qualities, while tweens tend more toward the group.

Gloria Baume, fashion director for *Teen Vogue* magazine says, "There is no distinction between what a woman of 40 wants and what a girl of 15 wants."[9]

A growing number of well-known designers and retailers hope to benefit through the trend by getting into the teen and tween business. The idea of families sharing a clothing label has long been the foundation for apparel empires such as Polo/Ralph Lauren, Rocawear, and the Gap. Moms and daughters are shopping the same racks. To satisfy this new trend, specialty chain J.Crew Group is selling tiny versions of its popular adult apparel. The kid's line, called Crewcuts, has done so well that J.Crew is expanding freestanding stores for Crewcuts.

## Merchandising and Marketing

Many of the features and activities of the children's wear industry are similar, if not identical, to those of the women's and men's apparel industries. For example, the trend of sustainable and organic fashions is now seen in children's wear too (see Figure 11.6).

However, sales promotion and advertising activities for children's wear are considerably more limited. The few giants in the industry—Carter's, Health-tex, and OshKosh B'Gosh—ad-

**FIGURE 11.6** Kids are even taking part in sustainable fashion. These dresses from Kicky Pants are made out of bamboo.

vertise aggressively to consumers. Smaller firms—the majority of firms producing budget and moderately priced children's wear—leave most consumer advertising to retailers. Firms producing higher priced, name-designer merchandise do a limited amount of consumer advertising. The high cost of this advertising is often shared with textile firms.

In general, the industry limits its advertising to the trade press. Specialized publications concerned with children's wear include *Children's Business*, *Earnshaw's*, and *Girls' and Boys' Wear Review*. Trade publications that report on adult fashions, such as *Women's Wear Daily* and the *Daily News Record*, also carry children's wear advertising and news reports of interest to retailers on a regular basis. More and more companies are going on the Internet, often combining information about the company with a catalog.

## Market Centers

Most of the children's wear firms are located in the North Atlantic states, particularly in New York City. As is the trend in the women's and men's apparel industries, some factories have moved farther south in order to obtain lower production costs. Many goods are produced in foreign countries—outerwear, jeans, woven shirts, and sweaters primarily in the Far East; infants' knits and apparel items in Greece, Spain, and Israel. These countries offer lower production costs than do France, Italy, and

Switzerland, which produce prestige merchandise. But the design, sales, and distribution centers of such firms remain in New York City. While New York continues to be the most important market center for children's wear, many producers maintain permanent showrooms in the large regional apparel marts, especially in Miami, and schedule showings there. Los Angeles, too, has emerged as a children's apparel center not only because of its enormous manufacturing base but also for the fashion trends that originate there. Dallas has Anthony Mark Hankins, for example, who sells his budget line of children's wear to Target Stores, among other retailers.

## Trade Shows

The California Market in Los Angeles promotes through direct mail, floor displays, and caravans that bring in retailers from surrounding counties (see Figure 11.7). It also sponsors MAGIC Kids, held three times a year. The huge MAGIC International shows for men's, women's, and children's apparel and accessories are held in Las Vegas twice a year.

Other popular children's wear trade shows include the Children's Club trade show in New York City, produced by ENK International; and an annual Women's and Children's Apparel Market in Chicago.

**FIGURE 11.7** Trade show booths are an important place for children's apparel manufacturers to reach retail store buyers.

# Fashion Focus

Fashion Focus

## Babes in Denimland
### *Going Gaga*
#### *for Denim*

Left page: Seven for All Mankind kids denim (top center); Even the youngest tots sport denim (bottom left); Right page: Design by Lilica Ripilica/Marisol, 2005 (top right); Denim is the perfect apparel for outdoor play (bottom right).

Famous names like Diesel, GUESS, Ernest Sewn, Chip & Pepper, and True Religion have launched their own babies' and children's denim lines, and Seven for All Mankind has joined with presenting a full children's sportswear collection for girls and boys, with denim items retailing from $75 to $224.

The people buying the kids' clothing are typically already loyal adult customers of the brand. Not surprisingly, moms are spearheading the trend. According to Cotton Incorporated's *Lifestyle Monitor*, women with children under the age of 18 own an average of eight pairs of jeans themselves. This high level of knowledge and intimacy with one product is impacting how moms shop for their kids.

"Today's stylish moms are definitely seeking that same fashionable edge and attention to detail in their children's wardrobes that they demand in their own, as evidenced by the growing number of premium denim brands entering the market," said a *WWD* report.

Just as celebrities have driven the adult premium market, so too have celebrity kids. Tweens, teens, and adults are all interested in what the hottest celebrities are wearing, so of course their children's wardrobes are getting scrutinized as well.

Celebrity designers such as Sean "P. Diddy" Combs, Tory Burch, and Kimora Lee Simmons have entered the children's wear race with their lines of kids' wear. Other big names such as new mom Gwen Stefani, and even the team of Victoria Beckham and Katie Holmes, have reportedly shown interest in designing kids' apparel.

Brands and designers are becoming increasingly aware of the impact creating a children's line can have on their overall sales. By the time children reach their teenage years, they have developed their own sense of style and know what they want and what they don't want. But the denim industry is finding out that kids have a much larger say in what they wear at an even earlier age.

Retailers are enjoying the babies' and kids' denim boom. Shops such as Scoop, Barneys, Bloomingdale's, Nieman Marcus, and Saks Fifth Avenue have opened their door to these

### Designer Labels

Children's designer-label clothing and accessories are highly visible in stores across the country. The appeal of these items seems to rise above income levels. Designer labels are available in stores geared to middle-income as well as high-income customers. Although designer wear for children has been around for a while—Izod introduced a boys' line in the late 1960s—the explosion in designer-label children's wear took off in the late 1970s with the designer jean craze.

Designer labels are expected to continue to grow in children's wear (see Figure 11.8). An interesting British Lifestyle Survey by Mintel in 2001 showed that parents continue to indulge their children with brand-name clothing even when the economy is slow and they have less money for themselves. The study found that many parents sacrificed their own wardrobe to buy designer labels for their children.

Well-known brand names in children's wear include Flapdoodles, Gymboree, Little Me, Absorba, Joe Boxer, Cotton Caboodle, and, of course, GUESS and the Gap. Because they have designer-name status, some children's wear designers, following in the pioneering footsteps of Florence Eiseman and Ruth Scharf, have acquired celebrity status, such as Hanna Andersson.

Adult designers have also entered the children's

brands, as have specialty boutiques such as Babesta in New York, Naked Baby Boutique in Los Angeles, and Psychobaby in Chicago. Out of the mouth of babes: Give us denim!

**FIGURE 11.8** Just like apparel for adults, designer labels for children's wear are seen on the runway (Ming and Aoki, left) and in fashion spreads (Poesia, right).

wear arena. As David Wolfe, creative director of Doneger Group, a New York buying office, said:

> Status is definitely trickling down to kids. They are looking at their mothers and older sisters, and they want to wear the same brands. They are also looking at pop icons and want to dress just like them.[10]

Several companies, including Esprit, GUESS, Patagonia, Ralph Lauren, and Jessica McClintock, have launched separate divisions of children's wear. Other designers offering children's lines are Gucci; Donna Karan; Armani; Marc Jacobs; and Moschino, which markets Moschino Bambino for infants and toddlers and Moschino Junior for 2 to 15 year olds.

Status names are also changing the shape of the boys' wear industry. It is difficult to tell which came first, though—the boys' demand for designer clothes or the designers' efforts to enter the boys' wear market. Whatever the case, well-known fashion designers are now competing for space alongside traditional branded merchandise in boys' wear departments. Boys' wear, in fact, has become a prime area for designers such as Pierre Cardin, Yves Saint Laurent, Ralph Lauren, Tommy Hilfiger, and Calvin Klein. Of course, not all designers actually design and manufacture all the products sold under their labels.

### Licensing

Like designer labels, other kinds of licensed names provide a sense of fashion rightness, in addition to giving a garment or line instant identification in consumers' minds. As a result, as the children's wear industry became more fashion-conscious, manufacturers were quick to produce licensed goods. Today, in addition to designer names, the ever-popular cartoon and toy character licenses share the spotlight with a growing number of sports and corporate licenses.

## Character Licensing

The first licensed cartoon character was Buster Brown in 1904. Licensed cartoon and toy characters, long a staple with children, are still thriving in the 21st century. Younger children especially enjoy wearing representations of their favorite characters. A widespread example is Dora the Explorer, whose picture adorns children coast to coast.

Character licenses dominate in children's T-shirts, sweatshirts, and sleepwear and are also strong in accessories and sportswear (see Figure 11.9). Their impact is not as great in dresses, suits, and outerwear, but some of these items are available. Even with the recent boom, children's character licenses, especially those associated with feature-length movies, tend to be short lived, like the Dick Tracy merchandise. Only a few reached the ranks of true stardom (and big profit). As a result, many retailers, particularly department store buyers, have become cautious about overinvesting in them. Department stores, whose promotion is necessary if a licensed character is to be truly successful, tend to stick with classics like Pooh, Snoopy, and Mickey Mouse. In the popular-priced lines of children's apparel, a licensing agreement between Kmart and Children's Television Workshop, creators of *Sesame Street*, is likely to be profitable to both parties for a long time.

**FIGURE 11.9** Character licenses are everywhere in the children's apparel industry, such as these T-shirts by Disney.

Two major studios that produce cartoons, Disney and Warner Brothers, have established their own retail outlets, where the mix of apparel, accessories, and toys may help to extend the lives of the movie characters. Warner Brothers owns both Superman and Batman, perennial favorites with boys on sleepwear, underwear, and T-shirts. Warner Brothers made a licensing agreement with Spalding Sports Worldwide to put its Looney Tunes characters (Bugs Bunny, Daffy Duck, Road Runner, and Wile E. Coyote) on its leisure products line, including backpacks. Warner Brothers also oversees licensing arrangements for the Hanna-Barbera studio (the Flintstones, Scooby Doo, and Tom & Jerry). Kmart's exclusive Disney Kids and Sesame Street clothing licenses have been so successful that the otherwise ailing discount chain store was the number two retailer in children's clothing in 2002.[11]

## Sports Licensing

Sports licensing is another prospering area of licensing. Sports figures and teams both have high media visibility and thus enjoy instant recognition among children and young adults. In areas with professional or school teams, college stores, airport shops, and stadium concessions increase the availability of licensed apparel at retail. Sports figures, who have successfully put their names on sports equipment for years, are now adding them to jogging and running suits, tennis clothes and accessories, as well as less active casual and sportswear lines, with great success. And producers of athletic shoes, sweatshirts, and sports equipment feature their names and logos on active sportswear.

Professional hockey, football, basketball, and baseball teams, as well as college and university athletic teams, now routinely license their names for use on clothes, mostly T-shirts and sweatshirts. The National Football League, to increase the already intense popularity of the game with children, launched a "Play Football" promotional campaign with competitions and programs for boys and girls in different age groups, advertising in *Sports Illus-*trated for Kids and at the Super Bowl, and promoting the campaign with forty-five national and regional retailers. The results: Kids are not only playing football, they are wearing millions of dollars worth of related apparel.

Sportswear companies are also quick to capitalize on trends. Over the past few years, soccer has been the fastest growing sport among young Americans. It's not surprising that Nike introduced a children's soccer line in 2001 to keep up with the trend.

## Industry Trends

Like women's apparel manufacturers, children's wear producers are constantly on the lookout for ways to increase productivity and reduce—or at least minimize—costs while still maintaining quality. Computerized operations have become the norm for manufacturers. Even portions of the design process are now computerized in children's wear, mostly because this technology helps producers respond more quickly to fashion trends in the industry.

Suppliers, manufacturers, and retailers of children's wear are also interacting on the Internet. Although freestanding e-commerce sites never reached the level of success projected in the late 1990s and still don't have a strong presence in the market, there are Web sites that offer multiple brands of clothing for children, such as Baby Style (www.babystyle.com). However, the e-commerce sites that attract the most traffic are already attached to a major retail brand, like The Disney Store (www.disneystore.com) and Warner Brothers (www.wbshop.com) for younger children and Abercrombie and Fitch (www.abercrombie.com) and Hot Topic (www.hottopic.com) for teens.

Production costs have risen in recent years, forcing producers of budget goods to move into moderate lines. Most of the budget-priced children's clothing is produced offshore in labor-cheap foreign countries, but even this expense is

# Then & NOW

## Paper Dolls
### Stardolls, Fame, Fashion, Friends

When was the last time you played with paper dolls? Years ago, paper dolls were a great favorite of young girls from 3 to 8 years old, and many paper doll books were published. In fact, a favorite song back in 1943 was called "Paper Doll" and was a popular hit by the Mills Brothers. It started with the line: "I'm gonna buy a Paper Doll that I can call my own. . . ."

Today, paper dolls have made a comeback, but this time around, they are the favorites of the teen queens! Stardolls.com is a favorite Web site for teens. The site features more than four hundred dolls to dress up, each and every one with a unique wardrobe. The dolls range from actors and actresses to singers, celebrities, superstars (VIPs), athletes, and a variety of "makeup" dolls. But how can teen queens live without designer duds for their dolls? They can't! So big names are coming to the virtual mall in Stardolls.

DKNY and Sephora recently opened virtual stores where the girls can see the brand's latest lines, try them on, and buy them for their avatars for about a dollar or two.

Stardolls has more than 10 million members and more than 6 million unique visitors a month, making it one of the largest sites of its kind.  Its team created a three-floor flagship that closely resembles DKNY's real-world stores. "Choosing different clothes and styles is very important for our users," said Stardolls Chief Executive Mattias Miksche. "They are expressing themselves online, and also it is the foundation of who you choose to connect with."

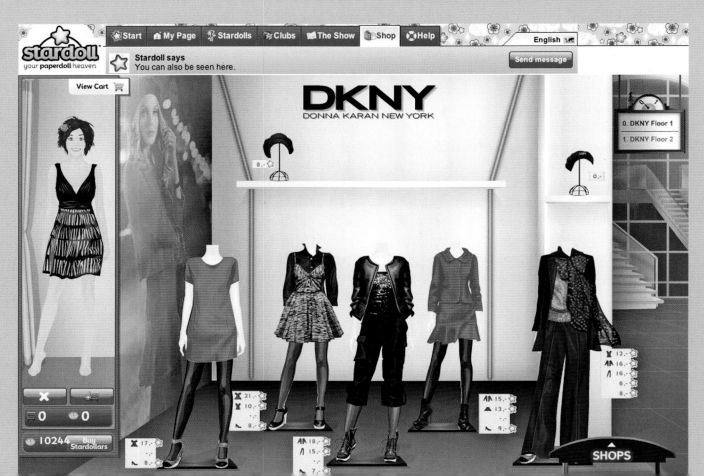

growing as the standard of living improves in developing nations.

## Price Lines

The clear distinctions that once existed between budget, moderate, and better-priced children's wear were eroded in an era of heavy inflation in the 1970s, and the disintegration has continued. Several major moderate-priced sportswear producers such as Pandora and Girlstown were driven out of business by inflation and rising operating costs.

Had they stayed in business, they would have been forced to raise their prices beyond the upper limits of the moderate price range. Doing so would have placed them in competition with established producers of higher-priced apparel and put them in a much smaller segment of the children's wear market—thus making it likely that they would ultimately fail anyway.

Although there was no room for expansion in the upper-priced categories during the upheaval of the 1970s, this was not the case in moderate-priced children's wear. To fill the vacuum created in this price range, many budget manufacturers opted to trade up. At the same time, many moderate-priced manufacturers such as Health-Tex and OshKosh B'Gosh, known as suppliers of children's basics, began to supplement their lines with more up-to-date, fashion-oriented garments, a gesture that moved them closer to the better-priced category. And to come full circle, the vacuum created in the budget market by the upgrading of companies such as Health-tex and OshKosh B'Gosh is now being filled to a large extent by lower-cost imports.

## Offshore Production

Promising low cost and decent quality, imports have made substantial inroads into children's wear. Of special interest to manufacturers of children's apparel are the White House Apparel Industry Partnership's age standards for child labor.

These standards are also of increasing concern for children in developed countries, who are dismayed to learn of the existence of child labor in many less-developed countries. Balancing the reliance of families in developing countries on their children's contributions to the family income against the protection of the children, the White House task force set the minimum age for hiring at 15 years, reduced to 14 only in countries that allow the employment of factory workers younger than age 15.

Buying foreign-made children's wear does have some drawbacks. Very early commitment—as much as 8 to 9 months' lead time, for example—is required, and there is usually no opportunity for reordering. Despite this limitation, children's retail buyers still favor imports, because foreign-made goods satisfy consumer demand. In fact, retail buyers not only have been buying imports but have often been ordering them to their specifications. In response, manufacturers have also sought out global sourcing.

## Specialty Retail Outlets

Increasing attention is being given to children's wear by apparel retailers whose main lines are men's and women's clothing (see Figure 11.10). A related trend is the prominence of clothing in the merchandise mix of retail outlets carrying a broader array of children's goods. Even among clothing stores that have not opened freestanding children's outlets, distinctive stores-within-stores are now selling children's wear exclusively. Carrying the trend to its logical conclusion, the infants' and toddlers' departments of the children's stores and stores-within-stores are being set up as separate outlets.

### Separate Stores

Typical of this trend are the Gap's GapKids and BabyGap. Begun in 1969 as a retailer of jeans for adults, the Gap expanded into a private-label spe-

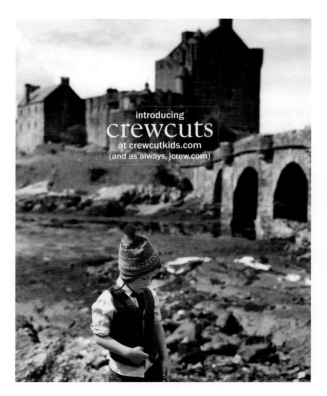

**FIGURE 11.10** After receiving a positive response from customers, J.Crew brought back their line of children's wear, Crewcuts.

cialty store featuring casual wear for men and women. In 1986, the first GapKids store opened, offering Gap customers basic but fashionable children's wear that catered to the same tastes as the adult lines. The BabyGap line, begun in 1990, became a separate department within GapKids stores and departments, and in 1996, the flagship freestanding BabyGap store opened in New York. However, the Gap's overall sales started to decline in 2001, perhaps because the company's core customers felt alienated by the store's fashion-forward merchandise. The decreasing traffic also hurt the label's children's wear.

Benetton is another producer/retailer that has developed a successful chain of children's wear stores. Called Benetton 0–12, they are packed with miniversions of the same stylish merchandise sold to adults. In the late 1980s, Laura Ashley began translating her classic English clothing for adults into **children's sizes** and opened stores called Mother and Child, which effectively cater to two major markets. Gymboree has used other concepts to build its business. Its Outlet division, started in 2005, now operates forty-two stores. The Janie and Jack stores, which sell clothing at higher prices than the company's original Gymboree children's stores, now number eighty-one stores since their 2002 launch. The company plans to open more than ninety new stores, consisting of twenty Gymboree stores, forty-five Gymboree Outlet stores, fifteen Janie and Jack shops, and a minimum of ten stores that involve a new concept.[12]

## Catalogs

Major catalog retailers such as Lands' End, Eddie Bauer, Talbots, and L. L. Bean have also increased their offerings for children in recent years. They offer specialized catalogs, such as Talbots Kids and Talbots Baby. JCPenney has long had a separate "kids' book": it now also offers JCPenney for "school uniforms." Marketing clothes to a group who, for the most part, is too young to drive or hold down full-time jobs is a risky proposition. But who

said dealing with teenagers was easy? dELiA's is a company whose target customer is in the 12- to 19-years-old demographic. dELiA's is a collection of three marketing brands—dELiA's and Alloy, both targeted to teenage girls, and CCS, which is geared toward teen boys. For the dELiA's and Alloy brands, it aims to appeal to "trendsetting, fashion-aware teenage girls."[13] Its prime customer is the alpha fashionista—high school juniors who are often copied in style and dress by younger kids. CCS uses skateboard culture and other tie-ins to appeal to boys. The company's strongest suit is its online presence: two-thirds of its sales are through the Internet.

## The Internet

Although children and teens are generally very Internet savvy, they still spend a good deal of their time shopping off-line. Web sites for companies like Disney, Nike, Hollister, American Eagle Outfitters, and Hot Topic offer merchandise online, but their most important role is to push the store's image and establish a relationship with their young shoppers so they will be enticed to buy more products from brick-and-mortar retailers.

## *Resale of Children's Wear*

Another important trend in children's wear retailing is the growth of secondhand resale or consignment stores. For parents who are concerned about the price of their children's wardrobe basics, secondhand clothes received as hand-me-downs or purchased at garage sales or nursery school bazaars have always been a good source of clothing Since children—especially infants and toddlers—so quickly outgrow their clothes, increasing numbers of budget-minded parents are using this kind of outlet.

Resale shops have emerged as a popular source of "lightly used" children's wear. Two franchise chains, the Children's Orchard and Once Upon a Child, have become prominent resale outlets (see

**FIGURE 11.11** K.I.D.S. (Kids in Distressed Situations) is the children's apparel manufacturers' national charity. It is a way that the industry can demonstrate its concern for the welfare of its market. Members provide brand new clothing and other essentials for disaster victims and other children in need at home and abroad.

Figure 11.12). The first Children's Orchard store opened in 1980. The company now has more than 100 stores and has grown its business to over $20 million a year in sales. One way Children's Orchard boosts sales is by allowing customers to bring in used clothing in return for store credit, which gives customers an incentive to take store credit over cash for their goods. This strategy promotes the virtuous cycle of buying, selling, and returning to the store for more.[14]

**FIGURE 11.12** Children's Orchard, a franchiser for resale shops for children's clothing and accessories, supplies its franchisees with ads they can run in local newspapers. The franchisee just needs to add the store's address, phone number, and business hours.

The appeal of these stores to budget-conscious parents is twofold: they can sell their children's outgrown clothing and get paid for it immediately. This practice distinguishes resale shops from consignment shops, which pay a percentage of the retail price only when the item is sold.

Once Upon a Child (www.ouac.com), Children's Orchard (www.childrensorchard.com), and similar stores also have successful online businesses. Interestingly, resale of children's clothing has become a very popular form of online shopping. There are hundreds of small and large Web sites that offer "gently used" children's clothing.

## School Uniforms

The number of schools requiring school uniforms continues to increase (see Figure 11.13).[15] School officials believe uniforms have contributed to improved behavior, including reductions in lateness, class cutting, fighting, and robberies and other crimes. As the principal of a middle school in Long Beach, California, said: "Uniforms are an effective method of reducing unwanted behavior, because the more formal clothing puts students in the right mind-set to learn. It's about dressing for success."[16]

President Clinton's 1996 State of the Union address included a pitch for school uniforms. The U.S. Department of Education sent every school district in the United States a *Manual on School Uniforms*, which began with a section called "School Uniforms: Where They Are and Why They Work." Uniforms have become so common at elementary and middle schools that in many areas of the country they are the rule, not the exception.

Supporters of uniforms point out that uniforms also help students identify with their school and make intruders not in uniform easier to spot. They cite the positive associations of children with other uniformed groups, such as scouts, teams in children's athletic leagues, children in private and parochial schools, and children in public schools in other countries. Stylish but functional uniforms are

**FIGURE 11.13** Traditional school uniforms (top) and today's fashionable interpretations on *Gossip Girl* (bottom).

presented as a superior alternative to the unofficial uniforms of street gangs.

Answering the objections of opponents, supporters point out that uniforms equalize affluent and low-income students and that a set of uniforms need not be more expensive than an ordinary school wardrobe. Children can be encouraged to participate in the selection of uniforms as a way of expressing their tastes. In 2007, Time Inc., in its magazine *Parenting*, polled readers on the question,

*Should kids wear uniforms to school?* More than 11,000 families responded, and 76% said yes.[17]

As uniforms have become more common, many schools have updated the traditional (and itchy) blue blazers, plaid skirts, and white knee socks. An increasing number of students are sporting "business casual" clothes like pants, jumpers, and denim shirts from brands like Lands' End, Old Navy, Target, and Wal-Mart instead.

JCPenney, in partnership with Izod, is the year-round headquarters for school uniforms. Through izoded.com and select JCPenney stores, customers can receive school uniform specifications and purchase their local school district–approved apparel that is stylish, comfortable, and easy to care for. In addition, JCPenney can accommodate all special-size uniform needs with its vast assortment of fits for all kids and teens in stores and at jcp.com.[18]

For manufacturing, some stores are turning to French Toast, whose large presence and experience in the market allows for a broad assortment of styles and colors and good depth in sizing. Other respected resources are Girls Will Be Girls! and Longstreet's Genuine School Uniform collection. School Apparel, Inc., sells its products only through authorized school uniform dealers, which sell mainly to schools. The company does not sell to department or discount stores. Some schools are using traditional dealers/distributors of adult uniforms, since these companies have long made quality clothes designed and constructed for daily wear.[19]

## Summary and Review

The children's wear market is segmented by gender and by size categories. The special features of infants' and toddlers' apparel must be taken into consideration by designers and manufacturers.

Designer labels, which are often licensed to manufacturers that specialize in children's products, are becoming increasingly important in this industry, as are character and sports licensing.

Established trends that bear watching are multiple price lines offered by manufacturers and steady offshore production. Retail trends include establishing separate stores, the widespread use of catalogs, and establishing Internet sites. The trend toward school uniforms for grade school students and some high school students also demands attention.

Most experts are optimistic that the two prevalent trends—a move toward greater fashion in children's and teens' wear and another move toward buying better children's and teens' wear—are unlikely to reverse themselves in the coming years. This situation should make this industry one of the more stable divisions in the fashion industry. The segment that has simply been called children's wear can now rightly be called children's and teens' fashion.

## Trade Talk

Define or briefly explain the following terms:

| | |
|---|---|
| boys' sizes | children's sizes |
| girls' sizes | infants' sizes |
| preteen sizes | teens' sizes |
| toddlers' sizes | young men, prep, student, or teen sizes |

## For Review

1. How did the children's wear industry adjust to demographic changes between the 1980s and 1990s?
2. What three developments occurred after World War I to cause the growth of the children's wear industry?
3. Name and briefly describe the seven size categories of children's wear. What distinguishes girls' from preteen sizes and boys' from young men's sizes?
4. Explain the statement "Children's wear . . . must still be viewed as a business that is a fashion-

able rather than a fashion business." Do you agree with this statement? Explain your reasons.

5. How is consumer advertising handled by different types of firms in the children's wear business?

6. What accounts for the popularity of character licensing in children's wear?

7. What is the appeal of designer-label children's clothing?

8. What has been the attitude of U.S. retailers and manufacturers toward the growth of imports in the children's wear industry?

9. Describe the current trend toward specialty retail outlets for children's wear.

10. Explain the popularity of resale shops for children's wear.

## For Discussion

1. Discuss the importance of licensing in today's children's wear market. How does the licensing system work? Why is it particularly popular with children?

2. Discuss the pros and cons of school uniforms. What impact does this issue have on the children's wear industry?

3. What trends do you see in the young adult market today that have filtered into the design of children's clothing?

unit four

No matter how chic, exquisite, or hip your apparel may look, it is the finishing touches that make your outfit something special, something that says . . . YOU! For years, intimate apparel, accessories, and cosmetics and fragrances were simply something that you thought of as "maybe yes, maybe no." They were not the most important part of your fashion look. Things have really changed.

Today, producers of accessories, innerwear, cosmetics and fragrances, and home fashions must stay on the cutting edge of fashion trends that affect apparel, because the customer expects them to support and refine each new fashion trend. These producers have evolved from their original role of coordinating with apparel, becoming fashion innovators and trendsetters on their own. What we wear underneath is as important to fashion as what we wear outside. How we choose our accessories, cosmetics, and fragrance, and the items we surround ourselves with at home, all add up to our own personal fashion feel and look. The four chapters in this unit explore the history and current activities of these other producers.

# THE SECONDARY LEVEL: THE OTHER PRODUCERS

# chapter twelve

KEY CONCEPTS

- History of the women's intimate apparel industry
- Categories of intimate apparel
- Merchandising and marketing of intimate apparel
- Merchandising of men's and children's underwear and sleepwear
- History and organization of the hosiery industry
- Branding of women's legwear
- Trends in the hosiery industry

*Everything you always wanted to know*

*about the innerwear, bodywear,*

*and legwear industries.*

# Innerwear, Bodywear, Legwear

Innerwear, bodywear, and legwear used to be personal and secret choices, hidden from everyone except our closest and dearest. What supported our bodies, glorified our figures, and made us feel wanted was a secret weapon we shared with no one. Today, all that has changed! Men, women, and children flaunt the "intimate apparel" that was once hidden from view. What is hidden under clothing can never make a name for itself, so innerwear, bodywear, and legwear designers decreed that it should all "hang out." Today, bras, corsets, slips, nightgowns, underwear, and hosiery are a very important part of a person's total fashion look. People enjoy the luxurious array of styles and colors provided by these industries and consider them an important part of their wardrobes. The importance of designer names in these industries has helped to ensure that the interpretation of changes in silhouette, fabrication, and color is reflected in the innerwear, bodywear, and legwear industries.

When you shop for boxers, do you think of Calvin Klein or Joe Boxer? Do you associate Nike or Russell with activewear? And is Hanes or Donna Karan your choice for hosiery? If you are looking for a leotard, do you think of Danskin or Capezio? Do you buy "no brand" socks or Gold Toe? All these manufacturers are vying for your business. They and their competitors also want their names in the forefront of your mind. Manufacturers and retailers have long recognized that the intimate apparel and hosiery segments of the fashion industry operate in support of the women's, men's, and children's apparel segments. Consumers maximize the versatility of their wardrobes and enhance the look of each outfit by coordinating their underwear and legwear with their clothing. Therefore, the way for a designer, manufacturer, or retailer to grow is to provide the components of a total fashion statement.

## An Overview of the Underwear and Innerwear Industries

In the past, the manufacturing and marketing of men's and children's underwear was driven by considerations of practical functionality, but lately, these segments of the apparel industry have also felt the impact of fashion. Through mergers and acquisitions, producers of men's and children's underwear have become divisions of more diversified apparel firms. This trend is discussed later in this chapter.

Women's underwear or **innerwear**, sometimes called "inner fashions," "intimate apparel," or "body fashions," is the trade term for women's underwear, usually divided into foundations (bras, shapewear, lingerie, and loungewear). Originally these three groups of products were separate industries. In recent years, a single industry called **intimate apparel** has evolved as a result of business mergers, diversification of products, technological advances in fibers and fabrications, and a growing relationship between these industries and women's ready-to-wear.

### Innerwear or Intimate Apparel

The wearing of undergarments probably grew out of practical need as people sought something to protect their skins from the chafing of harsh animal skins. And indeed, for many years the purpose of underwear was primarily utilitarian. Foundation garments were for shaping and support, lingerie provided warmth and protection, and loungewear marked the boundaries of propriety for at-home entertaining. As the distinctions among these categories have blurred, new fashion features of intimate apparel, new types of undergarments, and new uses of innerwear as outerwear, have emerged—literally.

### *History and Development*

The foundations industry began after the Civil War with the opening of the Warner Brothers' corset factory in Bridgeport, Connecticut (see Figure 12.1).

WARNER BROS. CORALINE CORSETS,
THE LATEST ÆSTHETIC CRAZE.

**FIGURE 12.1** An advertisement for the Warner Brothers' Coraline corset.

The bell-shaped silhouette was then at the height of its popularity. To achieve the tiny waist demanded by the bell and its successors, the bustle-back and Gibson Girl silhouettes, women wore corsets made of sturdy, unyielding cotton. Reinforced with vertical stays of whalebone or steel, the corsets laced up the front or back. They were tightly laced to achieve the extreme (in many cases) constriction of the waist and internal organs that fashion required.

Variations on these stiff corsets were worn by all women until the 1920s, when the rounded and bustled silhouettes that had prevailed for decades gave way to the straight, loose styles of the "boyish" flappers. Stiff, full-torso corsets were no longer required. The new silhouette demanded that the bosom and hips be minimized. Bandage-like bras were created to flatten the bust, and new girdlelike corsets controlled any conspicuous bulges below the waist.

By the 1930s, soft, feminine curves were back in style. Rubberized elastic was introduced, and the corset became known as the "girdle." Women now coaxed their bodies into two new types of foundations, the two-way stretch girdle and the cup-type brassiere, both of which were more comfortable than any of their predecessors.

These innovations set a precedent in the foundations industry and in women's lives. Women would henceforth wear inner garments that molded the figure more gently. Undergarments would now permit freedom of movement.

The 1930s also marked the introduction of rayon, changing the face of the intimate apparel industry. Until then, most mass-produced lingerie and loungewear were made of cotton, with wool being used in extremely cold climates. Silk, which was expensive and tedious to care for, appeared in custom-made, luxury styles affordable only by the rich. Rayon had the luxurious feel of silk, but it was washable and inexpensive.

Similar fibers followed, culminating in the 1950s with the reintroduction of nylon, a synthetic fiber that was softer and longer wearing than rayon and even more easily maintained. (Its use had been limited during the war years—1940 to 1945.) Innovations in fabrics continued over the next four decades, with the introduction of polyester, acrylics, microfibers, Tencel, and Lyocell. Stronger sheer fabrics, more pliable leathers, and Ultrasuede also helped transform the intimate apparel industry, especially loungewear.

Repeated improvements in elasticized fabrics have led to softer, more comfortable, and increasingly lightweight foundation garments that retain their shape even after many washings. Spandex body shapers mixed with nylon or polyester microfibers are the latest episode in this ongoing saga and Nancy Ganz, whose Lycra Bodyslimmers were introduced in 1990, is the heroine. Depending on the area they want to reshape, women can rely on her hipslip, thighslimmer, buttbooster, or knee beater.

Brassieres offer the best example of the massive style changes that the intimate apparel industry has undergone in the past half-century. They have evolved from the original bandage-type bra to a cup form; from plain-weave cotton, to polyester fiber-filled, to spandex; from the "no-bra" (unconstructed) look to the molded (unseamed) bra.

An important development of the 1940s was the introduction of padded bras to enhance the figure. In the 1960s, feminist activists rebelled against this focus on creating a standard of female beauty, which they characterized as treatment of women as sex objects. Bra burning became a symbol of the social revolution of the decade (see Figure 12.2). As the movement matured and women felt less compelled to demonstrate their independence from physical stereotypes in such dramatic ways, they

adopted natural-looking soft cups and seamless styles of bras that became available in the 1970s. Gradually, more structured styles of foundations were reintroduced to support the power dressing of the business woman of the 1980s.

In 1986, the Wacoal Company of Japan, a leading manufacturer of foundations, pioneered the computer "mapping" of the female body, which permitted them and other manufacturers to design undergarments that truly supported and enhanced the female figure. The push-in-and-up bra, introduced in 1994 by Sara Lee Foundations as the Wonderbra, was the foundation fashion story of the 1990s.

In 2006, the Barely There brand conducted a survey in which 75 percent of the women respondents claimed that wearing a bad bra can result in a bad mood. It's called the Bad Bra Syndrome (BBS), and it's currently affecting three out of four American women. To help remedy the problem, Barely There Intimates introduced the Invisible Look bra collection (see Figure 12.3).

"Starting with the right intimate apparel, and specifically a great-fitting bra, is one of my number one fashion tips for women," says Stacy London, style expert and cohost of TLC's *What Not To Wear*. "With the new Invisible Look Bra, women can wear anything from a tight-fitting white tank top to a strapless black dress and feel completely confident

**FIGURE 12.2** Women protesters took off their bras to place on the bra-burning pile in honor of the social revolution of their time.

that how incredible they look in their clothes is the only thing people will notice."[1]

Innerwear has become increasingly luxurious over the decades. And fashion has finally invaded this segment of the market, so much so that some beautifully designed undergarments are now worn as outer garments. A lacy silk camisole is used as a dressy top to wear under a suit jacket—or alone. A sexy slip becomes an evening garment, and lounging pajamas are elegant components of any ensemble (see Figure 12.4). Driving the market are teenage and young adult shoppers, who demand variety to meet their disparate needs from sports bras for the gym to body shapers for form-fitting fashions. Today's innerwear also meets the needs of aging baby boomers, who want to retain a shapely, sexy look.

## Categories of Intimate Apparel

Items traditionally classified as **foundations** support either the bust (brassieres) or the lower torso (girdles, which have evolved into shapewear). **Lingerie** is the term for less structured innerwear and sleepwear, and **loungewear** refers to the loose-fitting apparel designed for home entertaining and, more recently, an evening out.

### Bras

Brassieres are the most important foundation item for the bust. Their practical features are designed to fit different body types and suit a variety of purposes and occasions. Wide straps, banding or underwires under the cups, and closures with three or more hooks offer extra support and comfort for buxom women. Padding adds shaping and increased size for women with smaller bustlines, and the Wonderbra lifts the bust, creating a different silhouette. Cups cover the breasts completely or not, sides are wide or narrow, and straps are positioned strategically or removed so that the bra will not show unintentionally under the top.

In addition, materials and design accommodate

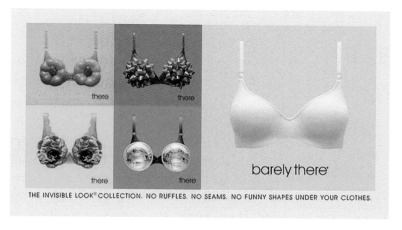

**FIGURE 12.3** The Invisible Look bra collection by Barely There provides comfort and a good fit .

special needs: *training bras* gently support the developing breasts of young teens; *sports bras* move with the body, give support, and absorb perspiration; *nursing bras* have cups that unfasten to allow a mother to breast feed without undressing; and *mastectomy bras* have pockets for prostheses. A *bustier* is a foundation garment that extends over the waist or hips. It serves more often as outerwear, making a

**FIGURE 12.4** Glamorous sleepwear often resembles evening wear.

provocative fashion statement for evening wear when covered with satin, crushed velvet, or sequins.

Bras are complicated to make, and their production requires careful management. They may contain twenty pieces and come in more than a dozen sizes and colors for each style. Fit is critical; no one wants to have a bra altered. Bra manufacturers have to wring the most they can out of each component—such as getting the same kind of strap to work for five different bras. The major offshore bra production center is the Philippines, followed by Costa Rica.

Although its ability to provide actual support as a bra is debatable, who cares, if one's décolletage can get a $6.5 million lift? That's the estimated value of Victoria's Secret's Hearts on Fire Diamond Fantasy Bra (see Figure 12.5). For over 10 years, Victoria's Secret Fantasy Bras collection has been a sensation on the runways.[2]

Lingerie bearing the Badgley Mischka Couture name has followed up on this trend. Its line of signature embroidered and beaded bras and coordinating undies are a progression from its couture clothes. "The beauty in the collection is, it's meant to be shown, not hidden," James Mischka said. "It's

**FIGURE 12.5** Victoria's Secret's Hearts on Fire Diamond Fantasy Bra costs nearly 6.5 million dollars!

meant to interpret our product and enhance our gowns. The goal was to find the right undergarments to go with each gown."[3]

## Shapewear

Girdles, corsets, and *corselettes* (one-piece combinations of a brassiere and girdle) are traditional foundation items designed to smooth and flatten the lines of the stomach, buttocks, hips, and thighs. As with *garter belts*, they also have fasteners to hold up a woman's stockings. With the advent of pantyhose and a growing casualness in everyday dress, these items have been replaced in many women's wardrobes by **shapers**, or shapewear, lightweight undergarments that control problem areas with spandex. Control briefs serve the purpose of the old-fashioned girdle; and for more focused control, waist-cincher briefs, butt boosters, tummy toners, and thigh trimmers are available.

## Lingerie

The lingerie segment of intimate apparel has typically been divided into daywear (slips, petticoats, camisoles, and panties) and nightwear (nightgowns, sleepshirts, nightshirts, chemises, baby dolls, pajamas, wraps, and robes). *Chemises* are sleep gowns with no waistlines, while *baby dolls* are short, sheer gowns with matching panties. *Wraps* are short robes that cross and tie in front.

The latest revolution in lingerie is the rise of the thong panty. Thongs have come a long way from being a slightly scandalous item that could be found only on showgirls and Brazilian carnival dancers: today they have become a mainstream lingerie basic worn by women of all ages. Clever new products, like the "control thong" from Donna Karan, hold in the tummy and eliminate bumps and lumps of underwear lines.

Another new product is Nundies, a single-use disposable panty that adheres to the front of pants. Designed as an alternative to underwear, thongs, or G-strings, Nundies are shaped like a small tulip, made of nylon and Lycra spandex, and feature a

**FIGURE 12.6** Wonderbra's collection Wonderstar aims to link innerwear with the outer garment.

**FIGURE 12.7** The market for plus-size lingerie is expanding, with better fitting garments and more available styles.

proprietary medical-grade adhesive tape to avoid allergic reactions or skin rashes.[4]

Wonderbra has created a new collection called Wonderstar (see Figure 12.6). The collection is made up of bra and panty sets with matching dresses. The collection consists of four looks: Diamonds Forever, Flower Power, Jungle Fever, and Wonder Geisha. Each represents a Hollywood icon: Marilyn Monroe, Brigitte Bardot, Elizabeth Taylor, and Sophia Loren. "We wanted to turn each one into a personality," said the designer, Jenny Packham.

"It's a premium launch, moving Wonderbra away from the mainstream," said Tracy Hayward, marketing manager at Wonderbra. Hayward said the idea of linking the outer garment with the innerwear ties in with a theme already in the brand's existing marketing strategy. "It's nice because you get a little glimpse on occasions, so the bra becomes part of the whole garment."[5]

In the nightwear classification, styles also range from sporty and casual to romantic and seductive. Chenille robes, seemingly dead since the 1950s, revived in the late 1990s, as TV sitcom stars began wearing updated versions decorated with amusing motifs, such as coffee cups and cats with fish bones. At the elegant end of the style spectrum are the *peignoir* (a sheer robe, often with lace detail) and gown set, popular as a Valentine's Day gift, and the *kimono*, an adaptation of the traditional Japanese garment. The Westernized version is often made of rich silk or less expensive synthetics that imitate silk's luxurious appearance; the kimono can also serve as loungewear.

This market is also expanding with added styles and better fitting lingerie for plus-size women and women who are categorized as wearing "in-between" sizes (see Figure 12.7). Women who are sizes 12 and 14 were often left without many lingerie choices in the past. Standard lingerie frequently didn't come in a size above 10, and plus-size lingerie didn't start until sizes 14 and 16. Today, many plus-size lingerie manufacturers have realized and remedied this gap in the market.[6]

## Loungewear

Loungewear is the trade term for robes, lounging pajamas, hostess gowns, bed jackets, and housecoats or dusters. *Dusters*, which usually have buttons or

# Fashion Focus

Fashion Focus

## Its All in the Family—Now
### *The House of Natori*

On its thirtieth anniversary, in 2007, the Natori Company and its portfolio of expanding brands embarked on a new era of glamour and luxury in lingerie. "It's never been so glamorous and luxurious," said Josie Natori.

Among the projects are four new categories: a line of ready-to-wear that will be produced in-house, and licenses for fragrance, jewelry, and tabletops. Already launched is a line of men's luxury sleepwear and loungewear made in-house, and a lifestyle-oriented line of home accessories licensed to JLA Home Distribution for all categories is aimed at twenty-five countries.

In 1977, Natori, who was the first woman vice president of Merrill Lynch and Company, made the decision to leave her job—to be a designer of unique and upscale apparel and lingerie. For starters, she developed a signature collection of peasant-inspired blouses embroidered in her native Philippines with handmade appliqués. These were a quick hit with top retailers like Bloomingdale's and Saks Fifth Avenue.

The word *natori* in Japanese means the "highest form of art," and the company's namesake made it her mission to live up to the highest standards by transforming lingerie and related brands into something of an art form.

"I knew it would be a brand from day one, but after five years, I knew the focus of the business would be not the concept of design and lingerie but building a platform for home accessories, fragrance and jewelry," said Natori, whose personal style is as impeccable and discerning as her designs. "Today, I am really quite proud of what each brand I've created represents."

Burt Tansky, chairman and CEO of Neiman Marcus Group, Inc., is a Natori fan, as is Stephan I. Sadove, chairman and CEO of Saks, Inc., and Michael Gould, chairman and CEO of Bloomingdale's. They all agree that she has a great fashion sense, an ability to listen, understands her customers, and seeks out other people's counsel and thoughts.

Since the sale of Natori's first blouse, in her living room in the 1970s, the Natori Company, cofounded with her husband Ken, has weathered the ups and downs of consolidations at retail and within the industry. Ken Natori, a former managing director of Shearson Lehman, joined his wife as business partner in 1985. He now oversees the company's finances, licensing, and partnerships.

The couple's only child, Kenneth Cruz Natori, joined his parents in the family business in 2007 as vice president of finance. He was an associate in international equities at Lehman Brothers.

Josie Natori said she's been in and out of a variety of licenses and private-label projects over the years. But all of the cards seem to have fallen in place for the privately owned company that generates an annual wholesale volume of $80 million. Sales growth is projected to increase 30 to 40 percent by 2012, Natori said.

Regarding the firm's longevity, Natori said: "I am so pleased there is not an ounce of private label in our business. What makes me excited after thirty years is that we are totally

Left page: Josie Natori and son Ken (top center); Natori's mix of lace and printed foundations at Josie foundations (bottom). Right page: Natori silk Kyoto kimono (top);

focused on brands and luxury and the department store business, while all of the others are going into mass. Today, you have to stay the course, and brands are the place we have a niche. It is very clear I wanted to build brands that would stand the test of time. I want brands that are constant. And it's exciting to know that with my son, we are here to stay as a family company."

**FIGURE 12.8** Activewear is also worn as leisurewear.

snaps down the front, are especially popular with the elderly and handicapped, because they are easy to put on and take off. Leggings and fleece pants and tops are also popular attire for at-home wear for women of all ages, especially in cold areas. Activewear is also increasingly worn as leisurewear (see Figure 12.8), especially by the young and fashionable, influenced by TV shows such as *Hannah Montana*.

Designs from other cultures are also popular, such as the Hawaiian *muumuu* or float, a short-sleeved garment that slips on over the head and comes in several lengths. *Caftans*, ankle-length garments with long sleeves, came originally from Turkey and are widely worn throughout the Middle East. The African *dashiki*, a loose-fitting pullover garment, is also seen increasingly in the United States.

### Market Centers
New York City is the principal market center for the intimate apparel industry. The major firms maintain permanent showrooms there, as well as in most

of the regional apparel marts, like Dallas, Chicago, Los Angeles, and Atlanta. Market weeks are held five times a year:

- Early Spring—August
- Summer—January
- Fall and Holiday—May
- Spring—November
- Early Fall—March

The Intimate Apparel Council is a trade group that is part of the American Apparel Manufacturers Association that organizes subsidiary, promotional activities for market weeks. One of their endeavors is Intimate Apparel Market Week, which is held five times a year and has greatly increased business. The Intimate Apparel Council also organized the first-ever industry-sponsored lingerie fashion show in the Bryant Park tents during the Mercedes-Benz Fashion Week in September 2001. In recent years, the August market in New York has become the focal point for many buyers. Besides the action of buying at the Madison Avenue showrooms, the Lingerie Americas and Boutique Lingerie by Samantha Chang trade shows have become very successful.[7] In 2007, two intimate apparel trade shows, Curve NY and Boutique Lingerie, merged for a February market. The partnership, called Curve NY Featuring Boutique Lingerie, is staged annually during New York Fashion Week in February and runs again in Las Vegas in late February.[8]

### Merchandising and Marketing

In the merchandising and marketing of innerwear, an emphasis on brand names is concurrent with a trend toward greater promotion of individual styles, colors, fabrics, textures, and designer names (see Figure 12.9). Producers and designers aim to coordinate their innerwear and outerwear lines and to offer a range of images that offer a complete look for a variety of occasions and moods. Market segmentation by age groups enables producers and

**FIGURE 12.9** Revealing the latest fashions in intimate apparel, the Victoria's Secret Fashion Show is one of the biggest in the industry.

retailers to target their merchandising and marketing efforts.

### Brand Names

Since Warner Brothers opened its first factory in 1874, brand names have been important in the intimate apparel industry. (Warner's is now one of the brands of Warnaco, which also produces Olga.) Many of its merchandising and marketing activities, such as cooperative advertising with retailers in consumer publications and advertisements in trade publications, are geared toward promoting brand names.

These strategies have met with considerable success, as women have identified intimate apparel as a category in which they rely on brand names as an indicator of durability and consistency of fit. As mergers, acquisitions, and licenses of designer names join several brands under a corporate umbrella, parent companies are retaining the individual names to keep their loyal customers. Jockey, the men's and boys' underwear firm, started Jockey for Her in 1982. In 1997, it acquired Formfit seamless panties and the Formfit name, relaunching FormFit in the summer of 2000 under the slogan "Fashion, Fit, Comfort."

## Market Segments

Teenagers and young adults are a very influential segment of the intimate apparel business. In leisurewear, their interests in working out—or looking as if they do—has popularized such fabrics as fleece, jersey knit, flannel, and flannelettes, all of which inject a sportswear attitude into these casual styles. The trend is carried out in underwear in cotton-crop tops and matching boyleg briefs or boxers, and in sports bras. Such companies as Natori, with its popular Josie line, and Intimate Resources, with its Max and Eddie and Everlast store brands and Jordache for the mass market, cater to this segment. The trend toward wearing briefer briefs under formfitting pants has boosted sales of junior-size hiphugger styles with bikinis, thongs, and high French-cut legs.

The under-25 shopper has also supported the metamorphosis of the girdle into a variety of body shapers. In the market for these products, baby boomers—who are gaining weight as they age, are also an influential segment. Despite increasing interest in health food and exercise, many women find it easier, faster, and more comfortable to shape up with the help of spandex.[9] The plus-size woman is a focus of many designers, who are creating attractive and form-fitting leotards, sports bras, and shorts for this emerging market. Playtex has added both the Eighteen Hour Comfort Strap bra and the Cross Your Heart bra with side shaping to its very successful lines to appeal to the plus-size woman.

## Visual Merchandising

In-store displays for innerwear departments and specialty stores demonstrate the importance of brand names and the close connections between product classifications. In contrast to earlier eras, when intimate apparel was stocked in closed drawers rather than displayed, contemporary fixtures allow for the grouping of bras and panties by brand and, within a brand display, by style and color. Price tags color-coded by size help the customer select her size within each style and color grouping. Although bras and panties are sometimes displayed by size, with different brands and colors on the same rack, this practice is giving way to the more visually appealing displays arranged by brand, style, and color, which promote the fashion features of the merchandise (see Figure 12.10).

Victoria's Secret stores are a good example of the role of visual merchandising in producing a coordinated fashion image. The interior design of the stores, with elegantly appointed alcoves, allows for separate displays of related items in an intimate space, and the Victorian-style dressers that serve as storage and display fixtures reinforce the upscale, feminine look of the merchandise.

## Industry Trends

Variety is the watchword in every aspect of the intimate apparel industry. Not only are firms that once specialized in foundations, lingerie, or loungewear joining together to produce complete and complementary lines of intimate apparel, but these companies are becoming part of larger firms with other

**FIGURE 12.10** Visually appealing displays promote the fashion features of the merchandise.

# &Then NOW

## Made to Be Seen
### *The Bra and Panty Set— Bust-See TV*

Since 1968, when feminists trashed their bras in protest of the televised Miss America Pageant, women and their innerwear haven't exactly shied away from the camera. In the television series *The Brady Bunch*, Carol Brady's episodes wrapped up over a good book in the boudoir. When Chrissy and Janet of *Three's Company* romped around in short shorts and camisoles in the late 1970s, they paved the way for *Dynasty* diva Alexis Carrington Colby to regularly breakfast in a teddy that suggested the previous night's activities.

Let's not forget *Laverne and Shirley* and their innerwear and sleepwear in the 1980s, and our favorite *Golden Girls* of the 1990s showing that "mature" women also love sexy lingerie! That was then!

Now we have *Desperate Housewives*, with Marcia Cross and her friends saluting the subtle powers of lingerie. She and Eva Longoria aren't the only actresses prancing around in bra and panties on TV. They are now joined by *Army Wives*, a drama about home life on a military base, where leading ladies Catherine Bell, Kim Delaney, Sally Presman, and Wendy Davis don a whole lot less than fatigues.

But the 21st-century lingerie items have become "display pieces." Lingerie's cachet as a sexy, emphatically visible component of a woman's outfit has contributed to rising sales. The category known quaintly as intimate apparel has climbed to the top of women's shopping lists because showing off your lingerie has become very much a fashion trend.

Figleaves, the popular lingerie Web site, sells waist-cinchers and embroidered bras from makers like Wacoal, Elle Macpherson Intimates, Calvin Klein, and Le Mystère that are worn to be seen. Consumers are delighted. They are talking about lingerie like they talk about their shoes and handbag.

Bralets, a decorative hybrid of bra and camisole, have become very popular. Women are wearing them to be seen under pretty chiffon blouses and transparent layers. They blur the line between a bra and outerwear. Today's lingerie is designed for display, and clothes are cut to show it.

holdings in related segments of the apparel industry. For example, Playtex, Bali, and Wonderbra are siblings of Champion activewear and hosiery manufacturers Hanes and L'eggs, under the umbrella of the parent corporation of Sara Lee. Intimate Brands operates 1,799 specialty stores through Victoria's Secret and Bath and Body Works brands, in addition to Victoria's Secret's tremendous catalog business.

These alliances allow the parent corporation to coordinate its appeals to different market segments, offering styles and price points that attract different age and income groups and retain brand loyalty.

## Market Expansion

Intimate apparel producers are expanding their markets in aggressive and innovative ways, including launching crossover product lines and licensing. Crossover products include the Hanes Her Way brand of underwear, which was spun off the Hanes men's underwear brand in 1986. Hanes Her Way has become a big hit, especially in the panty line, which is now the best-selling panty line in the entire Sara Lee organization (see Figure 12.11). The equally famous Jockey for Her underwear crossover is being further extended to include lines of hosiery and sleepwear.

Through the licensing of designer names, producers are coordinating their products with ready-to-wear. Licensing is equally advantageous to the designer in associating his or her name and fashion image with this apparel category. For example,

**FIGURE 12.11** Christina Applegate, featured in this ad, thinks Hanes Her Way is a perfect fit!

Oscar de la Renta's lingerie line is completely licensed to Carole Hochman, a small, family-owned company that started in 1930. Besides the de la Renta line, Carole Hochman produces a signature collection of sleepwear. The company has also signed a licensing agreement with Lilly Pulitzer to produce and distribute a collection of sleepwear and intimate apparel bearing the Lilly Pulitzer name. Lilly Pulitzer "is uniquely different than everything else we have," said Carole Hochman. "My concept is to license iconic brands that are specific and noncompetitive."[10]

As in the ready-to-wear departments, sections of intimate apparel departments feature the lines of individual designers and manufacturers such as Vanity Fair, Chanterelle, La Perla, Eileen West for Charles Romar and Sons, and Donna Karan Intimates by Wacoal.

Paradoxically, as conglomerates are expanding through acquisitions and mergers of producers that serve various segments, the brands, whether part of a larger organization or not, are focusing on precisely defined segments to increase market share. Rapidly changing selections of colors and prints appeal to the desire for something new among these young customers. For the same market segment, Hanes Her Way offers high-cut and bikini panties in bright colors and retro prints and styles the garments to fit the not-yet-curvy preteen figure.

More and more designers and manufacturers are using TV home shopping channels like QVC and the Home Shopping Network (HSN) to sell their products. Many women appreciate the detailed product information these channels offer; in addition, they like listening to other women calling in to discuss similar purchases.

## Junior Innerwear Departments

Recognizing the growing influence of teenage and young adult shoppers (ages 13 to 32) on the intimate apparel market, department stores as well as national chains and discounters are starting to merchandise junior innerwear as collection con-

cepts, much like the shops-within-a-shop for designer label outerwear. Although consumers in this segment typically have less income than their elders, they are more prone to impulse buying of items they consider "fun." They want merchandise they will not find in their mothers' wardrobes. Growing up with the idea that fashion features as well as functionality are important criteria for their innerwear buying decisions, young shoppers are responding favorably to the junior innerwear departments.

## Catalogs and the Internet

Manufacturers such as Vanity Fair are marketing their brands directly to retail customers through catalogs. Many department stores send out special intimate apparel catalogs, and they regularly include high-fashion intimate apparel in their seasonal catalogs. The Victoria's Secret catalog, with its provocatively posed models, is a separate company from the stores of the same name. It has a distribution of 365 million and releases fifteen to twenty catalogs a year. Private Lives by Spiegel, the giant mail-order house, marked that company's entrance into the intimate apparel specialty-catalog field. Even L. L. Bean, with its focus on the great outdoors, features silk and thermal long underwear for men and women in its winter catalogs.

Another growing form of nonstore retailing for intimate apparel is the Internet (see Figure 12.12). Even the smallest producer cannot afford to be without a Web site through which it can market directly to consumers as well as communicate with its retailer customers. Virtually every fashion magazine ad for a brand of intimate apparel includes an invitation for a virtual visit to the producer's Web site.

## Men's and Children's Underwear and Sleepwear

Even more than women's intimate apparel, men's and children's underwear have been considered utilitarian rather than fashion apparel categories.

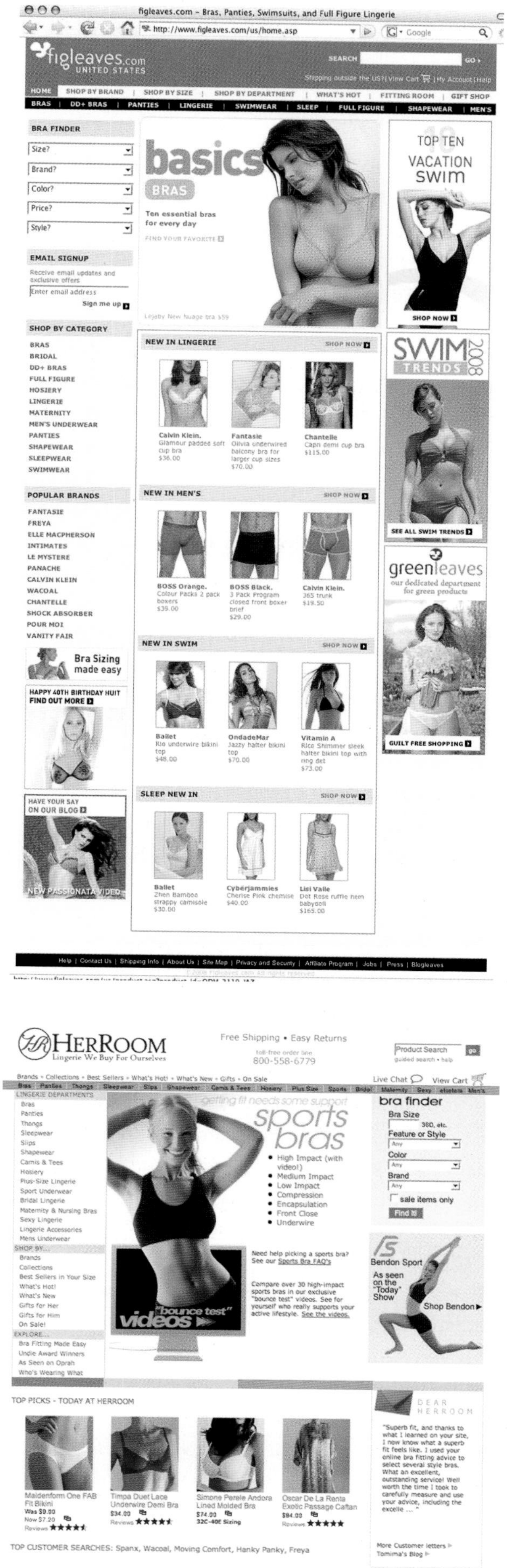

Today, however, the fashion influence has taken hold (see Figure 12.13).

## Men's and Children's Underwear

Much of the history of men's underwear is the history of the biggest name in the industry, Fruit of the Loom.[11] Founded as Union Underwear in 1926, the company began with one-piece underwear known as "union suits." The company was one of the finished-garment licensees of the Fruit of the Loom textile company, and it introduced boxer shorts and knit underwear under that label in the 1940s.

The knit styles of briefs and undershirts were also produced by two famous manufacturers of men's and boy's underwear: Jockey, founded in the late 1800s, and Munsingwear, founded in 1909. Undershirt styles were limited to short-sleeved crew- and V-necks and sleeveless, U-necked ribbed vests. Virtually all men's knit underwear was white, and woven boxers were made in limited colors and patterns.

Not until the 1970s did a wide choice of colors and patterns become available. About the same time, bikini styles in briefs were introduced to the newly fashion-conscious male shopper. In 1982, Calvin Klein's men's underwear collection made white seem boring. By the mid-1990s, casual pants styles with low-slung waists allowed men to show their allegiances to their favorite designers and brands by revealing the elastic waistbands of their underpants, inscribed with such names as Calvin, Tommy Hilfiger, or Jockey.

A trend to watch is the crossover of shapers from women's foundations. Tummy-toners have already won some adherents among men who want to maintain a fit, trim silhouette. Young men have adopted loose-fitting, comfortable boxer shorts and have made them a fashion item for at-home and sleepwear. Boxers are made in a limitless variety of colors and prints and in woven silks, cotton flannel, and jersey knit cotton/polyester blends, as well as the traditional lightweight woven cotton. Women have incorporated boxers into their own wardrobes.

**FIGURE 12.12** The Internet is a popular form of nonstore retailing for the intimate apparel industry.

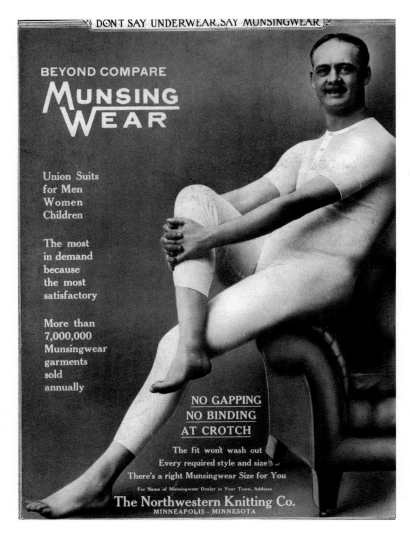

**FIGURE 12.13** Men's underwear styles change more slowly than women's but still are under the influence of fashion.

In addition to the established men's underwear brands, Joe Boxer enjoys a large market for this item, as does the licensed Tommy Hilfiger Intimates at Bestform, a unit of VF Corporation.

Men's underwear is making a new and dynamic name for itself as a wired community. One of its largest players is Freshpair.com, a Web-only underwear site that carries major brands, including Hanes, Champion, Perry Ellis, and Calvin Klein. The balance of its large men's inventory comprises new boutique, fashion-oriented brands such as C-IN2, Baskit, and Papi, that specialize in technical fabrics, sexier cuts, and whimsical colors and fabrics.

Web retail also provides shoppers with two other commodities guys like: privacy and simplicity. "We've got the consumer looking for more-fashionable underwear, and because of that he is not necessarily comfortable shopping in a retail environment. Underwear, with its uncomplicated sizing, also lends itself to the Web. If you're a medium in one brand, you're likely a medium in the next. It's probably easier to sell on the Web than anything else," says Marshal Cohen, NPD Group's chief industry analyst.[12]

The marketing of men's underwear as a fashion item benefits retailers' private-label merchandise as well as national and designer brands. A study of men's shopping habits found that 24 percent of dollar sales and 15 percent of unit sales of men's underwear, sleepwear, and loungewear went to private-label brands. Since customers see the merchandise as a brand, comparable to national brands but available exclusively through a particular store, loyalty to private labels translates into store loyalty.

Children's underwear has also evolved from merely functional to fashionable. Girls' panties were available in pastel colors for decades, but the range of colors and prints has exploded to match the variety available to adult women. Thanks to Fruit of the Loom's Underoos line, which first appeared in 1978, little boys also have the chance to express their tastes and to sport the images of favorite cartoon charac-

**FIGURE 12.14** An organic baby look from Peau-Ethique's permanent collection. A crop of emerging brands are paving the way for innerwear's green future.

ters, like Batman and Superman. Today, Fruit of the Loom, working under a licensing agreement with Marvel Entertainment, will develop and manufacture children's underwear lines based on several premier Marvel character franchises. Fruit of the Loom will develop products inspired by a diverse range of Marvel heroes and villains including Spider-Man, Wolverine, Captain America, Daredevil, Thor, Fantastic Four, Black Panther, Blade, Dr. Octopus, Dr. Strange, Elektra, Venom, and Sandman.[13] Other manufacturers have joined this trend; for example, Hanes features *Toy Story* characters on its briefs for boys. Little girls also have cartoon characters, like Minnie Mouse and dogs from *101 Dalmatians,* made by Hanes Her Way.

The Web site Ecobaby (www.ecobaby.com) exemplifies another trend in children's underwear: parents' preference for natural, environment-friendly products for infants. Companies such as Ecobaby and Peau-Ethique are paving the way for organic innerwear (see Figure 12.14).

## Men's and Children's Pajamas and Robes

Cotton, batiste, flannel, and silk, all in a variety of colors and patterns, have added a fashion element to men's sleepwear. Perhaps the most ubiquitous robe of the last 50 years is the terry cloth robe—worn by men, women, and children and as famous for its comfortable cotton fabric as for its loose fit and easy belt. At the other end of the price spectrum is the classic men's silk robe, by designers such as Fernando Sánchez and by private labels such as Saks Fifth Avenue.

Children's sleepwear, like adults', includes pajamas, nightgowns, and nightshirts, as well as *Dr. Denton's.* This brand name for sleepers with feet—and sometimes with a back flap for convenience in using the toilet—has come to be used as a generic term for such garments. Special finishes are applied to children's sleepwear to improve its flame resistance, in compliance with the Flammable Fabrics Act. However, the Consumer Products Safety Commission loosened its regulation in 1996, allowing the use of cotton and cotton blends and holding tight-fitting sleepwear in sizes 9 months to 14X and infants' sizes 0 to 9 months to general apparel standards rather than the more stringent children's sleepwear standards.

## Bodywear

The physical fitness boom of the 1980s and 1990s, which lured millions of Americans into aerobic classes and bodybuilding activities, also was responsible for producing a new fashion category, **bodywear.** It encompasses coordinated leotards, tights, unitards, wrap skirts, sweatsuits, leg warmers, shorts, T-shirts, and crop tops. The line between bodywear and activewear is constantly shifting—especially as stretch fabrics find their way into more and more activewear.

Originally, bodywear was sold in hosiery departments, but most stores are now selling it in separate shops or boutiques. Some department stores, such as Nordstrom and Dillard's, have focused even more

**FIGURE 12.15** A look from the Danskin Heritage Collection. Commemorating Danskin's 125th anniversary, Iconix Brand Group unveiled a collection of ten limited edition styles, redone in luxurious fabrics.

attention on bodywear by staging fashion shows, scheduling personal appearances by designers, and even sponsoring in-store exercise and dance classes. More sporting goods stores and specialty stores are adding bodywear, especially if it has performance features, such as anti-moisture fabric. Some gyms have become bodywear retailers as a sideline to their exercise businesses.

Many fashion-conscious women insist on being stylish while they stretch, strain, and sweat to get in shape. Longtime bodywear manufacturers, such as Danskin, capitalized on this market by creating new, exciting leotards with coordinating tights, cover-ups, and other workout apparel necessities (see Figure 12.15). Many designers, including Ralph Lauren, created bodywear lines that have sold very well. Another manufacturer, Carushka, Inc., of California,

sells its line of bodywear and yogawear for women on the Internet.

Yoga has become increasingly popular, and according to recent reports, 15 to 18 million Americans practice it regularly.[14] This trend has naturally launched new lines of yogawear, with garments like cotton tank tops, stretching pants, and cashmere shorts and cardigans. In 2001, supermodel Christy Turlington launched the upscale yogawear line Nuala with Puma, and Nike released the yoga-inspired clothing line Tek Zen for women in 2002 and added Mahanuala in 2007.

In the dancewear category, Capezio, long famous as a manufacturer of ballet and pointe shoes, added lines of leotards, unitards, and dance dresses for women, as well as tights, body warmers, and leg warmers. Capezio products, available in more than 3,000 stores or "doors," have been expanded to include lines for figure skating, ballroom dancing, yoga and Pilates, and drill team and cheerleading.

### Legwear

The ancient Greeks were among the first to wear cloth legwear. By the late 1500s, European men and women wore stockings made from a single fabric width that was knitted flat, with the two edges sewn together to form a back seam. This technology remained essentially unchanged for centuries. Because of wear at the heels and toes, socks often developed holes that had to be mended, a process called *darning*. For centuries, darning socks was an everyday task for women.

Today, legwear is an $83-billion-a-year business. New generations of teenagers and young adults who never wore hose are discovering legwear (see Figure 12.16). Marshal Cohen, chief industry analyst, the NPD Group says, "The industry needs to take advantage of that. It's a gift from the fashion gods to get a young consumer who will embrace this for the first time in her life, and could be a customer for the rest of her life if the industry responds properly."[15]

## The Evolution of Women's Hosiery

Until World War I, women's legs were concealed under floor-length skirts and dresses. When skirt lengths moved up and women's legs became visible, interest in adorning them increased, and the hosiery industry began to grow. Hanes, Trimfit, Berkshire, and Round the Clock were all introduced in the 1920s. But it was not until the introduction of nylon that hosiery as we know it today became a fashion accessory. Before the introduction of nylon in 1938, women wore seamed silk, cotton, or rayon stockings. Because of its easier care and greater durability, the new nylon hosiery was eagerly accepted despite its high price. Still, a "run" or "ladder" in a nylon stocking was an expensive accident, and women went to great lengths to prevent them. Saleswomen routinely donned gloves before showing stockings to a customer.

Fashion first entered the hosiery picture in the 1950s with the introduction of colors other than black or flesh tones. But it was not until the 1960s that hosiery became a major fashion accessory. To accessorize the shorter skirt—eventually evolving into the miniskirt and micromini—colors, textures, and weights of stockings were created in great variety. Women wore "pettipants" in the early 1960s to cover the garters of their garter belts or girdles—and to show a bit of lace under the shorter skirts. Then pantyhose were introduced and became a fantastic success. In turn, their popularity led to the introduction of seamless pantyhose and figure-control or support pantyhose (see Figure 12.17).

In the 1970s, when women began wearing pants to work, knee-high and ankle-high hosiery were introduced. Together with pantyhose, they captured the major share of the hosiery business. The sale of stockings plummeted and has never recovered. In addition, with elasticized bands on knee-high and over-the-knee hosiery, garters became unnecessary, and garter belts and pettipants became passé.

In the 1980s, changes in lifestyle produced a new set of customer needs and wants that were met with textures in pantyhose and tights. Socks in ribs and

**FIGURE 12.16** Hosiery comes in a variety of colors and patterns (top). **FIGURE 12.17** A group of girls who work in a hosiery factory help out the factory chemist by wearing the stockings for a waterproofing test for nylon's introduction in 1938 (bottom).

knits, leg warmers, and many kinds of athletic socks revitalized the industry.

The 1990s saw a drop in the sales of pantyhose, brought about in part by the advent of casual dress days in 90 percent of U.S. businesses. Even with more tailored pants, women may opt for *trouser socks*, a type of knee-high hosiery that is slightly heavier than sheer knee-highs and is available in a variety of colors and textures. In the 2000s, another influence is the impact of teenage customers, who shop for hosiery more frequently than adult women. Reacting to the latest fashion news on MTV, the young shoppers have boosted the sales of brightly colored tights and designer brands. Teens and adults are also wearing hosiery with patterns at the ankles, known as "docks."

Hosiery continues to evolve away from the basic item it was 20 years ago. Consumers are seeking and willing to pay more for the right product. Hosiery is considered an accessory as important as shoes and handbag.

## The Recent History of Socks

The influence of teenage shoppers has also boosted the women's sock business. Women of all ages have responded well to the combination of fashion design and comfort features offered in socks for casual wear and for extensive physical activity, such as sports (see Figure 12.18). Dress-down Fridays have also led women to expand their sock wardrobes. Women's socks generally come in three lengths: ankle, crew, and knee.

For work and athletic socks, the comfort features are also emphasized. Cushioning may be designed for very specific activities, with differences between,

say, tennis and running. **Wicking**, the ability to carry the moisture of perspiration away from the skin, is offered by various synthetic fibers. Cotton and wool are often combined with nylon, acrylic, and spandex to add elasticity, shape retention, and ventilation.

These comfort features are also an important selling point for men's athletic socks. A new development to reduce blister-causing friction is the interweaving of Teflon fibers with polyester and cotton at pressure points in socks. Inventor Bob Gunn has worked with DuPont's Teflon and Chipman Union, a sock making firm, to market Blister Guards socks.

*Tube socks*, which are knit without a defined heel, are popular as a functional everyday sock. The one-size-fits-all design is almost impossible to outgrow. Tube socks are less expensive to produce than conventional socks, and the savings are passed on to the consumer. Packaging of three or six pairs at a reduced per-pair price also appeals to the budget-minded shopper.

More expensive *ragg socks*, which are very thick, warm socks designed for wear with boots or sandals, are increasingly popular for work or winter sports. Similarly, Polar fleece socks in various lengths are also good for keeping the feet warm, even when wet.

In the 2000s, socks stepped to the forefront of their category. The re-emergence of legwear as a fashion item is allowing designers to branch out and be more creative. Many manufacturers are expanding their sock collections and using new materials. For now, to tie socks in with their fashion-forward hosiery collections, they have added metallic threads and also moved toward texture with ribs, pointelles, and cables that stretch out to reveal design elements. Today, socks can be a key part of putting one's best foot forward!

Here's a sock alert: pity the sock that becomes separated from its mate. Pity the sock that says farewell to its match in the overflow of the washer or is sucked into a black hole by the exhaust vent in

**FIGURE 12.18** Socks come in a variety of styles and colors.

the dryer. Well, pity the stray sock no more! Little Miss Matched, a San Francisco–based company, has embraced the dilemma of the missing sock. Today, preteen girls are collecting these individual mix-and-match socks. A red-and-blue striped sock with a red-and-blue sock with hearts? Why not? In the 21st century, individuality counts—so the mismatched sock pair is here to stay.[16]

## Organization and Operation

The hosiery industry consists primarily of large firms, many of which are divisions of huge textile or apparel conglomerates. The largest concentration of hosiery plants is found in the Southern states, with more than half of them in North Carolina.

Since hosiery is knitted in the greige (unfinished) state, most manufacturers can produce branded and unbranded hosiery in the same mill. The greige goods are then dyed, finished, stamped, and packaged to specification for national brand, private brand, or unbranded hosiery.

## Merchandising and Marketing

Traditionally, the women's hosiery industry concentrated its merchandising activities almost exclusively on the promotion and sale of nationally advertised brands. Recently, however, the industry has been merchandising its products for private labeling or for sale from self-service displays in supermarkets and drugstores. Designer labeling has also become increasingly important. The world's largest hosiery manufacturer, Sara Lee Hosiery, has annual sales of over $1.5 billion with its designer (Donna Karan), national (Hanes), and mass-merchandise (L'eggs) brands. Hanes alone is the largest hosiery brand in the world. Parent company Sara Lee Corporation is also a major marketer of socks; L'eggswear is just one of its lines of socks and tights. At Dillard's, Spanx and other upscale shapewear lines have eclipsed more moderate, promotional resources to become "the backbone of the intimate apparel busi-

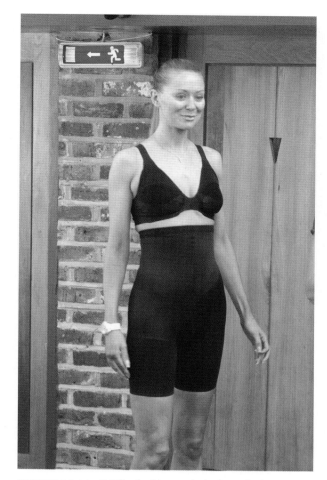

**FIGURE 12.19** At Dillard's, Spanx and other upscale shapewear lines have eclipsed more moderate, promotional resources to become "the backbone of the intimate apparel business."

ness," said William Dillard III, vice president of intimate apparel, accessories, and shoes (see Figure 12.19). "Spanx has revolutionized undergarments and the way clothes fit."

### National Brands

Major hosiery producers sell their brand lines to retail stores across the country. Producers aggressively advertise their lines in national magazines and newspapers and on television. They also usually supply cooperative advertising, display aids, and fashion assistance to help promote these national brands at the store level. Major national brands include Hanes, Burlington, Round the Clock, Trimfit, and Kayser-Roth.

### Designer-Label Brands

Because designer labeling adds an aura of couture and prestige to any item, designer labels have

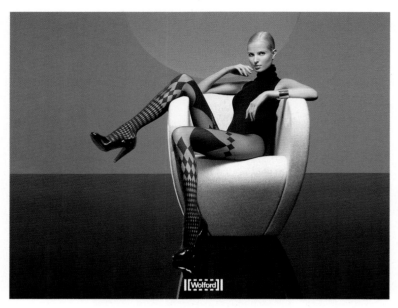

**FIGURE 12.20** Designer labels, like Wolford, adds an aura of couture and prestige to hosiery.

appeared on a variety of hosiery items, including pantyhose, socks, and leg warmers. Almost all of the designer-label hosiery is the result of licensing agreements between the designer and manufacturers of national brands. In hosiery and pantyhose, Kayser Roth uses Calvin Klein, GBT Group uses Givenchy, and Leg Resource uses Betsey Johnson. In socks, Gold Toe Brands uses Perry Ellis.

Hue, the Kayser-Roth–owned hosiery firm, tapped contemporary designer Tracy Reese as a partner for its Guest Designer Collection. Reese was the first of a long stream of designers who will create limited-edition hosiery collections.

Hue is not the first to partner with a designer for an exclusive collection. Wolford, the 56-year-old Austrian luxury hosiery and bodywear maker, signed agreements with fashion houses Missoni, Kenzo, Antonio Berardi, and Zac Posen for exclusive collections (see Figure 12.20).[17]

### Private Brands

Chain organizations, retail stores, and some individual stores have developed their own private or store brands that compete with nationally advertised brands. A private label offers many advantages for the retailer. The cost of the hosiery is usually less because there is no built-in charge for advertising as there is for national brands. The private brand can be made up in colors and con-

struction that will match customer profile specifications. Because the private brand is not available elsewhere, price promotions are easier. Customer loyalty can also be built upon the exclusivity of the private brand. Charter Club hosiery, tights, and socks, for example, are the private label of Macy's, Inc.

### Mass-Merchandised Brands

For self-service stores such as supermarkets, discount stores, and drug chains, hosiery manufacturers have developed low-priced, packaged hosiery. Each mass-merchandised brand offers a good choice of styles and colors. Each manufacturer supplies attractive, self-service stock fixtures and promotes its brand through national advertising. When L'eggs pantyhose, made by Hanes, were introduced, their distinctive packaging in plastic eggs brought immediate name recognition, but by the early 1990s, a more conventional package was adopted to meet the objections of environmentalists. By then, the name was nationally established as one of the best-selling mass-merchandised brands along with competitor Kayser-Roth's No Nonsense pantyhose. Surprisingly, nearly half of the doors that distribute No Nonsense are food stores, drugstores, and other mass merchandisers.

### *Industry Trends*

Trends in the legwear industry are similar to those in the innerwear industry. Licensing agreements enable designers and manufacturers to produce and market lines of legwear that coordinate with a designer's ready-to-wear lines. Special packaging also promotes brand loyalty. Manufacturers assist retailers with visual merchandising to help them stimulate sales. In manufacturing, the trend is toward offshore production.

### Fashion Trends

Fashion trends have a tremendous influence on sales in the hosiery industry (see Figure 12.21). For

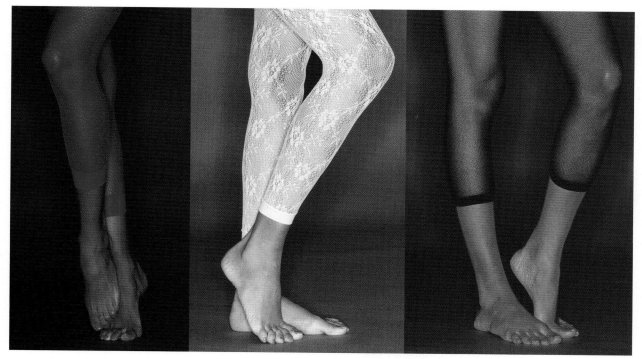

**FIGURE 12.21** When footless tights became the hottest trend, sales in the hosiery industry skyrocketed.

example, when skirts are shorter or have leg-revealing silhouettes, texture and color in hosiery become important. Apparel manufacturers work with hosiery manufacturers to design pantyhose that are both texture- and color-coordinated to their sportswear. The hosiery is displayed with the apparel to promote a total fashion look.

The inventory of most hosiery departments includes ankle-length, knee-high, and over-the-knee stockings; sheer and opaque pantyhose; leg warmers; bodywear; and casual footwear. Bodywear and casual footwear are relatively high-priced retail items, while packaged hosiery is low priced. As a result, some stores have made separate departments out of these two different categories.

The needs and wants of customers prompt hosiery manufacturers to design entirely new items. Control-top pantyhose, support hose, and queen-sized pantyhose cater to the demands of an aging population that is also growing heavier. A new nylon and Lycra (spandex) hosiery by Victoria's Secret is promoted as wearing longer and not running easily—even when a tack is pushed through it.

Men's, women's, and children's sock sales are predicted to increase steadily in the next decade. Athletic, sport, and work socks are the sources of growth in the men's area. New textures, colors, and patterns are fueling the market in women's socks, as more spandex content is added to tights and pantyhose. Children are emulating their sports heroes and requesting their specific brand of sport socks.

## Special Packaging

Manufacturers turn to special packaging as a way to make their products stand out in this very competitive industry. Susan Spindell, sales manager for Hot Sox, said its sales have been strong, helped by the Hot Sox Comfort Line. The company recently revamped its packaging, which now calls attention to individual product attributes, such as seamless toe, and makes selection easier (see Figure 12.22)..[18]

Bonuses are popular in sock merchandising. Hue marketed its sport socks through a 3-for-12 program, which allowed customers to pick and choose three pairs of socks at a discounted price. While each pair retailed for $5, a selection from any of the sport sock lines cost $12. Some of the special packaging success stories include the Gold Toe gift-with-purchase program of Gold Toe Brands The company packaged a one-ounce radio with a six-pair pack of boy's crew socks. This promotion was

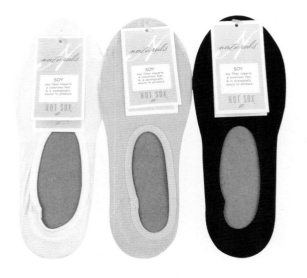

so successful that the package was prominately displayed at the entrance of many legwear stores.

### Visual Merchandising

In-store displays and other point-of-purchase materials are being offered by manufacturers to retailers to add some color to hosiery departments. While increasingly casual dress codes among office workers have caused a decline in sales of sheer pantyhose, the women's sock market has blossomed. Fishnets, animal prints, luxury yarns, and novelty styles, such as the super-low sock traditionally used only by athletes, have given new life to the category. This lighthearted approach has also inspired sock vendors to promote holiday- and Halloween-themed socks with matching retail displays. When Hanes introduced Donna Karan's new Evolution line of hosiery,

which offers waist-to-toe compression, it offered retailers a videotape of Donna discussing her view of hosiery; the video was widely played in hosiery departments across the country.

### Summary and Review

The categories of women's intimate apparel, men's and children's underwear and sleepwear, and hosiery for all three market segments were long considered strictly utilitarian, but today all of these categories have taken on fashion features. A consumer can develop a wardrobe that is coordinated from the inside to the outside and from head to toe.

Women's intimate apparel includes foundation garments (bras and shapewear), lingerie (such as panties, camisoles, slips, and sleepwear), and loungewear. These formerly separate categories are now coordinated and are often promoted as distinctive designer or producer lines.

Men's underwear and sleepwear also features a broad choice of colors and a variety of styles, ranging from bikini briefs to loose boxers, and children's underwear and sleepwear is decorated with favorite cartoon characters.

The growing awareness of the need for exercise to be physically fit has generated the development of a separate apparel category called bodywear, which includes spandex shorts and tops for both women and men, leotards, and other apparel suitable for wearing while working out.

Hosiery categories include women's pantyhose and tights and a variety of styles of socks for men, women, and children. Through licensing, apparel designers have gained customer loyalty for brands of hosiery coordinated with their apparel lines. Private labels and mass-merchandised brands also have their adherents among consumers, who identify brand names with a particular fashion and quality image. Hosiery manufacturing is carried out wholly or partly overseas by many producers.

## Trade Talk

Define or briefly explain the following terms:

| | |
|---|---|
| bodywear | foundations |
| innerwear | intimate apparel |
| legwear | lingerie |
| loungewear | shapers |
| wicking | women's underwear |

## For Review

1. How does the foundations industry respond to trends in ready-to-wear?
2. How does the intimate apparel industry relate to the ready-to-wear industry?
3. How does the display of women's underwear and intimate apparel demonstrate the growing influence of fashion features? How do current visual merchandising practices differ from those of the past?
4. Why is the junior market important to the women's intimate apparel industry?
5. What fashion features have been emphasized in the merchandising and marketing of men's underwear?
6. What is bodywear, and how did it grow into a separate apparel category?
7. Why is the development of new fibers so important to the women's hosiery industry?
8. Identify and describe four categories of brands of women's hosiery.
9. What is the influence of fashion trends in ready-to-wear on the fashion features of women's, men's, and children's hosiery?
10. How does special packaging help hosiery producers increase market share?

## For Discussion

1. Discuss current trends in the intimate apparel industry as they relate to (a) mergers, (b) diversification of product lines, and (c) styling.
2. How has the increasing informality of dress in the 1990s affected the innerwear and hosiery industries?

# chapter thirteen

*Everything you always wanted to know about the classifications of accessories. These include footwear, handbags, gloves, belts, millinery, eyewear, and jewelry.*

**KEY CONCEPTS**
- History and development of the accessory industries
- Organization, operation, merchandising, and marketing of the footwear and jewelry industries.
- Manufacturing, merchandising, and marketing of handbags, belts, gloves, hats, neckwear, and eyewear
- Trends in the various classifications of accessories

# Accessories

Accessories in the 21st century continue to create excitement and sizzle at retail, and whether in the luxury, mid-tier, or mass markets, they provide customers with a jolt of fresh fashion, instant access to the latest trends, and in many cases, a piece of a designer dream.

The manufacturers of accessories must constantly forecast the changes in cycles of fashion so that their accessories are perfect for new fashions. This includes not only the changes in silhouette but also in fabrications and color. The marketing of accessories gained an enormous boost with the entrance of well-known designers' names into the business. Today, the fame of the accessories designer is as important as the fame of the clothing designer; and in many cases, it is the same famous name. It is only through constant alertness to trends and degrees of customer acceptance that fashion accessory designers succeed. They must be prepared to design and produce styles that blend, follow or lead, and innovate. The fashion accessories category includes footwear, handbags, gloves, hats, neckwear, eyewear, and jewelry.

## Footwear

Footwear has always conjured up exciting, glamorous, and amusing times in history and literature. We read about gallant heroes in seven-league boots, princesses in glass slippers, Mercury with winged feet, and, of course, the magic red shoes that took Dorothy from the land of Oz back home to Kansas.

Feet, the base upon which our bodies stand, have been wrapped, covered, or left uncovered since the beginning of time (see Figure 13.1). Primitive people wrapped their feet in fur, and later people strapped them into sandals. Chinese women bound their feet. Footwear often was—and still is—dictated by profession: Arctic trappers wore snowshoes, while ballet dancers wore pointes, or toe shoes; cowboys wore leather boots, and firefighters wore rubber boots.

Making shoes was once a painstaking handicraft. But the commercial production of shoes has developed into an industry providing over 300 variations in shoe lengths and widths and over 10,000 different shapes and styles. The footwear category includes shoes, slippers, athletic shoes, and boots. Most shoe styles originated in Europe, keeping pace with the growth of European fashion. However, a classic shoe style that originated in America is the moccasin. Favored by both men and women and adored by most children, the moccasin style of shoe still retains its popularity and stands as one of the first examples of unisex fashion.

### Organization and Operation

Footwear production was once a major industry in New England, but many of that region's factories have downsized or closed (see Figure 13.2). Among those remaining are Nine West of Stamford, Connecticut, primarily a manufacturer of women's shoes, and Timberland of Stratham, New Hampshire, best known for its work boots. Timberland boots have become the signature footwear of the hip-hop community and are immensely popular with young men and women worldwide. The shoe industry moved west when the Midwest became an important source of hide supplies and cheaper labor, and another large center of production grew around St. Louis, Missouri. Brown Shoe Company, producer of Buster Brown children's shoes, Regal shoes for men, and Air Step shoes for women, is based there.

The largest shoe producer in the United States today is Nike. Nike actually does not own any of the manufacturing facilities that produce the shoes and apparel it sells; rather it acts more like a wholesaler and focuses on marketing its products.

Imports are also a factor in dress shoes at higher price points. A longstanding reputation for quality craftsmanship and styling has contributed to the

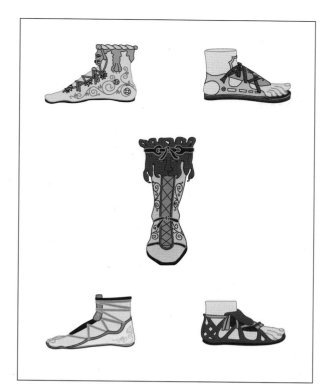

**FIGURE 13.1** Ancient Roman styles of sandals.

**FIGURE 13.2** Lining stitcher in an old Massachusetts shoe factory, 1895.

success of Italian manufacturers such as Ferragamo, Prada, Gucci, and Diego Della Valle. Italy is the number one producer of high-end designer shoes, with world-famous designs and quality craftsmanship. The bulk of less expensive imported shoes comes from Asia, mainly China. Other countries that export low-priced shoes are Brazil, Portugal, and Spain. The domestic shoe production declined considerably over the second half of the 20th century. American shoe factories now produce less than 25 percent of the merchandise that was made here in the 1960s. Most of the surviving U.S. manufacturers in the 21st century that have been successful have turned to niche markets.

Shoe production begins with a last. Lasts were originally wooden forms in the shape of a foot, over which the shoes were built. Today most modern factories, American and foreign, make lasts of plastic or aluminum. Lasts made from these materials provide more exact measurements and are easier to handle than the old wooden ones.

The variety of lasts, the quality of materials, and the number and type of manufacturing operations required determine the quality and price of the finished shoe. As many as 200 to 300 operations per-

formed by highly skilled workers are required to make an expensive, high-quality shoe. Shoe manufacturers produce shoes in an enormous range of sizes. The normal range of women's shoe sizes involves 103 width and length combinations. And this does not include sizes shorter than 4, longer than 11, or wider than E.

Inventories, production problems, and capital investments in the shoe business are tremendous compared with those of other fashion-related industries. Thus, it is not surprising that giant companies dominate the industry. Among the fashion industries, only cosmetics has a higher percentage of production by giant companies.

## Women's Shoes

For centuries, little attention was paid to the styling of women's shoes. Their purpose was regarded as

**FIGURE 13.3** Styles of women's shoes run the gamut from pointed to open toes, d'orsay to stiletto heels, and sandals to ankle boots.

purely functional. Since the 1920s, however, women's feet have been plainly visible, and shoes have developed both in fashion importance and variety. After World War II, the black or brown all-purpose shoes designed to be worn with any wardrobe disappeared. New and varied leather finishes, textures, plastic and fabric materials, and ranges of colors provided shoe styles that not only kept pace with changes in fashion but in many cases originated fashion trends.

Styles have run the fashion gamut from pointed to square toes, from high to flat heels, and from naked sandals to thigh-high boots (see Figure 13.3). Typically—but not always—broad toes and low, chunky heels go together, and narrow, pointed-toe shoes are more likely to have stiletto heels. The slim, elegant designs have been popular when apparel fashions have emphasized formality, and the heavier, more down-to-earth styles have been the rage in seasons when more casual clothing styles prevailed.

Recently, the market has segmented along age and income lines. The tapered lines featured in high-fashion designer shoes have won some favor with society leaders, while Hollywood stars and models favor the stiletto heel. Working women and younger women, the customers of such manufacturers as Nine West and Kenneth Cole, opted for comfort and solid footing. Even the once outré Hush Puppies returned—in wild new colors. In

London, Patrick Cox designed the Wannabe loafer, a chunky, square-toed, unisex shoe that was an immediate hit with movie and TV stars and fellow designers. Perhaps the warnings of orthopedists and fitness trainers have gained attention: constant wearing of high heels shortens the Achilles tendon, "hammer toes" can result from wearing shoes with very pointed toes, and feet that become accustomed to wide, roomy shoes resist being stuffed into narrower styles. Nevertheless, stiletto heels and pointed toes have made a huge comeback. Young fashion-conscious women eagerly follow the example of Sarah Jessica Parker's character, Carrie, in the popular TV series *Sex and the City*, and wear fragile stiletto shoes and sandals as their everyday footwear, regardless of weather and temperature.

## Men's Shoes

A shift in thinking and lifestyle on the part of American men has had a dramatic effect on the merchandising of men's shoes. Dress shoes were once the most important sales category in men's shoe departments in retail stores. They are now being replaced by dress/casual and casual shoes, which were once considered appropriate only for the 18-to-25 age group but now are preferred by men of all ages (see Figure 13.4). The dress shoe business is now considered a niche market.

Timberland, Sebago, and Rockport are examples of casual shoe manufacturers whose reputation for durable work shoes has benefited from this trend. Sperry Top-Siders, made by Stride Rite, were once limited to boat owners; today they are much more widely worn for casual wear. Red Wing Shoes of Red Wing, Minnesota, continues to grow in its niche: specialized work shoes for letter carriers, loggers, welders, firefighters, and electrical linemen.

Well-known U.S. brand names for men's dress and casual shoes include Florsheim, Johnston & Murphy, Allen-Edmonds, and Alden. L. B. Evans has been making slippers and sandals in New England since 1804. At the high end of the market are Gokey boots and shoes, which are handmade in the United

 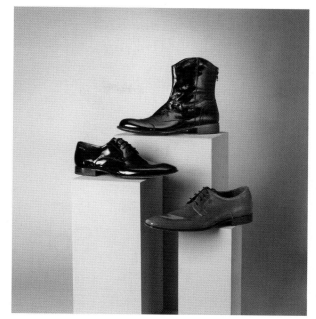

**FIGURE 13.4** To keep up with the mainstream of fashion, manufacturers of men's dress shoes have branched into casual styles.

States to customers' exact specifications; they are sold by Orvis through its catalog and stores.

American designer dress and dress/casual shoes are also predominately produced abroad. High-end imports from Europe include Clark's of England, Bally of Switzerland, and Ferragamo, Gucci, and Bruno Magli of Italy.

### Children's Shoes

From an early age, both boys and girls take a serious interest in their shoe wardrobes (see Figure 13.5). Perhaps they are influenced by stories about shoes with magical powers, as in Cinderella, Puss in Boots, and The 12 Dancing Princesses.

Shoes, especially everyday shoes, are subject to wear and tear, so even though they are outgrown as quickly as apparel, they are not as suitable for handing down or buying secondhand. Furthermore, a professionally fitted new pair of shoes is more likely to ensure health and comfort than are used shoes. Children thus must be active participants in the purchase decision. Having a deciding vote on the comfort of their shoes, children can easily make the next step to expressing opinions on appearances. Dressing in conformity with their peers and older children is an obvious way of showing that they fit into their social group.

The styles of children's dress shoes are adapta-

tions of adult styles, with oxfords being popular for boys and the classic Mary Janes for girls. The use of leather distinguishes higher priced lines from less expensive lines of vinyl and other leather substitutes. For casual wear, a popular low-priced choice is jellies, a sturdy sandal in brightly colored plastic. Jellies are a rare example of a children's style that became popular for adults. Many teens wear Doc Martens, work boots with lug soles.

As athletic shoes evolved from canvas sneakers, they became the preferred shoe for school wear. Practical features, such as Velcro fastenings; purely decorative features, such as the popular light-up shoe; and brand and style identification, such as that provided by Nike's Air Jordans, all influence

**FIGURE 13.5** Even though they grow out of them quickly, kids take a big interest in their shoe wardrobes.

**FIGURE 13.6** *Footwear News* provides inside perspective on news, fashion trends, and business strategies relating to the footwear industry.

children's preferences (see Figure 13.6). But the trend to school uniforms for public school students is slowing the switch to athletic shoes for school wear, and leather oxfords or T-straps are re-emerging.

## Athletic Shoes

Sneakers, the original athletic shoe, were made possible by Charles Goodyear, who invented the vulcanizing process for rubber in the late 1800s. Keds were the first shoes to use this process, bonding rubber soles to canvas tops. In 1917, Converse, Inc., of North Framington, Massachusetts, introduced the All Star, which has sold more than 500 million pairs! From these humble beginnings, a huge industry has grown—and shod the world.

Perhaps the most significant development in shoes since the 1980s—affecting men's, women's, and children's shoes—has been the proliferation of athletic footwear. Spurred by the trend toward more casual dressing, this separate category is now considered a mature market (see Figure 13.7).

Athletic shoes have become ever more specialized. Manufacturers make special shoes for virtually any sports activity—walking, running, climbing, aerobics, racquetball, biking, hiking, golf. Most of the "super-specialty" shoes are carried in specialty sporting goods stores, while department stores and other general retailers stock a less specialized and more fashion-oriented range of athletic shoes.

## Merchandising and Marketing

As with most fashion industries, New York City is the major U.S. market center for shoes. It is there that most producers maintain permanent showrooms, and it is also home to the industry's trade shows. The Fashion Footwear Association of New York (FFANY), with a membership of 300 corporations and 800 brand names, stages the international footwear trade show New York Shoe Expo three times a year.

The American Apparel and Footwear Association (AAFA) was formed in 2000 through the merger of two highly regarded trade associations: the American Apparel and Manufacturers Association and Footwear Industries of America. Drawing from a broad, strong membership base, AAFA is the national trade association representing apparel, footwear, and sown products companies, which compete in the global marketplace.[1]

Brand names are important in the footwear industry, and manufacturers advertise extensively in national fashion magazines and on national television. Designer names are also growing in importance, especially at the mid-price to high end of the market. In 2007, three shoe companies came

**FIGURE 13.7** Whether you are walking, running, jumping, or hiking, there are fashionable and specialized athletic shoes for every activity.

together through Payless Shoe Source's acquisition of Collective Licensing International, a brand management and global licensing company, and the acquisition of the Stride Rite Corporation, the leader in lifestyle and athletic branded footwear and high-quality children's footwear.

Collective Brands, Inc., now ranks as the largest nonathletic footwear company in the Western Hemisphere and the largest footwear company based on retail stores.[2]

In contrast with most other fashion industries, many of the large shoe manufacturers operate retail chain organizations of their own. This practice is known as dual distribution. Another industry that practices dual distribution is the men's wear industry (see Chapter 10). Examples of dual distribution in the shoe industry include the Brown Group and Nine West. All of these shoe brands are sold in retail stores owned by the shoe manufacturers (see Figure 13.8). Frequently these shoe chains also stock related accessories, such as handbags and hosiery.

Some shoe manufacturers also operate in the retail field through leased departments in retail stores. Because of the tremendous amount of capital required to stock a shoe department and the expertise needed to fit and sell shoes, many department and specialty stores lease their shoe departments to shoe manufacturers. Surveys by the National Federation of Retailers have repeatedly shown that women's shoe departments are among those most commonly leased by its member stores. Examples of manufacturers of shoes who operate leased shoe departments in stores are Nine West and Jones New York, which features Joan & David, Enzo Angiolini, Joan & David, Pappagallo lines, and the Brown Shoe Company, which features Buster Brown shoes for children, Naturalizer shoes for women, and Regal shoes for men. The Bakers Footwear Group is a chain-store retailer that imports shoes and also operate leased shoe departments in other stores.

For most men's shoe retailers, space limitations make meeting consumer demands a challenge.

**FIGURE 13.8** A rotating conveyor belt of sneakers sits in the front window of A Bathing Ape store in New York. The Japanese clothing company specializes in urban and hip-hop fashion and has made the expansion from Japan to cities worldwide.

Even stores that deal exclusively in men's shoes tend to be small, with less than 1,700 square feet of space for both selling and stocking. The manufacturers' retail outlets that predominate among freestanding units cannot compete on availability of many brands. Catalog retailers such as L. L. Bean, Lands' End, and Orvis, who have less of a space problem, are realizing a golden opportunity to attract customers, so long as they maintain an easy return policy.

Because of the tremendous consumer demand for athletic shoes, many retailers have begun paying extra attention to the category, often creating a separate department for athletic shoes. Athletic shoe stores, such as The Athlete's Foot, Foot Locker, and Foot Action chains, which carry a variety of brands and related fashion-oriented merchandise, have sprung up across the country.

American designer dress and dress/casual shoes are also commonly produced abroad.

## Industry Trends

Americans purchase more than 2.2 billion pairs of shoes a year, and at least 98 percent of them are manufactured overseas, mainly in Asia. Like apparel manufacturers, some U.S. shoe companies rely on factories overseas, particularly in developing countries where the labor is cheaper. About 84 percent of the footwear worn by Americans is made in China.[3]

Whether in athletic or other footwear, there is a strong relationship between shoes and the clothes with which they are worn. Increased emphasis on fashion continues to be the major trend in the footwear industry. Shoe designers and manufacturers regularly attend the MICAM Shoevent, in Milan, Italy, or the GDS International Shoe Show in Germany. They also attend European apparel openings, as do shoe buyers from retail stores, gathering information on international trends in styling. More and more, apparel fashions influence both the styling and color of footwear. Skirt lengths, silhouette, pants, and sporty or dressy clothes are the fashion keys to women's shoe designs. It is therefore essential for retailers to coordinate shoes and apparel wherever and whenever they can.

Clothing designers designing shoes is a growing trend. Back in 1986, Donna Karan launched her own label, and she was one of the first clothing designers to make a statement about having their own shoes to finish off the total look. On the heels of Donna, designers Tom Ford and Marc Jacobs also put their design stamp with influential footwear collections.

While the shoe market in a very lucrative one, it's also highly competitive. The new *garmentos*-cum-cobblers are up against massive shoe brands, including Gucci, Prada, Louis Vuitton, Ferragamo, as well as true shoemakers like Manolo Blahnik and Christian Louboutin.[4]

## Handbags

Handbags are continuing their reign as the best-selling classification within the accessories industry. Once again, many retailers have expanded their space to accommodate more and/or new brands. Fashion continues to drive handbag sales, both in branded and private-label product. Consumers show little price resistance for the "right design"—especially at luxury level. Designer "it" bags drew even more attention to the classification—even

**FIGURE 13.9** Some customers will pay anything to have this original Chanel bag.

with retail prices exceeding $1,000 (see Figure 13.9).

As fashion statements, handbags are used to dramatize, harmonize, or contrast with whatever else one is wearing. Styles vary from the most casual, used for sportswear, to the more formal, used for dress-up evening occasions. A handbag may be small or large; its shape, a pouch or a tote, draped or boxy. So important are handbags as fashion accessories that most women own a wardrobe of them. The late Princess Grace of Monaco favored the Hermès bag, now called the Kelly bag in her honor. The late Princess Diana was often photographed with one of her more than twenty Ferragamo clutch purses. Perhaps the most-copied handbag of this century was Chanel's "2.55" diamond-quilted bag, with the shoulder strap that slides through golden chains.

As personal statements, handbags also send a message. A woman who chooses to carry a leather briefcase, for example, sends a professional message, while a woman who uses a backpack sends one of functionalism. Whether a woman opts for a small, delicate beaded handbag at night or something far more exotic, perhaps a gold box set with unusual jewels, says something about her. The woman who carries a tailored, expensive leather purse creates an image that has more chic than that of the woman who settles on a vinyl tote (see Figure 13.10).

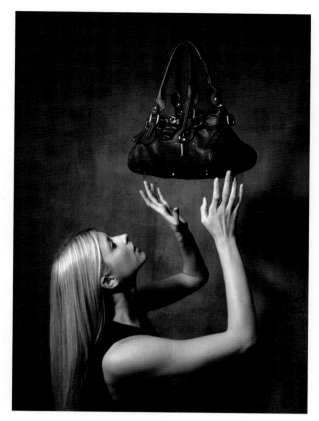

**FIGURE 13.10** Chloé's Paddington bag is a much coveted accessory.

**FIGURE 13.11** Handbag and accessory displays at Saks Fifth Avenue (top) and Dolce & Gabbana (bottom).

## Organization and Operation

Compared with other fashion industries, the handbag industry is small. The number of domestic firms producing handbags diminishes each year, as imports made in Europe, South America, and the Far East increase. Although U.S. manufacturers' brand names are relatively unimportant in the handbag industry (except for certain classics such as Coach Bags, Le Sportsac, and Dooney & Bourke), designer handbags have become popular (see Figure 13.11). Famous names like Anne Klein, Ralph Lauren, Donna Karan, and Marc Jacobs have entered licensing agreements with handbag manufacturers. Judith Leiber, is still famous for her handmade beaded bags in animal shapes and her metal minaudières (small evening bags). Kate Spade is a U.S. designer who has won several awards for her striking handbag designs. Today, not all quality handbags are made of leather; microfiber and nylon are key materials, with minibags popular.

Several foreign manufacturers, such as Louis Vuitton, Hermès, Ferragamo, Bottega Veneta, and Gucci, have always enjoyed enormous status at the high end of the market, and the names of Chanel and, more recently, Prada are associated with distinctive styles of handbags.

## Backpacks

Some of the larger manufacturers have recently diversified their lines, reaching out to men, who have flirted with the idea of carrying handbags since the 1960s. The backpack has gained favor with men who do not have enough room in their pockets

## On the Rocks
### *Chakra Calmed*
### *In Color*

Chakra 1 is believed to heighten creativity and focus and encourage friendship and love.

**JASPER**

Diamonds may be a girl's best friend, but the luckiest gals are the ones with rocks in shades of yellow, pink, and blue. Colored diamonds are attracting more attention than ever, spurred by celebrity purchases, explosions of wealth in China and Russia, and the general desire to own the exceptional.

Diamonds form and surface over millions of years when carbon comes under high levels of pressure and temperature; naturally occurring colored diamonds get their hue from unusual chemical compositions. One of every 10,000 diamonds mined is a color other than white. Yellow diamonds occur when nitrogen atoms replace some carbon atoms in the formation process. Blue diamonds benefit from too much boron, and green diamonds sparkle thanks to natural radiation. Fancy brown, gray, and black diamonds are the most price friendly, followed by fancy yellow, orange, and olive, then pink, blue, and green. The rarest and most expensive of colored diamonds come in pure shades of purple or red and can easily cost $1 million per carat, though it's nearly impossible to find a purple stone that is larger than a carat.

Ladies who enjoy wearing massive chunks of ice on their finger may not care for fancy colored diamonds because they are rarely found in double-digit carat size. A colored diamond is "not for somebody who needs everybody else to know what it is," says the famous jeweler Graff.

Although diamonds are a girl's best friend, white or colored, can they help a girl get rid of her phobias? Or make her beauty treatments work better? Spas across the country are tapping into the use of gemstones by adding them to their beauty treatments. But can a stone perched on a person's forehead during a facial achieve even the tiniest miracle? Let's find out.

Chakra 7 is known for its healing and calming powers.

**AMETHYST**

**LEPIDOLITE**

Chakra 6 is believed to drive away negative influences, dispel anxiety and melancholy, and enhance self-confidence.

**TURQUOISE**

Chakra 5 is believed to alleviate phobias and bring love to lonely hearts and fidelity to marriage.

FIGURE 13.12 Backpacks are a popular way for students, and even adults, to transport valuables.

or briefcases for everything they want to carry. Perhaps the backpack's acceptance is a carryover from its use as a school bookbag. For that purpose, it remains popular with boys and girls from kindergarten through college (see Figure 13.12). Canvas is the most popular material, and names such as L. L. Bean, Lands' End, and Jansport carry status as well as school supplies. Meanwhile, smaller leather backpacks or Prada's nylon backpack have become a trendy handbag style among women.

## Small Leather Goods/Personal Goods

The category called small leather goods or personal goods includes wallets, key cases and chains, jewelry cases, briefcases, and carrying cases for cellphones and laptop computers (see Figure 13.13). Similarly, men and women with busy schedules are increasingly seen with leather-covered appointment books or "organizers." Of course, despite the name, not all of these items are made of leather. Fabrics, particu-

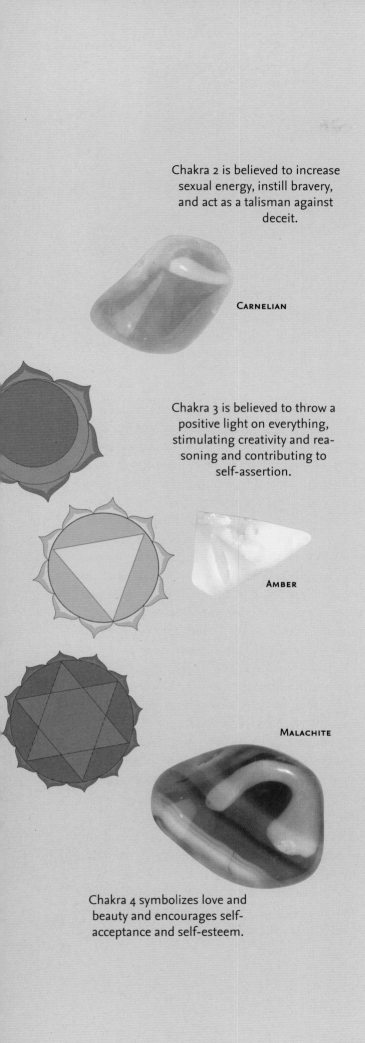

Chakra 2 is believed to increase sexual energy, instill bravery, and act as a talisman against deceit.

CARNELIAN

Chakra 3 is believed to throw a positive light on everything, stimulating creativity and reasoning and contributing to self-assertion.

AMBER

MALACHITE

Chakra 4 symbolizes love and beauty and encourages self-acceptance and self-esteem.

FIGURE 13.13 The wristlet and clutch bags are good options if you have just a few things to carry, or want to look fashionable!

larly nylon and microfibers, have assumed great importance in this category. Leading manufacturers of these items in the United States include Coach, Nine West, and Dooney & Bourke. More and more designers are moving into this category; among them are Kate Spade and Anne Klein.

### Merchandising and Marketing

Few handbag manufacturers are large enough to advertise on a national basis in newspapers and television. The customer's impression of what is new and fashionable in handbags is mostly gleaned through store displays and advertising in magazines. Catalogs, home shopping networks, and the Internet are also increasingly popular ways of reaching customers.

### Industry Trends

Faced with severe competition from foreign imports, many domestic handbag manufacturers have themselves become importers of foreign-made handbags. These importers employ American designers to create styles and then have the handbags made in countries with low wage scales.

The industry's trade organization—the National Fashion Accessories Association (NFAA)—has worked closely with government agencies to promote the domestic handbag industry both here and abroad. The NFAA also formed the Fashion Accessories Shippers Association (FASA) to support the interests of importers as well as manufacturers of handbags and related accessories (including belts, small leather goods, gloves, and luggage).

The leather goods trade fair, Mipel, held in spring and autumn in Milan, attracts handbag buyers from all over the world.

## Belts

For dressing an outfit up or down to suit the occasion, a belt is an easy solution. Since belts are not

**FIGURE 13.14** The right belt can dress up any outfit.

absolutely essential—if you need one to hold up your pants, you can have your pants altered or buy a better-fitting pair—their appeal as a fashion accessory is of primary importance (see Figure 13.14). Although belts are categorized and sold with small leather goods, they are also made of a host of other materials including cloth, plastic, metal, and straw.

The price of a belt can be less than $10 or more than $500, depending on the materials, the precious metals or jewels used in the belt buckle, and the amount of hand-craftsmanship involved in its production. Designer names and logos—often appearing on the buckle or other metal trim—add to the fashion status of a belt and often to its price.

The fashion district of New York City is the home of belt manufacturing, though manufacturers like Tandy Brands in Fort Worth, Texas, can be found across the country. Manufacturers who produce belts to be sold as separate fashion accessory items are said to be in the "rack trade." They are distinguished from the cut-up trade, which manufactures belts to be sold as part of a dress, skirt, or pair of trousers. Self belts, with bands and sometimes buckles covered in the same fabric as the apparel item with which they are sold, are produced by this segment of the industry.

In the rack trade, most men's and women's belts are sized according to waist measurements, with women's belts ranging from 22 to 32 inches and men's, from 28 to 44 inches. Sometimes they are grouped as small, medium, large, and extra large. Plus sizes in belts have become more important. Belts manufactured for the cut-up trade are made in lengths to fit the size of the garment.

The U.S. belt industry generates over $713 million annually at wholesale, according to industry analysts. Refer to Chapter 7 for more information on leather belts.

## Gloves

Crude animal-skin coverings were the forerunners of mittens, which, in turn, evolved into gloves with individual fingers. Gloves are not new, though; leather gloves were discovered in the tombs of ancient Egyptians (see Figure 13.15).

Gloves have enjoyed a long and varied history, at times even taking on symbolic value. To bring them luck, knights once wore their ladies' gloves on their armor as they went into battle. So long as women wore modest dress, men often cherished the gloves of their beloved as erotic objects. Gloves were once exchanged when property was being sold as a gesture of good faith. And in dueling days, one man would slap another across the face with his glove as an invitation to a duel. Gloves have also been used to denote rank or authority. Until the 16th century, only men of the clergy or of noble rank were allowed to wear them.

For centuries, gloves were coordinated in styling, detail, and color with current apparel styles. To be specific, glove styles correlated to the currently popular sleeve length, especially in coats and suits.

In the first half of the 20th century, the glove business flourished largely because no self-respecting, let alone fashionably dressed, woman went out without wearing gloves. The untrimmed, white, wrist-length glove was de rigueur for dress occasions, as was the suit glove, which extends a few inches above the wrist, often made up in leather and used for general wear. The 1960s, which saw the onset of a long period of casual dress, also saw the end of gloves as a requirement for a well-dressed woman. White cotton gloves as an accessory for dress or business wear disappeared. When leather became expensive in the 1980s, manufacturers began to make gloves of knit and woven fabrics, which now dominate the market. Currently, in winter, when gloves are worn for warmth, they are coordinated with dress or casual outfits (see Figure 13.16).

**FIGURE 13.15** Leather gloves were discovered centuries ago but are still a trendy and functional accessory.

**FIGURE 13.16** Gloves are often coordinated with clothing and other accessories.

# Then & NOW

## Salvatore Ferragamo
### A Big Footprint Walking the Walk

Left page: Salvatore Ferragamo, 1953 (top center); Ferragamo Atelier collection (bottom left); Right page: Designs by Ferragamo from 2006 (top) and 2005 (bottom).

The house of Ferragamo has left its footprint in Hollywood history, creating hundreds of styles designed for dozens of films starting in the early 1920s and adding glamour in the 1930s, 1940s, and 1950s. From Lana Turner, Marilyn Monroe, Greta Garbo, and Audrey Hepburn to today's Eva Longoria and Keira Knightley, the Ferragamo style and glamour live on. In 2006, the legendary Italian brand was awarded the Walk of Style award that the city of Beverly Hills and the Rodeo Drive Committee presented to Ferragamo. This permanent plaque on Rodeo Drive joins other famous names, including Armani, Tom Ford, Herb Ritts, and Edith Head, all celebrated for their lasting contribution to Hollywood fashion.

Ferragamo's history runs from rural Italy through the sets of Hollywood to a worldwide luxury empire. At age 14, Salvatore Ferragamo was a successful shoemaker in Italy, and at 16 he crossed the ocean to Boston and joined the Queen Quality Shoe Company where shoes were machinemade.

Appalled by the low quality of the machine-made footwear and firmly believing that luxury shoes had to be made and stitched by hand, Ferragamo headed west to join his three brothers in Santa Barbara, California, where they started making handmade boots and shoes for the American Film Company and the budding film business.

In 1923, Ferragamo moved to Los Angeles and became part of the growing movie business, traveling in glamorous circles and hobnobbing with stars of the 1920s and 1930s, including Rudolph Valentino, John Barrymore, Jean Harlow, and the crème de la crème of Hollywood stars.

Ferragamo's fascination with the foot led him to study human anatomy at the University of California.

Feet, he said, spoke to him and communicated a person's character. He wrote that feet, regardless of the social class of their owners, were covered with corns, bunions, and calluses, and toes were cracked, all of which he attributed to machine-made shoes. He became obsessed with making pretty footwear that was comfortable and did not damage the wearer's feet.

Years later, in a bid to ease the pain of as many bad feet as possible, he applied his expertise to machinery. He discovered new fittings and designed shoe casts with different widths.

Today, Salvatore Ferragamo Italia S.P.A. is one of the most prestigious and internationally well-known luxury brands, with more than 450 stores in over fifty-five countries. Footwear, handbags and small leather goods, scarves and ties, men's and women's ready-to-wear, bijoux, watches, fragrances, and eyewear are the products created and marketed by Ferragamo.

Ferragamo was always recognized as a visionary, and his designs ranged from the strikingly bizarre objet d'art to the traditionally elegant, often serving as the main inspiration to other footwear designers of his time and now. His most famous design is the "Cage Heel," and his daughter Fiamma inherited her father's great talent and came up with the "Vara Pumps" in 1978. The Ferragamo family is still actively involved with the business; Salvatore's wife Wanda chairs the board of directors.

A famous and lasting memorial is the Salvatore Ferragamo Museum that opened in 1995 in Florence, Italy. Located on the second floor of Palazzo Spini Feroni, the museum extends over four rooms and comprises a collection of over 10,000 models of shoes created by Ferragamo throughout his career, from the 1920s until his death in 1960. The museum also has a small collection of period shoes from the 18th and 19th centuries, a collection of clothing from 1959 and later, a collection of handbags from 1970, and a huge document archive.

As Nancy Sinatra sang in her hit record, "These Boots Are Made for Walking," she was paying her respects to the finest boot and shoemaker ever.

## Organization and Operation

The production of gloves varies, depending upon whether they are made of leather or fabric. Leather gloves are among the most difficult accessories to manufacture. Most leather gloves are made, at minimum, with hand-guided operations, and some are still made entirely by hand.

Leather gloves are typically made in small factories, since few machines and workers are required to run such a factory. Glove producers tend to specialize, performing only one manufacturing operation, such as cutting or stitching. Other operations are farmed out to nearby plants, each of which, in turn, has its own specialty.

In contrast to the methods used to make leather gloves, the fabric-glove industry is much more mechanized. The cheapest gloves and mittens have only two parts—a front and a back—sewn together. More expensive gloves have separate small pieces that fit the fingers and thumbs. Most fabric gloves are made of some kind of double-woven fiber because this gives them great durability. Knit gloves and mittens are made of wool, acrylic, and cotton—even cotton string—usually in one-size-fits all. Chenille and Polar Fleece are popular for cold weather wear, along with fake fur.

New York City was once the center of the glove-manufacturing industry. Today, glove manufacturers have turned to offshore production, and most gloves are made in China, the Caribbean, and the Philippines. One well-known specialist glove manufacturer in the United States is the totes»ISOTONER Corporation, which makes the Isotoner line of fabric leather gloves. Other fashion glove makers in the United States are Fownes, Grandoe, and LaCrasia.

## Merchandising and Marketing

Compared with the dollars spent on consumer advertising for other accessories, the industry outlay for glove advertising is quite modest. Only a few large producers with nationally distributed brand names actively promote their products or offer even limited merchandising support services to retail stores.

Manufacturers have learned to make gloves more creatively. Gloves are lined with—and sometimes even made of—a wide array of knitted fabrics, lace, cashmere, fur, and silk. Wonderful colors—like orange, purple, acid yellow, and lime green—are often matched to winter hats or scarfs.

Finally, while many fashion industries have turned to diversification, the glove industry has moved in the opposite direction, toward specialization. Glove manufacturers, for example, have created markets for gardening gloves, driving gloves, and gloves for specific sports. Men and women can choose from an array of gloves designed for use at tennis, baseball, bicycling, and golfing—to name just a few. Gloves for skiing and winter gloves and mittens are made of high-tech materials, like Gore-Tex, Thinsulate, and Polartec, to maximize their insulating properties.

### Industry Trends

Sales of domestically produced leather gloves have suffered considerably in recent years from the competition of less expensive imports. To meet this challenge, the industry is trying to improve manufacturing procedures in order to reduce costs. Manufacturers have reduced the number of glove sizes, preferring to sell gloves in only small, medium, and large. Stretch-fabric gloves, in which one size fits all, are made as well. In addition, improved materials are resulting from product research and development in the leather industry. These are expected to increase the market potential of domestically produced leather gloves. For example, many leather gloves today are hand washable and come in a wide range of fashion colors.

The fabric-glove industry is exploring innovative packaging techniques, such as packaging matching

hats and gloves (or mittens) together, or matching scarfs and gloves, or matching headbands and gloves for winter wear.

## Millinery

According to an old saying, whatever is worn on the head is a sign of the mind beneath it. Since the head is one of the more vulnerable parts of the body, hats do have a protective function. But they are also a fashion accessory (see Figures 13.17 and 13.18).

The man's hat of the 19th and 20th centuries in Europe, which was derived from the medieval helmet, protected its wearer both physically and psychologically. The heavy crown kept the head safe from blows, and the brim shaded the face from strong sunlight and close scrutiny. In 19th-century America, the cowboy hat became an enduring national icon. Late in the century, the top hat was a status symbol of a special kind. This was the time of European immigration, and those who wanted to distinguish themselves from the immigrant peasants took care to wear hats.

After decades of prosperity and popularity, the men's hat industry began to collapse in the years following World War II. This was soon true for the women's hat industry, called the millinery industry, as well. Because of the more casual approach to dressing and the popularity of women's beehive and bouffant hairstyles, men's and women's hat sales hit

**FIGURE 13.17** A milliner fitting and adjusting a glamorous hat.

**FIGURE 13.18** Men and children are increasingly conscious of their accessory choices, including hats, jewelry, sunglasses, and shoes.

1990s, which led to the increased popularity of all types of winter hats and caps. David Chu of Nautica designed a polyester fleece cap and scarf that provide warmth while wicking away moisture. The fleece stocking cap for kids was a runaway best-seller. A variation like a jester's cap was also popular on the ski slopes and city streets.

With the rise of hip-hop fashion and "ghetto fabulous" clothing styles, a new range of headwear, from streetwise Kangol hats, berets, and caps, to elegant fedoras, have become must-haves among young fashion addicts (see Figure 13.19). Many leading luxury houses like Gucci, Louis Vuitton, and Burberry are enjoying tremendous success with their logo-embellished newsboy caps, bucket hats, and fedoras.

Another factor was the featuring of flamboyant hats in designer shows, especially on the runways of Paris and Milan. Although these extreme styles are presented more as a display of the designer's imagination than as an attempt to introduce a trend, they remind fashion arbiters and consumers that hats can be a fun accessory and can make or break an outfit. Philip Treacy, a well-known British hat designer, has designed hats for the runway shows of Chanel, Valentino, and Versace (see Figure 13.20). Treacy has also expanded into handbags.

Well-known U.S. millinery designers include Patricia Underwood, Eric Javits, and, at a lower price point,

bottom in 1960. During the freewheeling 1960s and 1970s, a hat was worn only on the coldest days—strictly for warmth, not for fashion.

During that time, the millinery industry and its active trade association, the National Millinery Institute, researched, publicized, and campaigned in an extensive effort to reverse the trend, with little success. This was not surprising, since, as we have already learned, no amount of sales promotion can change the direction in which fashion is moving.

However, the pendulum has begun to swing back toward the popularity of hats for men, women, and children. Several factors have contributed to this development. One was the fierce winters of the late

**FIGURE 13.19** Hats have become a must-have item for hip-hop wear.

**FIGURE 13.20** Philip Treacy design on the runway, 2002.

with young consumers. In this instance, boys and young men have worn them as a mark of support for their favorite teams. Soon the caps became promotional items for businesses, clubs, and other organizations. Designers took up the trend, putting their names and logos on this activewear accessory, often adding sequins, beading, or braid trims. Caps have proliferated, worn backwards or forward, by men, women, and children.

The men's felt hat industry in the United States is still alive. Cowboy hats and "Indiana Jones" hats are the most popular styles, though derbies, pork pies, homburgs, snap brims, and fedoras are being made by a few firms. The largest manufacturer is Hatco of Garland, Texas. It owns the famous Stetson brand of cowboy or western hats as well as the Dobbs and Resistol brands. A few men's custom hatters can still be found; among them are Colorado Mountain Hat Company in Fairplay, Colorado; Rand's Custom Hatters in Billings, Montana; and The Custom Hatter in Buffalo, New York. Well-known European brands for men include Kangol and James Lock & Co. of England and Borsalino of Italy.

The center of the women's millinery industry is in New York City in the West 30s, between Fifth and Sixth Avenues, with some smaller firms in Los Angeles and St. Louis. One-person millinery shops can be found in many cities, since millinery involves a great deal of handwork and is ideal for custom work.

Betmar. Makins Hats designs for both men and women; its clients include Bill Cosby and Arsenio Hall. August Accessories of Oxnard, California, uses neoprene in a line of reversible, weatherproof hats.

The third factor contributing to the increased popularity of hats is the awareness of the dangers of overexposure to the sun. Dermatologists recommend wearing hats for protection in all seasons. Straw and canvas hats with large bills or brims offer shade without undesired warmth. Also available are hats made of fabrics with an SPF (sun protection factor). Baby hats that tie under the chin, or bonnets, have long been popular for infants; they are now widely used for toddlers as well. Along with the popular safari hat for men, hats with neck guards, once seen only in French Foreign Legion movies, have become popular in retirement communities across the country.

As with many fashion trends, the growing popularity of baseball caps as a fashion accessory started

## Neckwear

With the introduction of foreign designer's signature scarfs in the 1970s, women's neckwear began an upswing, which continued in the 1990s. (Note that the industry uses the unusual spelling of scarfs rather than scarves.) Customers are wearing scarfs to change the look of an outfit. Squares and oblongs of varying sizes can be tied in different ways, sometimes with the help of specially designed scarf clips. Neckerchiefs, the hottest trend in the late 1990s, energized the scarf category by bringing women from 20 to 35 years old into the department. Often entire walls were devoted to displays—much like socks and tights.

Echo is one of the largest manufacturers of scarfs in the United States. In addition, a number of leading American designer names have become associated with neckwear, further enhancing the category's appeal. Among them are Perry Ellis and Anne Klein, Ellen Tracy, Oscar de la Renta, and Liz Claiborne. Some high-end imported scarfs, like those of Hermès (France) and Pucci and Gucci (Italy), are famous worldwide (see Figure 13.21).

For men, ties have been a standard accessory for business suits for more than a century. They have provided an opportunity to brighten the business uniform with a small splash of bright colors and lively patterns (see Figure 13.22). The necktie, or four-in-hand, and the bowtie are the two most common styles. The bolo, or string tie, is popular in the southwester United States. The ascot, or broad neck scarf, is rarely seen today.

Among patterns, the regimental stripes have been popular for decades; they began with military regiments in England. Club ties have small embroidered emblems. Today most ties are made of woven silk or polyester. Knit ties and ties of leather or other specialty fabrics account for only a small percentage of total production.

At the height of power dressing in the late 1970s and 1980s, the color, print, and fabric of a necktie became a silent language, communicating the wearer's status. In the more casual office of the 1990s, where ties are not always required, "conversational" or whimsical ties—shaped like a fish or printed with cartoon characters—can contribute to the informal atmosphere.

Top names in the United States include Countess Mara, Ralph Lauren (who began his career designing ties), Salant Corporation, Tabasco, and Ralph Marlin (of fish tie fame), which is now the leader in licensed neckwear.

In addition to neckties, men wear neck scarfs of wool in winter. The knit variation of these scarfs is

**FIGURE 13.21** High-end imported scarfs by Hermès (top). **FIGURE 13.22** A colorful or patterned tie can brighten up any business suit (bottom).

called a muffler. Some men wear silk neck scarfs with formal dress coats.

The Men's Dress Furnishings Association is a 100-member international trade association of tie manufacturers and suppliers.

## Eyewear

In recent years, consumers have become increasingly aware of the need to protect their eyes from the sun's harmful ultraviolet (UV) rays. Even for children, sunglasses are now considered more than a cute, wearable toy. Bausch and Lomb has added ten new designs to its children's sunglasses line, called Covers. The line features UV protection, impact-resistant lenses, and durable plastic frames in a wide range of colors. Swiss Army Brands entered the high-tech sunglass market with a print ad campaign that said: "Navy Seals bring our knives on every one of their underwater missions. Now they'll be equipped to hit the beaches too."

At the same time, manufacturers of sunglasses have made a concerted effort to produce styles that are high fashion. Wraparound frames, clear frames, and lenses that are reflective or tinted different colors are some of the distinctive design features. Combine these factors with the high visibility of sunglasses on prominent celebrities and on MTV, and it is no wonder that sales in this category exploded (see Figure 13.23).

Italian firms dominate the world of eyewear. The biggest of them, Luxottica, has annual sales of over $6 billion dollars.

"Ten years ago, sunglasses were a functional device," says Andrea Guerra, chief executive of Luxottica. Today, sunglasses have colored lenses, oddly shaped frames, and all kinds of adornment, including loud logos in silver and gold, and clusters of diamonds.

Luxottica has won the most lucrative contracts, including licenses from Burberry and Polo Ralph Lauren. Luxottica attributes success to the strength of its in-house brands and to its control of the retailers where they are sold. Luxottica bought Lens Crafters in 1995, and then acquired Sunglass Hut. The brands it owns, such as Ray-Ban, acquired in 1999, are the backbone of the business. In 2007, Luxottica announced the purchase of another portfolio of brands with the takeover of Oakley, a California-based maker of sunglasses.

The latest plan is flagship stores for ILORI, its new retail chain for ultra-fashionable shades. Over the next two to three years, the firm plans to open 150 ILORI shops in America.

Luxottica thinks it can persuade Americans to spend $250 to as much as $10,000 for a pair of sunglasses. Michael Hansen, vice president and general manager of ILORI, is confident that clients will enjoy the ILORI "experience" in the shops. They will be able to relax in a "VIP lounge" and model prospective purchases on a special runway. Sunglasses are the third-fastest growing category in luxury goods after handbags and shoes, says. Hansen. So, he asks, why not spend $10,000 on a pair of sunglasses, which will be just as visible as a Hermès $140,000 handbag to gawking bystanders?[5]

Prescription eyeglasses (see Figure 13.24) are

**FIGURE 13.23** The market for designer sunglasses has exploded.

**FIGURE 13.24** Licensing for eyewear, such as these Disney frames, is an important part of the industry.

another important segment of the fashion eyewear category. Despite the popularity of contact lenses, optometrists now fit their customers to improve their looks as well as their vision. Aging baby boomers have spurred growth in the market for nonprescription reading glasses, or readers. The industry has responded with fashionable styles available at different price points. Designer readers are available from such famous names as Donna Karan, Hugo Boss, Perry Ellis, and Calvin Klein. Lower-priced readers are available in drugstores.

Marchon Eyewear is the largest manufacturer and distributor of prescription and sunglasses frames in the world. The firm has stayed ahead of the curve, accurately predicting when eyeglasses would move from the directly functional to the glamorously fashionable and pursuing licensing agreements with globally recognized brands such as Calvin Klein, Coach, Diane von Furstenberg, in addition to the superstars of fashion.[6]

## Jewelry

Jewelry has always played a significant and varied role in people's lives. In ancient times, some articles of jewelry were worn as amulets to ward off evil. Jewelry was popular among ancient Greeks, Romans, and Africans. The beautiful Roman women featured in the old frescoes wore long, thin necklaces that encircled their necks two or three times, strands of pearls braided in their hair, and engraved belts decorated with precious stones.

A symbol of wealth and importance, jewelry was at certain times worn only by nobility. Laden with gold chains, their clothing adorned with gems, their fingers covered with rings, they carried on their persons the fortunes of their ruling houses. Medieval noblemen displayed elaborate heraldic emblems symbolizing their knighthood, and military men, another privileged class, used to make a great display of their decorations, which were once jewel-encrusted. Jeweled tiaras were in vogue among the upper classes in the Napoleonic era, because they simulated the laurel wreaths of antiquity. Tiaras saw an unexpected revival among brides in the early 1980s when Lady Diana Spencer wore a Spencer family heirloom tiara at her wedding to Prince Charles. Tiaras resurfaced again in the late 1990s, when designers like John Galliano and Vivienne Westwood featured them in their fashion shows. Suddenly tiaras were seen at proms and debutante balls around the United States.

### Organization and Operation

Methods of making jewelry have changed little over time. Modern jewelers melt and shape metal, cut and carve stones, and string beads and shells much as jewelers have been doing for centuries. Jewelry designers have always used enamel, glass, ceramic, and natural mineral formations as their raw materials (see Figure 13.25).

Based on the quality of their products, the jewelry industry in the United States can be divided into two primary groups: fine jewelry and costume or fashion jewelry. A third group, bridge jewelry, has gained in importance, as has a fourth group, ethnic jewelry.

**FIGURE 13.25** Big, elaborate necklaces make a comeback as top accessories looks on the Lanvin fall 2008 runway.

## Fine Jewelry

Fine jewelry is the counterpart of haute couture. Only precious metals such as gold and platinum are used to make fine jewelry. Sterling silver is also considered a precious metal, although its intrinsic value is far less than that of gold or platinum. Too soft to be used alone, these precious metals are alloyed, or combined, with one or more other metals to make them hard enough to be fashioned into jewelry.

Platinum (which includes palladium, rhodium, and iridium) is the most expensive metal. It was first used for jewelry by Cartier and became a hallmark of the Art Deco movement of the 1920s and 1930s.

The gold content of jewelry is measured by weight in karats, abbreviated as K. An item called solid gold actually has only 24 karats of gold, or 1/24 gold to 23/24 alloy. Less costly 14K gold is popular in the United States, while 18K gold is popular in Europe, and 22K gold is popular in India. Gold-filled jewelry is made of an inexpensive base metal with a heavy layer of gold on top. White gold is a substitute for platinum; it is an alloy of gold and another metal, usually nickel. Vermeil (pronounced ver-MAY) is a composite of gold over sterling silver. The term sterling silver is used for jewelry (and flatware) with at least 92.5 parts of silver; the remaining 7.5 parts are usually copper. Not all sterling silver is equal; thicker items are generally more valuable than thin ones.

The stones used in fine jewelry are called gemstones to distinguish them from lower-quality stones that are used for industrial purposes. Gemstones, which always come from natural mineral formations, have traditionally been classified as either precious or semiprecious. Precious stones include diamonds, emeralds, rubies, and sapphires. Stones are measured by weight, in a unit of measure called a carat, which equals 200 milligrams, or 1/142 of an ounce. Carats are subdivided into points; there are 100 points to a carat. Thus a half-carat stone is a 50-point stone.

Diamonds are the hardest substance known and are in limited supply. From 250 tons of ore, only one carat of rough diamonds can be recovered, and only 20 percent of them are suitable for gemstones. Diamonds are found in South Africa, Siberia, Australia, and Arkansas. The world supply is dominated by the DeBeers cartel of South Africa. It has spent millions to promote the romance of diamonds with its ad slogan "A diamond is forever."

Diamonds are usually cut into 58 facets, which are small, polished planes that are precisely placed to reflect the maximum amount of light (Figure 13.26). Traditional cuts or shapes of diamonds are round, emerald, marquise, pear, oval, and heart (see Figure 13.27). A relatively new cut, called the radiant cut, was developed in 1976. It has about 70 facets and was originally developed to hide flaws.

Advanced technology in the new millennium has unleashed a new crop of innovative cuts. Among them is the square-shaped Context cut, which is not cleaved but based on the natural twelve-sided rough diamond crystal. Other new cuts include the circular Spirit Sun cut and the triple-brilliant Gabrielle cut, which has 105 facets (compared to the traditional 58) and is available in a wide range of classic shapes.[7] For centuries, diamond briolettes and faceted diamond heads were used in some of the world's most famous jewelry. Historians believe the briolette cut originated in India. The Crown Jewels of Iran, the tiara worn by the Grand Duchess Xenia Alexandrovna of Russia, and the diamond briolette necklace that Napoleon gave his second wife, Empress Marie Louise, were all made with briolette diamonds.

Briolette began to gain popularity in commercial jewelry designs in the 1990s and remain a hot trend today. Laser-cutting and drilling tools make it easier for jewelry designers to use them, and, with color on the frontline of fashion, designers are using these fancy color diamond briolettes. Most fancy color diamond briolettes are one of a kind, and designers cannot guarantee that shapes and colors will always be available.[8]

A solitaire is the mounting of a single gemstone; a diamond solitaire is the traditional engagement ring. A Tiffany setting refers to a four- or six-prong setting that flares out from the base to the top, with long slender prongs that hold the stone. A baguette is a rectangular-shaped small stone used with a larger stone. A pave setting is one in which a number of small stones are set as closely together as possible, so that no metal shows between them, and they appear as an all-stone surface.

Real, or oriental, pearls are of animal origin but are still considered precious stones. Tahitian and South Sea pearls are the most expensive real pearls. Cultured pearls are pearls formed by an oyster around an irritant placed in the oyster's body by man. They are not considered precious stones, although they can only be raised in limited parts of the world's oceans. Freshwater pearls are nugget-shaped pearls that grow in lakes or rivers; they are more abundant and less expensive than real or cultured pearls.

Pearls are measured in millimeters of circumference and length. Size contributes to the value of pearls; large pearls are hard for oysters to grow and so are more expensive. Pearls cannot be cut or shaped like other gems. The more symmetrical the pearl, the more expensive it is. Pearls with irregular and asymmetrical shapes are called baroque pearls. The rarest—and most expensive—pearls are black; other natural tints are cream, a pinkish hue, or a bluish one.

The so-called semiprecious stones include a host of other natural stones that were once more costly and less rare than precious stones but are still quite beautiful (see Table 13.1). The Jewelers of America Association

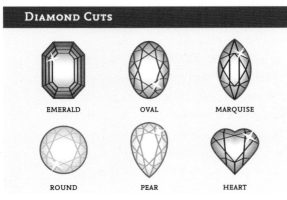

**DIAMOND CUTS**

EMERALD   OVAL   MARQUISE

ROUND   PEAR   HEART

**FIGURE 13.26** Even though there is a limited supply, diamonds are still a girl's (and rap star's) best friend! (top)
**FIGURE 13.27** Traditional diamond cuts (bottom).

**TABLE 13.1** *Fine Gemstones*

| | |
|---|---|
| Alexandrite | |
| Amber* | |
| Amethyst | |
| Aquamarine | |
| Chrysoberyl | |
| Citrine | |
| Garnet | |
| Iolite | |
| Jade | |
| Kunzite | |
| Lapis lazuli | |
| Moonstone | |
| Opal | |
| Peridot | |
| Rubellite | |
| Spinel | |
| Tanzanite | |
| Topaz | |
| Tourmaline | |
| Tsavorite | |
| Turquoise | |
| Zircon | |

*Vegetable, not mineral, in origin.
Source: Jewelers of America, *What You Should Know about Gems*. New York: Jewelers of America, Inc.

holds that the division of gems into precious and semiprecious is invalid, because discoveries have added new varieties that are higher priced, because of their rarity, than the more well-known gems. For example, fine jade is more valuable than a lesser quality emerald. Tanzanite, first discovered near Mount Kilimanjaro in 1967, is a deep purple gemstone that Tiffany & Co. has popularized. Although it is considered a semiprecious stone, it is being used by fine-jewelry designers in very expensive pieces.

Chemists have succeeded in creating synthetic stones that are chemically identical to real stones. Synthetic stones are now used in combination with 14-carat gold and sterling silver. The most popular of the synthetics is zirconia, which offers the dazzle of diamonds at a fraction of the cost. Other synthetic stones include synthetic spinel, which looks like emeralds or aquamarines, and synthetic corumdum, which looks like amethysts.

Fine-jewelry production is still a handcraft industry. A lapidary, or stonecutter, transforms dull-looking stones in their natural states into gems by cutting, carving, and polishing them. Then the jeweler creates a setting for the stones to bring out their brilliance.

In the established fine-jewelry houses, as in haute couture houses, design, production, and retail sales typically take place under one roof—and one management. Many fine-jewelry firms sell only the jewelry they create, much of which is custom designed for them. Names such as Cartier and Tiffany have always been used to sell jewelry, but in the past, the designers, who were in the employ of these companies, were not well known. In the past few decades though, individual designers have taken on new importance, and customers now look for jewelry designed by their favorite designers.

Paloma Picasso and Elsa Peretti designs are sold at Tiffany & Co. Other leading independent designers with large followings include Angela Cummings, Barry Kieselstein-Cord, Robert Lee Morris, David Yurman, and Steven Lagos. As another example, Bergdorf Goodman's fine-jewelry department carries the work of seventeen designers, including the established designers listed above and newcomers

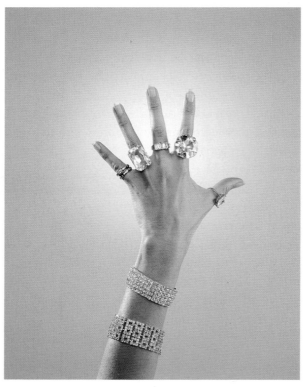

**FIGURE 13.28** Costume jewelry allows the customer to have the look of luxury for a lower cost.

Christopher Walling, Julie Baker, Stephen Dweck, Stephen Webster, and Angela Pintaldi of Italy.

## Costume Jewelry

Costume or fashion jewelry is like mass-produced apparel. A wide range of materials—wood, glass, and base metals such as brass, aluminum, copper, tin, and lead—are used to make it (see Figure 13.28). Base metals are sometimes coated with costlier precious metals such as gold, rhodium, or silver. The stones and simulated (fake) pearls used in costume jewelry are made from clay, glass, or plastic. While they are attractive and interesting in their surface appearance, they are less costly and lack the more desirable properties (durability for one) of natural stones.

Before the 1920s, costume jewelry as we know it did not exist. Most jewelry was made from gold or, more rarely, silver set with precious or semi-precious stones. Jewelry was worn for its sentimental or economic value and was never used to accessorize one's clothing.

The age of costume jewelry began with designer Coco Chanel. In the 1920s, she introduced long, large, and obviously fake strands of pearls to be worn with her clothes. This new accessory was called costume jewelry because it was meant to coordinate with one's costume. The pearls were called simulated in English and faux, which means false, in French.

Chanel, it might be noted, not only helped to create an industry but also continued to wear her trademark pearls for the rest of her life. Today, simulated pearls—indeed Chanel-style pearls—are a staple of the costume jewelry industry. Two first ladies also contributed to the popularity of pearls: Jackie Kennedy Onassis (see Figure 13.29) and Barbara Bush.

Costume jewelry has always gone through phases. At times, it is intended to look like fine jewelry; at other times, frankly fake-looking jewelry is in style. Beginning in the 1960s and continuing to today, Kenneth Jay Lane designed costume jewelry

**FIGURE 13.29** When the estate of the late Jacqueline Kennedy Onassis auctioned the set of simulated pearls she wore in this widely reproduced photograph, they fetched the amazing price $211,500! Copies were made by Carolee Jewelry; they sold for $300.

so real-looking that socialites and other fashion leaders favored it over their own authentic jewels.

There is always a market in costume jewelry for products that look like the real thing; most mass-produced jewelry, in fact, falls into this category. Large, popular-priced costume jewelry houses employ stylists who design seasonal lines or adapt styles from higher-priced lines. Mass-produced costume jewelry is made in Providence, Rhode Island, where small jewelry manufacturing firms are still located, though the industry there has shrunk considerably. Facilities are geared toward producing jewelry to the specifications of individual firms, much as apparel manufacturers contract out their work and use jobbers.

Mass-production methods are employed in contrast to the handwork that exemplifies the making of fine jewelry. While a fine jeweler pounds and hand shapes metal, manufacturers of costume jewelry cast metal by melting it and then pouring it into molds to harden. Designs are applied to the hardened metal surface by painting it with colored enamel or embossing it by machine. Electroplating is the name of a process that coats inexpensive base materials with a thin coat of silver or gold.

Large firms dominate the industry. Examples are the Monet Group (Monet, Trifari, and Marvella) and Carolee. Victoria & Co Ltd. is a leading designer and marketer of branded and private-label costume jewelry. Victoria manufactures and markets the licensed jewelry collection for Givenchy and Tommy Hilfiger and also creates jewelry under Napier and Richelieu, its own brands, as well as under the Nine West brand. While most large firms work with multiple price lines and many different materials, some companies do specialize. An example is Swarovski Jewelry U.S., which specializes in crystal jewelry, made under the company name and the Savvy label.

Still, more than 90 percent of U.S. jewelry producers are small, family-owned companies. Individuals with creative talent often open successful small retail or wholesale operations that cater to customers who are interested in individualized styling and trend-setting fashions. Such operations are an outgrowth of the handcraft movement of the 1960s and 1970s. Handmade jewelry had a major comeback at the beginning of the new millennium, which launched a rise of small, independent jewelry designers across the country.

### Bridge Jewelry

Dramatic increases in the price of gold and silver in the early 1980s left jewelers seeking new ways to meet the public's demand for reasonably priced authentic jewelry. The solution was bridge jewelry, that is, jewelry that forms a bridge—in price, materials, and style—between fine and costume jewelry. Prices at retail range from about $100 to $2,500 for bridge jewelry. (Also see the discussion of bridge apparel in Chapter 9.)

The development of bridge jewelry led to increased use of sterling silver and its subsequent elevation to a precious metal. The boom in Native American jewelry in the early 1970s also helped to create interest in bridge jewelry. Many department stores and specialty stores created bridge departments to handle sterling silver and Native American jewelry, and when interest in it faded, they were open to other kinds of bridge jewelry that would help them keep the customer base they had developed.

Bridge jewelry departments at such stores as

Neiman Marcus now carry gold-filled, vermeil, sterling silver, and some 14K gold fashion jewelry set with semiprecious stones. Sterling silver jewelry continues to grow rapidly in popularity. Bridge designers include Zina and M & J Savitt. Judith Jack specializes in marcasite (crystallized mineral) jewelry, which attracts both costume and fine jewelry customers.

### Ethnic Jewelry

The category of ethnic jewelry includes pieces from all over the world at all price points, although some of these items are not made of intrinsically valuable materials, but rather of shells, stones, wood, or fabric (see Figure 13.30). The artistry is so remarkable that these items can command a higher price than costume jewelry. As previously mentioned, Native American jewelry in silver and turquoise has been popular for decades. Two famous styles of silver

**FIGURE 13.30** Ethnic jewelry is worn as everyday fashion.

necklaces, the squash blossom necklace and the liquid silver necklace, continue to be reinterpreted by modern Native American designers.

Ralph Lauren popularized African jewelry with his 1997 collection that was inspired by the Masai of Kenya; it included arm cuffs, bead chokers, and hoop earrings. Similarly, traditional ethnic jewelry from India, made from 22K gold and decorated with ornate patterns and precious gemstones, became popular in the late 1990s after Nicole Kidman and Goldie Hawn began wearing these styles. Most people, however, buy far less expensive designs in glass, brass, and silver. Chinese-inspired jewelry made of jade, coral, and mother-of-pearl is perennially popular, as is the yin-yang symbol. Moroccan beads, the Egyptian ankh, Guatemalan string figures, Greek worry beads, Caribbean shell necklaces, Peruvian hammered copper earrings—all have fans worldwide.

Another category of ethnic jewelry involves wearing religious or spiritual symbols in necklaces, earrings, rings, or pins, such as the Jewish Star of David, the Christian cross, the Buddhist lotus blossom, the Native American eagle feather, and the New Age crystal. The famous Indian "Navratan Haar" ring is made of nine gems with astrological significance: a diamond in the center, circled by eight rainbow-colored stones: ruby, emerald, cinnamon, coral, cat's eye, blue and yellow sapphires, and pearl.

Designers must show sensitivity when adapting these powerful symbols into jewelry. A storm of protest arose when Madonna wore a cross as part of her on-stage costume during the early part of her career; it was interpreted by many as irreverent, even blasphemous.

Many people wear their so-called "birthstone," to which folklore attributes good luck, according to their sign of the zodiac. In fact, the concept of the birthstone was introduced in the United States in 1912 by the predecessor of the Jewelers of America association and is matched to calendar months rather than the zodiac.

Another interesting development in ethnic jewelry is the growing number of firms making licensed copies or reproductions of museum pieces of jewelry. Museums around the world, from the State Historical Museum of Moscow, to the Vatican Library, to the Metropolitan Museum of Art in New York, are selling vast amounts of inexpensive reproductions of museum pieces in their stores and through catalogs. These pieces come from many different eras and many different cultures; what they have in common is that they have been preserved because of their beauty and power.

## Watches

The useful, dependable wristwatch is a relative newcomer to the 500-year history of mechanical timepieces. Nineteenth-century craftsmen made the pocket watch efficient—and a thing of beauty. In 1904, Louis-Joseph Cartier introduced the first modern wristwatch, the Santos-Dumont, named for a Brazilian aviator. By 1997, Cartier was selling 40,000 Santos-Dumonts a year! And by 2004, on its 100th anniversary, Cartier was selling over 100,000 Santos-Dumonts a year.[9]

There are three basic types of watches made today: the mechanical, the self-winding, and the quartz movement. Mechanical watches are driven by a balance wheel and powered by a spring, which must be hand wound. Automatic or self-winding watches wind themselves as the wearer moves a wrist. The quartz movement, invented in the 1970s, offers very accurate timekeeping at a low cost. Most quartz watches have removable batteries that last about one year.

Analog watches have faces with hands that sweep around the numbers "clockwise" (see Figure 13.31). Digital watches display the time in numbers, generally using a liquid crystal display (LCD). Extra features available in some watches include night-light buttons, calendars, moon-phase indicators, stopwatch (or chronograph) features, alarms, and chimes. Some watches also give the time in other countries or time zones. But watches

**FIGURE 13.31** These luxurious analog watches by Chanel, Piaget, and Louis Vuitton have unique designs, giving customers a fashionable way to tell time.

have always been a fashion statement as well as a useful device.

The inexpensive Timex watch of the 1960s, which "took a licking, but kept on ticking," broadened the market to include a huge number of people who could not afford even the mass-market watches of previous decades.

During the 1980s, Swatch made a splash in the market with its casual watches and has now spread its name and contemporary look into a number of other product categories such as jewelry. The Swatch lines have become so popular that some retailers have created Swatch boutiques. Other well-known companies include Movado, Fossil, and Armitron.

In the 1990s, many companies jumped onto the sports-watch bandwagon by adding resistance to water, wind, dust, shock, and magnetic fields.

Chronograph watches that measure small fractions of a second were best-sellers; some are used to measure speeds, distances, and altitudes.

There has never been a better time for luxury watches. Such statements come from most of the leading brands, from Rolex and Omega to Patek Philippe and Cartier, all of which consistently introduce new models. Officials from these firms, as well as from Tag Heuer, Hubot, Audemars Piquet, Ebel, Van Cleef & Arpels, Jaeger-LeCoultre, Baume & Mercier, Chaperel, de Grisogono, Bulgari, Chanel, Harry Winston, David Yurman, and Montblanc, all anticipate strong double-digit growth through 2012. Watches costing more than $100,000 were plentiful at the Jewelry & Watch Fair in Hong Kong, and timepieces costing in excess of $1 million emerged as the new benchmark for the extraordinary, largely because of demand from Asia, Russia, the Middle East, and the United States.[10]

At the other end of the market are children's watches. The Mickey Mouse watch for children was introduced in the 1930s. Today Timex makes watches for Disney, Joe Boxer, Nautica, and others. In 2001, Timex introduced TMXessories, a line aimed at tween and teen girls that includes colorful, decorative watches disguised as bangle bracelets, rings, and pendant necklaces. Armitron is another maker of cartoon-character watches, such as Tweety, Bugs Bunny, Garfield, and Scooby Doo. Mattel, the giant toy maker, has a line of Barbie watches.

But, have cell phones and iPods made watches obsolete? Many news and blog reports worldwide claim that the widespread use by young people of cell phones and iPods has reduced the interest in watches. By an overwhelming majority, manufacturers and retailers believe the watch business is thriving. They cite three reasons: fashion, status, and convenience.[11]

## Merchandising and Marketing

Jewelry manufacturers present their new styles and, in the case of costume jewelry manufacturers, their new lines at semiannual shows, JA New York, sponsored by the industry's trade association, the National Jewelers Network. One of the largest trade shows is the Accessories The Show, held in New York in January, May, and August. Other major trade associations include the American Gem Society, the Diamond Council of America, the Fashion Jewelry Trade Association, the Gemological Institute of America, and the Jewelers of America.

Fine-jewelry manufacturers traditionally have concentrated on providing a wide range of basic pieces, most notably, diamond rings and watches. They support their lines with a variety of services offered to stores. Some advertising assistance is offered, but this has not been common in a business where brand names have been relatively unknown. However, with the emergence of designer jewelry names, this is changing.

For all types of jewelry, but especially diamond rings, the Christmas holidays and Valentine's Day are especially busy. Birthdays and anniversaries provide a steady year-round business, while watches show a sales spurt around graduation time. The renewed popularity of vintage clothing in the 1990s led to a renewed interest in "estate pieces," or fine jewelry of earlier eras, still in its original settings.

Costume jewelry firms offer seasonal lines designed to coordinate with what is currently fashionable in apparel. Most costume jewelry is produced on a contract basis, which offers the advantage of fast turnaround on individual items. When a particular item is suddenly in demand, costume jewelry manufacturers can switch gears and produce it quickly in a large quantity. One example is the colorful beaded or carved pendant necklaces that exploded on the market in the summer of 2002, after similar styles had been sported by famous actresses and models on the pages of *People* and *InStyle* magazines.

The larger firms also market their goods under their nationally known brand names and advertise widely in national consumer publications. In addition, they offer cooperative advertising to retail outlets. Some manufacturers provide guidance and sales training to retailers.

Major jewelry store chains include the mall-oriented Zale's, Helzberg Diamond Shops, and the Fred Meyer chain. Tiffany's, Cartier, and Gumps occupy the high end of the market. Ross-Simons is a leading retailer-cataloger. Most department stores have extensive jewelry departments, carrying fine, bridge, and costume lines, with varying amounts of ethnic specialty items. Finlay Enterprises, Inc., operates over 800 leased shops, including those in Macy's, Lord & Taylor, Bloomingdale's, and Dillard's stores. Many thousands of small jewelry stores also exist across the country.

Industry research reveals that the largest segment of the jewelry market is women buying it for themselves. This has led the World Gold Council, among others, to advertise directly to women. Their strategy has paid off—women now buy 90 percent of all silver jewelry, 60 percent of all gold jewelry, and 30 percent of all platinum.[12] Retailers have also begun to focus their advertising on women. Zale's used the slogan, "Just because they're solitaires, doesn't mean you have to be alone when you wear them." The romantic TV ads that promote diamond anniversary gifts that "tell her you'd marry her all over again" are directed to men—and subliminally to women.

All retailers report increasing problems with balancing the need for displaying jewelry with the need for keeping it secure. Shoplifting and armed robbery are real threats. Special locked display cases, drawers, and vaults have been used increasingly in major cities worldwide, as have a number of small antitheft tags attached to the merchandise.

### Industry Trends

Today, all branches of the jewelry industry emphasize the production of designs that complement currently fashionable styles (see Figure 13.32). For example, when turtlenecks are popular, jewelry companies make long chains and pendants that

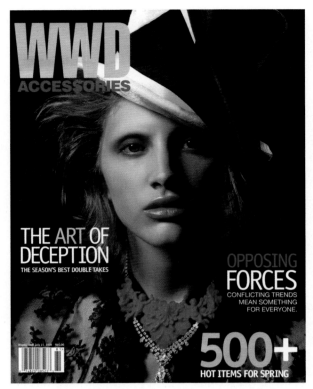

**FIGURE 13.32** *WWD Accessories* provides updates on the latest styles and trends in the accessories market.

look graceful on high necklines. When sleeveless dresses are in fashion, bracelets become an important piece of jewelry. When French cuffs are in fashion, both men and women wear cufflinks. When prints are popular, jewelry styles become tailored; but when solid or somber colors are popular, jewelry often moves to center stage with more complex designs and bright colors.

Masculine and unisex designs in gold chains, earrings, rings, shirt studs, nose studs, and fashion/sports watches are popular. More men are also wearing colored gemstones.

To compete with costume jewelry, which has gained broad acceptance over the past few decades, fine-jewelry companies have begun to diversify. Some have broadened their lines by moving into bridge jewelry. Others have also diversified into complementary nonjewelry areas. Swank, for example, which for years has manufactured men's small jewelry items, now produces colognes, sunglasses, travel accessories, and a variety of men's gifts.

Designer jewelry is another major market force,

especially in costume jewelry. Designers are thought to have been a major contributing factor to expanding sales. Chanel, Kenneth Cole, Anne Klein, Donna Karan, Yves Saint Laurent, Dior, Liz Claiborne, Givenchy, Pierre Cardin, and Ralph Lauren are some of the apparel designers who have been successful in licensing jewelry lines.

Celebrities, like Joan Rivers, Ivana Trump, and Heidi Klum, who sold more than 11,000 pieces of new jewelry on channel QVC in a half hour, have also launched successful jewelry lines that are sold on the TV home shopping networks. Television home shopping is the fastest-growing distribution channel for jewelry, because of its convenience and values, and because it lets the viewer see the item both up close and worn by a model, so the viewer gets a clear idea of its proportionate size.

## Other Accessories

There are many categories of accessories—and much variation within categories—from dress shoes to jellies, from briefcases to lunch boxes, from hard hats to snoods, from anklets to ankhs. Other ornaments, like ribbons, bows, feathers, and fabric flowers, come and go in popularity. The accessory maker needs to move quickly in and out of these trends (see Figure 13.33). Three other categories of accessories deserve mention; they are handkerchiefs, umbrellas, and hair ornaments.

That most functional of accessories—the handkerchief—has had its main function usurped by paper tissues. Today most women's handkerchiefs are produced in China or Japan, where they are a fashion item. Most men's handkerchiefs are packaged by the dozen (or baker's dozen—13) in all cotton or cotton-polyester blends. Some high-end stores provide monogramming for an additional charge. Silk "show" handkerchiefs, called pocket squares, are produced for both men and women. They are puffed casually, not worn square, like standard cotton handkerchiefs. Children's handkerchiefs are a novelty item.

**FIGURE 13.33** Different fashion accessories come and go with the trends.

## Trends in the Fashion Accessories Industries

For accessory manufacturers, being supporters of apparel fashions does not necessarily mean being followers. In fact, accessory manufacturers must often be fashion leaders. In the fashion business, which always moves in the fast lane, accessory manufacturers must move in a faster lane than anyone else. They have to be able to adapt or change a style in mid-season if that is what is required to stay on top of current trends.

### Market Weeks and Trade Shows

New accessory lines are shown during the five major fashion market weeks in New York so that merchants can buy a coordinated look. These include:

- Summer, January
- Transitional, March
- Fall, May
- Holiday, August
- Spring, November

In the United States, the Femme Show, held in New York's Javits Center in January, May, and September, is the largest trade show for accessories. The Fashion Jewelry World Expo and Providence Expo both take place in Rhode Island.[13] Paris Premiere Classe, the Fashion Accessories Trade Show, is held in Paris in March and October. These shows are a reflection of the growing importance of accessories to retailers and consumers.

### Retailing Accessories

Accessories are sold in every kind of store, ranging from the largest department stores to smaller boutiques to specialized stores carrying only one kind of accessory or a limited array of related accessories. Retailers have traditionally viewed accessories as impulse items—products that customers typically buy on the spur of the moment. A person who may not want to or is not able to update a wardrobe with the latest apparel styles each season can use accessories to look fashionable. As Denise Filchner, Accessories Coordinator at Macy's, says:

> Now, more than ever, accessories play a pivotal role in fashion. Today, accessories are accents on a background of ready-to-wear. They are meant to be noticed, not necessarily to match or even to blend, but to stand out for a more interesting look. Last year's little black dress is updated instantly with the latest patterns in textured hosiery. It's an easy and inexpensive way to take what you had and give it new life.[14]

Also, less expensive accessories are still purchased when there is price resistance to costlier items of apparel. Accessories are chosen because of their color, style, and newness or simply because one wants to give one's wardrobe—and spirits—a lift.

**FIGURE 13.34** Claire's sells less expensive accessories to a younger market.

In recognition of this "impulse" buying pattern, most department stores position accessories on the main floor, or near the door or cash register in the case of small stores. More recently, they have experimented successfully with outposts, small accessory departments located next to apparel departments, and with movable kiosks, or large carts.

Some stores have begun to feature one-stop shopping with boutiques (often stocked exclusively by one designer) that allow customers to buy everything they need—apparel and accessories—in one department. One-stop shopping has proven especially successful with working women who have little time to shop. It also appeals to the women who are a little unsure of themselves and like the added help that one-stop shopping provides in coordinating their outfits. Designer signature stores featuring apparel have become a mainstay.

Some chains, like Icing and Claire's, sell only accessories (see Figure 13.34). Some chains sell only subspecialties, like Tie Rack, which sell men's ties, or the Sunglass Hut. Many stores, of course, sell only shoes, or only jewelry. Catalogs are also increasingly popular places to sell accessories; every major apparel catalog also offers selected accessories. Specialty catalogers include Nature's Jewelry, Coldwater Creek, and Horchow. In addition, many catalogers selling accessories are on the Internet, like Ross-Simons. Other general merchandisers, from L. L. Bean to Spiegel to Talbots to the giant Service Merchandise, also offer substantial selections of accessories over the Internet.

## Summary and Review

Specific accessories wax and wane in popularity, but some accessories are always popular because most people do not consider themselves fully dressed until they have accessorized an outfit. In recent years, the business has boomed overall. Many people feel the accessory business, like many other fashion categories, has been given a boost by its association with designer names.

And the benefits are mutual. At the haute couture shows of Paris and Milan, the clothing has become the designer's fashion statement, and accessories have generated the financial support—as well as supporting the look of the season—to allow designers to experiment. Made-to-order gowns and ensembles are individually produced by hand, whereas accessories can be machine-made in larger numbers and sold at higher margins. Similarly, American ready-to-wear designers literally display their names or logos on licensed accessories such as belts, scarfs, caps, handbags, and sunglasses. For the purveyors of fashion as much as for the consumer, accessories support a complete, coordinated image. In addition, they are the source of a more attractive bottom line.

## Trade Talk

Define or briefly explain each of the following terms:

| | |
|---|---|
| alloyed | bridge jewelry |
| carat | costume or fashion jewelry |
| cut-up trade | electroplating |
| ethnic jewelry | millinery |
| minaudieres | outpost |
| personal goods | rack trade |
| readers | self belt |
| small leather goods | solid gold |
| sterling silver | synthetic stones |
| vermeil | |

## For Review

1. Why have U.S. shoe producers moved their factories offshore? How has this trend affected the footwear industry?
2. How do changes in lifestyle and activities affect the shoe industry? Give examples.
3. Describe the merchandising and marketing of handbags in the United States today.
4. What are the current trends in the millinery industry?
5. What are the major types of neckties sold today?
6. Why are shoe and fine-jewelry departments often leased?
7. What three metals are considered precious? What is the difference between solid gold and 14-karat gold?
8. What are the major gemstones used in the production of jewelry?
9. Give several examples of how women's apparel fashions influence jewelry fashions.
10. What categories of merchandise are to be found in fashion accessory departments today? In outposts?

## For Discussion

1. How has the increasing informality of dress in the last decade affected the accessories industries?
2. List each of the current important fashion accessory items and discuss why they are important to the total fashion look. At which stage of the fashion cycle is each item positioned? Give reasons for your answers.

# chapter fourteen

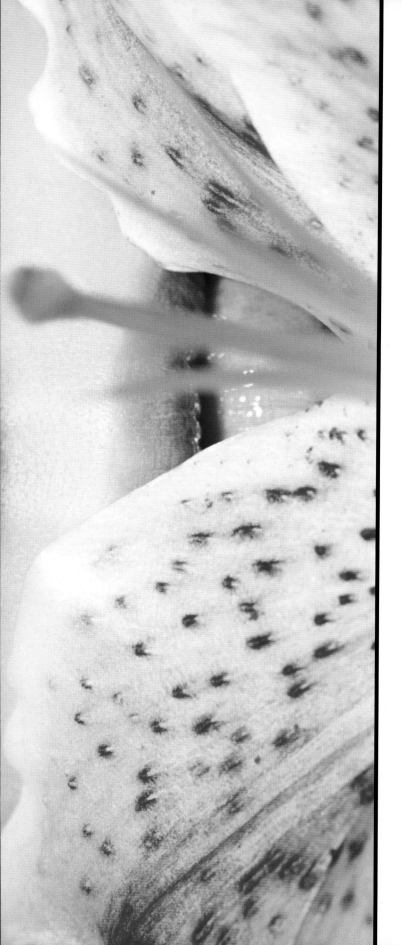

KEY CONCEPTS

- History and development of the cosmetics and fragrance industry
- Categories of cosmetics and fragrances
- Federal laws and environmental issues affecting cosmetics and fragrances
- Seven major market segments in the cosmetics and fragrance industry
- Distribution of mass and class cosmetics and fragrances
- Advertising and promotion of cosmetics and fragrances
- Trends in cosmetic and fragrance products

*Everything you always wanted to know about cosmetics and fragrances.*

# Cosmetics and Fragrances

To be or not to be?—that is the question. Should we be bemused, bothered, and bewildered about our looks? Or should we revel in the beauty that is natural and nurtured? Whichever way you choose, the cosmetics and fragrance industry will meet your needs and wants with exciting new colors and potions, in both exotic test-tube creations or drawn from the world's natural fauna and flora. This quest for beauty is hardly new. For thousands of years people have smeared themselves with lotions and potions of every kind in the hope of making themselves as attractive as possible (see Figure 14.1). As far back as 100 B.C., Cleopatra rubbed her face with lemon rinds, took milk baths, accentuated her eyes with kohl, and set her hair with mud. When Queen Elizabeth I of England died in 1603, her face was caked with a thick layer of chalk, the foundation of her day, which she wore to cover the pock marks of an early illness. Before modern hygiene dictated daily bathing, natural body odors were masked by perfumes. In the days of the Roman Empire, spices and scents were imported from Africa and Asia. A popular Greek scent called Susinum is evidence of the existence of brands.[1] In the American colonial era, Caswell-Massey, predecessor of the modern drugstore, sold cologne to then-colonel George Washington.

Today, the cosmetics and fragrance industry is big business and getting bigger. It turns out hundreds of new products annually, each of which must compete for a share of the market. These days, the fashion-apparel business plays an important role in building the business of the cosmetics industry. Many designers have introduced their own cosmetic and fragrance lines, and they often work with the cosmetic manufacturers to help them design new products that will coordinate with each season's new styles.

Thanks to the new link to designers' new season's styles, cosmetics, like fashion, are now cyclical. For example, when sports clothes are popular, and a no-makeup look is in, the cosmetics industry, eager to maintain sales, has learned to respond with appropriately low-key cosmetics and fresh, country-like scents. When bright colors and elaborate clothes are in style, the industry touts more makeup, brighter palettes, and heavier scents.

## History and Development of the Cosmetics and Fragrance Industry

For centuries, the pursuit of beauty was the prerogative of the rich. Special beauty aids concocted in temples, monasteries, alchemists' cells, and kitchens were available only to the privileged few. Makeup was called *maquillage*, and used only in court circles—and by the demimonde. Only in the past 75 years has the pursuit of beauty found its way into modern laboratories and brought with it an ability to manufacture and distribute cosmetics on a widespread basis for ordinary people. Max Factor, the Hollywood makeup artist, is credited with popularizing the terms *lipstick*, *makeup*, and *eye shadow* (see Figure 14.2). Before he made it respectable, nice girls just did not wear makeup.[2]

Although an elite segment of the market has survived, cosmetics and fragrances are now available to anyone who wants to use them. What were once luxuries are now viewed by many as necessities. This perception, in turn, has led to more innovation in mass production, advertising, and package design. The market has also become increasingly segmented as different kinds of cosmetics and scents are made available to customers based on their age, gender, ethnic group, lifestyle, and ability to pay.

### Dreams Versus Science

With the move to the laboratory came a new emphasis on the scientific development of cosmetics. Whereas for decades the word "moisturize"

FIGURE 14.1 Egyptians used kohl as eyeliner around the entire eyes and on their brows. Kohl was used to brighten and beautify the eyes as well as protect them from outside contaminants.

alone was enough to sell a skin cream, new, improved creams were now promoted for their abilities to "nourish" and "renew" the skin. Today, one takes a "daily dose" of skin care products, which are likely to be "pH-balanced." Cosmetics salespersons no longer help their customers select a make-up shade; they are trained technicians who can "diagnose" the customer's needs and prescribe the right "formula." Fragrances, too, are regarded with a more scientific approach despite the romantic allure that is attached to their use. One way of keep-

ing down costs of mass-merchandised fragrances is the laboratory production of synthetic substitutes for expensive natural ingredients.

Until the 1960s, most women's use of colored makeup was limited. The development of easy-to-apply powders, gels, and glosses and the marketing of attractive packages brought about a change of buying habits. Estée Lauder's promotional brainstorm, offering a gift sample with a cosmetics purchase, is still a popular way of luring customers to the cosmetics counter.

The 1970s saw the emergence of *natural* products made from such ingredients as aloe vera, honey, musk, almonds, and henna. Incense moved beyond the "head shop" into respectability. The trend toward natural cosmetics in the 1980s turned into a full-blown consumer preoccupation with health and self-image. The new emphasis was on the protective aspects of cosmetics. The buying public began to seek products that maintained and protected their skin rather than merely enhanced them cosmetically. Skin care products became the fastest-growing segment of the cosmetics industry. Although fashion and beauty have remained the driving force behind most cosmetics sales in the 1990s, more consumers than ever before are willing to spend money for products that enhance their overall health.

In the early 2000s, every year saw more than 100 women's and men's scents being launched. According to the Fragrance Foundation in New York, a good share of them were celebrity- and designer-branded potions (see Figure 14.3). Among them were Kylie Minogue's Darling, Marc Jacobs's Splash Cucumber, Michael Kors's Island Hawaii, and Tom Ford's line of a dozen unisex fragrances sporting names like Purple Patchouli, Tuscan Leather, and Velvet Gardenia. Mary Ellen Lapansky, executive director of the Fragrance Foundation, said, "We're seeing lush, full-bodied, women's fragrances, to focus on the floral, that are heavily concentrated and longer-lasting and make a statement." She drew a distinction between current blends and the sometimes-overpowering

FIGURE 14.2 Max Factor demonstrating his product with Clara Bow, American actress, at the St Louis Exposition, 1920s.

scents of the 1980s. "No one should smell you beyond your scent circle," she said.[3]

## Legends Versus the New Entrepreneurs

The cosmetics and fragrance industry has always been dominated by personalities, a trait that shows little sign of abating. What has changed is the nature of the personalities and their purposes in their businesses.

An early worldwide celebrity associated with fragrance was Coco Chanel. More than 75 years ago, she introduced a perfume that, despite its unpretentious name, became associated with designer fashion: Chanel No. 5 (see Figure 14.4). Decades later, another French designer linked fragrance with designer fashion; he was Christian Dior. His Miss Dior accompanied his famous post–World War II New Look.

But the big names in cosmetics and fragrances were not all French. From the 1950s through the 1970s, a few flamboyant personalities in the United States, most notably, Elizabeth Arden, Helena Rubinstein, Max Factor, and Estée Lauder, dominated the industry and virtually dictated its shape and scope. Less well known but equally innovative were Dorothy Gray, Hazel Bishop, and Harriet Hubbard Ayer. The drive, intuition, foresight, and promotional ability of these pioneers is still felt in the industry and has rarely been duplicated in other industries. By the mid-1980s, most of the companies founded by these individuals had become public corporations or part of multinational conglomerates.

Only Estée Lauder survived with her beauty empire still intact and run by her personally (see Figure 14.5). This famous "nose" personally developed her fragrance lines while overseeing her cosmetics empire. Instead of being swallowed up by a larger organization, she built her own conglomerate with the Aramis, Clinique, and Prescriptives brands. Not until 1995, after she had turned man-

Roberts, Mary Kay Ash, and Don Bochner, soon emerged. Unlike the old stars, though, these new entrepreneurs relied less on personality and more on sound business strategies. In England, Anita Roddick opened her first Body Shop in 1976, making environmental protection the guiding force of her business decisions.

A third generation of cosmetics personalities includes the late Frank Toskan of the Canadian firm MAC (Make-up Art Cosmetics) and Bobbi Brown. Besides being makeup artists for the fashion industry who brought their expertise to the public, Brown and Toskan had in common their parent company, Estée Lauder.

## Organization and Operation of the Industry

The cosmetics and fragrance industry has undergone significant changes in recent years in terms of its organization and operation. Once made up entirely of many small firms, none of which controlled a significant share of the market, it is now dominated by a few huge, global firms that command large market shares. Although the industry still supports 600 companies, many are now owned by conglomerates that also produce other consumer goods, such as processed foods, health care products, and household cleaners. The largest companies in the world with holdings in the cosmetics and fragrance industry are L'Oréal, in which Nestlé has a substantial interest; Procter & Gamble; Unilever; and Estée Lauder. Complicating the issues are licensing of designer brands and cosmetics, and the constant changes in mergers, sales, and acquisitions that take place according to changes in the market and the economy. For example, in 2000, Unilever entered a 5-year-growth strategy that would reduce its brands from 1,600 to 400.[4] In 2000, Unilever sold its Elizabeth Arden division to FFI Fragrances, and in 2002 announced that it was selling off its entire upmarket fragrance business (including Calvin Klein, Nautica, Vera Wang, Chloé, and Karl Lagerfeld) to concentrate on core high-yield brands.

**FIGURE 14.5** Estée Lauder, Inc. (top) was founded by Estée Lauder (bottom), one of the first-generation superstars of the American cosmetics industry.

agement of the company over to her son, did it go public, and even then, the family retained control of 85 percent of the stock.

The cosmetics industry seems destined to be run by personalities, and a second generation, with names like Adrien Arpel, Madeleine Mono, Christine Valmy, Georgette Klinger, Merle Norman, Flori

# Fashion

Fashion

## A Game of Musical Celebs
### Sing a
### Song of
### Scent

It may seem that hitching your star to the celebrity wagon is a wonderful idea, given the public's fascination with fame and fortune. But star power does not guarantee a blockbuster! Remember Cher's fragrance? Or Linda Evans's? Well, maybe! In 2002, Jennifer Lopez's Glow by JLO ignited a celebrity fragrance craze, and her scent stayed a bestseller for 12 months, but then quietly disappeared. With more and more musical artists jumping into the fragrance business, it feels like companies and pop stars are pairing off in an industry of musical chairs. Maybe their talent for singing sweet notes gives them an extra-sensatory talent for fragrance notes.

Jennifer Hudson for
IMARI
SEDUCTION

Where desire leads

IMARI
SEDUCTION

Exclusively from

AVON
Call Your Avon Representative 800-FOR-AVON
or visit avon.com/jenniferhudson

| Celebrity | Company | Fragrance Name |
|---|---|---|
| Beyoncé | Emporia Armani | Diamonds |
| Jennifer Hudson | Avon | Imari |
| Gwen Stefani | Coty | L, L.A.M.B. |
| Prince | Revelations Perfume | 3121 |
| Usher | Liz Claiborne Cosmetics | Usher for Men and Women |
| | | |
| Kylie Minogue | Coty | Darling |
| Sean "Diddy" Combs | Estée Lauder | Unforgivable for Men and Women |

Left page: Gwen Stefani's L fragrance (top center); Jennifer Hudson's Imari Seduction for Avon (bottom left); Mariah Carey at the launch of her fragrance M by Mariah Carey (bottom right); Right page: Gwen Stefani's Harajuku Girls fragrance.

The World of
HARAJUKU ♥ LOVERS
FRAGRANCE

Following this strategy, Unilever unveiled plans in 2002 to enter the hair color market with a major new product launch, and compete with L'Oréal and Procter & Gamble, which had previously owned the bulk of the hair color market.[5]

## A Global Business

The joining of cosmetics and fragrance firms in multinational conglomerates is part of the same trend that is manifested in the changing role of heads of companies from product development artists to master marketers. The giant parent companies can offer their cosmetics and fragrance industry subsidiaries clout and expertise in the consumer marketplace. As packaging, promotion, and distribution become as much a part of the product as the ingredients, the giant corporations develop global marketing strategies to get each product line into the hands of its targeted group of consumers.

Western Europe has a global cosmetics and fragrance industry of its own. Their marketing practices are similar to those in the United States, with subsidiaries and lines catering to various market segments. For example, German-based Wella, known for its hair care products, has expanded by acquiring a fragrance company and developing new lines within the subsidiary's brands. In 2002, Wella boosted its Parfums Rochas subsidiary division by acquiring the Escada Beauty Group.[6]

## The Main Categories

All large, nationally advertised cosmetics firms produce hundreds of items. For sales and inventory purposes, products must thus be divided into broad categories. The typical order form of one large firm, for example, lists all the company's products, in the various sizes or colors available, under end-use categories such as:

- Fragrances
- Color cosmetics (facial makeup, including lip and cheek color, eye makeup, and liquid and powder foundations)

- Skin care
- Sun care
- Nail care
- Hair care

If a firm produces men's as well as women's cosmetics, each of the two lines is given its own distinctive brand name, and, of course, separate sales and inventory records are kept for each brand line. We discuss all but hair care in more detail.

Because of fashion and product obsolescence, as well as customer boredom, manufacturers are constantly updating and shipping new items to keep cosmetics customers buying new products, or new colors, or both. Manufacturers update formulas when they become aware of new technology and new ingredients to improve their products.

A system of product returns, unique to the cosmetics industry, aids the retailer in keeping the inventory current. The industry refers to this system as **rubber-banding**, which means that cosmetic products not sold within a specified period of time may be returned to the manufacturer to be replaced with others that will sell. This guarantees that the cosmetics retailer will never have to take a markdown on this merchandise. Only if a cosmetics company is discontinuing an item does it permit markdowns by a store. (Other industries allow returns to vendors only for damages, over shipments, or wrong shipment.)

## Fragrances

The term **fragrance** includes (in increasing order of strength, lasting power, and price) cologne, toilet water, eau de parfum, and perfume. Other forms of fragrances are spray perfume, after-shave lotion, and home fragrances. Scents are also added to other beauty products, such as soap, shampoo, bubble bath, and hand and body lotions, but the items in the fragrance category are designed specifically to enhance the smell of the person wearing them.

The scent of a fragrance is a combination of essential oils, often from plants, including a variety of trees, flowers, grasses, herbs and spices, and edible extracts—like the very popular vanilla. Other scents are concocted in the perfumer's laboratory. Each scent is called a **note**, and, like musical notes, they vary in strength and duration. The perfumer, like the composer, combines them in a harmonious whole. Alcohol carries the scent to the skin. The more alcohol, the less concentrated the fragrance.

Fragrances are affected by the body chemistry of the wearer; they may smell different on different people or even on the same person at different times. Table 14.1 lists the top five women and men's fragrances found in department stores. For example, diet may make one's skin more or less oily, and fragrance is more intense on oily skin. In addition, the scent of a single application of a fragrance changes over time. Virginia Bonofiglio, who teaches in the unique Fragrance Knowledge course at the Fashion Institute of Technology in New York, describes "three major stages in the life of a perfume":

First, the top note—what you smell when you take a whiff from a bottle—usually a citrus or green smell, which lasts about fifteen minutes on the skin. Then the middle note, often a floral or wood, which lasts three to four hours. And finally the bottom note, usually a musk or vanilla, which lasts four to five hours.[7]

Cosmetics manufacturers produce fragrances with their own brand names and, under licensing agreements, the names of designers and celebrities. Tommy and Tommy Girl, Tommy Hilfiger's fragrance lines, are manufactured by Estée Lauder, which also produces, under its own name, (such scents as Beautiful, Pleasures, and Youth Dew) and, under the names of its subsidiaries, Aramis and Clinique's Happy Aromatics, among others.

Continual innovation in fragrances is necessary to maintain growth in a fashion-conscious market. As many as 100 new fragrances may be launched in a season in various concentrations. Fragrances are

**FIGURE 14.6** Fragrances often come in a range of sizes and intensities.

**TABLE 14.1** *Top 5 Scents for Men and Women*

| TOP MEN'S SCENTS | TOP WOMEN'S SCENTS |
| --- | --- |
| 1. John Varvatos | 1. Chanel Coco Mademoiselle |
| 2. HM by Hanae Mori | 2. Ralph Lauren Romance |
| 3. L'Eau d'Issey Pour Homme | 3. Max Azria BCBGirls |
| 4. Armani Black Code | 4. Lancôme Trésor |
| 5. Armani Acqua Di Gio Pour Homme | 5. Michael by Michael Kors |

also bottled in a range of sizes, making even expensive perfumes available to a larger market (see Figure 14.6).

Perfumes are worn predominantly by women 25 to 44 years old—a group that is both fashion-conscious and affluent enough to buy this luxury product. Toilet waters and colognes, also worn by the aforementioned group on informal occasions, have great appeal for younger women because they are lower priced. They appeal to men because they are more subtle than most perfumes. These lower-priced products also are used to entice the male or female customer from any economic level to try a new product.

## Color Cosmetics

The term **color cosmetics** usually refers to facial makeup; nail color is categorized with other nail care products. Color is the primary feature of facial makeup, but the substance into which the pigment is mixed is also important. The oils, wax, and talc that are used in the bases of color cosmetics affect the wearer's skin and the finish of the makeup. The pigments also interact with the ingredients in the bases, so manufacturing products that are consistent from batch to batch require a well-equipped factory staffed by experts.

Lip coloring is produced in the form of lipstick and solid or gel-like glosses. It may be opaque or transparent, and the finish may be matte, glossy, or even glittery. This variety and the range of colors allows for mixing to achieve a look suitable to the occasion and the colors in one's outfit. A smash hit

in 2002 were the triplet launches of Outlast from Revlon, Lipfinity from Max Factor, and Endless from L'Oréal. All three products were variations on lip color and gloss combinations that stayed on all day, even during activities such as eating or kissing.

Liquid, gel, and powder blushes, in addition to the more traditional rouge, provide similar variety in cheek color cosmetics. Liquid and powder foundations not only give the skin an even surface and color; the various formulations provide skin care for dry, oily, and normal skin.

Eye makeup, especially eye shadow, is available in a broad range of colors, not all of them natural, to set off this most expressive facial feature.

Estée Lauder, Lancôme, and Clinique are called "The Big Three" because they dominate color cosmetics. In addition to these prestige lines, mass-marketed color cosmetics manufacturers are influential in certain product categories, although most produce the full range. For example, Cover Girl, a division of Procter & Gamble, is noted for foundations, while Maybelline, a subsidiary of L'Oréal, is a big name in eye makeup. See Table 14.2 for a list of the top ten cosmetic companies.

## Skin Care

Soap, long the basis of skin care, is no longer the only product used for bathing. In a market that is constantly demanding new choices, alternatives to the familiar bar of soap are turning a bath or shower into a new experience. Bar soap is still the largest selling product for bathing, but the growth of sales is challenged by liquid soap, syndet bars (Dove, among others), and body washes and gels. The

**TABLE 14.2** *Top 10 Cosmetic Companies*

| COMPANY | SUBSIDIARIES/ MAIN BRANDS |
|---|---|
| **L'Oréal** Clichy, France | Pléntitude, Féria, Elséve, Garnier, Maybelline, Club des Créateurs de Beauté, La Scad, Laboratoires Ylang, Lancôme, Biotherm, Parfums Armani, Cacharel, Ralph Lauren Fragrances, Paloma Picasso, Kiehl's, Guy Laroche, Vichy, La Roche-Possay, Shu Uemura, Technique Professionnelle, Kérastase, Redken, Inné, Matrix, Galderma, Soft Sheen Carson, The Body Shop |
| **Procter & Gamble** Cincinnati, Ohio | Cover Girl, Max Factor, Clairol, Olay, Hugo Boss, Pantene, Physique, Vidal Sassoon, Infusium 23, Aussie, SK II, Old Spice, Head & Shoulders, Herbal Essences, Noxzema, Pert Plus |
| **Unilever PLC** London/Rotterdam | Unilever HPC: Axe, Impulse, Rexona, Dove, Lux, Pond's, Vaseline, Suave, Sunsilk, Organics, Thermasilk, Unilever Cosmetics International: Calvin Klein, Contradiction, Calvin Klein Color, Cerruti, Lagerfeld, Chloé, Valentino, 1881, Cerruti Image, Vendetta, Nautica, BCBG Max Azria, Vera Wang |
| **The Estée Lauder Cos. Inc.** New York | Estée Lauder, Prescriptives, Stila, Clinique, Origins, Bobbi Brown, MAC Cosmetics, Jane, La Mer, Aramis, Jo Malone, Tommy Hilfiger, Aveda, Bumble and Bumble, Donna Karan, Kate Spade Beauty, Darphin, Michael Kors, Fragrances |
| **Shiseido Co. LTD** Tokyo | Shiseido The Makeup, Shiseido The Skincare, Cle de Peau Beatue, Carita, Joico, Benefiance, Pureness, Vital Perfection, Shiseido Suncare, Shiseido Hair Care, BOP, Eudermine, Relaxing Fragrance, Energizing Fragrance, ZEN, IPSA, Ettusais, 5S, FSP, Za, FT Shiseido |
| **Avon Products Inc.** New York | Anew, Avon Color, Skin-So-Soft, Avon Solutions, Advanced Techniques Hair Care, Avon Wellness, Mark |
| **Beiersdorf AG** Hamburg, Germany | Nivea, 8x4, Atrix, Labello, Basis PH, Juvena, Personal Skin Collections, Rejuven Q10, Body Results, Sunsation, Discover, Color Cosmetics, La Prairie, Hidrofugal, Eucerin, Florena |
| **Johnson & Johnson** New Brunswick, NJ | Neutrogena, Aveeno, RoC, Clean & Clear, Johnson's (baby skin and hair care), Renova, Retin-A, Ambi, Biapharm |
| **Alberto-Culver** Melrose Park, IL | Alberto VO5, TRESemm, Consort, St. Ives Swiss Formula, TCB, Soft & Beautiful, Just for Me, Comb-Thru, Motions, Family Fresh. |
| **Limited Brands** Columbus, OH | Victoria's Secret Beauty, Bath & Body Works, White Barn Candle Co. |

Source: "Beauty's Top 70." *Beauty Biz.* September 8, 2006.

washes and gels are marketed as a way of avoiding the skin-drying effects of soap; they rely on mild detergents for cleansing, and net puffs packaged with the product help to make bathing an invigorating experience (see Figure 14.7).

Perhaps because bathing is a routine daily activity rather than a luxury, mass-merchandise products sold at low price point are at the forefront of the market. Some popular brands of washes are White Rain and Caress. Prestige products are also being marketed. Procter & Gamble, Gillette, Colgate Palmolive, Nivea, and Unilever all offer body washes (without puffs) targeted to men in Europe.

Of course, the skin care category is wider than just soap or soap substitutes. It includes hand, face, foot, and body lotions, as well as creams, scrubs, masks, moisturizers, and anticellulite treatments. The enormous impact of alpha hydroxy acids (AHAs) on these products cannot be overestimated. This emerging segment of skin care products is based on dermatology and promises to correct the visible signs of aging and promote new cell growth. (See the discussion under Federal Laws, later in

**FIGURE 14.7** Washes, gels, and lotions help avoid the skin-drying effects of soap.

this chapter.) The addition of antibacterial agents to skin care products is discussed later in this chapter under Trends, as is the antiallergenic versions of these products.

## Sun Care

Sun care has become a major category of the cosmetics industry, as consumers have become increasingly aware of the health dangers—and aging effects—of the sun's rays. As a result, even the prestige manufacturers have rushed to produce a wide range of scientifically formulated sun products. An important feature of a sunscreen is its SPF, or sun protection factor. The SPF number, which indicates how long the screen will protect the wearer from burning, may go as high as 45, but most people are adequately protected by a sunscreen with an SPF of 15.

What once was a category dominated by drug stores and mass merchants has now become a major business for department stores as well. Despite the efforts of the medical community, most consumers continue to get too much sun. To keep them protected, marketers have rolled out an array of new products: sunless tanning lotions, sprays, and foams (see Figure 14.8). They are waterproof, hypoallergenic, quick-drying, non-greasy, and oil-free and are claimed to provide broad-spectrum UVA/UVB protection.[8]

Product innovation, in conjunction with consumers' growing concern about sun damage, has fueled the sunless tanner market in the United States and will continue to do so over the next few years. Driving the growth in the sunless tanner category is an increase in consumer awareness that dangerous rays not only can be deadly but also can damage the skin and cause signs of aging. It is no secret that today's beauty shopper desperately wants to ward off future wrinkles and diminish the ones she already has. A recent release by Pennsylvania Medical Society's Health and Wellness division quoted dermatologist John Faskas Jr. as saying, "There is no such thing as a healthy tan. UV rays can kill you.... If you're bald,

**FIGURE 14.8** Neutrogena's sunless tanning products allow you to get a tan without the harmful rays of the sun.

wear a hat, and if you absolutely have to be tan, try some of the new self-tanning products to get that 'golden glow.'"[9]

## Nail Care

Nail care products really took off in the 1990s; according to industry experts, nail polish became a $350 million-a-year market. In addition to transparent nail enamels and colors echoing the range of lipstick colors, dramatic blues, greens, blacks, and yellows are now available for women—and men. The rapid growth of the 1990s flamboyant nail care trend launched a new slew of independent, style-savvy nail care companies like Hard Candy and Urban Decay. These companies specialized in funky colors and provocative product names like Libido and Pothole.

An equally flamboyant style of nail decoration is artificial nails, available in a selection of lengths, shapes, and colors. A popular brand is Flo Jo, named for the late Florence Griffith-Joyner, the Olympic champion runner, who pioneered the decorated fingernail style. Independent nail salons, where manicures are not merely a service added on to hair care, have sprung up around the country. In these salons, one can acquire a set of nails painted in multicolor designs, including gold decorations.

## Packaging

Packaging plays a vital role in marketing fragrances and cosmetics (see Figure 14.9). Often it is the pack-

age rather than the contents that leads the customer to buy one product over another. Manufacturers have historically tried for unique packaging. In the early 1900s, when Coty perfume was the most expensive in France, Coty tried to get the exclusive rights to a newly invented—and enormously expensive—packaging material: cellophane.[10]

It often seems that the bottle and packaging take on incredible significance. In the next decade, according to the Fragrance Foundation, for every $100,000 in expected gross sales, a manufacturer should plan to spend $20,000 on the bottle (and the perfume in it) and $35,000 on advertising and promotion. An interesting example of a successful perfume marketing concept where the bottle played a vital role is Parfums Christian Dior's blockbuster scent J'Adore. Launches in 1999, at a time when best-selling fragrances were packaged in minimalist bottles like CK and cK One, J'Adore set a new trend with a voluptuous amphora-shaped bottle with a golden Masai-like "collar" around the neck. Patrick Choel, president of the Perfumes and Cosmetics Division at LVMH, which released J'Adore, claims that the bottle is actually more important than the juice itself.[11]

Efforts to preserve natural resources by recycling packaging materials have had a mixed influence on the packaging of cosmetics and fragrances. (See Recyclable Packaging later in this chapter.)

## *Private-Label Manufacturers*

Although dominated by giant producers of nationally advertised brand lines, the industry has many private-label manufacturers, producing merchandise to specification under the brand names of chain stores, mass merchants, department stores, small independent stores and hair salons, and direct-to-the-home marketers (see Figure 14.10). The famous scent Giorgio was born in the Rodeo Drive Giorgio store. It was such a success that, although an original private label, it is now sold in fine stores from coast to coast. Competitors Avon

**FIGURE 14.9** Some customers may purchase Jean-Paul Gaultier (top) and the Fendi (bottom) fragrances for the packaging alone.

**FIGURE 14.10** Bond No. 9 teamed up with the Andy Warhol Foundation to produce the Andy Warhol-inspired fragrances sold at their boutiques and Saks Fifth Avenue.

Products and Mary Kay Cosmetics both sell products produced and packaged for them by the same private-label manufacturer.

Some of the better-known private-label manufacturers are Kolmar Laboratories of Port Jervis, New York; Quest International of Mount Olive, New Jersey; Douglas Cosmetics of Westport, Connecticut; and Private Label Cosmetics of Fair Lawn, New Jersey. Kolmar sells mass quantities to large users, but not all private-label producers are big enough to meet large orders. Small private-label manufacturers, such as Olin (a division of the House of Westmore), supply small distributors. A beauty salon owner can walk into a private-label distributor's office, and in less than ten days and for about $500, have a complete private-label line in his or her shop. Or a dermatologist may want a private-label line of products to sell to patients. However, this line is based on what the private-label house has already been manufacturing. Private-label manufacturers do not develop new products for individual clients.

Retailers get little help from their private-label suppliers. Private-label firms do not share advertising costs, provide gift-with-purchase offers, or accept returns.

A serious threat to the private-label industry is posed by federal ingredient-label requirements. Packaging is usually kept to a minimum by private-label firms in order to keep prices low. To get the government-required ingredient label on a small lipstick, however, an additional package is required. Through its lobbying group, the Independent Cosmetic Manufacturers and Distributors Association, the private-label industry is fighting labeling requirements.

## Copycat Scents

The conspicuous consumption of expensive designer fragrances in the 1980s gave rise to a new industry segment, producers of **copycat scents**. These products are unabashed imitations of the packaging as well as the aromas of popular designer fragrances. Comparison advertising highlights the price difference to assure customers who cannot afford the prestige brand that they are getting value for their dollar. In the more economically cautious 1990s, copycats thrived in mass-merchandise and off-price outlets, flea markets, and direct mail. Knockoff fragrances that appeal to young consumers, such as cK One and Tommy, have fared especially well.

The leading producers of fragrances have been fighting this "copycat" category. There have been many lawsuits, and the international courts have upheld copyright lawsuits for the first time. A court in the Netherlands has ruled that a fragrance called Female Treasure, marketed by Dutch company Kecofa, is so similar to Lancôme's Trésor that it constitutes a deliberate and unlawful copy infringement. A court in Paris handed down a similar judgment against Belgian company Bellure for imitating the composition of twelve L'Oréal fragrances, including Trésor, Miracle, Anaïs Anaïs, Drakkar

# &Then
# NOW

## Mission Possible
### CEW Builds
### *Leaders*

Cosmetic Executive Women, Inc., commonly known as CEW, has more than 4,000 members in the beauty, cosmetics, fragrance, and related industries, not including more than 500 members in France and the United Kingdom, comprising the most talented women in the industry. A lot has changed since CEW's formation in 1954, but now, what remains is a dedication to developing the careers of women working in the cosmetics industry with Access, Advancement, and Achievement.

As a result of the enormous growth in membership, CEW conducted extensive research to better understand new members and identify programming that would address their critical issues. The results established that CEW now has three distinct generations of members: entry level, mid-career, and senior executives, each with unique needs.

Young executives increased from 12 percent of the membership to one-third in 3 years. CEW found that these young people were looking for jobs, connections, and exposure. As a result of that information, CEW created special events that encourage making new contacts. Their Speed Networking events ensure that each member makes five or six new connections.

Members in the middle-management group are looking for an "edge," the advantage that will help them get to the next level in their careers. The Women in Beauty Series and the new CEW Learning Communities support professional development by focusing on peer-to-peer access and learning opportunities.

The social aspect comes back into play at the senior level.

CEW provides high-level executives with opportunities to reconnect with colleagues, meet other senior women, and give back to the industry.

CEW offers more than sixty programs, including its Young Executive Parties, Women in Beauty Series, Speed Networking events, Learning Communities, Newsmaker Forums, Beauty Awards Programs, Achievers Awards, and Holiday Luncheon and Auction. One of the biggest issues facing the beauty industry today is finding talent. CEW sees this need as an opportunity to address the industry's problem and serve its members at the same time.

The Beauty Career Center is an important resource connecting women with cosmetic companies. The key to the success of the site is its exclusivity—the CEW career center is the only Web site dedicated to listing cosmetic industry jobs.

The Beauty Career Center offers a number of unique services, such as anonymous resume posting, an online library of articles, one-on-one coaching, and career advice. The Beauty Career Center also serves as a reflection of the job market as a whole, allowing members to see companies in a competitive framework.

Noir, Emporio Armani, and Ralph Lauren Romance.

These judgments mark the first time courts in European Union (EU) member states—and possibly the world—have ruled that a fragrance could be protected by copyright, just like other original works of authorship, such as music or artwork.[12]

### Federal Laws

Because chemicals are the basis for most cosmetic products, the Food and Drug Administration (FDA) is the federal agency that polices and regulates the cosmetics industry. The Federal Trade Commission defines a **cosmetic** as any article other than soap that is intended to be "rubbed, poured, sprinkled, or sprayed on, introduced into, or otherwise applied to the human body for cleansing, beautifying, promoting attractiveness, or altering the appearance without affecting the body's structure or functions."[13]

Manufacturers are prevented by FDA regulations from using potentially harmful ingredients and from making exaggerated claims regarding the effects of their products. An example of the results of these regulations is the use of **alpha hydroxy acids (AHAs)**—which are extracted from fruits, vegetables, and sugar cane—in facial creams intended to prevent wrinkles. When they were introduced in 1994, AHAs came under federal scrutiny as the FDA considered whether to regulate their use as a drug. Drugs are subject to time-consuming independent tests of their potency and possible harmful side effects, which can delay approval to market a product. In manufacturers' tests, AHAs showed effectiveness, but while they awaited the FDA's decision, many producers limited the amount of AHAs in their product so that they could sell it as a cosmetic. Ultimately, the FDA decided not to regulate products with AHAs as drugs.[14]

The 1938 Federal Food, Drug, and Cosmetic Act was the first federal law controlling cosmetics. It prohibited the adulteration and misbranding of cosmetics. Amendments added to the law in 1952 made it more stringent. More amendments in 1960 required government review and approval of the safety of color additives used in cosmetics.

The Fair Packing and Labeling Act of 1966 prohibits unfair or deceptive methods of packaging and labeling. This act covers many consumer industries in addition to the cosmetics industry. All cosmetics labeled since April 15, 1977, must bear a list of their ingredients in descending order of weight. To help identify potentially dangerous ingredients for manufacturers, the Cosmetic Ingredient Review, an independent research group funded by the industry trade organization, the Personal Care Products Council (the Council) [formerly the Cosmetic, Toiletry and Fragrance Association (CTFA)], was established in the early 1980s.

In any event, the major ingredients of most cosmetics in any price range do not vary much and mostly consist of fats, oils, waxes, talc, alcohol, glycerin, borax, coloring matter, and perfumes.

Constant surveillance by consumer and industry groups and advisory boards keeps the cosmetics industry sensitive to product liability. The FDA Modernization Act of 1997 focused on modernizing the regulation of medical products, food, and cosmetics. This act includes provisions for global harmonization of standards. Since the European Federation of Associations of Health Products Manufacturers (EHPM) has more stringent standards than the United States does, U.S. manufacturers expect to be required to register their products and formulas and to establish their safety before selling them to the European customer.

The Campaign for Safe Cosmetics, a coalition of health and environmental organizations, has been pressuring personal-care product and cosmetics companies to phase out chemicals they say have been linked to cancer, birth defects, and other health problems for several years. This effort has aided a newly enacted California chemical ingredient disclosure law for cosmetics and a 2007 EU policy requiring all companies, including cosmetic firms that produce or use chemicals, to collect extensive data on possible human health risks of the substances.

The consumer coalition has persuaded about 500 companies to sign a compact agreeing to remove all toxic chemicals and replace them with safer alternatives. Many of the companies are part of the "natural products" industry, including the Body Shop, Burt's Bees, Avalon Natural Products, and Aubrey Organics. But the coalition has met resistance from the big names in cosmetics and personal care products, including Estée Lauder, Revlon, Chanel, Clinique, L'Oréal, Unilever, and Procter & Gamble.[15]

## Environmental Concerns

Environmentalism, as a major issue of political and social concern, has had a strong effect on consumer buying habits and on industry practices to meet consumer's demands. Attention to health and fitness influences what people are willing to put on their skin and hair, so a demand for natural products and ingredients has arisen in the cosmetics and fragrances industry, just as it has in the food industry. Consumers are also becoming more educated about the effects of their behavior on natural resources.

### Natural or Botanical Products

Although everything on earth has a chemical composition, many people prefer products made from substances grown by nature to products produced by chemists in a laboratory (see Figure 14.11). The cosmetic and therapeutic benefits of essential oils derived from plants prove that Mother Nature's recipes are effective, and many consumers do not believe that scientists can improve upon—or even equal—these ingredients. Perhaps there is also a connection in some people's minds between the natural look in today's fashion and natural ingredients in the cosmetics that help them achieve that look.

Table 14.3 lists some oils that are harvested from nature for use in cosmetics. Some companies, notably The Body Shop, Aveda, and Origins, use only natural ingredients in their cosmetics. Adding

**FIGURE 14.11** Aveda and Kiehl's sell organic products that are good for the environment and your skin.

**TABLE 14.3** *Some Popular Oils Used in Cosmetics*

| OIL | COSMETICS IN WHICH IT IS USED |
| --- | --- |
| Aloe leaf gel | Sun care products, shampoos, hair rinses |
| Apricot kernel oil | Hair preparations, bath oils |
| Avocado oil | Burn treatments, shaving cream |
| Babassu oil | Skin care products, suntan products |
| Black currant seed oil | Treatments for dry skin |
| Borage oil | Moisturizers |
| Castor oil | Lipstick |
| Cocoa butter | Sun care products |
| Coconut oil | Shampoo |
| Djarak oil | Products to treat skin diseases and wounds, products to promote hair growth |
| Groundnut oil | Skin cleansers |
| Japan wax | Makeup sticks, mascara |
| Jojoba oil | Sun care products |
| Keku nut oil | Treatments for dry skin, sunburn, and acne prevention; conditioning shampoos |
| Kiwi oil | Products to support cell growth |
| Macadamia nut oil | Baby oil |
| Mexican poppy oil | Treatments for dry skin |
| Sea buckthorn oil | Antiaging preparations |
| Wheat germ oil | Hair and skin care products |

AVOCADO · BLACK CURRANT · COCONUT · MACADAMIA NUT

## Animal Testing

The issue of testing cosmetic and fragrance formulas on animals to ensure that they are safe for human use reached the height of controversy in the late 1970s when animal rights activists protested the testing of eye makeup on rabbits. Outraged that animals should be subjected to painful and blinding tests so that people could enjoy a luxury product, the protesters threatened boycotts of the offending manufacturers' products and picketing of their headquarters. The tests were eventually suspended when less controversial and equally reliable computerized analyses were developed to acquire the same kind of information.

Cosmetics manufacturers and ingredient suppliers will be prohibited from conducting any test that involves the placing of a cosmetic or cosmetic ingredient in an animal's eye or on an animal's skin to

to the appeal of the products themselves is the satisfaction consumers derive from knowing that their purchases benefit the populations of countries where the ingredients are found.

measure its irritant effects, according to legislation passed in New York State in 2007. The FDA, which regulates the cosmetic industry, does not require the use of animals for safety testing, though some manufacturers continue the practice. Alternatives to the use of animals for eye and skin irritancy tests of cosmetics and their ingredients are widely available and in use by many corporations, including Avon, Noxell, Revlon, Paul Mitchell, Fabergé, Mary Kay, and Whole Foods Market (see Figure 14.12).[16]

### Recyclable Packaging

Packaging of cosmetics has been greatly influenced by interest in recycling. Refillable glass bottles at lower cost are available from The Body Shop, among others. But the elaborate glass bottles used for designer fragrances are not the object of serious recycling efforts because the product is a luxury item, which is often saved as an art object.

The cardboard outer packaging of many luxury cosmetics and fragrances are more of an issue. Many of the coatings used to give the packages an elegant appearance render the cardboard unsuitable for recycling. Cargo Cosmetics has come up with the answer to this problem: Plant-Love's Botanical Lipstick is packaged in a lipstick tube made entirely of corn—a renewable, abundant resource. This environmentally friendly innovation also emits less greenhouse gases. The outer carton, which is also biodegradable, is made of flower paper embedded with real flower seeds. Simply moisten, plant, and wait for a bouquet of wild flowers to grow![17]

Mass-merchandised lines of such products as liquid soap, shampoo, and hand and body lotions are typically packaged in recyclable plastic containers.

BODY CARE HAS A BRAND NEW STANDARD. **OURS.**

BE GOOD TO YOUR WHOLE BODY

**FIGURE 14.12** Whole Body by Whole Foods Market offers high-quality products that are not tested on animals.

## Market Segments

The success of a perfume or cosmetic depends on accurate identification of the target customer and recognition of the product features, packaging, and promotional activities that will attract that customer's attention. Women have long been recognized as the primary market for cosmetics and fragrances, but six other major market segments have been identified. These segments overlap, but in defining the target for each product or line, the marketer focuses on particular characteristics. Currently, the most promising market segments are the male market, the teen market, the children's market, the ethnic market, the home market, and the export market.

### The Male Market

The market for cosmetics and fragrances for men has expanded and is expected to experience above-average growth in the future. Changing male images are opening up new and larger markets in hair care, face and body care, and fragrances (see Figure 14.13). Men are buying more diversified products, such as moisturizers, cleansers, and skin toners.

Men, like women, are concerned about aging. Unlike women, they have done little about it until recently. Today, however, it has become socially acceptable for men to treat skin to retard the aging process. Many male baby boomers, concerned about keeping their jobs, are resorting to cosmetic surgery. There is also a growing trend for male grooming, and the demand for male grooming products is of increasing importance to the cosmetics industry.

Many market-leading companies targeted the growing male consumer market early on. L'Oréal, for example, launched its comprehensive men's skin care and personal care range, Men's Experts, in the global market in late 2004.

Increasingly sophisticated products that have traditionally catered to female vanities are being marketed to men, with manufacturers like Biers-

**FIGURE 14.13** Sean John targets the male market with his Unforgivable fragrance for men.

dorf and Shiseido launching products such as anti-wrinkle creams, bronzing products, and toning gels. France-based company L'Occitane launched a mass-market male cosmetic range, Cade Male Cosmetics, in 2005. Companies are no longer choosing to manufacture the stereotypical male grooming product, such as shaving foam and razors, but are now focused on developing increasingly new products.[18]

The world today is referred to as the metrosexual era, with male role models such as David Beckham and Robbie Williams professing to use products such as concealer and mascara. The launch of the M Cover concealer product by Clinique, its first foray into male cosmetics, pushes the company further into the public eye as a trendsetter. Premium cosmetics company Jean-Paul Gaultier launched Le Male Cosmetics, and though the trend is still relatively new, there is customer interest.

However, with mass retail stores such as H&M launching male mascaras, it is probably only a matter of time before customer demand drives dedicated male cosmetic segments in most beauty retail outlets and stores.

Despite the upsurge in male cosmetics in stores, today the Internet has become a prime retail area for the more self-conscious male consumer. The Internet enables men to browse and explore products within a nonthreatening environment. Another male grooming market includes institutions, such as gyms and spas, where men can learn how and why to use cosmetics.[19]

In 2007, the male grooming industry was esti-

mated to be worth over $9 billion and was expected to grow by 6 percent by 2010.[20] All indications are that men have accepted cosmetics and fragrances as an integral part of their lifestyle.

## The Teen Market

Buying a first tube of lipstick has been a rite of passage for teenage girls for generations, but the teenager of today has gone far beyond this initial plunge into cosmetic and fragrance purchases. The U.S. youth spending on cosmetics and toiletries is estimated to $8 billion annually.[21]

Furthermore, today's typical teen customer has her own tastes—literally. Bonne Bell, the pioneer in cosmetics lines for teens, features Lip Lix lipsticks in flavors as trendy as their colors. Some of the products in the line, such as Manic Melon and Mad About Mocha, are available in both matte and shimmer finishes.

Bonne Bell's success has inspired other producers to offer cosmetics lines specifically for the teen market segment. Among them are M Professional, Fun Cosmetics, Jane, and Sel-Leb. They go after their target customer by following her into the mass-merchandise store, the apparel specialty store, and the record store. They speak to her on MTV and on the Internet. Besides flavored lipstick, they offer her eye makeup and nail enamel in attention-getting colors. Jane, for example, added a nail enamel line called Hot Tips in 1997, shipping to 6,000 stores, or doors, to start. Thus Jane became the first manufacturer of teen-oriented products to offer a full nail program.[22] (Jane was subsequently bought by Estée Lauder to expand its offerings to teens and to give Lauder an entry to the mass market).[23]

Prestige cosmetics and fragrance producers appeal to the teenage customer with light and unisex scents. The ecologically oriented lines, such as those offered by The Body Shop, are also popular with this segment.

With more than 31 million teenage girls spending an average of $2 per week, it is no surprise that the cosmetics and fragrance industry courts their business.[24] And the benefit is mutual: for a fraction of the price of a new dress or pair of jeans, a teen can express her style and indulge her shopping impulses.

Of course, both boys and girls spend heavily on acne treatments and concealers to help them deal with their teenage complexion problems. A success story was Bioré's wildly popular—and quickly imitated—dermal patch designed to remove blackheads.

## The Children's Market

The children's market, which has existed since the 1950s, is now expanding. Actually, this segment can be regarded as two markets: parents and the children themselves. Parents, particularly the parents of infants, want only the best to protect their children's sensitive skin. Dual wage-earner couples who have postponed parenthood have more income to spend on their children and a willingness to invest at least as much on their children's skin- and hair-care products as they spend on their own.

More than 200 personal care products for children have hit the market since 1994, many of them taking advantage of parental largesse. A proliferation of sunscreens is part of the fashion industry's response to consumers' concern about protection from ultraviolet rays. Today, parents are more aware of the dangers of excessive sun exposure, and products geared to infants and children constitute one of the most vibrant segments of the skin care business. Kimberly-Clark Corporation has extended its well-known Huggies Little Swimmers brand by launching a collection of three sunscreen lotions with the only patented self-adhesive sun sensors for measuring exposure to ultraviolet B (UVB) radiation, which causes sunburn. Other suppliers include Solar Cosmetics, Inc., which offers a collection of kids' sunblocks called Disney Sun Pals under its No-Ad brand. The line features a number of Disney characters, including Nemo, Ariel, and Winnie the Pooh.[25] California Baby and Aromather-

apy for Kids even offer bath soaps and oils to soothe cranky babies' spirits.

Whatever influence children have on their parents' purchases is directed toward products that are fun. For 2- to 8-year-olds, fun means bubble bath, lip balm, printed bandages, candy-flavored toothpaste, and licensed products featuring their favorite cartoon characters and television celebrities (see Figure 14.14). Mattel, manufacturer of the ever-popular Barbie, also markets through Avon's direct-to-the-home sales force a line of Barbie cosmetics, fragrances, and toiletry products for children.

## The Ethnic Market

The complexion of the U.S. population is changing as the birth rates for African Americans, Asian Americans, Hispanics, and Native Americans exceed that of Americans of European ancestry. Nearly one-third of the population of the United States is made up of African Americans, Asian Americans, and Hispanics, representing $1.2 trillion in joint purchasing power. By 2040, those groups will make up half the population. Thus, retail sales to these groups are one of the fastest growing segments of the cosmetics and fragrance industry.

Differences in skin shades and tones and hair texture among African American women have stimulated the development of special products for this segment of the ethnic market. In the 1960s, companies such as Libra and Astarte pioneered in creating mass-market lines for black women. Another early pioneer, Flori Roberts, produced the first prestige cosmetic line for African Americans. Still a major force in the cosmetics industry, she also introduced the first fragrance within a black cosmetics line, initiated in-store seminars on careers for black women, and began in-store makeup demonstrations.

The multicultural market in the United States presents many opportunities for suppliers to increase their presence in categories as varied as personal care products, cosmetics, and fragrances

**FIGURE 14.14** Cosmetics and fragrances for kids often come in fun packaging, with bright colors, sparkles, and popular celebrities or cartoon characters.

(see Figure 14.15). These are bound to grow as ethnic groups account for an increasingly larger share of the general public and have significant spending power as well. According to the NPD Group, more than three-quarters of women across ethnic groups currently use basic beauty products such as skin care, makeup, bath, and fragrances. According to Karen Grant, senior beauty analyst for the NPD Groups, "In beauty, the future is today—not in 10, 20, or 50 years from now. Today's ethnic population is already exerting an impact across all beauty categories. That is a fact the beauty industry must recognize right now. And, just as all boomers cannot be lumped together and marketed as one homogeneous group, 'women of color' are diverse, rapidly changing, and defy generalization. To tap into the power of this ever-expanding group, beauty manu-

facturers and retailers must understand the nuances of differences and adapt strategies to be identified as 'for someone like me.' That is a key statement for leading brands that resonates well with these increasingly important groups of beauty consumers."[26]

According to "The Multicultural Economy 2006," a report by the Selig Center for Economic Growth at the University of Georgia, ethnic groups, including African Americans and Hispanics, wield formidable economic clout today. African American's buying power is projected to increase from $318 million in 1990 to $1.1 trillion in 2011. Similarly, the buying power of Hispanics, who will account for about one in six people in the United States by 2011, will grow at a similar rate.[27]

The challenge that retailers and product marketers face in coming up with the right product mix and selling strategies is daunting. In the personal care product category, discount stores, chain drug stores, and supermarkets have been at the forefront of finding effective ways to reach them. Ethnic products, once comprising a relatively narrow niche, have now gotten the attention of large consumer product companies eager to capitalize on a growing market.

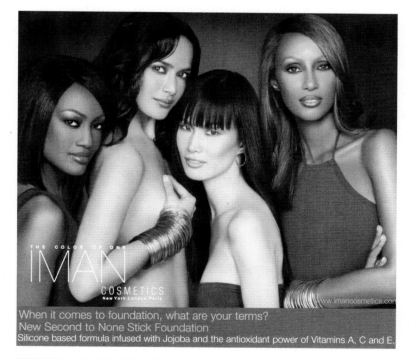

**FIGURE 14.15** IMAN Cosmetics designs cosmetics and skincare products specifically for multicultural women with different skin tones.

But, just as chain retailers are getting a firm handle on the ethnic mix of each store, consumers are throwing a wrench into micromarketing by buying items they like rather than those targeted to them. Two examples include Activate Beauty, a line of hair care products created and promoted by Latina women, and Milani, a cosmetics line intended for women with diverse shades of skin. Another is HIP from L'Oréal, which sources said was initially intended to reach women of color but had such high appeal in testing that it was launched as a general market line.[28]

For retailers, the challenge now is to determine how to merchandise the blurred categories. Many still want larger selections in stores with a high concentration of ethnic consumers. Others, however, are using these smaller brands as a way to provide shoppers more choices. Many chains are open to taking on brands with more ethnic heritage and using these niche brands as a point of difference between competitors.

## The Home Fragrances Market

Many industry experts feel that **home**, or environmental, **fragrances** will be the next major breakthrough in the perfume industry. The public's growing awareness of fragrance is not restricted to personal use but includes their homes as well.

Many consumers are gaining satisfaction from enhancing their environment and are taking in-home activities, such as gourmet cooking and home entertaining, more seriously.

Fashion designers were quick to pick up on the interest in environmental fragrances, and many have already produced scented candles, silk flowers, paperweights, and holiday gifts. The pioneer is Ralph Lauren, whose collection has been available since the late 1970s. Donna Karan, Oscar de la Renta, and Marc Jacobs also have designer home fragrance lines (see Figure 14.16).

The green movement has candle manufacturers making consumer education a key marketing priority as arguments for or against the benefits of certain wax ingredients heat up the marketplace. A broadening of "other" home fragrance delivery methods, such as diffuser reeds, scented oils, and potpourri, also has many vying for their share of the market.

Home fragrance today is as much an accessory to interior design as any piece of art, furniture, or lamp placed into a perfectly decorated room. It isn't the price point that matters, but rather how the home fragrance object will complement the environment. As we become aware that these little luxuries help improve our mood and help us to sleep better, the future for home fragrances is very bright.[29]

**FIGURE 14.16** Fashion designers, like Marc Jacobs, quickly recognized that they could expand their lines to the home fragrances market.

## The Export Market

The export market for U.S. cosmetics has grown in recent years partly because the "Westernization" of much of the world has made the wearing of cosmetics acceptable. Until 1980, China had a law that banned the wearing of cosmetics, and in what was once the Soviet Union and its Eastern Bloc satellites, American products were hardly known until recently. That has now changed. Japan, China, Western Europe, and South America have emerged as strong markets for U.S. cosmetics and fragrances.

Fortunately, American cosmetics and fragrances usually need little or no adjustment in formulas and packaging in order to succeed in the international market. An exception is Japan, where cosmetics are basically treated the same as pharmaceuticals and require licensing for import and sale. The Japanese list of approved ingredients restricts some formulas and specifies strict labeling requirements. But in the rest of the world, American products have enough variety for marketers to edit their offering to suit the demands of their customers abroad. Superior ingredients, promotion, and distribution work as well abroad as at home, and American companies have the expertise and money to ensure that their products continue to be best sellers the world over.

The U.S. Commerce Department has promoted efforts by small cosmetics companies to export to the more affluent third-world countries where per capita expenditures on cosmetics products are growing rapidly. Direct distribution, private-label products produced for foreign firms, and licensing specialties for foreign production are considered the most productive prospects for this international market.

U.S. companies cashing in on the opening of the vast Chinese market to imported cosmetics include Revlon and direct sellers Avon and Amway. As the infrastructure improves and the Chinese become more familiar with these foreign products, demand is expected to increase.

A trade bloc of Asian–Pacific nations is emerging as another potential major market because of the standardization of import rules and the invitation to the United States to join the bloc. In contrast, India, despite its dense population and substantial middle class, has placed itself off limits with duty rates exceeding 100 percent.[30]

## Merchandising and Marketing

The cosmetics and fragrance business is a highly visible one. Its products are used nearly every day by millions of people. In the prestige cosmetics market, competition for restricted distribution to quality department and specialty stores is keen. All of the prestige brand manufacturers want to sell their lines in the most prestigious store in each town. They offer these stores exclusives, specials, and cooperative advertising to guarantee that their products will receive prime locations. Limiting the doors where their products are available adds to the aura of exclusivity and uniqueness the manufacturer of each line wishes to convey to its target customers. Such merchandising techniques are used by most prestigious cosmetics brands, including Estée Lauder, Elizabeth Arden, Clinique, Orlane, Lancôme, Borghese, and Ultima II.

## Distribution

The structure of distribution techniques in the cosmetics area is both distinctive and complex, involving such elements as class versus mass distribution, limited versus popular distribution, mass-market distribution, and distribution limited to in-store salons. The use of behind-the-counter brand-line representatives or direct selling techniques are also popular in the cosmetics and fragrance industry.

### Class Versus Mass

Another name for "class" is "franchise," so when industry insiders talk about "class versus mass," they mean franchise versus mass. In **franchise distribution**, the manufacturer or exclusive distributor sells directly to the ultimate retailer. No wholesalers, jobbers, diverters, rack jobbers, or intermediaries of any kind are involved. Each vending retailer is on the books of the manufacturer or distributor as a direct-receivable account. A good example of this is Estée Lauder, which sells directly to stores such as Neiman Marcus and Saks Fifth Avenue. In contrast, third-party vendors, such as wholesalers, diverters, and jobbers, play a role in mass distribution. These third parties may sell to any one of a number of retailers of any type. No control is exercised over these intermediaries. Manufacturers may not know their retailers. Furthermore, territory or other definable exclusivity does not run from manufacturer to retailer in mass distribution as it does in the franchise or class relationship. A good example of this is Revlon's line, which is sold in mass-merchandise outlets such as variety stores, drugstores, and chain stores.

## Limited Versus Popular

The franchise cosmetics business is described as being either limited or popular in its distribution pattern. In the industry, any line distributed to more than 5,000 doors is considered popular; any line distributed to fewer than 5,000 doors is limited.

## Counter Brand-Line Representatives

Since a need exists to inform and educate cosmetics customers about the many products that are available to them, prestige cosmetics companies place their own **brand-line representatives** behind the counter as line salespeople. These line salespeople, also called "beauty counselors," are well equipped to perform this important function. They are trained in the end-use of the hundreds of items carried in each specific line. In many instances, the salaries of these salespeople are paid by the cosmetic company directly. Sometimes, in an arrangement called **joint merchandising**, the store shares in the payment of their salaries. These salespeople are also responsible for stocking inventory. They keep detailed records that show what items are and are not selling. The cosmetics companies constantly keep their brand salespeople informed about new items, new colors, and new promotions through updated training and materials. As might be expected, the limited-door stores have the best-trained salespeople.

## Mass-Market Distribution

The **mass-distribution** cosmetics market involves drugstores, discount stores, variety stores, and large national chains such as Sears and JCPenney. The volume of business done in these stores is growing. As they have become increasingly interested in distribution to these types of retail outlets, large cosmetics companies have planned and implemented new merchandising activities. Until a few years ago, the mass-distribution outlets were limited to selling lines such as Cover Girl, Maybelline, or a store's own label line. Now large, nationally advertised brands such as Max Factor and Revlon have introduced their medium-priced lines into these outlets, enabling customers to select products more easily and thus increase sales. Mass-market retailers are turning to open-access display systems and mass-marketing displays.

## In-Store Salons

In-store salons that provide a full range of hair, skin, and body services are another trend (see Figure 14.17). Customers can now obtain specialized advice and beauty care right on the department store floor from such lines as Lancôme, Orlane, Payot, and Adrien Arpel. In-store salons have helped to introduce American women to the beauty regimens (routines) long favored by European women, and in turn, the products and regimens have been simplified to fit in with Americans' fast-paced lives. Regimens will become increasingly personalized as computers tailor them to individual customer's needs.

**FIGURE 14.17** Christian Dior's in-store salon provides a full range of skin and cosmetic services.

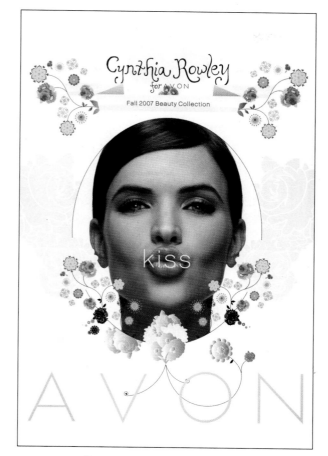

**FIGURE 14.18** Avon's sales representatives sell its products directly to groups or individuals.

## Direct Selling

A few companies sell their products to consumers only through individual or group presentations by their own salespeople. Three well-known examples are Avon, Mary Kay, and BeautiControl (see Figure 14.18).

## *Advertising and Sales Promotion*

National advertising budgets of cosmetics companies are immense, especially in comparison to sales. Fierce competition for retail shelf space forces companies to spend an average of $10 million annually to support a single fragrance line, even more if it is a new product. And national advertising is not the only type of sales promotion in which a company must engage.

The expense of promotion and advertising is well worth the effort. A campaign combining direct mail, television, and print exposure often results in three times the usual amount of business generated by a particular product in any given week.

Television has become *the* medium for cosmetics that are sold by mail or phone order. Extended broadcast advertising is accomplished on QVC and the Home Shopping Network (HSN) and through "infomercials" on cable channels. Magazine ads continue to be the traditional way of reaching a targeted segment of the cosmetics market, while many retail store catalogs regularly push cosmetics and fragrances in their catalogs.

## Premiums

An extensive publicity campaign is also mounted to introduce new products. These are often promoted by a celebrity, providing yet another basis for a publicity campaign. Many companies also promote their products with **premiums**, a gift-with-purchase or a purchase-with-purchase offer, a concept that originated with Estée Lauder. These premiums range from samples of products to cosmetic "paint boxes," umbrellas, tote bags, scarfs, and even small duffel bags.

## Direct Mail

Because of the breadth and depth of its reach, many stores are finding direct mail one of the most successful forms of advertising for both promotions and regular-price cosmetics. Another advantage to the store is that direct mail campaigns are generally vendor-funded. The most common formats are order forms in four-color vendor mailers, bill insertion leaflets, and remittance envelope stubs. Estimates of sales volume from mail-order average about 2 to 3 percent of all cosmetics sales per year.

## Scent and Color Strips

Another promotional tool that has gained a foothold in the cosmetics industry is the use of scent and color strips, sometimes as bill insertions, but more often as part of a company's advertisement in

**FIGURE 14.19** Fragrance advertisements in magazines often feature scent strips to allow the consumer to sample a whiff of their product.

**FIGURE 14.20** Sephora.com allows customers to shop online and learn about the latest beauty products on the market. Through their collaboration with Stardoll.com, customers are able to try on virtual beauty products.

a magazine (see Figure 14.19). A method of sampling made possible by modern technology, scent and color strips allow consumers to experiment with new eyeshadow colors or try out new fragrances in the privacy of their own homes.

New technology has improved scent and color strips. Much to the relief of people who are ultra-sensitive to odors, scent samples can now be encapsulated so that they must be opened for the smell to be released. Liquids and creams can also be encapsulated in foil packets and distributed in magazines or bill inserts. Multiple-color samples can now be sealed under a plastic patch that peels away.

### Computerized Displays

A number of cosmetics companies offer computerized assistance to help customers choose the products that are best suited to them. Computers create a virtual reality makeover in which the customer can see how various products will look on her. Less elaborate programs prepare a collection of cosmetics for a customer according to information about her coloring and skin type that she has typed into the computer.

### The Internet

For mass-merchandised cosmetic lines, the Internet provides virtual counter space. Teens and young adults, who make up a large portion of the market for these lines, can go directly to the producer's Web page to find out about the latest colors or get other information about the company (see Figure 14.20). Virtually every cosmetics and fragrance company now has its own Web site to promote and sell its products as well as provide chat rooms, information about company history, and locations of nearby retailers.

### Trade Associations, Shows, and Publications

The Personal Care Products Council (the Council) is a major cosmetics trade association. Its membership markets 90 percent of all cosmetics, toiletries, and fragrances sold in the United States. The Council coordinates the industry commitment to scientific and quality standards (see Figure 14.21). It is the industry vehicle for information exchange about scientific developments among association members, consumers, and those who regulate the industry at federal, state, and local government levels. The Council also keeps members informed on government regulations and offers advice on interpretation and compliance. Through its home page on the Internet, the Council offers members access to government agencies, product safety resources, international trade organizations, and the Web sites of other members.

**FIGURE 14.21** CosmeticsInfo.org is an information Web site that includes factual and scientific information on ingredients most commonly used in cosmetics and personal care products in the United States. It is sponsored by The Personal Care Products Council (the Council) and its members.

## Industry Trends

As noted earlier in this chapter, the cosmetics and fragrance industry is now a global one. This trend will accelerate in the coming decades. In the United States, sales of skin care products are expected to grow at a faster pace than color cosmetics, due to an older and more affluent population and the increasing popularity of men's products.

The market for fragrance will remain strong, in part because of the steadily increasing number of working women, who prefer a lighter fragrance when at work to the heavy perfumes they may wear in the evening. The concept of a **fragrance wardrobe** to suit the various roles a woman (or man) assumes is being promoted and has boosted demand. Men are also adapting (though more slowly) to the idea of one fragrance for the office, another for sports, and another for evening.

Five other sectors predicted to continue solid growth include: (1) antiaging products, (2) antibacterial and antiallergenic products, (3) aromatherapy products, (4) spa products, and (5) individualized products.

### Antiaging Products

Antiaging products are enjoying booming sales thanks to the baby boom generation (see Figure 14.22). When the oldest members of this group turned 50 in 1996, they raced to the cosmetics counter for skin care products to ward off or lessen the appearance of wrinkles. About the same time, laboratory tests confirmed the effectiveness of AHAs for this purpose, and the FDA decided to regulate AHAs as cosmetics rather than as drugs.

America's quest for youth shows no signs of aging, as research predicts that the U.S. antiaging skin care treatment segment will experience triple-digit growth through 2011.[31] Aging consumers, particularly female baby boomers, are the primary force driving sales in the antiaging treatment market. But baby boomer women aren't the only ones driving the growth. Younger women seeking pre-

Another helpful organization is the Fragrance Foundation in New York, founded in 1949. Manufacturers, suppliers, designers, packagers, retailers, and media and public relations personnel who are involved in the industry are members. The Fragrance Foundation maintains a library of print and video materials and a Web page, and publishes industry reports and educational and sales training materials. It sponsors National Fragrance Week in June and honors an American and a European with "FiFi" awards. The Fragrance Foundation also sponsors a program at the Fashion Institute of Technology (FIT), in New York City, which offers a bachelor's of science degree in cosmetics and fragrance marketing. The program includes mentoring, an internship, and placement assistance.

International trade shows bring together visitors and exhibitors from all facets of the cosmetics and fragrance industry—manufacturers, suppliers, packagers, retailers, and advertising and promotion specialists. The largest trade show in the United States is the HBA Global Expo, held in the Jacob K. Javits Center in New York. Bologna, Italy, is the site of the mammoth Cosmoprof, with around 130,000 visitors. Cosmoprof is the perfect occasion to launch a new line in front of the entire worldwide industry, and many producers do so.

**FIGURE 14.22** Aveeno and Dove offer lines of antiaging products that keep skin soft and free of wrinkles, while also taking a more positive approach toward aging.

ventative solutions and men who consider antiaging as a regular aspect of their grooming routine also are fueling sales.

### Antibacterial and Antiallergenic Products

Antibacterial and antiallergenic cleansing products have been available in both mass-merchandised and prestige lines for a long time. Almay and Clinique exemplify the two ends of the market. Functional cosmetics and targeting beauty from the inside are among the fastest growing segments in the cosmetics and nutraceuticals market, with antiaging, antiwrinkle, and anticellulite among the top claims made for many products containing a variety of mostly natural substances. As natural and organic beauty items continue to trickle onto the beauty scene, items bearing the U.S. Department of Agriculture organic seal have launched in stores, including items by Origins and Nature's Gate.

What makes these launches so newsworthy is that each brand was able to concoct formulas for lotions worthy of the seal. Mass retailers are beginning to acknowledge the importance of separating natural and organic items from mainstream items in order to demonstrate their point of difference. Stores such as Target, Walgreens, Duane Reade, CVS, and Longs are planning to showcase the natural and organic ingredient items separately.[32]

### Aromatherapy Products

**Aromatherapy** involves fragrant oils distilled from plants, herbs, and flowers; these oils have been used for centuries to stimulate or relax. So important has the study of the physiological effects of fragrance on humans become that Annette Green, former executive director of the Fragrance Foundation, coined the term *aromachology* to describe the modern, research-based phenomenon. Dr. Alan Hirsch of the Smell and Taste Treatment and Research Foundation in Chicago explains that specific feelings can be transmitted through odor because the olfactory nerve of the nose attaches directly to the limbic system of the brain, which influences emotions, memory, hormone secretion, appetite, and sexuality. This connection explains the association of smells with memories of people and places. Some scents that promote emotional responses and behaviors are listed in Table 14.4. Notice that food scents are especially influential.

The fragrance industry uses this research in the development of home fragrances, and that segment of the market has consequently been thriving. The association that actively promotes aromatherapy research is the Sense of Smell Institute.

### Spa Products

The ultimate indulgence in personal care is a visit to a health spa. The word "spa" originally referred to a European institution built around a thermal spring, where doctors sent the chronically ill for

**FIGURE 14.23** Bliss spas offer a full range of facial and body treatments, as well as shops that allow the spa-goer to take a bit of "bliss" home with them.

**TABLE 14.4** *The Effects of Scents*

| SCENT | EFFECT |
|---|---|
| Spiced apple | Lower blood pressure, ward off panic attacks, reduce stress |
| Plum, peach | Reduce pain |
| Jasmine, green apple | Lift depression |
| Geranium | Dispels anxiety |
| Peppermint, lemon | Restore energy |
| Chamomile, rose, vanilla | Relax the spirit |
| Cloves, cinnamon, oriental spices | Increase sensuality |
| Seashore, cucumber | Combat claustrophobia |
| Floral scent | Promotes faster puzzle-solving |
| Lavender | Increase sensuality, promotes alertness |

LAVENDER        CHAMOMILE        PEPPERMINT

Source: Renee Covino Rouland, "The Bath and Shower Experience," *Discount Merchandiser*; and Maxine Wilkie, "Scent of a Market," *American Demographics*.

treatments lasting weeks. Today, spas are springing up in health clubs, department stores, and beauty salons across the country, where they offer treatments lasting a day, or a few hours (see Figure 14.23). Most modern **spas** offer a wide range of services, including massages, manicures, pedicures, waxings, and facials, which often are combined with aromatherapy. In addition, one can, for a price ranging from $20 to more than $200, be completely covered in a body wrap, which is thought to cleanse and heal the skin and relax the body. In a **body wrap**, herbs, seaweed, or mud is applied directly to the body, which is then wrapped like a mummy to allow the substances to penetrate the pores. In a similar procedure, the wrapping cloths are soaked in the substances and then wrapped around the body. Body wraps date back to Biblical times and came to America by way of Europe, where they have been popular for centuries. The muds and other substances used in spa products still have many of the same sources, like the famed Dead Sea salts. The experts who administer these therapies and the special equipment available at spas give them an aura of alternative medicine, providing a rationale for the consumer's investment. Spa products fit in with the trend in cosmetics toward products that promote the health of the skin.

Treatments with fango, a mud rich in minerals, are popular, as are exfoliation treatments, which remove dead cells, smooth the skin, and promote circulation. Anticellulite treatments are frequently available. Many spas also offer **thalassotherapy**, which involves sea water, seaweed, or sea algae and is believed to hydrate and rejuvenate the skin.

## Individualized Products

Another trend relies on modern technology, particularly on computers. Personalized toiletries, makeup, and fragrances are being developed at the cosmetics counter for—and sometimes by—the customer. For example, a computer at General Nutrition Company's Alive store in Altamonte Spring, Florida, allows the customer to program a set of products using a base—say, shampoo or liquid soap—and various additives. Sample scents are available at the counter, and the computer provides information about the benefits of various ingredients so that the customer can tailor the recipe to her needs and tastes. A machine mixes the product on the spot, and the computer's database stores the formula for easy reordering.

**TABLE 14.5** *Fashion Trends in Apparel and Accessories to Cosmetics and Fragrances*

| TREND | APPAREL AND ACCESSORIES | COSMETICS AND FRAGRANCE |
|---|---|---|
| Health and fitness | Activewear, workout apparel, summer hats, and sunglasses to protect from sun's rays | Skin care products, spas and spa products, sun-protection products, hypoallergenic and antiaging products |
| Casual lifestyle | Dress-down Fridays and informal office dress codes | Light fragrances, light makeup for no-makeup look |
| Individuality | Easing of business dress codes, mix-and-match separates, size lines for different figure types, and custom-fit jeans | Customized cosmetics and fragrances, marketing in record stores and sporting goods stores |
| Internationalism | International corporations and conglomerates, global marketing, marketing on the Internet, breakdown of trade barriers, international sourcing | Same as apparel and accessories |
| Multiculturalism | Adaptation of ethnic themes by designers; textiles and patterns from around the world; Native American, Indian, and African jewelry and other accessories | Ethnic cosmetics lines, ethnic hair care products and hairstyles (hair extensions, dreadlocks), menhadi, shiatsu, reflexology, and thalassotherapy |

A more low-tech manifestation of product personalization is the promotional makeover by a brand-line representative at the department store counter. Like the do-it-yourself displays, the activity on the sales floor attracts the attention of passing shoppers and builds brand loyalty on the part of customers who acquire a customized cosmetics and fragrance collection.

## *Reflections of Trends*

The focus of the cosmetics and fragrance industry in the 2000s echoes trends in other segments of the fashion industry. New and newly popular cosmetics products respond to the same trends as apparel and accessories, as the examples in Table 14.5 show.

## Summary and Review

Over the past 10 years, cosmetics and fragrances have proliferated in the global marketplace, sparked by advances in science and technology. Today's consumer selects a cosmetic or fragrance not only for its ingredients, but also for its packaging, its promotion, and where it can be bought. Some stores are perceived as having higher status, and therefore many product lines are only sold in these types of stores, through a manufacturer's own sales force, through direct mail, or on the Internet.

The main categories in this industry are fragrance, color cosmetics, skin care, sun care, and nail care. While the U.S. cosmetics industry is regulated by a number of state and federal laws, it is currently less regulated than Europe or Japan. The increasingly global nature of the industry will doubtless mean increased regulation in the coming decades. Also, environmental concerns like animal testing, recyclable packaging, and "natural" or botanical ingredients are leading to higher industry standards worldwide.

As the industry continues to expand, new market segments beyond the traditional women's market have attracted increased attention. These segments include the male market, the teen market, the children's market, the ethnic market, the home fragrances market, and the export market.

Trends in cosmetics and fragrances follow those in apparel and accessories, and bear close attention. The major trends include antiaging products, antibacterial and antiallergenic products, aromatherapy products, spa products, and individualized products.

## Trade Talk

Define or briefly explain the following terms:

alpha hydroxy acids (AHAs)
body wrap

copycat scent
fragrance

aromatherapy
brand-line representatives
cosmetics
fragrance wardrobe

franchise distribution
joint merchandising
premiums
rubber-banding
spa

home fragrances
mass distribution
private label
   manufacturers
thalassotherapy

## For Review

1. How do the heads of the major cosmetics and fragrance firms today differ from their predecessors in the first decades of the 20th century?

2. What distinguishes perfume from cologne and toilet water?

3. How does the cosmetics industry relate to the ready-to-wear industry?

4. Summarize the Food and Drug Administration's laws in regard to cosmetics.

5. Where are the international growth opportunities for cosmetics and fragrance producers?

6. Describe the products of the home fragrance market.

7. Outline the major distribution methods used by the cosmetics industry.

8. Describe the various advertising and promotion activities currently engaged in by the cosmetics industry.

9. Identify the major professional organizations of the cosmetics and fragrance industry and describe their activities.

10. Briefly discuss the most significant trends in cosmetics products today.

## For Discussion

1. Discuss current trends in the cosmetics and fragrance industry as they relate to: (a) mergers, (b) diversification of product lines, and (c) global marketing.

2. Discuss the recent growth in men's cosmetics and ethnic cosmetics lines.

3. Cosmetics salespersons, or brand-line representatives, exercise much more control over the products carried in their stock than do salespeople in other departments in a store. Discuss the system used and its advantages and disadvantages.

# chapter fifteen

*Everything you always wanted to know*

*about the home fashions industry.*

KEY CONCEPTS

• History of the home furnishings industries

• Organization, operation, and product categories of soft goods and tabletop goods industries

• Market segments of the home fashions industry

• Market centers and resources of the home fashions industry

• Fashion influences in the home fashions industry

• Influences of technology on the home fashions industry

# Home Fashions

It is said that your home is your castle. Whether that home is a spacious, sprawling mansion or just one room that you can call your own, it is your space. It is a place to relax, be solitary, entertain friends, and establish an environment that supports your lifestyle. Therefore, creating a sanctuary that you look forward to coming home to has become the dream of people in the 21st century.

As Americans spend more time at home, they are also spending more of their money on home decorating—and redecorating—and less on their personal wardrobes. This trend is especially apparent in the dominant markets segment for fashion goods—baby boom women. So fashion designers, textile manufacturers, and retailers are turning their attention to the home furnishings and home accessories business. **Home fashions** is the umbrella term used frequently today to describe the two fashion-driven industries that have long been called *home furnishings* and *home accessories* (see Figure 15.1). In this text, we use all three terms, since that is what you will see and hear in the field.

In this market, fashion exerts its greatest influence in the soft goods lines, including bed, bath, and table linens; curtains and draperies; upholstery fabric; and area rugs, and in the **tabletop** categories of dinnerware, glassware, flatware, hollowware, and giftware (see Figure 15.2). (Furniture, electronic equipment, home appliances, and wall-to-wall carpeting have slower fashion cycles; these items are typically one-time purchases or long-term investments. They are beyond the scope of our discussion.)

A serious problem for both manufacturers and retailers of home furnishings is the vast amount of product knowledge required to sell these products. The challenge of sales staff education is a great one; the most successful manufacturers share the burden with retailers by providing extensive sales aids.

## History of the Home Furnishings Industries

The types of furnishings and household accessories in contemporary American homes are based primarily on models and ideas that the early European immigrants brought with them. Most of our beds and eating utensils, for example, are Western. But many of the fabrics and other material, the decorative patterns, and the objects themselves originated in the East and came to America *through* rather than *from* Europe. The rugs that covered the floors in medieval European castles were imported by the crusaders, and when later Europeans established their own rug factories, the designs evolved from patterns developed in Turkey, Persia, India, and China. China was also the source of the finest quality of clay for ceramic dinnerware. Before there were Wedgwood and Royal Doulton potteries in England, British nobles imported their custom designed dinnerware with the family crest from China through the British East India Company.

### The Role of Linen

From ancient times, linen was used in the Middle East and Europe for clothing and bedding. When medieval Europeans began sitting at a table for meals rather than reclining, they wiped their hands on remnants of linen cloth covering the table. The association of linen with sheets, tablecloths, and towels was so strong that even today, when these household accessories are usually made of other textiles, we still refer to bed, table, and bath linens.

Today, linen household accessories are being revived by such designers as Ralph Lauren, Donna Karan, and Calvin Klein; sheer weaves are appearing as curtains; and Turkish rug producers are experimenting with the fiber.

The history of tabletop goods is more varied that that of linen and so is discussed under each category.

**FIGURE 15.1** Home fashions reflect your personality and style just as much as your dress.

## *The Evolution of Global Home Fashions*

Travelers since Marco Polo have brought home examples of native crafts and handwork to beautify their homes and impress their friends. Today materials, designs, and finished goods move simultaneously in both directions between East and West and beyond. African kente cloth patterns appear on American bed linens; sisal from Brazil and Tanzania is imported into the United States for rugs; Japanese apartments feature Western rooms; and Americans buy their bedding from specialized futon shops. Home fashions retain their distinctive local character, but they are enjoyed in homes far from their point of origin.

## Organization and Operation of the Industries

Manufacturers of soft goods and tabletop merchandise can be found all across the country. Their showrooms, however, are centered in New York, like the showrooms for other categories of fashion merchandise. And as in other fashion businesses, the home fashions industry involves the widespread and growing use of licensing agreements.

## *Size and Location of Soft Goods Manufacturers*

As the United States grew from an agricultural nation to a vast industrialized one, textile mills and manufacturers of textile home furnishing products

**FIGURE 15.2** Choices of dinnerware, glassware, and flatware can change the look of a tablesetting from modern and casual (top) to traditional and formal (bottom).

were established in the cotton-growing South. The major American textile mills are also the largest manufacturers of goods produced from their fabrics. Some mills specialize in apparel textiles and products or in home furnishing textiles and products, and others manufacture both.

Because household linens are essentially flat sheets of cloth, they require little work beyond the manufacturing of the textiles, perhaps hemming or the addition of decorative trim. Bedspreads, comforters, blankets, and curtains are also manufactured by the same vertically integrated companies and may be coordinated with bed or bathroom linens. Similarly, area rugs are often manufactured by carpet mills.

## Size and Location of Tabletop Manufacturers

The fashion influence on the marketing of household linens and other soft goods for the home is also apparent in the hard lines of home furnishings. Everything from furniture to kitchen appliances has a fashion cycle. Our discussion focuses on the categories of tabletop goods because the role of fashion is most apparent in these segments of the home furnishings industry. From the time the medieval Europeans began to use forks instead of fingers, the basic items in a table setting have not changed significantly in function. Design criteria drive the consumer's buying decision. Today, when home entertaining has become a widespread leisure-time activity, the selection of fashionable tabletop goods is part of the fun.

Because the three categories of tabletop goods—dinnerware, glassware, and flatware—are used together, manufacturers in each category have grown through expansion as well as mergers and acquisitions into the other categories. Some large firms also include companies or divisions that produce table linen and products outside of the home furnishings industry. For example, Lenox, the leading U.S. manufacturer of china dinnerware, also produces crystal and giftware. The company's parent corporation since 1983 is Brown-Forman, which also owns such other manufacturers of tabletop goods as Dansk Contemporary Tabletop, Gorham, and Kirk Stieff, as well as producers of wine and spirits (Jack Daniels, Southern Comfort, Bolla) and Hartmann, maker of upscale luggage and leather goods. There is no single geographic center in the United States or elsewhere for these companies that manufacture so many different products.

Other leading tabletop manufacturers include Fitz and Floyd, Syracuse China Company, Mikasa, Pfaltzgraff, Johnson Brothers, Villeroy & Boch, and Ralph Lauren. The Homer Laughlin China Company is the largest china manufacturer in the United States. Its Fiesta product line is one of the most collected china products in the world, and dozens of the company's other patterns are sold through retail outlets and to numerous restaurants, hotels, and institutions. In 1992, Homer Laughlin became one of the first china manufacturers to completely eliminate lead from its products. The popularity of Homer Laughlin's Fiesta line has helped the company remain successful and to keep the company's jobs in the United States.[1]

Popular imports of tabletop products include Wedgwood, Franciscan (a division of Waterford Wedgwood USA), Royal Albert, Royal Doulton, Royal Worcester, Portmeirion, and Spode from England. Limoges, Lalique, Baccarat, and Cristal d'Arques are famous French manufacturers. Orrefors crystal from Sweden is world famous, as is Waterford crystal, which has been made in Ireland since 1731. In Italy, Silvestri and Bormioli Rocco E Figlio produce beautiful glassware. Versace and Armani, also from Italy, have a large collection of tabletop products, in addition to their world famous apparel collections. Rosenthal and Meissen glassware china come from Germany, while Noritake, Sango, and Morimura are very popular lines from Japan.

## Licensing

Designer names are not the only commodity licensed in the home furnishings industry. Colonial Williamsburg presents an example of the stringent conditions of licensing by a cultural institution.

Character licensing is the main form of licensing in the industries that manufacture tabletop goods, and most of the licensed characters appear on lines of dinnerware and glassware for children. Not surprisingly, Disney rules in the licensing of animated movie "stars" for glasses and dinnerware, as it does for sheets. The marketing campaigns for children's movies typically include a 3- to 6-month selling period for related merchandise, and the release of the movie in video form may add to the life of these products. In addition to sales through conventional retail channels, glassware featuring characters from movies and children's television shows is given away as promotional items by fast-food chains. Classic Disney characters—Mickey, Minnie, Donald, and friends—and classic literary characters like Winnie the Pooh have longer careers as licensed decorations.

### Designing a Soft Goods Line

To meet and encourage the demand of cocooning consumers, manufacturers are designing coordinated lines of bedroom accessories. Sheets and pillowcases match or complement bed covers and window treatments; bath linen sets may also be coordinated with the bedroom lines (see Figure 15.3). These fashionable products generate replacement sales long before the replaced items wear out. However, the soft goods fashion cycle is slower than the apparel fashion cycle, lasting years rather than seasons. New colors and designs may be introduced annually or in two seasonal showings, but previous years' fashions are not totally replaced by new offerings. Some lines stop selling only when the producer discontinues them.

The need for color forecasting for home accessories is a 20th-century phenomenon. Earlier, bed linens were undyed, then they were bleached white, and finally colors and prints began to come on the market. Since the 1990s, the color cycle has been reduced from 10-year periods of recent decades to colors remaining fashionable for just a few years. Ironically, environmentalism has made the neutral hues of undyed textiles one of the hottest new color trends. Trends in color are monitored and predicted by organizations such as the Color Association of

**FIGURE 15.3** Coordination of sheets and pillowcases encourage replacement purchases and makes fashion a consideration in the buying decision.

the United States (CAUS) and the International Colour Authority (ICA) and by companies such as Color Box and the Color Marketing Group.

The success of a new line of household linens depends on accurate forecasting of fashions in prints, weaves, and fabrics, as well as color, and on production processes that ensure timely availability. With computers, textile designers can create decorative prints or translate their hand-drawn designs into repeated patterns. Computer-aided design (CAD) programs allow them to produce a print design in several color combinations, thereby expanding their lines at a minimal increase in cost. CAD programs even produce decorative stitching patterns for quilts and "instruct" computerized quilting machines in how to sew them more quickly and accurately than conventional equipment.

Other consumer demands that manufacturers must consider in designing a line include finishes that enhance the products for their intended purposes. For example, table linens may be treated for stain resistance, and wool carpeting may be treated for protection from mildew, molds, and moths. Filling for pillows and comforters can be treated with chemicals that protect allergy sufferers from bacteria and dust mites. Techniques for decorating linens with print patterns affect the feel—and price—of sheets and bath and kitchen towels.

The demand by ecology-minded consumers, mostly Gen Xers, for natural products has given rise to lines of 100 percent cotton bed and bath linens not treated with the bleaches that normally set dyes or the formaldehyde in permanent-press finishes. These natural features create a fashion statement with their characteristic limited palette and wrinkles. The Gen Xers are the first true high-technology generation and the first Internet-shopping generation. It is now they, not boomers, who drive the adoption of new products and create new trends. There are two fronts on which home textiles product developers can best appeal to them: environmentally friendly goods and technology. A few items are beginning to appear that claim to employ nanotechnology in their fibers, but for the most part, there is no evidence of how that technology improves the product in a significant and perceivable way. Time to put on your thinking caps, home fashions industry. Gen X is waiting. Here are a few ideas that could really make a difference. What about a comforter or a sheet that could change patterns? What about a reactive window panel that could help heat or cool a room? What about an area rug that could shift sizes? What about a bath towel that could warm itself up?[2]

### Importance of Name Designers

Whether the entry of apparel designers into the home furnishings industry made it a fashion business, or consumer interest in home decorating lured the designers into the home accessories market, is a chicken-or-egg question. The important fact is that home fashions from name designers satisfy a consumer need. The designer's name on the label is assurance of a consistent look that the consumer recognizes from the designer's apparel lines (see Figure 15.4). This is true even though the designer's involvement may be limited to providing—or merely approving—the print patterns and colors. Many licensing agreements leave textile selection and other production decisions, as well as the marketing plan, to the manufacturer.

Bill Blass was the first major American apparel designer to design a home fashions line in the 1960s. Laura Ashley followed in the 1970s, and Ralph Lauren in the 1980s. Since then, Ralph Lauren has become the largest supplier of sheets, towels, and pillows to department stores, with annual sales exceeding $250 million. A number of designers have followed, among them Calvin Klein, Liz Claiborne, Ellen Tracy, Jessica McClintock, Donna Karan, Tommy Hilfiger, Josie Natori, and Vera Wang.

### Importance of Brand Names

If a designer's name conjures up a particular fashion image, brand names suggest other qualities that consumers also consider when they shop, such as textile selections and price points. The major textile mills that produce household linens are known to the public primarily by the brand names of their sheets and towels because consumers buy these end products more than they buy

**FIGURE 15.4** Designer labels such as Ralph Lauren are making their way into the home fashion market.

curtains, upholstery fabric, or bolts of fabric for home sewing.

Store brand names are also influential. When the Federated Department Stores conglomerate took over Macy's, one of the major attractions of the acquisition was Macy's expertise in marketing its private brands, such as the Charter Club brand of apparel and home accessories. By circumventing the middleman, retailers can sell their private brands for a lower price than comparable brand-name merchandise, even virtually identical goods manufactured by the same supplier. And the exclusivity of the private brand builds store loyalty.

Two high-end European manufacturers of bed linens are Porthault of France and Pratesi of Italy. Pratesi has seven "salons" in the United States, where a king-size sheet of Egyptian cotton sells for $3,000!

### Designing a Tabletop Line

Tabletop goods respond to the same trends that affect other segments of the home furnishings industry and other fashion industries. Producers rely on resources such as the Color Marketing Group for forecasts of color, design themes, and other changing consumer preferences. This information leads to the introduction of new patterns and sometimes the discontinuation of old ones. Public interest in ecology, combined with the promotion of gardening by Martha Stewart and others, has given rise to the decoration of tabletop products with floral patterns and gardening themes.

Producers also base technical production decisions and the allocation of resources to particular product categories on their analyses of trends in the marketplace. When consumers are cautious about investing in high-ticket purchases, manufacturers may promote giftware items and introduce more new pieces in that category rather than focusing on lines of formal china dinnerware or sterling flatware. Another strategy, exemplified in the manufacturing of dinnerware, is to improve productivity and reduce costs through technological advances. A new heat transfer processes for applying multicolor decorations to ceramic wares has enabled manufacturers to offer a more salable product in moderately priced lines.

A special feature in the *Tabletop Market Report* is a psychographic study of four different personality types that make up the tabletop market: Neoconservative Connie/Conrad, Casual Carol, Formerly-Formal Frances, and Helena the Hostess with the Mostest.

Neoconservative Connie/Conrad is the largest consumer segment. They are rather traditional about their use and preferences for the tabletop. Connies/Conrads agree that their lifestyle is more casual than formal, so they prefer to set the table with more casual, less formal tableware. This group has an equal representation of men and women, thus the gender-neutral name.

Casual Carol makes up the second-largest segment in the tabletop market. She wants nothing to do with a formal tabletop because it doesn't fit her lifestyle.

Formerly-Formal Frances used to be a traditionalist, but today she is marching to her own drummer when it comes to her tabletop. She has relegated her formal dinnerware to the china cabinet and instead sets her table with the casual luxury style she much prefers.

Helena the Hostess with the Mostest is the smallest and oldest segment. While she also lives a casual lifestyle, Helena leans toward a more formal table presentation, especially when entertaining. She is also the most likely to own holiday dinnerware to set a festive holiday table.

As you can see, consumers' tastes have shifted toward a more casual, but luxurious way of setting the table. Pam Danzinger, president of Unity Marketing, says, "People want tableware they can dress up and dress down depending on the occasion. This affects marketers at both ends of the pricing spectrum, as people want tabletop that is better than everyday, but more casual than formal dinnerware."[3]

# Fashion Focus

Fashion Focus

## The Fashion 50
### *The Most Powerful People in Home Fashions*

When Meryl Streep's Miranda Priestly character in *The Devil Wears Prada* tells her new assistant that the sweater she is wearing is a result of a complex series of events orchestrated over a several-year period by a cast of characters too numerous to mention, it is the quintessential Fashion 101 in making business happen. The close coordination of many people is the driving force, whether the product is sweaters or sheets, dresses or dishes, tops or toasters. In 2007, *HFN, Home Furnishing News*—the industry "bible"—presented its annual list of the fifty most powerful and influential people in home furnishing design and style. Among the fifty listed, fifteen are designers, fifteen are retailers, nine are manufacturers, and the other eleven are people who influence home fashions in a myriad of ways, in color, support, magazines, and public relations.

Here are just a few of the top fifty who have defined the trends in home fashions.

### 1 Martha Stewart
Chairperson, Martha Stewart Living Omnimedia

This domestic diva now defines the home departments of two of the nation's biggest retailers: Macy's and Kmart. The launch of Martha Stewart's exclusive collection at 800 Macy's stores gives her an unrivaled influence in the home fashions area. She also influences how Americans eat with the rollout of her exclusive line of food at Costco. Stewart's print and TV media empire continues to shape the way Americans think about—and carry out—the domestic arts.

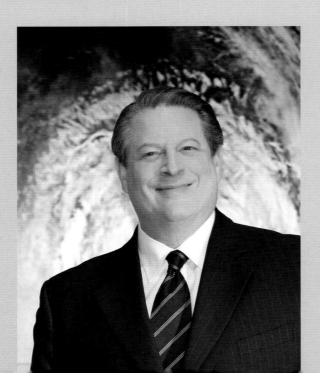

### 3 Gordon Segal and Barbara Turf
Founder and Chief Executive Officer; President, Crate & Barrel

The clean, crisp Crate & Barrel look is coming into more dining rooms, living rooms, kitchens, and bedrooms than ever before. Crate & Barrel is taking its lifestyle retailing across the USA and into Europe and Japan.

### 5 Ralph Lauren
Designer

Powerhouse Lauren is still a master of home fashion and is one of the few designers able to successfully balance luxury and moderately priced merchandise. Once basically restricted to department stores and his own boutiques, Lauren has expanded into Kohl's and is revitalizing JCPenney with the American line.

### 13 Al Gore
Green Movement

He never did become president, but Al Gore has been a tireless champion for global warming. Consumers are voting with their dollars in favor of earth-friendly products.

### 21 Chris Madden
Designer

Chris Madden is gaining ground as Middle America's decorator. The designer's exclusive home collection for JCPenney is the retailer's marquee brand. Madden's traditional take on home design will inform the decorating tastes of moderate shoppers.

**25** Joe Laneve and Kevin Harter
Senior Vice President;
General Merchandise Manager, Bloomingdale's

Laneve and Harter are leading the fashion and merchandising vision of the nation's only upscale, total home department store chain. The new home concept is segmented by lifestyle as opposed to brand and product category.

**29** Lou Scala
Chief Merchandising Officer of Waterford Wedgwood USA
President of Rosenthal and Wedgwood USA

The design aesthetic and creativity of Lou Scala is credited with developing the successful program for Lenox, and now he has his hand in several Waterford, Wedgwood, and Rosenthal projects.

**42** Aaron Stewart
Creative Director, Sferra

Aaron Stewart has helped the high-level company launch its new, more accessible Sferra 1891 line, named after the year the company was founded. A lower point makes it more accessible to a younger demographic, introducing Sferra to a whole new generation of consumers.

**49** The Container Store Team

The design team at The Container Store actually consists of the retailer's merchandising, creative, and marketing departments, and all under the direction of Sharon Tindell, chief merchandising officer, and Mona Williams, vice president of buying. Together, this group works with vendors to create some of The Container Store's unique products.

## Importance of Brand Name

Although manufacturers of tabletop goods produce a variety of products, many of the larger firms are associated with the category that was their initial specialty. Indeed, some names conjure up a particular segment of a category or even the name of a pattern. The name Wedgwood is so closely identified with its most famous design that the background color is called Wedgwood blue (see Figure 15.5).

Some manufacturers capitalize on their image in one home accessories category by developing coordinated or complementary lines in related categories. Waterford is using its reputation for fine lead crystal to gain entry into the market for table linens. It is having lines produced at different price points to attract different market segments. At the high end are lines for collectors of its glassware; and for newlyweds who want to own something with the Waterford name, the lower-priced lines are affordable. Lalique (glassware and jewelry) and Puiforcat (handcrafted silverware) have also entered the dinnerware market and offer glassware, flatware, and porcelain lines.

## Product Categories of Selected Soft Goods

Textile fabrics and other materials, such as fur, leather, straw, cork, paper, and metal wire are used to decorate walls, floors, windows, and furniture. We focus on the seven main categories of soft goods

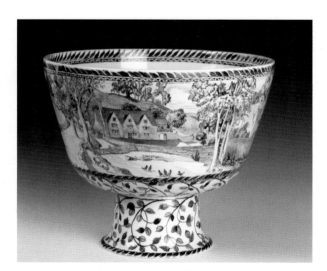

**FIGURE 15.5** Wedgwood blue punchbowl, 1928.

that bring fashion to home interior wardrobe (see Table 15.1).

### Bed Linens

For several reasons, bed linens, especially sheets and pillowcases, are one of the most frequently purchased categories of home accessories (see Figure 15.6). For a weekly change of freshly laundered sheets and pillowcases, a stock of three sets is recommended: one set on the bed, one in the wash, and one in the closet. Furthermore, a change of bedding is a relatively inexpensive way to achieve a dramatic change in the look of a room, especially if the colors and patterns of various items are mixed and matched. Buying a new bed often means buying new bed linens to fit—for example, when a baby outgrows its crib or adults in the family opt for a larger bed. New mattresses, which may be as thick as 14 inches, may require new fitted sheets and mattress pads with more generous corner pockets than the bedding designed for older 8-inch-thick mattresses.

Although linen and even silk are used for luxury sheets, most sheets are made of cotton/polyester blends or cotton of a tight, smooth weave called percale. Two criteria are used to judge their quality: thread count and cotton content. Thread count refers to the number of threads per square inch. A higher count indicates a finer, softer sheet. Thread counts range from 180 to 350 or more; 200 is considered standard.

**FIGURE 15.6** Bed linens, especially sheets and pillowcases, are one of the most frequently purchased categories of home accessories.

Cotton/polyester blends are common in mass-merchandised sheets and offer a no-iron finish and moderate price, but 100 percent cotton is preferred for its softness. Pima cotton sheets are woven with at least 8 percent of a high-quality cotton fiber from Arizona. Supima sheets are made of 100 percent pima cotton. The finest cotton for sheets and pillowcases is imported Egyptian cotton. In harsh winter climates, soft flannel (cotton brushed to raise the nap) sheets are often used for additional warmth.

There are many subcategories of bed linens, including sheets, pillowcases, bedcovers, blankets, and pillows. Some of the latest fashions involve the choice of bed covers. Replacing bedspreads with a cozier, less formal look are quilts, comforters, and

**TABLE 15.1** *Seven Major Categories of Soft Goods*

| CATEGORY | EXAMPLES | |
|---|---|---|
| Bed linens | Sheets, pillowcases, bed covers, blankets, pillows | |
| Bath linens | Towels, washcloths, floor coverings | |
| Table linens | Tablecloths, napkins, placemats | |
| Window treatments | Curtains, shades, blinds, valences | |
| Upholstery fabric | Slipcovers, pillows | |
| Miscellaneous | Throws, kitchen towels, appliance covers | |
| Area rugs | Scatter rugs, runners | |

duvets. The **duvet** (pronounced doo-VAY), a down-filled quilt in a cover, can serve as an all-in-one top sheet, comforter, blanket, and decorative covering. Some bedding sets include coordinated sheets and pillowcases, pillow shams (covers that go over the pillowcase when the bed is not in use), a duvet cover, and a dust ruffle or bed skirt (which tucks between the mattress and box spring and hangs to the floor). Sets of coordinated sheets, pillowcases, comforter, shams, and dust ruffle, called Bed-in-a-Bag, were introduced by Dan River; customers responded enthusiastically to the convenience of this product.

Sheets and pillowcases are sized to fit standard-sized mattresses and pillows. Note that a **California king** is an extra-long, extra-wide sheet, and that an extra-long twin sheet is the size usually found in dorm rooms.

A version of traditional Japanese bedding has been adapted to Western use and sizing. In Japan, where people remove their shoes on entering a home and floors are covered with thick *tatami* mats, bedding is placed on the *tatami* for sleeping and rolled up for storage during the day. A densely filled futon serves as a mattress, and a top futon as a comforter. The Western version, the heavier bottom or mattress futon, is often sold with a hinged wooden frame. For sleeping, the futon is placed on the flat frame. The frame can be folded, and the futon draped over the back and seat to convert the bed into a couch.

### Bath Linens

The most distinctive characteristic of bath linens is the cotton terry cloth that is used for virtually all towels. The loop construction of the threads creates a spongy fabric that holds water, thus enhancing the natural absorbency of cotton. The base from which the loops project may have a small amount of polyester woven with the cotton to prolong the life of the towel. The fabrication of textiles for other bathroom accessories, such as rugs and covers for toilet

seat lids and toilet tanks, typically echoes the texture of terry cloth.

Because towels are a staple item produced in standardized sizes, they are a natural candidate for automated manufacturing. Machinery in some large mills can measure, cut, hem, and even fold towels. The plain-textured towels that make up the largest portion of the market are produced this way. The major manufacturers subcontract to smaller companies to produce towels with decorative features, such as embroidery (see Figure 15.7).

Adding fashion to function is the rainbow of choices in single colors and patterns. Sculptured towels provide another design detail. Textures include waffle-weave, corduroylike ribbing, chevrons, and other patterns. Along with the proliferation of soaps, body washes, shampoos, and lotions, giant fluffy bath sheets and other attractive bath linens add an element of luxury to personal hygiene.

**FIGURE 15.7** Bath towels come in a variety of colors and sometimes have decorative features, such as embroidery. They are often coordinated with other merchandise such as soap dishes and furniture.

### Table Linens

The informality of the contemporary American lifestyle has reduced the everyday use of table linens. Placemats and paper napkins are the norm at many dinner tables. On the other hand, this informality has elevated the dinner party to the level of a state occasion, even when the guests are close friends and the atmosphere is casual. For the sizeable segment of the population who enjoy home entertaining as a leisure pastime, attractive table linens lend elegance to the meal.

Tablecloths are manufactured in a variety of sizes and shapes, and matching napkins are usually sold separately so that customers can buy as many as they need. The choices of textiles and weaves range from fine damask and cotton/linen blends, usually in white or off-white, for formal settings to more colorful synthetics for an informally decorated table (see Figure 15.8). Stain-resistant and no-iron finishes are especially appealing to customers with small children. Several kinds of table coverings that may be placed over a tablecloth for protection from spills and crumbs (like vinyl cloths) also vary the table setting.

### Window Treatments

As the link between a room and the outside world, windows are a focal point of interior design. There are so many ways of accenting a window with textiles—not to mention wooden shutters and plastic, metal, or wooden blinds—that labels like curtains or draperies are too limited. Interior decorators refer to this vast category as window treatments (see Figure 15.9), which encompasses many important subcategories and items. Each contributes to the character of the window and the room, creating an atmosphere of openness or pri-

**FIGURE 15.8** With a mix of solids and stripes, these tablecloths create an inviting setting, while protecting the table underneath.

**FIGURE 15.9** Window treatments encompass curtains, draperies, and other window adornments.

vacy, casualness or formality, streamlined simplicity or ornateness.

The main distinction between curtains and draperies is in the weight of the fabric. Draperies are made of heavier, opaque material and are often lined. Typically, they are hung from rods by hooks and can be opened or closed by pulling a cord. Curtains are made of lighter weight, translucent fabric and are unlined. They may be hung from rods, like draperies, or they may frame the window. Some window treatments combine curtains and draperies. Either may have a matching **valance**, a horizontal strip across the top of the window, or a valance may be used alone.

Today, window treatments are often made of acrylic, polyester, nylon, and other synthetics that are more resistant than some natural fibers to the fading effects of sunlight. Curtains, especially, are easy to maintain; they may be laundered at home and changed to coordinate with bed linens. Draperies and Roman shades are more often selected to match fabric wall coverings or complement the fabrics of upholstered furniture, so these window treatments may be replaced less frequently than curtains.

## Upholstery Fabric

Furniture is expensive, making the selection of upholstery fabric an infrequent decision but an important one for fashion-conscious consumers. Whether they are purchasing a single piece or decorating an entire room, they shop for furniture that works well with other pieces and with the window treatments, floor coverings, and other home furnishings to achieve a coherent decor. In response to recent consumer demand for increased decorating options, **slipcovers** have reemerged as a home fashion item. They can protect the permanent upholstery and give a chair or sofa a new look. They are also often machine washable. A wide range of plastic gadgets has been developed to improve the fit of slipcovers.

The choice of material also has a significant influence on the look of upholstery, as well as its durability and ease of maintenance. In the 1990s, polyester and other synthetics gained the acceptance of interior designers, who, for many years, favored cotton, linen, and silk. Nontextiles, such as leather and vinyl, are also available for upholstery. Some new nontextiles, such as metallic yarn and thinly sliced cork, are being used in combination with textiles for upholstery, window treatments, and other home decorating purposes.

## Miscellaneous Soft Goods

A whole host of miscellaneous items are sold as accessories to the major categories of home furnishings. For example, the firms that manufacture bath linens and the stores and departments that sell them to consumers also produce and sell beach towels, even though they are not intended for use in the home. Other items may be associated with several major categories, such as decorative pillows, which are featured with both bed linens and upholstered furniture.

**Throws**, small woven blankets about 50 by 60 inches, became "hot" during the "cocooning" 1990s. In the beginning of the 2000s, throws were often made of luxury fabrics that echoed ready-to-wear runway trends. Popular materials for throws included cashmere, pashmina, silk, velvet, and faux fur. An earlier kind of throw, called an "afghan," was a knitted or crocheted item, often handmade, and frequently displayed over the back of a sofa. Probably the most famous afghan is the multicolored one on the sofa in the TV sitcom *Roseanne*, now in reruns.

## Area Rugs

In the category of soft floor coverings, **area rugs**, which cover most of the floor of a room but are removable, offer greater flexibility in decorating than carpets, which are permanently tacked to the floor (see Figure 15.10). The distinction between

stores changed its fixtures to hold and display more products in the same square footage. Macy's has also experienced a growth in the area-rug business. In the e-commerce channel, which previously exhibited little growth, Home Shopping Network plans to grow its online assortment on the basis of customers' response to its early-rug category.[4]

## Product Categories of Selected Tabletop Goods

A well-appointed table sets the stage for fine dining and demonstrates the host's mastery of the art of gracious home entertaining. Today's consumers can choose from broad selections of dinnerware, glassware, and flatware to suit their needs, no matter what their taste or budget. Some of the most commonly used items in each category are listed in Table 15.2. Two other important categories—hollowware and giftware—are often combined at the retail level.

### Dinnerware

The term **dinnerware** refers to the whole range of serving vessels for presenting food to diners and the cups, bowls, and plates for holding individual portions (see Figure 15.11). These pieces are sometimes collectively called *dishes*, but that term also has the narrower meaning of plates. The generic term *china* also has a more limited meaning, labeling only one of the materials of which dinnerware may be made. We use the industry term dinnerware to avoid confusion.

### Categories of Dinnerware

Dinnerware is available in glass and, in response to consumer concerns about breakage and price, in melamine and other plastics. However, most dinnerware is ceramic, that is, made of baked—or *fired*—clay. The quality of the clay is a major factor in the quality of the product. In ascending order of quality, the major clay bodies used for dinnerware

**TABLE 15.2** *Dinnerware, Glassware, and Flatware*

| DINNERWARE | GLASSWARE | FLATWARE | |
|---|---|---|---|
| *Place Setting* | *Stemmed* | *Four-Piece Place Setting* | |
| Dinner plate | Brandy snifter | Knife | |
| Salad plate | Champagne flute | Dinner fork | |
| Cup | Cocktail | Teaspoon | |
| Saucer | Cordial | Salad fork | |
| Bowl | Sherry | | |
| | Water | *Five-Piece Place Setting* | |
| *Accessory Pieces* | Wine | Soup spoon | |
| Bread plate | | | |
| Soup bowl | *Tumblers* | *Accessory Pieces* | |
| Rimmed soup bowl | Iced tea | Iced tea spoon | |
| Mug | Beer mug | Steak knife | |
| | Juice | Butter spreader | |
| *Serving Pieces* | Double old-fashioned | | |
| Vegetable dish (some covered) | | *Serving Pieces* | |
| Platter | *Serving Pieces* | Salad fork and spoon | |
| Coffeepot | Decanters | Salad tongs | |
| Teapot | Pitchers | Serving spoons | |
| Sugar bowl | | Meat fork | |
| Creamer | | Pie server | |
| Cake plate | | Cake rack | |

**FIGURE 15.11** Maidenhair Fern table setting by Martha Stewart Home.

place settings. Service for four is common in casual patterns for everyday family use. The number of serving pieces may be limited, and the place settings may include only a dinner plate and cup and saucer. Five-piece place settings add a salad plate and a bowl or bread and butter plate to the basic items.

Customers can expand their sets of dinnerware or replace broken pieces by purchasing additional place settings or individual items. Pieces sold individually are called open stock. The most elaborate sets of dinnerware include plates, bowls, and cups that vary in size and shape according to very specific use. For example, a coffee cup is larger than a tea cup and has straighter sides. Most modern patterns, however, include fewer types of items, and contemporary consumers, with their informal lifestyle, do not demand such fine distinctions. In fact, a common practice is to build a set of dinnerware from open stock, coordinating items in the same pattern but different colors.

### Glassware

Glass has long been recognized as a versatile material with properties suitable for many uses. Essentially, glass is sand, melted in a furnace and molded or blown into the desired shape and allowed to harden. Because the main component is nonporous, glass is ideal for vessels for storing and serving food and beverages. Examples of beautifully colored opaque glass vessels from ancient Egypt, Syria, and Rome have survived for thousands of years.

The English colonists brought the manufacturing of glass to America. In the 19th century, Americans made several technical contributions to the industry. A pressing machine, introduced in 1825, allowed for the production of pressed-glass patterns. The production of the first electric light bulbs by Corning Glass Works in 1879 was an early example of this company's focus on innovations in industrial uses of glass. But later Corning also developed glass products for oven-to-table use, including Pyrex and Corning Ware.

are peasant pottery, earthenware, ironstone, stoneware, china (or porcelain), and bone china. Peasant pottery is most often used only for serving pieces or decorative objects. Hand-decorated Delft pottery from Holland and Majolica from Italy are valued as craft objects for display. Stoneware is common for everyday dinnerware, and china and bone china, with more formal decorative patterns, for serving guests.

Glazes and other decorative features of dinnerware also affect their value and durability and raise safety issues. In formulating glazes, manufacturers must balance the desired colors against the resistance of the glaze to the chemicals in detergent. Decorative gold trim renders a piece unusable in a microwave, and other aspects of the chemical composition control whether a product is oven-proof, dishwasher-safe, and suitable for the refrigerator or freezer.

### Sets of Dinnerware

Dinnerware is usually sold in sets of service for four, eight, or twelve, including serving pieces and basic

At the end of the century, Michael J. Owens of the Libbey Company invented an automatic bottle machine that greatly improved production processes. Now the largest glassware manufacturer in the United States, Libbey makes more than two thousand products, including its popularly priced lines of drinking glasses.

The top quality is leaded glass, which has a minimum of 5 percent lead oxide. Full lead crystal has at least 24 percent lead oxide. The softness of lead crystal makes it easy to hand cut, and it is the most brilliant crystal. Some questions have been raised, however, about the leaching of lead into wine decanters, because the wine usually remains in the decanter for long periods.

## Place Settings

Three types of glassware categorized by shape are **tumblers**, cylindrical glasses; **footed tumblers**, tumblers with a heavy bottom; and **stemware**, bowl-shaped glasses on a stalk or, as the name suggests, stem. The various shapes are designed to hold specific beverages (see Figure 15.12). Water may be served in any of the shapes. Milk, fruit and vegetable juices, and sodas are typically served in tumblers or footed tumblers, and cocktails, in footed tumblers.

Drinking wine from the correct glass enhances enjoyment because the shape captures the bouquet. At a formal table, appropriate stemware may be set out for red and white wine. But modern society is not strict about the rules. Although manufacturers of fine crystal offer sets in matched patterns, many customers prefer to buy glassware from open stock and to set their tables with just one or two glasses at each place.

## Flatware

The use of flatware is a relatively recent phenomenon, and it is not as widespread as the use of dinnerware or glassware. Think of all the Asian countries where chopsticks are used and the not-so-primitive societies that have developed ways of eating neatly without utensils. In fact, hors d'oeuvres, sandwiches, and other finger foods are common in cultures that serve other foods with flatware.

In medieval Europe, a banquet invitation was a "bring your own flatware" occasion. People of high

**FIGURE 15.12** Glassware comes in various shapes, and each piece is designed to hold a specific beverage.

social status acquired a personal silver knife, fork, and spoon set at birth and used their own utensils—in addition to their hands—wherever they ate. The Italians of the 16th century were the first to eat their meat with a knife and fork, and the practice was not widely accepted elsewhere in Europe for a hundred years. But once the idea of having a variety of knives, forks, and spoons took hold, the choices became overwhelming. Different spoons were designed for coffee and tea and for cream soups and clear soups.

Today flatware contributes to the style of a table setting. It can be formal or casual, traditional or modern, elegant or utilitarian. Ideally it makes eating easier and more pleasant.

### Categories of Flatware

Like "china" that is actually stoneware, "linens" made of cotton, and plastic "glasses," not all "silverware" is silver. Only sterling silver can accurately wear that label. It must be 92.5 percent silver and only 7.5 percent alloy metal (copper, for example, which is added for strength). If the flatware is silver plate, the proportions of silver to alloy are more or less reversed: the silver is a coating over an alloy core. *Vermeil* (pronounced ver-MAY), silver flatware dipped in gold to prevent corrosion of the silver by the chemicals in certain foods, may be made up in whole sets of flatware or in a few pieces. Stainless steel flatware is manufactured for everyday use, but some of it is of high enough quality to be used with fine china. The best-known American manufacturers of flatware—Oneida, Reed & Barton, Gorham, Towle, and Kirk Steiff, among them—offer patterns in all four categories.

### Place Settings and Serving Pieces

Like other tabletop goods, flatware is sold in sets for four, eight, and twelve as well as open stock. The typical place setting consists of a knife, dinner fork, salad fork, and teaspoon, and in some sets, a soup spoon. Serving utensils are designed to facilitate transfer of a portion from the serving dish to the individual's plate. Slotted vegetable spoons drain the vegetables; a pie server slides neatly under the slice; and so on.

### Hollowware

The term **hollowware** covers a variety of metal service items such as trays, candlesticks, sugar bowls and creamers, coffeepots, and teapots. Common materials for hollowware include sterling silver, silver plate, and pewter. Some items may be kept on display in the living room or dining room and used for buffet service.

### Giftware

Giftware is a thriving segment of the home accessories industry because of recurring gift-giving occasions. Some gifts may be made from any of a number of materials. Picture frames in wood, ceramic materials, a variety of metals, and even leather and papier-mâché are all popular. Giftware can be displayed on coffee tables, desks, and shelves, adding decorative accents to a room. Table 15.3 lists some of the more frequently given gift items.

**TABLE 15.3** *Giftware*

| All Occasions | Baby Gifts | Desk Sets |
|---|---|---|
| Picture frames | Cups | Blotters |
| Mirrors | Spoons | Bookends |
| Vases | Rattles | Pencil holders |
| Flower pots | Teething rings | Note pad holders |
| Candlesticks | Porringer | Letter holders |
| Candles | Comb and brush set | Letter openers |
| Clocks | | Pen holders |
| Figurines | | |

An interesting aspect of the gift market is the proliferation of museum reproductions now available from institutions worldwide. In the United States, reproductions have become available not only from the Museum of Fine Arts, Boston, the Art Institute of Chicago, the Smithsonian, and the Metropolitan Museum of Art of New York, but also from smaller institutions like the Winterthur Museum in Delaware, Historic Natchez Foundation, the Henry Ford Museum, and Greenfield Village. Some of these museums also have set up free-standing stores outside the museum.

All of the cultural institutions named, both great and small, are members of the Museum Store Association (MSA), an organization of retail personnel at cultural institutions across the country. Museum stores offer unique shopping opportunities that can't be experienced anywhere else, and MSA represents more than 1,600 stores in every kind of cultural institution from art museums and science centers to zoos, botanic gardens, and nature parks to performing arts centers, libraries, halls of fame, historic houses, and other cultural institutions.[5]

## Market Segments

New homes, whether they are the first apartment of a newly married couple, the expanded home of a growing family, or the vacation home that is the prize of financial success, provide a dependable market for the home furnishings industry. Replacement purchases, spurred by the cocooning of baby boomers, add a direction for growth. Other huge market segments, beyond the scope of this text, are the institutional and military markets.

### Bridal

Marriages are a source of celebration for the home furnishings industry as well as for the newlyweds because they generate spending disproportionate to the small percentage of households—less than 3 percent in the United States—they represent. Many

**FIGURE 15.13** Brides- and grooms-to-be can browse JCPenney's top registry picks and create their own wish lists.

couples experience a sudden surge of money as they combine their incomes and reduce the costs of separate housing. They spend their windfall on setting up their new home, and well-wishers among their friends and family buy them gifts. The fact that half of all purchases of sterling silver flatware and giftware are for the bridal market is a dramatic indicator of the impact of this segment.

**Wedding** or **bridal registries** in department stores and specialty stores give the retailer an opportunity to establish a good relationship with the customer by offering a service. They provide a record of the customer's taste and attract the business of gift-givers who want to be sure of making the right selection. Today, most department stores and mass-market retailers have added online registrations to complement their computerized in-store registry programs. Condé Nast Bridal Media has married something old (print) with something new (a microsite) in a program put together for JCPenney. At the center of the program is a virtual-room gift registry Bridal Media created called "Click It. Pick It. Love It." There, the bride and groom can make a wish list; browse JCPenney's top registry picks for the kitchen, bedroom, dining room (see Figure 15.13); and even monogram their towels. The microsite, which will be housed at Brides.com, also taps into couples' growing desire to customize their weddings. Beside the new Brides.com, The Knot and Wedding Channel are established sites that already have audiences of over 1.5 million.[6]

### New Home/Vacation Home

When a family or individual moves into a new home, at whatever stage of the life cycle, possibilities open up for sellers of home furnishings. New housing starts tend to increase the demand for bedroom and bathroom products because the new homes typically have more bedrooms and bathrooms. Moves to accommodate the growth of a family feed the market for baby giftware as well as the market for bed linens. Going away to college involves buying bed and bath linens, perhaps even window treatments. Even a move into a retirement community involves home furnishing purchases—new window treatments, for example, when the old ones do not fit.

Vacation homes are often initially furnished with castoffs from the main residence. But the informal nature of life at the beach, in the mountains, or at a country retreat usually dictates a less formal style of decorating, with emphasis on easy upkeep. It is the rare vacation home that does not gradually get redecorated!

### Replacement

The replacement market exists at many levels. Many young people begin their first apartments with hand-me-downs from relatives and friends. As their earnings grow, they replace the worst of the used items. Some households seek inexpensive replacements for broken or worn items. Many of these people shop at garage sales, flea markets, thrift stores, or discounters. Others trade up to slightly more expensive items. Thanks to cocooning

baby boomers, redecorating has expanded the home furnishings market. This generational segment was a large proportion of the population in childhood, and as life expectancy increases, boomers will continue to have a significant influence on the replacement market.

## Market Resources

The producers and marketers of home furnishings have both common and unique interests, and resources are available to meet the needs of the industry as a whole and those of the various segments. As a world fashion capital, New York is the location of manufacturers' showrooms for home textiles and other home furnishings products and the site of major industry trade shows. The Atlanta Market Center, with 600 showrooms and proximity to the large textile mills, is also important in the international home furnishings scene. North Carolina is the center of the furniture industry in the United States and has showrooms that include upholstery, pillows, and other decorative objects. The vast Merchandise Mart in Chicago is devoted to furniture and various soft goods and tabletop merchandise.

### Trade Associations

Organizations that promote all home furnishings industries include the Home Furnishings Independents Association in Dallas; the National Home Furnishings Association in High Point, North Carolina; the Home Fashion Products Association in New York City; and the International Housewares Association in Rosemont, Illinois.

The home textiles industry is served by trade associations that are also involved in apparel textiles. Cotton Incorporated and the Wool Council promote specific textiles, and the American Textile Manufacturers Institute has a more generalist mission. The Decorative Fabrics Association and the National Association of Decorative Fabrics Distributors focus on home textiles.

Because High Point, North Carolina, is the center of furniture manufacturing, it is also the home of the American Home Furnishings Alliance and the Upholstered Furniture Action Council. Other associations that promote specific industry segments include the Carpet and Rug Institute in Dalton, Georgia, and the National Association of Floor Covering Distributors in Chicago.

### Trade Shows

New York, Chicago, and Atlanta, with their large numbers of permanent showrooms and vast convention facilities, host the biggest trade shows (see Figure 15.14). The New York Home Textiles Show comes to the Javits Center each January and August. The New York Tabletop Market is also a major event.

The International Home and Housewares Show in Chicago attracts thousands of buyers from around the world every March; the Chicago Merchandise Mart also draws buyers all year because of the huge number of showrooms it contains. In Atlanta, the Atlanta International Area Rug Market features exhibitors and products from all over the world.

Another trade show is the Pacific Home Fashion Fair, which also provides opportunities for manufacturers, designers, jobbers, and retailers to meet.

### Trade Publications

Weekly magazines for the home furnishings industry, such as *HFN, Home Furnishings News* and *Home Accents Today*, provide broad coverage. *Home Textiles Today* and *LBD Interior Textiles* have a slightly narrower focus on home textiles. Other trade publications, such as *Ceramic Industry*, indicate by their name which segment of the market they serve. See Table 15.4 for a more complete list of trade publications.

### Merchandising and Marketing

Home furnishings can take many routes from manufacturer to consumer. Depending on the product, there may be a few or many stops along the way.

The distribution of textile products for the home is particularly complex and involves a number of professionals, each of whom adds service and expertise to the process. The major manufacturers display their household linens in their New York showrooms, and their sales representatives bring sample books with fabric swatches and photos of products to customers.

**TABLE 15.4**
*Trade Publications for the Home Furnishings Industry*

| BROAD COVERAGE | SEGMENTS OF THE HOME FURNISHINGS INDUSTRY |
| --- | --- |
| FDM—Furniture Design and Manufacturing | Ceramic Industry |
| HFN—Home Furnishings News | Floor Covering Weekly |
| Home Accents Today | Residential Lighting |
| Home Furnishings Review | Furniture Today |
| Interior Design | |

**FIGURE 15.14** Maison et Objet, the vast, semi-annual home furnishings trade fair, gives people from around the world a preview of upcoming trends.

## Retail Channels of Distribution

Consumers have a variety of resources to meet their home furnishings needs. For customized upholstered furniture and window treatments, as well as expert advice and access to goods not otherwise available, consumers can turn to professional interior designers. Some designers have their own firms, and others are on staff at home furnishings and department stores.

Consumers who are making their own selections turn to different types of stores for different categories of goods. For example, mass merchandisers are the main source of household linens. The top sellers in this category are Wal-Mart, JCPenney, Kmart, and Target. Together they account for about 90 percent of the sales in this category.[7]

Some vendors see home centers as the fastest-growing channel. Many home center retailers are moving boldly into soft goods once thought incompatible with their hard lines and building products mix. One example is Home Depot's Right At Home decor program for its warehouse stores, which is growing rapidly.

For consumers who are bargain conscious but want more upscale merchandise than is available through the mass merchandisers, the category killer in home furnishings is the discount superstore. The leading chains are Bed, Bath & Beyond and Linens 'n Things. Overlapping their market is Williams-Sonoma, which is primarily a retailer of housewares and appliances but also offers casual tabletop goods and other home fashion products. HomeGoods is the off-price chain of TJX Companies, which owns Marshalls and T.J.Maxx. Bath & Body Works At Home is the Limited's entry into this field. IKEA, a Swedish superstore chain, offers low-price furniture (some of which the customer assembles), home furnishings, and housewares. Manufacturers' factory outlets also appeal to this segment of the market.

The broad assortments in different product lines offered by the superstores have cut into the business of the traditional department stores. Some of the ways the department stores are holding onto their customers are by offering exclusive merchandise, including private brands; featuring designer lines in model room displays; and matching competitors' prices through periodic "white sales."

In categories in which the superstore discounters do not compete or where their offerings are limited, department stores continue as dominant players. They account for 40 percent of giftware purchases and about one-third of sterling silver flatware sales.

Specialty stores in this market segment compete by offering exclusive merchandise, often imported goods. Well-known examples are Crate & Barrel, Pottery Barn, and Domain. Specialty stores, with almost half the sales in the giftware segment, are the competitors to beat.

Nonstore retailing is another resource for consumers. Some stores, both specialist and general merchandise retailers, do a significant portion of their home furnishings business through catalog divisions (see Figure 15.15). Bloomingdale's, Crate & Barrel, Eddie Bauer Home, Tiffany, and Gumps are a few examples that convey the range of retailers who have followed this route. Catalog retailers like Spiegel, Lands' End, and L.L. Bean have also added home furnishings to their lines. Specialty catalogs include Chambers (a high-end catalog from Williams-Sonoma/Pottery Barn), Ross-Simons Gift & Home Collection, the Horchow Collection, Domestications, Smith & Noble Windoware, and Country

**FIGURE 15.15** Anthropologie, Crate & Barrel, and Pottery Barn advertise their home products through catalogs.

Curtains. All these companies also have their own Web sites that showcase and sell their products, as well as provide information about them.

Cable television retailers have entered this lucrative market. The latest development in the home furnishings market is part of the larger trend to take advantage of the Internet. As the virtual neighborhood of the Web home pages grows, all segments of the market can play host or visitor to each other. The home page can be a store, an in-house public relations agency, and an advertising agency all rolled into one.

### Advertising and Publicity

What could be more natural to cocooners and home decorating enthusiasts than to curl up with a magazine directed right at them? Home decorating magazines, known in the trade as "shelter magazines," include *Architectural Digest, Better Homes and Gardens, Domino, House Beautiful, Metropolitan Home, Country Living, Elle Decor, Martha Stewart Living,* and *Vogue Living* (see Figure 15.16). They are a great medium for manufacturers to advertise to the public and build demand for their brands. Retailers, especially national chains, also advertise in these periodicals. Other magazines that feature ads for home furnishings include the bridal magazines like *Modern Bride,* women's magazines like *Woman's Day* and *The Ladies Home Journal,* and upscale magazines like *Town and Country* and *The New Yorker.* There are also a newer crop of magazines, including *Wallpaper, Surface,* and *City,* with content that focuses on avant-garde trends in interior designs as well as fashion.

Magazines are perhaps even more beneficial as a source of publicity than as an advertising medium. They provide favorable mention by a presumably disinterested authority and show attractively photographed examples of a product or line in use.

Local newspapers are another advertising medium advantageous to both producers and retailers, who share the costs through cooperative advertising agreements. And local media can provide pub-

**FIGURE 15.16** Trade magazines like *Architectural Digest, Domino,* and *Vogue Living* feature the latest home trends and products, plus decorating tips.

licity to retailers for in-store events such as the opening of a new unit of a chain; a lecture by a home furnishings star; a home fashion show, perhaps featuring a designer; or a cooking demonstration that culminates in the presentation of a meal at a beautifully set table.

Coordinated, mix-and-match choices are more popular than ever. Croscill Home Fashions, for example, offers a premerchandised display concept to both department stores and home centers.

### Industry Trends

In the home furnishings industry, as in other aspects of daily life in the new millennium, fashion, technology, and environmentalism have been important influences. Responses at all levels to issues in these three areas will continue to affect each other for the rest of the 21st century.

### Growing Fashion Influence

We have already observed how baby boomers have turned their fashion interests toward their homes

and how apparel designers, alert to the trend, have responded.

In some ways, the cycle is speeding up. The collection of home furnishings designed by Martha Stewart, icon of gracious living, is now sold by Kmart and in all 800 Macy's stores. Anyone, class or mass, who wants to know the latest news from designers, producers, or marketers of home fashions can find out on the Internet. The products themselves are available at affordable prices through discount superstores and factory outlets.

We have also seen how the life cycle of home fashion products has speeded up as consumers spend their money on replacement purchases that can give them a new look at relatively little expense. As producers use new technology to develop faster, more economical ways of manufacturing and delivering goods, their response has generated even greater demand.

## Increased Automation in Design and Production

CAD has arrived in both the hard and soft sides of the home furnishings industries. Hand-drawn designs can be scanned and patterns can be generated electronically. Manufacturing equipment can be programmed to reproduce these designs on dinnerware or upholstery fabrics. Employees are retrained to oversee automated production equipment rather than operate older machinery. American manufacturers have invested heavily in new automated equipment; for example, an automated hemming machine can hem all four sides of a flat sheet faster than manual sewing can (see Figure 15.17).

Automated production speeds up manufacturing and thereby enables producers to fill orders more quickly. Borrowing from the apparel industry, home furnishings manufacturers, especially textile producers, have instituted quick response procedures. Basically, quick response is a service that allows retailers to avoid the expense of excess

**FIGURE 15.17** This machine enables manufacturers to produce embossed goods at a high speed.

inventory by placing orders on short notice. The retailer can keep enough stock to meet immediate demand but not be stuck with items that have passed their fashion peak. It is the computerized connection between retailer and supplier that enables both to analyze sales trends and adjust stock levels accordingly. Automation in the U.S. textile industry has had such a favorable impact on production costs that there is little impetus to reduce labor costs through offshore production.

## Growth of Exports

One area in which the home furnishings industry is bucking a trend is international trade. Imports have focused on high-end merchandise, such as Egyptian cotton bed linens, Indian rugs, and fine china and crystal from famous European companies. Many of these products are valued for the tradition of artistry and craftsmanship they exemplify and for their distinctive designs. But the United States continues to lead the world in the design, manufacture, and export of midrange bed and bath linens, rugs and carpets, and tabletop goods.

## Increased Use of High-Tech Fabrics

New technology not only means faster and more highly automated production and delivery of products but sometimes means changes in the very nature of the product. In the manufacturing of bedding, especially pillows, high-tech fibers now protect consumers from allergy-producing molds, mildews, fungi, and dust mites. **Antimicrobials**, compounds that are spun into acetate fibers, break down the cells of microbes that lurk in the moist atmosphere of bedding.

Other treatments of textiles include no-iron finishes on bed linens, antifungal finishes on drapery fabric, and pesticides in wool carpeting.

## Increased Awareness of Ecological Issues

According to a report from the NPD Group, nearly 65 percent of consumers surveyed believe it is important to purchase environmentally friendly products for their home. Additionally, the report shows purchasing "green-related" home products becoming more important to consumers as they grow older. "The information in the report is somewhat contrary to the belief that it's the younger generation who is more concerned about going 'green.' It may be that the older generation is now looking to leave the planet in better shape for their children and grandchildren," said Mark Delaney, director, home improvement, NPD.[8]

Countering the trend toward the use of high-tech fabrics is a demand for untreated natural materials (see Figure 15.18). Manufacturers are responsive to this backlash, a manifestation of the growing concern about protecting the environment. Ecological issues affect both the processes of producing home furnishings and the resulting products.

For example, in the early 1990s, a chemical in the glue used on the back of carpeting was linked to a high incidence of leukemia among workers in a Georgia carpet factory. The chemical was also suspect in the sick feelings experienced by some consumers when their carpets were installed. Environmentalists called on the federal government to regulate the use of the glue or at least investigate its possible effects. The environmentalists also conducted tests of their own. They publicized recommendations that consumers replace carpets with area rugs made of untreated natural fibers.

This tale is one of many that demonstrate the interrelationship of fashion, technology, and ecology in shaping the home furnishings industry. With growing environmental awareness and a return to domesticity in the new millennium, there are an increasing number of companies that offer ecologically sound products and how-to tips for a healthy lifestyle. Gaiam (www.gaiam.com) is a Web site that offers eco-friendly products as well as editorial content on everything from nontoxic cleaning methods to yoga exercises.

## Summary and Review

A trend toward spending more leisure time at home has prompted interest in home decorating and has speeded up the fashion life cycle of home furnishings in such categories as household linens, window treatments, upholstery fabrics, area rugs, and tabletop goods. Clothing designers have developed home fashions lines, often through licensing agreements with major textile manufacturers. National and store brands of household linens and tabletop goods have taken on distinctive fashion images. Computer-aided drafting has enabled designers and manufacturers to provide consumers with new patterns of soft goods and tabletop items to meet growing demand.

**FIGURE 15.18** There is a growing trend for organic, eco-friendly home products, such as these bed linens by Organic Style.

Major market segments for home accessories include the bridal market, the new home and vacation home segments, and a growing market for replacement merchandise. This last segment is propelled by home-centered leisure activity and the availability of relatively inexpensive purchases that can bring new looks to home decor.

The home furnishing industry is served by trade associations, trade shows, and trade publications that address both the collective interests of all segments and the specialized interests of the home textiles industry and other product line segments. New York is the main market center, and the Atlanta market is also important. Textile manufacturing and the production of household linens are centralized in the South. The production of tabletop goods is not centralized but is dominated by a few large producers.

Channels of distribution at the retail level include discount superstores, department stores, manufacturers' outlets, specialty retailers, and catalog retailers. Electronic shopping resources are becoming more important. Shelter magazines are a major medium for retail advertising and publicity.

The interplay of fashion, technology, and environmentalism dominates trends in the home furnishings industry. Some fashion trends are a casual lifestyle and a preference for natural fibers and other natural materials. Technological trends include computer-aided drafting, automated production, quick-response ordering systems, and the use of high-tech fabrics. Environmentalism is manifest in concern about the environmental impact of production processes and the effect of chemicals in home furnishing products on consumers and the environment.

## Trade Talk

antimicrobials
California king
duvet
area rug
dinnerware
footed tumbler
hollowware
shelter magazine
slipcover
tabletop
tumbler
wedding or bridal registries
home fashions
sisal
stemware
throw
valance

## For Review

1. Why have apparel designers branched out into home furnishing lines?
2. Why are the names of textile mills important in the merchandising of household linens?
3. What benefits do natural fibers offer in household linens? What benefits do synthetics offer?
4. What do window treatments contribute to interior design?
5. Why have slipcovers become fashionable?
6. Name five shelter magazines.
7. What role do stages of the family life cycle play in defining market segments for home furnishings?
8. Name the major trade associations in the home furnishings industry. What services do they provide for their members?
9. Name five retail channels of distribution for home furnishings and describe the market of each of these types of retailer.
10. Identify three trends in the home furnishings industry.

## For Discussion

1. Why is the home furnishings industry considered a fashion industry? Discuss the influence of fashion on the manufacturing, merchandising, and marketing of home furnishings.
2. Discuss the influence of computerized manufacturing on the home furnishings industry.
3. Discuss the influence of concern for environment on the fashion features of home furnishings. What role do ecological issues play in the selection of materials and treatment of textiles?

unit five

The explosion of fashion markets and marts across America has been repeated not only in European markets but also in Canada, South America, and several Asian countries, including Japan and China. With the emergence of so many international markets, fashion has truly become global!

The most important market center for fashion in the United States is New York City. For many years it was the only center, but today Los Angeles, Miami, Dallas, Chicago, and Atlanta have captured large shares of the fashion business. Paris, which has reigned as the fashion capital of Europe for many years, now has competition from Italy, England, Belgium, Germany, and Spain. Global sourcing—the buying of foreign goods—is perhaps the most significant development in the fashion industry in many decades.

American manufacturers and retailers now routinely do direct importing and product development around the world. In addition to fashion fairs they hold in their own countries, foreign sellers and producers schedule fashion fairs in the United States to showcase and sell their goods. Popular kinds of buying that are the most successful are specification buying, private label, and product development.

This unit focuses on the elements of fashion marketing and reveals how markets operate to help manufacturers sell their products.

# THE RETAIL LEVEL: THE MARKETS FOR FASHION

# chapter sixteen

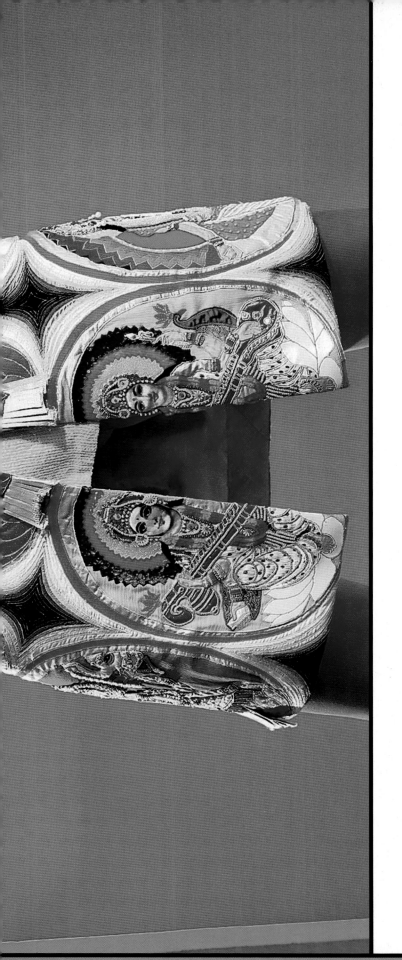

**KEY CONCEPTS**

- Meaning of the terms market, market center, mart, and trade show, and the function of each in bringing fashion from producers to consumers
- Locations and activities of markets, marts, and trade shows in the United States
- Locations and activities of foreign fashion markets
- Trends in U.S. and foreign fashion markets

*Everything you always wanted to know*

*about markets, market centers, marts, and trade shows.*

# Global Fashion Markets

As the popular children's poem states, "To market, to market, to buy a fat pig; home again, home again, jiggety jig." Going to market can be an exciting and different experience, whether it is going to buy food, candy, sporting goods, or clothes. Most of us go to market with great expectations and plans—and once home from market, sometimes the purchase is perfect and other times it is just not right. Regardless of the outcome of the trip, it is your money and can be spent however you wish. However, this is not the case when you spend someone else's money, as is the case for store buyers. When buying for a store, you are using its money, which requires an exhausting amount of planning, organization, and hard work before you can even go to market.

## Market Terminology

Markets, market centers, marts—what are they? You will hear these terms used frequently and even interchangeably, which makes them that much harder to sort out.

### Market

The word *market* has several meanings. We have already spoken of the market, or demand, for a specific product, for instance, how much people want to buy athletic shoes, dress casual trousers, or coordinated bed linens. In this chapter, the word takes on yet another meaning. A **market** is the place where goods are produced and sold at wholesale prices to store buyers. It is an important step in the pipeline that takes clothes and other fashion items from manufacturer to customer. Buyers attend markets, in effect, to choose the styles we will all be wearing within a few months.

You may hear the term **domestic market**; it refers to the market in one's own country. For example, in the United States it refers to the places throughout the United States where goods are sold to retail buyers. The **foreign market**, then, refers to places outside the United States. If you live in Canada, Canada is your domestic market, and the United States is considered a foreign market. (Both domestic and foreign markets are discussed in detail later in this chapter.)

### Market Center

Actually, there is no one giant shopping mall that serves as a market for the entire American fashion industry. Instead, several **market centers**, or geographic locations, exist throughout the country, and what are—to Americans—foreign market centers dot the globe. A market center is a city where fashion is produced and sold wholesale.

The first market center in the United States that comes to mind is New York City. For many people in and out of the fashion industry, New York City epitomizes the allure and excitement of the fashion world. Indeed, New York is the oldest market center in the United States and in many ways the most challenging to visit.

But in recent years, fashion has become regionalized, and while New York still produces much of America's fashion, it no longer produces all of it. In the past few decades, Los Angeles, Dallas, and Miami all have become flourishing market centers. Other cities that are not major apparel production centers, such as Chicago, Atlanta, and Denver, are considered markets rather than market centers, although the line between the two sometimes blurs. Chicago, for example, has always promoted itself as a market center.

### Mart

A **mart** is a building or complex of buildings that houses a wholesale market, that is, an exhibition of fashions that are ready to be sold to retail stores (see Figure 16.1). Most marts are owned and operated by independent investors. Some marts are operated by

**FIGURE 16.1** The granddaddy of all the marts is the Chicago Merchandise Mart built in 1930.

the cities themselves, and at least one, the Carolina Mart in Charlotte, North Carolina, is operated by a trade association. A permanent, professional staff operates the mart, although a large number of temporary employees are hired for market weeks.

Like convention centers, marts consist almost entirely of exhibition space. Some space is rented out as full-time corporate showrooms, but in many marts, the space is rented only during market weeks. These marts often balance their income by sponsoring other shows and conventions.

New York City, which, despite the rise of regional marts, in many ways still reigns as the country's premiere market center, is ironically the only market center without a mart. Part of the aura of a New York market week is the trek through the garment district from showroom to showroom.

The granddaddy of marts is the Merchandise Mart in Chicago, which opened its doors in the early 1930s, making Chicago New York's only rival for years. Because the Merchandise Mart was cen-

trally located, buyers from across the country found it convenient to meet in this huge building on the Chicago River several times a year to do their wholesale buying. The Mart is still very much in use today for other goods, such as home furnishings, contract (office/institutional) furnishings, kitchen and bath, and gifts and decorative accessories.

### Market Weeks

Buyers can and do travel to market centers and to some marts at any time during the year to visit individual producers, but several times a year, they also gather for market week (see Table 16.1). Few buyers are willing to forego the glamour and excitement of **market week**. During market week, market centers and marts are filled to the rafters with producers and designers, all of whom exhibit their new lines with as much style and panache as possible. The atmosphere is electrifying, heady with new, innovative ideas and the latest trends.

**TABLE 16.1** *A Basic Market Week Calendar*

| MONTH | MERCHANDISE SHOWN |
| --- | --- |
| January | Summer market |
| Late March–early April | Early fall market |
| Late May–early June | Late fall market |
| August–early September | Resort market |
| Late October–early November | Spring market |

As a purely physical convenience, it is immeasurably easier for buyers to take in new trends and make their buying decisions when they can see lots of clothes all at once. But beyond that, market week also gives everyone a chance to talk to each other and generally take in what is new in the industry.

### Trade Shows

**Trade shows** are periodic exhibits that are scheduled throughout the year in regional market centers and some marts. Smaller than market weeks, trade shows are typically attended by buyers from one region of the country. Exceptions are a few huge trade shows, such as MAGIC, which attract buyers from all over the world.

### History and Development of Market Centers in the United States

New York City was the first market center in the United States. When design and production clustered in New York, it followed that it would become a center for buying, too. That New York was the most cosmopolitan and fashion-conscious of American cities also helped. Even when travel was a strenuous undertaking, buyers at major stores tried to travel to New York twice a year. To service them, manufacturers set up showrooms near their factories in the garment district.

But for many, twice-a-year buying trips were not enough to service a store properly. And many owners and buyers for small stores across the country could not afford to travel to New York. To handle accounts between New York buying trips and to help those who did not come to New York at all, manufacturers hired **sales representatives**.

### The Role of Sales Representatives

Sales representatives played an important role in transforming other cities into market centers. For years, in addition to being the only link between apparel manufacturers in New York and the rest of the country, these jobs were filled by men. Traveling at first by train, and later by car, sales reps, as they were familiarly called, mailed advance notices to key customers in each city to announce the date of their arrival. In the early days of the fashion business, sales reps carried only one line. Later, as the fashion business became more sophisticated, they carried several noncompeting lines so they could offer their clients more variety. Once a rep arrived in a city, he rented one or more hotel rooms, which he used to exhibit his line of apparel.

For company more than anything else (the life of a sales rep was lonely), reps began to travel in groups. Soon, groups of sales reps were jointly renting clusters of adjoining rooms, so their customers could visit not just one but several exhibits at once. When they learned that this was good for business, the next step was to rent a large hotel ballroom or exhibition hall. This gradually led to the development of regional market centers, such as the Chicago Merchandise Mart.

### The Role of Marts

The Chicago Merchandise Mart had little competition until the 1960s, when other cities began to build their own marts, and regional markets took a giant step forward in their development. California had become a recognized center for selling sportswear by the 1940s, and it would soon become the second-largest market center outside New York

City. In 1964, the CaliforniaMart opened in Los Angeles, giving that city the capacity to sponsor a major market show rather than just sportswear shows. That same year, the dazzling Dallas Market Center opened and began servicing the western half of the country. The successes in Dallas and Los Angeles prompted other cities to open their own marts, and throughout the 1970s, Atlanta, Seattle, Miami, Denver, Pittsburgh, Minneapolis, and Charlotte, North Carolina, became important regional market centers.

Sales reps employed by large producers operate out of corporate showrooms in a fashion mart. If the rep can write up $1 million in orders, maintaining a permanent base at a mart is advantageous for the rep, the corporation, and their retail buyer customers. Apparel producers whose sales in a region do not warrant the investment in a corporate showroom often rely on multiline sales reps. These reps rent showroom space at the regional mart during market weeks.

## Services of Market Centers and Marts

A market week is organized by manufacturers' associations, in cooperation with the market center or mart staff. It is the prime selling opportunity for market center or mart staffs, fashion producers, and sales reps, all of whom devote themselves to making the visit as easy and convenient as possible for the buyers. Keeping buyers interested, comfortable, and happy encourages them to write orders.

Market weeks are scheduled several months before the clothes will be needed in the stores. Four or five market weeks are held each year for women's and children's wear, three to five for men's and boy's wear, and two to five for shoes. Separate market weeks are held in many market centers or marts for accessories, infants' and children's wear, lingerie, Western wear, sportswear, and bridal apparel. Table 16.1 lists the seasonal fashions shown at market weeks throughout the year. The chapters in Units Three and Four include more specific market week calendars for the various categories of fashion merchandise.

## Physical Facilities

As discussed later in this chapter, the physical facilities vary between New York and the rest of the market centers and marts in the United States. The physical facilities of marts are designed for buyers' convenience. Exhibition space is arranged by fashion category; for example, handbags, small leather goods, and jewelry are typically located together; women's sportswear occupies another area, and lingerie still another.

Marts include an array of meeting rooms, ranging from auditoriums and theaters for fashion shows to smaller rooms for seminars and conferences. The newer marts even have office space where buyers can take a quiet moment to relax—and add up what they have spent.

## Publicity

A market week is only as successful as the exhibitors it manages to attract, so most regional markets and marts mount an ongoing publicity program to draw interesting and exciting exhibitors (see Figure 16.2). So the chemistry will be mutual, market centers and

FIGURE 16.2 An advertisement promoting Moda Manhattan as the place to be for fashion and accessory trends.

marts also do what they can to attract buyers. Flyers and brochures touting market weeks go out to stores and individual buyers several times a year. Buyers are also treated to buyers' breakfasts, luncheons, and cocktail parties throughout market week—all courtesy of the market center, mart, or a supporting organization.

The most popular form of publicity is the fashion shows that highlight every market week. The shows are hectic because they are so huge and so much activity is going on. They are also among the more extravagant and interesting fashion shows ever staged, primarily because they are the work of many different designers, all of whom enter their most beautiful or interesting designs. In order to give some coherence to a market week fashion show, it is often organized around a theme, such as a particular color or, more often, an exciting new trend.

## Special Services for Market Week

The market center or mart staff does everything in their power to make viewing and buying of seasonal lines easy for buyers who travel to market week. The endless rounds of exhibits are exhilarating but exhausting, and no one wants to lose buyers because they were not offered enough support.

Support services begin even before the buyer leaves home. Buyers are sent information on hotels with special rates, shuttle service to and from the fashion shows, and screening procedures. Only authorized manufacturers and buyers are admitted to market week, and security is high throughout.

Specialized support services are also planned. For example, models are hired to work in the showrooms in case a buyer wants to see someone wearing a particular garment. Beyond this, buyers are provided with an array of information, educational, and between-show services.

### Information Services

Once the buyers arrive, they are given a **buyer's directory** and a calendar to help them find their way

around and schedule events they want to see. A steady flow of daily publications—trade newspapers, flyers, brochures, and newsletters—continues throughout the week and keeps buyers abreast of breaking market week news.

### Educational Services

An orientation program is typically scheduled for the first day, and consultants are on call throughout the week to discuss and deal with specific problems. Seminars and conferences are held to supply buyers with the latest information on fashion. Typical topics are new advances in fiber and fabrics, trends in fashion colors, the latest merchandising techniques, advertising and promotion ideas, and sales training hints.

### General Services

The level of life and services between market weeks varies from place to place, but the trend is for both market centers and marts to stay open year-round. At the Miami International Merchandise Mart, for example, many tenants operate their showrooms year round.

## The New York Market

As a market, New York belongs in a category by itself, not only because it is the city with the most resources to offer the fashion world but also, as mentioned earlier, because it has no central mart building.

### Trading Area and Economic Impact

The New York market is made up of literally thousands of showrooms, which line the streets of the garment district. Generally, similar-quality apparel is grouped together. In the women's wholesale market, for example, the couture (pronounced koo-TUR) or higher-priced lines are situated primarily along Seventh Avenue in elegant showrooms. Moderate-priced lines and sportswear firms are housed around the corner on Broadway. Obviously, time and coordination are required to shop the New York market—as is a comfortable pair of shoes.

The lack of a central mart is a minor drawback compared to what many buyers consider the glory of shopping this crème de la crème of markets. New York, after all, is the fashion leader, the place where American fashion originates. Whatever is new will be seen here first. New York, most industry people agree, is the most dynamic and creative market center. Any buyers servicing stores of any size must come to New York to do so, regardless of the other markets they add to their schedule.

New York offers a wide range of shopping. Every kind of fashion can be found here in every price range. Men's, women's, and children's wear, accessories, intimate apparel, and cosmetics are located within the garment district. Textile and fiber companies and home furnishings producers maintain showrooms in or near the garment district. Most local manufacturers feel they must maintain a New York showroom, and many regional manufacturers sponsor one as well, if only during market weeks. Many foreign manufacturers participate in the New York market, and high-fashion European designers like Helmut Lang, Alexander McQueen, and Nicolas Ghesquière of Balenciaga have recently staged fashion shows here. Lang, who moved his business headquarters to New York at the end of the 1990s, has described it as "the most modern and urban place."[1]

Originally, New York Fashion Week was under the auspices of CFDA (Council of Fashion Designers of America) and organized by CFDA's offshoot "7th on Sixth." In September 2001, CFDA sold the 7th on Sixth trademark and operations to the sports management and marketing agency International Management Group (IMG). While 7th on Sixth still coordinates the event scheduling and registrations, it now operates under the auspices of IMG. You can look up fashion show schedules and general information on 7th on Sixth's Web site, www.mbfashionweek.com.[2]

The New York market is open year-round, but specific times are still set aside for market weeks.

(Chapters 6 through 15 contain specific listings of New York market weeks by industry.)

## Advantages of the New York Market

Buyers who come to New York can shop not only the market but also the department stores and boutiques for which the city is known. New York is home to the flagship stores of Macy's, Bloomingdale's, Lord & Taylor, Barneys, Bergdorf Goodman, and Saks Fifth Avenue. There is also a high concentration of national and international flagship designer stores. Areas like the Upper East Side, SoHo, and the Meatpacking District (see Figure 16.3) are brimming with elegant flagship boutiques like Marc Jacobs, Donna Karan, and Ralph Lauren. Because New York is one of the fashion capitals of the world, practically every important international fashion house has a flagship store here.

The city is also the hub of the fashion network. Many national organizations have headquarters here and stand ready to provide assistance and support services to buyers. Even on a personal level, the networking possibilities are good. Local New York buyers attend market weeks, as do buyers from all over the country. Buyers who can attend only a few market weeks each year generally head for New York.

Last but hardly least, part of the draw of New

**FIGURE 16.3** The N.Y.C. Meatpacking District is full of elegant flagship boutiques like Diane von Furstenberg, Marc Jacobs, Donna Karan, and Ralph Lauren.

York is that it is the fashion capital of the United States. The fashion publishing industry is located there. The Fashion Institute of Technology (FIT), founded in 1944 and located in the garment district (see Figure 16.4), provides training in fashion design, production, and merchandising, and since the 1940s, its graduates have been making their mark on American design. The Metropolitan Museum of Art houses one of the world's largest archives of historic fashions. New York is also home to opera, theater, and ballet—all sources of inspiration to those in the fashion world. Here, too, are the restaurants and nightclubs where celebrities of the media and the international political scene present their own unofficial fashion shows.

### Disadvantages of the New York Market

The city is also not without its disadvantages, particularly with regard to its ability to maintain its preeminence as a market center in the face of competition from regional markets. To retail merchants and buyers who have shopped at the newer marts, the lack of a central mart is

sometimes considered a drawback. Many manufacturers, however, oppose the idea of a central mart, arguing that the garment district itself is the mart. They question whether the huge selection of merchandise—over 5,500 women's and children's lines alone—could ever fit into one building. The closest thing New York offers to such a site is the Jacob K. Javits Convention Center, and it does house a number of trade shows for various segments of the fashion industry (such as the men's wear shows, the National Shoe Fair, and the New York Home Textiles Show). Bryant Park is the site of the women's wear shows and some men's shows.

Some fashion producers—mostly those who have moved their businesses out of the city—complain that many of the buildings that house showrooms are old and deteriorating. Moving stock through New York's crowded streets and nonstop rush hour is a major undertaking. The cost of doing business in New York is among the nation's highest. Rents are constantly spiraling, space shortages are a fact of life, and local taxes are high.

To counter these conditions, the Fashion Business Improvement District (BID) has been estab-

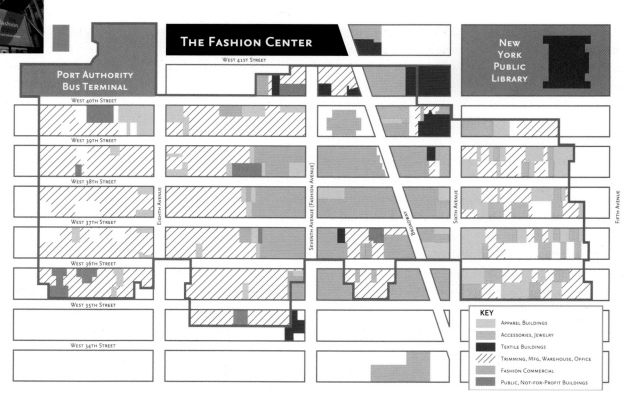

**FIGURE 16.4** In New York, the design and marketing of most fashion goods are done in an area known as the Garment District or the Fashion Center.

lished to reenergize the garment district, which contains over 34 million square feet.

## The Regional Market Centers

Each market center has its own unique flavor, as does each city, and buyers look forward to the varied experiences they will have at different markets. Many small retailers attend New York market weeks less often than they once did, relying instead on regional market centers closer to home. Travel costs are lower, less time is spent away from the stores, and for many, the atmosphere feels more personal. As regional markets become more sophisticated, thus drawing more exhibitors, New York loses even more of its allure. If regional markets can meet their needs, buyers ask, then why struggle through what many consider to be a grueling week in New York? Some retailers have cut out New York entirely, while others have reduced the number of trips they make and fill in with trips to regional markets in Los Angeles, Dallas, or Miami. They can visit them year-round or during special market weeks.

### The Los Angeles Market

Much of the look and style of California's markets revolves around its casual lifestyle, which it seems to sell almost as much as it sells its clothing. California leads the nation in retail apparel sales, and Southern California is the nation's largest apparel manufacturing center. Los Angeles' fashion industry alone supports 66,000 jobs. The ninety-four-block fashion district in downtown Los Angeles is responsible for 80 percent of California's apparel production.[3]

Since the 1930s, when California introduced pants for women, the West Coast has been the source of many important trends in sportswear. Today, Los Angeles is home to some of the country's largest sportswear manufacturers, GUESS, L.A. Gear, and Speedo. Other recent Los Angeles successes are Bisou Bisou, Moschino, Laundry by Shelli

Segal, Richard Tyler, St. John's Knits, and Rampage. Bob Mackie, who designs for Hollywood stars and is frequently seen on television home shopping shows, is also based in Los Angeles.

Surf-fashion firms include companies such as Hurley, Billabong, and Blake Kuwahara's KATA Eyewear.

Apparel design, production, and distribution is spread out along the entire West Coast, but the heaviest concentrations are in Los Angeles, with more than 4,000 garment manufacturers, and San Francisco.[4] West Coast apparel producers have experienced phenomenal growth, in part because of the activities of the CaliforniaMart, the nation's largest apparel mart, located in downtown Los Angeles. With an expansion completed in 1996, the mart has permanent and temporary exhibition space not merely for California's lines but for New York and Dallas lines as well, along with a growing number of foreign producers. The CaliforniaMart is open year-round and offers five market weeks and twenty specialty trade shows, such as ISAM (the International Swimwear & Activewear market), the Los Angeles International Textile Show, the Los Angeles Shoe Show, and the California Collections Preview.

San Francisco is also home to about 500 apparel companies, including Levi Strauss, Esprit, the Gap, Banana Republic, Old Navy, and Jessica McClintock.[5] Since the San Francisco Mart closed in the early 1990s, many of these companies now show in Los Angeles.

### The Dallas Market

The mood at Dallas market weeks is strongly Southwestern. Handcrafted clothes, or clothes that look handcrafted, with bright, vibrant colors are seen here. Once a center for budget garments, Dallas has become an important production and market center. Now the third-largest center in the country, it advertises itself as the "marketplace for the Southwest, the nation, and the world." Dallas-pro-

duced fashions are shown alongside fashions from New York, California, and around the world. Designers Anthony Mark Hankins and Victor Costa, the firms Jerrell and Poleci, and jewelry designers Elizabeth Showers, Dian Malouf, and Joan & Co. are based in Dallas.

The Dallas Apparel Mart and the separate Menswear Mart are part of a multibuilding complex that offers more than 2 million square feet of exhibition space (see Figure 16.5). The Menswear Mart is the only mart in the world devoted exclusively to men's wear.

### The Miami Market

The Miami market weeks have a highly international—mostly Hispanic and South American—flavor. Colors and styles are lively. The Miami market is also known for an outstanding selection of children's wear.

Greater Miami has become one of the most dynamic, cosmopolitan, and international fashion-producing centers in the country. Drawn by the temperate climate and quality labor force (many Cuban immigrants), many apparel designers and manufacturers now call South Florida home. Retailers find that Miami-produced clothing is well made, reasonably priced, and perfect for the semi-

tropical weather that prevails in the Sun Belt. In Miami, three strong selling seasons—cruise wear, spring, and summer—are available year-round. In addition to cruise and resort wear, Miami design and production centers around budget and moderate-priced sportswear, swimwear, and children's clothing. Miami-based designers of better-priced daytime and evening wear are becoming known for their work.

The Miami International Merchandise Mart, Florida's only wholesale mart, features more than 300 U.S. and international wholesale merchandise showrooms in 286,000 square feet of space, adjacent to Miami International Airport. Established in 1968, it is the premiere trade destination for local, national, and international retail buyers.[6]

## The Regional Marts

Although they are not major centers of fashion apparel production, several cities, such as Charlotte and Denver, have proven they can hold their own against larger marts. They do so primarily by emphasizing local design and production. Regional marts sponsor market weeks and in other ways operate much as the larger marts do.

Local marts have made inroads in servicing the stores in their trading area, and many department store buyers who regularly go to New York and Los Angeles feel they now must supplement these major buying trips with trips to their local regional market. Smaller store buyers often find the regional market is all they need to attend. In the early 1990s, both the San Francisco and Kansas City marts closed, victims of high-priced real estate and strong competition from the larger regional markets.

## Trade Shows in the United States

Trade shows, which are held in market centers throughout the year, are sponsored by **trade associations**—professional organizations of manufacturers and sales representatives. A few of these events are major extravaganzas that attract buyers from across the country and even from abroad. MAGIC International, held twice a year at the Las Vegas Convention Center, has the atmosphere of an apparel mart market week minus the permanent facilities.

The typical U.S. trade show, however, is much smaller than a mart show and lasts two to four days. Regional trade shows are held in hotels and motels, civic centers, and small exhibition halls. Specialized trade shows cover areas of fashion that might otherwise get lost at major market weeks. The Big & Tall Associates (BATA) shows suits and outerwear for big and tall men, for example, and the Surf Expo features surf equipment and surf-inspired sportswear.

These small trade shows show every sign of being able to hold their own against the proliferation of marts and market weeks. Trade shows are especially popular with small retailers and exhibitors because they are typically less expensive than market weeks for both groups of participants to attend. Small retailers like to deal with sales reps who are personally familiar with their needs and can cater to them at these smaller exhibits. Buyers from boutiques find that trade shows are their best outlet for the kind of unique and unusual merchandise they seek. Trade shows are known for displaying the work of unusual or small designers who do not ordinarily exhibit at the major marts.

The disadvantage of trade shows is that the exhibitors are limited in number. Buyers have difficulty doing across-the-board buying that is easily accomplished during market weeks at major marts. Trade shows also cannot feature the ongoing service that marts offer, as marts are increasingly open year-round.

## Foreign Fashion Markets

For several centuries, the foreign fashion market consisted entirely of French designers' high fashions. In the 1960s, the ready-to-wear market emerged first in Italy and then in France. Today, cultural and economic changes and a renewed interest in nationalism and ethnicity have combined to encourage the development of fashion markets worldwide. American buyers no longer travel exclusively to France and Italy; they journey to fashion markets all over the globe.

At the opposite extreme from the fashion buyers who stick close to home are those who make a twice-yearly ritual of visiting the dazzling and often frenzied foreign fashion markets. As Americans have become increasingly fashion conscious, the foreign shows have taken on greater importance. Particularly for the retailers who cater to an upscale and fashion trend-setting clientele, even faithful attendance at the New York market weeks is not sufficient for staying at the forefront.

Foreign fashion markets are designed to show off the fashion industries around the world. In the leading foreign markets, clothing is typically designed and presented on two different levels. First in prestige and cost are the **haute couture** (pronounced "oat-koo-TUR") clothes. A French expression originally meaning "fine sewing," haute couture is today synonymous with high fashion. These original designs, which use luxury fabrics and are known for their exquisite detailing, are expensive out of necessity and thus are made in very limited numbers. With prices that start in the thousands of dollars for a single garment, haute couture design is affordable to only a small group of wealthy women.

The next layer of fashion design is called **prêt-à-porter** (pronounced "pret-ah-por-TAY"). A French term meaning "ready-to-wear," prêt-à-porter is produced in far larger numbers than haute couture. Like haute couture, it is introduced in foreign fashion markets at semiannual shows where design collections are revealed to the fashion world. Haute couture and designer prêt-à-porter provide the inspiration for the inexpensive mass market designs that dominate the fashion market.

## France

France first emerged as a fashion showcase during the reign of Louis XIV (1643–1715), often called the Sun King, partly because of his lavish lifestyle. The elaborate clothing worn by his court was widely copied by royalty and the wealthy throughout Europe. The splendor of his court at Versailles created a market for beautiful fabrics, tapestries, and lace. Textile production in Lyons and lace works in Alençon were established to meet these needs. Paris, already an important city and located only a few miles from Versailles, became the fashion capital.

Paris is still considered the cradle of the fashion world. New fashion is born there. After it is seen there, it is adopted and adapted by others around the world.

### Paris Couture

France has been the center of haute couture since 1858, when the house of Charles Frederick Worth, generally regarded as the father of Paris couture, opened its doors. Beginning about 1907, Paul Poiret became the second great fashion legend of Paris. Poiret was the first to stage fashion shows and to branch out into the related fields of perfume, accessories, fabric design, and interior decoration.

A **couture house** is an apparel firm for which a designer creates original designs and styles. The proprietor or designer of a couture house is known as a **couturier** (pronounced "koo-tour-ee-AY") if male or **couturière** ("koo-tour-ee-AIR") if female. Most Paris couture houses are known by the names of their founders—Yves Saint Laurent, Givenchy, and Chanel, for example. The name may survive even after the original designer's retirement or death, but the signature style changes with his or her successor. In recent years, rapid changes of personnel and licensing of designer names has blurred the identity of the fashion houses and focused attention on individual designers. For example, Karl Lagerfeld designs for Chanel, Fendi, and Chloé, as well as for himself.

In 1868, an elite couture trade association, called the Chambre Syndicale de la Couture Parisienne, came into being. Membership in the Chambre Syndicale (pronounced "shahmbrah seen-dee-KAHL") was by invitation only and was restricted to couture houses that agreed to abide by its strict rules. In 1973, Fédération Française de la Couture, du Prêt-à-Porter des Couturiers et des Createurs de Mode was established. La Fédération is the executive organ of all the trade associations (or Chambre Syndicales) of each fashion division. Haute couture, ready-to-wear, and men's wear each has its own Chambre Syndicale. You can look up fashion show schedules and general information on the federation's Web site: www.modeaparis.com.[7]

The Chambre Syndicale is a strong force in the French fashion industry. From the foreign visitors' point of view, its most valuable contribution is the organization and scheduling of the twice-yearly market shows. It handles registration and issues the coveted (and limited) admission cards. It also registers and copyrights new fashion designs. It is illegal in France to copy a registered fashion design without making special arrangements and paying a fee. (In the United States, there is no copyright protection for clothing designs.) From its members' point of view, the Chambre Syndicale's most valuable contribution is that it represents its members in arbitration disputes and seeking regulation of wages and working hours.

**Couture Shows.** The Paris couture house trade shows are held twice yearly: the spring/summer collections are shown in late January, and the fall/winter ones in late July (see Figure 16.6). These shows have evolved into a promotional outlet for the couturiers. Today they are an expense rather than a source of income, as in the past. All the clothes in an haute couture collection are made-to-measure. Customers select a sample from the runway show, then make an appointment with the fashion house's atelier to get the garment custom made for them. This is, of course, outrageously expensive. The wealthy private customers in the audience, who order the clothes for their personal wardrobes, are too few in number for

**FIGURE 16.6** Dior's couture show in Paris, fall 2007.

their purchases to exceed the costs of producing the samples and the show. The fashion press, who comprise the remainder of the audience, perform the mutually beneficial job of publicizing the exciting, glamorous news about the designers' creativity.

## Other Couture Business Activities

The sales of haute couture clothing have steadily declined in recent years as prices have risen and customers have turned to the designer ready-to-wear lines. To survive, couture houses have expanded into other, more lucrative activities, such as the development of ready-to-wear collections and the establishment of boutiques and the ever-present (and profitable) licensing arrangements.

**Couturiers' Ready-to-Wear.** Most couturiers' ready-to-wear clothes are sold to department and specialty stores, which often set aside special areas or departments to display these prestige items.

The exclusivity and cost of producing haute couture lines, in combination with declining crafts-

manship skills among designers and atelier staff, have changed the Parisian fashion climate. The ready-to-wear business has completely eclipsed haute couture on the French prestige designer market. Ready-to-wear lines are not ordered directly by the customer but are bought in bulk by buyers who select the styles they like from the runway and then order them in various sizes and quantities. Although some houses still have a haute couture atelier and participate in haute couture fashion shows, it's the ready-to-wear lines that are featured in their advertising, showrooms, and stores. Today, many famous fashion houses, like Balenciaga, Chloé, Louis Vuitton, and Yves Saint Laurent, produce only ready-to-wear lines.

**Couture Boutiques.** The French word for *shop*, **boutique** (pronounced "boo-TEEK"), has come to mean, more specifically, a shop that carries exclusive merchandise. In the past, many couturiers installed boutiques on the first floor or a lower floor of their design houses. Most famous fashion labels also have their own flagship ready-to-wear stores in key cities around the world. Goods sold in these shops are usually designed by the couture house staff and are sometimes even made in the couture workrooms. All bear the famous label.

This was where the haute couture customers made their appointments. Some of these boutiques still exist; for example, Chanel's ready-to-wear flagship store on Rue Cambon in Paris, is still adjoined to the Chanel atelier. Today, most French fashion houses have several flagships boutiques that sell their ready-to-wear collections as well as accessories. These stores are designed to reflect the image of the house and create an atmosphere that expresses the spirit of the label.

**Licensing Agreements.** The most lucrative business activities for couturiers are the numerous licensing arrangements they establish to sell their accessories and ready-to-wear lines and also a variety of goods produced by others on their behalf. The most popular prestige licenses include perfume, shoes, bags, sunglasses, and watches.

# Fashion Focus

## Stella McCartney
### *A Stella Attraction*

**S**tella McCartney was born in London in 1971 to Beatle Paul McCartney and his photographer wife, Linda. Thanks to her maternal grandfather, entertainment lawyer Lee Eastman, she grew up with a love and appreciation of art, represented by the de Koonigs and major abstract Expressionists he collected. "We grew up with art around as kids," McCartney says.

(Despite going to a fashion design school, she wrote her college thesis on de Koonig.) She graduated from the famous St. Martin Design School in London in 1995, and her senior year collection had the rare accolade of being bought by influential stores such as Browns, Bergdorf Goodman, and Neiman Marcus. McCartney launched her own fashion line immediately on leaving college. Her style of combining sharp tailoring with humor and sexy femininity was immediately apparent in her first collection. In 1997, after only two collections, she became the creative director of the house of Chloé in Paris, following the famous Karl Lagerfeld.

McCartney laid the groundwork for Chloé's winning boho sorority-girl signature, so the industry was completely unprepared when, for her first show under her own name for the Gucci Group for Spring 2002, she showed a hard, dressed-down, sexed-up affair that crossed over from racy to raunchy. The reviews were scalding. Looking back, McCartney acknowledges a too-aggressive approach, although she maintains she never aspired to a tough, rock-chick sensibility.

A life long vegetarian, McCartney does not use any leather or fur in her designs. Her collections include women's ready-to-wear, accessories, eyewear, fragrance, and skincare. Her first perfume, Stella, was launched successfully in September 2003.

McCartney operates three flagship stores in Manhattan's Meatpacking District, London's Mayfair, and L.A.'s West Hollywood. Her collections are distributed in over forty countries through 300 wholesale accounts, including specialty stores and better department stores. In addition to the main line collection, Adidas by Stella McCartney, has grown to include several sports categories, including running, gym, yoga, swimming, and dance.

In 2005, the hugely successful one-off collection Stella McCartney for H&M sold out worldwide in record time. In

2006, Stella In Two, a new interpretation of her successful fragrance Stella, introduced a new way to customize fragrance by splitting the notes of the original fragrance into the liquid Peony and the solid perfume, Amber, which can be either worn alone or layered.

In 2007, McCartney unveiled CARE by Stella McCartney, the first luxury organic skincare line, containing 100 percent organic active ingredients. The line took more than 3 years to develop, in collaboration with YSL Beauté.

McCartney has received many awards recognizing her achievements in fashion and social awareness: VAI/*Vogue* Fashion and Music 2000 Designer of the Year award (2000, New York), the Woman of Courage award for work against cancer at the prestigious Unforgettable Evening Event (2003, Los Angeles), the *Glamour* award for Best Designer of the Year (2004, London), the *Star* honoree at the Fashion Group International Night of the Stars (2004, New York), the *Organic Style* Woman of the Year award (2005, New York), and the *Elle* Style award for Best Designer of the Year (2007, London).

McCartney is a designer whose success developed over time, during which she learned to focus her talent with intelligence, perseverance, and a strong work ethnic. When as a student she realized that her St. Martins experience had emphasized creative development at the expense of actual skills, she apprenticed herself to a Savile Row tailor, and she has retained that sense of self-education. "Stella has put a lot of time and a lot of energy into researching what makes a brand successful, and you can see all of those elements," says Bergdorf Goodman fashion director Roopal Patel.

McCartney is at the top of her game. After a decade of tireless work, super-scrutiny and no small amount of criticism, she has earned card-carrying membership in the exclusive club of the world's most important designers.

## French Ready-to-Wear

The burgeoning French ready-to-wear (or prêt-à-porter) fashion has two distinct sources: designers and mass-market producers. Young, innovative ready-to-wear designers such as Dries Van Noten, Olivier Theyskens, and Junya Watanabe have added much-needed excitement to the French fashion industry. These and other nonnative designers, like Alexander McQueen of the United Kingdom, are showing along with French designers. Thus they have changed the image of Paris as the center of French fashion to the French center of international fashion leadership.

To meet the needs of these ready-to-wear designers, the Chambre Syndicale created an autonomous section for designers who work exclusively in ready-to-wear, designating them créateurs (pronounced "kray-ah-TERS") to distinguish them from "couturiers." Among the créateurs are such important names as Karl Lagerfeld, Sonia Rykiel, Christian Lacroix, and Jean-Paul Gaultier.

Although their prestige is great, the couturiers and créateurs represent only a small part of the French fashion industry in terms of numbers and revenue. The remaining 1,200 companies are mass producers of ready-to-wear

**Prêt-à-Porter Trade Shows.** The French ready-to-wear producers present their collections at two market shows a year. The first, for the fall/winter collections, is held in March, and the second in October, for the spring/summer collections. Actually, two large trade shows take place simultaneously. The runway shows, sponsored by the Chambre Syndicale for the prêt-à-porter designers, take place at Carousel du Lourve. At the other, sponsored by the Fédération, the mass-market prêt-à-porter collections are exhibited at the Porte de Versailles Exhibition Center. This trade show, known as the *Salon du Prêt-à-Porter Féminin*, brings together more than a thousand exhibitors from all over the world.

With each succeeding show, the press pays more attention and provides more coverage of this end of the French fashion business. About 40,000 buyers

attend the prêt-à-porter shows, which are rivaled only by the ready-to-wear shows in Milan.[8]

A semiannual men's ready-to-wear show, *Prêt-à-Porter Mode Masculin*, traditionally held in January and July, is as important to the men's fashion industry as the women's ready-to-wear shows are to the women's fashion industry.

## Italy

Italy is France's most serious rival in the fashion industry. In certain areas, such as knitwear and accessories, Italian design is considered superior to the French. Italy has long been recognized as a leader in men's apparel, knitwear, leather accessories, and textiles.

A centuries-old tradition of quality craftsmanship and a close relationship between designers and manufacturers are common features of Italy's otherwise disparate fashion houses. Ermenegildo Zegna, a firm that markets three lines of men's wear, also produces men's textiles. Rather than economize on labor costs through offshore manufacturing to the extent that designers in other developed countries do, Italian designers rely more on domestic factories. Consequently, much of their output is in the luxury price ranges. Italian manufacturers are also the sources for materials and production for many foreign designers, among them Hugo Boss, Calvin Klein, Helmut Lang, and Ralph Lauren.

### Italian Couture

Italy has long had couture houses named for the famous designers who head them—Valentino and Mila Schön (see Figure 16.7). Its designers are members of Italy's couture trade group (a counterpart to the Chambre Syndicale) known as the Camera Nazionale della Moda Italiana. The Camera Moda organizes the biannual ready-to-wear fashion week runway shows that take place in Milan each year in March and September. You can look up schedule and general information at the association's Web site: www.cameramoda.com.

**FIGURE 16.7** Valentino's couture show in Italy, spring 2008.

Unlike French couture houses, however, Italian couture designers are not all located in a single city. Although Milan is the biggest fashion center, couture designers may be found in Rome, Florence, and other Italian cities.

Both Italian and French couture depend heavily on Italian fabric and yarn innovation and design. Most of the excitement today in print and woven textile design is created and produced in the fabric mills of Italy. Italian knits are also known for their avant-garde styles.

Only a handful of Italian houses have an haute couture business today. There are no haute couture runway shows in Italy. Valentino and Versace show their haute couture collections in Paris. They are scheduled one week prior to the Paris shows so that foreign buyers can cover both important fashion markets in a single trip.

Like their Paris counterparts, many Italian couture houses have set up boutiques for the sale of exclusive accessories and limited lines of apparel.

The designs are usually those of the couture house staff, and the apparel and accessories are sometimes made in the couture workrooms. All items offered in boutiques bear the couture house label.

Italian couture designers also have established licensing agreements with foreign producers. Some design and produce uniforms for employees of business firms, most notably airlines and car rental agencies. Some accept commissions to create fashion products ranging from perfume to men's wear to home furnishings.

## Italian Ready-to-Wear

Italy began to develop both its women's and men's ready-to-wear industries along with its couture fashions. As a result, it started exporting earlier than France, and today its economy relies heavily on its exporting program. The textile, apparel, footwear, and leather goods industries account for one-fifth of Italy's exports. Much of this exported merchandise is in the medium- to high-price range, especially in knitwear and accessories.

**Designers.** Innovative Italian ready-to-wear designers make their shows as exciting as the Paris ready-to-wear shows have become. Giorgio Armani and Versace are considered the standard-bearers for two very different definitions of Italian design (see Figure 16.8). Versace is noted for brightly colored prints, and Armani, for classic elegance combined with comfortable styling. Other well-known Italian ready-to-wear designers are equally protective of their reputations for distinctive, recognizable signature styles. Among the leading designers are Dolce & Gabbana, Gianfranco Ferré, Krizia, Missoni, and Miuccia Prada. Ferragamo and Gucci are major names in shoes and accessories, and Fendi in fur.

**Trade Shows and Market Centers.** Until the late 1960s, the most important Italian ready-to-wear shows were staged at the elegant Pitti and Strossi palaces in Florence. Milan grew as a fashion center in the 1970s, and many designers began to show there, in addition to or instead of Florence.

In addition to the ready-to-wear shows, Italy hosts a number of shows featuring the categories of apparel, accessories, and textiles for which Italian

**FIGURE 16.8** Versace's ready-to-wear design, fall 2007.

# &Then NOW

## Giorgio Armani
### A Man for All Worlds!

Left page: Giorgio Armani (top); Armani's designs for spring 2007 (bottom left) and spring 2008 (bottom right); Right page: Armani's flowing design in Milan, 1979.

He may not be immortal, but Giorgio Armani is nothing if not fashion's great survivor. His rivals—Yves Saint Laurent, Calvin Klein, Valentino, Donna Karan—quit their front-line design roles, but he remains at the helm of a company that announces record results almost every year.

The year 2004 marked the 30th anniversary for Armani. The fashion house is reportedly worth US$3 billion and has over 400 shops and 5,000 employees. Armani is one of the most successful designers in the global fashion business.

It may be over 30 years since he founded his business, but Armani was a late starter. Now he is over 70 in an industry where you are considered old at 40. But not Giorgio!

If there is one designer who has the right to an opinion on Hollywood style, it's the 74-year-old Armani, the designer who single-handedly ended the embarrassing chapter of Hollywood's freakish costume processions of the 1980s and ushered in a completely new, utterly modern way of dressing for the spotlight. "He professionalized the red carpet," observes fashion historian Harold Kode, who co-organized the 25-year Armani retrospective exhibit at the Guggenheim in 2000. "He made it a place where actresses could present the kind of glamour that historically the movie studios would orchestrate."

In 2004, Armani unveiled the Giorgio Armani Atelier couture collection—modern evening wear made to haute couture standards. The collection debuted during the Paris haute couture shows. The lure of haute couture for Armani is its red-carpet appeal. Armani is extremely well connected to the fashion and entertainment glitterati.

Armani has outlined an ambitious plan for expansion in the United States, which includes a mega store on Manhattan's Fifth Avenue. The fashion house will spend $100 million to grow its U.S. wholesale and retail operations, renovate existing stores, open new stores, and relaunch the Armani Jeans line in better department stores. The crowning glory is the 47,000-square-foot store on Fifth

Avenue, offering the brands Giorgio Armani, Emporio Armani, Armani Jeans, Armani Junior, and Armani Casa, as well as offering Armani and Emporio Armani accessories, watches, eyewear, jewelry, and perfumes.

Armani will be expanding his emporium and opening an online boutique on the 3-D virtual world Second Life. The store will allow viewers to purchase the brand's top ten products virtually via Second Life currency, the Linden dollar, or in actuality.

Also, Armani started selling all Emporio Armani products online in the United States as part of a strategy of expanding e-commerce.

"In the last seven years, I have seen mounting enthusiasm for online fashion shopping in the United States through the growing success we have had with our A|X Armani Exchange site," Armani told *Women's Wear Daily*. "Over this same period I have also observed the increasing sophistication of fashion consumers shopping online, which has encouraged me to develop this site for my Emporio Armani lifestyle."

In an interview in *Women's Wear Daily* in November 2007, Armani was asked, "Your plans, then, are to stay put?" to which he replied, "I would rather say that I'm staying on, but not staying still!"

Armani is a man for all worlds. Today he is the major fashion idol in Europe, America, China, Japan, India, South America, and many other nations—where he intends to keep making his customers happy with his designs.

designers and manufacturers are internationally renowned. Leather shoes, handbags, gloves, and small leather goods are one major segment of Italy's fashion industry. Other accessories that are world famous are knitted hats, scarfs, and gloves; and silk scarfs and ties. There are 731 companies producing accessories in Italy. Como, the hub of Italy's silk industry, has two hundred companies that finish raw silk imported from China. Together they produce 90 percent of Europe's silk export.

Trade shows are held in the regions where the respective industries are centralized.

### Great Britain

For many years, London's Savile Row was for men's wear what Paris has been for women's apparel—the fountainhead of fashion inspiration. Savile Row is a wonderful place where each suit is handcrafted for its new owner, a process known as "bespoke tailoring." (*Bespoke*, an archaic word meaning to have reserved in advance, is applied in England to men's clothing that is made to measure, a process that takes 6 to 10 weeks.)

In the 1980s, Italy became the main source of European-styled men's wear, and Britain's fashion reputation focused on the craftsmanship of its tailoring and the quality of its tweeds and woolens rather than on trend-setting designs. Then, in the late 1990s, the British fashion industry, harking back to its daring hippie, mod, and punk styles of the late 1960s and 1970s, began to revive its image as a place for cool, new designs. Today, London is the place to look for innovative, although not always wearable, designs.

### London Couture

Although Britain has never supported a couture industry the way that France and Italy have, it does offer famous design schools, such as the Royal College of Art, the London College of Fashion, and Central St. Martin's. St. Martin's alumni include internationally famous names John Galliano, Alexander McQueen, Hussein Chalayan, Julien

MacDonald, Stella McCartney, and Clements Ribeiro. In addition to their own lines, these designers have or have had designer posts at leading French fashion houses. Other recent graduates of these schools, both British and foreign, are bringing design back to London. Philip Treacy is a five-time winner of the British Accessory Designer of the Year award for his striking hats.

### British Ready-to-Wear

Ready-to-wear was a minor industry in Britain until after World War II (see Figure 16.9). The fact that it

**FIGURE 16.9** Jasper Conran's ready-to-wear design, fall 2006.

entered a period of expansion after the war is largely due to the efforts of the government. According to one English fashion authority, the government became "the fairy godmother" responsible for "the survival of [British] couture and the rapid development of [Britain's] large and excellent ready-to-wear trade."[9]

Vivienne Westwood is a talent who has sparked and shocked the London fashion scene with her unorthodox clothes and lifestyle since the mid-1970s. Today, she continues to be an innovator and leader of the avant-garde pack.

### Trade Shows

After a dormant period in the late 1980s and early 1990s, the British runway shows and trade shows are once again a required stop on the European fashion circuit. British and foreign designers are showing, and British and foreign audiences are looking.

### *Canada*

The development of a group of new and innovative designers has given the Canadian fashion industry a growing sense of confidence that has paid off in real growth. The fashion industry is the fifth-largest employer in Canada and gets bigger every year. It has two important centers: the largest is Montreal, in Quebec; second is Toronto, in Ontario. With Montreal's strong economy and unemployment at an all time low, Canadian trade shows continue to grow and prosper. The North American Fur and Fashion exhibition is celebrating its 25th anniversary. "We're still trying to be more creative to become part of the global fashion world," said Chantal Durivage, co-president of Sensation Mode, which operates Montreal Fashion Week.

Fashion week in Toronto is now considered part of the international fashion weeks, with L'Oréal as a sponsor. Fashion week appears to have caught the attention of the international media and foreign buyers, according to Robin Kay, president of show and organizer of the Fashion Design Council of Canada.[10]

Well-known Canadian designers from Montreal include Hélène Barbeau, Marisa Minicucci, Marie Saint Pierre, Nadya Toto, and Simon Chang. Designers from Toronto include Brenda Beddone, Brian Bailey, Pat McDonagh, and Alfred Sung. Internationally successful Toronto-based manufacturers and retailers include Club Monaco, M.A.C., and Roots. Roots made the uniforms for the Winter Olympics in 2002. It was the first time the Winter Olympics used a company outside sportswear giants like Nike and Adidas.

Most Canadian apparel manufacturing is located in Montreal, but every province has a stake in the industry, and shows in each province bring local goods to the attention of other Canadians and to buyers from the United States and around the world. Montreal and Toronto each has its own fashion week twice a year, where local men's and women's wear designers showcase their new collections in runway shows. Other women's apparel and accessories shows include Western Apparel Market in Vancouver, the Alberta Fashion Market in Edmonton, the Prairie Apparel Markets in Winnipeg, the Saskatoon Apparel Market, and Toronto's Mode Accessories show. Children's wear markets take place in Vancouver and Alberta, and the North American Fur and Fashion Exposition is featured at the Place Bonaventure in Montreal. Alberta, Montreal, Vancouver, and Toronto all host gift shows.

## Other European Countries

For leadership in Europe, the fashion industry definitely focuses on France, Italy, and Britain. Other countries do attract international interest, however. In the 1990s and the 2000s, the Belgian town Antwerp has become somewhat of a high fashion mecca. Antwerp natives, such as Dries Van Noten, Ann Demeulemeester, Martin Margiela, Veronique Branquinho, AF Vandevorst, and Raf Simons, have achieved great success with their innovative and creative clothes. Although all these designers show and have their business headquarters in Paris, some of them still live in Antwerp. Other European countries that have a presence on the global fashion market are Ireland, with its traditional garments and fine linen, and Spain, with its swimwear, lingerie, and bridal fashion tradeshows. As the European Economic Community and other factors globalize the economy, however, national boundaries assume less significance than they once had.

## Germany and Scandinavia

Until the mid-1980s, most American fashion buyers skipped Germany on their European buying trips. The country was still divided into East and West, and few West German designers were well known outside Europe. But a new wave of high-fashion women's designers is changing this. Two apparel firms, Escada and Mondi, are noteworthy successes with their high-fashion lines. Designers Hugo Boss and Wolfgang Joop have developed international followings.

Although Germany's fashion industry is relatively small, its international trade fairs have become a major source of fashion inspiration for new fabric and designs. The Igedo Company produces the CPD women's wear and men's wear fashion shows twice a year in Düsseldorf (see Figure 16.10). Interestingly, this company has exported the fashion trade show through joint ventures with exhibition producers in Hong Kong, London, and Beijing. For textiles, the major international show is Interstoff in Frankfurt, and Cologne hosts shows of men's wear, sportswear, children's wear, and apparel production machinery.

Each of the four Scandinavian countries—Norway, Sweden, Denmark, and Finland—has its own fashion industries and specialties. However, even though each country has its roster of designers, the styles tend to be alike, with emphasis on simple silhouettes and sturdy materials like wool, leather, and linen.

Leather apparel, primarily in men's wear, is a

**FIGURE 16.10** Igedo in Düsseldorf is the largest European fashion fair for women's ready-to-wear. Around 2,150 exhibitors from 40 countries, including Markam (above), present their collections during the fair.

popular Swedish product. Both Sweden and Norway are among the important suppliers of mink and other furs to countries around the world. Birger Christensen and Saga are leading furriers.

Scandinavia also offers some interesting textile designs. The best known, internationally, are the work of Finland's Marimekko.

Excellent jewelry in all price ranges is available in Scandinavia. The area has long been known for its clean-cut designs in gold and silver. Some well-known, Swedish-born contemporary designers include expatriates Lars Nilsson and Richard Bengtsson.

### Mexico and South America

For buyers and producers from the United States and Canada, the signing of the North American Free Trade Agreement (NAFTA) in 1994 brought new possibilities in the Mexican market. The rest of Central and South America and the Caribbean countries began to press for inclusion in this trading pact. (NAFTA is discussed more in detail in Chapter 17.)

By the mid-1970s, the Central and South American market could be added to the growing list of international fashion markets. The fashion world began visiting market centers in Rio de Janeiro, Buenos Aires, São Paulo (see Figure 16.11), and Bogotá.

Two factors contributed to this new presence in the fashion world. The first was the appeal to Americans and entrepreneurs from other developed countries of cheap sources of materials and labor. The second was the conveniently corresponding development of a fashion industry in Mexico and Central and South America. We examine American outsourcing of production in this region in Chapter 17.

From the perspective of Mexico and the Central and South American governments, the fashion industry become a means of increasing their gross national product and their status in the world marketplace.

### Fashion Products

The fashion industry in Mexico and South America offers fashion on three levels. First, several countries have developed their own high-fashion industries, many of which are ripe for import to the United States and Europe. The second level revolves around the development of fashion products that reflect each country's national heritage of crafts. With a renewed interest in ethnicity throughout the world, such products are welcome. Third and finally, Central and South America and Mexico have become important "offshore" sources of products made to North American manufacturers' specifications.

Handbag buyers seek out the better-quality goods of Argentina and go to Brazil for moderate-quality goods. Uruguay is another important source of moderate- to high-quality handbags.

The most important shoe center is Brazil, where manufacturers concentrate on creating a stylish product made from lasts that fit North American feet. Belts and small leather goods are the specialty of Brazil, Argentina, and the Dominican Republic.

Costume jewelry is another important product from this region. Ecuador, Peru, and Mexico export silver and gold jewelry of native design.

## Trade Shows in Mexico and South America

The single most important market center in South America is São Paulo, Brazil. At the turn of the millennium, the emergence of designer talents like Alexandre Herchcovitch, Rosa Chá, and Icarius de Menezes coincided with a major Brazilian boom in fashion in general. The appearance of superstar models like Gisele Bündchen in these designers' shows attracted enough attention to put São Paolo fashion week on the map. Since then, São Paolo fashion week has been steadily growing in importance, and it may become one of the most attended and publicized fashion events in the world.[11] Other important international fairs featuring textiles and textile products as well as fashion accessories are held in Bogotá, Colombia; Lima, Peru; San Salvador, El Salvador; and Santiago, Chile.

These shows offer not only an opportunity for buyers from North America and elsewhere but also a place for U.S. textile producers to be seen by potential customers in the region. As the rampant inflation of the 1980s has been reduced in many Latin American countries, their fashion industries have become better able to satisfy the desire for textile products made in the United States. The efforts of the World Trade Organization (WTO) to end textile and apparel quotas by 2005 and the possibility of the expansion of NAFTA into Central and South American countries suggest that trade among the countries of the Americas will grow in the coming years.

### The Far East

The United States imports more apparel from the Far East than from any other area in the world. However, the major portion of these imports has been low-priced, high-volume merchandise, and hardly any of the apparel has qualified as "designer merchandise." There are definite signs that this situation is beginning to change, and now fashion buyers can find exciting, innovative styles offered by new design-oriented Asian stylists.

**FIGURE 16.11** Models present creations by Do Estilista during São Paulo's Fashion Week 2008.

Buyers have used certain countries in the Far East as a market in which to have fashions they saw in the European fashion centers copied and adapted. A fashion buyer needs to know which areas in the Far East are best equipped to handle specific types of manufacturing. Japan and Hong Kong were once the two major contract, or copyist countries. But Japan has upgraded its fashion image so that today it is a producer of outstanding high-styled, high-priced fashion apparel. Hong Kong is working to develop the apparel industry of China and promoting Chinese goods in its international trade fairs.

FIGURE 16.12 Comme des Garçons ready-to-wear.

## Japan

The Japan Fashion Week keeps growing in importance every year. The growing attention being paid to Japan Fashion Week, according to retailers and executives at Japanese fashion brands, is the uniqueness of design from Japan is the main factor (see Figure 16.12). In 2007, the show drew 22,200 visitors, including 160 journalists from countries such as the United States, South Korea, China, Taiwan, England, Italy, France, Spain, Holland, Russia, Australia, Argentina, and Israel.

Japan Fashion Week has been financially backed by the Ministry of Economy, Trade, and Industry and is looking for more sponsors from outside the fashion industry. Nobuyuki Ota, public relations director of Japan Fashion Week, said, "This is the event to incubate the new generation after Comme des Garçons. Young designers are actually growing. For a bigger and better Japan Fashion Week, more investment will be required."[12]

**Japanese Ready-to-Wear.** In the 1950s and 1960s, the Japanese faithfully copied Western trends. Ironically, in the 1970s, as Western dress had finally won acceptance in Japan, a group of highly original Japanese designers—Hanae Mori, Kenzo Takada, Issey Miyake, and Kansai Yamamoto—emerged. They first worked in Paris, where their lines were design sensations that rivaled the French prêt-à-porter designers. For over a decade, in fact, these daring designers were thought of as French rather than Japanese. Some of them still show in Paris.

**Japanese Designers.** In the early 1980s, a mostly new wave of avant-garde designers—Rei Kawakubo of Comme des Garçons, Yohji Yamamoto, and Matsuhiro Matsuda—stormed the American fashion scene.

Although these Japanese designers continue to be a force in the American fashion world, and no one disputes their creative brilliance, their clothes never became commercially successful in America. U.S. retailers had trouble mass merchandising the designs, which appeal mostly to customers who are looking for strikingly unusual shapes and fabrics. Today, although their work is highly revered and regarded as a source of great inspiration for the fashion industry, they remain niche players on the market.

In the 1990s, the latest generation of Japanese designers, catering to a domestic market, have, like their British contemporaries, focused on retro pop cultural influences such as hippie beads and T-shirts and 1970s punk. Today, young Japanese designers, such as Shinichiro Arakawa, Hiroaki Ohya, Kosuke Tsumura, Masaki Matsushima, and Gomme, tend to create technically ingenious designs based on theme, a gimmick, or a concept. For example, Ohya produced a limited edition of dresses packaged in books that were sold in bookshops. To these designers, the concept is more important than commercial results, which is why these talents often work for major design houses or commercial clients, (e.g., Arakawa collaborates with Kawasaki motorcycles) in order to finance their own label.

## China

The recent history of trade between China and the United States has been a story of steady but uncertain expansion. The issues of whether the United States should use the threat of cutting trade to pressure China to end human rights abuses was only one of the problems that complicated relations between the two countries. However, in 2000, the United States entered a trade agreement with China that gave China normal trader status. This paved the way for the country's entry into the WTO. Since then, China's growth in the apparel industry has been clear—it's pulling ahead of Mexico as the number-one supplier of imported garments to the United States.[13]

Among the products that China exports, one of the most sought after is silk. Although it is the world's largest silk producer, China is just beginning to acquire the modern technology need for quality weaving, printing, and dyeing. As the Chinese have been more proficient in these finishing processes, they have exported more finished silk

**FIGURE 16.13** Various fabrics are displayed at the Intertextile Beijing show.

fabrics and apparel products (see Figure 16.13). Cotton and polyester production, once big exports, now barely meets China's domestic needs. Inexpensive plastic shoes are another major export. Leather and fur are also important exports. Several trade shows in Beijing and Shanghai have been instituted by Western-owned exhibition producers to promote Chinese leather to the international market.

**Hong Kong.** In July 1997, Hong Kong rejoined mainland China after 156 years as a British Crown colony. The world held its collective breath, waiting to see what would become of this quintessentially market-driven world trading center when it came under Communist rule. The agreement between Britain and China calls for the governing of Hong Kong as a Special Administrative Region for 50 years, and local businesses are reassuring their international customers that Hong Kong will continue to offer all the advantages they have enjoyed plus more. In addition to the political change, Hong Kong has experienced a move in its economy from manufacturing to trade and service industries, and its trade shows, once focused on promoting its own goods, now concentrate on serving as an international marketplace. Some of the advantages of participating in Hong Kong trade shows include the following:

- A duty-free port where exhibitors can bring in their samples and sell them from the exhibition.

- A newly expanded convention and exhibition center.
- A central location in Asia, easily reached by air.
- A thriving hospitality industry with a growing number of hotel rooms and world-class restaurants.

As trade shows continue to grow to accommodate China's continuing prominence in the global market, Hong Kong is still relevant as a safe window to the mainland. Since 1997, Hong Kong's economy has changed dramatically for the better.[14]

Hong Kong Fashion Week has long focused on design. "Though the global fashion trend is still largely led by European designers, we do see that Asian designers are getting more attention and making a strong influence in recent years," said Anne Chick, senior exhibition's manager for the Hong Kong Trade Development Council. Chick cited Anna Sui, Issey Miyake, and Hong Kong's Vivienne Tam, Flora Cheong-Leen, and Barney Cheng as well known in the international fashion scene.[15]

The Hong Kong Trade Development Council[16] sponsors over twenty exhibitions. Among the most well known are Hong Kong Fashion Week, Fall/Winter and Spring World Boutique, Hong Kong International Jewelry Show, Hong Kong Toys & Games Fair, Hong Kong Houseware Fair, and the Inno Design Tech Expo.

## Other Asian Countries

The other countries of Asia, being smaller and, in many cases, less industrialized than those discussed above, have less influence on the American apparel industry, but their roles as trading partners and sites of offshore production grow increasingly important.

Singapore has many of the advantages of Hong Kong—an easily accessible location, a multinational population, and expertise in international trade. It is Hong Kong's chief rival as a center for trade shows.

Korea, with a design history similar to Japan's, has some exciting young designers creating for the Korean fashion-conscious market. Much of the production of ready-to-wear in Korea is still contract work. But because of the fashion design movement among young Koreans, this is slowly beginning to change.

Indonesia, Thailand, Malaysia, Vietnam, and the Philippines are regarded by many Americans in the apparel industry as sites of offshore production, but that is only part of the story. As these developing countries become more industrialized and the standard of living improves, their own industries and markets are taking their place in the global economy. Thailand, for example, has for many years been a producer of fine printed silk and cotton.

India's centuries-old textile industry continues to make it a major force in the Asian textile market. India also has its own rapidly expanding fashion industry. Homegrown designers are a relatively new phenomenon in India. Most set up their businesses at the end of the 1990s in response to India's growing upper class and its appetite for global styles. New Delhi has had its own Lakme Indian Fashion Week since 1999, which draws tremendous attention and is produced by IMG, the same event-marketing conglomerate that runs New York's Fashion Week.

India is also the home of the largest handloom industry in the world—over 13.5 million handlooms are in operation in India. Cotton and silk are the strongest growth areas of the Indian textile industry. India is the only country in the world that produces all four silk varieties: mulberry, tussah, eri, and muga. Its textile industry employs more than 10 million people, second only to the number who work in agriculture.

With "India Inc." being the latest buzzword in just about every industry from software to pharmaceuticals, the country's fashion industry is not about to be left behind. India Fashion Week is now a semi-annual event with both fall and spring shows (see Figure 16.14). The Trade Development Council of India conducts promotions and fashion events. The Indian designer market is still small by international standards, but the FDCI estimates that it will grow by 100 percent over the next decade. Designer Namrata Joshipura, who sells her designs to Henri Bendel, Bergdorf Goodman, Neiman Marcus, and Anthropologie, said the key to success internationally for her has been to look beyond just being profiled as an Indian designer. "I don't sell India, I sell Joshipura," she said. "You can't be just an Indian designer. You have to be a global designer with a global aesthetic sense."[17]

## Trends in Global Fashion Markets

The fashion industry survives through change. International fashion markets are working furiously to keep up with the five major changes that are necessary to remain viable in a highly competitive global market. Fashion is increasingly becoming a global business. Presently, there are international fashion weeks in Australia (see Figure 16.15), Brazil, New Zealand, Canada, Columbia, Mexico, Iceland, Hong Kong, Thailand, Japan, and South Africa. Most of these fashion weeks are geared toward promoting the local designer industry with the eventual goal of competing with the dominant world fashion capitals—New York, Milan, and Paris. Many also receive government sponsorships because they help promote trade and taxes and boost the local economy with big business for hotels and airlines. But there are also other important industry changes.

First, mart managements and trade associations in the United States have responded to industry growth, shifts in population, and changes in buying habits. Marts have also of necessity become more competitive with one another. Elaborate promotions designed to lure buyers now routinely include offers of reduced airfare and hotel rooms. Seminars and cocktail receptions are further enticements. The move toward year-round service is another response to competition. Many facilities expanded their exhibition space and provided access to secretarial and clerical services.

Second, the expense of attending markets and

**FIGURE 16.14** Manish Arora design at Indian Fashion Week (top). **FIGURE 16.15** The Australian trade shows are growing each year. Designer Kaat Tilley shows her designs at Fashion Exposed (bottom).

trade shows has had an impact on buyers and exhibitors at home and abroad. For example, the haute couture showings in Paris have become promotional events; buyers attend them vicariously by reading the fashion press. Economic globalization has made fashion capitals like Paris, Milan, and New York showplaces for designers from all over the world, not just from the home country. Retail buying trips to the national and international market centers have become the province of senior staff, who must make decisions for more departments or store units. Designers and other vendors carefully weigh the costs and benefits of several less elaborate exhibitions against fewer, more lavish ones.

Third is another aspect of globalization: developing countries are now becoming major players in the fashion industries, primarily as sources of materials and production but also as importers and exporters of finished goods.

Fourth is the increased worldwide use of computers and the Internet for buying, especially the basics. The Internet also provides buyers, press, and

**FIGURE 16.17** A booth at the WWDMAGIC show in Las Vegas. Contacts made at WWDMAGIC can lead to sales contracts during and after the show.

consumers with instant information. For example, American Publisher Condé Nast's fashion Web site Style.com publishes runway reviews and photographs of a collection only hours after it has been shown on the catwalks in Paris, New York, London, or Milan (see Figure 16.16). Some people argue that all this product information has made the consumer's attention span for trends shorter. Pictures of collections are now shown so quickly that the clothes look old by the time they hit the stores.

Fifth is the U.S. Commerce Department's International Buyer's Program, which does the research needed to find likely buyers for American products and bring them together with American companies at trade shows. This program has greatly increased the foreign attendance at shows such as the International Fashion Boutique Show in New York and the MAGIC shows in Las Vegas (see Figure 16.17).

## Summary and Review

A market is a meeting place of buyers and sellers. Retail buyers of fashion goods go to market several times a year during market weeks, at the market centers of New York, Los Angeles, and Miami, and regional marts in other cities, including Atlanta, Chicago, Dallas, and Denver. With the exception of New York, where an entire district serves as a marketplace, markets are located in large convention centers with exhibition halls called marts. In addi-

**FIGURE 16.16** Style.com publishes runway reviews and photos of the latest Paris, New York, London, and Milan collections.

tion to visiting the manufacturers' sales representatives in their showrooms or multiline sales reps in temporary exhibition spaces, the buyers may attend trade shows and seminars sponsored by trade organizations.

In Europe, market weeks are semiannual. Designers' haute couture (custom designs) and ready-to-wear collections are shown in the market centers of Paris, Milan, and London. Numerous trade shows for apparel, accessories, and textiles are presented in other cities.

Quebec is the province with the largest fashion industry, but all the provinces have apparel manufacturers, and market weeks and trade shows are held in major cities across the country. Mexico and Central and South America are developing as centers for the production of wool and wool products, leather goods, and costume jewelry.

Japan's fashion designers and producers operate on an international scale with showings, boutiques, and manufacturing facilities at home and abroad. The biggest international market for fashion goods in Asia is Hong Kong. Apparel businesses there are using their manufacturing and marketing expertise to develop the silk, leather, and fur industries on the Chinese mainland. Singapore is also emerging as an important market center. The fashion industry is truly operating in a global economy.

## Trade Talk

Define or briefly explain the following terms:

| | |
|---|---|
| boutique | buyer's directory |
| créateur | couture house |
| couturier/couturière | domestic market |
| foreign market | haute couture |
| market | market center |

| | |
|---|---|
| market week | mart |
| prêt-à-porter | sales representative |
| trade association | trade show |

## For Review

1. What criteria must be met for an area to be considered a market center?
2. What support services for buyers are offered by the marts during and between market weeks?
3. What distinguishes New York City as the major fashion market center in the United States?
4. Describe the distinctive characteristics of the three regional market centers.
5. What are the advantages and disadvantages of trade shows?
6. What business activities have the Paris couture houses undertaken to offset the decline in sales of haute couture clothing?
7. Name the fashion products for which Italy and Britain, respectively, are considered leaders.
8. Name the fashion products for which Canada is considered a leader.
9. Name the fashion products for which Japan is considered a leader.
10. What role does Hong Kong play in the international fashion market?

## For Discussion

1. Discuss the importance of the Far East to producers and retailers of fashion goods.
2. The reputation of Paris as a prime source of fashion inspiration began to develop several centuries ago as the result of many interrelating factors. Identify those factors and discuss their importance in the development of any major fashion design center.

# chapter seventeen

*Everything you always wanted to know*

*about the international balance of trade.*

# Global Sourcing and Merchandising

Because nations are no longer able or willing to produce all the goods and services they need and want, they rely on one another to supply them with what they cannot or choose not to produce themselves. In the process, the world's nations are becoming economically interdependent in ways they have never been before. The world is, in effect, becoming one huge global market. We are less a universe made up of individual nations and more one world in ways that were unimaginable even 20 years ago. Political scientists call this process—whereby the nations of the world become more interlinked with one another—*globalization*. The fashion industry is very much a part of the global economy, so much so that those who work in the business invented a term to describe the process of shopping for and purchasing imported goods: **global sourcing** (see Figure 17.1). When a firm in a country, such as the United States, buys foreign goods, it **imports** them (see Figure 17.2). The country that furnishes the goods, such as Italy, exports them. Most countries are both importers and exporters, although, as we shall see, they do not necessarily do each activity in equal amounts.

Fashion producers, retailers, and consumers in the United States have learned to expect the variety and sophistication that imports provide. The world of international trading is undeniably a fascinating one; this is its great appeal. Long gone are the days when foreign buying in the fashion industry consisted of buyers traveling to France a few times a year for the haute couture shows. Even then, very few U.S. retail store buyers actually bought haute couture. They bought ideas and patterns—and then came home to have them produced by American manufacturers. Eventually, as the world experienced a strong and growing post–World War II economy, other European countries—Italy at first, and then other Western European nations—developed their own fashion industries and began luring foreign—that is, American—buyers.

The rest of the world soon followed. Asia, long a source of import goods in home furnishings and a few other specialized areas, went after the U.S. fashion market. Mexico and the Central and South American countries have been the most recent to tap into the mother lode that many consider the American fashion consumer market to be. In sub-Saharan Africa, the manufacture of textiles presents a promising prospect for export; the establishment of this industry would help rebuild the economies of nations recovering from decades of political and military upheaval.

Apparel and textile executives operating in more than 116 countries shipped goods worth $93.3 billion to the United States in 2007, making fashion one of the most globally integrated industries.[1]

Today, American buyers have expanded their sources to cover, quite literally, the globe. There is no place in the world that American apparel buyers do not travel to in order to obtain goods. Where the Far Eastern circuit once meant shopping the markets in Hong Kong and Taiwan for raw materials, it now also means traveling to Japan for high fashion and places such as Sri Lanka, Indonesia, Malaysia, and the Philippines for their growing number of fashion specialties. American buyers have learned to use a global market to their advantage, molding it to current trends such as private-label manufacturing and specification ordering. They have learned to work their way through the labyrinth of federal and international restrictions that regulate international trade.

Adding to the complexity of global sourcing is the increasing reliance of textile and apparel producers on **offshore production**, the use of foreign workers in one or more countries to complete the steps of manufacturing the goods that bear the producer's label. U.S.-owned firms, as well as companies based in Canada, Western Europe, and other industrialized nations, use a variety of arrangements to take advantage of the resources available

**FIGURE 17.1** Traveling the globe is an everyday experience for today's buyers. Tsim Sha Shui, in Kowloon, is a neon-lit shopping district for expensive jewelry and clothing from around the world (left). **FIGURE 17.2** The United States often imports foreign goods from other countries (right).

in countries with developing textile and apparel industries. Company-owned factories abroad, contracts with factories owned by citizens of the foreign country, and joint ownership are all options. A garment may be made of fibers grown in one country, woven into fabric in another, cut in a third, and assembled in a fourth. Decisions of where and how such multinational goods will be made have implications for quality, production costs, and a host of legal issues involving import taxes and quotas.

## Importing by Retailers

Retailers are the primary importers of foreign goods in the fashion industry, although manufacturers also seek global sourcing. Retailers like imports for several reasons: their uniqueness, quality, cost, and the variety they add to their stock. They constantly seek merchandise that makes their stores stand out in special and unique ways that set them apart from the competition. Foreign merchandise often fits that bill.

Global sourcing is a complex and often complicated business. What makes a foreign source attractive—its low cost and promise of higher profits—can be lost or diminished in a matter of minutes if something goes wrong.

Anyone who intends to buy goods from a foreign country needs a thorough knowledge of its local laws and regulations, particularly the laws that regulate exporting and importing, the efficiency of the transportation system, and the availability and skill of the labor force. The buyer must be well versed on the tax system and exchange rates. He or she must understand local and national customs and must be well informed about the current political and economic climate. Finally, the buyer must be up-to-date on U.S. import–export regulations, including any pending legislation, and must know all this for any country in which he or she intends to do business. This is why importing is best done by someone with access to good suppliers and extensive experience in dealing with foreign manufacturers and import regulations.

To gain entry to foreign fashion markets, as well as to cover them extensively, U.S. buyers rely on the help and experience of intermediaries. These specialists help U.S. buyers shop in the international markets successfully. Foreign-made goods can be purchased:

- In foreign fashion markets
- By store-owned foreign buying offices
- By commissionaires or independent agents
- At import fairs held in the United States
- By importers

## American Buyers' Visits to International Fashion Markets

Buyers like and need to travel to foreign fashion markets so they can observe new trends first-hand and buy goods suited to their customers. The international markets offer a variety of goods, but not all of them are suited to the American marketplace. By personally shopping in international markets, often during market weeks, American buyers can be sure that they are obtaining goods that will sell at home. They are also able to soak up the cultural and social climates of the countries to which they travel, which, in turn, helps them translate what is new and exciting to their customers.

## Store-Owned Foreign Buying Offices

Some stores—those that are large enough to do so or whose image is very special—maintain company-owned foreign buying offices. Buyers who work in these offices support and advise store buyers by surveying the market for new trends, supervising purchases, and following up on delivery. Because they are an extension of the store, buyers in foreign buying offices are often authorized to make purchases just as store buyers are when they shop in foreign and domestic markets.

If the purchase is part of a new trend, stores need the goods when they are still new and customers are still eager to buy them. If it is part of a foreign theme promotion, goods must be delivered while the promotion is in progress. Delivery—especially timely delivery—has been a major problem with imported goods.

Stores generally locate their buying offices in major fashion capitals such as Paris, Rome, London,

Hong Kong, and Tokyo, from which their buyers can travel to smaller markets around the world.

Saks Fifth Avenue and Neiman Marcus maintain store-owned foreign buying offices, as do the big general-merchandise chains such as Sears, JCPenney, and Wal-Mart. Some stores that cannot afford their own foreign buying offices subscribe to the services of independently owned buying offices with foreign facilities, which shop exclusively for their member stores. Examples include the Doneger Group and the Associated Merchandising Corporation.

## Foreign Commissionaires or Agents

In contrast to store-owned foreign buying offices are **commissionaires**, or foreign-owned independent agents. Commissionaires, whose offices are also located in key buying cities, tend to be smaller than store-owned offices. Commissionaires also represent both retailers and manufacturers.

Apart from these differences, though, they provide many of the same services as store-owned foreign buying offices. They often have specialized buyers, or market representatives, who work closely with clients, keeping them abreast of what is generally available and helping them locate specific goods. As is the case with store-owned buying offices, a substantial part of the staff's time is spent following up on purchases to make sure they are delivered when they are needed.

Unlike store buyers, who are authorized to purchase on the store's behalf, commissionaires do not purchase unless they have been authorized to do so.

Commissionaires are paid on a fee basis. Usually, they take a percentage of the **first cost**, or wholesale price, in the country of origin.

## Foreign Import Fairs in the United States

Another way to buy foreign goods is to attend one or more of the foreign import fairs that are now regularly held in the United States. Many foreign countries participate in such shows or stage their own fashion fairs in the United States (see Figure 17.3).

These shows perform two important functions. First, they give foreign manufacturers and designers the same chance to observe American culture that Americans get when they buy in foreign fashion markets. The result is usually closer collaboration between buyers and manufacturers to adapt styles and quality to American tastes. Second, they increase the size and depth of the import market by giving buyers of small- and intermediate-sized stores who would not ordinarily tap into the foreign market a chance to do so. To provide their customers with imported merchandise, these buyers need not maintain foreign representatives or shop in the foreign markets, neither of which would be cost-effective for their operations.

### American Importers

Last but hardly least in a market that relies increasingly on foreign goods, American buyers purchase from American-owned importing firms. Import firms shop in the international markets to purchase their own "lines," which they put together and display to retailers. Shopping these lines gives small retailers an opportunity to purchase foreign fashion merchandise that would not otherwise be available to them. The only drawback to this method is that it does not allow for the customized ordering that buyers from big stores and chains have come to expect.

**FIGURE 17.3** For the small to midsize retailer, foreign import fairs, such as the China Sourcing Fair (top) and the Global Sources Show (bottom) bring merchandise to the U.S. buyers' doorstep.

### Importing by Manufacturers

American manufacturers, initially upset about the growth of direct importing done by retailers, have increasingly turned to offshore sources for the same reasons that retailers do: price advantage, exclusivity, and workmanship. Like retailers, they often cite high domestic labor costs as a primary reason for resorting to imports. But labor costs must be viewed in the light of the other considerations if a manufacturer is to maintain control of its brands' images. For example, a sportswear manufacturer may combine fine-quality knitwear produced overseas with domestically produced skirts or pants to create a line of separates. A classic example of this is American Apparel. The company, known for trendy, undecorated T-shirts, underwear, jeans, and other apparel sold in more than 140 American Apparel stores around the world, continues to apply current trends by manufacturing exclusively in its Los Angeles facility and paying the highest wages in the industry at $100 a day (see Figure 17.4). While that might be more than what some companies pay for offshore labor, the total costs are not much different when you factor in other indirect costs—such as the $300,000 to $400,000 annual salaries that other companies pay their employees to "keep flying back and forth to China."[2]

## Product Development: Specification and Private Label Buying

In addition to importing unique or distinctive goods, many retail operations use product development to set their assortment apart from those of their competitors. They may rely on domestic manufacturers or foreign sources for specification and private-label buying.

As discussed in Chapter 8, these two terms may be used to describe the same items of merchandise, but the meanings are slightly different. If the retailer agrees, the manufacturer may design private-label merchandise for the retailer. On the other hand, **specification buying** is a type of purchasing that is done to the store's rather than the manufacturer's standards. Retailers provide the standards and guidelines for the manufacture of clothes they order.

As they grow more successful with specification buying, stores are also using it for their private-label lines. Initially intended as a way to keep production at home, a growing amount of private-label stock is now purchased offshore. When stores began to pit their private-label merchandise against national brands, they often found that foreign manufacture was one way to control the cost. In the apparel sector, private-label brands now generate nearly half of all sales. Their importance has grown since the World Trade Organization–required import quotas on textiles and apparel were ended on January 1, 2005. "Most retailers and multinational brands have seen the way to reduce cost, shorten time to market, and improve quality is to develop closer partnerships with fewer suppliers," said Walter Wilhelm, president and chief executive of Walter Wilhelm Associates, LLC, a retail consultancy.

The growth of private labels is already being

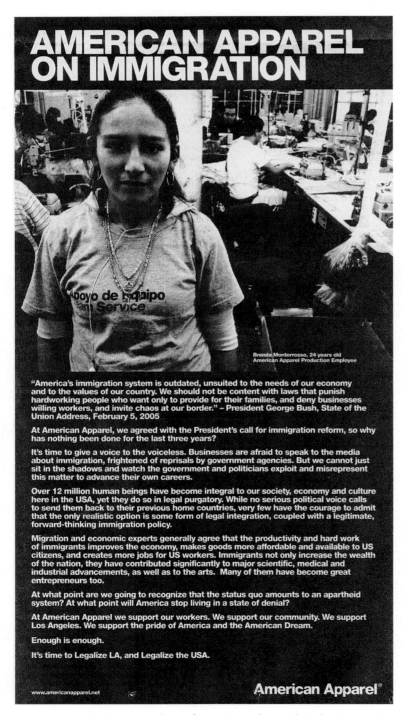

FIGURE 17.4 American Apparel manufactures its products exclusively in Los Angels and pays its workers the highest wages in the industry.

reflected in supply chains. In the apparel sector, the traditional import sourcing chain for apparel retailers began to change about 5 years ago. Until then, most major retailers relied on foreign-based agents to provide valuable services for their overseas production, including order tracking, product inspection, and management of post-production shipping.

Gradually, however, as retailers squeezed costs out of their supply chains to remain competitive with giants such as Wal-Mart, they forged closer relationships with a handful of foreign suppliers who can meet their low-cost, high-quality requirements on the larger scale they require.

In the future, Wilhelm said, intermediaries will count even less. By 2010, he predicts, fewer overseas contract manufacturers will provide an even broader range of services, saving more money for retailers of private labels.3

## International Balance of Trade

Just as there are two sides to every coin, there are also two sides to the global market. Throughout the early 1980s, the expanding international market seemed to work to everyone's advantage. The global market came about largely because the early 1980s were a period of prosperity at home and abroad. There was nothing wrong with a fashion market that was truly international so long as a balance was maintained between exports—what Americans sold abroad—and imports—what they bought abroad. For several decades, foreign countries were eager to import American-made goods, which were much sought-after for their high quality.

Unfortunately, by the mid-1980s, the downside of a global market—what happened when the trade balance shifted—revealed itself. The U.S. dollar grew weak, which meant that American goods became expensive, often too expensive to be of interest for export. The American reputation for producing quality goods suffered by comparison as other nations learned how to turn out quality prod-

ucts. The Japanese were soon beating Americans at their own game—cars and electronics. And the clothing industry proved itself woefully inept at competing at all. At first, Americans bought foreign clothes because they were so much cheaper than domestically produced goods. Eventually, though, they began to buy them because of their excellent workmanship and distinctive design.

When the dollar weakened, foreign countries only increased their exports to the United States. The resulting tidal wave of imports caused severe trauma to American industry generally and to the U.S. apparel manufacturing industry specifically. As foreign producers gained ground, domestic producers lost out.

These few cold facts seem to paint a discouraging picture for the U.S. fashion industry, but a closer examination of the situation from several perspectives shows that the outlook is far from uniformly bleak. To understand the present state of the import–export market, it is important to know something about the **balance of trade**. This is the difference between the value of exports and the value of imports. When the value of goods that a country imports exceeds the value of its exports, it experiences a **trade deficit**. When a country's exports exceed its imports, it has a **trade surplus**.

In recent years, the United States has become the world's largest clothing importer, buying nearly one-third of all the imported clothing in the world. In contrast, for many of the world's developing countries, the manufacturing of clothing and textiles for export is the first step toward a sound national economy. The U.S. trade deficit hit a record $36.6 billion, including apparel and textile imports that increased 2.6 percent, valued at $93.3 billion. The deficit between how much more the United States buys from abroad and how much it sells grew 65 percent. China captured 35.7 percent of the apparel and textile import market and widened its trade gap in all goods by 15.4 percent to $ 232.5 billion, the largest U.S. deficit ever with a single country.4

# Fashion Focus

# Fashion Focus

## Counterfeiting
### Faking It!
### Real Money
### for Fake Goods

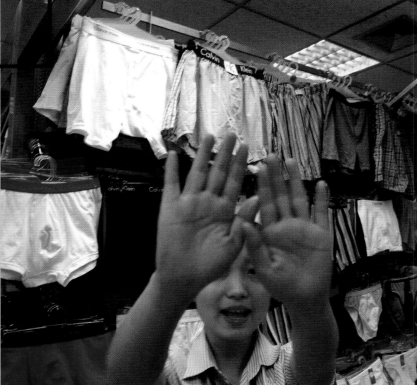

Maybe you can't afford the real thing. Maybe you think you deserve a bargain. So you go to an online auction or a street corner to buy a fake handbag. After all, the fakes (also called copies, knockoffs, replicas, and counterfeit goods) now are so good that even pros have trouble telling the difference. You get the bags, shades, shirt, or watch that you wanted and saved hundreds of dollars. What's the harm? Here are just a few of the ways counterfeiting is affecting you.

Counterfeiting robs the United States of taxes. The counterfeit market is huge and growing. Estimates of worldwide global sales of counterfeit products—including everything from apparel to music and DVDs to cigarettes to pharmaceuticals—range between $600 billion and $700 billion. Apparel and accessories accounted for over 50 percent of the counterfeit goods seized by U.S. Customs and Border Control. Statistics show that apparel, footwear, handbags, wallets, backpacks, and computer hardware were the top commodities seized by value. Julie L. Myers, assistant secretary of Homeland Security for Immigration and Customs Enforcement, said in a statement, "Counterfeiting has risen to the level of an economic pandemic costing the legitimate U.S. economy more than $200 billion annually. Targeting these illicit networks will remain one of the most important crimes we pursue."

Most counterfeit goods are produced in China, making it the counterfeit capital of the world. Joining China is Korea and Taiwan, producing copies of such coveted brands as Cartier, Dior, Louis Vuitton, Rolex, Coach, Gucci, Nike, Prada, and Chanel, among others.

However, because of the stepped-up vigilance of our border and customs divisions, with their constantly improving record of finding and destroying foreign-made counterfeits, we are now faced with counterfeiters in the United States stepping up domestic manufacturing.

A federal crackdown on counterfeit imports is driving an increase in domestic output of fake merchandise, according to investigators and industry executives. Raids carried out in New York City resulted in the seizure of an estimated $200 million in counterfeit apparel bearing the logos of brands such as the North Face, Polo, Lacoste, Rocawear, Seven for all Mankind, and Fubu. The raids also uncovered a large assortment of tags, buttons, and labels of brands such as Baby Phat, Tommy Hilfiger, Nike, Adidas, and Enyce.

One of the largest seizures was a joint operation in Arizona, Texas, and California that seized seventy-seven containers of

fake Nike Air Jordon shoes and a container of Abercrombie & Fitch clothing valued at $69.5 million. The stepped-up oversight of U.S. ports has made a significant impact on counterfeit imports.

Another current method of attacking counterfeits is at the retail level. In a recent case, Fendi sued the Sam's Club division of Wal-Mart Stores, Inc., for selling fake Fendi bags and leather goods in five states. Sam's Club agreed to pay the Italian luxury firm a confidential amount to settle the dispute and dismiss the action, which had charged the retailer with selling "significant quantities" of counterfeit items valued "in the millions of dollars."

Design houses are constantly plagued by high-end fakes being sold on e-commerce sites. Tiffany & Co. sued eBay, the world's largest online auction site, for allowing the sale of counterfeits, and Gucci filed suit against some thirty Web sites in the United States and is currently tackling at least 100 more.

Counterfeiting has become the crime of the 21st century. But behind the seemingly innocent façade of a fake handbag lies the tragic world of child labor and sweatshops and of crime syndicates and gangs who profit from selling counterfeit merchandise.

The United States is not the only country with trade deficit problems. Around the world, trade statistics show that the industrial countries are relying more and more on imports while the developing countries are becoming the exporters. Although indications are that the growth in the U.S. trade deficit has slowed, the United States remains the single largest contributor to the world trade imbalance.

The conditions that traditionally encouraged consumers to purchase domestic goods—a devalued dollar and heightened tariffs—seem to have done little to turn the American public away from foreign merchandise. While the promotion "Crafted with Pride in the U.S.A.," which urges Americans to buy American, has created a sentimental support for domestic goods, at the point of purchase, consumers seem less interested in the origin of the goods than in getting the best value at a given price point. Furthermore, the distinction between domestic and foreign goods is clouded by the widespread practice of offshore production. The name of a U.S.-owned company on a label does not indicate anything at all about the nationality of the workers who made the product or the origin of the materials they used.

Some people believe that sterner measures—higher tariffs and stricter import quotas among them—are necessary to protect American industry from imports. Others oppose such measures. They argue that the real problem is the inefficiency of American industry, which will not be made stronger by import restrictions. These two groups support two opposing ideologies regarding the conduct of American business.

**Protectionism** is the name given to an economic and political doctrine that seeks to exclude or limit foreign goods. The opposing doctrine, **free trade**, supports the free exchange of goods among nations. Since the balance of trade affects the nation's economic health, and the federal government is constantly passing and revising legislation about importing and exporting, advocates of both doctrines are well represented in Washington, D.C., by lobbyists who seek to promote legislation supporting their views.

## Protectionism

The first import restrictions on goods brought into the country date back to 1789, when the United States, a newly founded republic that was still mostly rural, feared that it would not be able to compete with the world's industrial powers. To reduce its considerable reliance on imported goods, it slapped a 50 percent tariff, or import tax, on seventy different articles imported from France and England. Tariffs have come and gone, but the debate over whether protectionism is good—or necessary—has persisted for more than 200 years.

In the fashion industry, the leading supporters of protectionist legislation are manufacturers, who are most hurt when Americans buy imported rather than domestic goods. Industry trade associations and UNITE, the apparel and textile workers' union, offer the most organized support for protectionism. Most consumers recognize their work through their campaigns, "Crafted with Pride in the U.S.A." and "Made in the U.S.A.," which encourage people to buy American (see Figure 17.5). But the manufacturers have also mounted a behind-

the-scenes campaign designed to inform retailers about the advantages of buying domestically produced goods.

The industry has also changed its attitude in recent years, moving from a "Here's what we can do for you" stance to a "What can we do for you?" posture. Among the advantages of domestic buying promoted by the industry are quality, Quick Response, and flexibility.

## Free Trade

Free traders believe that restrictions on trade will threaten the nation's ability to grow and compete in the global marketplace. Retailers and most consumers are among those who support free trade. They believe the buying public should be free to buy imported as well as domestic goods.

Except for those times when protectionists are active, free traders do not do much to promote their cause. In many respects, they already have the support of the federal government. The history of the United States as the model of a capitalistic economy, the financial interests of powerful U.S. businesses in multinational conglomerates, and the interrelationship of the nation's role in international politics with its position as an economic power all favor a free trade stance.

The struggle over free trade versus protectionism is played out in several arenas, such as international trading laws, U.S. regulations, and preferential programs sponsored by various trading nations.

## International Trading Laws

In the global economy, trade is truly international, not merely a set of bilateral agreements among pairs of nations. (A *bilateral agreement* is one in which two countries reach a separate agreement.) The trade relationship between any two nations affects the relationship of each party with its other trading partners as well. International trade laws have therefore developed out of need.

**FIGURE 17.5** Americans are encouraged to buy and support domestic goods.

## The General Agreement on Tariffs and Trade (GATT) and the World Trade Organization (WTO)

In 1947, the United States and twenty-three other nations met in Geneva, Switzerland, to write an agreement known as the **General Agreement on Tariffs and Trade (GATT)**. This agreement played a major role in reducing trade barriers and unifying trading practices among member nations. Membership grew to ninety-two, and representatives met every few years to negotiate new trade arrangements among member nations. In 1995, GATT was succeeded by the **World Trade Organization (WTO)**, which has continued to adjust member agreements to meet the changing needs of the global economy. Some of the agreements apply specifically to the textile and apparel industries.

However, the free trade agreements have come under a lot of criticism. One of the arguments is that the interest of powerful nations and corporations are shaping the terms of world trade. This could mean that the interest of the people would be compromised, while a decreasing number of people would prosper. It could also threaten the domestic industries of industrialized countries, whose production costs can't compete with those of developing nations. There are also special agreements made between large companies and leaders of poor countries that are eager to attract foreign businesses. For example, billions of dollars in imports from poor countries enter the United States duty-free through preferential trade agreements and free trade pacts.[5]

Free trade agreements have caused a lot of friction worldwide. China's entry to the WTO in 2001 was seen as a huge threat to the domestic industries in many nations. China's seemingly unlimited supply of low-cost labor makes it a very attractive place for foreign corporations, and many textile and industry workers in countries with higher wages fear that this will cause them to lose their jobs.

## Multi-Fiber Arrangement (MFA)

In 1973, the United States and fifty-three other nations signed the first multinational agreement specifically regulating the flow of textile products. A primary purpose of the **Multi-Fiber Arrangement (MFA)** was to establish ground rules for bilateral agreements and unilateral actions designed to restrict the free flow of these products. The United States, Canada, and some of the industrialized nations of Western Europe wanted to protect their textile industries from cheaper imports from less developed countries.

The MFA was renewed twice without any essential changes in its stated purpose or goals. It was also renewed in 1986, but this time not without controversy. The 1986 renewal attempted to deal with two changes in the status of textile trade:

1. Growing pressure in the United States to enact tighter quotas on textile imports
2. The United States' insistence that the Big Three textile-exporting nations—Hong Kong, Korea, and Taiwan—revise their bilateral agreements with the United States.

Despite the substantial revision, many American producers felt it did not give them the measure of relief they sought. They pointed out, for example, that the MFA limits the number of units that can be brought into the country rather than the cost value of merchandise. Faced with quantity limits, many foreign producers have merely shifted to higher-priced merchandise, a move that hurts the domestic market even more than limiting cheap imports does.

The textile exporters were dissatisfied for the opposite reason. They did not want their fledgling textile export industries to be singled out for quotas at all. Particularly galling to these less developed nations was the imposition of protectionist policies by an organization that was supposedly formed to promote free trade. Like David battling Goliath, the exporters won, and the MFA was phased out in three stages over the period between 1995 and 2005.

## U.S. Regulation of Textile and Apparel Imports

Some of the specific measures the United States—or any other country—is liable to undertake or has undertaken to promote its own trade interests are quotas, tariffs and duties, and preferential programs.

### Import Quotas

Under the provisions of the MFA, the United States negotiated bilateral agreements to impose quotas on textile imports from certain countries. In determining where quotas are needed to protect domestic textile production, the United States considers the price of textile imports from each potential trading partner.

Part of the analysis is an assessment of the stage of development of the country's economy. **Developed countries (DCs)**, such as Canada, Japan, and members of the European Union, and **less developed countries (LDCs)**, including, among others, Haiti, Bangladesh, and many sub-Saharan African nations, are usually not targeted for quotas; the DCs, with their high standards of living and well-paid labor forces, are unlikely to undersell domestic producers, and the LDCs, if they have an export market, do not have a large enough one to compete seriously. It is the **newly industrialized countries (NICs)** that are typically subject to quotas by the United States and other DCs. Examples of NICs include Malaysia and the Philippines.

The United States has negotiated bilateral trade treaties over the past few years with its five major Asian suppliers—Hong Kong, Taiwan, China, South Korea, and Japan. (Although Japan is a DC, its protectionist policies have influenced its trade agreements with the United States.) These treaties have been successful in reducing the general level of imports to the United States from these countries, but at the same time, other countries such as Indonesia, Malaysia, and the Philippines have taken up the slack as they grew from LDCs to NICs, so there have been no overall reductions in imports from these areas.

**Import quotas** are limits set to restrict the number of specific goods that may be brought into the country for a specific period of time. Quotas, which are established either by presidential proclamation or legislation, are either absolute or tariff-rate.

### Absolute Quotas

**Absolute quotas** limit the quantity of goods that may enter the United States. When the limit is reached, no more goods of that kind may be imported until the quota period ends. Absolute quotas may be global or directed to specific countries. Imports in excess of a quota may be exported or detained for entry during the next quota period. To keep accurate and consistent records of apparel and other textile imports, these items are counted in terms of square meter equivalents (SMEs).

### Tariff-Rate Quotas

**Tariff-rate quotas** set a limit after which a higher duty is charged on goods entering the country. When a certain number of goods have entered at the lower rate, customs raises the duty on any additional goods, which, in effect, also raises their price in the market.

### Taxes: Tariffs and Duties

Most fashion merchandise is subject to an import tax, called a **duty** or **tariff**. This is a fee assessed by the government on certain goods that it wishes to restrict or limit. Tariffs and duties are imposed on imported goods that the government wishes to make more competitive in price with domestically produced goods. The tax varies depending on the category of merchandise, but it is usually a percentage of the first cost.

### Antisweatshop Commitments

The downside of relying on offshore production for cheap labor (see Figure 17.6) became apparent to American fashion producers when sweatshop conditions in third-world countries—and even in some domestic factories employing illegal aliens—came to light in the mid-1990s. Horror stories of workers held in virtual captivity, required to work long hours for less than subsistence wages, and subject to corporal punishment for the slightest infraction of inhumane work rules made front-page news. Realizing the threat to their reputations as good corporate citizens, many apparel manufacturers were quick to recognize the need for self-regulation.

The Gap has also been accused of using sweatshop labor. In February 2002, the protestors surrounding the World Economic Forum in Manhattan singled out the Gap as a symbol of globalism gone bad. The demonstrators charged that one of the factories that produce the Gap's apparel in Guatemala underpays and abuses its workers.

The American Apparel Manufacturers Association of Arlington, Virginia, formed a twelve-member labor task force to address the sweatshop problem, and in August 1996, representatives of eighteen organizations, including human rights advocacy groups and labor unions, as well as apparel manufacturers and retailers, joined together in the White House Apparel Industry Partnership.

This advisory panel established voluntary standards for the working conditions in factories where members of the U.S. apparel industry do business. Among the provisions are a maximum 60-hour work week, including overtime; one day off from work per week; and pay meeting or exceeding the minimum wage in countries where the firms operate. Balancing the reliance of families in developing countries on their children's contributions to the family income against the protection of the children, the standards set the minimum age for hiring at 15 years, reduced to 14 only in countries that allow the employment of factory workers younger than age 15. Prison labor and other forced labor may not be employed. Workers are protected from abuse or harassment, and they have the right to form unions and bargain collectively. To ensure compliance,

**FIGURE 17.6** Sewing is a major cost for most garments, which has led to global sourcing for cutting costs.

monitoring by the apparel companies and independent observers from labor, human rights, and religious groups are part of the agreement.

These standards are called the WRAP (Worldwide Responsible Apparel Production) principles. Global support for WRAP continues to grow monthly. So far, manufacturers' organizations in Guatemala, Sri Lanka, Turkey, and twelve other countries that have been known to have factories with substandard worker conditions have endorsed WRAP.

In 2000, the American Apparel Manufacturers Association merged with the Footwear Industries of America and The Fashion Association to become the American Apparel and Footwear Association (AAFA). The AAFA continues to demonstrate its commitment to responsible business practices.

## Counterfeit, Black Market, and Gray Market Goods

Both importers and exporters are plagued by the illegal importing of counterfeit, black market, and gray market goods. Counterfeit goods, like counterfeit currency, are inferior imitations passed off as the genuine article. Luxury goods and designer brands are the chief objects of counterfeiters.

Counterfeiting flourishes for two main reasons. First, it is considered a high-return, low-risk business: counterfeiters can earn millions of dollars and are rarely caught. Counterfeiters are among the world's most ruthless criminals. They are known to have smuggled workers from Asia into places such as New York and Los Angeles and kept them locked up to assemble fakes that are imported in pieces.

While the U.S. government and many European governments are focusing on ways to catch and punish counterfeiters, the real challenge is learning how to rehabilitate the child labor force that the industry helps create. According to UNICEF's Geoffrey Keele, "We need to look at why children become laborers to begin with. That comes down to issues of poverty. Access to education and to health care will help keep them from being vulnerable to exploitation in the labor field, sexual exploitation, and trafficking."[6]

The sale of counterfeit goods at "bargain" prices devalues the real brand and deprives legitimate businesses of their fairly earned profits. U.S. Customs officials are authorized to seize imported counterfeit goods.

Another problem for manufacturers is **bootleg goods** (See Figure 17.7 and 17.8). Many of these goods are not cheap rip-offs; rather, they cannot be distinguished from the real ones. They are made by the same manufacturers who make the real ones but who sell some goods to the black market. An example is a Prada shoulder bag sold in the Prada store in Manhattan for $390; the bootleg copy sold on the streets of Rome for $117.

**Gray market goods** are those that were not intended for sale in the country in which they are being sold. Sometimes called parallel imports, gray goods are legitimate products that are distributed through channels not authorized by their original manufacturer. An authentic sneaker manufactured for distribution in Europe, for example, is considered "gray" if it is sold in the United States instead.

However, gray market goods can cause problems for vendors and consumers, especially in cases where legitimate gray market goods are mixed in with counterfeit products. The flood of gray market goods can also weaken sanctions against counterfeits.[7]

**FIGURE 17.7** These accessories may look real, but they are counterfeit products sold for a much lower price (top). **FIGURE 17.8** An elephant crushes pirated Mickey Mouse products. Disney has issued a stern warning to Indian firms infringing on copyrights. Pirating of international brand names is a big business in India (bottom).

## Preferential Programs

Over the years, the United States has been a proponent of aid to developing countries. Among the incentives offered in its many preferential programs are arrangements that permit the imports from certain nations to enter the country quota- and duty-free and that allow other countries low tariffs or generous quotas.

## Most-Favored Nations

The term *most-favored nations* may seem almost self-contradictory because it is applied to trading partners that are not necessarily regarded with favor by the United States. In the era when the Soviet Union dominated Eastern Europe, "favored" status in trade relationships was part of the political and diplomatic efforts to win countries over to a market economy. Since the breakup of the Soviet Union, the term is heard mostly with reference to trade negotiations between the United States and China. The debate within the federal government focuses on whether to tie granting of most-favored nation status to correction of China's human rights abuses. So far, trade has continued to expand, and there is no clear evidence to indicate whether the ongoing negotiations have any influence on China's treatment of its political prisoners.

## Tariff Schedules 807 (9802) and 807A

Tariff schedules 807 (9802) and 807A provide for preferential access of goods that originate or are partly manufactured in the United States and are also partially made abroad. These tarrif schedules favor American manufacturers. Item 807 of the United States tariff schedule (renumbered 9802 in 1989 but still referred to by its old number within the apparel industry) allows cut piece goods and trim items to be exported from the United States, assembled or sewn abroad, and then returned to United States with duties owed only on the value that was added abroad. In other words, duty is paid only on the labor that was done abroad—not the materials.

A revision, 807A, requires that the piece goods taken out of the country be of U.S. origin. Approximately 80 percent of the value of 807A exports comes from the United States. Item 807A is also referred to as Super 807, because it provides special access for goods that are domestically cut and made of U.S. fabrics.

## Caribbean Basin Initiative (CBI)

Latin American imports have been an area of growing concern to Americans. While U.S. manufacturers worry that a flood of imports from Latin America will hurt domestic industry, Americans also see these countries as customers for U.S.-made goods and have a special interest in promoting their neighbors' economic development. The Caribbean Basin Initiative (CBI) was designed to do two things: offer trade protection to U.S. manufacturers at the same time as it encourages the growth of an import industry in Latin America. One major feature of the CBI—duty-free entry of goods into the United States—was not applied to apparel and textile products, but 807 and 807A production favors the CBI countries in these industries.

However, since the NAFTA passage in 1994, these countries have found themselves at disadvantage with Mexico (see discussion on NAFTA in the following section). While continuing to lobby for NAFTA-like treatment, Central American countries like the Dominican Republic, Honduras, and Costa Rica looked for new ways to compete with Mexico, such as developing full-package capabilities and higher quality production facilities. In 2000, the Caribbean Basin Trade Partnership Act (CBTPA) granted NAFTA-type duty treatment to U.S. imports of footwear from eligible Caribbean and Central American countries. U.S. industries believe that the CBTPA will facilitate U.S. investments in the region.

## North American Free Trade Agreement (NAFTA)

The **North American Free Trade Agreement (NAFTA),** which went into effect in January 1994, eliminated quotas and tariffs for goods shipped between the United States and Canada and Mexico. Its effects have been hotly debated. Canada, long the United States' largest trading partner, is still the largest. Since NAFTA entered into force, the Canadian economy has grown by an annual average of 3.8 percent.

## Sweatshops
### *Product Safety, Environmentalism, and Human Rights*

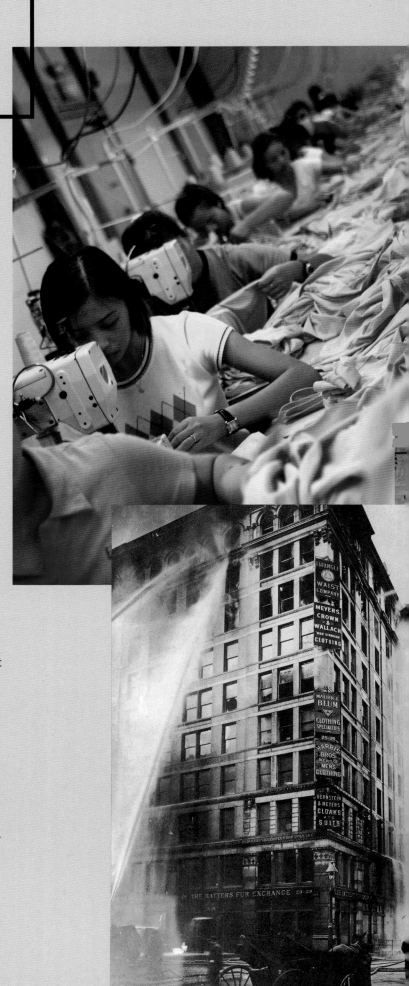

The term sweatshop was coined in the United States in the late 1800s to describe factory environments where managers used harsh, deceptive, and inhumane treatment to sweat as much profit from their workers' labor as was humanly possible.

Sweatshops became a household word at the beginning of the 20th century when the tragic death of over 140 garment workers become headline news across the United States. On March 25, 1911, a fire broke out on the ninth floor of the Asch Building in New York City, owned by the Triangle Shirtwaist Company. Unable to escape through the narrow aisles between crowded sewing machines and down the building's only stairway, these young workers, mostly women and children, burned to death, suffocated, or leaped to their doom on the pavement below. Firefighters and bystanders who tried to catch the young women and children in safety nets were crushed against the pavement by the falling bodies. That was then!

In the decades that followed, government regulation and union-organized drives—particularly in the post–World War II period—resulted in significant improvements in factory conditions. This period, in which many—but not all—garment workers in North America enjoyed stable, secure employment with relatively decent working conditions, was short-lived. Globalization and free trade have negated some of the hard-earned gains of garment workers. This is now!

To lower production cost, garment companies began to outsource the manufacture of their products to subcontract factories owned by Asian manufacturers in Hong Kong, Korea, and Taiwan. Retailers and discount chains quickly followed the garment manufacturers' lead and began outsourcing to offshore factories. Competition heightened. Asian suppliers began to shift their production to even lower-wage countries in Asia, Latin America, and Africa. A race to the bottom for the lowest wages and worst working conditions went into high gear.

We are now in the 21st century and have fallen back into the horrors of the 19th and 20th centuries of slave labor and unspeakable conditions for workers. The worst sweatshops are in third-world countries, but sweatshops still exist in the United States.

In the past decade, examples of sweatshop horrors have come to light in California, Florida, and New York. The U.S. General Accounting Office investigated New York City's garment industry and found many sweatshops still operating, particularly in the city's Chinatown.

Recent changes in global trade rules (the end of the quota system) are once again speeding up the race to the bottom. Although some major brands have "company code-of-conduct compliance staff" who answer complaints almost immediately, promising to investigate the situation and report back on what they are willing to do to "remediate" the problems, the same companies pressuring suppliers to meet code-of-conduct standards are also demanding their products be made faster and cheaper. Recent examples have been Nike and Gap. Conflicting pressures make suppliers hide abuses or subcontract to sewing workshops and home workers. The name of the game remains the same: more work, less pay.

Globalization and relentless retail competition among the likes of Wal-Mart, Target, H&M, Kohl's, Gap, and Macy's might have turned supply chain "efficiency" into a high art, but the pressure on factories has spurred a slew of sweatshops, industrial pollution, and consumer safety concerns that many expect ultimately will increase prices.

Recent safety recalls of Chinese-made toys, bibs, toothpaste, and Christmas trees prompted consumer outcries and governmental reviews in both the United States and China. The intertwining of product safety, environmental, and human rights' concerns marks a significant evolution in the sourcing landscape navigated by fashion brands, retailers, and importers in general. The combination of the three issues might be enough to awaken the consumer in ways that worker conditions alone rarely has done.

The impact of the agreement on trade with Mexico has been a subject of great controversy. The U.S. textile and apparel manufacturing sector has lost more than 1 million jobs since the implementation of NAFTA in 1999. Breaking down the numbers, the U.S. textile industry lost 360,600 jobs (52% employment loss), and the U.S. apparel industry lost another 640,500 jobs (75% employment loss) over the period. The American Manufacturing Trade Action Coalition believes the job losses are due to an uncontrolled flood of imports, often heavily subsidized, and that the implementation of NAFTA was asymbolic of a sea change in U.S. trade policy.[8]

### Central American Free Trade Agreement (CAFTA)

In 2006, CAFTA (Central America Free Trade Agreement) was signed into law. The trade pact was the focus of intense debate. Proponents saw CAFTA as an opportunity for the United States to get improved access to the Central American market for U.S.-made goods and to strengthen poor countries. Opponents argued that the United States would impose unfair trading conditions on neighbors. Textile lobbyists who helped to get the deal through Congress and signed by President Bush see CAFTA as one fight among many to keep U.S. producers afloat.

"CAFTA has been very helpful in some products and not quite as helpful in others," said Missy Branson, senior vice president of the National Council of Textile Organizations. "I wouldn't say it has had a negative effect. It's been over ten years since NAFTA was implemented, and I don't think people could tell you what the final outcome is going to be. These things are kind of moving targets as the global trade dynamic changes."[9]

In 2007, Susan Schwab, U.S. Trade Representative, signed a customs cooperation agreement with Mexico, taking an important step toward integrating apparel trade between North America and Central America. The pact laid the groundwork for cumulation between Mexico and the countries of the CAFTA, which would allow producers in Central America to make apparel with Mexican materials and still get duty-free access to the U.S. market.

Julia Hughes, senior vice president of international trade at the U.S. Association of Importers of Textiles and Apparel, said these conditions might all be met soon. "This is one of those unusual circumstances where a textile and apparel provision is indeed breaking new ground in trade policy," said Hughes. "It's the first step toward what we were calling the North American Platform, or an integrated North American industry that would bring the yarns, the fabrics, the apparel manufacturers all together without barriers between borders.[10]

## Penetration of the U.S. Market by Foreign Investors

Direct investment in U.S. properties and businesses is extremely attractive to foreigners. Because so many textiles and apparel items are imported into the United States, foreign investors have long been interested in buying into American textile and apparel manufacturing companies. Only recently have they succeeded in doing so. Foreign investors, mostly from Europe and the Far East, have taken three routes to ownership: joint ventures, total ownership, and licensing.

For example, L'Oréal of France purchased three important U.S. cosmetic labels: Maybelline, Redken, and Helena Rubinstein. While the purchasing of manufacturers is a relatively new form of foreign investment, many retail operations have been foreign-owned for some time, and there is even more activity in this sector than in manufacturing.

A new example, Who.A.U., a South Korean brand with a passion for the California lifestyle, has entered the already crowded teen and young adult category. The unusual name Who.A.U. stands for Who Are You. The company is in direct competition with Abercrombie & Fitch, Hollister, and American Eagle Outfitters. Who.A.U.'s, original plan was to

open twelve to eighteen stores, but Daniel Pang, executive vice president of U.S. operations for the South Korean group, said, "Who.A.U. could eventually be as big as Hollister, and Hollister has 416 stores in the U.S."[11]

Aioli, a $100 million South Korea apparel maker, has launched stateside contempory brands, Plastic Island and McGinn. Aioli kicked off a third contemporary brand, Egoist, in 2007 and plans to open retail stores selling its brands.[12]

The arrival of the South Korean groups follows the launch in the United States of Japan's UNIQLO Chain, as well as continued expansion of such European Chains as H&M, Mango, and Zara, with Topshop of the United Kingdom also looking to expand in America.

New York's Madison Avenue, Chicago's Michigan Avenue, and Los Angeles's Rodeo Drive are lined with the boutiques of such Italian designers as Valentino, Armani, Ungaro, Dolce & Gabbana, Missoni, and Prada. Their presence in the United States is just a part of their global retailing strategy.

## Licensing

Investment by foreign manufacturers in the fashion industry is not entirely new. Licensing arrangements, which often involve ownership of domestic companies, were initiated over 25 years ago by companies such as Christian Dior, Pierre Cardin, and Hubert de Givenchy. Today, the European presence is widespread. For example, Donna Karan's and Marc Jacobs's collections are financed by the French LVMH-Louis Vuitton Moet Hennessy family.

## Penetration of Foreign Markets by U.S. Companies

To counterbalance foreign investment, American businesses have been interested in investing in foreign countries, where U.S. management is often welcomed because American know-how and standards for high quality are much-respected commodities. U.S. investment in foreign countries also helps the balance of trade.

### Licensing

Just as foreign manufacturers first penetrated the U.S. retail market with licensed products, so too have American companies been able to license products abroad. American character licenses such as Mickey Mouse, Kermit the Frog, Superman, and Miss Piggy have been great successes abroad, as have sports licenses and brand names, such as Nike, and designer names, such as Calvin Klein, Donna Karan, and Ralph Lauren (see Figure 17.9).

Today, many companies are switching from licensing to importing strategies in order to establish and strengthen brand identity. As international distribution continues to develop, particularly in Asia, U.S. manufacturers are finding that a mix of locally licensed product and U.S.-manufactured apparel is the most effective way to sell locally.

### Joint Ownership

While the United States permits total ownership by foreign investors, most other countries only allow foreign investors to be partners or joint owners. Among the American companies that are joint owners in foreign manufacturing firms is Blue Bell, producer of Wrangler jeans, in Asia, Italy, and Spain.

### U.S. Exporting

Because the "Made in the U.S.A." label is desirable all over the world, the United States can export its fashion products around the globe. Increased U.S. exports, in fact, are seen by many industry experts as the solution to the U.S. trade deficit. The United States does not need to keep out foreign competitors as much as it needs to sell and promote its products abroad.

Although U.S. designer fashions are available in upscale department stores around the globe, a common strategy is to establish a presence in a new foreign market with a freestanding "signature store," or boutique. The ability to monitor consumer reac-

**FIGURE 17.9** Products that feature American licensed characters, such as this backpack with Mickey Mouse, are popular abroad.

tion to the designer's merchandise allows for rapid adjustment to local tastes and preferences, just as is true at home. Bud Konheim, chief executive officer of Nicole Miller, predicts that: "By the end of the century, the term 'going global' will have lost its meaning. Foreign sales will just be another part of every firm's account list."[13]

Meanwhile, as U.S. exporters await the easing of trade barriers, their goods are often subjected to the same kinds of trade restrictions that the United States imposes on other countries. U.S. manufacturers seeking to export their products must work their way through a maze of foreign country quota, duty, and tariff regulations.

Because the United States is a major industrial giant, it is not the beneficiary of foreign-sponsored preferential programs such as it frequently sponsors for other nations. But recently, many domestic programs have been developed to help U.S. manufacturers become more successful exporters. The new programs are usually sponsored by the federal and state departments of commerce.

## Summary and Review

Through imports, offshore production, and exports, the U.S. textile and apparel industry is a major player in the global economy. Importing is a major source of merchandise for retailers, who rely on visits to foreign markets, store-owned foreign buying offices, commissionaires, import fairs, and U.S. import firms. Apparel manufacturers are also purchasers of foreign products, especially fabrics and other materials and trimming. Retailers may develop products bearing their private label by having their designs produced by foreign manufacturers.

U.S. apparel manufacturers have turned to offshore sources for all or part of the production of their goods. To improve the unfavorable balance of trade that has resulted from this extensive import activity, the government has imposed quotas and tariffs on selected goods from countries whose products have a competitive advantage. The United

States participates in multinational agreements such as those of the World Trade Organization and in separate trade agreements with individual countries or groups of countries.

U.S. and foreign businesses mutually penetrate each other's markets through licensing arrangements, investments in manufacturing, and establishment of retail outlets. Export of U.S.-made fashion goods is a growing aspect of the country's role in the global economy.

## Trade Talk

Define or briefly explain the following terms:

| | |
|---|---|
| absolute quota | balance of trade |
| bootleg | Central American Free Trade agreement (CAFTA) |
| commissionaire | developed countries (DCs) |
| duty | export |
| first cost | free trade |
| General Agreement on Tariffs and Trade (GATT) | global sourcing |
| gray market goods | import |
| import quota | less developed countries (LDCs) |
| Multi-Fiber and Textile Agreement (MFA) | Newly Industrialized Countries (NICs) |
| North American Free Trade Agreement (NAFTA) | offshore production |
| protectionism | specification buying |
| tariff | tariff-rate quota |
| trade deficit | |

## For Review

1. What advantages do imports give retailers?
2. Name the five ways foreign-made fashion merchandise can be purchased.
3. What are the two important functions of foreign import shows in the United States?

4. What concerns arise when retailers do specification buying of private-label merchandise?
5. Who are the advocates of protectionism in the fashion industry? Why?
6. Who are the advocates of free trade in the fashion industry? Why?
7. What is the purpose of WTO? MFA? NAFTA? CAFTA?
8. What are the provisions of Tariff Schedules 807 and 807A?
9. What rules has the Apparel Industry Partnership established for U.S. apparel manufacturers who do business with offshore factories in order to eliminate sweatshops?

10. What are the forms of American investment in foreign fashion industries?

## For Discussion

1. As a fashion consumer, do you advocate protectionism or free trade? What major items of your current wardrobe would you have been unable to purchase if broad protective legislation prohibiting imports had been in place?
2. What are the advantages of using a store-owned foreign buying office? A commissionaire?

# chapter eighteen

*Everything you always wanted to know*

*about the organization, operation, differences,*

*and new trends in various types of retail organizations.*

KEY CONCEPTS

- History and development of fashion retailing in the United States
- Organization for buying and merchandising in department stores, specialty stores, and discount stores
- Organization for buying and merchandising in chains, leased departments, and franchises
- Operation of off-price retailers, factory outlet stores, category killers, boutiques, and showcase stores
- Operation of nonstore retailers, including direct sellers, catalog stores, TV home shopping, and Internet sites
- Trends in retail patterns

# Fashion Retailing

484

The business of everybody in the fashion business is store business, whether one designs, manufactures, buys, sells, promotes, displays, reports, or photographs clothes, shoes, accessories, or beauty products. Eventually, the goods must be where the people are, and the people must come to where the goods are, and what is in the stores must be desired and bought by people—people continuously "shopping"; seeing, desiring, paying, and possessing. That is store business, and, in one way or another, it is the business of everybody in the fashion business.

—Estelle Hamburger,
"*Fashion Business*—
*It's All Yours*," Harper & Row, 1976

Retailing is the business of buying and selling goods to those who will use them, the ultimate consumers. Retailing is a vital industry in the United States today. With over 2 million retailers, the nation generates about $3.8 trillion in sales annually.[1] **Fashion retailing** involves the business of buying and selling—or merchandising—apparel, accessories, and home fashions. It is the way fashion products are moved from the designer or manufacturer to the customer.

Retailing is in many ways the heart of the fashion industry. It is the most challenging end of the fashion business, existing as it does in a constant state of change. Retailers must, for example, be among the first to spot and act on new trends. They must be attuned to their customers' needs and desires to a degree that is required in few other businesses. Retailers must react to a constantly changing and often unsettled economic climate.[2] See Table 18.1 for a list of the top ten global retail leaders.

An extraordinary amount of planning and effort goes into the merchandising of fashion products. For people who are not in the fashion business, the process of merchandising fashion products can look very easy. Fashion moves from concept to customer; that is, it moves from designer to manufacturer to retailer to you—the customer! The most intricate part lies in the merchandising and retailing of the goods. As mentioned previously, an old adage among fashion retailers, called the five R's, stands for choosing:

- The Right merchandise
- At the Right price
- In the Right place
- At the Right time
- In the Right quantities

If any one of these R's is incorrect, it will collapse all the R's. Think of it as smoothly juggling five balls at once. You must keep them all in the air at the same time; constantly moving, never touching. Your timing must be flawless. If you let one ball slip, they will all fall. And you must keep smiling and make it look effortless. That is like fashion merchandising—it looks easy but is hard to do!

## History and Development of Fashion Retailing

People have been swapping, trading, or selling each other various goods for thousands of years. In the Orient and eastern Mediterranean, bazaars and marketplaces still operate on the sites they have occupied for centuries. Not until the mid-1800s and the opening of the first department store—the Bon Marché in Paris—did modern merchandising as we know it begin to develop (see Figure 18.1). Even then, it developed differently in the United States than in Europe. In this chapter, we explore the development of retailing in the United States.

Retailing in the United States grew directly out of the frontier. It was an attempt to meet the needs of countless numbers of settlers who were moving west to populate a huge country. The first settlements in the United States were situated along its eastern coast. There, settlers built cities and towns that resembled what they had left behind in Europe. Philadelphia, New York, and Boston were soon pop-

TABLE 18.1 *Top 10 Global Retail Leaders*

| COMPANY | COUNTRY OF ORIGIN | RANK 2005 | RANK 2004 | RANK 2003 | RANK 2002 | RANK 2001 | RANK 2000 | RANK 1996 |
|---|---|---|---|---|---|---|---|---|
| Wal-Mart | US | 1 | 1 | 1 | 1 | 1 | 1 | 1 |
| Carrefour | Fr | 2 | 2 | 2 | 2 | 2 | 2 | 8 |
| Home Depot | US | 3 | 3 | 3 | 3 | 4 | 4 | 24 |
| Metro | Ger | 4 | 4 | 4 | 5 | 6 | 5 | 4 |
| Tesco | UK | 5 | 5 | 6 | 8 | 13 | 13 | 18 |
| Kroger | US | 6 | 6 | 5 | 4 | 5 | 3 | 13 |
| Target | US | 7 | 8 | 7 | 6 | 7 | 10 | 12 |
| Costco | US | 8 | 7 | 9 | 9 | 12 | 14 | 23 |
| Sears Holdings* | US | 9 | 33 | 17 | 17 | 9 | 7 | 7 |
| Schwartz | Ger | 10 | 11 | 16 | 24 | 27 | 29 | 33 |

*Ratings prior to 2005 represent predecessor company, Kmart.
Sources: Published company data and Planet Retail, www.planetretail.net.

ulous centers of commerce and culture. Their shops were patterned after those in London and Paris. No one is sure who should be credited with the founding of the first department store in the United States. Most authorities claim it was R. H. Macy in about 1860 (see Figure 18.2). Others claim the first department store was The Fair in Chicago in 1874, or Wanamaker's in Philadelphia in 1876. On the frontier, however, such sophistication was not possible, nor would it have served the needs of western buyers. Instead, three elements—general stores, peddlers, and mail-order sellers—each uniquely geared to life on the frontier, combined to give birth to modern retailing in the United States.

### General Stores

When the West was in the very early stages of settlement, there were no stores—and very few women to buy anything in them anyway. Apart from the settled areas along the East Coast, most of North America was populated by Native Americans, fur traders, and explorers. Groups of Native Americans had long traded goods among themselves, and the Europeans who traveled west soon learned to follow suit. They began by trading with Native Americans, but soon European traders opened trading posts. There, fur traders swapped furs for basic supplies.

**FIGURE 18.1** Modern merchandising began with the first department store in Paris, the Bon Marché, 1880 (top). **FIGURE 18.2** R.H. Macy's in New York City, 1908 (bottom).

Gradually, as the West became more settled, and pioneer men and women moved across the country, trading posts evolved into **general stores**. Where trading posts had carried only such basics as guns, gun parts, and food supplies, general stores sought to expand their stock by adding such goods as saddles, salt pork, lamp oil, and even ladies' bonnets. Money was a scarce commodity on the frontier, so general stores were still willing to take goods as well as cash for payment. A farmer's wife might make bonnets or lace collars to exchange for the few supplies she needed from the general store. As people became more settled, they became interested in buying more than basic supplies, and general stores were soon stocking a greater variety of items such as dress fabric, sewing notions, and fancier bonnets.

Not surprisingly, in a place where life was spartan and store-bought goods were one of life's few pleasures, people liked to linger over their purchases. As a result, general stores also functioned as community social centers as well as gathering places for political debate. To this day, general stores still serve many small communities in rural areas of the United States.

Gradually, as settlers became more prosperous, the general stores stopped bartering and began to operate on a cash-only basis. The new influx of capital could be used for expansion. Over time, some general stores—such as Meier & Frank in Portland, Oregon, and Filene's in Boston—grew into full-fledged department stores.

## Peddlers
Even with general stores located in communities and trading posts scattered along well-traveled trails, many homesteads were too isolated to make regular use of them. Itinerant peddlers began to service these remote customers. A peddler visited some areas only once a year, so he was accorded a warm welcome.

In many ways, peddlers were the first marketing experts. In addition to their wares, which typically

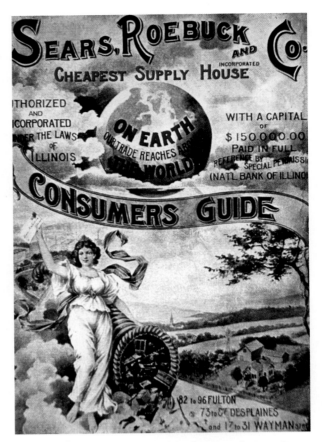

FIGURE 18.3 In the latter part of the 19 century, the Sears, Roebuck and Co. catalogs opened a whole new world of fashion to rural Americans who lived far away from shops.

consisted of pots and pans, shoes and boots, sewing notions, and a few luxury items such as lace, combs, and ribbons, they carried news of the latest fashions being worn in the cities back east. The reverse was also true, and they carried word back east about specific items that pleased or displeased customers in the Midwest or West.

## Mail-Order Sellers
The final element in the development of modern retailing was the mail-order seller. Mail-order companies, which began in the late 1800s, serviced the rural areas of the United States. At that time, the United States was largely rural, so almost everyone was a mail-order customer. Montgomery Ward, which mailed its first catalog in 1872, was the first company to do the bulk of its business by mail. By 1893, it had a competitor, Sears, Roebuck and Co., and the mail-order business was in full swing (see Figure 18.3). Such companies were only able to operate after the establishment of rural free delivery

(RFD), a system of free mail delivery to rural areas, and later, parcel post, a system of low-cost mail delivery that replaced RFD.

The mail-order catalog brought a new and expansive world to the lives of rural Americans. Hundreds of fashion items, furnishings for the home, and tools for the farm were offered in the catalogs. The illustrations were clear, goods were described in detail, and best of all, from a farm woman's point of view, prices were reasonable. The catalogs did not offer high fashion, but to rural women their variety and prices were still enough to delight. Women who had been limited to the scant provisions that a peddler was able to carry on his wagon or the barely filled shelves of general stores now felt as if the world was at their fingertips.

With the expansion of the catalog in 1894, the fledgling company posted astonishing sales of $750,000.[3]

## Traditional Types of Fashion Retailers

As the frontier turned into towns and cities, peddlers became sales representatives, and general stores and mail-order businesses evolved into something entirely different from their ancestors. Today, hundreds of thousands of retail stores exist to serve the over 300 million consumers in the United States.[4]

Today retailers usually can be classified into one of two broad categories—general and specialized—depending on the kinds of merchandise they carry. In each of these categories are many different kinds of retail operations: department stores, specialty stores, chain operations, discount stores, and leased departments, to name a few. Almost all retail stores offer some form of mail-order or telephone or fax buying service, and there are also retailers that deal exclusively in mail order. Most retailers also have Internet sites. Some stores have grown into giant operations, but many others are still small, independently owned and operated business.

The retail scene is dominated by **general merchandise retailers**, such as JCPenney, Sears, and Target. These retailers typically sell many kinds of merchandise in addition to clothing. They try to appeal to a broad range of customers. Most general merchandisers very broadly target their merchandise to several price ranges, and only a few limit themselves to narrow price ranges.

**Specialty retailers**, in contrast, offer limited lines of related merchandise targeted to a more specific customer. They define their customers by age, size, or shared tastes. Their customers are more homogeneous than those of general merchandisers. Examples are Crate & Barrel, Tiffany's, and Talbots.

Today, the differences between types of retailers are not as clearly defined as they used to be. It has, for example, become increasingly difficult to distinguish a department store from a chain operation, a discounter from an off-pricer, a franchiser from a chain. In this section, we look at three traditional types of fashion retailers: department stores, specialty stores, and discount stores.

## Department Stores

The **department store** is the type of general retailer most familiar to the buying public. Many are even tourist landmarks. Few people, for example, visit New York without seeing Macy's or Bloomingdale's. In London, Harrods is a big tourist attraction, as is Le Printemps in Paris (see Figure 18.4).

Department stores are in a state of flux that makes them difficult to define. The Census Bureau defines a department store as a retail store carrying

**FIGURE 18.4** Le Printemps in Paris is not only a department store but also a tourist attraction.

a general line of apparel, home furnishings, and housewares, and employing more than fifty people. Despite this official definition, however, many department stores have eliminated their appliances and furniture departments.

Department stores reigned as the kings of retailers well into the 1960s, when there was only about 4 square feet of retail space per person in the United States. They had long dominated downtowns with main stores called "flagships." In the 1960s and 1970s, department stores anchored malls. But in the turbulent 1980s, department stores failed all across the country, victims of overexpansion, mergers and acquisitions, and increased competition. By 2000, there was 20 square feet of retail space per person, much of it occupied by chain specialty stores and category killers.

Department stores strengthened in the mid-1990s. As Arnold Aronson of Kurt Salmon Associates, a management consulting firm, put it: "Department stores have been the main targets of new formats, because they basically have it all. Everybody has targeted a piece of the department store, but nobody has been able to target the entire package. In the end, department stores are the dominant concept under one roof."5 Table 18.2 lists the survivors.

Before getting into the ways in which stores are changing, let us look at how various kinds of traditional retailers operate and merchandise themselves. As general merchandisers, department stores typically serve a larger portion of the community than other stores and often offer a variety of quality and price ranges. A department store usually offers a category of apparel at several price points, each in a different part of the store. Figure 18.5 shows that typical department stores offer dresses on many floors, in many departments, with varying rates of return.

Department stores have also traditionally enjoyed a certain prestige that often extends even beyond the communities they serve. They are usually actively involved in their communities. A department store, for example, will eagerly stage a fashion show for a local charity, knowing that such activities create goodwill and enhance the store's overall reputation.

## Organization for Buying and Merchandising

Department stores are organized into special areas, or departments, such as sportswear, dresses, men's clothing, and furniture. Generally, buyers purchase for their departments, although in very large department stores, even the departments may be departmentalized, with individual buyers purchasing only part of the stock for a department (see Figure 18.6). In some sportswear departments, for example, one buyer may purchase tops, while another buys bottoms.

**TABLE 18.2**

*Top 10 Department Stores in the United States*

| COMPANY | SALES | NO. OF STORES |
|---|---|---|
| Sears Holding | $53,012,000 | 3,835 |
| Macy's | $26,970,000 | 1,360 |
| JCPenney | $19,903,000 | 1,033 |
| Kohl's | $15,544,200 | 817 |
| Nordstrom | $8,560,698 | 191 |
| Dillard's | $7,849,400 | 328 |
| Neiman Marcus | $4,063,900 | 59 |
| Belk | $3,150,000 | 300 |
| Mervyn's | $3,000,000 | 172 |
| Saks | $2,940,003 | 165 |

Adapted from "*Stores*' Annual Report on the Nation's Retail Power Players," www.stores.org/pdf/07TOP100Chart.pdf, *Stores*, July 2007, pp. S5–S13.

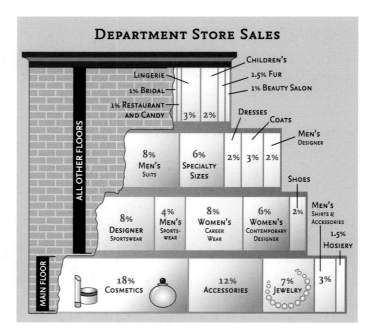

**FIGURE 18.5** This diagram of a typical flagship store for a department store chain shows the percent of business it gets from each department.

**FIGURE 18.6** The traditional department store look features separate, departmentalized classifications, as in these distinctively styled women's wear departments.

## Entertainment Values

The weaving of entertainment into modern retailing is reshaping the shopping experience. Entertainment values in retailing are defined in a number of ways. The most traditional way is by "simply having a compelling, often changing, merchandise assortment." Many retailers think of their stores as theaters that provide entertainment. The walls are the stage, the fixtures are the sets, and the merchandise is the star.

Other popular entertainment strategies include providing video walls and interactive Internet sites, arranging store visits by celebrities, presenting designer trunk shows, sponsoring charity fund raisers, and on and on.

Contrary to the rumors that the department store is a dinosaur, many department stores are fighting back by adding entertainment value. One way that department stores have built relationships with their customers is through award and loyalty programs. These programs reward high-spending customers with bonuses and make members feel like they are part of a VIP club. The stores arrange

events that range from meet-the-designer product launches to luncheons and cocktail parties. Neiman Marcus, for example, hosts lunches for its InCircle program and has featured guests such as Robin Leach and Larry King. Jeff Henry, vice president of San Francisco–based retail design firm Gensler, offers his vision of what successful contemporary retail should look like: "Retailing in the new millennium will have a 'deliberate calmness' about it. The heavy emphasis on entertainment during the previous decade will give way to experiences that are simple, direct and authentic. Artifice will not be welcomed. Service and caring for customers will be the rule."[6]

### Specialty Stores

A **specialty store** carries a limited line of merchandise, whether it is clothing, accessories, or furniture (see Figure 18.7). Examples of specialty

**FIGURE 18.7** Ralph Lauren's Rugby specialty store is classically iconic but maintains a unique look.

# Fashion Focus

Fashion Focus

## JCPenney
### *Still Raising the Bar*

The decline of the department store, the format that put mass in market, seemed to prove that middle-class shoppers had all but disappeared and no amount of innovation could bring them back. But the rumors of disaster turned out to be highly exaggerated. The American middle class is back, thanks to the exclusivity, experience, value, quality and ego-satisfying brands of a revitalized Macy's, Kohl's, and JCPenney.

JCPenney did not supersize or specialize into narrow niches. The hundred-year-old, traditionally mid-priced retailer is the talk of the turnarounds.

Since 2000, the company has transformed itself from an uninspired mall placeholder, selling rather dowdy basics to the department store of choice for the moderate customer. Its merchandising and marketing efforts have received accolades within the industry. After achieving the goals of a 5-year plan within 2 years, JCPenney unveiled an aggressive new strategy in 2007 that upped the ante.

JCPenney has publicly stepped forward with a plan that calls for adding 250 stores by 2011, mostly off-mall, posting overall sales gains of 9 percent. In addition to the new units, some 300 stores will also be renovated by 2011, resulting in an 18 percent increase in square footage.

As chairman and CEO Myron (Mike) Ullman III said in a recent speech, "The goal is to reach an industry leadership position by 2011." Ullman categorized 2006 as "a very busy and successful year. JCPenney has a major competitive advantage: we have 600 mall stores paired with 400-plus off-the-mall stores . . . 45 percent private label and 55 percent national brands . . . for a total of 1,000-plus stores working in synergy with our Web site and catalogs."

JCPenney has successfully created "an emotional connection" with its customers by adding new, exclusive brands such as Concepts by Claiborne and Solitude, while enhancing its eight private-label "power brands"—Ambrielle, a new women's lingerie label; a.n.a., a women's sportswear brand; Chris Madden and Cooks for home; St. John's Bay and Stafford for the traditional customer; Arizona, for young men's, juniors', and children's wear; and Worthington, a women's career label.

But that's not all. JCPenney made headlines when it signed on as the first retailer with Polo Ralph Lauren's newly formed Global Brand Concepts to develop and market a new brand, American Living. When the label debuted in spring of 2008, it was the largest launch in JCPenney's history.

Other drivers of JCPenney's aggressive growth plan include the further development of Jcp.com—currently a $1.3 billion business.

In 2004, Myron (Mike) Ullman became the ninth chairman and CEO. His skills were well honed, having served as president of Macy's, group managing director of luxury giant LVMH Moet Hennessy Louis Vuitton, and CEO of DFS Group. Ullman is now firmly entrenched in JCPenney's culture, and although he's clearly enjoying the company's recent success, he's hardly resting on his laurels. Acknowledging that his "goals and aspirations are aggressive," he maintains that the JCPenney team is up to the challenge. He summed it up this way: "We truly believe retail is a contact sport, and you have to take something away from somebody else to win."

### JCPenney Milestones

**1898** James Cash Penney opens his first business, the James C. Penney Meat Market and Bakery. It quickly failed when he refused to bribe a local cook who worked for his biggest client.

**1902** At 26, J.C. Penney opens the Golden Rule Store in Kemmerer, Wyoming, with partners Thomas M. Callahan and William Guy Johnson. Annual sales were $28,898.11 with a first-year profit of $8,514.36. The store is still in operation today.

**1907** Penney buys out Johnson and Callahan and begins rolling out a chain of Golden Rule stores.

**1911** Combined sales of the twenty-two stores reach $1 million.

**1913** With thirty-six stores, J.C. Penney is incorporated in Utah.

**1914** J.C. Penney moves its offices to New York City to simplify the buying, financing, and transportation of goods.

**1922** Big Mac Works, the company's oldest private brand, launches in stores.

**1924** The company opens its 500th store, in Hamilton, Missouri.

**1942–45** More than 5,500 J.C. Penney associates serve in the Armed Forces.

**1951** Sales surpass $1 billion.

1959 Based on a positive test, plans are announced to offer credit in all stores.

**1963** The J.C. Penney catalog is introduced for the first time.

**1966** The opening in Honolulu, Hawaii, marks a J.C. Penney in all fifty states.

**1969** J.C. Penney hires its first advertising agency.

**1971** James Cash Penney dies, and the stores are closed for a half-day. The logo (still used today) is introduced.

**1979** Catalog sales top $1 billion.

**1981** The Stafford brand is launched. The Stafford wrinkle-free dress shirt line is the best-selling men's dress shirt in America.

**1982** St. John's Bay is launched.

**1984** First National Bank of Harrington, Delaware, is acquired and renamed JCPenney National Bank, allowing the company to offer its own Visa and MasterCard.

**1986** Arizona brand is launched after the name was purchased from Aalfs. Products hit stores 2 years later.

**1992** JCPenney home office and museum opens in Plano, Texas.

**1993** JCPenney becomes the largest catalog retailer in the United States after Sears, Roebuck closes its catalog.

**1997** Eckerd was purchased and merged into JCPenney's drugstore division with Thrift Drugs.

**1998** JCPenney's Web site is launched; annual sales total $15 million.

**1999** Vanessa Castagna becomes COO of JCPenney stores, merchandising, and catalog after being lured from Wal-Mart. Internet sales increase almost 600 percent to $102 million in the site's second year.

**2000** Allen Questrom hired as CEO.

**2001** Arizona brand sales top $1 billion.

**2002** JCPenney celebrates its 100th anniversary.

**2004** Eckerd is sold, marking the end of JCPenney's drugstore division. Myron (Mike) Ullman III becomes JCPenney's ninth chairman and CEO.

**2007** Introduction of Web access at 35,000 cash registers in its stores.

**2008** Launch of American Living.

stores include shoe stores, jewelry stores, maternity-wear stores, and boutiques. As noted, specialty merchandisers tend to target a more specific customer than do general merchandisers. They may offer a single line; just shoes, for example. Or they may offer related limited lines, for example, children's apparel, shoes, and other accessories. Or they may offer a subspecialty, like just athletic shoes, or just socks!

Another variation of the specialty store is the private-label retailer, which sells only what it manufacturers itself. The Gap, Ann Taylor, and Brooks Brothers are leading examples.

Most of us are familiar with specialty stores but do not realize how varied they are. A specialty store can be one tiny hat shop, or it can be a chain of large, multidepartment stores such as Saks Fifth Avenue, which specializes in apparel. The latter is the type that *Stores* magazine reclassified as full-fledged department stores.

Most specialty stores in the United States are individually owned and have no branches. The composite sales of these single-unit specialty stores, however, represent only somewhat less than half of the total sales volume of all specialty stores. These stores are having an increasingly difficult time as harried consumers have less time to spend on shopping and want convenience and low prices.

Specialty stores such as Asprey's Jewellers in London, Gucci in Rome, and Hermès in Paris attract customers all across the world.

## Organization for Buying and Merchandising

In small specialty stores, the buying and merchandising are done by the owner or a store manager, sometimes with the assistance of a small staff. Large multidepartment specialty stores are organized along the lines of department stores, with buyers purchasing merchandise for their own departments. Multiunit specialty stores belonging to chain organizations are set up in a unique way that is described under chain organizations, later in this chapter.

## Entertainment Values

Entertainment is a natural activity for specialty stores. In addition to exciting visual merchandising, many specialty stores now offer related entertainment. Niketown began the trend with its video wall and then expanded to a Town Square with a staffed counter, banks of video monitors, and information about local and national sports teams. Galyan's Trading Company, the sports division of The Limited, offers indoor and outdoor climbing walls and an inline skating area. Contempo Casuals "The Girl's Room" is an in-store boutique that features magazines, incense, black lights, and photo booths. A small chain of specialty stores called Hot Topic features a so-called Rock Wall, a 30-foot-long display of T-shirts of alternative musicians such as Nine Inch Nails, and computer stations that allow customers to surf the Internet.[7]

## *Discount Stores*

The discount business got its start after World War II, when servicemen and servicewomen came home with a well-thought-out agenda for their lives: get married, establish a home, and start a family. Within a few years, with the help of the G.I. bill, which funded both education and mortgages, they had managed to achieve at least one of their wishes. Millions of new houses had been built in "new" suburban towns. The next step was to furnish them.

Discounters saw a need and began to fill it. The first discounters sold household goods. They ran weekend operations, usually setting up shop in an empty warehouse, barn, or lot just out side the city limits. Their stock varied from week to week, but they managed to have what people needed. One weekend, toasters were featured; on another, bath and bed linens were on sale. The selection was not particularly good, but the prices were right, so people came to buy. Through word-of-mouth, discount businesses began to grow. Some even expanded into permanent stores.

The discounters sold name-brand merchandise at less than retail prices. They did it by keeping their overhead low and offering minimal services— two facets of discount selling that prevail to this day. Cash-and-carry was the rule.

Fair trade laws made the sale of goods at more than retail or "list" price illegal. Discounters discovered, however, that the fair trade laws did not apply to selling lower than list price. Soon they were doing exactly that. In a sense, the fair trade laws, designed to prevent gouging by retailers, made the discounter's low price more recognizable and reputable.

Today, a **discount store** is any retail operation that sells goods at less than full retail prices (see Figure 18.8). Discounters are called *discount stores, mass merchandisers, promotional department stores,* and *off-pricers*. Discounters, which may be either general or specialty merchandisers, sell everything from cosmetics, accessories, and apparel to health and beauty aids to major appliances (see Table 18.3).

**FIGURE 18.8** Discounters, like Century 21, make a profit by keeping their overhead low.

**TABLE 18.3**

**CHAPTER EIGHTEEN**
**FASHION RETAILING**

**493**

*Top 10 Discount Stores in the United States*

| RANK | CHAIN (HEADQUARTERS) | SALES ($) |
|------|----------------------|-----------|
| 1. | Wal-Mart (Bentonville, AR) | 139,131,000 |
| 2. | Kmart (Troy, MI) | 37,000,000 |
| 3. | Costco (Issaquah, WA) | 34,797,037 |
| 4. | Target (Minneapolis, MN) | 32,588,000 |
| 5. | Sam's Club (Bentonville, AR) | 29,395,000 |
| 6. | Meijer (Grand Rapids, MI) | 11,450,000 |
| 7. | Dollar General (Nashville, TN) | 5,322,895 |
| 8. | BJ's Wholesale (Natick, MA) | 5,161,164 |
| 9. | Fred Meyer (Portland, OR) | 3,724,839 |
| 10. | Consolidated (Columbus, OH) | 2,647,500 |

Source: SAP top 100 Retailers, http://www.stores.org.
Accessed July 2007.

Discount stores are operated in different formats, as follows:

**Discount department stores** are retailers that offer well-known branded apparel at 20 to 60 percent off regular department store prices. The store format resembles that of a department store.

**Discount general merchandisers** are retailers like Wal-Mart and Carrefour that carry a broad range of products, from apparel to electronics, typically private label and basics. Their prices are lower than department stores or specialty stores.

**Warehouse clubs** stock a limited number of apparel SKUs—generally whatever brands they can buy. The top warehouse clubs globally in 2006 were: Costco with $16 billion total retail, $1.14 billion in apparel; Sam's Club with $39.80 billion total retail, $637 million in apparel; and BJ's with $7.95 billion total retail, $151 million in apparel.

**Discount/off-price specialty stores** offer low-price apparel from private labels and typically lower-end brands, with the exception of H&M and similar stores that are partnered with designers and labels like Karl Lagerfeld and Stella McCartney to create exclusive lines that drive traffic and give the perception of higher quality and value at reasonable to inexpensive prices.

**Hypermarkets** typically discount off-brands that are not necessarily designer or well-known name brands. The hypermarket environment also offers grocery or superstore items, and apparel is not necessarily the focus of this category.[8]

## Organization for Buying and Merchandising

Early discounters searched the marketplace for closeout and special-price promotions. Their inventories consisted almost entirely of this type of goods. Today, discounters specialize in low-end open-market goods or special lines made exclusively for them. Most conventional retail operations do not want their buyers to purchase goods that will be sold to discounters, but this has not stopped manufacturers from making special lines for discounters. Some designers and manufacturers use discount outlets to sell their overstocks or slow-moving items.

Independently owned and nonchain discounters follow the same buying and merchandising practices as other retailers of similar volume and size. Chain discounters follow the usual practices of their business, with one exception. In chain discount buying, buyers are usually responsible for several departments rather than a single category of merchandise.

Experts estimate that 30 percent of all retail and 19 percent of all apparel sales in the country take place in discount stores.[9] Ninety million people—or approximately one-third of the U.S. population—walk into a Wal-Mart every week. The large and widespread customer base is one reason analysts and economic observers look to the retail giants as an indicator of the economic condition. Discounters have a tremendous stake in the future of fashion retailing.

## Entertainment Values

Discounters added "greeters" early on to welcome people to their vast stores and direct them to the

# Then & NOW

## 100 Years of Neiman Marcus

### May They Live Happily Ever After— For Another 100 Years

In 1907, Herbert Marcus, his sister Carrie Marcus Neiman, and her husband, A. L. Neiman decided to invest $25,000 in a speculative venture. After much study, they came down to two choices: the Missouri franchise for a new-fangled bottled drink called Coca-Cola or opening a women's upscale fashion store on the dusty plains of Texas. Open they did, and for 100 years, Neiman Marcus has been the beacon of style and luxury through the country's good times—and bad.

A hundred years is a milestone worth celebrating, especially in the high-stakes game of fashion retailing. Surviving ten decades—through eras when many retailers have suffered bankruptcy, consolidation, and business failure—is a testament to the strength of the brand and the constant vision of Neiman Marcus management. *Women's Wear Daily* looks back at the Neiman Marcus century.

**1907**: Neiman Marcus opens on September 10 at Elm and Murphy Streets in Dallas.

**1913**: Fire destroys the original store and all inventory.

**1914**: Store is rebuilt at Main and Ervay Streets, the current location of the chain's flagship.

**1926**: Stanley Marcus leaves Harvard Business School and assumes his first responsibilities with the family-run retailer as secretary, treasurer, and director.

**1926**: The store launches the first weekly retail fashion show in the United States at the Baker Hotel in Dallas.

**1927**: The Sports Shop opens in the downtown Dallas store in conjunction with the rise of the women's sportswear category.

**1928**: A men's wear department opens, featuring such items as French-made ties and English shirtings rarely found west of the Hudson.

**1934**: Neiman's becomes the first apparel store outside of New York to advertise in national fashion magazines.

**1936**: The retailer stages its first charity fashion show for the Texas Centennial Celebration.

**1938**: The Neiman Marcus Award for Distinguished Service in the Field of Fashion is founded by Stanley Marcus to bring the names of European and American designers into public awareness.

**1939**: Neiman's dispatches a magazine-size holiday catalog that becomes an annual mailer.

**1950**: Stanley Marcus is promoted to president of the company upon the death of his father, Herbert Marcus.

**1951**: Neiman's opens its second Dallas store in Preston Center.

**1951**: Stanley Marcus commissions Mariposa, a large-scale mobile by Alexander Calder and, with that, the Neiman Marcus Art Collection is born.

**1957**: The first Neiman Marcus Fortnight is staged, honoring France.

**1959**: Edward and Stanley Marcus draw worldwide press attention for the Christmas Book, offering a Black Angus steer delivered "on the hoof" or in steaks.

**1960**: The His & Hers gift becomes an annual tradition with a pair of Beechcraft airplanes.

**1969**: Neiman Marcus is sold to Broadway-Hale.

**1971**: Neiman Marcus builds its first store outside Texas in Bal Harbour Florida.

**1972**: Carter Hawley Hale Stores buys Bergdorf Goodman.

**1973**: Stanley Marcus is promoted to chairman of the board and chief executive officer.

**1979**: The Beverly Hills branch opens.

**1982:** The eighth and ninth floors are added to the downtown Dallas flagship, which receives historical institutional landmark status the same year.

**1984:** Neiman's establishes inCircle, the industry's first customer-loyalty program.

**1986:** The last fortnight is staged at the downtown Dallas store. The subject nation is Australia.

**1987:** General Cinema buys Neiman Marcus and Bergdorf Goodman from Carter Hawley Hale.

**1988:** The company buys The Horchow Collection catalogue of home furnishings.

**1989:** Neiman's reaches $1 billion in sales.

**1991:** Horchow and the Neiman Marcus Mail Order business are merged to form Neiman Marcus Direct.

**1994:** The NM Holiday Express Train, a store on rails, gets on track for the Christmas season, visiting 16 cities in the South and Midwest.

**1994:** Burt Tansky is named president and chief executive of Neiman Marcus Stores.

**1995:** Stanley Marcus celebrates his 90th birthday with a gala in the Dallas flagship, where he's presented with the Neiman Marcus Award for Distinguished Service in the Field of Fashion. The award is also given to Miuccia Prada, Grace Mirabella, and Jean-Paul Goude.

**1996:** *The Book*, a fashion magazine presenting Neiman Marcus merchandise, makes its debut.

**1998:** The retailer opens the first Galleries of Neiman Marcus store in Beachwood Place in Beachwood, Ohio.

**1999:** NM Direct launches neimanmarcus.com, offering customers access to the largest collection of current designer merchandise and luxury brands on the Internet.

**1999:** Harcourt General spins off Neiman Marcus stores, NM Direct, and Bergdorf Goodman as a separate entity, dubbed The Neiman Marcus Group. Burt Tansky is named president and chief operating officer.

**1999:** Neiman's revives the spirit of Fortnight with Festa d'Italia, a four-week exposition of Italian goods and culture. It is held at the flagship and cosponsored by the Italian Trade Commission.

**2002:** Stanley Marcus dies on January 22 at age 96.

**2005:** The Neiman Marcus Group goes private with a majority of the equity ownership held by TPG and Warburg Pincus.

**2006:** The group launches Cusp, a smaller store format targeting a younger fashion customer, in Tysons Corner, Mclean, Virginia.

**2007:** Neiman's officials announce aggressive store expansion plans, including units in Topanga, West Los Angeles, in fall 2008; Bellevue, Washington, in Fall 2009; Oyster Bay on Long Island, New York, in fall 2010; and Princeton, New Jersey, in 2010.

**2007:** Neiman Marcus celebrates its 100th anniversary in grand style, and the Dallas Market Center, parent of the FashionCenterDallas wholesale market, honors Neiman Marcus with its Fashion Excellence Award. The company's 39th store opens in Massachusetts.

correct spot within the store. Some early discounters also used "blue light" specials to stimulate customer interest. Discounters in malls usually rely on the mall to draw and entertain customers, while they focus on keeping prices low. As people tire of plain stores with rows of fluorescent lights, and hundreds of counters in rigid rows, some discounters are upgrading their visual merchandising and looking for related entertainment values.

## Forms of Ownership

There are four types of ownership commonly found in U.S. retailing today: sole proprietors, chains, leased departments, and franchises. Partnerships, once a very popular form of retail ownership (Sears, Roebuck and Co., Abraham and Straus, etc.), are seldom found today because of liability issues and tax considerations.

Owners use many different formats, including the traditional department store, specialty store, or discount store, or the newer off-price, factory outlet, or category killer formats.

### Sole Proprietors

Sole proprietors, or owners, are the entrepreneurs who shaped American retailing. Many of the retailing greats, James Cash Penney, John Wanamaker, Adam Gimbel, and Isaac and Mary Ann Magnin, began as sole proprietors with a great idea and went on from there to found great retailing empires.

Today, over 90 percent of all U.S. retailers own and operate a single store. Sole proprietors usually have small stores because of the huge amount of capital required to support an adequate inventory for a large business. These **mom-and-pop stores** are usually single stores, managed by the owner with a few assistants. They are most frequently specialty stores, because department stores require more space and more inventory. If the owner prospers and expands to more than four stores, he or she is said to have a "chain."

## Chain Organizations

A **chain organization** is a group of centrally owned stores, four or more according to the Bureau of the Census definition, each of which handles similar goods and merchandise. A chain organization may be local, regional, or national, although it is the national chains that have had the largest impact on retailing. They also may be general or specialty merchandisers, and depending on the kind of stores they are, they will target their customer broadly or narrowly. A chain organization can be a mass merchandiser known for its low prices; a department store known for high-quality, mid-priced goods; or a specialty merchandiser selling exclusive designs at high prices. Apparel chains may focus on a special size, age, or income group.

The oldest and best-known chain organizations are JCPenney and Sears, Roebuck and Co., which *Stores* magazine categorizes as department stores (see Figure 18.9). Newer chains include Kmart and Wal-Mart, which are categorized as discount stores. Prestigious specialty chains are Talbots and Eddie Bauer. Wet Seal is a juniors' specialty chain.

## Organization for Buying and Merchandising

Most chain stores are departmentalized, but not in the same way as department stores. Chain-store buyers are typically assigned to buy a specific category or classification of apparel within a department instead of buying all categories for a department the way a department-store buyer does. This practice is called **category buying** or **classification buying**. Buyers in department stores, in contrast, are said to be responsible for **departmental buying**.

A departmental buyer in a sportswear department, for example, would buy swimwear, tops, jeans, sweaters, and slacks. A chain-store buyer who bought in the sportswear department might buy only swimsuits or only swimwear accessories. Category buying is necessary because huge quantities of goods are needed to stock the individual stores of a chain operation. Some chain operations have merchandise units numbering in the hundreds of thousands.

In addition to centralized buying and merchandising, most chains also have a system of central distribution. Merchandise is distributed to the units from a central warehouse or from regional distribution centers. Computer systems keep track of stock so that it can be reordered as needed; they also keep buyers informed of what is selling.

Like department and discount stores, specialty stores are searching for ways to set themselves apart by adding entertainment value. Wet Seal was one of the first stores to add video walls to its stores to entertain both its female customers and the boyfriends who accompany them. The company's latest innovation is the "Limbo Lounge" concept, a store that offers both men's and junior's apparel and accessories, along with several virtual reality stations and a juice bar. Both teenage and older couples are drawn to these stores.

**FIGURE 18.9** Sears, Roebuck and Co. is one of the oldest chain organizations.

## Leased Departments

**Leased departments** are sections of a retail store that are owned and operated by outside organizations. The outside organization usually owns the department's stock, merchandises and staffs the department, and pays for its own advertising. It is, in turn, required to abide by the host store's policies and regulations. In return for the leasing arrangement, the outside organization pays the store a percentage of its sales as rent.

Leased departments work best where some specialized knowledge is required. Jewelry, fur, and shoe departments are often leased, as are beauty salons. Glemby Company and Seligman and Latz, for example, lease many of the beauty salons in stores.

Department stores, chains, and discount organizations will lease both service and merchandise departments, while specialty stores usually restrict leased operations to services, such as jewelry or shoe repair or leather and suede cleaning.

## Organization for Buying and Merchandising

Leased operations vary from the independent who operates in only one store to major chain organizations that operate in many stores. In chain organizations, centralized buying and merchandising prevail. Supervisors regularly visit each location to consult with local sales staff and department store managers. At such meetings, they assess current sales, deal with any problems, and plan for the future.

As the buying and selling functions have become increasingly separate from one another, operators of leased departments enjoy a unique—and at this point, rather old-fashioned—position within the fashion industry. Most operate in a variety of stores. They are furthermore buyers who maintain daily contact with their markets and their suppliers, which allows them to make excellent projections about future trends as well as to give outstanding fashion guidance to their customers.

## Franchises

Franchises established themselves as a viable form of retailing when shops featuring fast food, bath linens, cookware, fabrics, unfinished furniture, electronics, and computers were successfully franchised. In a **franchise** agreement, the franchisee (owner-operator) pays a fee plus a royalty on all sales for the right to operate a store with an established name in an exclusive trading area. The franchiser (parent company) provides merchandise and assistance in organizing and merchandising, plus training. Customers often think that franchises are chains because they look alike.

With the exception of one or two bridal wear franchises and the maternity shop Lady Madonna, the fashion industry was not part of the initial franchise boom. It seems to have made up for lost time, however, in the second wave of franchising that proliferated during the 1980s. Firms as diverse as Benetton and Gymboree have adopted this form of ownership. Athletic footwear, tennis apparel, and men's sportswear have all produced lucrative and popular franchises. Athlete's Foot, for example, which sells athletic footwear and activewear, has 750 locations in 45 countries.

The latest trend is for designers to get in the act. Examples of successful worldwide franchises by designers are Ralph Lauren's Polo Shops, Calvin Klein shops, and Yves Saint Laurent's Rive Gauche shops.

Industry experts see no signs that franchising will slow its pace, and many feel that this form of retailing will continue to grow.

## Other Types of Fashion Retailers Today

In addition to the traditional retail formats discussed above, a new group of businesses have evolved over the past 30 years that adapt some of the attributes of the traditional retailers with some new ideas, as retail formats continue to evolve.

Types of retail formats popular today include off-price retailers, factory outlet stores, convenience stores, category killers, catalog showrooms, and boutiques or showcase stores, among others. Many overlap with existing traditional formats. Many are chains. We focus on those that are most important to apparel, accessories, and home furnishings.

## Off-Price Retailers

One area that is experiencing strong growth is **off-price retailing**, the selling of brand-name and designer merchandise at lower-than-normal retail prices when they are at the late rise or early peak in the fashion cycle. In contrast, regular discounters sell merchandise in the late peak and decline stages of the fashion cycle.

Off-price retailers attribute part of their success to their providing an invaluable service to manufacturers and price-conscious customers. Because manufacturers must commit to fabric houses so far in advance (up to 18 months before garments will be in the stores), they risk not having enough orders to use the fabric they have ordered. For many years, manufacturers took a loss when this happened. Then in the 1980s, when they had fewer orders than anticipated, they turned to off-pricers, who often pay full price for the fabric if the manufacturers will make it into garments at a lower cost. The manufac-

turers can more easily afford to cut their production costs than the cost of material they have already paid for. Off-pricers have in effect helped to smooth out the cyclical and often financially disastrous course of apparel manufacturing. Customers, in turn, benefit from being able to buy garments very similar to those that are being sold in exclusive stores for less than they would pay in those stores.

The first major off-price retailer in the United States was Loehmann's, which set up shop in Brooklyn in 1920 to sell "better" women's wear. Until then, high-quality women's garments had been available only through exclusive department stores. The regular-priced stores, for their part, did not fail to notice the arrival of Loehmann's on the retail scene. Department stores demanded that the discounter remove the labels so customers would not know what they were buying. That convention held for decades, but labels are rarely removed today.

The growth of off-price retailing in the 1980s drew other retailers into the market. The Zayre Corporation started the off-price chain T. J. Maxx. Today TJX, which now owns T. J. Maxx and Marshalls, is the second-largest apparel chain in the United States (see Figure 18.10). Dress Barn is another off-price chain that has enjoyed great success, offering moderately conservative fashion for customers with limited incomes. Even small off-pricers, such as Syms, experienced phenomenal growth in the 1980s and 1990s.

Off-pricers managed to capture an important share of the brand-name market. The success of brand names such as Donna Karan, Bill Blass, and Calvin Klein meant that designers no longer had to give department stores exclusives, and they were soon selling their products to off-pricers. More recently, however, many designers have begun to prefer selling their overstocks in their own stores. This has put severe pressure on off-pricers like Loehmann's and Syms to get enough inventory.

One other disadvantage seems to be built into off-price retailing: off-price retailers get the goods later than regular-priced retailers. While a depart-

**FIGURE 18.10**   T. J. Maxx stores successfully fill the consumer's appetite for brand-name and designer clothes at discounted prices.

ment store puts designer spring and summer clothing on the selling floor during the winter, the off-pricer does not get the same merchandise until several months later. As a result, the off-pricer has a shorter selling season than the regular-price retailer.

Industry experts worry that off-pricers will overextend themselves, as retailers did during the mid- to late 1980s, in the rush to cash in on a strong market. Other signs indicate that off-price retailing has still more muscle to flex. Burlington Coat Factory turned in $2 billion in sales in 1999, a remarkable demonstration of the consumer's appetite for brand-name and designer garments at reduced prices.

## Factory Outlet Stores

**Factory outlet stores**, discount operations run by a manufacturer, or increasingly these days, by a designer, are another booming area of discount retailing (see Figure 18.11).

Factory outlet stores began in the 1920s in New England. For many years, they experienced little or no growth. A manufacturer would open a little store in one corner of a plant to sell company products—slightly defective goods and overstocks—at reduced rates to company employees. Kayser-Roth and William Carter Co. were among the first to sponsor factory outlet stores. Other manufacturers followed suit, usually opening their outlets on the premises, which also always meant in the Northeast where the apparel factories were

**FIGURE 18.11** The popularity of outlet malls continues to increase.

located. Over time, manufacturers opened their stores to the buying public—that is, those who drove by their often obscure locations.

The proliferation of factory outlet stores can be traced to a recession in the early 1980s, which created a market for stores that could meet the demand for bargain-hungry shoppers. Not only did the already-established factory outlets, such as Warnaco, Inc., Manhattan Industries, and Blue Bell, continue to operate, but big-name designers such as Calvin Klein, Anne Klein, and Bill Blass and brand-name organizations like Adidas, Bass Shoes, and Van Heusen men's wear opened factory outlet stores.

Factory stores also left the factory, often to band together with one another in malls. The latest development is the emergence of entire communities, such as Freeport, Maine; Manchester, Vermont; and Secaucus, New Jersey, devoted almost exclusively to the selling of factory outlet goods. (The draw in Freeport was the presence of L.L. Bean, an established force in mail-order retailing that expanded its factory store outlet throughout the 1980s from a small outpost to a huge multibuilding operation.) See Chapter 19 for a discussion of retail locations.

Like off-price discounters, factory outlets offer certain advantages to manufacturers and customers. Most important is that they provide manufacturers and designers with a backup channel of distribution, which improves inventory control. Canceled orders and overstocks can be funneled into discount stores, which, if run correctly, also can be enormous image enhancers. Not to be underestimated is the possibility of strong profits. An outlet buys merchandise from the parent company for 30 percent off the regular wholesale prices and sells it for the same markup percentage as regular-priced retailers.

Designers and brand-name manufacturers use their outlets for overstocks and canceled orders. Some better sportswear manufacturers have 100 to 150 outlet stores, but to avoid offending the department stores, they do not publicize them. Large manufacturers, such as Kayser-Roth and Carter, are careful to use their outlets only for closeouts and seconds.

The latter are unwilling to risk offending department stores and other major customers with more direct competition. But now even the department stores have opened outlet stores: Saks Fifth Avenue has Saks Off 5th, while Nordstrom has The Rack.

Originally, most outlet stores were pipe-rack operations in dingy surroundings. Many looked like the factories out of which they had originally operated. Today, factory outlets resemble regular-priced retailers more and more, offering attractive merchandise displays and customer service that compares to that offered by full-priced retailers.

Factory outlet malls proliferated in the 1980s, but poor site selection and insufficient numbers of stores led to widespread failures. As with all real estate and merchandising, a chief success factor is location. Manufacturers have always been reluctant to open outlets in locations that compete with their retail partners, so most factory outlet centers were located outside metropolitan areas and away from the nearest regional mall. Developers are now learning that is not correct. Fifteen years ago, outlet malls were at least 50 miles from a regional mall, 10 years ago that distance dropped to 25 miles, 5 years ago it dropped to 15 miles, and today it is as little as 5 miles.[10]

Experts speculate on how well factory outlets will do when the market cools off, as it inevitably will, and as already appears to be happening. In the late 1990s, for example, customers' expectations regarding factory outlets were raised by the proliferation of attractive, full-service, professionally run designer shops. Yet, ironically, factory outlet customers are not people who must look for bargains. Instead, they are people with incomes far above average. Their motto is "NPR" or "Never Pay Retail." For these customers, bargain hunting is a leisure pastime, one that could easily be given up if factory outlet stores had to raise prices or cut services.

## Category Killers

Superstores or category specialists carry one type of goods that they are able to offer in great depth at low prices because of volume buying. They so dominate a market that they drive out or "kill" smaller specialty stores and so are known as **category killers**. They offer a narrow but deep assortment of goods in stores 8,000 square feet or larger. Because of their buying power they can get not only rock-bottom prices but also excellent terms and an assured supply of scarce goods.

The first category killer was Toys"R"Us, in the 1970s, which wiped out thousands of mom-and-pop toy stores. It then went on to affect the toy departments of major department stores to the point where few survived the 1980s. By 1995, it accounted for over 40 percent of all toys and games sold in the United States. However, competition from discount rivals eroded Toys"R"Us's market share, and by 2000 it relinquished the overall "biggest in the business" toy crown to Wal-Mart.[11]

Examples of category killers include Bed, Bath and Beyond; Home Depot; Barnes & Noble; and Best Buy. Typically these are huge, freestanding stores, often called "big boxes." They are rarely located in malls. They carry thousands of related products, at low prices, which they think offset no-frills service and decor.

Barnes & Noble is famous for adding entertainment value to its stores through its kids' theaters, coffee bars, poetry readings, and book signings.

## Boutiques/Showcase Stores

Although boutiques originated as small shops with French couture houses, they really came to life as small, individually owned shops in the antiestablishment 1960s. The first freestanding boutiques opened in London and quickly spread to the United States. Their appeal lies in their potential for individuality. These stores are often owned and operated by highly creative persons who are eager to promote their own fashion enthusiasms. Their target customers are like-minded souls who share their unique attitudes about dressing.

Some boutique owners design their own mer-

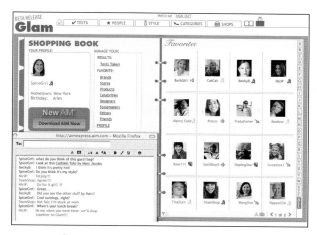

Established online players—including specialty sites such as Neiman Marcus and Net-a-Porter—and department stores such as JCPenney and Macy's report large profits and growth rates in their online business.

Key reasons for the growth of apparel, accessories, and footwear online are new sites; liberal shipping policies; and better, richer, sharper imaging. High-speed broadband access at home is now common, enabling users to navigate quickly through shopping sites. Some sites allow customers to zoom in on and see multiple views of products—a virtual examination that compensates somewhat for the lack of hands-on shopping.

Retailers are always looking for ways to make the shopping experience more interactive. Many have added next-generation content, including video and user-generated content such as customer-written product reviews, blogs, profiles, and social networking (see Figure 18.15).

JCPenney has been online since 1996 and is constantly moving forward with new technologies to enhance the customer experience at its $1.3 billion site. It has added social networking, user reviews, and video.

Neiman Marcus has also added interactivity to its site. It is adding video to its virtual trunk stores and is planning live chats with designers and store executives. The retailer had great growth in its online sales. A big reason for the booming business is that the Internet has enabled it to extend its brand to customers who live outside its store areas.[18]

## Mergers and Acquisitions

Until the 1930s, most department stores in the United States were independently owned. Most, in fact, were owned by the families whose names they bore, names such as Marshall Field, John Wanamaker, Gimbel Brothers, and J. L. Hudson. By the 1980s, most of these long-established stores had changed hands, and with these changes in ownership came new images and sometimes even new names.

So much change has occurred in the retail

**FIGURE 18.15** Glam.com features customer-written product reviews, blogs, profiles, and social networking to enhance the shopping experience.

business recently that you need a scorecard to track the remaining players. Consolidations, changes in distribution channels, bankruptcies, altered buying organizations, and foreign investments have all caused the retail scene as we knew it to change.

Although mergers have taken their toll on the department stores, causing some old, established stores to close their doors, some good has been served. Without mergers, many of the established department stores would not have survived the onslaught of competition from chains and discounters. In fact, mergers generally occur for one of two reasons: a need to reorganize for greater efficiency and a need to expand.

## *Merging for Efficiency and Expansion*

Like everything in life, the only thing that has remained constant in the retail business over the last century is change. The trend toward mergers and consolidations started in 1896 when John Wanamaker acquired A. T. Stewart. But it was Fred Lazarus Jr. of the founding family of the original Lazarus Store in Columbus, Ohio, who consolidated the first retail giant with the purchase of the Shillito Store in Cincinnati and Filene's of Boston, Abraham-Straus in New York joining them to form Federated Department Stores in 1930.

### The 1970s and 1980s

In the 1970s and 1980s, the big corporate merger trend picked up momentum with some of the most famous names in the business changing hands.

Among the most memorable deals: Dayton Hudson bought Mervyns in 1978 and Marshall Field's at the beginning of 1990. Crown American Corp. bought Hess's Department Stores in 1979. Allied Stores Corp. picked up Garfinckels's, Raleighs, and Miller & Rhoads in 1981. Taubman bought Woodward & Lothrop in 1984 and John Wanamaker in 1986. P. A. Bergner acquired Boston Stores in 1985 and Carson Pirie Scott in 1989. May Department Stores acquired Associated Dry Goods in 1986 and Filene's and Foley's in 1986. L. J. Hooker, an Australian real-estate developer, bought Bonwit Teller, B. Altman, Sakowitz, and Parisian in 1987. Harcourt General bought Bergdorf and Neiman's in 1987. Dillard's acquired Joske's in 1987, half of Higbee's in 1988, D. H. Holmes in 1989, and Ivey's in 1990. Macy's added Bullock's, Bullock's Wilshire, and I. Magnin in 1988. Marks & Spencer bought Brooks Brothers in 1988, and Investcorp bought Saks in 1990.

### The 1990s

The mergers and acquisitions of the 1970s and 1980s led to the restructuring and reorganization of the 1980s and 1990s, when many of these firms wound up in bankruptcy court or simply disappeared from the scene. Among the best known were the liquidation of B. Altman in 1989, Federated/Allied's Chapter 11 filing in January 1990, Carter Hawley Hale's bankruptcy in 1991, and Macy's bankruptcy in 1992.

### 2000 and Beyond

The mergers and acquisitions movement had a resurgence in the early 2000s with one of the biggest happening in 2005. The two most notable deals include the acquisition of May Department Stores by Federated Department Stores in 2005 and the purchase of Neiman Marcus Group by Texas Pacific Group/Warburg Pincus.

Other high-profile retail deals in 2006, 2007, and beyond include Saks Incorporated selling its Parisian unit, Federated Department Stores (now known as Macy's since 2007) selling Lord & Taylor, Burlington Coat Factory sold to Bain Capital Partners, and Sports Authority, Inc., sold to an investor group. The merger and acquisition story is not over yet —stay tuned.[19]

## Trends: Changing Retail Patterns

Retail operations not only must constantly respond to change in their environments, but they themselves must change if they are to survive. One theory, suggested by Malcolm P. McNair, retailing authority and professor emeritus at the Harvard Business School, describes the way in which retail organizations naturally change or evolve.

According to McNair's theory, called the Wheel of Retailing, most retail organizations begin life as lower-priced distributors. They offer strictly functional facilities, limited assortments, and minimal customer services. As time elapses, the successful businesses need to grow in order to survive, so they begin to trade up in an effort to broaden their customer profile. Facilities are modernized. Store decor becomes more attractive. Assortments become more varied and of higher quality. Promotional efforts are initiated or increased, and some customer services are introduced.

The process of trading up, however, involves considerable capital investment in the physical plant, equipment, and stock. Operating expenses spiral. As a result, retailers are forced to charge higher prices to cover the increased cost of doing business. To justify the higher prices, they also begin to stock more expensive merchandise.

According to McNair's theory, as retailers move out of the low-priced end of the market into the moderate-to-high-priced field, they create a vacuum at the bottom of the retailing structure. The vacuum does not exist for long, though. Enterprising new retailers move quickly to fill the vacated and temporarily uncompetitive low-priced area to meet the demands of customers who either need or prefer to patronize low-priced retailers. This pattern keeps repeating itself as successful retailers trade up and new ones move into the vacuum. This theory also applies to catalog companies—Spiegel is one example of a firm that moved upscale.

Even those who move up must still constantly cope with the ever-changing nature of the fashion business. In Chapter 19, the most important challenges and trends confronting today's retailers are discussed, along with strategies to overcome them.

## Summary and Review

The history of fashion retailing in the United States is an interesting one. From general stores and peddlers to the earliest mail-order sellers, all early retailers sought customer satisfaction. Today's retailers seek the same goals through a variety of formats.

Three traditional retailing formats are the department store, the specialty store, and the discount store. Newer formats include off-price retailers, factory outlet stores, category killers, and boutiques and showcase stores. All of these formats can be owned in one of four ways: sole proprietors, chains, leased departments, or franchises.

Four types of nonstore retailing are popular today: direct selling, catalog or mail-order selling, TV home shopping, and Internet sites.

Mergers and acquisitions have changed the face of retailing as we knew it and will probably continue to do so. Malcolm McNair's theory of how retailers evolve and change proposes that most retailers begin as lower-priced distributors and then move upscale, creating an opportunity for new retailers to fill the lower-priced niche. McNair calls this the Wheel of Retailing.

## Trade Talk

Define or briefly explain the following terms:

big boxes

category killer

classification buying

department store

discount/off price
 specialty store

fashion retailing

category buying
 or factory outlet store

chain organization

departmental buying

discount department store

discount store

franchise

general merchandise
 retailer

general store

warehouse clubs

## For Review

1. Name and briefly explain the characteristics and importance of three early forms of retail distribution in the United States.
2. How is the buying function handled by a department store?
3. What is a specialty store? How are buying and merchandising handled in a specialty store?
4. What is a chain organization? How are buying and merchandising handled in chain operations?
5. How do successful discounters make a profit?
6. What is a leased department, and how does it operate? Name the departments in a retail store that are frequently leased.
7. What is a category killer?
8. What stage or stages of the fashion cycle would most likely be emphasized by (a) a specialty store, (b) a department store, and (c) a discount store?
9. What is the difference between home TV shopping and shopping on the Internet?
10. According to Malcolm P. McNair, how do retail organizations typically evolve?

## For Discussion

1. Compare and contrast the organization for buying and merchandising among (a) prestigious chain organizations, department stores, and large specialty stores; (b) discounters and off-price mass merchandisers; and (c) franchises and leased departments. Give examples of different types of retailers in your community.
2. What examples in your community can you cite that support McNair's theory of trading up by retailers?

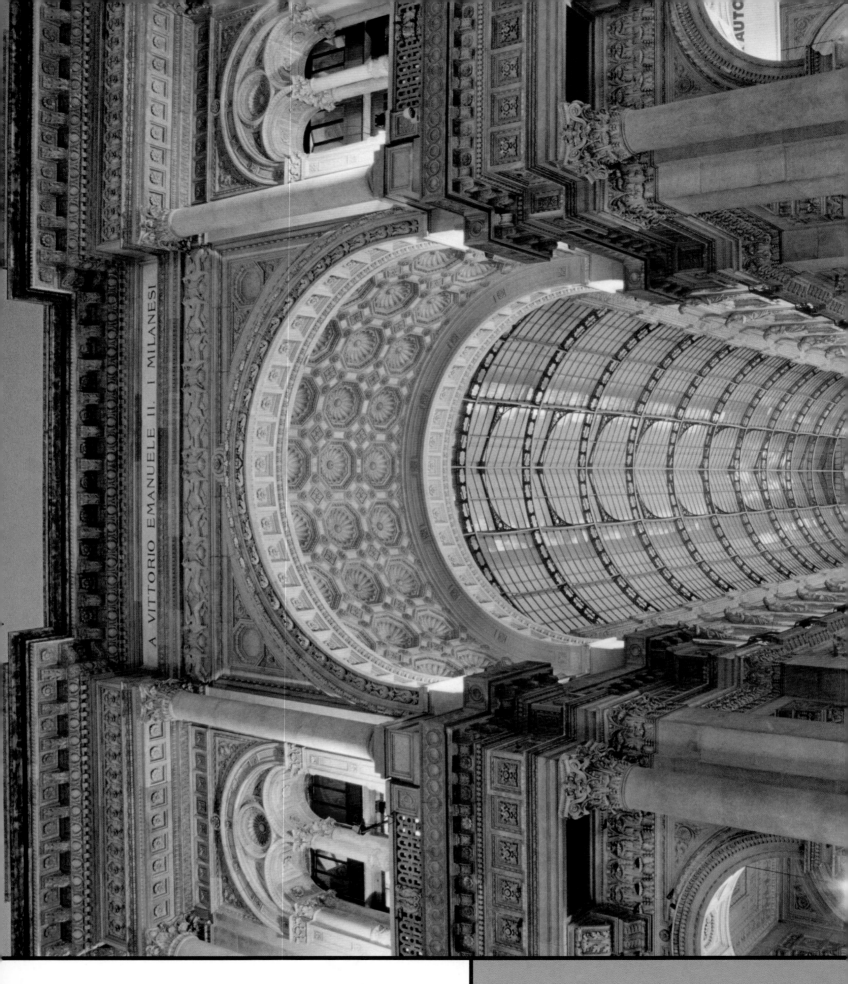

# chapter nineteen

*Everything you always wanted to know*

*about the major merchandising, operational,*

*and location policies of retailers.*

**KEY CONCEPTS**

- The six major merchandising policies that must be set by each retailer
- The five operational policies that must be set by each retail store
- The major strategies retailers are using to respond to customer concerns
- The major trends in merchandising and operational policies

# Policies and Strategies in Fashion Retailing

Retailing is ruled by imitation. A successful new retailing format or concept will soon be duplicated. Yet, certain retail innovators continue to flourish despite the intensifying competition. One reason is the innovator's knowledge that is difficult to imitate. Competitors can duplicate Wal-Mart's large stores, cross-selling of food and general merchandise, even its use of "people-greeters," but few, if any, can match the productivity of its core competencies: inventory management and distribution. The former are visible to the eye, the latter are knowledge-based and invisible.

—*Chain Store Age*

Stores use their merchandising, operating, and location policies to differentiate themselves from the competition and to attract different kinds of customers. Successful retailers realize that "you cannot be all things to all people," as the old saying has it. So they carefully craft a unique mix of merchandise, policies, and store locations to attract a loyal customer following. At the same time, they must respond to changing trends—a challenging balancing act.

## Merchandising Policies

Regardless of whether a retailer is a chain or a mom-and-pop operation, a general or specialty merchandiser, it seeks to maximize its profits by going after a target group of customers. In order to better target their customers, retailers establish **merchandising policies**. These are general and specific guidelines and goals established by store management and adjusted according to current trends and marketplace needs to keep the store on target.

Of the many elements that go into a store's merchandising policies, the six most important are the store's overall general goals regarding:

1. Stage of the fashion cycle that will be emphasized
2. Level of quality that will be maintained
3. Price range or ranges that will be offered
4. Depth and breadth of merchandise assortments
5. Brand policies
6. Exclusivity

### *Fashion Cycle Emphasis*

As a means of establishing its image, every retailer decides to emphasize one phase of the fashion cycle over others. It then chooses its merchandise to fit that phase. Most stores want to ride the tide of new fashion. Few knowingly highlight styles once they have reached the decline stage, but stores still must choose whether to emphasize styles in their introductory, rise, culmination, or peak stages.

A retailer who chooses to buy styles in the introductory phase is opting to be a fashion leader, while a store that waits for the styles to become slightly established, that is, to enter the rise stage, has decided to aim for being a close second to the fashion leader. Finally, a retailer may buy clothes in the culmination or peak stages, thus making itself a follower of fashion trends—as indeed most women are. The majority of stores across the country probably fall into this category.

Naturally, a store's choice about fashion emphasis must accord with its targeted customers' needs and wants. Henri Bendel in New York, which for many years had a reputation for extreme trendiness, knew that its target customers were a small, elite group of young and very stylish women who wanted to be the first to wear whatever was new. When The Limited bought Bendel, management changed Bendel target customer and shifted the store's emphasis, moving from a position of fashion leadership to one of pursuing a broader market. In the late 1990s, it changed back to the narrower, less competitive niche of the fashion leader customer. Today, Bendel has reestablished its reputation for featuring and nurturing young, fashion-forward talent, with exclusive in-store boutiques and "designer-in-residence" programs (see Figure 19.1).

FIGURE 19.1 Henri Bendel's target market has evolved over the years, starting with an emphasis on the niche, then expanding to a broader market, and finally back to a narrow focus.

## Quality

Retailers can choose from three general levels of quality:

1. The top level, which involves the finest materials and workmanship
2. The intermediate level, which exhibits concern for quality and workmanship but always with an eye to maintaining certain price levels
3. The serviceable level, which involves materials and workmanship of a fairly low level, consistent with equally low prices

Just as retailers are known for their chosen emphasis within the fashion cycle, they are also known for their decisions regarding quality. Quality and high fashion, however, do not always go hand in hand. Although most introductory styles are high priced, this is not always the case. Some stores that assert themselves as fashion leaders do not bother with high quality, preferring merely to push what is new and exciting. In contrast, retailers that emphasize the rise or culmination stage also often stake their reputations on the high quality of their merchandise. They are thus able to emphasize their apparel's lasting qualities in ways that fashion leaders often cannot and do not want to do. One example is Sears's boy's wear, which stresses sturdy workmanship.

Once a store has set its quality policies, it must make more specific decisions, such as whether it will accept nothing less than perfect goods or whether it will permit irregulars and second-quality goods to be offered.

## Price Ranges

What people earn affects what they can spend, especially for clothing, where a variety of choices regarding quality and price are available. As a result, pricing policies are an important merchandising decision (see Figure 19.2). A store's pricing policies play a major role in determining the kinds of customers it will attract.

There is actually no direct correlation between price and quality. Items of relatively low quality may carry a high price tag if there is a reason for them to do so, such as the presence of a designer's name or the fact that they are in the introductory phase of the fashion cycle. Despite the lack of a correlation, however, most retailers do attempt to tie their price ranges to quality standards. A store policy of buying only top quality also permits high price ranges, whereas a store that features intermediate quality usually sets some bottom limits that it will not go below. Stores that emphasize serviceable quality

FIGURE 19.2 Chadwick's offers special promotions and discounts on its merchandise.

**FIGURE 19.3** Too many sales may undermine customers' trust.

assortment in which it stocks relatively few styles but has them in many sizes and colors. Or it can stock a **broad and shallow assortment** in which it offers many different styles in limited sizes and colors.

The two are mutually exclusive because space and cost are limiting factors in retail operations. A policy of stocking a broad assortment usually limits the depth to which those items can be stocked, and conversely, if depth is desired, variety must usually be limited. Prestige stores tend to stock broad and shallow assortments, offering small stocks of many styles in limited sizes and colors.

In stores that cater to mid-range fashion and quality, assortments are broad and shallow early in a season when new styles are being tested. Once the demand for a style has become clear, the store begins concentrating on narrow and deep assortments of proven styles.

Mass merchandisers focus on narrow and deep assortments of styles in the culmination stage. Target, for example, has built an enviable reputation for fashionableness and fresh selection, yet its selections are not particularly deep. But its meticulous attention to housekeeping ensures that its counters and shelves give the impression of being well-stocked. Its apparel assortment is largely basics. But a handful of items in cutting-edge styles and colors give it an upscale look.

### Brand Policies

Stores also must establish policies regarding the brands they will carry. A brand is a name, trademark, or logo that is used to identify the products of a specific manufacturer or seller. Brands help to differentiate products from their competition. Some brands, those associated with designers like Ralph Lauren, for example, acquire a special status that permits them to be sold at higher prices. Status and price, however, are not the only things that help a brand sell well. National brands and private labels have also become important.

usually tend to also emphasize their low prices.

Ineffective pricing can drain a retailer's profits, muddle its image, and undermine customer trust (see Figure 19.3). Many stores now stress a "value pricing" policy. For example, JCPenney launched a line of value-priced jeans called the Arizona Jean Company. By contracting with its own manufacturers, JCPenney could buy cheap, set quality standards, and underprice Levis. The result was overwhelming sales and imitation of this strategy by Sears's Canyon River Blues jeans.

### Depth and Breadth of Assortments

An **assortment** refers to the range of stock a retailer features. A store can feature a **narrow and deep**

A national brand, which identifies the manufacturer of a product, is widely distributed in many stores across the country. National brands, which hold out the promise of consistent quality, have become the backbone of many retailers' stocks. Today the names of some designers, such as Tommy Hilfiger and Eileen Fisher, to name but two, have become so well known to consumers that their labels are considered national brands. These name brands have acquired a value in the consumers' mind that is distinct from any intrinsic value in the products themselves. To minimize competition over national brands, some major retailers insist on buying exclusive styles, or **confined styles**, from national brand manufacturers. Also, some manufacturers limit the number of stores that can carry their products. Nike, for example, allows only The Lockeroom and Belk's to sell its products in Newton County, Georgia, while the Russell Corporation allows only a few stores in the same county to sell its baseball and basketball uniforms.

Retailers are also riding the wave of popularity of brand names by promoting their own private labels or store brands. Store brands have proven to be an excellent way to meet price competition and achieve exclusivity. JCPenney's, for example, has seen its private label, Arizona Jeans Company, become a blockbuster success.

Prestige specialty stores tend to feature their own store labels and designer names, a strategy Bergdorf Goodman pursued with a private-label collection of classic but luxurious sportswear. Many department stores have adopted private labels with great success. Macy's with its I.N.C., Charter Club, M.T. Studio, and Arnold Palmer collections is a prime example. Mass merchandisers have always offered their own private labels, typically sold alongside unbranded merchandise, as a means of keeping prices low. Kmart, for example, sells "celebrity" lines, including apparel by Jaclyn Smith and Martha Stewart's linens and home fashions. Home Depot's spokesperson, Lynette Jennings, is a well-known interior designer with a highly rated

TV show. Target has established a slew of both clothing and beauty licenses through exclusive agreements and designer partnerships with Michael Graves, Stephen Sprouse, Mossimo, Sonia Kashuk, and Cherokee.[1] Wal-Mart sells a line by Kathie Lee Gifford. Even mass merchandisers, however, have been swept into the tidal wave of national brand names and now carry them.

## Exclusivity

**Exclusivity** is something many stores strive for but few are able to achieve. Several store policies can help retailers establish a reputation for exclusivity.

- They may prevail upon vendors to confine one or more styles to their store for a period of time and/or within their trading area.
- They can buy from producers who will manufacture goods to their specifications.
- They can become the sole agent within their trading area for new, young designers.
- They can seek out and buy from domestic or foreign sources of supply that no one else has discovered.

However, the first two policies (confined lines and specification buying) are options only when a store can place a large enough initial order to make production profitable for the manufacturer.

The last two policies do not necessarily demand high volume. They are thus invaluable to prestige stores who need exclusivity as part of their images but cannot hope to compete in volume with mass merchandisers or even big department stores.

## Operational Store Policies

After a retailer has defined its target customers and set its merchandise policies in a manner designed to attract them, it must next establish **operational policies.** Often more specific in nature than merchandising policies, these are primarily designed to keep the customers once they are attracted enough to come into the store. What merchandising policies do to establish a retailer's image, operational policies do to build a store's reputation. Operational policies also serve to enhance merchandising policies. They establish such things as the store's ambiance, its customer services, its selling services, its promotional activities, and last but hardly least, its frequent shopper plans.

## Ambiance

**Ambiance**, the atmosphere you encounter when you enter a store, does much to create the image of a store (see Figure 19.4). Prestige department and specialty stores work hard to provide pleasant and even luxurious surroundings. Decor matters and usually consists of carpeted or wood floors, wood counters and display cases, chandeliers and other expensive lighting. Dressing rooms are numerous,

**FIGURE 19.4** A store with good visual merchandising, displays, and lighting will send a positive message about the store's image to customers.

large, and private. The store is pleasing to the eye. Merchandise is attractively displayed on a variety of fixtures. Just think of the strong link between the store design of a Crate & Barrel and its displays and merchandise. Its use of textured woods, colorful textiles, and bright pottery has made its merchandise the stars of an exciting show.

Len Berry coined the term **sensory retailing**, which means in-store stimulation of all the customers' senses. Sensory retailing is becoming a more significant competitive weapon in retailing. Think of the sensuous aroma, mood music, and dramatic lighting of merchandise displays in a Victoria's Secret. In fact, the music played in Victoria's Secret stores has become a successful business in itself. In the history of classical music, eleven compact discs have sold over a million copies. The label that released five of them—Victoria's Secret! This success has led to other retailers selling their own albums; among them are The Limited, Express, Lane Bryant, Polo, the Gap, and Pottery Barn.

Retailers must create an experience and draw customers into it. Shoppers usually splurge on some items while attempting to save as much as possible on others. A retailer that maximizes customer involvement creates a unique experience for the shopper, drawing out the desire to splurge.

Retail environments that include education, allow sampling, and impart a feeling of pampering will entice the customer. Creating a welcoming atmosphere isn't simply about the lights and music—it must grow organically. By converging atmosphere, design, and merchandise, a retailer can create a unified story that sells its customer on the buying experience.[2]

In contrast, at low-range and discount stores, ambiance may count for little. The intention is to send the customer a clear message: shop here in less than luxurious surroundings, and we will give you the lowest possible price. Fixtures are usually plain, garments crowded on racks or "rounders," with supermarket style signage. Fitting room space may be limited or may consist only of a large, shared dressing room, commonly referred to as a "snake pit" by customers.

## Customer Services

Department stores pioneered in offering customer services. They were the first retailers to offer their customers store charge privileges and generous return policies. Their willingness to accept merchandise returns, in fact, originated with John Wanamaker and his Philadelphia store of the same name. His first store, opened in 1876 in an old railroad freight station, was a men's clothing store. A year later, he added departments for ladies' goods, household linens, upholstery, and shoes, for a then unheard-of total of sixteen departments. Wanamaker further shocked the retail world by advertising that if anything did not please "the folks at home" or was unsatisfactory for any other reason, it could be returned for a cash refund within ten days.

Today, it is commonplace for department and specialty stores to offer their customers an array of services designed to increase their edge over the competition. The more familiar customer services include several credit plans, liberal merchandise return policies, telephone ordering, free or inexpensive delivery, in-store restaurants, free parking, and a variety of services such as alterations and jewelry repair. As competition, particularly from chains and discounters, has increased, general merchandisers have met it by offering still more services, such as fax order facilities, online ordering, and extended shopping hours.

Discount stores, especially small ones, offer a more limited range of services than do department and specialty stores. Discounters took a lead in establishing extended hours. At small discount stores, transactions are usually on a cash-and-carry basis, although most accept major credit cards. Most large discounters offer their own credit plans, with greater emphasis on installment buying. Refund policies are less liberal than those of department stores; however, most discounters will accept

**FIGURE 19.5** A child in a ball crawl at IKEA demonstrates this chain's strong customer service policies. They realize that if a child is content, Mom shops longer!

unused goods (often for credit rather than cash) if they are returned in a specified period of time, usually seven to ten days. Delivery service, if available, is restricted to bulky items and usually costs extra.

Large discount chains like Target, proving Malcolm MacNair's theory discussed in Chapter 18, have raised their level of services. They have "guest amenity kiosks" with phones that shoppers can use to summon a salesperson or get a question answered. Target also has pint-sized shopping carts to help keep shoppers' children amused. The Swedish discount chain IKEA offers play areas (see Figure 19.5).

## Selling Services

In all but the higher-priced specialty stores these days, self-service is the rule. In discount stores and low- to moderate-priced chain stores, clerks are present on the selling floor to direct customers to merchandise and ring up sales. In most department and specialty stores, salespersons are available on the sales floor to answer some questions and complete sales transactions.

The old service of catering exclusively to one client at a time, bringing clothes into the dressing room, and offering fit and style advice is gone in most department stores, probably forever. An exception to this rule is Nordstrom, which has maintained a high degree of selling services. In fact,

# Fashion Focus

Fashion Focus

## Here,
## There,
## Everywhere
## *They are Coming!*

Left page: UNIQLO store interior (top); Zara advertising (bottom left); Topshop's New York City flagship (bottom right); Right page: H&M's Marimekko inspired line, 2008.

It is a small, small world—especially when it comes to retail stores. Designers from France, Italy, England, and America started the trend by opening stores around the world, selling only their designer labels—among them Chanel, Armani, Burberry, Ralph Lauren and many others, all who have opened internationally. But what about stores featuring clothes for those who aren't haute couture customers?

America has been the leader in retail store openings across the country, with only a small group of them opening their stores internationally. They will soon say "hello" to stores from Spain, Japan, England and Sweden, who have traveled internationally, arrived on the U.S. shores, and found great success.

Zara from Spain, UNIQLO from Japan, Topshop from England, and H&M from Sweden have arrived and successfully captured both the interest and dollars of American consumers.

### Zara

The Spanish retailer chain is an international fashion success story with a business model that allows it to replenish its stores with new on-trend merchandise every two weeks. The chain of over 1058 stores in 68 countries has its own design-to-distribution facility in Spain that handles much of its production. It introduces about 20,000 different items for its stores every year with a swiftness designed to stimulate customer traffic—and produces in small quantities designed to create a sense of scarcity and exclusivity about its clothes.

Zara is owned by Inditex SA, Europe's largest clothing retailer, with eight chains and 8.5 billion in revenue. The Zara stores account for about 66 percent of those sales.

Inditex operates 24 Zara stores in the United States and plans to open 10 more each year, for a target of 65 by 2010. Zara's prices are comparable to Banana Republic or Club Monaco.

### UNIQLO

The Japanese fashion chain is owned by Fast Retailing Co. Ltd. The first UNIQLO store opened in Hiroshima, Japan in 1984, and initially offered casual fashions such as denim and fleece. The chain expanded rapidly into Britain in the early 2000s, but found that its successful Japanese retail model couldn't quite compete with popular and trendy stores such as Topshop and H&M. Revamping itself as more fashion-forward—yet still offering sharp basics in strong colors—UNIQLO's second foray into expansion has taken off. The chain now has over 760 stores worldwide, including a flagship store on London's Oxford Street. In 2006, UNIQLO opened its first U.S. store in New York City's Soho neighborhood, and is planning to open many more by 2010.

Prices are competitive with Zara, Topshop, and H&M's high-end line, COS. In 2008 UNIQLO introduced its Designer Invitation Project, which taps rising talent for limited-edition collections that complement the store's other pieces.

### Topshop

When the fast-fashion British retailer Sir Philip Green unveiled his first Topshop/Topman unit in New York City, it was the opening shot in an ambitious plan to build an American-wide—and global—brand. In London each season, Topshop sponsors the shows and collections of a group of young designers and supports them toward creating exclusive collections for Topshop—a program called New Generation. In addition to building an American leg to his retail business, Green hopes, in the same vein, to find young American design talent to sustain and support.

Sir Green, a famously hands-on merchant and manager, said he is under no illusions about the chal-

lenge. Entering the American market and managing a retail operation 3,500 miles from his central London base will be no picnic. "We deliver one to three times a day at our Oxford Street flagship, and 100 new stockkeeping units every 14 days," he said. "I can already envision the 10:00pm phone call from New York about stock issues. I can see myself calling up the jet, and being in the sky by 1:00am with a truckload of merchandise. Opening in the U.S. is definitely going to mean less sleep for me," he said with a laugh.

### H&M (Hennes & Mauritz)

H&M was established in Västerås, Sweden in 1947 by Erling Persson. Today, H&M sells clothing and cosmetics in about 1500 stores in 28 countries. The business concept is "Fashion and quality at the best price."

H&M has more than 100 designers who work with a team made up of 60 pattern designers, 100 buyers, and a number of budget controllers to create H&M's clothing collections for men, women, children, and teenagers. H&M also sells cosmetics under its own brand. Though new goods are delivered to the stores every day, H&M does not have any factories of its own, but works with the over 700 independent suppliers primarily in Asia and Europe.

The Swedish cheap and chic fashion retailer made shopping news by presenting a series of successful, headline-grabbing partnerships including design collaborations with Madonna, Viktor & Rolf, Karl Lagerfeld, Stella McCartney and Roberto Cavalli. They proved to be a sensational success and helped H&M to produce record-breaking sales.

H&M's planned growth strategies include going into the home textiles market via its current stores; the company is also planning a new, more expensive chain called Collection of Style, or COS. (At the present time, however, there are no plans to open COS stores in the U.S.) Other growth avenues for H&M include an extended women's shoe assortment, which is opening in 200 H&M stores, and more links with celebrities and designers.

As you can see, they are coming! New stores, new strategies, and new designs are arriving on our shores. Is this good or bad? Only the future will tell us.

it is the success of its sales help that has made Nordstrom one of the most successful specialty stores in America. Other very high-end specialty stores, such as Bergdorf Goodman and Lord & Taylor, also offer highly personalized selling techniques, which include recording what individual customers have purchased in the past and alerting them by phone or mail to new merchandise that may interest them. Very often, these high-level salespeople work on commission, so they have a real incentive to offer personalized service.

Despite the abundant lip service paid to customer service by more retail executives, a new study finds that in-store service is the biggest negative experience, generating negative word-of-mouth and resulting in lost sales.

The Retail Customer Dissatisfaction Study was conducted by the Verde Granada and the Baker Retail Initiative at the University of Pennsylvania's Wharton School.

Based on the study's findings, analysts at Verde and the Baker Retail Initiative have identified four core competencies that store associates must have to inspire customer loyalty:[3]

- Educator: Explain products, make recommendations, and inform customers where products can be found.
- Energy: Approach customer, smile, make eye contact, and help them no matter what task they are doing at the time.
- Expeditor: Be sensitive to time constraints of customer and help them through checkout more quickly.
- Authentic: Let customers browse on their own, but be genuinely interested in helping, whether or not a sale is likely.

## Promotional Activities

All retailers engage in some promotional activities, whether it is advertising or publicity. Advertising and publicity are a store's two chief means of communicating with its customers. How much a retail organization promotes itself, however, varies depending on the type of retail operation.

Discount stores are the heaviest promoters, and they rely heavily on advertising as opposed to publicity or public relations. All kinds of advertising—newspaper, television, radio, and direct mail—are employed to get their message across. Their advertising emphasizes low prices and in many instances invites customers to comparison shop. Discount operations tend to run frequent sales or special promotions. In a very popular promotion, IKEA, the Swedish home furnishings retailer, cooperated with public health officials in Houston to offer a day of free vaccinations and dental checkups for children of shoppers.

Compared to the discounters, department and chain stores and specialty stores engage in a more moderate amount of promotional activity, although, of course, large budgets are allotted for this purpose. Department stores rely most heavily on newspaper advertising, although some prestigious department and specialty stores also advertise in the major fashion magazines, or local magazines, or local cable television. Specialty chains like the Gap, Esprit, and Pier 1 have begun to use general magazines as much as fashion magazines or shelter magazines to reach their target customers. Internet sites are being used more frequently by both large and small retailers as a new way to reach affluent customers interested in convenience.

The more prestigious stores use direct mail. Monthly bills, stuffed with advertising and special catalogs, are mailed regularly to charge customers. These retailers also do a moderate number of "special sale" and "special purchase" advertising campaigns. Sales are usually tied to special events, such as a holiday (the Columbus Day coat sales are one example), an anniversary, or an end-of-the-month clearance (see Figure 19.6). Department stores were the leaders in pioneering traditional seasonal sales: white sales in January and August, back-to-school promotions in late summer and early fall.

**FIGURE 19.6** In-store promotions and special events are a good way to advertise and attract customers.

The content of advertising varies with the type of retailer. Discount and mass merchandisers' ads are heavily product-oriented, displaying the product and its price in a direct manner. The prestige stores run some advertisements for individual items, but their advertisements are more likely to feature a designer or a new design collection. Advertisements may emphasize a new fashion look or trend at the expense of promoting the apparel in the ad.

## Frequent Shopper Plans

A policy that the airlines have used to great advantage—frequent flier plans—has been adopted by many other businesses. Also referred to as *loyalty marketing* or *customer retention programs*, this policy is also widely used by hotels, who reward frequent guests with special rates, their favorite newspaper, special easy checkout, and other "perks." In today's "overstored" environment, retailers are searching for ways to stand out. Some retailers are adapting this policy by rewarding frequent shoppers with special sales, special discounts, newsletters, and clubs. This trend is spreading as retailers see the advantages of keeping existing customers and encouraging them to shop more often.

However, when it comes to the rewards shoppers would like to earn through retailers' frequent shopper plans, one prize no longer fits all. New research from loyalty marketing consultancy Colloquy, in Milford, Ohio, reveals a great variance in preferences and participation across different demographic groups. Hispanics and young adults are interested in loyalty programs because they hope to gain better value when shopping. Over 40 percent of this group's members participate in loyalty programs. Meanwhile, the affluent are the most frequent participants, with 80 percent involvement, the study found. It attributes increased participation to familiarity with loyalty programs through this demographic's years of activity in the financial and airline worlds.[4]

Borders has rolled out a new option to reward its loyalty program members. The new Rewards Perk Program gives members deals and discounts via coupons on more than 2,000 products and services from noncompetitive merchants. Offers include everything from apparel and home furnishings to electronics and travel. For example, members can save up to 15 percent at Brooks Brothers or up to 10 percent at Hewlett-Packard and free FedEx shipping. Other participating companies include Lands' End, the Children's Place, Ann Taylor, Target, Philips Electronics, and Obitz.[5]

Conventional wisdom is that loyalty programs can help lure shoppers not currently frequenting their respective stores. But that's not the most effective use of money, according to Larry Aronson, former Revlon executive who has cofounded Cartwheel LLC, a company specializing in loyalty programs.

Aronson's work with chains and loyalty programs reveals customers really like rewards, especially easy-to-use cash deals. But instant rewards aren't the only benefits to loyalty programs. Retailers must do more than just offer the discounts. Further digging into the data can help retailers market specific items, services, or new products to shoppers who frequent those categories. "It is like scan data. You have to do more than let it accumulate. You have to use it," said Aronson.[6]

In the United States, food chains have been way ahead of other channels. However, drug stores are quickly catching up. Aronson added that loyalty programs are among several efforts retailers should use and that top management needs to be on board to make the efforts pay off. Now it's time for the fashion retailer to act.

## Location Policies

In addition to the ever-present neighborhood shopping center, retailers are exploring a wide range of locations, including larger malls, airports and train stations, downtowns, and resort areas. They are using carts and kiosks, and even setting up traveling, temporary shops. Experts classify shopping centers in many ways; for our purposes, we use the following simplified system.

### *Shopping Centers and Malls*

A **shopping center** is a coordinated group of retail stores, plus a parking area. By 2005, there were 48,695 shopping centers in the United States.[7] Those shopping centers that are enclosed and climate-controlled are known as **malls** (see Figure 19.7). While most malls have one floor, two- or three-floor malls are becoming more common. In central business districts, more **vertical malls**, multistory buildings taller than they are wide, have been built to conserve valuable land. Water Tower Place in Chicago was the first vertical mall; it has seven levels of prestige stores and is next door to a Ritz-Carlton hotel.

Customers are increasingly seen as bored with cookie-cutter malls and stores. Too many malls look the same, contain the same stores, and lack any regional flavor. If dropped into the average mall, a customer would not know if he or she were in Alas-

**FIGURE 19.7** Galleria Vittorio Emanuel II in Milan.

# Then & NOW

## Goodbye to the Mall?
## *Hello to the*
## *Lifestyle Center?*
## *To the Epicenter?*
## *Time Will Tell!*

I n late 2006, mall developers from as far away as Dubai and China met in Las Vegas for an International Council of Shopping Centers Forum. They learned about an environment that challenged the very principles underlying the mall concept. That concept is now known as the "lifestyle center" or "town center," and people fear it could drive the traditional mall to extinction.

Designed like elaborate outdoor movie sets, lifestyle centers are meant to look like real towns, with curbed streets, parking meters, and themed architecture. They are opening up on the fringes of big cities, from Washington, D.C., to San Diego: 150 centers have been built, with 100 more in the pipeline. The trend is being driven by baby boomers, who left the cities long ago but still remember singing Petula Clark's "Downtown."

Lifestyle centers are more in tune with the rise in Internet shopping. Because most lifestyle centers have walkways and parking next to each other, they offer shoppers the ability to get in and out quickly—a must when shoppers have already decided what they want through online browsing.

But traditional malls are fighting back: they are beginning to space their tenant formula beyond mainstays such as Macy's, JCPenney, Neiman Marcus, and Dillard's to fill vacant spaces left by retail consolidation, particularly the Federated–Macy's merger in 2005, which resulted in the closing of almost ninety mall-based anchor stores.

The democratization of malls includes national players such as Costco making into these empty anchor stores, allowing the mall customer to buy traditional goods at the mall as well as membership in the traditionally lower priced Costco. Now customers can accomplish in one trip to the "traditional mall" what would have taken two trips.

Another new idea for the traditional mall owner is a new futuristic format that can also replace dormant anchors in malls. This new concept, called the Epicenter Collection, is a "showcase" in the mall for online and catalogue companies as well as for branded manufacturers that usually do not have stores. The Epicenter is envisioned as luring to the mall people who otherwise shop electronically, and the Epicenter experience will be like walking through the Web or being in a "living catalogue."

Wherever you choose to shop—mall, lifestyle center, Epicenter—you can be sure the retailing of product to the consumer will always be an exciting adventure. Let's go shopping!

Left page: New World Shopping Mall in Beijing, China (top); Galleria Dallas, Texas (bottom); Right page: Friedrichstadt-Passagen in Berlin, Germany.

ka, Iowa, or Texas. Consequently, the number of Americans who shop frequently at malls is only 34 percent of the shopping public.

The competition for customers is so great that existing malls feel they must continually renovate and expand, just to keep larger, newer centers from moving into their territory. The Taubman Cos., a developer of malls, is turning the common areas in its malls into lounges that resemble plush hotel lobbies. "It's all part of entertainment," said Barbara Ashley of Taubman. Other entertainment-driven strategies include play zones for children and how-to classes for adults. (See Chapter 18 for other examples of entertainment values in retailing.)

**Power centers** or **power strips** are outdoor shopping centers that offer three or four category killers together, so a range of merchandise is available at highly discounted prices. They may be built close to existing regional malls and contain off-price apparel retailers or category killers like Filene's Basement, Mervyns, the Cosmetic Center, Toys"R"Us, or Burlington Coat Factory. In the 1990s, these centers cannibalized market shares so fast that the traditional malls had to reinvent themselves to keep up with the competition. Some of the strategies that malls are using to attract shoppers are featuring new, innovative retailers for shoppers who are looking for something other than the usual national chains and an interior, mazelike layout that guides shoppers throughout different departments of a store and connects to other shops on the property.

### Larger Malls

As older, small malls are ailing, larger and larger malls continue to be built. **Regional malls**, for example, usually contain at least two "anchor" department stores, as well as many specialty stores and a food court or restaurants. Their trading area is at least a 5-mile radius. Prestige regional malls like Northbrook Court near Chicago offer such services as weekend valet parking, free strollers, and free newspapers.

**Superregional malls** are, as their name implies, even larger than regional malls, often containing up to 1 million square feet (see Figure 19.8). They contain at least three department stores or major chain stores, with 100 to 300 specialty stores and services. Their trading area is up to an hour's driving time. An example is Oak Park Mall in Overland Park, Kansas, which recently added a new concourse and a new anchor, Nordstrom, as well as another Dillard's and an expanded JCPenney.

Another type of huge shopping center (4 to 5 million square feet) has emerged in the last decade—the **megamall**. The first megamall was built in West Edmonton in Alberta, Canada; it is still the world's largest, with over 800 stores. The world's second megamall is in the United States; it is The Mall of America, in Bloomington, Minnesota. With over 525 specialty stores, it is ten times the size of an average regional mall. It combines shopping with entertainment in a major way: with fifty restaurants, seven nightclubs, fourteen movie theaters, and

Camp Snoopy, an amusement park! To draw customers one weekend, the mall hired Ringo Starr and the Beach Boys to play at a "Jam Against Hunger" in its vast parking lot.

**Outlet malls**, like the various "Mills" developed by the Mills Corporation—Gurnee Mills, outside of Chicago; Ontario Mills, in suburban Los Angeles; and Potomac Mills, outside of Washington D.C.—are increasingly popular. Entertainment, like Sega Game Works and IMAX 3-D theaters, plays a key role in these developments.

### Air Malls

Airport retailing as a whole is certainly nothing new. Food concessions have been in airports for decades. What is new is the number of well-known retailers, from The Disney Store to the Gap to Victoria's Secret, that are opening in what are being called **air malls** (see Figure 19.9). With plane traffic booming, and delays more frequent,

**FIGURE 19.8** The Mall of America in Bloomington, Minnesota.

**FIGURE 19.9** London's Heathrow airport mall.

airports have become the busiest street corners in America. The length of time that an average person stays in an airport is 61 minutes, just 3 minutes shorter than the time spent in a typical shopping mall. Further, the typical air passenger is a high-end shopper. So average sales per square foot are more than $1,000 versus $225 for the typical suburban mall.

## Lifestyle Retail Centers

**Lifestyle centers** are open-air shopping areas anchored by a multiplex cinema (or two) and a big bookstore, and they contain a collection of better restaurants that enjoy the terrific traffic that the movie crowd presents. They are upscale outdoor shopping areas designed to look like city streets, with an emphasis on spaces for people watching and shopping.

Real estate developers say that the lifestyle center is the hottest new retail venue in America. There are over 150 across the United States, and more than 100 more are planned. The lifestyle center is designed in a zigzag pattern, so that from any given place, your eye catches a few more stores down the way. Placement is everything. Marketers have discovered that today's time-pressed consumer will spend more if she can easily comparison shop among similar stores, so lifestyle centers will group, say, Ann Taylor, Coldwater Creek, and Talbots within 50 feet of one another. And it's around gathering spots—fountains, benches, and kids' play areas—that you will find impulse purchase stores like Sunglass Hut or Build-a-Bear Workshop.

A mixture of uses, such as residences, office space, hotels, churches, and municipal facilities such as libraries, is typically included. In many ways, these new centers are attempting to recreate the traditional city center or "downtown" environment within the shopping center. As a result of the added amenities found in a lifestyle center, there are more reasons for consumers to visit and stay longer. The longer people stay, the more they spend.[8]

## Resort Retailing

Progressive retailers are positioning themselves where their customers are when they are relaxed. For many, this has meant catalogs. For some others, however, it means putting stores in resort areas (see Figure 19.10). In the ski resort town of Aspen, Colorado, for example, major retailers like Banana Republic and the Chanel Boutique have opened stores. Some resort towns have established themselves as unique shopping destinations. Seaside, a planned resort community in the Florida panhandle, is one such place. It has an open-air bazaar called Per-spi-cas-ity, which features the work of local craftspeople and retailers in intriguing displays of casual clothes and accessories.

## Carts and Kiosks

Carts and kiosks are selling spaces in common mall areas and airports and train stations. Smaller and often on wheels, thus more flexible than even the smallest shop, **carts** are increasingly popular for selling accessories, T-shirts, and caps. Kiosks, on the other hand, are larger than carts and more stationary. Like a newsstand, a **kiosk** offers movable shelves or racks for merchandise. It is very popular for sunglasses, jewelry, and legwear.

**FIGURE 19.10** Ralph Lauren's resort retailing store in Aspen.

### Temporary Sites: Pop-Up Stores

Temporary retailers, who typically set up shop in empty storefronts or kiosks or carts in malls, are a booming business. Temporary holiday shops became commonplace in the 1990s (see Figure 19.11). However, these days, in a world of Blackberries and instant messaging, there's a growing sense of haste in people's lives. Retailers trying to get consumers' attention attempt to create a sense of urgency to get people into stores to try out their clothes, their shoes, and any other new product. The store itself is the new limited edition—so limited, in fact, that it may last a mere 96 hours.

Retailers today are adopting the concept of a pop-up store with gusto. A **pop-up store** opens up with great fanfare at an empty retail location for a few days in a major city or mall. And then, poof! It's gone. Nike opened a pop-up store in SoHo, New York City, for just four days for the sole purpose of selling 250 pairs of Zoom LeBron IV NYC basketball shoes named after the popular NBA All-Star LeBron James. The special edition shoes were priced at $250 a pair.

Retailers use pop-up stores to generate buzz and excitement around a new product launch. Sometimes the stores are a great way for retailers to check the pulse of consumers and try out new products. Retailers have clearly discovered that pop-up stores bring brands to life and let people sample products in a great format.[9]

**FIGURE 19.11** Temporary holiday shops in Union Square, New York City, offer a wide variety of products and provide the opportunity for quick shopping.

### Emerging Retail Strategies

Customers are demanding more convenient shopping, more varied products, and lower prices at the same time that they are shifting their loyalty from retailer to retailer, shopping at Kmart one week and Macy's the next. Retailers have developed a number of strategies to respond to them. Perhaps the strongest response is to more clearly define the store's fashion image, "no longer trying to succeed through broad appeal, but by narrowing [the] product assortments to present a very distinct point of view."[10]

Let us examine retailer's responses in more detail.

### Responding to the Customers' Desire for Convenience

As life grows ever faster-paced, customers continue to look for easier ways to shop. The consumer has less time, is smarter, and is more demanding. There are more products. There is less sales help. As retail consultant Walter Loeb said, "The slogan of the 1980s was 'Shop till you drop'; now it's 'Find it, buy it, and get out.'" With this axiom in mind retailers are investing heavily in new technology, and in more sales help.[11]

Surveys have found that a large number of shoppers will walk out of a store if the checkout lines are too long, the store is too crowded, or a salesperson is surly. Over 22 percent of shoppers report leaving a store for lack of sales help.

The four dimensions of customer convenience that retailers must consider are:

- Locational—where customers have to go to make purchases
- Time of day—when customers can make purchases
- Process—ease and speed of shopping and returns
- Assortment—what they can buy here and where else they will have to go

## Responding to the Decline of Customer Loyalty

Remember that retailing is all about people, anticipating their needs, knowing their lifestyles, their preferences, their expectations, and taking the time to observe what they do and how they do it—to try to understand them, and then, when they come to your store, to give them just a little bit more than what they expected—that's the secret of success in retailing.

—Allen Questrom

Many types of retailers are experimenting with lifestyle and lifestage strategies to attract loyal customers. Lifestage marketing has long been the specialty of catalog retailers. Newport News, Spiegel's catalog aimed at younger customers, hired Jasmine Bleeth of *Baywatch* to promote its line of swimwear. The junior apparel chains like Wet Seal/Contempo and Rampage are well-known examples of lifestage retailers (see Figure 19.12).

**FIGURE 19.12** Rampage is a well-known example of a lifestage retailer.

## Responding to Customers' Complaints About Sameness

Differentiation and customer loyalty can be achieved through proper positioning and image creation. With the glut of brands, it's imperative to create a distinctive image and niche in the consumer's mind. This provides an emotional benefit as well as the real benefits of credible value, quality, and reduced shopping time.[12]

Private-label merchandise is growing at an astronomical rate, as retailers try to differentiate themselves and their merchandise in response to customers' complaints about the sameness of merchandise everywhere. Private labels are discussed in Chapter 18.

## Responding to the High Cost of Product Development by Forging Strategic Alliances

A **strategic alliance** is a form of business combination in which retailers and manufacturers join forces to operate more efficiently, thus improving both companies' profits while enabling them to give the customer a better product at a lower price. Although strategic alliances between retailers and manufacturers are difficult to form and to maintain, they are perceived as increasingly critical for success in today's highly competitive marketplace.

"Essentially, it now takes the entire supply chain working as a team to serve the consumers' mounting demands," says Robin Lewis, executive editor of *Women's Wear Daily's Infotracs on Strategic Alliances*. He cites as an example of a highly profitable alliance the agreement between Sara Lee Intimates and Wal-Mart, which has led from an initial $134 million account to a $1 billion partnership in 8 years. Both Wal-Mart and Sara Lee have teams of merchandise, operations, management information services, and marketing executives who are devoted to this alliance. They meet regularly to iron out problems and plan joint market share goals.

**TABLE 19.1** *Characteristics of Traditional Relationships and Strategic Alliances*

| TRADITIONAL APPROACH | ALLIANCE APPROACH |
|---|---|
| Individual goals | Shared common goals |
| Independent performance | Joint performance |
| Independently defined goals | Supply chain definitions |
| Sequential processes and activities | Simultaneous processes |
| Activities performed by individual companies | Partner with greatest competency performs the activity |
| Rewards competed for | Rewards shared |
| Penalties absorbed by supplier | Penalties or losses shared |
| Many suppliers | Few select suppliers |
| Sequential improvements | Continuous improvements |
| Information is kept secret | Information is shared |

Adapted from Robin Lewis, "Partner or Perish," *WWD Infotracs: Strategic Alliances.*

The characteristics of strategic alliances as opposed to traditional retailer/manufacturer relationships are outlined in Table 19.1.

In 2001, Wal-Mart set up a strategic alliance with America Online, through which it launched an Internet service called Wal-Mart Connect. The partnership between the world's largest retailer and the world's largest Internet service provider brought Wal-Mart Connect users Internet access for less than $10 a month, as well as instant-messaging service. The AOL deal was designed to bring Wal-Mart's Web site, www.walmart.com, greater visibility, more customers, and, of course, more sales dollars, while creating a new revenue stream for AOL through the low access fee.[13]

## Trends in Retail Policies

Merchandising and operational policies continue to change at a dizzying rate. As the economy cycles through periods of boom and bust, retailers scramble to interpret and respond to changing customer needs and preferences. Of the many trends discussed in this chapter, two seem dominant: (1) using new technology, and (2) creating new job opportunities. Let us look at each of these trends in more detail.

### *Using New Technology*

Retailers' use of new technology varies widely in sophistication and cost. It can be as simple as the Gap providing sales associates with wireless headsets so that they can get inventory information for a customer immediately. Or it may be equipping salespeople with beepers so that a customer can summon them to a dressing room with the touch of a button. Or the technology may be as complex as establishing a multibillion-dollar data warehouse of customer information, as Sears has done.

Four ways that retailers are using new technology are: in faster shipping, in videoconferencing, in starting data warehouses, and in using the Internet.

### Faster Shipping

To get the right product to the customer at the right time, manufacturers, shippers, and retailers are employing a variety of new technological developments. The widespread use of scanners and universal product codes (UPC) and electronic data interchange (EDI) was covered in Chapter 8. Some retailers have already moved beyond these technologies. For example, some apparel and cosmetics are already being shipped internationally and domestically using an extended EAN-128 code, which carries more information about the product's source and destination than the conventional UPC code. This code was developed at the request of shippers, who are looking to cut transportation time by reducing manual shipping documents.

### Videoconferencing

PictureTel, Microsoft, and 3Com are bringing videoconferences to desktop computers, which will vastly increase the market and lower the cost. Meanwhile, large companies such as JCPenney are already using **videoconferencing** for a variety of purposes, including staff training, vendor conferences, and product development. Since several sites can participate in a videoconference, videoconferencing is an effective, low-cost way of doing staff training for very large businesses (JCPenney's has

1,230 stores), because it cuts down on staff travel time and expenses. JCPenney uses videoconferencing in the design and production of its private-label lines by linking its in-house designers in Plano, Texas, with mills overseas. Also, videoconferencing is used for dealing with vendors about problems. As Ron Fazio, manager of communications for Penney's, said:

If we have a problem with a garment, for example, and we want to improve a collar or its fabrication, we can show it directly to the supplier without having to mail samples. We solve a lot of problems simply by setting a three-way conference between ourselves, a supplier, and his manufacturer in the Far East.[14]

### Data Warehousing

To squeeze more profit out of each store, retailers are increasingly turning to a new technique called data warehousing. A **data warehouse** is a group of superpowerful computers hooked together and filled with information about customers, transactions, and finances. Its role is to make this mass of data easily accessible by organizing it into categories like purchase history, vendors, sales promotions, and so forth. The data warehouse is typically separate from existing operational systems.

Retailers with the largest data warehouses include Wal-Mart, Sears, and Target. Target was one of the first companies to set up a data warehouse; the company is using it to try to tailor 30 percent of the merchandise mix to each individual store. Lands' End uses its data warehouse to track out-of-stock items that customers order. Burlington Coat Factory uses its system to target big and tall customers for special promotions.

At the North County Fair Mall in Escondido, California, mall managers can generate reports that show which stores mall patrons are shopping in, what they buy, and how much they spend. This information is then shared with the retailers in the mall.

Data warehousing can also be used as a powerful marketing tool. Customer profiling can help the retail staff target people who look like they fit the best-customer profile. Best-customer profiling also helps identify narrow targets within the highest revenue-generating customer base. With these tools, a store can identify clusters of customers and/or prospects who can be addressed with relevant messages and offers via e-mail or e-cards.[15]

### The Internet

The Internet is hastening the blurring of the line between store and nonstore retailing, which began decades ago when catalog companies opened stores and stores began sending catalogs. Now both catalogers, like Lillian Vernon and Spiegel, and stores, like Macy's and JCPenneys, have Web sites (see Figure 19.13). The customer information they gather on the Internet is fed into the customer portion of their

**FIGURE 19.13** Internet surfers can enjoy shopping through discounted excess inventory on overstock.com and JCPenney.com.

data warehouse. This information enables them to customize further approaches to this customer.

Stores and catalogers are already tailoring their Internet sites to fit their needs. The Lands' End Web site, for example, has an overstock area that is very popular among Internet surfers and that is moving excess inventory quickly. JCPenney offers special online discounts to attract customers to its photography services.

Retailers are also using the Internet to communicate with suppliers all over the world. "The clock runs much faster in apparel retail than in most any other kind of business, so being able to have information and react on a global basis will be crucial," said Mark Smith, a retail industry expert.[16]

The specialty retailer/cataloger Talbots is using a groupware computer program combined with the Internet to share critical information among members of its product development team: the product manager, who is responsible for developing new clothing lines; a source, who is responsible for getting an item manufactured once it has been designed; and a buyer, who decides on quantity and price. As Annie Stobbs, project manager at Talbots, said: "All these people need to collaborate on product development, and we need to be able to track the progress." Since Talbots designs and manufactures 90 percent of all the merchandise it sells, this tracking is especially crucial.[17]

## Creating New Job Opportunities

The human element remains a critical component of successful retailing (see Figure 19.14). To develop a business that is truly customer-focused requires a greater investment in workers than most retailers were willing to make in the 1980s and 1990s, when many retailers found themselves in a low-wage/high-turnover trap.

Since experts assume that technology will play a greater role in the sales clerk function, funds will be freed up to allow companies to hire more full-time sales associates, who can establish relationships with valued customers. These associates require more advanced training in product knowledge, suggestion selling, and conflict resolution so that they can act as "product advisors." Personal shoppers are becoming more prevalent, both in stores and on the Internet.

The role of the buyer is also changing, especially in situations where retailers have strategic alliances with suppliers. Freed from recordkeeping functions by computers, buyers can become trend analysts, trendsetters, and product developers.

Additional employment opportunities exist for visual merchandisers and store designers, as chain stores try to customize each location. Even category killers are placing less emphasis on mass presentations of products. Also, experts predict that fashion retailers in particular will frequently change their total store environment to keep customers' interest.

Retailers are beginning to place more emphasis on developing employee loyalty through higher incentives, and real career paths. Nordstrom has been joined by a growing number of other retailers in pursuing this goal.

FIGURE 19.14 The fashioncareers.com Web site lists employment opportunities in the fashion industry.

## Summary and Review

There are six merchandising policies that every retailer must establish: (1) fashion cycle emphasis, (2) quality, (3) price ranges, (4) depth and breadth of assortments, (5) brand policies, and (6) exclusivity. Five major operational policies must also be determined: (1) ambiance, (2) customer services, (3) selling services, (4) promotional activities, and (5) frequent shopper plans.

Retail location policies include sites such as shopping centers, malls, air malls, downtown sites, resorts, carts and kiosks, and temporary sites.

Emerging retail strategies include responding to (1) customers' desire for convenience, (2) the decline of customer loyalty, (3) customers' complaints about sameness, and (4) the high cost of product development by forging strategic alliances.

Trends in retail policies include using a number of new technologies, such as faster shipping, videoconferencing, data warehousing, and the Internet. Along with these new technologies come corresponding new job opportunities.

## Trade Talk

Define or briefly explain the following terms:

| | |
|---|---|
| air mall | ambiance |
| assortment | confined style |
| data warehouse | kiosk |
| lifestyle centers | mall |
| megamall | merchandising policies |
| narrow and deep assortment | operational policies |
| outlet mall | pop-up stores |
| power center or strip | regional mall |
| sensory retailing | superregional mall |
| shopping center | strategic alliance |
| vertical mall | videoconferencing |

## For Review

1. What are the six major merchandising policies that a retailer must establish?

2. What stage or stages of the fashion cycle would most likely be emphasized by: (a) a specialty store, (b) a department store, and (c) a discount store?

3. What are the five types of operational policies that a retail store owner must establish?

4. What are the major kinds of shopping centers in the United States today?

5. What is the difference between a cart and a kiosk? Where can they usually be found?

6. What strategies are retailers using to respond to the customer's desire for more convenient shopping?

7. How are retailers responding to the decline of customer loyalty?

8. What are strategic alliances? What are their goals? Give some examples of these agreements.

9. Explain how new technological developments in shipping, data warehousing, and videoconferencing are being used in the fashion industries.

10. Name some new job opportunities that are being created in retailing today as a result of the emerging trends mentioned in this chapter.

## For Discussion

1. Compare and contrast the selling and fashion services of: (a) department stores, (b) specialty stores, and (c) discount stores. Give examples of selling and fashion services offered by different types of retailers in your community.

2. Explain and discuss the following statement by Laurence Siegel, citing current examples to illustrate how it does or does not apply to your community:

Traditional malls are all the same. They all have three or four anchors, a bunch of specialty stores in between, and maybe a multi-screen movie theater. There's little reason to drive past one to get to another.[18]

unit six

Just as customers coordinate their fashion looks, including all the fashion products seen or not seen, the fashion industry also coordinates all auxiliary services, seen or not seen, to the successful selling of the latest fashion products to the customer. The auxiliary services that support and enhance all the other levels of the fashion industries have an interconnecting role in the big fashion picture.

Try to imagine a new fashion season without fashion shows, magazines, fashion stylists, trade shows, visual merchandisers, TV, advertising agencies, public relations agencies, and the myriad of other services that support and grow this phenomenon known as the fashion business. What would the fashion world be without these services?

Understanding the roles these individual and specific services play in completing the whole is important to an understanding of how and why the fashion business goes from design to consumer.

In this unit we explore the functions of magazines, newspapers, broadcast and TV media, fashion consultants, visual merchandisers, trade associations, and product development offices. These services may be auxiliary, but—just like the Oscar awarded to supporting roles—they deserve a place of honor in the fashion business.

# THE AUXILIARY LEVEL: SUPPORTING SERVICES

# chapter twenty

*Everything you always wanted to know*

*about the services and information provided*

*to producers and retailers.*

**KEY CONCEPTS**

- Differences among advertising, publicity, and public relations
- Services provided to fashion merchandisers by such media as trade and consumer publications and broadcast media
- Role of store designers and visual merchandisers
- Information provided to fashion producers and retailers by fashion consultants and research agencies, trade associations and trade shows, and buying, merchandising, and product development offices

# Fashion Auxiliary Services

As consumers we expect to find what we want, when we want it, and where we want it every day of the year. In the fall, back-to-school merchandise had better be in stores, and the colors must be new and up to date. During the holiday months, gift merchandise and new items for holiday parties are expected. During spring and summer months, we expect new colors, silhouettes, and fabrics to brighten up our wardrobes and take us through spring days to the hot, muggy days of summer. How do the stores see into the future and anticipate our needs and wants? How do they keep stocks peaked when we want them and marked down when we are tired of them? They do not have crystal balls, or fortune tellers leading the way; what they do have are the fashion auxiliary services.

As a professional in the fashion industry, you know that this marvelous spectacle did not occur by magic. In fact, it required elaborate planning and execution of plans for months in advance. As you enjoy the offerings for the upcoming season, you are well aware that preparations are already underway for the next season and for the seasons beyond.

Bringing you and your fellow consumers the styles you want to wear is so huge and all-encompassing a task that the fashion industry requires many support, or auxiliary, services. Some services—computer, bookkeeping, legal—are typical of those needed by any business and may not be particularly tailored to the fashion business. Others, though, are specific to the fashion industry. Either they have been created specifically to serve it, as in the case of buying, merchandising, and product development organizations, or their function has been tailored to the fashion industry's specific needs, as in the case of advertising and public relations agencies, fashion magazines, and the variety of consultants and marketing groups. In this chapter, you will learn about the most important auxiliary services, such as trade and consumer fashion publications; the broadcast media; advertising and public relations agencies; store design and visual merchandising services; consulting and market research groups; trade associations; and buying, merchandising, and product development organizations.

## Fashion Auxiliary Services Offered by the Media

The media offer three broad categories of fashion auxiliary services: advertising, publicity, and public relations. **Advertising**, which appears in everything from magazines and newspapers to radio and television, is space and time that is paid for. **Publicity** is the free and voluntary mention of a firm, product, or person in the media. Its purpose is to inform or enhance public interest about something specific. **Public relations**, a broader term than publicity, is also free and voluntary mention, but it is designed to enhance a long-term goal, such as the shaping of a company's public image. All three efforts are important elements of the remaining auxiliary services.

One difference between advertising and publicity/public relations is the amount of control a manufacturer or retailer can exercise over each. Since advertising is purchased, a great deal of control can be exercised over its execution. Public relations and publicity can be carefully developed and well presented to the media, but there is no guarantee that the material and information supplied will be used well—or used at all.

Some people think that the newer broadcast media—like cable TV and the Internet—will replace the more traditional media, like newspapers and magazines. Others strongly disagree. Marc Brownstein, writing in *Advertising Age*, said, "We all know that most newspapers are experiencing monthly declines in advertising and circulation. However, many of the readers are now captured online in the newspapers' websites, where the con-

**FIGURE 20.1** Billboards are an effective way to advertise goods to a wide range of people.

tent is current, often compelling, and the writing and presentation gets better every day."[1]

Some other low-tech print media have recently received a high-tech boost (see Figure 20.1). Billboards carrying a retailer's phone number receive calls from drivers using their cell phones; Golden Creations of Murrysville, Pennsylvania, reported increased jewelry sales from this kind of billboard.

## Fashion Magazines

Fashion magazines, which combine advertising, publicity, and public relations, came into existence about 150 years ago in the form of a single publication called *Godey's Lady's Book* (see Figure 20.2). Prior to that, women discussed the newest fashions with one another but had no authoritative source from which they could learn what was new and exciting. The magazine's first editor, Sara Josepha Hale, is now best remembered for her early feminism, especially her struggle to help women win acceptance in professions, but her influence on fashion was equally important. *Godey's Lady's Book* reported on the latest styles and was the forerunner

**FIGURE 20.2** *Godey's Lady's Book* was the first fashion magazine.

of today's fashion magazines, such as *Vogue, Harper's Bazaar, Glamour,* and *Seventeen* for young women (see Figure 20.3).

For years, these magazines held sway, and while they competed with one another, they were not subject to new competition. In recent years, though, fashion has become so important that *Women's Wear Daily* has spun off a successful monthly publication called *W* geared to general consumers. Several other magazines have also established themselves as fashion arbiters, most notably *Elle,* which competes with *Glamour* and *Marie Claire,* and *Nylon,* which specializes in avant-garde fashion. In the mid- to late 1990s, two new important lifestyle magazines appeared on the scene. The first was *In Style,* a monthly glossy that married celebrity and style editorial by covering fashion trends among celebrities and rigorously

**FIGURE 20.4** Popular fashion magazines for men include *Details* and *Esquire.*

**FIGURE 20.3** Popular fashion magazines for women include *Vogue, Harper's Bazaar,* and *Elle.*

reporting on red carpet ceremony dressing. *In Style* was launched in 1994 and quickly became hugely successful. In 2002, the magazine had a monthly circulation of 1.6 million copies. Another important newcomer was *Lucky,* a publication that called itself "the magazine about shopping." The concept behind *Lucky* was very close to that of a catalog. It is almost exclusively based on still life pictures of clothing and brief descriptions of what a garment is and where it is retailed. *Lucky* reached a rate base with 1,114,241 readers in 2002.[2] Magazines that appeal to specific ethnic markets include *Essence, Ebony,* and *Today's Black Woman* for African Americans and the bilingual *Latina* for Hispanics. Even more specialized are such magazines as *Modern Bride* and *Bride's,* which report on wedding fashions.

*Gentlemen's Quarterly (GQ)* is the largest circulating men's fashion magazine. *Esquire,* which covers topics beyond fashion, is still widely regarded as an authority on the latest trends in men's wear. Other men's magazines that cover fashion in addition to topics like health and sports include *Details, Men's Fitness, Men's Health, Playboy, Men's Journal, Outside, FHM,* and *Maxim* (see Figure 20.4). Some men's magazines, like *Maxim* and *FHM,* also have their own biannual men's fashion magazine editions, which tend to be considerably more upscale than their parent magazines.

The **shelter magazines** are devoted to home fashions. Among the better known are *Elle Decor, Metropolitan Life, Architectural Digest, House and Garden, House Beautiful, Martha Stewart Living, Wallpaper,* and *Surface.*

Fashion magazines' pages are filled with advertisements for apparel, cosmetics, and accessories. The business of reporting and interpreting the fashion news, however, is their primary function. Fashion editors visit manufacturers' showrooms to choose the latest fashions as subjects for articles and photographs in the editorial pages of their magazines. These visits provide opportunities for useful exchanges of information about trends in markets that the manufacturers and publications share. In addition, most magazines prepare reports of their market research for the manufacturers and retailers that are both the subject of their editorial copy and their advertising accounts. These reports include reader surveys, such as those conducted by *Glamour,* and fashion forecasts of colors and styles for upcoming seasons. Like the fashion producers and retailers, the magazines must plan well in advance of offering their product to the public, so their reports can be relied upon for timely information.

Fashions that appear in magazine articles are accompanied by an **editorial credit**, a unique form of publicity that names the manufacturer and lists retail stores where the clothes may be purchased (see Figure 20.5). Editorial credit benefits even stores that are not listed, for if they have seen a magazine in advance, they can often stock the fashions. For advertisers whose merchandise is featured and credited in the editorial pages of a magazine, this publicity reinforces the paid advertising message.

**Marc Jacobs**'s sequined polyester top, at Marc Jacobs, New York, Boston and Las Vegas, marcjacobs.com; **Maison Martin Margiela**'s nylon bodysuit, at Maison Martin Margiela, New York. Balenciaga sunglasses and shoes.

**Beauty Note:**
Sleek locks evade heat-styling damage with Paul Mitchell Super Skinny Serum.

**FIGURE 20.5** Editorial credits, such as these from *W* magazine, provide priceless promotion for designers and manufacturers, rather than targeting the consumer.

## General Consumer Publications

General interest consumer publications also play a role in disseminating fashion news to the public. Practically every newspaper reports on fashion, and some, such as the *New York Times, Los Angeles Times, Chicago Tribune,* and *Washington Post,* devote regular weekly sections to apparel and home fashion design (see Figure 20.6). Their fashion editors cover fashion openings, press weeks, and trade shows around the world. Twice a year, the *New York Times Magazine* has a second section for each of three fashion markets, *Fashions of The Times* for women's fashions, *Men's Fashions of The Times,* and *Home Design.* In *Paper, Time Out,*

naughty and nice · HOLIDAY 2006

**FIGURE 20.6** *T,* the *New York Times* style magazine, features news, images, and style discoveries about women's and men's fashion.

**FIGURE 20.7** The *New York Look* reports the latest fashion trends.

**FIGURE 20.8** The Spanish version of the consumer magazine *Cosmopolitan*.

*City*, and other magazines that deal with pop culture, fashion gets extensive coverage. *Time, Newsweek,* and *People* provide occasional but important fashion coverage, as do the traditional women's magazines such as *Good Housekeeping* and *Ladies' Home Journal. Cosmopolitan*, whose primary market is young singles, has a circulation of 2.6 million. Other women's magazines that are geared to women who are not full-time homemakers also carry fashion news for their market segments. Among the most influential are *Oprah* and *Working Mother. Cosmo Girl, Seventeen, Teen Vogue,* and *Elle Girl* are designed for young teenagers. Women's sports magazines, such as *Self, Shape, Fitness,* and *Sports Illustrated Women/Sport*, include articles that cater to the fashion interests of female athletes and sports fans. *Playboy* and *Men's Health* are among the men's magazines that cover men's fashions.

The *New Yorker, New York Look, Vanity Fair, Harper's,* and *Atlantic Monthly* occasionally bring fashion news to their urbane, sophisticated audiences (see Figure 20.7).

Spanish-language versions of *People, Playboy, Cosmopolitan, Harper's Bazaar, Elle,* and *Marie Claire* are also in the market (see Figure 20.8). The Spanish version of *Reader's Digest*, called *Selecciones*, is widely circulated. The publicity departments of most stores across America usually have no difficulty getting their messages across in local newspapers because apparel stores are a major source of advertising revenue for newspapers.

## Trade Publications

One of the most important aids to the merchandising of fashion is the **trade publication**. Unlike the fashion magazines, trade newspapers and magazines are published just for the industry. Many discourage subscriptions from people outside their field; few are available at newsstands, except in fashion markets and marts.

Just as general publications like city newspapers and national news magazines keep the public informed about what is going on in the world, trade publications keep their special readers informed about what is going on in the fashion world—from the acquisition of raw materials to reports on retail sales. These publications announce new technical developments, analyze fashion trends, report on current business conditions, and generally help all who work in the fashion industry keep up-to-date on a staggering number of new products, techniques, and markets (see Figure 20.9). Even government regulations are covered, as are personnel changes and classified ads for jobs.

The best-known fashion trade publication is *Women's Wear Daily*, often referred to as the bible of the industry. First published in 1910, it is one of the oldest publications of its kind. Beginning as a page in the *Daily Trade Record*, this newspaper quickly became a separate six-day-a-week publication. Since its inception, it has played a prominent

role in the fashion business. *Women's Wear Daily*, called *WWD* by those who read it, is now published five days a week. It covers every aspect of the fashion industry from fiber and fabric to apparel, from day-to-day developments to new directions and trends. In the past 20 years, *WWD* has even covered the social scene, reporting on fashions worn by trend-setters at social events and parties. In addition, it is an advertising vehicle, and business notices, employment opportunities, and arrivals of buyers in the New York market are also reported. The Monday, Thursday, and Friday issues highlight children's wear, innerwear, legwear, and fashion accessories. In addition, *Infotracs*, or special supplements devoted entirely to examining a critical issue in depth, are published from time to time as a joint venture by *WWD* and the *Daily News Record (DNR)*. Special *WWD/Global* issues are published, provid-

**FIGURE 20.9** *Women's Wear Daily, DNR,* and *Footwear News* are leading trade publications in the fashion industry.

ing an overview of the major international markets that prepares readers for the upcoming spring and fall fashion weeks.

Numerous trade publications serve the needs of specialized segments of the fashion industry. The *DNR*, published every Monday, specializes in textiles and menswear. *DNR*, the counterpart to *WWD*, is actually the older publication, established in 1892 as the *Daily Trade Record*, a mimeographed report distributed at the Chicago World's Fair.

*Footwear News* covers its specialty as intensely as *WWD* covers the women's market and *DNR* covers the men's market. The youth market is covered in *Earnshaw's*. Department store and specialty store management and merchandising executives read *Stores* and *Chain Store Age*. The fiber and fabric professionals read *Apparel Magazine* and *Textile World*.

## The Broadcast Media

Fashion merchandisers have a choice of standard broadcast mediums: television, cable television, and radio. Or they may choose the newest medium—the Internet. Unlike the print media, the broadcast media are time, rather than space, oriented. Radio and television stations sell three levels of commercials, in descending order of cost: network, spot, and local.

Broadcast media focused on children have received a good deal of critical attention in recent years, as advertising in children-specific media grew more than 50 percent, to $1.5 billion from 1993 to 1996 alone. Many new children's channels were launched, and the kid's market seemed like a place of golden opportunity for advertisers. However, the climate slowed down at the turn of the millennium, and the children channels that turned a profit were the already established and relatively inexpensive giants like Cartoon Network and Nickelodeon. Other children's channels include Fox Kids, Kids' WB, and ABC/Disney.

Today, programs are designed for children and tweens on the same principle as they're designed for grown-ups: as a way to sell eyeballs to advertis-

ers. Nickelodeon made $800 million on its programming, and that figure does not even include the various merchandising streams—the DVDs, the magazines, the toys, and more. However, strong competition from the Disney Channel with tween comedies such as *The Suite Life of Zack and Cody* (see Figure 20.10) and *Hannah Montana* keeps Nickelodeon on its toes. Efforts by Viacom, Disney, and others to grab youngster's attention boils down to a bunch of adults trying to figure out what kids will like.[3]

### Television

One cannot turn on the television today without learning something about current apparel fashions. The fashion industry obtains invaluable publicity from the simple fact that everyone who acts in a show or hosts or appears on a newscast or talk show wants to—and usually does—wear the latest fashions.

In addition to this general across-the-board exposure, short segments on fashion are generally presented in many news and talk shows. News of the fashion world is reported, as are the latest styles. Occasionally, manufacturers and designers get a chance to exhibit their work.

Network television advertising is expensive enough to be prohibitive to all but a few fashion giants. Until the early 1980s, only huge companies such as Sears, Roebuck and Co. and JCPenney or fiber firms like DuPont and Monsanto could afford to advertise on television. Increasingly, though, retailers and manufacturers have built television advertising into their budgets because they have seen that it is the best way to reach a generation reared on television. Manufacturers of sportswear—specifically, makers of jeans—were among the first to use television, but now designers such as Calvin Klein use television to transmit their fashion message. Sometimes designers or manufacturers offer retailers cooperative advertising with time for a "voice over" for store advertising of their brand. The manufacturer can thus get a local advertising rate for the brand while the retailer gets the professionally produced commercial.

**FIGURE 20.10** Television shows, like *The Suite Life of Zack* and *Cody*, influence teen fashion and create trends.

Because of the technical expertise and high level of quality required for network television, outside advertising agencies are usually hired to produce television advertising. Agencies develop an idea, present it in storyboard form to their client, photograph the advertisement, obtain or create the music, and provide tapes to individual stations for on-air viewing. Television commercials for national brands of apparel, such as Levi's jeans, are now being shown in movie theaters as well.

## Cable Television

Cable television has become an increasingly attractive option for fashion advertisers, largely because it costs so much less than network television. Many more outlets also exist for cable television, which reduces the competition to buy space. Cable television is also the home of the **infomercial**, the extended commercial in which a sponsor presents information about its product in a program format. Several celebrity-owned or celebrity-franchised cos-

metics lines have relied on this advertising medium. The 1982 debut of the Home Shopping Network (HSN) marked the beginning of a new outlet for sales as well as advertising. Another popular shopping channel, QVC, reaches more than 160 million homes worldwide and reports annual revenue of more than $7 billion. The West Chester, Pennsylvania–based retailer has shipped more than a billion packages in its 20-year history.[4]

Cable television has also made possible the launching of channels with programming devoted to the interests of niche markets. Fashion advertisers can target commercials for Spanish-language channels, for example. Fashion is also receiving more attention in programming. In 1998, the New York cable channel Metro TV launched *Full Frontal Fashion* in conjunction with the New York Mercedes-Benz Fashion Week. *Full Frontal Fashion* offers round-the-clock coverage of the runway shows as well as behind-the-scenes reportage, industry commentary, and designer interviews. *Full Frontal* was acquired by the WE network in 2003 from the New York cable channel Metro TV.[5] E! Entertainment television offers the Style network, a 24-hour channel devoted to fashion and beauty. Among the shows on Style are *Extreme Makeover* and *Fashion Police*, which feature makeovers.

One of the most successful and popular fashion shows on cable is *Project Runway*. Hosted by Tim Gunn and Heidi Klum, it has been a success since its beginning in 2004—so successful that Bluefly, the online retailer has teamed up with *Project Runway* as the reality show's exclusive retail sponsor. Under the agreement with the Weinstein Company and Bravo, Bluefly gives the winning designer the opportunity to sell his or her designs on bluefly.com; collaborate with bravotv.com for "Get the Look," where viewers can shop for clothing and accessories that reflect the winning outfit from that week's challenge; own the accessories wall that contestants use to accessorize their runaway looks; sponsor all live voting; team with *Elle* magazine in a sweepstakes; and air commercials during all first-run episodes of the season.[6]

# Fashion Focus

## The Doneger Group
### *Through the Decades, a Prominent Presence*

Left page: The Doneger clan: Jason, Rita, Valerie, Abbey and Adam. The late Henry Doneger is pictured above them (top); Doneger's top lieutenants, Tom Burns and Leslie Ghize (bottom).

On November 6, 2006, the Fashion Institute of Technology (FIT) honored the Doneger Group on its sixtieth anniversary. The event, attended by every important player in the fashion industry, attracted over 600 attendees. The celebration not only commemorated the Doneger Group's sixtieth anniversary but also benefited the Henry Doneger Scholarship Fund for FIT students enrolled in the Baccalaureate Fashion Merchandising Management program and supported by Abbey Doneger.

The privately held Doneger Group was founded in 1946 by Abbey's father, Henry Doneger, whose name is still on the front door of the company's offices at 463 Seventh Avenue, New York City.

The Doneger Group is a fashion merchandising, trend-forecasting, and consulting company. It provides business intelligence on global market trends and merchandising strategy to the retail and fashion industries. The company was founded as a buying office, but through acquisition and expansions has grown to encompass trend forecasting, consulting on customized projects, trend and merchandising publications, and a comprehensive Web site.

The firm's progressiveness has helped Doneger transcend the image of a traditional buying office, a format virtually extinct now, and evolve into the largest independent, modern, and well-rounded fashion merchandising consulting and trend-forecasting organization. There are various divisions at Doneger. The Henry Doneger Association, consisting of sixty market analysts who shop the fashion markets and counsel retailers on items, trends, key resources, and emerging classifications, remains the heart and soul of the company.

Doneger publications—*Style Insight*, *West Coast Insight*, *Euro Insight*, *First*, and *Investments*—are geared to reinforce information learned from visits to the office. The group also includes the Carol Hoffman division, a buying office purchased in 2001. It has seventy-five retail clients selling contemporary, better, and designer-priced women's clothes, giving Doneger an upscale orientation.

Tobe, publisher of the *Tobe Report*, was acquired in 2006. Tobe is a well-established brand with an international following and is run as a separate division of the Doneger Group.

There are also the Price Point Buying Off-Price Division and the Doneger Consulting Unit for special projects, such as product development and strategic initiatives.

The other dimension to Doneger is called Creative Services. It provides trend and forecasting publications and advice, and David Wolfe, the head of Creative Services, is famous for his international view and understanding of the fashion world. Creative Services has 450 subscribers and clients, including retailers, designers, and manufacturers

Wolfe's last acquisition was Here & There, a provider of fashion information and trend publications. Doneger's clients include Nordstrom, Dillard's, Belk, Kohl's, TJMaxx, Overstock.com, ShopNBC, Home Shopping Network, Bon-Ton, and Boscov's. International clients include Almacenes

Of special importance to the fashion industry are the channels that appeal to the youth market: MTV and VH-1 (see Figure 20.11). As part of its lifestyle programming, VH1 airs *America's Most Smartest Model*.

## Radio

While television is unsurpassed as a fashion advertising medium because of its visual qualities, radio is popular because it is inexpensive and can reach large but targeted audiences. Stations exist that serve only the youth market; others, such as classical radio stations, are geared to an older market. Others broadcast news and can deliver a virtual captive audience during the morning and evening commutes, the so-called drive time.

The use of radio to sell fashion was tied to the rise of rock music in the 1950s and the youth-oriented market it created. The youth market has remained strong, but radio advertising, if chosen carefully, also reaches adults and families.

In terms of cost per customer reached, spot commercials on local radio stations are economical; most of the advertiser's customers live and work within the range of the station's signal. Commercials announcing sales and other storewide events can use radio effectively because they do not depend on visual appeals. To attract advertisers, stations provide assistance with the preparation of copy, which may be delivered by disc jockeys and other announcers.

Paris in Chile, the Suburbia specialty division of Wal-Mart in Mexico, Sears Mexico, House of Fraser in the United Kingdom, and Robinsons in Singapore.

### Doneger Through the Decades

**1946:** Henry Doneger and partner Jack Lasersohn form the Lasersohn-Doneger resident buying office.

**1964:** Henry Doneger buys out Jack Lasersohn and forms Henry Doneger Associates.

**1973:** Abbey Doneger joins the firm as an assistant dress buyer.

**1980:** Henry becomes chairman and CEO; Abbey becomes president. The company commences a strategy of growth and acquisition with the purchase of the Gordon/Horowitz buying office.

**1985:** Doneger's most direct competitor, Steinberg-Kass, is purchased.

**1989:** Doneger Group is formed, following acquisition of the IRS buying office.

**1991:** David Wolfe is appointed creative director, spotlighting Doneger's evolving services and forward direction.

**1995:** Henry Doneger dies.

**2001:** The Carol Hoffman buying office is bought, and Doneger Consulting and Creative Services are formed.

**2005:** Tobe is purchased; Doneger opens an office in the California Market Center.

**2006:** Here & There is acquired.

**FIGURE 20.11** MTV's *The Hills* focuses on the lives of social fashionistas interning at L.A.'s *Teen Vogue* offices.

Radio is also a source of publicity because products and fashion news are discussed on regular shows.

As with television, most retailers and manufacturers rely on outside agencies to write and produce radio commercials, although some use their in-house talent to prepare commercials and then hire time-buying groups to place them.

## The Internet

Look at a fashion magazine ad for a designer or fashion retailer, and more often than not, you will see, in addition to location, a Web site address. As the Internet has expanded from a communication system for scholars and researchers to include the commercial world, fashion merchandisers have reached out to their markets with home pages on the World Wide Web. The chief advantage of the Internet as a promotional medium is that a company can address its audience directly. Furthermore, through Web pages accessible from the home page, the company can reach selected market segments and respond to their specific needs at any given moment. For example, retail customers can locate the nearest outlet of a favorite chain store, job applicants can find out about available positions and can submit their résumés, and employees can communicate with each other, as well as with customers and vendors.

In the fashion industry, even more than in businesses that do not market image, a well-designed Web page is a reflection of a firm's identity. Professionals—sometimes on the staff of the in-house advertising and promotion department, sometimes freelance Web site designers—design the Web site and keep it up to date.

Most of the leading fashion and general interest magazines now have Internet sites, as do hundreds of retailers. Many of these sites are linked to each other, so it is possible to spend hours online, just surfing from one fashion site to another.

*Fashion: The Life* is a Web-based reality series that features three young fashion designers preparing for a major trade show in Las Vegas. The show is promoted on air via "podbusters"—extended TV spots that appear in the middle of regular commercial breaks during the popular MTV reality program *The Hills*. The spots drive viewers to full episodes of the series on the network's new fashion site. www.thelookrightnow.com. The Web site also offers visitors the chance to upload fashion to a personalized "My Closet" profile page and to view a "Latest Looks Wall" of fashion trends. Enhancements include a "Rate This Look" voting feature and a friends feature called "I Like Your Style" that lets members add people to their profile. People who get added the most will be named "Fashion Icons" on the site.[7]

MenStyle.com is a popular Web site for men's wear. After each showing of a designer's line, they tabulate the number of visits to the site. The number of page views, or "hits," for the first 12 days after each show is then posted online. Following the Spring 2008 men's wear collections in Milan, the top five designers were

1. Dolce & Gabbana: 929,095 viewers
2. Prada: 713,202 viewers
3. Burberry Prossum: 698,296 viewers
4. Dsquared2: 685,074 viewers
5. Gucci: 666,143[8]

MySpace.com, the networking Web site, is inviting small, ambitious fashion companies seeking to promote their brands directly to young Internet surfers to join them. Designers and retailers have good reason to pay attention. MySpace has more than 100 million registered members around the world. "A third of teenagers have learned about new products and brands on community-based Web sites," said Michael Wood, vice president of Teenage Research Unlimited (TRU). Wood said social networks like MySpace have become fertile ground for teenagers scouting for trends and fashions. The TRU study said young people aged 10 to 19 spend an average of 9 hours a week online, and one in two teens shop online—with apparel topping the list of purchases.[9]

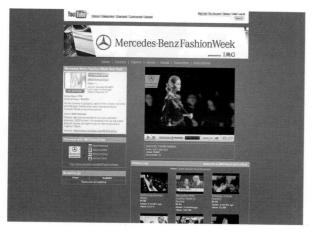

**FIGURE 20.12** YouTube broadcasts latest designer runway videos on special fashion week channels.

areas may be deeply involved in creating a multimedia campaign designed to shape the public's image of a client company. These campaigns are used for ongoing maintenance of a company's image as well as for an image change (see Figure 20.13).

Can fashion and luxury houses benefit from YouTube? You bet, according to Suzie Reider, head of advertising for YouTube. Since launching in 2005, YouTube has become the eighth most-trafficked Web site in the United States, with millions of daily viewers. And it's not just computer-savvy teens who frequent the site and post their clips. In fact, according its Reider, 19 percent of YouTube's audience is 55 or older (see Figure 20.12).

Judging by the positive reaction to YouTube, tomorrow's marketing will come from faceless masses who are online and shaping communication at a frenetic pace via Facebook, YouTube, and bottomless biogospheres. The fashion industry has acceded to the power of Internet marketing, but many businesses are unaware of how radically the Web has changed the game. Beyond access is the growing power of the Web to shape identity. Now people live out dreams and alternate realities in online worlds such as Second Life. Virtual space is having a greater impact on everyday life. Richard Tobaccowala, a digital marketing guru and chief executive officer of Denuo, an interactive marketing consultant firm, said "The Web is now a place of dream-making. The marketer's role in the new media is to help make those dreams a reality."[10]

## Advertising, Publicity, and Public Relations Agencies

Advertising, publicity, and public relations agencies do far more for the fashion industry than prepare and sell advertising. An agency in any of these three

**FIGURE 20.13** Successful ad campaigns for Marc Jacobs, Chanel, and the Gap ProjectRED.

# Then & NOW

## CFDA
### *Forty-Five Years of Glamour and Growth*

Left page: WWD's annual issue features CFDA's honorees for that year (top); right pagae: Ralph Lauren, Diane von Furstenberg, Rudolph Valentino, and Donna Karan attend a CDFA gala event (top); CFDA's charity t-shirt (bottom).

**W**hether by vote or, in some cases, persuasion, the Council of Fashion Designers of America (CFDA) has welcomed 10 presidents to lead its charge over the past 45 years.

Most who held the office checked in for two or three years, with Oscar de la Renta making a go of it twice—once from 1973 to 1976 and then again from 1987 to 1989. Stan Herman earned the badge for longevity, serving from 1991 until Diane von Furstenberg took over in 2006. In her short time at the helm, von Furstenberg is already seeing progress.

"I love to see the camaraderie and support that is happening through the CFDA," she says. "We are more powerful together than we are as individuals, and I see the CFDA as an organization that is as much about giving back as it is receiving. . . ."

De la Renta was instrumental in recognizing design talent. Looking back at his stints, he is most proud of establishing the CFDA awards in 1982. Prior to that, the Coty awards were the grand prize. "We felt we should be in control of the awards that were given to people in our industry," says de la Renta.

For Mary McFadden, persuading CFDA founder Eleanor Lambert to turn over all of the organization's papers was a feat. But unburdening Lambert and putting a secretary in place helped to give the group more autonomy, she says. "We were able to run it because now it was in the hands of the members."

McFadden, who held office from 1982 to 1983, began to host monthly CFDA luncheons at uptown restaurants to welcome in-the-know customers.

In those days, there were 50 to 60 members—a fraction of the roughly 300 who might turn out for a CFDA luncheon at the Condé Nast cafeteria today.

Stan Herman, who can remember when the CFDA had a little office with a $39 monthly phone bill, also recalls some of the livelier moments—Calvin Klein escorting Katharine Hepburn to the first awards, Karl Lagerfeld catching PETA's wrath in the early nineties, and Princess Diana introducing Liz Tilberis at the awards.

Herman came to office in a roundabout way. "When I became president, there was nobody who wanted to be president. We had just done the first 7th on Sale, and we were in a state of shock because it was so successful," he says.

With Carolyne Roehm, who was the president for two years

ALL THE HONOREES AND NOMINEES, INCLUDING RALPH LAUREN, PIERRE CARDIN, ROBERT LEE MORRIS AND PATRICK DEMARCHELIER, PLUS A LOOK BACK IN PICTURES

prior to Herman, and Donna Karan supporting it, the AIDS fund-raiser rang up more than $4 million in sales—well above the expected take of less than $1 million, Herman says. The Fashion Targets Breast Cancer, launched in 1994, was another initiative that CFDA members rallied behind.

Herman cites hiring Fern Mallis as the group's first executive director as another high point, but he still wonders if it would have been a better financial move to hold on to a piece of 7th on Sixth rather than sell the whole operation to IMG, as the organization did in 2001.

Herbert Kasper, president from 1977 to 1979,

notes how the CFDA has expanded from a local association into a global force. "People are producing and selling clothes all over the world today, and the CFDA has grown at that same level," Kasper says.

As the 2006–2009 president, Diane von Furstenberg has planned an extensive agenda for her initial 3-year tenure.

Von Furstenberg's agenda includes:

- Creating a business service network.
- Guiding designers on how to build export businesses and profiles abroad.
- Develop a permanent fashion center to serve a multitude of purposes, including fashion shows, events, and conferences.
- Reassessing the show calendars with her counterparts in Paris, Milan, and London.
- Lobbying for antipiracy laws to protect designers' original designs.

"My job as the president of the CFDA is to represent the designs," she said. "My first and main goal is really to increase the exposure of American fashion."

## Advertising Agencies

Advertising agencies provide many services, all of which are tied to the selling of commercial advertising space and/or time. Some agencies are specialized and deal only with one medium or one type of client, while others are general, offering a full range of services for many different types of clients. Agencies vary from a one-person shop to a giant agency that employs hundreds of people around the world. Small agencies claim to offer personal attention, but even large agencies divide their staff into creative teams so they, too, promise and often deliver a specialized service.

Small manufacturers and retailers and even fairly large department stores tend to rely on in-house advertising departments for all advertising except television and radio. Only the very large fiber and apparel companies regularly use advertising agencies, but those that can afford to do so find the investment worthwhile. For example, in an effort to expand their male market, Lee Jeans began a new marketing campaign with advertising agency Fallon targeted at teenage boys. The campaign used the Internet as its main tool. In July 2000, Fallon released unbranded home pages of fictional, ironic, pop-culture stereotypes, like the audaciously white-trash racecar driver Curry. At the same time the company also began circulating unbranded video clips starring the same characters on the Web, as well as plastering "wild postings" of them throughout college towns like Austin, Texas. By the time the commercials that connected these characters to Lee Jeans arrived on television, Curry and his friends had already gained underground notoriety among video game–playing young men. The campaign continued to work at an interactive media level. The Web sites featured video games that could be further enhanced by using codes that could only be found on the tag on a pair of Lee dungarees. The campaign paid off. Eighteen months later, Lee sales had doubled, and Lee's junior's carpenter pants became the top-selling blue jeans in the stores where they were carried.[11]

## Public Relations Agencies

Public relations firms are involved in the creation of publicity as well as in public relations. Publicity and public relations require that the agency work closely with its client, keeping abreast of what is new and newsworthy and announcing it to the world, either through press releases, often accompanied by photographs, or with story ideas presented to trade and consumer magazines and newspapers. As noted, public relations also involves, on a much deeper level, the shaping of a company's image. To this end, a public relations agency may suggest or help to plan and coordinate an event or activity, such as the rendering of a public service or gift to a charity or community, or the presentation of a scholarship or endowment to an institution or foundation. Examples include Piaget sponsorship of the opening night at Carnegie Hall's 106th season, and Miuccia Prada's Fondazione Prada supports exhibition projects by contemporary artists. Many of these events are produced and concepted by the New York public relations and creative services agency KCD. Fashion organizations also produce events with the backing of other glamour industries. For example, the presentation of the Cutty Sark Fashion Award, given annually to a designer, is an industrywide public relations activity. Similarly, Dom Pérignon has underwritten the awards ceremony of the Council of Fashion Designers of America.

The larger the company, the more likely it is to depend on an outside public relations firm. For example, KCD manages the public relations for the Victoria's Secret Fashion Show, a yearly event that is broadcast live on the Internet and on TV channels worldwide. Retailers, however, largely tend to have their own in-house publicity departments that work with top management to present the company's best face to the public. Among the well-known public relations agencies that specialize in the fashion industry are the huge Edelman, headquartered in Chicago; Cone Communications in Boston; the Hart Agency in Warwick, New York; and DeVries in New York.

## Other Advertising and Public Relations Services

Maintaining the corporate image of a fashion producer or retailer requires the services of a number of "creative" specialists, who may be company employees, agency employees, or freelancers. For example, **fashion stylists** may select and coordinate the apparel and accessories for store catalogs and print ads, for magazine articles, or for commercials. The job of the stylist involves juggling many tasks in one day, often including charming celebrities into posing in outfits they dislike. Many stylists work in either Los Angeles or New York, but more job opportunities are growing across the country. Hollywood's top stylists include Phillip Bloch, Jeannine Braden, Deborah Waknin, Lisa Michelle, and Stacy Young. Stylists must work cooperatively with the rest of the team: the photographers, the makeup artist, the hairdresser, the magazine editor, and the celebrity's agent or publicist.

Fashion illustrators' and photographers' work appears in advertising and in the editorial pages of consumer and trade publications. Skilled fashion photographers command creative control of a shoot as well as high pay.

Independent fashion show production companies offer their services to producers, retailers, and trade organizations.

## Store Design and Visual Merchandising Services

Two important onsite promotional activities that support the selling of fashion merchandise are store design and visual merchandising. The layout and design of any retail business have an impact on sales. Even catalog retailers and others who do not come face-to-face with their customers have to consider how much room they have for inventory and how stock should be arranged to expedite finding items and filling orders. For the traditional retailer operating in a store, the selling floor serves the critical purpose of presenting the merchandise to the customer, a function that is essential in selling fashion goods, for which appearance is a primary feature. Manufacturers' and designers' showrooms are their selling floors and thus require the same attention to interior design and visual merchandising.

## Store Design

Planning the layout for a store or department is even more daunting than designing the interior of one's own home. Some of the objectives are the same—visual appeal, ease of movement, and comfort, all within budget—but a space for the sale of merchandise must fulfill additional needs (see Figure 20.14). The designer must be attuned to the tastes of the target customer, and the environment not only must be pleasant but also must encourage shopping and buying. Shoppers may regard their visit as a recreational activity, but for the store, it is a business trip, and everything possible must be done to gain the customers' business. Placement of fixtures must take into account security considerations and easy access to exits in case of fire. Local building codes for commercial buildings must be met, and to comply with the Americans with Disabilities Act, certain features, such as ramps to ensure wheelchair access and Braille on the elevator buttons, may be required. Meeting all of these demands calls for the services of a professional, not just an architect or interior designer but one who specializes in store design.

Fortunately, a retailer who moves into a mall or a manufacturer with a showroom at an apparel mart may be renting space that has already passed inspection. Still, planning a selling area to maximize sales is not easy. Selecting fixtures that are suitable for the merchandise and the store image, choosing a color scheme, planning the lighting so that it will show off the merchandise in a flattering but accurate way—all these tasks and more must be considered. Major fashion designers, such as Ralph Lauren, have been known to supervise personally the furnishing and interior design of their boutiques within department stores as well as their freestanding outlets. As

**FIGURE 20.14** A store's layout is attuned to the tastes of its target customer.

apparel designers have extended their business into home furnishings and even furniture lines, the connection between store design and fashion image has become even more pronounced (see Figure 20.15). With the need for professional help as great as it is, the existence of trade shows and periodicals for store designers is not surprising.

## Visual Merchandising

The term **visual merchandising** includes the arrangement and presentation of merchandise in store windows and on the selling floor. It covers the arrangement of items that are for sale as well as the display of sample items on mannequins and other props. The term is broader than the older term *display*, reflecting not only the *showing* of merchandise but the *reason* for showing it—namely, to sell it.

Like all other successful promotional activities, a store's visual merchandising supports and exemplifies the retailer's image. For example, a designer boutique, though it may be small, is not cluttered. There is room for customers to step back and admire the exclusive merchandise. Coordinated and accessorized outfits are displayed to help customers assemble their own wardrobes. In the windows, no expense is spared to create an attention-getting environment for the featured merchandise. One or two outfits might be shown in a setting in which they could be worn, or they may be set off in

**FIGURE 20.15** This Lanvin store has a relaxing lounge setting.

an empty space with dramatic lighting and a few well-chosen props. Perhaps the price is indicated on a small, discreetly placed sign.

In contrast, the mass-merchandiser's windows and selling floor send a message of availability and affordability. Windows are crowded with mannequins wearing a variety of outfits. Brightly colored banners announce bargain prices. Inside, closely packed racks house a full range of sizes and colors for each style. No exclusivity is offered here, and none is desired.

What these two examples have in common is that each reveals an image carefully planned to appeal to the target customer. For retailers from single-unit specialty shops to giant department store chains, visual merchandising is an essential promotional service. In larger stores, the work is typically carried out by a staff under the leadership of a visual merchandising director. At the corporate, regional, or store level, window and interior managers may help to coordinate the visual merchandising plan with the merchandising and advertising plans. The staff who execute the plan must include employees who are skilled in carpentry, lighting, sign-making, collection of props, and dressing of mannequins—to name just some of their responsibilities. Small businesses, depending on their resources, may hire an independent visual merchandising firm or an individual freelancer. For help in deciding where to put merchandise on the selling floor, **planograms** are available. These computer-generated floor plans massage information about the sales of selected items or categories and factor those numbers in with other information about such items as the physical dimensions of the merchandise and the selling space. Feed that information to the computer, and it responds with a picture of the selling floor with merchandise in the best place.

## Fixtures

Display fixtures serve the dual purpose of showing and storing merchandise on the selling floor. Typically, they are purchased when the store is designed, but their use becomes part of the visual merchandising plan for each new selling season. The material and style of the fixtures should be selected to support the store image and the type of merchandise. See examples of fixtures in Figure 20.15. Three types of racks are typically used for hanging apparel: straight racks, rounders, and four-way fixtures.

- *Straight racks* may be installed in a recessed area against the wall, or they may be freestanding. Wall racks are ubiquitous for hanging dresses and other long garments, but freestanding straight racks tend not to be used for this purpose in upscale stores because the rack must be positioned high enough to keep the garments from dragging on the floor. Such racks take up considerable space and block the view of other merchandise. For a mass merchandise or factory outlet store, however, freestanding straight racks are appropriate for hanging all types of apparel. Rows of racks hold large amounts of merchandise, making it available for self-service selection. However, straight racks do not show a frontal view of the garments.
- *Rounders* are circular racks mounted on pedestals. Like straight racks, they hold a large amount of merchandise but do not provide a full view of it. Low rounders are suitable for tops, skirts, and folded trousers; they take up a fair amount of floor space, but because they do not obstruct the shopper's view, they do not make the selling floor look crowded.
- *Four-way fixtures* have two bars crossing at right angles. The customer can walk around the fixture for frontal views of four garments, and more apparel can be hung behind the item in front. An effective way of displaying merchandise on a four-way is to assemble an outfit on the outside hanger, for example, a shirt and jacket with the jacket buttoned to hide the shirttail. With pants or a skirt hanging below the jacket hem, the arrangement presents an indication of how the clothing will look when worn.

**FIGURE 20.16** Fixtures serve two purposes: They display the merchandise and make stock available to customers. Each retailer must select the best fixtures for the merchandise offered.

An important factor in using racks effectively is housekeeping. Usually, salespeople are responsible for arranging the merchandise by size, style, and color and hanging clothing neatly and in its proper place when it is returned from the fitting room. Maintaining order and neatness is important for the store's image and for the convenience of shoppers and salespeople who want to locate a garment in a particular size or color.

Another common fixture for apparel is the *gondola*, a freestanding island with a flat surface or bin on top and often with shelves or storage drawers below. It can be used to show stacks of folded tops or, if a bargain image is desired, a jumble of small items, such as socks, scarfs, or underwear.

Built-in cubicles have been used by the Gap and Benetton to show jeans and tops, decoratively sorted by style, size, and color. These fixtures are also suitable for displaying household linens. The stacks of merchandise create an attractive pattern, and it is easy to see the assortment and find the desired item.

## Signs and Graphics

Signs and graphics enhance merchandise presentations both in windows and on the selling floor. Temporary signs to announce a sale or special event or inform shoppers of a price can be produced easily with computer software. More permanent signage, such as directional signs for elevators, escalators, and rest rooms and signs identifying departments are more typically prepared by professionals. Like other aspects of visual merchandising, signs should be in keeping with the store's image.

## Information Resources

The fashion business is so huge and complex that no one individual or company can keep abreast of everything that is happening in it. It is a business made up in large part of trends and news in addition to its products. As a result, the auxiliary service provided by fashion consultants and research agencies, whose role is to supply information, is vital to the industry.

### *Fashion Consultants and Information Services*

Fashion consultants are individuals and groups who provide information and services to producers and retailers. Other well-known consultants today are Kurt Barnard and Walter F. Loeb. Marvin Traub, the former chairman and CEO of Bloomingdale's, is broadening his universe of consulting beyond his original Marvin Traub Associates. He is also chairman of SD Retail, a firm that centers on financial, operational, strategic, and supply-chain issues. Marvin Traub Associates mostly consults on merchandising, marketing, media, and branding issues, as well as licensing and mergers and acquisition activities, for retailers and consumer goods companies.[12] Other firms working in the fashion and retailing consulting area today include Kurt Salmon Associates in Atlanta; State Street Research in Boston; Retail Management Consultants in San Marcos, California; and WSL Strategic Retail in New York.

### The Fashion Group International, Inc.

Another vital source of industry information is The Fashion Group, Inc., a nonprofit global association of professional women who work in the

**FIGURE 20.17** FGI publishes a bulletin that focuses on trends and events in the fashion industry.

industry and the associated beauty and home fashions industries (see Figure 20.17). It was founded in 1930 to create executive jobs for women. Over the ensuing decades, however, it has become an important consulting and research agency. Its services are offered to members and, in some instances, nonmembers. Originally a group of seventeen fashion leaders in New York, it now has over 5,000 members in chapters in fashion centers across the world.

The Fashion Group is known for its exciting and prophetic fashion presentations. Through lavish fashion shows and fiber displays, it offers the fashion industry its expert and insightful analysis of upcoming trends. It covers the American, European, and Far Eastern fashion scene. The Fashion Group also publishes monthly news bulletins and maintains a valuable Web site (www.fgi.org), an online information service featuring directories of industry executives and professional services; calendars of events; trend reports and forecasts; classified job listings; and e-mail, public announcements, conferences, and Internet access.

## Specialized Information Services

A number of services disseminate reports on various segments of the fashion industry. For example, Nigel French, a British company, issues reports on fabrics, knitwear, and color. The *International Colour Authority*, a British publication, and the Color Association of the United States (CAUS) specialize in reporting on color trends in women's and men's wear.

## Market Research Agencies

Because knowing what is new and what is now at the very heart of fashion, businesses in all segments of the industry avidly consume the raw data and trend analyses published by market research agencies. The services of these professional prophets are expensive, but many of their findings are made public in time to be useful to a larger following. Among the better-known agencies is Kurt Salmon Associates (KSA), known for its extensive work with textile and apparel manufacturers and softgoods retailers.

The major accounting firms also have special divisions devoted to the fashion industries. Ernst & Young, Deloitte & Touche, and PricewaterhouseCoopers all offer respected management consulting services on a global basis.

A new breed of researchers and forecasters who rely on a variety of resources—including their own anecdotal observations and gut instincts as well as polls and surveys—is epitomized by Faith Popcorn. She has been called the Nostradamus of marketing. Popcorn started her career in advertising, and in 1974, she started BrainReserve. BrainReserve started from the understanding that in order to properly position a brand, one needs to understand the future of the brand in the environment in which it exists. Today, BrainReserve employs 10,000 people globally and has about ninety trend spotters across the world who are constantly searching for clues and ideas, which are the precursors to future trends.

Popcorn also started the Trend Bank in 1968. Through the Trend Bank, she has offered such hypotheses as Future Tense, EveVolution, 99 Lives, Cocooning, and AtmosFear, to name a few, which have proved to be right—now.

Faith Popcorn says this about what they do, "It's not about finding information, but being able to link the various clues and see the bigger picture. We are drawing the cultural map of 2017, not 2007."[13]

As consumers become more aware of trends, they become more aware that they are trendsetters, and the fashion industry, instead of attempting to dictate what will be worn next season, is actively seeking out the influential consumers and taking a cue from them.

## Trade Associations and Trade Shows

Associations of manufacturers and retailers assist fashion buyers in many ways. The nature and frequency of assistance available, though, are not uniform throughout the industry, and buyers soon learn how much assistance will be forthcoming from their particular trade. (See Units Two, Three, and Four for the names and activities of trade associations and trade shows for the major segments of the fashion industry.)

### Retailers Group

The National Retail Federation (NRF) is the largest retail trade association in the United States, counting among its members all the major department and specialty stores. It disseminates information and advice through its monthly magazine, *Stores*, and other periodicals and through regional and national meetings. An annual general convention is sponsored by the National Retail Federation in New York City in January. Vendors of products and services as diverse as market research, management software, and shopping bags exhibit at this meeting. Members gather at seminars and workshops to learn from retailing authorities and from each other. A special feature at this convention is a session devoted to outstanding fashion promotions during the previous year.

## Buyers Groups

Specialized associations or buying clubs provide an opportunity for an exchange of opinions and ideas among members. Retail buyers' groups also transmit the preferences of their members on matters as varied as the dates when lines should be opened and the appropriate sizes of stock boxes for specific products. Trade associations are often subsidized by outside sources, either the industry itself or a trade publication. Again, these associations are covered in Units Two, Three, and Four.

## Trade Shows

Retail and manufacturing groups, as well as independent organizations, sometimes sponsor trade shows at which many exhibitors gather to show their products and lines in one place, usually a hotel or convention center. Trade shows save time that would otherwise be spent trudging from showroom to showroom and also provide buyers with a chance to meet and exchange ideas with one another. They are especially helpful in fashion areas made up of many small firms. Exhibitors also find them a place to meet their counterparts from other regions or countries.

The shoe, notions, piece-goods, and men's sportswear industries regularly sponsor trade shows. (See Chapter 16 for a discussion of trade shows and market weeks at U.S. and foreign markets and marts.)

## Buying, Merchandising, and Product Development Organizations

Another type of auxiliary service—one developed especially for the fashion industry—is the **buying, merchandising, and product development organization**. This type of organization evolved from a service called a *resident buying office (RBO)*, and to understand the function of a buying, merchandising, and product development organization, one must first know something about RBOs. The buying offices came into being to serve the ongoing needs of a store or group of stores for a steady supply of new merchandise. Because a store's buyers worked out of the store and made only occasional market trips, they came to rely on a service located at the market centers for ongoing, daily attention to the store's needs.

Today these officers watch and report on fashion trends, help with strategic planning, make vendor recommendations, coordinate imports, and assist in product development. They help to organize fashion weeks and ensure that they go smoothly for their client stores' buyers. A good office continually adds to its list of services, and many have even expanded into areas such as sales promotion and advertising, personnel operations, and computer processing.

## Location

Most American offices, including the largest firms—The Doneger Group, Associated Target Sourcing Services/AMC, Macy's Merchandising Group—are headquartered in New York's garment center. But a number of buying offices are located in Los Angeles or have West Coast offices there. The organizations mentioned above all have Los Angeles offices. Marshall Kline Buying Service is an example of a Los Angeles–based buying office; it serves department stores and women's, men's, and children's apparel and home furnishings specialty stores. Some retail fashion chains, such as Ross Stores (a California off-price specialty chain), which maintain their own buying offices, have West Coast offices in Los Angeles.

The large buying, merchandising, and product development organizations also maintain branches abroad, and smaller companies have affiliates in the major foreign market centers.

## Types of Ownership

Buying offices are either independent or store-owned. An independent office works for noncompeting clients that it seeks out, while a store-owned office is owned by a group of stores, or—less often—one store, for whom it works exclusively.

**FIGURE 20.18** Fashion forecasting involves researching colors and styles and predicting what's next to come in the dynamic fashion world.

## Independent Offices

Independent offices are more numerous than store-owned offices simply because relatively few retailing giants can afford to own and manage such a resource. The number of buying offices has declined in recent years because of mergers and acquisitions among their retailer clients and among buying offices themselves.

Independent offices typically represent noncompeting moderate-priced department and specialty stores in mid-sized and secondary markets. To avoid conflicts, most independents restrict themselves to one client in each trading area, although they may have clients who serve different market segments within a single area. For example, a resident office's clients within a trading area may include a department store; a bridal shop; a shoe store; stores specializing in activewear, men's sportswear, and children's wear; and stores catering to customers at different price points.

The staff familiarizes themselves with each client's needs and attempts to meet those needs with as wide a range of services as possible. One aspect of service that buying offices are promoting to attract new clients is personal attention. Small operations, which offer exclusivity to their customers, claim that in a business consumed by "mergermania," they are better able to service their clients, who may themselves be expanding, by continuing to provide personalized and individual service.

Larger firms have responded by forming divisions that cater to the needs of different groups of clients. The largest independent resident buying office—in fact, the largest resident buying office of any type—in the United States is the Doneger Group. Its ten divisions include specialized buying offices for retailers in such markets as apparel for large women, apparel for tall women, children's wear, men's wear, home furnishings, and off-price retailing. Other divisions provide research and forecasting services and assistance in import and export.

Typically, an independent office charges each client store an annual, stipulated fee, which is based on the store's sales volume.

## Store-Owned Offices

Store-owned offices are either associated or corporate owned. An **associated** or **cooperative office** is cooperatively owned and operated by a group of privately owned stores for their mutual use. It never takes outside private clients; membership is by invitation only. It is considerably more expensive than if the store were a client of an independent office because members buy shares in the cooperative when they join. The amount of shares that must be purchased is keyed to member stores' sales volume.

One advantage of belonging to an associated office is that it provides members with an important exchange of information, often including financial information and merchandising experience. The best-known and largest associated buying office is Target Sourcing Services/AMC.

The **corporate-owned**, or **syndicated office** as it is sometimes called, is maintained by a parent organization exclusively for the stores it owns. One advantage of this type of organization is that it can be given more authority than an independent office, although some corporate-owned offices still require authorization from store buyers for major purchases. The Federated corporate office, which serves Bloomingdale's, the Bon Marché, Burdines, Goldsmith's, Lazarus, and Macy's, department stores and a number of smaller specialty shops, is an example of this type of office.

## Functions of the Buying, Merchandising, and Product Development Organization

Even with instant communication by electronic mail and faxes, the buying function benefits from the services of a representative and advisor who is actually at the market. Some of the functions that buying offices perform on behalf of their clients are purchasing, preparing for market weeks, importing, and developing products.

### Purchasing

Buying offices offer store buyers advice and support in various buying situations. For example, an office can place an order large enough to qualify for a manufacturer's quantity discount and then divide the goods among several small clients. The organization's staff can visit manufacturers' showrooms and make recommendations to their clients about specials, trends, and hot items. Size and location give the buying office clout with vendors when it comes to reordering in midseason or making sure that the right goods are delivered on schedule.

### Preparing for Market Weeks

As noted in Chapter 16, market weeks are hectic times for fashion buyers, with many showroom visits and other information-gathering events. A buying office can provide services similar to those of a tour guide to make the buying trip smooth and efficient. Staff members visit the showrooms in advance and assess each manufacturer's lines on behalf of their various clients. When the store buyers arrive, the buying office may give presentations to let them know what to expect. Sometimes personnel from a buying office accompany visiting buyers to vendors' showrooms and offer on-the-spot advice about orders.

### Importing

In response to the increasingly global nature of the fashion business, many buying offices maintain divisions in key foreign cities or affiliate with a *commissionaires* overseas. (A commissionaire is an agent that represents stores in foreign markets. See Chapter 15 for further discussion.) Overseas divisions and commissionaires work closely with the merchandising division and with client stores. In addition to performing the buying functions of a domestic buying office, these services deal with the unique challenges of importing, such as quotas, tariffs, long lead times for delivery, and interpretation of the buyer's orders for vendors who speak a different language. Having an advisor and consultant overseas is especially beneficial for buyers who are attending a market week or trade show or having private-label goods produced in a foreign country.

### Developing Products

Buying offices have played an important role in the development of private labels. Most corporate-owned buying offices have a private-label program for their member stores.

Target Sourcing Services/AMC has established a particularly strong retail presence developing private labels for its member stores. The company is known for its Preswick & Moore label, aimed at the high-end, traditional customer, and Architect, geared toward the young, career-oriented customer.

Corporate offices have also aggressively pursued private-label business. When the Federated conglomerate acquired Macy's, it expanded on the store's well-established product development program, placing the Charter Club apparel and home furnishing lines in its other mid-range department stores. Federated's product development program employs 400 people in eighteen countries to design, develop, and identify manufacturers for its private brands, which include its brands of cookware and other household goods as well as its fashion labels.

## Summary and Review

Fashion producers and retailers depend on a variety of auxiliary services to support the merchandising function. Depending on the size and resources of a company, it may rely on its own staff for these service or hire outside firms to perform them.

The media regard fashion businesses as clients and offer assistance in preparing and placing advertising (print ads in newspapers and consumer and trade magazines and commercials on television and radio). To attract advertisers, the media offer fashion businesses color and style forecasts and other trend information. Advertising and public relations agencies also provide auxiliary services in placing paid advertisements and free publicity in the media. Store design and visual merchandising are other promotional services that may be performed by staff members or independent suppliers.

For information about industry trends and fashion forecasts, retailers and producers can take advantage of the services offered by fashion consulting firms, market research agencies, trade associations, and trade shows.

A source of information unique to the fashion industry is the buying, merchandising, and product development organization. This type of business began as resident buying offices, representing out-of-town retailers in the major markets. Some firms were independent, selling their services to noncompeting retailers. Others were corporate-owned, either as cooperatives owned by several retailers or as divisions of large retail chains. Resident buying offices have evolved into businesses that include wholesalers and producers among their clients and that provide a full range of services, including liaisons with vendors, advice and assistance in buying, merchandising, forecasting, and other information services.

## Trade Talk
Define or briefly explain the following:

advertising

buying, merchandising, and product development organization

associated or cooperative office

corporate-owned or syndicated office

infomercial

public relations

trade publication

fashion stylist

planogram

publicity

visual merchandising

## For Review
1. What is the difference between advertising and publicity/public relations?
2. Describe the contents of *Women's Wear Daily.*
3. What are the advantages of television and radio for fashion exposure?
4. What tasks do public relations firms undertake for their clients?
5. What advantages does a Web site offer as a promotional medium?
6. How does a store design contribute to the store's image?
7. What resources are available to a small specialty store for effective visual merchandising?
8. Describe the research methods that trend forecasters use.
9. What is the major function of buying, merchandising, and product development organizations? What additional services do they perform?
10. What are the similarities and differences between independent and corporate buying, merchandising, and product development offices?

## For Discussion
1. As a consumer, where do you get your information about fashion? How does each medium influence your buying decisions?
2. You own a small boutique that caters to upscale young women. What services of a buying, merchandising, and product development organization would be most useful to you? Why?

| | NAME | DECADES OF INFLUENCE | DEFINING CHARACTERISTICS |
|---|---|---|---|
| 18 | Courrèges, André | 60s–70s | First couturier to raise hemlines to mid-thigh . . . white boots, tough chic |
| 19 | Connolly, Sybil | 60s–70s | Ireland's most prestigious designer . . . famous for fine wools and tweeds |
| 20 | de la Renta, Oscar | 60s–2000s | Luxury designer . . . opulent eveningwear, sophisticated daywear |
| 21 | Demeulemeester, Ann | 90s–2000s | Precision tailored suits . . . clever cutting of jersey fabrics . . . monochrome color palette |
| 22 | Dior, Christian | 40s–50s | The "New Look" in 1947 . . . cinched waist, pushed up bosom, short jacket emphasized hips, full long skirts |
| 23 | Dolce, Domenico, and Gabbana, Stefano | 90s–2000s | Inspired the young to dress up . . . sexy lingerie looks are their signature . . . glorification of female physique is the message of their designs |
| 24 | Ellis, Perry | 70s–80s | Added high-fashion pizzazz to classic looks . . . young in spirit . . . natural fibers, hand-knitted sweaters |
| 25 | Fath, Jacques | 40s–50s | Sexy clothes . . . hourglass shapes . . . plunging necklines |
| 26 | Ferré, Gianfranco | 80s–90s | Architectural look to his designs . . . was educated as an architect and he shows well-defined construction in his clothes |
| 27 | Fisher, Eileen | 90s–2000s | The empress of understatement . . . easy-fitting clothes for an imperfect figure |
| 28 | Fogarty, Anne | 50s–60s | Introduced fashion innovations to the junior-size world |
| 29 | Ford, Tom | 90s–2000s | New design voice of Gucci |
| 30 | Fortuny, Mariano | 20s–30s | Pleated artistry . . . his clothes are now collector's items |
| 31 | Galanos, James | 40s–50s | First American couturier . . . elegant haute couture designs |
| 32 | Galliano, John | 90s –2000s | Theatrical design . . . knitted lace dresses |
| 33 | Gaultier, Jean-Paul | 80s–2000s | Trendy and controversial . . . advocate of the "punk look" . . . daring and avant-garde |
| 34 | Gernreich, Rudi | 60s–70s | Topless swimsuit . . . the "no-bra" . . . see-through blouses |
| 35 | Givenchy, Hubert de | 50s–80s | His fashion muse was Audrey Hepburn . . . introduced chemise or sack dress |
| 36 | Grès, Alix | 30s–50s | The duchess of draping . . . her Grecian column dresses are draped to perfection |
| 37 | Halston | 70s–80s | Unconstructed separates, lush cashmeres . . . Studio 54 |
| 38 | Hartnell, Norman | 30s–40s | Biggest couture house in London in 1930s . . . designed coronation gown for Queen Elizabeth II |
| 39 | Head, Edith | 30s–50s | One of Hollywood's best-known designers . . . dressed Liz Taylor, Lana Turner |
| 40 | Herman, Stan | 60s–90s | President of the Council of Fashion Designers of America . . . leading uniform designer of the world . . . think airlines, McDonald's |
| 41 | Herrera, Carolina | 80s–2000s | Caters to high-society clientele . . . dressy eveningwear . . . luxurious fabrics |
| 42 | Hilfiger, Tommy | 80s–2000s | "Brand image" designer |
| 43 | Jacobs, Marc | 90s–2000s | Designed for the Perry Ellis label . . . exceptional in leather and fur design |
| 44 | James, Charles | 40s–50s | The Dali of Design |
| 45 | Johnson, Betsey | 60s–70s | The Betsey of "Betsey, Bunky, and Nini" . . . designed for "Paraphernalia" stores |
| 46 | Joop, Wolfgang | 90s | Leading 1990s designer from Germany |
| 47 | Kamali, Norma | 80s–90s | Sweatshirt clothes made high fashion news . . . appeals to the young |
| 48 | Karan, Donna | 80s–2000s | High-fashion elegant sportswear . . . simple silhouettes, sarong skirts, easy-fitting dresses |
| 49 | Kawabuko, Rei | 80s–90s | Avant-garde clothes challenged classic idea of femininity |
| 50 | Kenzo | 70s–80s | Attentive to the quality of fabrics . . . uses splashes of irreverent color . . . now into home fashions |
| 51 | Khanh, Emmanuelle | 60s–70s | One of the first major ready-to-wear designers in Paris . . . kicky, young clothes |
| 52 | Klein, Anne | 50s–60s | Classic American sportswear designer . . . "Junior Sophisticates" was her company |
| 53 | Klein, Calvin | 70s–2000s | King of the minimalism look . . . designer jeans . . . sexually-charged advertising |
| 54 | Kors, Michael | 90s–2000s | Strong on shape and line, devoid of ornamentation |
| 55 | Lacroix, Christian | 80s–90s | Introduced the "pouf" silhouette . . . fanciful apparel and elaborate wedding gowns |
| 56 | Lagerfeld, Karl | 80s–2000s | Produces 16 collections a year! . . . perfect technique and witty design resurrected the Chanel name |
| 57 | Lanvin, Jeanne | 20s–30s | One of the earliest Paris couturiers |
| 58 | Lauren, Ralph | 80s–2000s | Western look for men and women . . . creates upper-crust lifestyle looks . . . classic silhouettes |
| 59 | Mackie, Bob | 60s–70s–80s | Dresses TV and movie stars . . . lots of glitz |
| 60 | McCardell, Claire | 40s–50s | Introduced dirndl skirt as a high fashion icon . . . leading proponent of American sportswear look |

| | NAME | DECADES OF INFLUENCE | DEFINING CHARACTERISTICS |
|---|---|---|---|
| 61 | McFadden, Mary | 70s–80s | Fortuny successor . . . used pleats to emphasize her enticing looks |
| 62 | McQueen, Alexander | 90s . . . | Started as a Savile Row tailor in London . . . now designs couture for Givenchy |
| 63 | Mainbocher | 30s–40s | An American in Paris . . . introduced strapless evening gowns . . . designed the wedding dress of Wallis Simpson, the Duchess of Windsor |
| 64 | Miller, Nicole | 80s–2000s | Innovative prints . . . pure, simple designs for the 1990s |
| 65 | Missoni, Rosita and Ottavio | 50s–90s | Bold, multiple-color combinations in knitwear . . . simple but sophisticated knitwear designs |
| 66 | Miyake, Issey | 80s–90s | Developer of new fabrics and design techniques . . . produces innovations like oil-cloth clothes |
| 67 | Mizrahi, Isaac | 80s–90s | Flashed on fashion scene under Chanel backing . . . moved on to theatrical and movie works |
| 68 | Montana, Claude | 80s–90s | Wedge-shaped silhouette . . . architectural shapes in original designs |
| 69 | Moschino, Franco | 90s . . . | Fashion spoofs made him famous |
| 70 | Mori, Hanae | 80s | Mines the gap between East and West . . . Chanel inspired her designs |
| 71 | Mugler, Thierry | 70s–90s | Extravagant and innovative . . . spans from lots of ornamentation to rigorous minimalism |
| 72 | Muir, Jean | 60s–70s | Elegantly, intricately detailed classic clothes |
| 73 | Natori, Josie | 80s–2000s | Banished the borders between inner and outerwear . . . success based on mix of comfort, practicality, and style |
| 74 | Norell, Norman | 40s–60s | Winner of first Coty award in 1943 . . . his shimmering sequined dresses are worn and treasured forever |
| 75 | Oldham, Todd | 90s . . . | Whimsical mix of commercial and offbeat . . . designs sophisticated and youthful clothes with a sense of humor |
| 76 | Patou, Jean | 20s–30s | Elegant, ladylike couture clothes . . . successful businessman and showman |
| 77 | Piquet, Robert | 30s–40s | Influenced Givenchy and Dior, both of whom worked for him |
| 78 | Poiret, Paul | 20s–30s | First Paris couturier of 20th century to become a trendsetter . . . liberated women from corsets |
| 79 | Prada, Miuccia | 90s–2000s | Clothing and accessories global trendsetters . . . secondary line Miu Miu a rage with the young |
| 80 | Pucci, Emilio | 50s–60s | His colorful graphic prints on jersey revolutionized Italian fashion at that time |
| 81 | Quant, Mary | 60s–70s | Swinging sixties London scene . . . popularized miniskirts, colored tights, and football sweaters |
| 82 | Rabanne, Paco | 70s–80s | Produced clothes of plastic, chain metal, fiber-optic wire, and doorknobs . . . fashion's heavy metal guru . . . a revolution in fashion |
| 83 | Rhodes, Zandra | 70s–80s | Glamorized print designs . . . soft fabrics, handscreened prints . . . started as a textile designer |
| 84 | Rodriguez, Narciso | 90s–2000s | Designs for Loewe, a Spanish design company |
| 85 | Rykiel, Sonia | 70s–80s | Knitwear her forte . . . sense of fashion humor, mixing the outrageous with the feminine |
| 86 | Saint Laurent, Yves | 60s–90s | Exploded on scene in 1960s . . . "Infant Terrible" . . . famous for pantsuits, pea jackets, "le smoking," safari suits . . . Rive Gauche |
| 87 | Sander, Jil | 90s–2000s | Highest quality in materials and craftsmanship . . . expert tailoring in suits and coats |
| 88 | Simpson, Adele | 50s–60s | A durable of Seventh Avenue . . . known for conservative good taste in design |
| 89 | Schiaparelli, Elsa | 30s–40s | Avant-garde designer in Paris . . . famous for introducing "shocking pink" |
| 90 | Sui, Anna | 90s–2000s | Free-spirited approach to design . . . mix of hip and haute couture |
| 91 | Trigère, Pauline | 40s–80s | Pioneer American designer . . . her coat silhouettes are famous . . . attention to detail |
| 92 | Tyler, Richard | 90s | Custom tailoring, graceful cut . . . sophisticated styling and expert cut . . . appeals to the 1990s Hollywood crowd |
| 93 | Ungaro, Emanuel | 70s–80s | Space-age inspired . . . bold colors . . . sharp edged |
| 94 | Valentino | 60s–90s | His famous V-shaped emblems crown his collection . . . simple, subtle design |
| 95 | Versace, Gianni | 80s–90s | Kinetic, kaleidoscope prints . . . metallic mesh garments . . . king of fashion for the rock and roll set |
| 96 | Wang, Vera | 90s–2000s | Wonder of the wedding dress . . . besides bridal parties, has expanded to evening clothes |
| 97 | Weitz, John | 60s–90s | Women's sportswear with a menswear look . . . designs in all fields (once "designed" a cigar!) |
| 98 | Westwood, Vivienne | 80s–90s | Punk rock fashion . . . T-shirts with outrageous messages . . . named her boutique "Sex" |
| 99 | Worth, Charles Frederick | The originator of fashion | He created the "designer name" as we know it . . . established the pattern of regular seasoned fashion shows |
| 100 | Yamamoto, Yohji | 80s–90s | Sparse, understated fashions . . . dark, strong designs . . . asymmetrical cuts |

Adapted from a variety of sources, including WWD: *75 Years in Fashion 1910–1985*, *WWD Century*, September 1998.

# glossary

**Absolute quota** A limit to the quantity of goods entering United States. *Ch 17*

**Activewear** The sector of sportswear that includes casual attire worn for sports such as running, jogging, tennis, and racquetball. Sometimes called "active sportswear." *Ch 10*

**Adaptations** Designs that have all the dominant features of the style that inspired them but do not claim to be exact copies. *Ch 2*

**Advertising** The paid use of space or time in any medium. This includes newspapers, magazines, direct-mail pieces, shopping news bulletins, theater programs, catalogs, bus cards, billboards, radio, TV, and the Internet. *Ch 20*

**Air malls** Retailer stores in aiports. *Ch 19*

**Ambiance** The atmosphere encountered when entering a store. *Ch 19*

**Anchor** A design from a previous season reworked in a different color or fabric. *Ch 8*

**Apparel contractor** A firm whose sole function is to supply sewing services to the apparel industry. *Ch 8*

**Apparel jobber** (manufacturing) A firm that handles the designing, planning, and purchasing of materials, and usually the cutting, selling, and shipping of apparel, but does not handle the actual garment sewing. *Ch 8*

**Apparel manufacturer** A firm that performs all the operations required to produce a garment. *Ch 8*

**Aromatherapy** Fragrant oils are extracted from plants, herbs, and flowers, and used to stimulate or relax people. *Ch 14*

**Assortment** The range of stock a retailer features.

See also *merchandise assortment. Ch 19*

**Auxiliary level** Composed of all the support services that are working with primary producers, secondary manufacturers, and retailers to keep consumers aware of the fashion merchandise produced for ultimate consumption. *Ch 5*

**Baby-boom generation** People born in the United States between 1946 and 1954; the largest generation group ever recorded. *Ch 3*

**Balance of trade** The difference between the value of exports and the value of imports. *Ch 17*

**Big boxes** A concept for a store that presents a large selection of goods in a selling space oversized for its merchandise category. *Ch 18*

**Bodywear** Coordinated leotards, tights, and wrap skirts. *Ch 12*

**Body wrap** Herbs, seaweed, or mud is applied directly to the body, which is then wrapped like a mummy to allow the substances to penetrate the pores. *Ch 14*

**Bootleg goods** Quality products made by the same manufacturer that produces the genuine branded products; these are sold to the black market. *Ch 17*

**Boutique** A shop associated with few-of-a-kind merchandise, generally of very new or extreme styling, with an imaginative presentation of goods. French word for "shop." *Ch 16*

**Brand** A name, trademark, or logo that is used to identify the products of a specific maker or seller and to differentiate the products from those of the competition. Also called "brand name." *Ch 6*

**Brand-line representative** (cosmetics) A trained cosmetician who advises customers in the selection and use of a specific brand of cosmetics, and handles the sales of that brand in a retail store. *Ch 14*

**Bridal registry** See *wedding registry. Ch 15*

**Bridge** (apparel—women's and men's wear) A price zone that bridges the gap between designer and better prices. *Ch 10*

**Bridge jewelry** Merchandise ranging from costume to fine jewelry in price, materials, and newness of styling. *Ch 13*

**broad and shallow assortment** A store that offers many different styles in limited sizes and colors. *Ch 19*

**Bundling** Assembling the cut pieces of each pattern—sleeves, collars, fronts, and backs—into bundles according to their sizes. Usually done by hand. *Ch 8*

**Buyer's directory** A list (and often a map) of the manufacturers' showrooms in a particular market or mart; it is furnished to retail buyers to assist them in "working the market." *Ch 16*

**Buying, merchandising, and product development office** *Associated/Cooperative:* One that is jointly owned and operated by a group of independently-owned stores. *Private:* One that is owned and operated by a single, out-of-town store organization and that performs market work exclusively for that store organization. *Salaried, Fee, or Paid:* One that is independently owned and operated and that charges the stores it represents for the work it does. *Syndicate/Corporate:* One that is maintained by a parent organization that owns a group of stores and performs market work exclusively for those stores. *Ch 20*

**Carat** A measure of weight of precious stones; equal to 200 milligrams or 1/142 of an ounce. See also *karat. Ch 13*

**Career** A profession for which one trains and which is undertaken as a permanent calling. *Career Project 1*

**Career path or ladder** The order of occupations in a person's life. *Career Project 2*

**Category or classification buying** A practice whereby a chain store buyer located in a central buying office is usually assigned to purchase only a specific category or classification of merchandise instead of buying all categories carried in a single department. See also *departmental buying. Ch 18*

**Category killer** Superstores or category specialists who so dominate a market that they drive out or "kill" smaller specialty stores. *Ch 18*

**Chain organization** A group of twelve or more centrally owned stores, each handling somewhat similar goods, which are merchandised and controlled from a central headquarters office (as defined by the Bureau of the Census). *Ch 18*

**Chargebacks** Financial penalties imposed on manufacturers by retailers. *Ch 8*

**Classic** A style or design that satisfies a basic need and remains in general fashion acceptance for an extended period of time. *Ch 2*

**Collection** A term used in the United States and Europe for an expensive line. *Ch 8*

**Commissionaire** (pronounced "ko-mee-see-oh-NAIR") An independent retailers' service organization usually located in the major city of a foreign market area. It is roughly the foreign equivalent of an American resident buying office. *Ch 17*

**Computer-aided design (CAD)** A computer program that allows designers to manipulate their designs easily. *Ch 8*

**Computer-aided manufacturing (CAM)** Stand-alone computerized manufacturing equipment, including computerized sewing, pattern-making, and cutting machines. *Ch 8*

**Computer-integrated manufacturing (CIM)** Many computers within a manufacturing company are linked from the design through the production stages. *Ch 8*

**Confined style(s)** Styles that a vendor agrees to sell to only one store in a given trading area. See also *exclusivity. Ch 19*

**Consignment selling** A manufacturer places merchandise in a retail store for resale but permits any unsold portion to be returned to the wholesale source by a specific date. *Ch 7*

**Contemporary** A type of styling and a price zone that is often also referred to as "updated," "better," or "young." Applies to all categories of apparel and furnishings. *Chs 9 and 10*

**Contract buying** See *specification buying.*

**Contract tanneries** Business firms that process hides and skins to the specifications of converters but are not involved in the sale of the finished product. *Ch 7*

**Contractors** See *apparel contractor. Ch 8*

**Converter, leather** Firms that buy hides and skins, farm out their processing to contract tanneries, and sell the finished product. *Ch 7*

**Converter, textiles** A producer who buys fabrics in the greige, contracts to have them finished (dyed, bleached, printed, or subjected to other treatments) in plants specializing in each operation, and sells the finished goods. *Ch 6*

**Copycat scents** Imitations of the aromas (and sometimes the packaging) of popular designer fragrances; sold at much lower prices. *Ch 14*

**Corporate licensing** The use of a company's name on (sometimes) related merchandise. *Ch 8*

**Corporate-owned or syndicated office** See *buying, merchandising, and product development office. Ch 20*

**Cosmetics** Articles other than soap that are intended to be rubbed, poured, sprinkled, or sprayed on the person for purposes of cleansing, beautifying, promoting attractiveness, or altering the appearance (as defined by the Federal Trade Commission). *Ch 14*

**Costume jewelry** Mass-produced jewelry made of brass or other base metals, plastic, wood, or glass, and set with simulated or non-precious stones. Also called "fashion jewelry." *Ch 13*

**Couture house** (pronounced "koo-TOUR") An apparel firm for which the designer creates original styles. *Ch 16*

**Couturier** (male) or **couturière** (female) (pronounced "koo-tour-ee-AY" and "koo-tour-ee-

AIR") The proprietor or designer of a French couture house. *Ch 16*

**Créateurs** (pronounced "kray-ah-TOURS") French ready-to-wear designers. *Ch 16*

**Culmination** (stage) See *fashion cycle. Ch 2*

**Custom-made** Clothing fitted specifically to the wearer. *Ch 9*

**Cut-up trade** Manufacturers of belts that are sold as part of a dress, skirt, or pants. *Ch 13*

**Data warehouse** A group of super-powerful computers hooked together and filled with easily accessible information about customers, transactions, and finances. *Ch 19*

**Decline** (stage) See *fashion cycle. Ch 2*

**Demographics** Population studies that divide broad groups of consumers into smaller, more homogeneous market segments; the variables include population distribution, age, sex, family life cycle, race, religion, nationality, education, occupation, and income. *Ch 3*

**Departmental buying** A practice whereby a department buyer is responsible for buying all the various categories of merchandise carried in that department. See also *category buying. Ch 18*

**Department store** As defined by the Bureau of the Census, a store that employs twenty-five or more people and sells general lines of merchandise in each of three categories: (1) home furnishings, (2) household linens and dry goods an old trade term meaning piece goods and sewing notions, and (3) apparel and accessories for the entire family. *Ch 18*

**Design** A specific version or variation of a style. In everyday usage, however, fashion producers and retailers refer to a design as a "style," a "style number," or simply a "number." *Ch 2*

**Details** The individual elements that give a silhouette its form or shape. These include trimmings; skirt and pant length and width; and shoulder, waist, and sleeve treatment. *Ch 2*

**Developed countries** (DCs) Countries in the stage of economic development marked by a well-paid labor force and a high standard of living. *Ch 17*

**Discount store** A departmentalized retail store using many self-service techniques to sell its goods. It operates usually at low profit margins, has a minimum annual volume of $500,000, and is at least 10,000 sq. ft. in size. *Ch 18*

**Discretionary income** The money that an individual or family has to spend or save after buying such necessities as food, clothing, shelter, and basic transportation. *Ch 3*

**Disposable personal income** The amount of money a person has left to spend or save after paying taxes. It is roughly equivalent to what an employee calls "take-home pay," and provides an approximation of the purchasing power of each consumer during any given year. *Ch 3*

**Diversification** The addition of various lines, products, or services to serve different markets. *Ch 5*

**Domestic market** A fashion market center located in one's own country. *Ch 16*

**Downward-flow theory** The theory of fashion adoption which maintains that to be identified as a true fashion, a style must first be adopted by people at the top of the social pyramid. The style then gradually wins acceptance at progressively lower social levels. Also called the "trickle-down" theory. *Ch 4*

**Drop** (men's wear) The difference between the waist and chest measurements of a man's jacket. Designer suits are sized on a seven-inch drop; traditional suits are styled with a six-inch drop. *Ch 10*

**Dual distribution** A manufacturer's policy of selling goods at both wholesale and retail. *Ch 10*

**Duty** See *tariff*.

**Editorial credit** The mention, in a magazine or newspaper, of a store name as a retail source for merchandise that is being editorially featured by the publication. *Ch 20*

**Electronic Data Interchange (EDI)** The electronic exchange of machine-readable data in standard formats between one company's computers and another company's computers. *Ch 8*

**Entrepreneurs** People who start new business ventures. *Career Project 1*

**Entry-level job** One requiring little or no specific

training and experience. *Career Project 1*

**Environment** The conditions under which we live that affect our lives and influence our actions. *Ch 3*

**Erogenous** Sexually stimulating. *Ch 4*

**European styling** (men's wear) Features more fitted jackets that hug the body and have extremely square shoulders. *Ch 10*

**Exclusivity** Allowing sole use within a given trading area of a style or styles. An important competitive retail weapon. *Ch 19*

**Export** When a country provides goods to another country. *Ch 17*

**Fabrics** Materials formed from knitted, woven, or bonded yarns. *Ch 6*

**Factor** Financial institution that specializes in buying accounts receivable at a discount. *Ch 8*

**Factory outlet store** Manufacturer-owned store that sells company products at reduced prices in austere surroundings with minimum services. *Ch 18*

**Fad** A short-lived fashion. *Ch 2*

**Fashion** A style that is accepted and used by the majority of group at any one time. *Ch 2*

**Fashion business** Any business concerned with goods or services in which fashion is an element—including fiber, fabric, and apparel manufacturing, distribution, advertising, publishing, and consulting. *Ch 2*

**Fashion cycle** The rise, widespread popularity, and then decline in acceptance of a style. *Rise:* The acceptance of either a newly introduced design or its adaptations by an increasing number of consumers. *Culmination:* That period when a fashion is at the height of its popularity and use. The fashion then is in such demand that it can be mass-produced, mass-distributed, and sold at prices within the reach of most consumers. *Decline:* The decrease in consumer demand because of boredom resulting from widespread use of a fashion. *Obsolescence:* When disinterest occurs and a style can no longer be sold at any price. *Ch 2*

**Fashion industries** Those engaged in producing the materials used in the production of apparel and accessories for men, women, and children. *Ch 2*

**Fashion influential** A person whose advice is sought by associates. A fashion influential's adoption of a new style gives it prestige among a group. *Ch 4*

**Fashion innovator** A person first to try out a new style. *Ch 4*

**Fashion jewelry** See *costume jewelry. Ch 13*

**Fashion Retailing** The business of buying and selling—or merchandising—goods, apparel, accessories, and home fashions. *Ch.18*

**Fashion trend** See *trend.*

**Fiber** A threadlike unit of raw material from which yarn and, eventually, textile fabric is made. *Ch 6*

**First cost** The wholesale price of merchandise in the country of origin. *Ch 17*

**Floor-ready** Merchandise that has been ticketed with bar-coded price and packed in labeled cartons with all shipping documents attached. If the merchandise is a garment, it has been pressed and folded or hung on a hanger with a plastic bag over it. *Ch 8*

**Foreign market** Markets outside the domestic market; for example, to businesses in the United States, France is a foreign market. See also *market* and *domestic market. Ch 16*

**Foundations** The trade term for such women's undergarments as brassieres, girdles, panty girdles, garter belts, and shapers. *Ch 12*

**Fragrance** Includes cologne, toilet water, perfume, spray perfume, aftershave lotion, and environmental scents. *Ch 14*

**Franchise** A contractual agreement in which a firm or individual buys the exclusive right to conduct a retail business within a specified trading area under a franchiser's registered or trademarked name. *Chs 5 and 18*

**Franchise distribution** (cosmetics) The manufacturer or exclusive distributor sells directly to the ultimate retailer. *Ch 14*

**Free trade** The unrestricted exchange of goods between nations. *Ch 17*

**Fur farming** The breeding and raising of fur-bearing animals under controlled conditions. *Ch 7*

**General Agreement on Tariffs and Trade (GATT)** A 1947 agreement, between many countries, to reduce trade barriers and unify trading practices. It was replaced by the World Trade Organization (WTO) in 1995. *Ch 17*

**Generation X** The "baby boomlet" group, born from 1966 to 1976. *Ch 3*

**Generation Y** The second "baby bust" group, born from 1977 to 1987. *Ch 3*

**General merchandise retailer** Retail stores which sell a number of lines of merchandise—for example, apparel and accessories; furniture and home furnishings; household lines and drygoods; hardware, appliances, and smallwares—under one roof. Stores included in this group are commonly known as mass-merchandisers, department stores, variety stores, general merchandise stores, or general stores. *Ch 18*

**General store** An early form of retail store which carried a wide variety of mainly utilitarian consumer goods. *Ch 18*

**Generic name** Non-trademarked names assigned by the Federal Trade Commission to twenty three manufactured fibers. *Ch 6*

**Geographics** Population studies that focus on where people live. *Ch 3*

**Geotextiles** Manufactured, permeable textiles currently used in reinforcing or stabilizing civil engineering projects. *Ch 6*

**Global sourcing** The process of shopping for and purchasing imported goods. *Ch 17*

**Grading** Adjustment of a style's sample pattern to meet the dimensional requirements of each size in which the style is to be made. Also referred to as "sloping." *Ch 8*

**Gray market goods** Goods not intended for sale in the country in which they are being sold, often with an invalid warranty. *Ch 17*

**Greige goods** (pronounced "grayzh goods") Fabric that has received no preparation, dyeing, or finishing treatment after having been produced by any textile process. *Ch 6*

**Group** A subdivision of a line, linked by a common theme such as color, fabric, or style. *Ch 8*

**Haute couture** (pronounced "oat-koo-TOUR") The French term literally meaning "fine sewing" but actually having much the same sense as our own term "high fashion." *Ch 16*

**Hides** Animals skins that weigh over 25 pounds when shipped to a tannery. *Ch 7*

**High fashion** Those styles or designs accepted by a limited group of fashion leaders—the elite among consumers—who are first to accept fashion change. *Ch 2*

**High-fashion, or name, designer** A person who creates designs, chooses the fabric, texture, and color for each design. Often, this person is involved with the development of the production model as well as with plans for the promotion of the line. Name designers may work for fashion houses, own his or her own firm, or work for a publicly owned firm. *Ch 8*

**High-tech fabric** A fabric that has been constructed, finished, or processed in a way that gives it certain innovative, unusual, or hard-to-achieve qualities not normally available. *Ch 6*

**Home fragrances** Fragrances used to scent a place rather than a person; also called environmental fragrances. *Ch 14*

**Horizontal growth** A company expands on the level on which it has been performing. See also *vertical growth*. *Ch 5*

**Horizontal-flow theory** The theory of fashion adoption that holds that fashions move horizontally between groups on similar social levels rather than vertically from one level to another. Also called the "mass-market theory." *Ch 4*

**Import** When a country buys goods from a foreign country. *Ch 17*

**Import quota** Limits set to restrict the number of specific goods entering a country. *Ch 17*

**Inflation** A substantial and continuing rise in the general price level. *Ch 3*

**Innerwear** The trade term for women's underwear; usually divided into foundations, lingerie, and loungewear. *Ch 12*

**Inside shops** Garment factories owned and operated by men's wear manufacturers who perform all the operations required to produce finished garments. *Ch 10*

**Intimate apparel** The trade term for women's foundations, lingerie, and loungewear. Also called inner fashions, body fashions, and innerwear. *Ch 12*

**Item house** Contractors that specialize in the production of one product. *Ch 8*

**Jobber** A middleman who buys from manufacturers and sells to retailers. See also *apparel jobber*. *Ch 8*

**Joint merchandising** An arrangement in which a retail store pays part of the salary of the cosmetic/fragrance salespeople who represent one manufacturer's line. *Ch 14*

**Karat** A measure of the weight of the gold content of jewelry; abbreviated as "K." *Ch 13*

**Kiosk** A stand that offers shelves or racks for merchandise. *Ch 19*

**Kips** Animal skins weighing from 15 to 25 pounds when shipped to a tannery. *Ch 7*

**Knockoffs** A trade term referring to the low-price copies of an item that has had good acceptance at higher prices. *Ch 2*

**Leased department** A department ostensibly operated by the store in which it is found but actually run by an outsider who pays a percentage of sales to the store as rent. *Chs 7 and 18*

**Less developed countries** (LDCs) Countries in the early stages of economic development; they have a low standard of living and lack a well-paid labor force. *Ch 17*

**Let out** (furs) A cutting and resewing operation to make short skins into longer-length skins adequate for garment purposes. *Ch 7*

**Licensed trademark** (fibers) A fiber's registered trademark used under a licensing agreement whereby use of the trademark is permitted only to those manufacturers whose end products pass established tests for their specific end use or application. *Ch 6*

**Licensing** An arrangement whereby firms are given

permission to produce and market merchandise in the name of the licensor, who is paid a percentage of sales for permitting his or her name to be used. *Ch 5*

**Lifestyle centers** are open-air shopping areas anchored by a multiplex cinema (or two) and a big bookstore, and they contain a collection of restaurants. *Ch 19*

**Line** An assortment of new designs offered by manufacturers to their customers, usually on a seasonal basis. *Ch 5*

**Line-for-line copies** These are exactly like the original designs except that they have been mass-produced in less expensive fabrics to standard size measurements. *Ch 8*

**Lingerie** A general undergarment category that includes slips, petticoats, camisoles, bras, panties, nightgowns, and pajamas. Underclothing is considered "daywear," while nightgowns and pajamas are classified as "sleepwear." *Ch 12*

**Long-run fashion** A fashion that takes more seasons to complete its cycle than what might be considered its average life expectancy. *Ch 2*

**Loungewear** The trade term for the intimate apparel category that includes robes, bed jackets, and housecoats. *Ch 12*

**Mall** An enclosed, climate-controlled shopping center. *Ch 19*

**Manufactured fiber** A fiber invented in a laboratory; also called "man-made" or "synthetic." *Ch 6*

**Manufacturer** See *apparel manufacturer.*

**Marker** (apparel manufacturing) A long piece of paper upon which the pieces of the pattern of a garment in all its sizes are outlined and which is placed on top of many layers of material for cutting purposes. *Ch 8*

**Market** (1) A group of potential customers. (2) The place or area in which buyers and sellers meet for the purpose of trading ownership of goods at wholesale prices. *Ch 16*

**Market center** A geographic center for the creation and production of fashion merchandise, as well as for exchanging ownership. *Ch 16*

**Market segmentation** The separating of the total consumer market into smaller groups known as "market segments." *Ch 3*

**Market weeks** Scheduled periods throughout the year during which producers and their sales representatives introduce new lines for the upcoming season to retail buyers. *Ch 16*

**Marketing** A total system of business activities designed to plan, price, promote, and place (distribute) products and services to present and potential customers. *Ch 2*

**Mart** A building or building complex housing both permanent and transient showrooms of producers and their sales representatives. *Ch 16*

**Mass distribution** (cosmetics) Third-party vendors, such as wholesalers, diverters, and jobbers, often interposed between the manufacturer and the retailer. *Ch 14*

**Mass or volume fashion** Those styles or designs that are widely accepted. *Ch 2*

**Megamall** Larger than a superregional mall, it contains four to five million square feet. *Ch 19*

**Merchandise assortment** A collection of varied types of related merchandise, essentially intended for the same general end-use and usually grouped together in one selling area of a retail store. *Broad:* A merchandise assortment that includes many styles. *Deep:* A merchandise assortment that includes a comprehensive range of colors and sizes in each style. *Narrow:* A merchandise assortment that includes relatively few styles. *Shallow:* A merchandise assortment that contains only a few sizes and colors in each style. *Ch 19*

**Merchandising** The planning required on the part of retailers to have, for a specific consumer target group, the right merchandise at the right time, in the right place, in the right quantities, at the right price, and with the right promotion. *Ch 2*

**Merchandising policies** Guidelines established by store management for merchandising executives to follow in order that the store organization

**Sales representatives** Company representatives who exhibit merchandise to potential customers. *Ch 16*

**Sample hand** The designer's assistant who sews the sample garment. *Ch 8*

**Secondary level** Composed of industries—manufacturers and contractors—that produce the semifinished or finished fashion goods from the materials supplied by the primary level. *Ch 5*

**Section work** The division of labor in apparel manufacturing whereby each sewing-machine operator sews only a certain section of the garment, such as a sleeve or hem. *Ch 8*

**Sensory retailing** In-store stimulation of all the customer's senses, using pleasant aromas, mood music, dramatic lighting. *Ch 19*

**Shelter magazines** Home-decorating magazines. *Ch 20*

**Shopping center** A coordinated group of retail stores, plus a parking area. *Ch 19*

**Short-run fashion** A fashion that takes fewer seasons to complete its cycle than what might be considered its average life expectancy. *Ch 2*

**Showcase store** A manufacturer's or designer's store that sells merchandise at the introductory and early-rise stages of the fashion cycle.

**Silhouette** The overall outline or contour of a costume. Also frequently referred to as "shape" or "form." *Ch 2*

**Skins** Animals skins that weigh 15 pounds or less when shipped to a tannery. *Ch 7*

**Sloping** See *grading.*

**Slop shops** A name associated with the first shops offering men's ready-to-wear in this country. Garments lacked careful fit and detail work found in custom-tailored clothing of the period. *Ch 10*

**Small leather goods** A category that includes wallets, key cases and chains, jewelry cases, briefcases, and carrying cases for cell phones and laptop computers. *Ch 13*

**Source** (of supply) See *vendor.*

**Spa** Formerly "health spa," now a service business offering a wide variety of beauty treatments, including massages, manicures, pedicures, waxings, facials, aromatherapy, and thalassotherapy. *Ch 14*

**Specialty retailers** They offer limited lines of related merchandise targeted to a more specific customer. *Ch 18*

**Specialty Store** These stores carry a limited line of merchandise, whether it is clothing, accessories, or furniture.

**Specification buying** A type of purchasing that is done to the store's rather than to the manufacturer's standards. See also *private label. Chs 8 and 17*

**Specification manager** Manager who oversees the purchasing and manufacturing process for a private label. Also called "product manager." *Ch 8*

**Spinnerette** A mechanical device through which a thick liquid base is forced to produce fibers of varying lengths. *Ch 6*

**Spreader** A laying up machine that carries material along a guide on either side of a cutting table, spreading the material evenly, layer upon layer. *Ch 8*

**Sterling silver** A term used for jewelry and flatware with at least 92.5 parts of silver; the remaining 7.5 parts are usually copper. *Ch 13*

**Strategic alliance** A form of business combination in which a retailer and a manufacturer join forces to operate more efficiently, thus improving profits for both companies, while offering customers a better product at a lower price. *Ch 19*

**Style** A characteristic or distinctive mode of presentation or conceptualization in a particular field. In apparel, style is the characteristic or distinctive appearance of a garment, the combination of features that makes it different from other garments. *Ch 2*

**Style number** The number manufacturers and retailers assigned to a design. The number identifies the product for manufacturing, ordering, and selling. *Ch 2*

**Stylist-designer** A person who adapts or changes the successful designs of others. *Ch 8*

**Suit separates** (men's wear) Sports jacket and trousers worn much as the tailored suit used to be. *Ch 10*

**Sumptuary laws** Laws regulating consumer purchases, for example, dress, on religious or moral grounds. *Ch 4*

**Superregional mall** Even larger than a regional mall, they often contain up to one million square feet, with at least three department or major chain stores, and one hundred to three hundred specialty stores. Their trading area is a distance up to one-hour's driving time away. *Ch 19*

**Sustainable use** An environmental program that encourages land owners to preserve animal young and habitats in return for the right to use a percentage of the grown animals. *Ch 7*

**Tabletop** (goods) Categories of merchandise commonly found on tabletops, including dinnerware, glassware, flatware, hollowware, and giftware. *Ch 15*

**Tailored-clothing firms** Those men's wear firms that produce structured or semistructured suits, overcoats, topcoats, sportcoats, and or separate trousers in which a specific number of hand-tailoring operations are required. *Ch 10*

**Tanning** The process of transforming animal skins into leather. *Ch 7*

**Target market** A specific group of potential customers that manufacturers and retailers are attempting to turn into regular customers. *Ch 3*

**Tariff** A fee assessed by government on certain goods that it wishes to restrict or limit. *Ch 17*

**Tariff-rate quota** A set limit after which a higher duty is charged on goods entering the country. *Ch 17*

**Taste** The recognition of what is and is not attractive and appropriate. Good taste in fashion means sensitivity not only to what is artistic but to these considerations as well. *Ch 2*

**Textile fabric** Cloth or material made from fibers by weaving, knitting, braiding, felting, crocheting, knotting, laminating, or bonding. *Ch 6*

**Textile converter** See *converter.*

**Texture** The look and feel of material, woven or unwoven. *Ch 2*

**Thalassotherapy** A skin treatment involving sea water, seaweed, or sea algae. *Ch 14*

**Trade association** Professional organizations for manufacturers or sales representatives. *Ch 16*

**Trade deficit** When the value of goods that a country imports exceeds the value of its exports. *Ch 17*

**Trade publications** Newspapers or magazines published specifically for professionals in a special field, such as fashion. *Ch 20*

**Trade shows** Periodic merchandise exhibits staged in various regional trading areas around the country by groups of producers and their sales representatives for the specific purpose of making sales of their products to retailers in that area. *Ch 16*

**Trade surplus** When a country's exports exceed its imports. *Ch 17*

**Trend** A general direction or movement. See also *fashion trend. Ch 2*

**Trimmings** All the materials—excluding the fabric—used in the construction of a garment; including braid, bows, buckles, buttons, elastic, interfacing, padding, self-belts, thread, zippers, etc. *Ch 6*

**Trunk show** A form of pretesting that involves a designer or manufacturer sending a representative to a store with samples of the current line, and exhibiting those samples to customers at scheduled, announced showings. *Ch 9*

**Universal Product Code (UPC)** The most widely accepted of a number of bar codes used for automatic identification of items scanned at retail cash registers. *Ch 8*

**Upward-flow theory** The theory of fashion adoption that holds that the young—particularly those of low-income families as well as those of higher income who adopt low-income lifestyles—are quicker than any other social group to create or adopt new and different fashions. *Ch 4*

**Vermeil** (pronounced "vur-MAY") A composite of gold over sterling silver. *Ch 13*

**Vertical growth** A company expands on a different level than its original one. *Ch 5*

**Vertical mall** An indoor, multistory shopping center, taller than it is wide. *Ch 19*

**Videoconferencing** A system that combines the telephone with a television image of a meeting. *Ch 19*

**Visual merchandising** Everything visual that is done to, with, or for a product and its surroundings to encourage its sale. This includes display, store layout, and store decor. *Ch 20*

**Wedding or bridal registry** A store's list of a bridal couple's desired merchandise, upon which gift-givers' selections are recorded as they are purchased. Today it is often called merely a "gift registry" and is computerized. *Ch 15*

**Wicking** The ability of a fabric to carry the moisture of perspiration away from the skin. *Ch 12*

**Yarn** A continuous thread formed by spinning or twisting fibers together. *Ch 6*

**Yarn-dyed** Refers to dyeing yarns before they are woven or knitted; this process results in deep, rich colors. See also *piece-dyed*. *Ch 6*

# references & notes

**CHAPTER 1**

Regina Lee Blaszczyk, ed., *Producing Fashion: Commerce, Culture, and Consumers* (Philadelphia: University of Pennsylvania Press, 2007).

Amy Fine Collins, "The Lady, the List, the Legacy," *Vanity Fair*, April 2004, pp. 260-274, 328-333.

Kathleen Craughwell-Varda, *Looking for Jackie: American Fashion Icons* (New York: Hearst Books, 1999).

Jane Farrell-Beck and Jean Parsons, *20th-Century Dress in the United States* (New York: Fairchild Books, 2007).

Jenna Weissman Joselit, *A Perfect Fit: Clothes, Character, and the Promise of America* (New York: Holt, 2002).

Eleanor Lambert, *Ultimate Style: The Best of the Best Dressed List* (New York: Assouline, 2004).

Valerie Bernham Oliver, *Fashion and Costume in American Popular Culture: A Reference Guide* (Westport, CT: Greenwood Press, 1996).

Caroline Rennolds Milbank, *New York Fashion: The Evolution of American Style* (New York: Harry N. Abrams, 1996).

Thomas C. Reeves, *Twentieth-Century America: A Brief History* (New York: Oxford University Press, 2000).

Valerie Steele, *Fifty Years of Fashion: New Look to Now* (New Haven: Yale University Press, 1997).

Valerie Steele, *Women of Fashion: Twentieth-Century Designers* (New York: Rizzoli, 1991).

FASHION FOCUS

Amy Fine Collins, "The Lady, the List, the legacy" *Vanity Fair*, April 2004, pp. 260-274, 328-333. David Patrick Columbia's New York Social Diary, March 11, 2004, www.newyorksocialdiary.com.

THEN AND NOW

"The 68th Annual International Best-Dressed List." *Vanity Fair*, September 2007, p. 290.

**CHAPTER 2**

1. George P. Fox, *Fashion: The Power That Influences the World. The Philosophy of Ancient and Modern Dress and Fashion* (London: Lange and Hellman, Printers & Stereotypers, 1850–1860–1872), Introduction, p. 20.

2. Guy Trebay, "Whatever Happened to Now?" *New York Times Magazine*, February 4, 2007, p. 56.

3. Catherine Moye, "Wearable Chairs and Tower-Block Frocks: Catherine Moye Looks at the Link between Designing Clothes and Buildings." *Financial Times*, January 27, 2007, p. 9.

4. *Webster's Tenth New Collegiate Dictionary* (Springfield, MA: G. & C. Merriam Company, 1998), p. 450.

5. Peter F. Drucker, *Management Tasks, Responsibilities, Practices* (New York: Harper & Row, 1973), pp. 64–65.

6. Paul H. Nystrom, *Economics of Fashion* (New York: The Ronald Press, 1928), pp. 3–7; and *Fashion Merchandising* (New York: The Ronald Press, 1932), pp. 33–34.

7. Ibid., p. 7.

8. James Laver, *Taste and Fashion*, rev. ed. (London: George C. Harrop & Co., Ltd., 1946), p. 202.

9. Fathi Nazila, "Enforcing a Single Hue for Islamic Fashion in Iran: Black," *New York Times*, May 4, 2007, p. P6.

10. Ruth La Ferla, "What They Design Real Women Wear." *New York Times*, February 8, 2007, p. G1.

11. Irma Zandl, "How to Separate Trends from Fads," *Brandweek Online*, October 23, 2000.

12. Agnes Brooke Young, *Recurring Cycles of Fashion: 1760–1937* (New York: Harper & Brothers, 1937; reprint, New York: Cooper Square Publishers, Inc., 1966), p. 30.

13. Furukawa Tsukasa, "UNIQLO Increases Recycling Efforts," *Daily News Record* 37 (March 19, 2007), p. 28.

14. Terri Agins, "Women's Wear: The Gold in Your Closet: Investment-grade Bustiers; Online Bidding Wars Erupt for Second-Hand Designer Duds: $500 for an $80 Dress—from H&M." *Wall Street Journal*, March 24, 2007, p. 1.

15. Holly Haber, "Talking Trends," *Women's Wear Daily*, January 3, 2002.

16. Damien Mc Guinness, "Technology Speaking in Germany," WWD.COM (March 23, 2007).

FASHION FOCUS

Phoebe Carman, "Fashion's Number One," *Harper's Bazaar*, September 2005, pp. 406–414.

Michelle Edgar, "Ralph Lauren Looks to Fifth Polo Scent for a Little Adventure," *Women's Wear Daily*, June 29, 2007, p. 4

Paul Goldberger, "American Dreamer," *Vanity Fair*, September 2007, pp. 360–364.

Jeanine Poggi, "Highest-Paid Vendors: Ralph Lauren is No. 1, Earning 25.9M in 2006," *Women's Wear Daily*, August 2, 2007, pp. 1, 9.

Marc Karimzadeh, "Ralph Lauren Designs T-Shirt for Breast Cancer Initiative," *Women's Wear Daily*, June 19, 2007, p. 2.

Marc Karimzadeh, "Ralph Takes Tokyo," *Women's Wear Daily*, March 29, 2006, pp. 1–4, 5.

Robert Murphy, "Rendezvous in Russia: Ralph Lauren Launches First Stores in Moscow," *Women's Wear Daily*, May 10, 2007, pp. 1–12, 13.

Jeanine Poggi, "Ralph: Polo Just Beginning," *Women's Wear Daily*, August 8, 2007, p. 2.

THEN AND NOW

Lisa Armstrong, "Azzedine Alaia on Paul Poiret Influence," *Harper's Bazaar*, July 2005, pp. 132–134.

Alix Browne, "Hip, Hip Poiret," *New York Times*, April 22, 2007, pp. 64–70.

Rosemary Feitelberg, "A Studied Look at Poiret," *Women's Wear Daily*, May 18, 2007, p. 15.

Marc Karemzadeh, "A Modern View of Paul Poiret," *Women's Wear Daily*, May 4, 2007, p. 11.

Lesley Scott, "Paul Poiret, Modern Designer: A Fashion History Insider Fave Gets His 15 Minutes," May 4, 2007, http://french-fashion-designers.suite101.com/article.cfm/paul_poiret_modern_designer.

Anna Wintour, "Letter from the Editor," *Vogue*, May 2007.

CHAPTER 3

1. Michael Weiss, *The Clustered World* (New York: Little Brown and Co. 2000), c.1.

2. SRI Consulting Business Intelligence (SRIC-BI). "VALS: The Framework." No date. www.sric-bi.com/marketing/VALS/VALS-Framework2002-09.pdf (accessed February 4, 2008), p. 1.

3. Ibid., p. 1.

4. Ibid., p. 1.

5. Quentin Bell, *On Human Finery* (London: The Hogarth Press, Ltd., 1947), p. 72.

6. Gerald Prante, "New Census Data on Income Gives a Welcome Dose of Fact Checking to 'Middle-Class' Rhetoric," September 2007, www.taxfoundation.org/news/show/22600.html.

7. *Webster's Tenth New Collegiate Dictionary* (Springfield, MA: Merriam-Webster, Inc., 1998).

8. U.S. Census Bureau, Statistical Abstract of the United States—2008 (Washington: U.S. Department of Commerce, 2008).

9. Cecil Beaton, *The Glass of Fashion* (New York: Doubleday & Company, Inc., 1954), pp. 335, 379–381.

10. Jennifer Steinhauer, "A Minority Market With Major Sales," *New York Times*, July 2, 1997, p. D-1.

11. U.S. Census Bureau, "Census Bureau Projects Doubling of Nation's Population," *United States of Commerce News*, Washington D.C., January 13, 2000.

12. Ibid.

13. Carol J. DeVita, Population Bulletin, "The United States at Mid-Decade."

14. Linda S. Wallace, "As Income Rises, African Americans Go on High Tech Buying Binge," www.Diversity.com, September 13, 2001.

15. John Naisbitt's Trend Letter, September 12, 1996, p. 2.

16. William Frey, "Census 2000," American Demographics, June 2001.

17. Aseem Chhabra, "Asian Indian Population Doubles in a Decade," The Rediff US Special Online, May 16, 2001.

18. Marcia Mogelonsky, "Asian-Indian American," American Demographics, August 1995, p. 34.

19. U.S. Census Bureau, "Workers with Earnings, by Occupation of Longest Job Held and Sex: 2004," July 2006.

20. Edward Sapir, "Fashion," *Encyclopedia of the Social Sciences*, vol. VI (London: Macmillan & Co. 1931), p. 140.

21. Bell, *On Human Finery*, p. 72.

22. Editorial, "The Great Money Grab," p. 2.

23. Rachel Dardis, "The Power of Fashion," *Proceedings of the Twentieth Annual Conference, College Teachers of Textiles and Clothing*, Eastern Region, New York, 1966, pp. 16–17.

24. Paul H. Nystrom, *Economics of Fashion* (New York: The Ronald Press, 1928), pp. 66–81.

FASHION FOCUS

Courtney Colavita, "Roman Holiday—Time Again," *Women's Wear Daily*, January 9, 2007, pp. 4–7.

"Fairground," Couture Dynasty, *Variety Fair*, October 2007, pp. 193–195.

Cathy Horyn, "Where Emperors Strode, Fashion Royalty (and the Real Kind) Hails Designer," *New York Times International*, January 8, 2007, p. 11.

Alessandra Ilari, "Alessandra Facchinetti Takes

Reins at Valentino," *Women's Wear Daily*, September 6, 2007, p. 3.

Alessandra Ilari, "'The Chic' Rides Off: Valentino to Retire after January," *Women's Wear Daily*, September 5, 2007, pp. 1, 4.

Jessica Kerwin, "His Brilliant Career," *Women's Wear Daily*, January 7, 2006, p. 4.

J. J. Martin, "Valentino: Six Decades in Fashion—And Why His Absence May Leave Fans Seeing Red," *Harper's Bazaar*, July 2007, pp. 160–165.

Alice Rawsthorn, "Rome's No. 1 Fashion Son, Stages a 45th-Anniversary Coup," *New York Times*, January 8, 2007, pp. 48–53.

WWD Milestones, "Valentino, a Look at a Legend," June 27, 2007.

WWD Staff, "Fashion Intrigue in Italy: Jockeying for Position in the World of Valentino," *Women's Wear Daily*, May 24, 2007, pp. 1–45.

THEN AND NOW

Lisa Armstrong, "Galliano's Glorious Reign," *Harper's Bazaar*, March 2007, pp. 426–435.

Cathy Horyn, "At Versailles: Let Them Wear Cake," *New York Times*, July 5, 2007, pp. G1, G6.

Cathy Horyn, "The Magnificent Madness of King John," *Women's Wear Daily*, July 3, 2007, pp. 6, 7.

Jessica Kerwin, "Past Perfect," W, August 1, 2005, pp. 194–201.

Suzy Menkes, "Past Present: The New New Look," *New York Times*, August 28, 2005, pp. 148–149.

Miles Socha, "Dior Plans Big Bash for Couture," *Women's Wear Daily*, June 25, 2007, p. 2.

Miles Socha, "Galliano's Larger World: Designer in Kid's Deal as Own Label Takes Off," *Women's Wear Daily*, October 5, 2007, pp. 1, 11.

Jennifer Weil & Miles Socha, "Galliano to Do Signature Scent," *Women's Wear Daily*, March 2, 2007, p. 11.

WWD Milestones, "Dior: 60 Years of New Looks," *Women's Wear Daily*, February 27, 2007, pp. 1–3.

CHAPTER 4

1. James Laver, *Taste and Fashion*, rev. ed. (London: George G. Harrop & Co., Ltd., 1946), p. 52.
2. Pearl Binder, *Muffs and Morals* (London: George G. Harrop & Co., Ltd., 1953), pp. 162–164.
3. Elisabeth McClellan, *History of American Costume* (New York: Tudor Publishing Company, 1969), p. 82.
4. John Taylor, *It's a Small, Medium, and Outsize World* (London: Hugh Evelyn, 1966), p. 39.
5. The NPD Group, "NPD Reports on the Evolving School Uniform Industry," www.NPD.com (August 9, 2006).
6. Laver, *Taste and Fashion*, p. 201.
7. Clara Pierre, *Looking Good: The Liberation of Fashion* (New York: Reader's Digest Press, 1976), p. 149.
8. Agnes Brooke Young, *Recurring Cycles of Fashion: 1760–1937* (New York: Harper & Brothers, 1937; reprint New York: Cooper Square Publishers, Inc., 1966), p. 30.
9. A. L. Kroeber, "On the Principles of Order in Civilizations as Exemplified by Change in Fashion," *American Anthropologist*, vol. 21, July–September 1919, pp. 235–263.
10. Madge Garland, *The Changing Form of Fashion* (New York: Praeger Publishers, 1971), p. 11.
11. J. C. Flügel, *The Psychology of Clothes* (New York: International Universities Press, 1966), p. 163.
12. Laver, *Taste and Fashion*, p. 200.
13. Ibid., p. 201.
14. Flügel, *Psychology of Clothes*, p. 163.
15. Garland, *Changing Form of Fashion*, p. 20.
16. Ibid., p. 11.

17. Dwight E. Robinson, "Fashion Theory and Product Design," *Harvard Business Review*, vol. 36, November–December 1958, p. 128.
18. Paul H. Nystrom, *Fashion Merchandising* (New York: The Ronald Press, 1932), p. 94.
19. Gabriel Tarde, *The Laws of Imitation* (New York: Henry Holt and Company, 1903), p. 221.
20. Georg Simmel, "Fashion," *American Journal of Sociology*, vol. 62, May 1957, p. 545.
21. Charles W. King, "Fashion Adoption: A Rebuttal to the Trickle-Down Theory," *Proceedings of the Winter Conference*, American Marketing Association, New York, December 1963, pp. 114–115.
22. Dwight E. Robinson, "The Economics of Fashion Demand," *The Quarterly Journal of Economics*, vol. 75, August 1961, p. 383.
23. King, "Fashion Adoption," pp. 114–115.
24. Amy Larocca, "'Mr. In-Between,' Philip Lim," *New York Magazine*, August 6, 2007, pp. 62–64.
25. Quentin Bell, *On Human Finery* (London: The Hogarth Press, Ltd., 1947), p. 46.
26. Flügel, *Psychology of Clothes*, p. 140.
27. King, "Fashion Adoption," p. 124.
28. Flügel, *Psychology of Clothes*, p. 140.
29. Edward Sapir, "Fashion," *Encyclopedia of the Social Sciences*, vol. VI (London: Macmillan & Co., 1931), p. 140.
30. Jessica Daves, *Ready-Made Miracle* (New York: G. P. Putnam's Sons, 1967), pp. 231–232.
31. Simmel, "Fashion," pp. 543–544.
32. Flügel, *Psychology of Clothes*, p. 140.
33. Sapir, "Fashion," p. 140.

FASHION FOCUS

Bridget Foley, "Jacobs Blasts Back: Designer Tells Critics Shut Up or Stay Home," *Women's Wear Daily*, September 13, 2007, pp. 1, 10.
—— "Partners in Power: Marc Jacobs–Robert Duffy," *W Magazine*, October 2007, p. 232.

Application Solutions at Computer Generated Solutions, Inc., "PLM."

Peter Haas, "On the Rise: BlueCherry by CGS," *Fashion Manuscript*, March 2007, pp. 36–37.

Stephen M. Samuel, "About Product Lifecycle Management," Design Visionaries, www.designviz.com, September 23, 2007.

VNU Business Media (PLM Focus Series), "A Closer Look: Automating a Vendor Collaboration Process in a PLM Solution," *Apparel*, July 2007.

VNU Business Media (PLM Focus Series), "A Closer Look: Enabling a Line Planning Process in a PLM Solution," *Apparel*, July 2007.

"Solutions: Product Lifecyle Management," www.cgsinc.com/solutions/bluecherry/plm.html, September 30, 2007.

THEN AND NOW

"The WWD 100," *WWD Special Report*, July 2007.

CHAPTER 9

1. The Fashion Center Business District Office, *FCBID-2007*.

2. Whitney Beckett, "Survey: US Women Buying Up Activewear," *Women's Wear Daily*, August 10, 2006, p. 15.

3. Evan Clark, Activewear High-Tech Boost," *Women's Wear Daily*, March 7, 2007, p. 6.

4. Melanie Kletter, "Skiwear Gets Lift From Designers," *Women's Wear Daily*, March 3, 2005, p. 18.

5. Cecily Hall, "For Richer or Poorer," *Women's Wear Daily*, June 21, 2007, p. 12

6. Jeanine Poggi, "Teen Queens," *Women's Wear Daily*, June 28, 2007, p. 8

7. Jeanine Poggi, "Relaunching Petite Sophisticate," *Women's Wear Daily*, September 25, 2006, p. 14.

8. Whitney Beckett, "Building Its Practice: The-

ory Enters Bridge with Premise, *Women's Wear Daily*, September 27, 2006, pp. 1, 9.

9. Marc Karimzadeh and Whitney Beckett, "De la Renta's New Deal: O Oscar Line to Launce Exclusively at Macy's," *Women's Wear Daily*, September 19, 2006, pp. 1, 16.

10. Whitney Beckett, "Vera's New View," *Women's Wear Daily*, May 10, 2007, p. 6.

11. Whitney Beckett, "How We Shop Now," *Time*, March 13, 2006, p. 62.

12. Whitney Beckett, "Online Apparel Sales Take Off," *VNN Business*, July 2006, p. 10.

CHAPTER 10

1. Harry A Cobrin, *The Men's Clothing Industry* (New York: Fairchild Publications, 1970), p. 67.

2. Courtney Colavita, Contributions by Amanda Kaiser, "Acting on Impulse: Men's Shopping Habits Have Become More Spontaneous, Opening Up New Opportunities for Retailers," *Daily News Record*, January 8, 2007, p. 38.

3. Candice Choi, "Guys' Territory: Today's Metrosexual Goes Shopping without His Wife or Girlfriend in Tow," *Daily News* (Los Angeles), January 26, 2005, p. B1.

4. Just-style.com, "U.S. Tailored Clothing Drives Men's Wear Sales," www.just-style.com, February 3, 2006.

5. Antoinette Alexander, "Men's Grooming Products Serve Look of Youth to Aging Boomers," *Drug Store News*, March 6, 2006, p. 49.

6. Arnold Karr, "Tailor-Made 2005: Men's Jumps 5.2%: Tailored Clothing Sparks Increase in Men's Wear for the Year," *Daily News Record*, February 27, 2006, p. 5.

7. www.Hartmarx.com. Accessed August 19, 2007.

8. Barbara Ettoie, "Business and Buttonholes," *New York Times*, October 28, 2007, p. F1.

9. Ray A. Smith, "A Real Savile Row," *Wall Street Journal*, April 14, 2007, p. P6.

10. Jean E. Palmieri, "Retailing's Seismic Shifts," *Daily News Record*, April 24, 2006.

11. Herbert Blueweiss, "Clothing at Neiman-Marcus," *Daily News Record*, November 29, 2007, p. 10.

12. Ray A. Smith, "Men's Aisle Gets Crowded; More American Designers Target Guys with Luxury 'Classic' Lines, Trying to Tap Menswear Resurgence," *Wall Street Journal*, December 12, 2006, p. B1.

13. Ray A. Smith, "Style & Substance: GQ Jr.: Menswear Brands Launch Lines for Younger Buyers," *Wall Street Journal*, February 5, 2007, p. B1.

FASHION FOCUS

Peter Born, "Ford Names Product Chief," *Women's Wear Daily*, September 30, 2005, p. 2.

Peter Born, "Tom Ford Gets Steamy for Esteé Lauder," *Women's Wear Daily*, September 30, 2005, p. 23.

Courtney Colavita and Alessandra Ilari, "Tom Ford Brand Goes Global," *Women's Wear Daily*, June 11, 2007, p. 2.

Sharon Edelson, "Ford Chooses Milan for First Owned Unit," *Women's Wear Daily*, November 5, 2007, p. 26.

Eric Helbig, "Fashion & Style: Model Ford," *Town and Country*, November 2007, p. 128.

Colin McDowell, "The Beauty of Being Tom Ford," *Harper's Bazaar*, November 2005, pp. 236, 238, 240.

Julie Naughton, "Ford's Call to Action: Renew the Spark." *Women's Wear Daily*, May 26, 2006, p. 5.

Julie Naughton, "Ford's Full Plate: Stores, Films and Building a Beauty Brand," *Women's Wear Daily*, July 28, 2006, pp. 4–5.

Julie Naughton, "Tom's Lauder Touch: Amber Nude and Revamping Youth Dew," *Women's Wear Daily*, August 5, 2005, pp. 1–12.

Julie Naughton and Pete Born, "In the Nude: Ford's First Lineup for Lauder," *Women's*

*Wear Daily*, September 9, 2005, pp. 14–15.

Julie Naughton and Pete Born, "The Big Comeback: Tom and Don Return in Deal with Lauder—Tom Don: chapter Two," *Women's Wear Daily*, April 12, 2005, pp. 1–5.

Miles Socha, "Ford's New Gig: Made in the Shade," *Women's Wear Daily*, October 12, 2005, p. 2.

André Talley, "It's a Man's, Man's, Man's World," *Vogue*, June 2007, pp. 60–62.

Sarah Taylor, "Tom Ford's Latest : Top Chef?" *Women's Wear Daily*, May 23, 2007, p. 4.

THEN AND NOW

Jean Larkworthy, "Male Pattern Badness," www.wmagazine.com, November 2006, pp. 154–156.

CHAPTER 11

1. "Plaid City," *Woman's Wear Daily*, February 14, 2001.

2. Joanna Ramey, "Walk the Line," *Woman's Wear Daily*, February 13, 2007.

3. Joyce Brothers, "How Clothes Form a Child's Self-Image," *Earnshaw's Infants', Girls' and Boys' Wear Review*, November 1979, p. 48.

4. Tammy LaGorce and Kristen Bentz, "Coming of Age in the Kid's Business," *Earnshaw's Infants', Girls' and Boys' Wear Review*, November 1996, p. 152.

5. Jim Urban, "EMP Report Offers Window into Tween and Teen Lifestyle." *The Licensing Letter*, July 16, 2007, p. 2.

6. Gail Robinson, "Because Sizes Aren't Written in Stone: Clothes for Girls Who Just Can't Wait to Grow Up," *Los Angeles Times*, January 19, 1995, p. E-1.

7. Allison Golub, "Size Matters," *Earnshaw's*, February 2007.

8. Urban, "EMP Report," p. 2.

9. Elisabeth Butler Cordova, "Combining Closets; Kids, Parents Find Tastes Converging;

Designers Cashing In," *Crains New York Business*, July 30, 2007, p. 3.

10. Anne D'Innocenzio, "Designers Think Small: Kid's Wear Shaping Up As New Status Market," *Women's Wear Daily*, February 6, 1997, pp. 1–7.

11. "Top 10 Children's Wear Retailers (The Children's Business List.)," *Children's Business*, July 2002, p. 7.

12. "Gymboree Gains Ground; Shares of the Retailer Advanced Wednesday After It Posted Solidly Higher Sales," *Business Week Online*, March 15, 2007.

13. Jeff May, "Delia's Depends on Teens' Fickle Whims," *Star Ledger*, December 4, 2006, p. 22.

14. Ken Clark, "Child's Replay: Children's Orchard Cultivates on Upscale Second-Hand Concept," *Chain Store Age*, October 2004, p. 45.

15. "NPD Reports on the Evolving School Uniform Industry," *NPD Press Release*, August 9, 2006.

16. Kathlyn Swantko, "Students Go to the Head of the Class in Uniforms from School Apparel," *American Sportswear & Knitting Times*, October 1997, p. 12.

17. "Should Kids Wear Uniforms to School?" (For You; The Mom Exchange, Parenting/Mom Debate), *Parenting*, June 2007, p. 26.

18. "JCPenney Launches 2006 Back-to-School Season; Company Leads Back-to-School Season with New Marketing Campaign, Styles and Brands; National Retailer Is Destination for Denim, Special Sizes, and School Uniforms." *Business Wire*, July 11, 2006.

19. "Manufacturers Expand Accessories I.Q. (French Toast Uniform L.L.C.)," *DSN Retailing Today*, May 22, 2006, p. 18.

FASHION FOCUS

Cecily Hall, "Babes in Denimland," *Women's Wear Daily*, May 24, 2007, p. 20.

THEN AND NOW

"Memo Pad: Off The Wall... Where's My Couture?... New Look," *Women's Wear Daily*, September 26, 2007.

CHAPTER 12

1. "Fashion Alert: Bad Bra Syndrome Is Sweeping the Nation. This August: Look for the Cure—Barely There Intimates Launches New Invisible Look," *PRNewswire*, August 17, 2006.

2. Susan Thea Posnick, "Hearts on Fire Creates 'Fantasy' Bra with Bling," *National Jeweler*, November 16, 2006, p. 21.

3. Karyn Monget, "Badgley Mischka Sets Intimate," *Women's Wear Daily*, January 22, 2007, p. 9.

4. Rusty Williamson, "Nundies: Contemporary Product with Dual-Purpose Flair," *Women's Wear Daily*, March 19, 2007, p. 8.

5. Lucie Greene, "Wonderbra Reveals Premium Line," *Women's Wear Daily*, February 5, 2007, p. 24.

6. Karyn Monget, "August Innerwear Market Packed with Buyers," *Women's Wear Daily*, August 27, 2007.

7. Karyn Monget, "Lingerie Fairs Unite," *Women's Wear Daily*, August 6, 2007, p. 14.

8. Patricia Braus, "Boomers against Gravity," *American Demographics*, February 1, 1995, p. 50.

9. Karyn Monget, "Hochman, Pulitzer in Deal," *Women's Wear Daily*, May 7, 2007, p. 14.

10. Hoover's Company Profiles, 1997.

11. Brenner Thomas, "Buyingundewear.com: A Surging Online Market for Underwear Opens Doors to New Brands and Business," *Daily News Record*, April 30, 2007, p. 22.

12. Marshal Cohen, http://www.npd.com/beyondthedatalive. Accessed March 2008.

13. "Marvel Entertainment Bolsters Presence

in Apparel Arena through New Agreements with Fruit of the Loom," *Business Wire*, June 18, 2007.

14. Stephanie Loughran, "Retailers Fit Yoga Tapes into Whole Health Aisle," *Supermarket News*, December 3, 2001.

15. "Legwear, A Three Billion Dollar Baby," *Women's Wear Daily*, October 29, 2007.

16. Lori Borgman, "Socks Are Mixed Up and Washed Up," *Knight Ridder/Tribune*, September 11, 2007.

17. Sophia Chabbott, "Hue, Tracy Reese Collaborate on Guest Designers Line," *Women's Wear Daily*, February 1, 2007, p. 15.

18. Laura Klepacki, "Creativity Steps Forward for Spring," *Women's Wear Daily*, November 7, 2005, p. 8.

FASHION FOCUS

David Moin, "Designer Kimonos Up for Auction," *Women's Wear Daily*, October 22, 2007, p. 11.

Karyn Monget, "Natori at 30: Layering on the Luxe," *Women's Wear Daily*, October 22, 2007, p. 10.

Karyn Monget, "The Art of Natori," *Women's Wear Daily*, October 22, 2007, p. 11.

"Natori Fills the Room for Josie Foundation Launch," *Women's Wear Daily*, August 13, 2007, p. 8.

Brenner Thomas, "Natori to Launch Men's Line," *Daily News Record*, April 30, 2007, p. 5.

Amelia Vicini, "Fashion & Style, Josie Natori" *Town and Country*, November 2007, p. 113.

THEN AND NOW

Ruth La Ferla, "Now It's Nobody's Secret," *New York Times*, October 25, 2007.

Jenny Sundel, "Bra and Panty Set," *Women's Wear Daily*, July 2007, p. 49.

Court Williams, "Bust-See TV," *Women's Wear Daily*, July 2007, p. 48.

CHAPTER 13

1. American Apparel and Footwear Association home page, www.apparelandfootwear. org/aboutAAFA/HistoryandMission.asp. Accessed February 21, 2008.

2. www.collectivebrandsinc.com. Accessed March 2008.

3. American Apparel and Footwear Association, "ShoeStats 2006: U.S. Consumption of Footwear, Share of U.S. Footwear."

4. Michelle Baran, "Shoe-Ins? Ready-to-Wear Tenderfeet like Zac Posen and Proenza Schouler Are Seeing the Benefits of Adding Shoes to Their Mix, but Whether They Can Make Their Mark in the Footwear World Remains to Be Seen," *Footwear News*, January 22, 2007, p. 82.

5. Michelle Baran, "Spectacular Results . . . Italian Champions," *The Economist* (U.S.), August 18, 2007, p. 55.

6. Ambrose Mercy, "Melville-based Manufacturer and Distributor of Eyeglasses Is Confident in the Future," *Long Island Business News*, February 6, 2007.

7. "Revolutionary New Cuts Add Spice to Engagement Rings," Jewelry Information Center, www.jic.org. Summer. Accessed March 2008.

8. Kristina McKenna, "Briolettes Add Dimension to Design," *Jewelers Circular Keystone*, June 1, 2007, p. 178.

9. William George Shuster, "Cartier Celebrates Santo's 100th: Honors Modern-Day Pioneers," *Jewelers Circular Keystone*, August 1, 2004.

10. Robert Murphy, "Good Times Roll On: Luxury Watch Sales Reach Record Heights," *Women's Wear Daily*, April 23, 2003, p. 1.

11. William George Shuster, "Retailers Still High on Watches," *Jewelers Circular Keystone*, June 1, 2007.

12. Nanz Aalund, "Women Who Buy Jewelry for

Themselves," *Professional Jeweler Magazine*, March 2001.

13. Melanie Kletter, "As Boutique Bows Out, Buyers Upbeat," *Women's Wear Daily*, January 11, 2001.

14. Laura Klepacki, "Multiple Options; Accessories Shows Have Grown in Size and Number as Well as Importance," *Women's Wear Daily*, June 20, 2007, p. 115.

FASHION FOCUS

Jane Larkworthy, "Chakra Calm, How to Get Stoned," *W Jewelry*, Spring 2005, p. 51–52.

Karla M. Martinez, "On the Rocks," *New York Times*.

Jamie Rosen, "Color Wheel," W, November 1, 2007, p. 162–164.

THEN AND NOW

WWD Special Report, "A Big Footprint," *Women's Wear Daily*, September 25, 2006, pp. 1–18.

Salvatore Ferragamo, Wikipedia, http://en.wikipedia.org/wiki/Salvatore_Ferragamo. Accessed August 19, 2007.

Ilari Alessandra, "Ferragamo Taps Ortiz as Creative Head," *Women's Wear Daily*, August 31, 2007, p. 2.

Ricci Stefania, *Walking Dreams: SALVATORE FERRAGAMO, 1898–1960* (New York: D.A.P., 2006).

CHAPTER 14

1. Chris Tullett, "Global Goals," *Soap, Perfumery & Cosmetics*, October 1, 1995, p. 25.

2. Dorothy Carey, "Max Factor," *Economist*, June 15, 1966, p. 82.

3. Tony Case, "Dollars, Scents, and Eco-awareness," *Brandweek (Cosmetics and Fragrances)*, June 18, 2007, p. 32.

4. "Unilever Sells Off Fragrance Brands," *Marketing*, August 18, 2002, p. 4.

5. Andrea M. Grossman, "Unilever Enters Hair

Color Mix," *Women's Wear Daily*, June 28, 2002, p. 2.

6. "Wella Group Acquires Escada Beauty Group," *European Report*, March 20, 2002, p. 600.

7. Virginia Bonofiglio, Fashion Institute of Technology Professor, Cosmetics & Fragrance Department. Author correspondence.

8. Tom Branna, "U.S.: Sun Downer," *European Cosmetic Markets*, April 2006, p. 155.

9. Antoinette Alexander, "Sunless Tanners See Big Gains, Sales May Hit $500M by 2011," *Drug Store News*, July 23, 2007, p. 43.

10. Stephen Fenichell as interviewed by Scott Simon on "Plastic—The Dominant Material of the Time," *Weekend Edition—Saturday (National Public Radio)*, August 10, 1996.

11. Jennifer Wiel, "Innovation is Perpetual Driver," *Women's Wear Daily*, July 19, 2002.

12. Jess Halliday, "L'Oreal Ruling Sets Fragrance Precedent," *Cosmetics International*, August 13, 2004.

13. Federal Trade Commission, www.cfsan.fda.gov. Accessed April 2008.

14. Shari Roan, "Atop the Wrinkle-Cream Heap; Medicines: Renova Has the Backing No Competitor Does; the FDA's Blessing. Its No Wonder Drug, But It Does Reduce Facial Lines," *Los Angeles Times*, January 6, 1996, p. E-2.

15. Robert Cohen, "Cosmetics Safety Is a Gray Area," *Newark Star-Ledger*, May 27, 2007, p. 1.

16. Jessica Best, "Animal Testing Legislation Passes New York Assembly," *Women's Wear Daily*, June 15, 2007, p. 12.

17. Cargo Cosmetics, www.cargocosmetics.com/product. Accessed October 15, 2007.

18. Louise Prance, "Niche Male Cosmetics Market on the Rise," www.cosmeticsdesign.com/newsky_products/news. Accessed October 17, 2006.

19. Louise Prance, "Male Cosmetics Go Main-Stream," http://www.cosmeticsdesign-europe.com/news/ng.asp?id=75988-euromonitor-clinique-male-cosmetics-internet. Accessed April 24, 2007.

20. Louise Prance, "Niche Male Cosmetics."

21. Regina Molano, "Teen Beat: Wondering What Makes Teens Tick?" *Global Cosmetic Industry*, July 2001, p. 20.

22. Fay Brookman, "Nail Color Is Jane's Latest Tip," *Women's Wear Daily*, April 4, 1997, p. 11.

23. "Sassaby Deal Opens Mass Market to Estée Lauder," *New York Times*, p. D-5.

24. Regina Molano, "Teen Beat: Wondering What Makes Teens Tick?" *Global Cosmetic Industry*, July 2001, p. 20.

25. "Children Become Major Target Market for Sun Care," *MMR*, July 16, 2007, p. 22.

26. Christina Hilsenrath, "Ethnicity and Its Impact on the Beauty Business," NPD Goup press release, January 22, 2007.

27. Christina Hilsenrath, "Diversity Means Opportunity," *MMR*, June 18, 2007, p. 147.

28. Faye Brookman, "Mass Shoppers Blur Ethnic Lines," *Women's Wear Daily*, March 16, 2007, p. 7.

29. Susan Dickenson, "Greener, Broader Marketplace Fuels Candle Sales," *Home Accents Today*, September 1, 2007, p. 9.

30. Jim Ostroff, "A New World Order," *WWD/CFTA Special Report*, February 1997, p.23.

31. Antoinette Alexander, "Good News for Retailers—Consumers Continue to Wage War on Wrinkles," *Drug Store News*, June 25, 2007, p. 104.

32. Andrea Nagel, " Naturals to See Growth in 2008 with USDA Seals," *Women's Wear Daily*, July 6, 2007, p. 10.

FASHION AND FOCUS

"Scent of a Celeb," Women's Wear Daily Scoop, September 2007, p. 105.

THEN AND NOW

Cosmetic Executive Women (CEW), *Women's Wear Daily*, (Advertising Section), October 6, 2006, p. 1–23.

CEW, Beauty Career Center, ktroy@cew.org, or customer service, clientserv@jobtarget.com.

CEW, "Collective Intelligence Learning Communities," http://cew.org. Accessed April 2008.

## CHAPTER 15

1. Christine Grahl, "Dinnerware Market Overview," *Ceramic Industry*, October 1st, 2004.

2. Jennifer Marks, "Big Spenders Crave Innovation: Time to Put on Your Thinking Caps; GenX Is Waiting," *Home Textiles Today*, May 1, 2006, p. 18.

3. Pam Danziger, "Tabletop Market Report," Unity Marketing, 2006.

4. Cecile B. Corral, "Product Enhancements Buoy Area Rugs," *Home Textiles Today*, January 15, 2007, p. 10.

5. Museum Store Association (MSA), www.msaweb.org, 2007.

6. Lucia Moses, "Bridal Bounty: JCPenney and CN Say 'I Do' (Condé Nast Bridal Media Signs Deal with JCPenney Corporation, Inc.)," *Mediaweek*, August 20, 2007, p. 35.

7. Carole Sloan, "Top 50 Retailing Giants," *Home Textiles Today*, July 16, 2007, p. 1.

8. NPD Press Release, "NPD Reports When Purchasing Home Products Consumer Get Greener with Age," October 4, 2007.

FASHION AND FOCUS

"The Fashion 50: In Style and On Target," *Home Furnishings News*, November 12, 2007, pp. 6, 8, 10, 14.

THEN AND NOW

Peter Goldman, "Here Come the Brides! NPD

Survey Looks at Who Is Walking Down the Aisles," NPD Group Press Release, February 21, 2007 .

NPD Group, "Wedding Sells: Brides Say "I Do" to Housewares in 2006," *License! Global*, March 2007, p. 24.

Allison Zesbo, "Survey: Here Comes the Newest Bride," *Home Furnishings News*, November 12, 2007, p. 28.

## CHAPTER 16

1. Constance C. R. White, "Patterns," *New York Times*, June 3, 1997, p. 21.

2. Eric Wilson, "7th on Sixth Sold to IMG, Mallis to Resign as CFDA Director," *Women's Wear Daily*, February 5, 2001.

3. "Los Angeles—Always in Fashion," Los Angeles Chamber of Commerce www.lachamber.org (October 2007).

4. Ibid.

5. Business & Industry, "Fashion & Apparel Manufacturers," San Francisco Chamber of Commerce, www.sfchamber.com (October 2007).

6. Miami International Merchandise Mart, www.miamimart.net/VI/about_us/index.asp# (October 2007).

7. "Federation Activities," www.modeaparis.com. Accessed November 6, 2007).

8. Prêt-à-Porter Paris® Exhibition Report, February 2007, www.pretaporter.com/en/news/php. Accessed March 2008.

9. Madge Garland, *The Changing Form of Fashion* (New York: Praeger Publishers, 1971), p. 73.

10. Brian Dunn, "Growth Factor: The Canadian Fashion Industry Comes into Its Own," *Women's Wear Daily*, November 22, 2006, p. 14.

11. Mike Kapp, "Sao Paulo Rio Fashions Mirror Economic Realities," *Women's Wear Daily*, July 26, 2005, p. 14.

12. Koji Hirano, "Japan Fashion Week Gains Overseas Attention," *Women's Wear Daily*, August 24, 2007, p. 13.

13. Scott Malone, "Getting Ready for 2005," *Women's Wear Daily*, September 24, 2002.

14. George Wehrfritz, "Better Times Are Here: An Architect of Hong Kong's Recovery Talks about the City's Aspirations," *Newsweek International*, July 2, 2007.

15. Vicki Rothrock, "Niche Marketing: As Competition for Attendees Increases, Chinese Shows Offer Specialized Content," *Women's Wear Daily*, November 22, 2006, p. 16.

16. Hong Kong Trade Development Council, www.tdctrade.com. Accessed November 6, 2007.

17. Ritu Upadhyaya, "Indian Fashion Makes Global Statement," *Women's Wear Daily*, October 10, 2006, p. 14.

## FASHION FOCUS

W. B, "Adidas by Stella McCartney Adds Dance," *Women's Wear Daily*, March 13, 2007, p. 10.

Whitney Beckett, "Stella-Adidas Adds Golf for Spring," *Women's Wear Daily*, September 19, 2007, p. 8.

Sophia Chabbotto, "Le Sportsac, McCartney Come Together," *Women's Wear Daily*, November 2007.

Samantha Conti, "McCartney Lingerie Line Set for Spring," *Women's Wear Daily*, July 30, 2007, p. 20.

Samantha Conti, "Stella McCartney in Asia Deal," *Women's Wear Daily*, May 14, 2007, p. 2.

Bria Costello, "A Second Act for Stella McCartney Scent," *Women's Wear Daily*, July 7, 2006, p. 10.

Sharon Edelson, "Stella McCartney's at Barney's Naturally," *Women's Wear Daily*, October 19, 2007, p. 4.

Bridget Foley, "Stella Performance," *W Magazine*, October 2007, pp. 358–63.

Jessica Iredale, "Stella Attraction," *Women's Wear Daily*, May 7, 2007, pp. 4–5.

Stella McCartney biography, www.stellamc-cartney.com/int/en/stellasworld/biography/. Accessed February 2008.

Karyn Monget, "Stella McCartney Fulfills Her Passion for Lingerie," *Women's Wear Daily*, October 23, 2007, p. 6.

Sari Anne Tuschman, "Stella Hits the Slopes," *Women's Wear Daily*, March 23, 2006.

## THEN AND NOW

Giorgio Armani, "Giorgio Does Dallas: His Dairy," *Women's Wear Daily*, December 2007, pp. 118–24.

J. J. Martin, "Giorgio Armani's Hollywood," *Vanity Fair*, 2007, pp. 334–39.

Giorgio Armani, Italian Fashion Designer, Clothing, Style, Fashion, *Fashion United News*, www.fashionunited.co.uk/news/armani.htm. Accessed November 2007.

Luisa Zargani, "Ginza Guy—Armani Bets Big on Tokyo," *Women's Wear Daily*, November 6, 2007 pp. 1, 12–13.

## CHAPTER 17

1. Evan Clark, "Keeping Safe Oversees," *Women's Wear Daily*, March 20, 2007, p. 95.

2. Jordan K. Speer, "Where Globalization Is Getting Us: Executives at the AAPN Annual Meeting Explored the True Costs and Opportunities of Doing Business Globally," *Apparel*, May 2007, p. 5.

3. Alan M. Field, "Store Brands Take Over: Popularity of Private Labels Is Changing Retailers' Supply Chains," *Journal of Commerce*, February 20, 2006, p. 18.

4. Evan Clark and Kristi Ellis, "Trade Deficit Hits Record as Industry Imports Rise," *Women's Wear Daily*, February 14, 2007, p. 13.

5. Kristi Ellis, "Feeling the Aftershocks—A

World Trade Organization Reports Registers the Toll September 11 Has Taken on Oversees Trade," *Women's Wear Daily*, November 28, 2001.

6. Dana Thomas, "The Fake Trade: Wanted for Stealing Childhoods: Each Year Hundreds of Children Have No Choice but to Sacrifice Their Lives to Produce Counterfeit Goods," *Harper's Bazaar*, January 2007, p. 69.

7. Lisa Casabona, "Gray Goods Pose Problems," *Footwear News*, November 27, 2006, p. 10.

8. Just-style.com, "U.S. Textile and Apparel Jobs Losses since NAFTA Exceed 1m Mark," *www.just-style.com*, June 4, 2007.

9. Evan Clark, "CAFTA: A Long and Winding Road," *Women's Wear Daily*, February 8, 2007, p. 26.

10. Evan Clark, "U.S. and Mexico Trade Deal Sets Stage for CAFTA-NAFTA Integration," *Women's Wear Daily*, January 29, 2007, p. 6.

11. Sharon Edelson, "Coming to America: South Korean Group to Launch Teen Chain," *Women's Wear Daily*, August 30, 2007, p. 1.

12. Khanh T. L. Tran and Emili Vesilind, "New Label and Stores on Tap for Aioli," *Women's Wear Daily*, July 25, 2007, p. 14.

13. "Exports Hit Their Stride," *Women's Wear Daily*, August 7, 1996, p. 28.

FASHION FOCUS

Liza Casabona, "Busting Counterfeits: Feds Crack Major Ring, Seize $200 M in Fakes," *Women's Wear Daily*, December 6, 2007, pp.1, 12, 13.

Liza Casabona, "Counterfeiters' Holiday Payday: Real Money for Fake Goods," *Women's Wear Daily*, December 21, 2006, p. 1.

Jan Goodwin, "The Human Cost of Fakes," *Harper's Bazaar*, January 2006, pp. 53, 54.

Miles Socha and Sharon Edelson, "Attacking Counterfeiters: Wal-Mart Unit Settles with Fendi Over Fakes," *Women's Wear Daily*, June 7, 2007, p. 1.

Ross Tucker, "Busted! Feds Break Up Major Counterfeit Rings," *Women's Wear Daily*, June 27, 2007, pp. 1, 7.

Ross Tucker and Liza Casabona, "Making Fakes in the USA: Counterfeiters Step Up Domestic Manufacturing," *Women's Wear Daily*, October 3, 2007.

THEN AND NOW

American Apparel and Footwear Association, "Sweatshops," www.apparelandfootwear.org/LegislativeTradeNews/Sweatshops.asp. Accessed November 11, 2007.

"California Hustlin': Urban Hipsters love American Apparel's 'Sweatshop Free' clothes, Can the Quirky Company Find Investors?" *Newsweek*, June 26, 2006, p. 38.

Evan Clark, "China Pressure Cooker: Ethical Questions Grow Over Low-Cost Sourcing," *Women's Wear Daily*, October 2, 2007, p. 1.

Bob Jeffcott, "Sweat, Fire and Ethics: The Sweatshop Is Back," *New Internationalist*, April 2007, p. 20.

"New-WRAP® Mandate Expands Factory Certification Beyond Apparel," *Business Wire*, August 30, 2007.

Worldwide Responsible Apparel Production, http://wrapapparel.org/modules.php?name WRAP. Accessed October 31, 2006.

CHAPTER 18

1. U.S. Census Bureau, Statistical Abstract of the United States Current Business Reports, Annual Revision of Monthly Retail Services, 2007. Retail Trade.

2. "Retailers in America," *American Business Index*, February 12, 2002.

3. "Sears History." www.sears.com/ourcompany.

4. U.S. Census Bureau, Statistical Abstract of the United States, 2007. Population.

5. "The Major Chains: Dominance through More Doors," *Women's Wear Daily*, June 1997, p. 18.

6. Jeff Henry, "Truth, Not Artifice," *Visual Merchandising and Store Design*, February 2000.

7. Jennifer Pendleton, "Melrose Place: Hot Topic Brings Urban Hip to Suburban Malls," *Los Angeles Times*, April 12, 1997, p. B-1.

8. Stacey Baker, "chapter 2, The Global Market for Discount Apparel (Global Market Review of Discount Apparel Retailing—Forecasts to 2012), Industry Overview," www.just-style.com/management. Accessed June 2007.

9. "Industry Environment," *U.S. Business Reporter*, February 5, 2002.

10. Matt Hudgins, "Bigger Is Better for Outlet Malls," *National Real Estate Investor*, August 2007.

11. Cliff Annicelli, "Much More In Store," *Playthings*, July 1, 2007, p. 6.

12. Patricia Sellers, "Giants of the Fortune 500: Sears: The Turnaround is Ending; The Revolution Has Begun," *Fortune*, April 28, 1997, p. 106.

13. Stephanie Thompson, "Fashion Hits Home: Tupperware-Style Parties Yield $10 Billion in Sales for Apparel Marketers," *Advertising Age*, May 1, 2006, p. 4.

14. Direct Marketing Association, "Catalog Sales Growth Continues to Outpace Overall Retail Growth," About.com: Retail Industry, http://retailindustry.about.com/library/bl/q2/bl_dma060401a.htm. Accessed March 11, 2008).

15. Mike Antonucci, "Opting Out of Catalog Lists Is a Click Away: Web Site Helps Stop Unwanted Mailings," *San Jose Mercury News*, November 16, 2007.

16. http://www.hsn.com/info/ 2007.

17. Mike Farrell, "Attention Shoppers," *Multichannel News*, November 12, 2007, p. 10.

18. Cate T. Corcoran, "Apparel Now No. 1

Online," *Women's Wear Daily*, May 14, 2007, p. 3.

19. Jean E. Palmieri, "Retailing's Seismic Shifts: From the Wal-Mart Rollout to the Nationalization of Macy's, Retailing Has Undergone Dramatic Changes," *Daily News Records*, April 24, 2006, p. 98.

FASHION FOCUS

Sharon Edelson, "The Big Shift," *Women's Wear Daily*, July 10, 2006, pp. 4–5.

Jean E. Palmieri, "The Department of Innovation: Stores at the High and Low Ends Have Gotten Credit for Innovation, Now the Middle Steps Out of the Shadows," *Chain Store Age*, August 2007, p. 6A(2).

Jean E. Palmieri, "JCPenney: Making Every Day Matter: The $20 Billion Retailer Continues to Identify Opportunities to Increase Market Share," *Daily News Records*, May 28, 2007, p. 26.

THEN AND NOW

"Neiman Marcus at 100," *Women's Wear Daily*, Special Milestone Issue.

David Moin and Holly Haber, "Neiman's Two-Day Dallas Hoedown," *Women's Wear Daily*, October 16, 2007, pp. 4–5.

Holly Haber, "Neiman Marcus Feted at DFAs," *Women's Wear Daily*, October 24, 2007, p. 9.

CHAPTER 19

1. Jill Rivkin "On Target? Target Looks to Hit the Mark in Cheap-Chic and Grocery," *Private Global Buyer*, September 2006, p. 16.

2. Tracey Sherwood, "Selling the Experience: Customers Want Retailers to Appeal to Their Ideas of Luxury with Interactive Experience and Electric Atmosphere," *Global Cosmetic Industry*, September 2007, p. 68.

3. "Shoppers are Ranked by Inadequate Service," MMR, May 28, 2007, p. 8.

4. Amanda Baltazar "Study: Customers' Reward Preferences Vary," *Supermarket News.* September 24, 2007.

5. Amy Johannes, "Borders Beefs Up Loyalty Program with Perks," *Promo Online Exclusive*, September 19, 2007.

6. Faye Brookman, "Former Revlon Exec Creates Firm to Reward Loyalty" *Women's Wear Daily*, September 7, 2007, p. 12.

7. National Research Bureau, Inc., Chicago, Data published by International Council of Shopping Centers, http://www.icsc.org.

8. Cybele Weisser, "A Whole New Mall Game," *Money*, November 2006, p. 156.

9. Gogoi Pallavi "Pop-up Stores: All the Rage; The Latest Trend in Retailing: Shops That Open for a Few Days in a Major City or a Mall—And Then Are Gone," *Business Week* February 12, 2007.

10. "Apparel Stores: Narrower Strategies Lead to Upward Growth," *Chain Store Age*, August 1997, p. 12A.

11. Bill Botteget, "What's Happening," *Shoe Retailing Today*.

12. Robin Lewis, "Partner or Perish," *Women's Wear Daily Infotracs: Strategic Alliances*, February 24, 1997, p. 7.

13. Don Yaeger, "Wal-Mart to Spend $9 Billion," *Women's Wear Daily*, June 4 2001.

14. Jeanette Hye, "Penney's Designing by Video Conference," *Women's Wear Daily*, July 9, 1997, p. 18.

15. John M. Coe, "A Road Map for B-to-B—Database Marketing," *Target Marketing*, June 2001, p. 65.

16. Kim Ann Zimmermann, "Internet: The Vital Link in Global Supply Management," *Women's Wear Daily/Global*, July 1997, p. 78.

17. Kim Ann Zimmermann, "Talbots' Groupware Strategy," *Women's Wear Daily*, July 7, 1997, p. 18.

18. Reda, "Mills Find Cure for Outlet Dol-

drums by Focusing on Entertainment Theme," *Stores*, April 1997, p. 106.

FASHION FOCUS

Donna Goodison, "Fast-fashion Chain Zara to Add Zip to Bay State," Boston Herald.com, February 8, 2007.

Samantha Conti, "UNIQLO's New Looks," *Women's Wear Daily*, November 8, 2007, p. 10

Samantha Conti, "Topshop Going Global: NYC First Step in Chain's Aggressive U.S. Rollout," *Women's Wear Daily*, November 28, 2007, pp. 1 and 6.

Robert Murphy, "How Swede It Is: H&M Profits Up 17%, New Formats on Horizon," *Women's Wear Daily*, January 26, 2007, p. 1.

Sharon Edelson, "Wild About Cavalli: H&M Launches Collection," *Women's Wear Daily*, November 9, 2007, pp. 12-13.

Sharon Edelson, "UNIQLO's Latest Young Designers," *Women's Wear Daily*, March 5, 2008.

Eric Newman, "Why H&M is Teaming With Roberto Cavalli," *Brandweek*, June 26, 2007.

THEN AND NOW

Pat Broderick, "Shopping Mall Blazed a Trail for Downtown's Revitalization," *San Diego Business Journal*, August 20, 2007, p. 34.

Rachel Brown and Aune Riley-Katz, "Democracy at the Mall: Giant Costco Moving in to Fill Anchor Store Void," *Women's Wear Daily*, December 19, 2007, p. 1, 16.

Holly Haber, "Galleria and NorthPark Battle to Be Top High-End Mall," *Women's Wear Daily*, March 13, 2008, p. 14.

Greg Lindsay, "Say Goodbye to the Mall," *Advertising Age*, October 2, 2006, p. 13.

David Moin, "Reconfiguring the Mall: Federated Takes Stake in 'Epicenter' Format," *Women's Wear Daily*, May 15, 2007, p. 1, 16.

Jamie Reno, "Scenes From a New Mall: Shoppers Can Now Find 'downtown' in Suburbia," Newsweek, December 4, 2006, p. 60.

**CHAPTER 20**

1. Marc Brownstein, "Stop Writing Those Obituaries for the Newspaper Industry," *Advertising Age*, October 24, 2007, p. 23.
2. Magazine Publishers of America, "Fact Sheet—Average Circulation," Magazine Publishers of America, 2006.
3. Jonathan Dee, "Tween on the Screen," *New York Times Magazine*, April 8, 2007, p. 33.
4. Dianna Dilworth "QVC.com Adds User Reviews," *DMNews*, June 4, 2007, p. 10.
5. Richard Linnett, "The Big: L'Oreal Exposed on 'Full Frontal' (*Full Frontal Fashion* Television Show Launches on WE Network)," *Advertising Age*, April 14, 2003, p. 41.
6. "In Brief: Bluefly Sponsors 'Perfect Runway,'" *Women's Wear Daily*, November 6, 2007, p. 2.
7. "MTV and Pepsi Cross-Promote Fashion Series," Penton Business Media Promotion, October 11, 2007.
8. "Hit Parade," *Daily News Record*, July 30, 2007, p. 25.
9. Mengly Taing, "Young Designers Build Business Network on MySpace," *Women's Wear Daily*, September 5, 2006, p. 12.
10. Marc Karimzadeh, "Global Reach: YouTube Offers Companies a Chance to Spread This Message to the Online Community," *Women's Wear Daily*, November 14, 2007, p. 28.
11. Kayte VanScoy, "Can Bust 'Em—For Its Ambitious Ad Campaign, Lee Jeans Took to the Web," *Smart Business for the New Economy*, July 2001.
12. David Moin and Lisa Casabona, "Balance Sheet Winners and Losers on the Fiscal Battlefield," *Daily News Record*, November 6, 2006, p. 9.
13. Rajiv Banerjee, "Keeping the Faith," *Economic Times*, October 5, 2006.

FASHION FOCUS

Lisa Casabona, "A Prominent Presence: Walking the Show Floor with Abbey Doneger," *Women's Wear Daily*, April 16, 2007, pp. 18, 19.
David Moin, "Doneger Group at 60, Adapting Is Key," *Women's Wear Daily*, November 6, 2006, p. 18.
"New Doneger Division," *Women's Wear Daily*, January 10, 2007, p. 2.

THEN AND NOW

Kimberly Cutter, "Personal Style: Diane Von Furstenberg, the Fashion Legend and New CFDA President, Invites Bazaar for a Day in her Whirlwind Life," *Harper's Bazaar*, February 2007, pp. 87–91.
Rose Cysodaca, "Westward Expansion," *Women's Wear Daily* (CFDA Fashion Awards supplement), May 2005.
Rosemary Feitelberg, "Lifetime Achievement Award: Stan Herman," *Women's Wear Daily*, (CFDA Fashion Awards supplement), May 2006, pp. 30–31.
Rosemary Feitelberg, "Presidential Reflections, "CFDA president recall their time at the helm," *Women's Wear Daily* (CFDA Fashion Awards supplement), May 2007, p. 46.
Marc Karimzadeh, "CFDA Launches Business Services Network," *Women's Wear Daily*, July 30, 2007, p. 17.
Marc Karimzadeh, "Fashion Fund Finalists Cover All Bases," *Women's Wear Daily*, July 25, 2007, p. 2.
Marc Karimzadeh, "President Von Furstenberg Sets Agenda," *Women's Wear Daily*, January 19, 2007, p. 9.

# credits

ENDPAGES: RICHARD BURBRIDGE/ © ART+COMMERCE

UNIT ONE: COURTESY OF FAIRCHILD PUBLICATIONS, INC.

CHAPTER ONE: HENRY CLARKE/ COPYRIGHT © CONDÉ NAST PUBLICATIONS INC.

7 (top): Photo by Allan Grant/Time Life Pictures/Getty Images

7 (bottom): Photo by Steve Granitz/WireImage.com

9 (top): © Bettmann/Corbis

9 (middle): Renè Bouèt-Willaumez/Copyright © Condé Nast Publications Inc.

9 (bottom): A. Keller/Copyright © Condé Nast Publications Inc.

11 (top): Library of Congress

11 (bottom right): Courtesy of Fairchild Publications, Inc.

11 (bottom left): Photo by W & D Downey/Getty Images

13 (top left): © Hulton-Deutsch Collection/Corbis

13 (top right): © Private Collection/Archives Charmet/The Bridgeman Art Library

13 (bottom): Library of Congress

15 (top): PARAMOUNT/THE KOBAL COLLECTION/ RICHEE, E.R.

15 (middle): Horst P. Horst/Copyright © Condé Nast Publications Inc.

15 (bottom): Horst P. Horst/Copyright © Condé Nast Publications Inc.

17 (top): John Rawlings/Copyright © Condé Nast Publications Inc.

17 (middle): George Hoyningen-Huenè/Copyright © Condé Nast Publications Inc.

17 (bottom): Courtesy Everett Collection

19 (top): AP Photo

19 (left): Library of Congress

21 (left): WARNER BROS/THE KOBAL COLLECTION

21 (right): Courtesy Everett Collection

23 (top right): Henry Clarke/Copyright © Condé Nast Publications Inc.

23 (bottom left): AFP/Getty Images

23 (bottom right): Courtesy Everett Collection

23 (center): Photo by Express/ Express/Getty Images

25 (top left): Francesco Scavullo/ Copyright © Condé Nast Publications Inc.

25 (top right): AP Photo/PA

25 (bottom): Helmut Newton/ Copyright © Condé Nast Publications Inc.

29 (top): Photo by Frank Micelotta/Getty Images

29 (middle): Photo by Tim Graham/Getty Images

29 (bottom): Courtesy Everett Collection

31 (left): Photo By Trevor Gillespie/Getty Images

31 (right): © MATTEI MICHELE/ CORBIS SYGMA

33 (top): Courtesy Everett Collection

33 (middle): Photo by Chris Moore/ Catwalking/Getty Images

CHAPTER TWO: © STEPHANE CARDINALE/PEOPLE AVENUE

Figure 2.1: © 2007 TESTA & WEISER, LOS ANGELES

Figure 2.1: Courtesy of Yoshiki Hishinuma

Figure 2.2: Courtesy of Fairchild Publications, Inc.

Figure 2.3: Courtesy of Fairchild Publications, Inc.

Figure 2.4: Photo by Majid Saeedi/Getty Images

Figure 2.5: Courtesy of Fairchild Publications, Inc.

Figure 2.6: Photo by Bryan Bedder/Getty Images

Figure 2.7: Royalty-Free/Veer

Figure 2.9: Courtesy of Fairchild Publications, Inc.

Figure 2.10: Courtesy of Fairchild Publications, Inc.

Figure 2.12: Courtesy of Fairchild Publications, Inc.

Figure 2.13: Sarah Silver for Target; Courtesy of Fairchild Publications, Inc.

Figure 2.15: Courtesy of Fairchild Publications, Inc.

Figure 2.16: Courtesy of Motorola

Figure 2.17: Courtesy Everett Collection

Figure 2.18: Courtesy of Fairchild Publications, Inc.

Figure 2.19: Courtesy of Fairchild Publications, Inc.

Figure 2.20: Photo by Karl Prouse/Catwalking/Getty Images; Photo by Chris Moore/Catwalking/Getty Images

CHAPTER THREE: CHRIS MOORE/CATWALKING

Figure 3.1: Courtesy of VALS

Figure 3.2: © image100/Corbis; © Danny Lehman/Corbis; Photo by MIKE CLARKE/AFP/Getty Images

Figure 3.4: Copyright © Condé Nast Publications Inc.; George Hoyningen-Huenè/Copyright © Condé Nast Publications Inc.; Serge Balkin/Copyright © Condé Nast Publications Inc.; Jean-Jacques Bugat/Copyright © Condé Nast Publications Inc.; Photo by GERARD JULIEN/ AFP/Getty Images; Courtesy of Fairchild Publications, Inc.

Figure 3.7: Courtesy Everett Collection

Figure 3.8: Courtesy of Fairchild Publications, Inc.

Figure 3.9: Photo by Tim Mosenfelder/Getty Images

CHAPTER FOUR: FRANCOIS GUILLOT/AFP/GETTY IMAGES

Figure 4.1: Courtesy of Nicole Miller

Figure 4.2: Library of Congress

Figure 4.3: Photo by Selwyn Tait//Time Life Pictures/Getty Images

Figure 4.4: Courtesy of Fairchild Publications, Inc.

Figure 4.5: Courtesy of Fairchild Publications, Inc.

Figure 4.6: © Hulton-Deutsch Collection/Corbis

Figure 4.7: Courtesy of Fairchild Publications, Inc.

Figure 4.8: Courtesy of Fairchild Publications, Inc.

Figure 4.10: Photo by Karl Lagerfeld for Bambi via Getty Images

Figure 4.11: © 2006 Robb Scharetg

Figure 4.12: Management Artists Syndication

Table 4.1: © Bettmann/Corbis; © Bettmann/Corbis; ASSOCIATED PRESS

Figure 4.13: © Nicolas Guerin/ Corbis

Figure 4.14: Photo by Scott Gries/Getty Images

Figure 4.15: © Andrew Goetz/Corbis

CHAPTER FIVE: COURTESY OF FAIRCHILD PUBLICATIONS, INC.

Figure 5.2: Courtesy HSN.com

Figure 5.3: Courtesy the Gap, Inc.

Figure 5.4: Courtesy of Fairchild Publications, Inc.

Figure 5.5: Courtesy United Colors of Benetton

Figure 5.6: PRNewsFoto/Kenneth Cole Productions, Inc.

Figure 5.8: Photo by Sylvain Gaboury/FilmMagic

Figure 5.9: Photo © Erin Fitzsimmons

Figure 5.10: Courtesy Nordstrom

Figure 5.10: Courtesy Macy's Incorporated

Figure 5.10: Courtesy Wal-Mart

UNIT TWO: STEWART SHINING/ © ART+COMMERCE

CHAPTER SIX: COURTESY OF FAIRCHILD PUBLICATIONS, INC.

Figure 6.1: John Cowan/Copyright © Condé Nast Publications Inc.

Figure 6.2: © Luca Tettoni/Corbis

Figure 6.3: AP Photo/Heribert Proepper

Figure 6.4: Courtesy of Fairchild Publications, Inc.

Table 6.2: Getty Images/Science-Foto; Photo Researchers; Photo Researchers

Figure 6.5: Courtesy of Fairchild Publications, Inc.

Figure 6.7: Courtesy of Fairchild Publications, Inc.

Figure 6.9: Getty Images/Science-Foto

Figure 6.11: Courtesy of DuPont

Figure 6.12: Courtesy of Cotton Incorporated

Figure 6.13: DEX IMAGE

Figure 6.14: Library of Congress

Figure 6.15: Courtesy of Fairchild Publications, Inc.

Figure 6.16: Courtesy of Pantone

Figure 6.17: Courtesy of Fairchild Publications, Inc.

Figure 6.19: Photo by Matt Cardy/Getty Images

Figure 6.20: AP PHOTO/Lionel Cironneau

Figure 6.21: Courtesy of Fairchild Publications, Inc.

Figure 6.22: Getty Images/ Glowimages

CHAPTER SEVEN: COURTESY OF FAIRCHILD PUBLICATIONS, INC.

Figure 7.2: Photos by Guang Niu/Getty Images

Figure 7.3: STR/AFP/Getty Images

Figure 7.4: © Scott McDermott/ Corbis; Photo by Chris Moore/Catwalking/Getty Images

Figure 7.5: Courtesy of Fairchild Publications, Inc.

Figure 7.6: Library of Congress

Figure 7.7: Library of Congress

Figure 7.8: © Craig McDean / Art + Commerce

Figure 7.9: Courtesy of PETA; Photo by Eric Ryan/Getty Images

Figure 7.10: Courtesy of Fairchild Publications, Inc.

Figure 7.11: STR/AFP/Getty Images

Figure 7.12: Photo by John Chiasson/Liaison

Figure 7.14: © Craig McDean / Art + Commerce

Figure 7.15: Photos by Karl

Prouse/Catwalking/Getty Images

Chapter Eight: Photo by Feng Li/Getty Images

Figure 8.1: REUTERS/ Charles Platiau

Figure 8.2: Courtesy of Fairchild Publications, Inc.

Figure 8.4: © Jean Pierre Amet/BelOmbra/Corbis

Figure 8.5: Photo by David McNew/Getty Images

Figure 8.9: Courtesy of Macy's Incorporated

Figure 8.11: Courtesy of Fairchild Publications, Inc.

Figure 8.12: Courtesy of Fairchild Publications, Inc.

Figure 8.14: Photo by Tim Boyle/Getty Images

Figure 8.15: Photo by Mark Peterson/Corbis SABA

Figure 8.16: Courtesy of Fairchild Publications, Inc.

Chapter Nine: Nathaniel Goldberg / © Art+Commerce

Figure 9.2: Library of Congress

Figure 9.3: Courtesy of Fairchild Publications, Inc.

Figure 9.4: PRNewsFoto/Nike, Inc.

Figure 9.5: Courtesy of Adidas

Figure 9.6: Courtesy of Fairchild Publications, Inc.

Figure 9.7: PRNewsFoto/Mimi Maternity; Courtesy of Fairchild Publications, Inc.

Figure 9.8: PRNewsFoto/Lane Bryant

Figure 9.9: Courtesy of Fairchild Publications, Inc.

Figure 9.10: Courtesy of Fairchild Publications, Inc.

Figure 9.13: Photo by Mark Von Holden/WireImage

Figure 9.14: Courtesy of Fairchild Publications, Inc.

Figure 9.15: Courtesy Prada.com

Figure 9.16: Courtesy Shopbop.com

Chapter Ten: Photo by Karl Prouse/Catwalking/Getty Images

Figure 10.1: Library of Congress

Figure 10.2: Photo by Hulton Archive/Getty Images; Photo by Bob Thomas/Popperfoto/Getty Images; Photo by David Mcgough/DMI/Time Life Pictures/Getty Images; Photo by Clive Brunskill/Getty Images

Figure 10.3: © Bettmann/Corbis; Photo by Hulton Archive/Getty Images

Figure 10.4: © Rèunion des Musèes Nationaux/Art Resource; Image copyright © The Metropolitan Museum of Art/Art Resource; AP Photo; Photo by Karl Prouse/Catwalking/Getty Images

Figure 10.5: Courtesy Everett Collection

Figure 10.6: Photo by Chris Moore/Catwalking/Getty Images

Figure 10.7: © Randy Faris/Corbis

Figure 10.8: Photo by Astrid Stawiarz/Getty Images

Figure 10.9: Photo by PierreVerdy/AFP/Getty Images

Figure 10.11: Photo by Chris Condon/PGA; Courtesy Adidas

Figure 10.13: Photo by Johannes Simon/Getty Images

Figure 10.14: © Anna Peisl/zefa/Corbis

Figure 10.15: Courtesy of Fairchild Publications, Inc.

Chapter Eleven: Veer

Figure 11.1: Photo by Brad Barket/Getty Images

Figure 11.2: Photo by Dimas Ardian/Getty Images

Figure 11.3: Library of Congress; Library of Congress; Library of Congress; Photo by Hulton Archive/Getty Images; Photo by Bernard Hoffman/Time Life Pictures/Getty Images; Photo by Cornell Capa/Time Life Pictures/Getty Images; Courtesy Everett Collection; Photo by David Kennedy/Hulton Archive/Getty Images; Courtesy Everett Collection; Courtesy Everett Collection; Courtesy Everett Collection

Figure 11.4: Courtesy of Fairchild Publications, Inc.

Figure 11.5: Courtesy of Fairchild Publications, Inc.

Figure 11.6: Courtesy of Kicky Pants

Figure 11.7: Photo by Thorsten Overgaard/WireImage

Figure 11.8: Courtesy of Fairchild Publications, Inc.

Figure 11.9: Photo by MN Chan/Getty Images

Figure 11.10: Courtesy of J.Crew

Figure 11.11: Courtesy of Kids in Distressed Situations, Inc.

Figure 11.12: Courtesy of Children's Orchard

Figure 11.13: Alamy; Courtesy Everett Collection

Chapter Twelve: © Plush Studios/Brand X/Corbis

Figure 12.1: Library of Congress

Figure 12.2: Image by © Bettmann/Corbis

Figure 12.4: Courtesy of Fairchild Publications, Inc.

Figure 12.5: PRNewsFoto/Hearts On Fire Co.

Figure 12.6: Courtesy of Fairchild Publications, Inc.

Figure 12.7: Courtesy of Fairchild Publications, Inc.

Figure 12.8: Courtesy of Fairchild Publications, Inc.

Figure 12.9: Courtesy of Victoria's Secret

Figure 12.10: Courtesy of Fairchild Publications, Inc.

Figure 12.11: PRNewsFoto/Hanes, Butch England

Figure 12.13: The Advertising Archives/Courtesy Calvin Klein

Figure 12.14: Courtesy of Fairchild Publications, Inc.

Figure 12.15: Courtesy of Fairchild Publications, Inc.

Figure 12.16: Courtesy of Fairchild Publications, Inc.

Figure 12.17: Photo by Arthur Tanner/Fox Photos/Getty Images

Figure 12.18: altrendo images/Getty Images

Figure 12.19: Courtesy of Fairchild Publications, Inc.

Figure 12.20: Courtesy of Wolford

Figure 12.21: Courtesy of Fairchild Publications, Inc.

Figure 12.22: Courtesy of Fairchild Publications, Inc.

CHAPTER THIRTEEN: COURTESY OF FAIRCHILD PUBLICATIONS, INC.

Figure 13.2: Library of Congress

Figure 13.3: © Leonard Mc Lane/Digital Vision/Veer

Figure 13.4: Courtesy of Macy's

Figure 13.5: AP Photo/Charlie Riedel

Figure 13.6: Courtesy of Fairchild Publications, Inc.

Figure 13.7: Courtesy of Fairchild Publications, Inc.

Figure 13.8: Courtesy of Fairchild Publications, Inc.

Figure 13.9: Courtesy of Fairchild Publications, Inc.

Figure 13.10: Lars Klove/The New York Times

Figure 13.11: Courtesy of Fairchild Publications, Inc.

Figure 13.12: Courtesy Macy's Incorporated

Figure 13.13: Courtesy of Fairchild Publications, Inc.

Figure 13.14: Courtesy of Fairchild Publications, Inc.

Figure 13.15: Courtesy Macy's Incorporated

Figure 13.16: John French for Harper's Bazaar/V&A Museum

Figure 13.17: Photo by William West/AFP/Getty Images

Figure 13.18: Veer/Getty Images

Figure 13.19: © Ben Baker 2007/Redux

Figure 13.20: Photo by Alan Davidson/WireImage

Figure 13.21: Courtesy of Fairchild Publications, Inc.

Figure 13.22: Courtesy of Fairchild Publications, Inc.

Figure 13.23: Courtesy of Fairchild Publications, Inc.

Figure 13.24: AP Photo

Figure 13.25: Courtesy of Fairchild Publications, Inc.

Figure 13.26: Getty Images/Veer/AP

Figure 13.28: Courtesy of Fairchild Publications, Inc.

Figure 13.29: Photo by Cecil Stoughton/Time Life Pictures/Getty Images

Figure 13.31: Courtesy of Fairchild Publications, Inc.

CHAPTER FOURTEEN: © IMAGE SOURCE/GETTY IMAGES

Figure 14.1: The Art Archive/Egyptian Museum Cairo/Dagli Orti

Figure 14.2: The Art Archive/Culver Pictures

Figure 14.3: Courtesy of Fairchild Publications, Inc.

Figure 14.5: Courtesy of The Advertising Archives/© William Coupon/Corbis

Figure 14.6: Courtesy of Fairchild Publications, Inc.

Figure 14.7: Courtesy of Fairchild Publications, Inc.

Figure 14.8: Courtesy of The Advertising Archives

Figure 14.9: Courtesy of Fairchild Publications, Inc.

Figure 14.10: Courtesy of Fairchild

Publications, Inc.

Figure 14.11: Courtesy of Fairchild Publications, Inc.

Figure 14.13: Courtesy of The Advertising Archives

Figure 14.14: Courtesy of Fairchild Publications, Inc.

Figure 14.15: Courtesy of Fairchild Publications, Inc.

Figure 14.16: Courtesy of Fairchild Publications, Inc.

Figure 14.17: Courtesy of Fairchild Publications, Inc.

Figure 14.18: Courtesy of The Advertising Archives

Figure 14.20: PRNewsFoto/Stardoll

Figure 14.21: CosmeticsInfo.org

Figure 14.22: Courtesy of Fairchild Publications, Inc.

Figure 14.23: Courtesy of Fairchild Publications, Inc.

CHAPTER FIFTEEN: © FERNANDO BENGOECHEA/BEATEWORKS

Figure 15.1: © Fernando Bengoechea/Beateworks/Corbis

Figure 15.2: Veer; © Michel Arnaud/Beateworks/Corbis

Figure 15.4: Photo by Tim Boyle/Getty Images

Figure 15.5: © Cheltenham Art Gallery & Museums, Gloucestershire, UK/The Bridgeman Art Library

Figure 15.7: Courtesy of Macy's

Figure 15.8: Rachael Hale/Red Cover

Figure 15.9: © Brad Simmons/Beateworks/Corbis

Figure 15.10: © Abode/Beateworks/Corbis

Figure 15.11: Courtesy Macy's Incorporated

Figure 15.12: Courtesy Macy's Incorporated

Figure 15.13: Courtesy JCPenney

Figure 15.14: AP Photo/High Point Enterprise, David Holston

Figure 15.17: Courtesy of Fairchild

Publications, Inc.
Figure 15.18: organicstyle.com

UNIT FIVE: PHOTO BY MJ
KIM/GETTY IMAGES
CHAPTER SIXTEEN: COURTESY OF
FAIRCHILD PUBLICATIONS, INC.
Figure 16.1: Courtesy Merchandise
Mart Properties, Inc
Figure 16.3: Courtesy of Fairchild
Publications, Inc.
Figure 16.5: Courtesy of Fairchild
Publications, Inc.
Figure 16.6: Courtesy of Fairchild
Publications, Inc.
Figure 16.7: Courtesy of Fairchild
Publications, Inc.
Figure 16.8: Courtesy of Fairchild
Publications, Inc.
Figure 16.9: © Catwalking.com
Figure 16.10: Photo by VOLKER
HARTMANN/AFP/Getty
Images
Figure 16.11: Photo by MAURICIO
LIMA/AFP/Getty Images
Figure 16.12: Courtesy of Fairchild
Publications, Inc.
Figure 16.13: Courtesy of Fairchild
Publications, Inc.
Figure 16.14: Courtesy of Fairchild
Publications, Inc.
Figure 16.15: Courtesy of Fashion
Exposed
Figure 16.16: Courtesy of Fairchild
Publications, Inc.
Figure 16.17: Courtesy of Fairchild
Publications, Inc.

CHAPTER SEVENTEEN:
©EIGHTFISH
Figure 17.1: © Guy Vanderelst/
Getty Images
Figure 17.2: Courtesy of Fairchild
Publications, Inc.
Figure 17.3: Courtesy of Fairchild
Publications, Inc.
Figure 17.5: © John Van
Hasselt/Sygma/Corbis
Figure 17.6: Photo by
STR/AFP/Getty Images
Figure 17.7: Courtesy of Fairchild

Publications, Inc.
Figure 17.8: Photo by DOUGLAS
E. CURRAN/AFP/Getty Images
Figure 17.9: Photo by Robert
Nickelsberg/Getty Images

CHAPTER EIGHTEEN: DAVID
NOTON/TAXI/GETTY IMAGES
Figure 18.1: © Snark/Art Resource
Figure 18.2: Courtesy of Macy's
Incorporated
Figure 18.3: AP Photo/Sears, Roe-
buck and Co.
Figure 18.4: Courtesy of Fairchild
Publications, Inc.
Figure 18.6: Courtesy of Fairchild
Publications, Inc.
Figure 18.7: Courtesy of Fairchild
Publications, Inc.
Figure 18.8: Courtesy of Fairchild
Publications, Inc.
Figure 18.9: Courtesy of Fairchild
Publications, Inc.
Figure 18.10: AP Photo/Elise
Amendola
Figure 18.11: Courtesy of Fairchild
Publications, Inc.
Figure 18.12: Courtesy of Fairchild
Publications, Inc.
Figure 18.14: AP Photo/Chris
O'Meara
Figure 18.15: PRNewsFoto/Glam
Media, Inc.

CHAPTER NINETEEN: © GUY
VANDERELST/GETTY IMAGES
Figure 19.1: Photo © Erin
Fitzsimmons
Figure 19.3: AP Photo/Richard
Lewis; Courtesy of Fairchild
Publications, Inc.
Figure 19.4: Courtesy of Fairchild
Publications, Inc.
Figure 19.5: © Najlah Feanny/
Corbis
Figure 19.6: PRNewsFoto/Apple
Computer, Inc.
Figure 19.7: © John Harper/
Corbis
Figure 19.8: Courtesy of Fairchild
Publications, Inc.

Figure 19.9: Courtesy of Fairchild
Publications, Inc.
Figure 19.10: Courtesy of Fairchild
Publications, Inc.
Figure 19.11: Courtesy of Fairchild
Publications, Inc.
Figure 19.13: Courtesy of Over-
stock.com; Courtesy of
JCPenney
Figure 19.14: Courtesy of
Fairchild Publications, Inc.

UNIT SIX: JOHN D
MCHUGH/AFP/GETTY IMAGES
CHAPTER TWENTY: COURTESY OF
FAIRCHILD PUBLICATIONS, INC.
Figure 20.1: Photo © Erin
Fitzsimmons
Figure 20.2: Library of Congress
Figure 20.5: Copyright © Condé
Nast Publications Inc.
Figure 20.6: © The New York Times
Agency
Figure 20.8: © Cosmo en Español
Figure 20.10: Courtesy Everett
Collection
Figure 20.12: Courtesy of Fairchild
Publications, Inc.
Figure 20.13: Courtesy of The
Advertising Archives
Figure 20.14: Courtesy of Fairchild
Publications, Inc.
Figure 20.15: Courtesy of Fairchild
Publications, Inc.
Figure 20.16: Courtesy of Fairchild
Publications, Inc.
Figure 20.17: Courtesy FGI
Figure 20.18: Veer

FASHION FOCUS
01 © Bettmann/Corbis
02 Courtesy of Fairchild Publications, Inc.
03 Courtesy of Fairchild Publications, Inc.
04 Todd Heisler/The New York
Times; Courtesy of Fairchild
Publications, Inc.
05 Courtesy of Fairchild Publications, Inc.
06 Courtesy of Fairchild Publica-

tions, Inc.; Courtesy of Linda Loudermilk; Eros Hoagland/Redux

07 © Craig McDean / Art + Commerce; Chris Moore/Catwalking; Courtesy of Fairchild Publications, Inc.

08 Courtesy of Siemens

09 Courtesy of Fairchild Publications, Inc.

10 Courtesy of Fairchild Publications, Inc.; FRANCOIS GUILLOT/AFP/Getty Images

11 Courtesy of Fairchild Publications, Inc.; Frazer Harrison/Getty Images; Veer; Fernanda Calfat/Getty Images

12 Courtesy of Fairchild Publications, Inc.

14 Courtesy of Fairchild Publications, Inc.

15 AP Photo/Ric Feld; © Najlah Feanny/Corbis; © Franck Robichon/epa/Corbis

16 Courtesy of Fairchild Publications, Inc.

17 Romain Degoul/REA/Redux; Pierre Bessard/REA/Redux

18 Courtesy of Fairchild Publications, Inc.

19 Courtesy of Fairchild Publications, Inc.

20 Courtesy of Fairchild Publications, Inc.

### Then and Now

01 John Kobal Foundation/Getty Images; Jared Milgrim/Everett Collection; © Francine Fleischer/Corbis; George Karger/Pix Inc./Time Life Pictures/Getty Images

02 Library of Congress; Courtesy of Fairchild Publications, Inc.; © Victoria & Albert Museum, London/Art Resource; Scott Wintrow/Getty Images

03 © Bettmann/Corbis; Courtesy of Fairchild Publications, Inc.; Pat English/Time Life Pictures/Getty Images; Courtesy Fairchild Publications, Inc.

04 Ben Baker/Redux; Don Arnold/WireImage; Sergio Dionisio/Getty Images; Courtesy of the Fairchild Archive

05 Courtesy of Fairchild Publications, Inc.

06 Courtesy of Fairchild Publications, Inc.; © Jack Fields/Corbis; KEVIN P. CASEY/*The New York Times;* Keystone Features/Getty Images

07 © Bettmann/Corbis; Robert Mora/WireImage; Courtesy of Fairchild Publications, Inc.

08 Courtesy of Fairchild Publications, Inc.

09 Gordon Munro/Time Magazine/Time & Life Pictures/Getty Images; Courtesy of Fairchild Publications, Inc.

10 Courtesy Everett Collection/Courtesy Everett Collection; AP Photo/Columbia Picture/ AP Photo/Matt Sayles; Courtesy Everett Collection © John Springer Collection/Corbis; Courtesy Everett Collection/Evan Agostini/Getty Images; © John Springer Collection/Corbis/Brad Barket/Getty Images

11 Courtesy Stardolls.com; © Christel Gerstenberg/Corbis

12 Courtesy Everett Collection; ABC-TV/THE KOBAL COLLECTION

13 © David Lees/Corbis; Courtesy of Fairchild Publications, Inc.

14 Courtesy of Fairchild Publications, Inc.

16 Image by © Phil McCarten/Reuters/Corbis; David Lees/Time & Life Pictures/Getty Images; Courtesy of Fairchild Publications, Inc.

17 Charles Pertwee/*The New York Times;* David McNew/Getty Images; Keystone/Getty Images

18 AP PHOTO/Amy Conn-Gutierrez; Courtesy of Fairchild Publications, Inc; © Bettmann/Corbis

19 © Atlantide Phototravel/Corbis; Courtesy of Fairchild Publications, Inc.; © Jean-Pierre Lescourret/Corbis;

20 Courtesy of Fairchild Publications, Inc.